BLOOD'S A ROVER

BLOOD'S A ROVER

James Ellroy

C

Century · London

Published by Century 2009

4 6 8 10 9 7 5

First published in Great Britain in 2009 by
Century
Random House, 20 Vauxhall Bridge Road,
London SW1V 2SA

www.randomhouse.co.uk

Addresses for companies within The Random House Group Limited can
be found at: www.randomhouse.co.uk

The Random House Group Limited Reg. No. 954009

A CIP catalogue record for this book
is available from the British Library

HB ISBN 9780712648158
TPB ISBN 9781846056420

The Random House Group Limited supports The Forest Stewardship
Council (FSC), the leading international forest certification organisation.
All our titles that are printed on Greenpeace approved FSC certified paper
carry the FSC logo. Our paper procurement policy can be found at:
www.rbooks.co.uk/environment

To

J. M.

Comrade: For Everything You Gave Me

Clay lies still, but blood's a rover;
Breath's a ware that will not keep.
Up, lad: when the journey's over
There'll be time enough to sleep.

A. E. Housman

THEN

Los Angeles, 2/24/64

S*UDDENLY:*
The milk truck cut a sharp right turn and grazed the curb. The driver lost the wheel. He panic-popped the brakes. He induced a rear-end skid. A Wells Fargo armored car clipped the milk truck side/head-on.

Mark it now:

7:16 a.m. South L.A., 84th and Budlong. Residential darktown. Shit shacks with dirt front yards.

The jolt stalled out both vehicles. The milk truck driver hit the dash. The driver's side door blew wide. The driver keeled and hit the sidewalk. He was a fortyish male Negro.

The armored car notched some hood dents. Three guards got out and scoped the damage. They were white men in tight khakis. They wore Sam Browne belts with buttoned pistol flaps.

They knelt beside the milk truck driver. The guy twitched and gasped. The dashboard bounce gouged his forehead. Blood dripped into his eyes.

Mark it now:

7:17 a.m. Winter overcast. This quiet street. No foot traffic. No car-crash hubbub yet.

The milk truck heaved. The radiator blew. Steam hissed and spread wide. The guards coughed and wiped their eyes. Three men got out of a '62 Ford parked two curb lengths back.

They wore masks. They wore gloves and crepe-soled shoes. They wore utility belts with gas bombs in pouches. They were long-sleeved and buttoned up. Their skin color was obscured.

Steam covered them. They walked up and pulled silencered pieces.

The guards coughed. It supplied sound cover. The milk truck driver pulled a silencered piece and shot the nearest guard in the face.

The noise was a thud. The guard's forehead exploded. The two other guards fumble-grabbed at their holsters. The masked men shot them in the back. They buckled and pitched foreword. The masked men shot them in the head point-blank. The thuds and skull crack muffle-echoed.

It's 7:19 a.m. It's still quiet. There's no foot traffic and car-crash hubbub yet.

Noise now—two gunshots plus loud echoes. Muzzle flare, weird-shaped, blasts from the armored car's gun slit.

The shots ricocheted off the pavement. The masked men and the milk truck driver threw themselves prone. They rolled *toward* the armored car. It blitzed firing range. Four more shots popped. Four plus two—one revolver load.

Masked Man #1 was tall and thin. Masked Man #2 was midsized. Masked Man #3 was heavyset. It's 7:20 a.m. There's still no foot traffic. This big blimp up in the sky trailed department-store banners.

Masked Man #1 stood up and crouched under the gun slit. He pulled a gas bomb from his pouch and yanked the top. Fumes sputtered. He stuffed the bomb in the gun slit. The guard inside shrieked and retched very loud. The back door crashed outward. The guard jumped and hit the pavement on his knees. He bled from the nose and the mouth. Masked Man #2 shot him twice in the head.

The milk truck driver put on a gas mask. The masked men put gas masks on over their face masks. Gas whooshed out the back door. Masked Man #1 popped gas bomb #2 and lobbed it inside.

The fumes flared and settled into acid mist—red, pink, transparent. A street hubbub started perking. There's some window peeps, some open doors, some colored folks on their porches.

It's 7:22 a.m. The fumes have dispersed. There's no second guard inside.

Now they go in.

They fit tight. It was a cramped space. Cash bags and attaché cases were stacked in wall racks. Masked Man #1 made the count: sixteen bags and fourteen cases.

They grabbed. Masked Man #2 had a burlap bag stuffed down his pants. He pulled it out and held it open.

They grabbed. They stuffed the bag. One attaché case snapped open. They saw mounds of plastic-wrapped emeralds.

Masked Man #3 opened a cash bag. A C-note roll poked out. He tugged on the bank tab. Ink jets sprayed him and hit his mask holes. He got ink in his mouth and ink in his eyes.

He gasped, he spit ink, he rubbed his eyes and tripped out the door. He shit in his pants and stood around flailing. Masked Man #1 stepped clear of the door and shot him twice in the back.

It's 7:24 a.m. *Now* there's hubbub. It's a jungle din confined to porches.

Masked Man #1 walked toward it. He pulled four gas bombs, popped the tops and lobbed them. He threw left and right. Fumes rose up red, pink and transparent. Acid sky, mini–storm front, rainbow. The porch fools whooped and coughed and ran inside their shacks.

The milk truck driver and Masked Man #2 stuffed four burlap bags tight. They got the full load: all thirty cash sacks and cases. They walked to the '62 Ford. Masked Man #1 opened the trunk. They dumped the bags in.

7:26 a.m.

A breeze kicked up. Wind swirled the gas clouds into wild fusing colors. The milk truck driver and Masked Man #2 gawked through their goggles.

Masked Man #1 stepped in front of them. They got pissy—*Say what?*—don't block the light show. Masked Man #1 shot them both in the face. Slugs blew up their goggle glass and gas-mask tubes and doused their lights in a second.

Mark it now:

7:27 a.m. Four dead guards, three dead heist men. Pink gas clouds. Acid fallout. Fumes turning shrubs gray-malignant.

Masked Man #1 opened the driver's side door and reached under the seat. Right there: a blowtorch and a brown bag stuffed with scald-on-contact pellets. The pellets looked like a bird feed/jelly bean hybrid.

He worked slow.

He walked to Masked Man #3. He dropped pellets on his back and stuffed pellets in his mouth. He tapped his blowtorch and blazed the body. He walked to the milk truck driver and Masked Man #2. He dropped pellets on their backs and stuffed pellets in their mouths and blowtorched their bodies.

The sun was way up now. The gas fumes caught rays and made a small stretch of sky one big prism. Masked Man #1 drove away, southbound.

He got there first. He always did. He bootjacked niggertown robbery squawks off patrol frequencies. He packed his own multiband squawk box.

He parked by the armored car and the milk truck. He looked down the street. He saw some coons eyeballing the carnage. The air stung. His first guess: gas bombs and a faked collision.

The coons saw him. They evinced their standard "Oh shit" looks. He heard sirens. The overlap said six or seven units. Newton and 77th Street—two divisions rolling out. He had three minutes to look.

He saw the four dead guards. He saw two scorched dead men near the east curb back a few car lengths.

He ignored the guards. He checked out the burned men. They were deep-scorched down to crackle skin, with their clothes swirled in. His first guess: instant double cross. Let's fuck up IDs on expendable partners.

The sirens whirred closer. A kid down the street waved at him. He bowed and waved back.

He had the gestalt already. Some shit you wait your whole life for. When it lands, *you know.*

He was a big man. He wore a tweed suit and a tartan bow tie. Little 14's were stitched into the silk. He'd shot and killed fourteen armed robbers.

NOW

AMERICA:
I window-peeped four years of our History. It was one long mobile stakeout and kick-the-door-in shakedown. I had a license to steal and a ticket to ride.

I followed people. I bugged and tapped and caught big events in ellipses. I remained unknown. My surveillance links the Then to the Now in a never-before-revealed manner. I was there. My reportage is buttressed by credible hearsay and insider tattle. Massive paper trails provide verification. This book derives from stolen public files and usurped private journals. It is the sum of personal adventure and forty years of scholarship. I am a literary executor and an agent provocateur. I did what I did and saw what I saw and learned my way through to the rest of the story.

Scripture-pure veracity and scandal-rag content. That conjunction gives it its sizzle. You carry the seed of belief within you already. You recall the time this narrative captures and sense conspiracy. I am here to tell you that it is all true and not at all what you think.

You will read with some reluctance and capitulate in the end. The following pages will force you to succumb.

I am going to tell you everything.

THEN

Part I

CLUSTER FUCK

June 14, 1968–September 11, 1968

Wayne Tedrow Jr.

(Las Vegas, 6/14/68)

EROIN:

He'd rigged a lab in his hotel suite. Beakers, vats and Bunsen burners filled up wall shelves. A three-burner hot plate juked small-batch conversions. He was cooking painkiller-grade product. He hadn't cooked dope since Saigon.

A comp suite at the Stardust, vouchered by Carlos Marcello. Carlos knew that Janice had terminal cancer and that he had chemistry skills.

Wayne mixed morphine clay with ammonia. A two-minute heating loosened mica chips and silt. He boiled water to 182°. He added acetic anhydride and reduced the bond proportions. The boil sluiced out organic waste.

Precipitants next—the slow-cook process—diacetyl morph and sodium carbonate.

Wayne mixed, measured and ran two hot plates low. He glanced around the suite. The maid left a newspaper out. The headlines were all *him*.

Wayne Senior's death by "heart attack." James Earl Ray and Sirhan Sirhan in stir.

His front-page ink. No mention of him. Carlos had chilled out Wayne Senior. Mr. Hoover chilled out the backwash on the King/Bobby hits.

Wayne watched diacetyl mass build. His blend would semi-anesthetize Janice. He was bucking for a big job with Howard Hughes. Hughes was addicted to pharmaceutical narcotics. He could cook him up a private blend and take it to his interview.

The mass settled into cubes and rose out of the liquid. Wayne saw photos of Ray and Sirhan on page two. He'd worked on the King hit. He'd worked it high up. Freddy Otash ran fall guy Ray for King and fall guy Sirhan for Bobby.

The phone rang. Wayne grabbed it. Scrambler clicks hit the line. It had to be a Fed safe phone and Dwight Holly.

"It's me, Dwight."

"Did you kill him?"

"Yes."

" 'Heart attack,' shit. 'Sudden stroke' would have been better."

Wayne coughed. "Carlos is handling it personally. He can frost out anything around here."

"I do not want Mr. Hoover going into a tizzy over this."

"*It's chilled.* The question is, 'What about the others?' "

Dwight said, "There's always conspiracy talk. Bump off a public figure and that kind of shit tends to bubble. Freddy ran Ray covertly and Sirhan up front, but he lost weight and altered his appearance. All in all, I'd say we're chilled on both of them."

Wayne watched his dope cook. Dwight spieled more news. Freddy O. bought the Golden Cavern Casino. Pete Bondurant sold it to him.

"We're chilled, Dwight. Tell me we're chilled and convince me."

Dwight laughed. "You sound a little raw, kid."

"I'm stretched a bit thin, yeah. Patricide's funny that way."

Dwight yukked. The dope pots started boiling. Wayne doused the heat and looked at his desk photo.

It's Janice Lukens Tedrow, lover/ex-stepmom. It's '61. She's twisting at the Dunes. She's sans partner, she's lost a shoe, a dress seam has ripped.

Dwight said, "Hey, are you there?"

"I'm here."

"I'm glad to hear it. And I'm glad to hear we're chilled on your end."

Wayne stared at the picture. "My father was your friend. You're going in pretty light with the judgment."

"Shit, kid. He sent you to Dallas."

Big D. November '63. He was there that Big Weekend. He caught the Big Moment and took this Big Ride.

He was a sergeant on Vegas PD. He was married. He had a chemistry degree. His father was a big Mormon fat cat. Wayne Senior was jungled up all over the nut Right. He did Klan ops for Mr. Hoover and Dwight Holly. He pushed high-line hate tracts. He rode the far-Right zeitgeist and stayed in the know. He knew about the JFK hit. It was multi-faction: Cuban exiles, rogue CIA, mob. Senior bought Junior a ticket to ride.

Extradition job, with one caveat: kill the extraditee.

The PD suborned the assignment. A Negro pimp named Wendell Dur-fee shivved a casino dealer. The man lived. It didn't matter. The Casino Operators' Council wanted Wendell clipped. Vegas cops got those jobs. They were choice gigs with big bonus money. They were tests. The PD wanted to gauge your balls. Wayne Senior had clout with the PD. He had JFK hit knowledge. Senior wanted Junior there for it. Wendell Durfee fled Vegas to Dallas. Senior doubted Junior's balls. Senior thought Junior should kill an unarmed black man. Wayne flew to Dallas on 11/22/63.

He did not want to kill Wendell Durfee. He did not know about the JFK hit. He got paired up with an extradition partner. The cop's name was Maynard Moore. He worked Dallas PD. He was a redneck psycho doing gofer jobs on the hit.

Wayne clashed with Maynard Moore and tried not to kill Wendell Dur-fee. Wayne blundered into the hit plot in post-hit free fall. He linked Jack Ruby to Moore and that right-wing merc Pete B. He saw Ruby clip Lee Har-vey Oswald on live TV.

He knew. He did not know that his father knew. It all went blooey that Sunday.

JFK was dead. Oswald was dead. He tracked down Wendell Durfee and told him to run. Maynard Moore interceded. Wayne killed Moore and let Durfee go. Pete B. interceded and let Wayne live.

Pete considered his own act of mercy prudent and Wayne's act of mercy rash. Pete warned Wayne that Wendell Durfee might show up again.

Wayne returned to Vegas. Pete B. moved to Vegas for a Carlos Mar-cello gig. Pete followed up on Durfee and logged tips: he's a rape-o shit-bird and worse. It was January '64. Pete heard that Wendell Durfee had fled back to Vegas. He told Wayne. Wayne went after Wendell. Three col-ored dope fiends got in the way. Wayne killed them. Wendell Durfee raped and murdered Wayne's wife, Lynette.

It was his very own free fall. It started in Dallas and spun all the way up to Now.

Wendell Durfee escaped. Wayne Senior and the PD worked to get Wayne a walk on the dope fiends. Mr. Hoover was amenable. Senior's old chum Dwight Holly was not. Dwight was working for the Federal Bureau of Narcotics then. The dope fiends were pushing heroin and were targeted for prosecution. Dwight squawked to the U.S. attorney. Wayne Junior fucked up his investigation. He wanted to see Wayne Junior indicted and tried. The PD fabricated some evidence and snowed the grand jury. Wayne got a walk on the killings. It left him hollow. He quit the PD and entered The Life.

Soldier of fortune. Heroin runner. Assassin.

Lynette was dead. He vowed to find Wendell Durfee and kill him. Lynette was his best friend and sweetheart and the wall to shut out his love for his father's second wife. Janice was older, she watched him grow up, she stayed with Senior for his money and clout. Janice returned Wayne's love. The longing went both ways. It stayed there and plain *grew*.

Wayne fell in with Pete and his wife, Barb. Pete was tight with a mob lawyer named Ward Littell. Ward was ex-FBI and the point man for the JFK hit. He was working for Carlos Marcello and Howard Hughes and playing both ends back, front and sideways. Wayne had Pete and Ward as teachers. He learned The Life from them. He blew through their curriculum at a free-fall pace.

Pete was hopped up on the Cuban exile cause. Vietnam was getting hot. Howard Hughes was nurturing crazy plans to buy up Las Vegas. Wayne Senior got in with Hughes' Mormon guard. Ward Littell developed a grudge against Senior. A rogue CIA man recruited Pete for a Saigon-to-Vegas dope funnel, profits to the Cuban cause, vouchsafed by Carlos Marcello. Pete needed a dope chemist and recruited Wayne. Ward's hatred of Wayne Senior grew. Ward fucked with Senior. He informed Wayne that his father sent him to Dallas.

Wayne reeled and grabbed at air and barely stayed upright. Wayne fucked Janice in his father's house and made sure that Wayne Senior saw it.

"The Life," a noun. A haven for Mormon burnouts, rogue chemists, coon killers.

Wayne Senior divorced Janice. He beat her with a silver-tipped cane to offset the cost of the settlement. Janice limped from that day on and still played scratch golf. Ward Littell sold Howard Hughes Las Vegas at the mob's inflated prices and began a sporadic love affair with Janice. Wayne Senior increased his pull with Howard Hughes and sucked up to former veep Dick Nixon. Dwight Holly left the Bureau of Narcotics and went back on the FBI. Mr. Hoover directed Dwight to disrupt Martin Luther King and the civil rights movement. Dwight deployed Wayne Senior in anti-Klan mail-fraud ops, a sop to sob sisters at Justice.

Wayne cooked heroin in Saigon and ran it through to Vegas. Wayne chased Wendell Durfee for four years. The country blew up with riots and a shitstorm of race hate. Dr. King trumped Mr. Hoover on all moral fronts and wore the old man down just by *being*. Mr. Hoover had tried everything. Mr. Hoover whined to Dwight that he had done all he could. Dwight understood the cue and recruited Wayne Senior. Wayne Senior wanted Wayne Junior to be in on it. Senior thought they needed a recruitment wedge. Dwight went out and found Wendell Durfee.

Wayne got a pseudo-anonymous tip. He found Wendell Durfee on L.A.

skid row and killed him in March. It was a put-up job. Dwight gathered forensic evidence and coerced him into the hit plan. Wayne worked with his father, Dwight, Freddy Otash and pro shooter Bob Relyea.

Janice was diagnosed with last-stage cancer. Her beating injuries cloaked early detection of the disease. The Saigon dope deal factionalized and blew into chaos. On one side: mob ghouls and crazy Cuban exiles. On the other: Wayne, Pete and a French merc named Jean-Philippe Mesplede. April and May were pure free fall. The election hovered. King was dead. Carlos Marcello and the boys decided to clip Bobby Kennedy. Pete was coerced in. Freddy O. waltzed over from the King hit. Ward Littell was still working angles on Carlos and Howard Hughes. Ward had inherited an anti-mob file. He left it with Janice for safekeeping.

Wayne went to see Janice on June 4. The cancer had taken her strength and her curves and had rendered her slack. They made love a second time. She told him more about Ward's file. He searched her apartment and found it. The file was very detailed. It specifically indicted Carlos and his New Orleans operation. Wayne sent it to Carlos, along with a note.

"Sir, my father was planning to extort you with this file. Sir, could we discuss that?"

Robert F. Kennedy was shot two hours later. Ward Littell killed himself. Howard Hughes offered Wayne Senior Ward's job as mob fixer/liaison. His first assignment: purchase the loyalty of GOP frontrunner Dick Nixon.

Carlos called Wayne and thanked him for the heads-up. Carlos said, "Let's have dinner."

Wayne decided to murder his father. Wayne decided that Janice should beat him dead with a golf club.

Carlos kept a mock-Roman suite at the Sands. A toga-clad geek played centurion and let Wayne in. The suite featured mock-Roman pillars and sack-of-Rome art. Price tags drooped from wall frames.

A buffet was laid out. The geek sat Wayne down at a lacquered table embossed with SPQR. Carlos walked in. He wore nubby silk shorts and a stained tuxedo shirt.

Wayne stood up. Carlos said, "Don't." Wayne sat down. The geek spooned food on two plates and vanished. Carlos poured wine from a screw-top bottle.

Wayne said, "It's a pleasure, sir."

"Don't make like I don't know you. You're Pete and Ward's guy, and you worked for me in Saigon. You know more about me than you should, plus all the shit in that file. I know your story, which is some fucking story compared to the other dickhead stories I heard lately."

Wayne smiled. Carlos pulled two bobbing-head dolls from his pockets. One doll represented RFK. One doll represented Dr. King. Carlos smiled and snapped off their heads.

"*Salud,* Wayne."

"Thank you, Carlos."

"You're looking for work, right? This ain't about a handshake and a thank-you envelope."

Wayne sipped wine. It was present-day liquor-store vintage.

"I want to assume Ward Littell's role in your organization, along with the position in the Hughes organization that my father has just inherited from Ward. I have the skills and the connections to prove myself valuable, I'm prepared to favor you in all my dealings with Mr. Hughes, and I'm aware of the penalties you dispense for disloyalty."

Carlos speared an anchovy. His fork slid. Olive oil hit his tux shirt.

"Where's your father going to be throughout all of this?"

Wayne toppled the RFK doll. A plastic arm fell off. Carlos picked his nose.

"Okay, even if I'm fucking susceptible to favors and prone to like you, why should Howard Hughes go outside his own organization full of suck-asses he feels comfortable with to hire a fucked-up ex-cop who goes around shooting niggers for kicks?"

Wayne flinched. He gripped his wine glass and almost snapped the stem.

"Mr. Hughes is a xenophobic drug addict known to inject narcotics into a vein in his penis, and I can concoct—"

Carlos yukked and slapped the table. His wine glass capsized. Pepper chunks flew. Olive oil spritzed.

"—drugs that will stimulate and sedate him and diminish his mental capacities to the point that he will become that much more tractable in all his dealings with you. I also know that you have a very large envelope for Richard Nixon, should he be nominated. Mr. Hughes is putting in 20%, and I plan to raid my father's cash reserve and get you another five million cold."

The toga geek walked in. He brought a sponge and swabbed the mess presto-chango. Carlos snapped his fingers. The toga geek disappeared.

"I keep coming back to your father. What's Wayne Tedrow *Senior* going to be doing while Wayne Tedrow *Junior* sticks him the big one where it hurts the most?"

Wayne pointed to the dolls and back up to heaven. Carlos cracked his knuckles.

"Okay, I'll bite."

Wayne raised his glass. "Thank you."

Carlos raised his glass. "You get two fifty a year and points, and you jump on Ward's old job straight off. I need you to oversee the buyouts of legitimate businesses started with Teamster Pension Fund loans, so we can launder it and funnel it into a slush fund to build these hotel-casinos somewhere in Central America or the Caribbean. You know what we're looking for. We want some pliable, anti-Communist *el jefe* type who'll do what we want and keep all the dissident hippie protest shit down to a dull roar. Sam G.'s running point now. We've got it narrowed down to Panama, Nicaragua and the Dominican Republic. That's your main fucking job. You make it happen and you make your hophead pal keep buying our hotels, and you make sure we get to keep our inside guys, who just might help us out with some skim."

Wayne said, "I'll do it."

Carlos said, "Daddy won't see you coming."

Wayne stood up too fast. His mock-Roman world swirled. Carlos stood up. His shirt was spattered working on soaked.

"I'll see that you're covered on it."

Janice kept a mock-casbah suite at the Dunes. Wayne supplied round-the-clock nurses. Janice stuck to the hotel now.

The p.m.-shift nurse was on the terrace, smoking. The view was half light show, half desert haze. Janice was bundled up in bed, with the air conditioner blasting. Her system was schizy. She either half-froze or half-broiled.

Wayne sat with her. "There's some golf on TV."

"I think I've had all the golf I can take for a while."

Wayne smiled. "Touché."

"The Hughes meeting. Isn't that coming up?"

"In a few days."

"He'll hire you. He'll figure you're a Mormon, and that your father taught you some things."

"Well, he did."

Janice smiled. "Who are you meeting with? The Hughes man, I mean."

"His name's Farlan Brown."

"I know him. His wife was the club champ at the Frontier, but I closed her out nine and eight the one time I played her."

Wayne laughed. "Anything else?"

Janice laughed. It made her cough and sweat. She tossed off her covers. Her nightgown flew up. Wayne saw new slack spots and hollows.

He wiped her brow with his shirtsleeve. She nuzzled his arm and play-bit it. Wayne made a play Ouch! face.

"I was about to say that he drinks and chases women, like all good Mormons. There's a trinity for men like that. Showgirls, cocktail waitresses and stews."

The room was ice-cold. Simple talk had Janice soaked. She bit her lip. Her temples pulsed. She touched her stomach. Wayne tracked the circuit of pain.

Janice said, "Shit."

Wayne opened his briefcase and prepped a spike. Janice held her arm out. Wayne found a vein, swabbed it and made a hand tourniquet. Needle and plunger, there now.

In one beat—

She tensed and lulled. Her eyelids fluttered. One yawn and out.

Wayne took her pulse. It tapped light and ran steady. Her arm weighed almost nil.

The *L.A. Times* was open on the nightstand. It showed a photo triptych: JFK, RFK, Dr. King. Wayne folded them out of sight and watched Janice sleep.

Don Crutchfield

(Los Angeles, 6/15/68)

WOMEN:

Two bevies walked by the lot. The first group looked like shop girls. They wore Ivy League threads and modified bouffants. The second group was pure hippie. They wore patched-up jeans, peacenik shit and long straight hair that swirled.

They came and went. The wheelmen waved. The shop girls waved back. The hippie chicks flipped off the wheelmen. The wheelmen wolf-called.

The Shell Station lot, Beverly and Hayworth. Four pumps and a service bay/office. Three wheelmen sprawled in their sleds.

Bobby Gallard had a Rocket Olds. Phil Irwin had a 409 Chevy. Crutch had a '65 GTO. He was the rookie wheelman. He had *the* boss ride: 390, Hurst 4-speed, coon maroon paint.

Bobby and Phil were midday-blitzed on high-test vodka. Crutch was residual torqued on the girl show. He scanned the street for more walk-bys. Ziltch—just some old hebes loping to shul.

Back to the paper. Yawn—more jive on James Earl Ray and Sirhan Sirhan. Snore—"America Grieves"/"Accused Assassin's Lair." Ray vibed pencilneck. Sirhan vibed towelhead. Hey, America, I got your grief swingin'.

Crutch flipped pages. He hit flyweights at the Forum and a grabber—*Life* magazine offers million scoots for Howard Hughes pix! A redhead walked by. Crutch waved at her. She scowled like he was a dog turd. Wheelmen emitted *baaaad* vibes. They were low-rent and indigenously fucked-up. They perched in the lot. They waited for work from skank private eyes and divorce lawyers. They tailed cheating spouses, kicked in doors and took photos of the fools balling. It was a high-risk, high-yuks job with female-skin potential. Crutch was new to it. He wanted to groove the job forever.

The paper called Howard Hughes a "billionaire recluse." Crutch got a brainstorm. He could starve himself down to bones and shimmy up a heat shaft. Snap—one Polaroid and vamoose.

The lot dozed. Bobby Gallard skimmed beaver mags and slurped Smirnoff 100. Phil Irwin wiped his 409 with a chamois cloth. Phil worked tail jobs and stooge gigs for Freddy Otash. Freddy O. was a shakedown artist and freelance strongarm. He was ex-LAPD. He lost his PI's license behind some horse-doping caper. Phil was his pet wheelman/lapdog.

The lot dozed. No work, no walk-by cooze, gas station ennui.

It was hot and humid. Crutch yawned and aimed the AC vent at his balls. It perked him up and got him head-tripping. Gas station blahs, adieu.

He was twenty-three. He got expelled from Hollywood High for candid-camera stunts in the girls gym. His old man lived in a Goodwill box outside Santa Anita. Crutch Senior panhandled, bet all day and ate pastrami burritos exclusive. His mom vanished on 6/18/55. Crutch was ten. She up and split and never returned. She sent him a Christmas card and a five-spot every year, different postmarks, no return address. He built his own missing person file. It filled up four big boxes. He killed time with it. He called around the country and ran PD checks, hospital checks, obit checks. He kicked off the quest in junior high school.

Nothing—Margaret Woodard Crutchfield was still stone *gone.*

The wheelman gig fell on his head. It happened like this:

He kept up with his high-school pal Buzz Duber. Buzz shared his passion for pad prowls. *Soft* prowls, like this:

Hancock Park. Big dark houses. Preppy girls' lairs. Knock, knock. Nobody's home? *Good.*

You enter undetectably, you carry a penlight, you dig some plush cribs. You walk through girls' bedrooms and exit with lingerie sets.

He did it a few times with Buzz. He did it *a lot* by himself. Buzz's dad was Clyde Duber. Clyde was a big-time PI. He did divorce jobs and got celebs out of the shit. He installed college kids in left-wing groups and got them to rat out subversion. The fuzz popped Crutch on a panty prowl. They snagged him with some black lace undies and a sandwich he glommed from Sally Compton's fridge. Clyde bailed him out and got his record expunged. Clyde got him wheelman and chump surveillance gigs. Clyde said window-peeping was kosher, but nixed B&E. Clyde said, "Kid, I'll *pay* you to peep."

The lot dozed. Bobby Gallard spray-painted an iron cross on his Olds.

Phil Irwin popped some yellow jackets with an Old Crow chaser. Crutch daydreamed per Howard Hughes. Brainstorm: assault his swank penthouse! Gain entry by grappling hook!

An unmarked cruiser pulled in. The lot revitalized. Crutch caught a flash of a red tartan tie and smelled pizza.

Beeline—Crutch followed Bobby and Phil. Scotty Bennett got out of the car and kicked blood in his legs. He was six-five. He weighed 230. He worked LAPD Robbery. His tie had 18's stitched in the weave.

The backseat was stuffed with six-packs and pizza. Bobby and Phil jumped in and helped themselves. Crutch looked in the car and checked the dashboard. Still there: the crime-scene photos, all taped up and yellowed.

Scotty's fixation: that big armored-car job. Winter '64. Still unsolved. Dead guards and scorched heist men—still unidentified. Looted cash bags and emeralds.

Scotty pointed to the photos. "Lest I forget."

Crutch gulped. Scotty always *loomed*. He carried two .45's and a beaver-tail sap on a thong. Bobby and Phil guzzled beer and snarfed pizza. They turned the backseat into a zoo trough. Crutch pointed to Scotty's tie.

"You had 16's last time."

"Two male Negroes robbed a liquor store at 74th and Avalon. I just happened to be in the back, holding a Remington pump shotgun."

Crutch laughed. "It's the record, right? Fatal shootings in the line of duty?"

"That's correct. I'm six up on my closest competitor."

"What happened to him?"

"He was shot and killed by two male Negroes."

"What happened to *them*?"

"They robbed a liquor store at Normandie and Slauson. I just happened to be in the back, holding a Remington pump shotgun."

The air smelled like ripe cheese and sud spray. Scotty wrinkled his nose. Phil was hunkered down to nosh, legs on the pavement. His pants rode low. His ass crack was exposed. Scotty pulled him up by his waistband.

Phil went airborne. Phil got that "Save me" look that Scotty inspired. Phil came to earth feetfirst and snapped to attention. Bobby gulped and snapped to. Scotty winked at Crutch.

"I'm looking for two male Caucasians driving a powder blue '62 T-Bird with dark blue fender skirts. They're clouting steak houses, they're robbing cash receipts, they're holding patrons hostage and forcing women to give them blow jobs. I'd appreciate it if you'd keep your eyes peeled."

Crutch said, "Physical descriptions?"

Scotty smiled. "They wore masks. The female victims described them as being 'normally endowed.' "

"Endowed"—*huh?*—Bobby and Phil slack-jawed it. Crutch smirked. Scotty grabbed the beer and pizza debris and fobbed it off on him. A sausage morsel hit Scotty's suit coat. Phil trembled and flicked it off.

Scotty got in his car and peeled out eastbound. Crutch eyeballed a blonde at the gas pumps.

Phil said, "He thinks he's tough, but I know I could take him."

The lot re-dozed. Bobby landed a rope job. His pet Jew lawyer came by and fed him the gist. It's a horny hubby-hooker parlay. The wife's the client. Rent a hot-sheet room and find hubby at his favorite gin mill. Facilitate a chance meeting. Get me snapshots and film.

Buzz Duber cruised by. Crutch ran the Hughes deal by him. Buzz got a brainstorm. He said he knew this nigger midget. The guy played pygmies in jungle flicks. They could send him up to Howard Hughes' lair in a room-service cart.

Freddy Otash cruised by. He'd lost some weight. He bragged up this low-roller hotel he'd bought in Vegas. He threw Phil a tail job. Phil drove off, half-blitzed.

Crutch and Buzz got dozy from too much beer and pizza. Crutch got doze blips of Dana Lund, softly window-lit.

A horn blared way too loud. Crutch opened his eyes. Shit—there's Phil's pet shyster, Chick Weiss.

With his kike-kayak Cadillac. With his frizzy-ass hairdo and his British fop suit. With his fucked-up Caribbean-art fixation.

Weiss said, "I got a fruit gig for you. The guy likes to brown well-hung Filipinos, and I got a mutant packing 10½ inches. The wife wants a divorce, and who can blame her?"

The hubby had a fuck pad at the Ravenswood. Crutch brought a Rolleiflex with a flashbulb bar. Buzz wore door-kicker shoes.

The Mutant met them in the lobby. He had a door key. Crutch was miffed. He craved some kick-the-door-in action. They huddled. Crutch told the Mutant to get hubby in the sack pronto. Buzz told him to provide decent lighting. The Mutant told them to get his *schvantz* in the pix. He serviced spouses of both genders. He wanted more divorce work. He wanted his heavy-hung status proclaimed.

They cooked up a four-minute countdown. The Mutant skedaddled to apartment 311. Crutch futzed with the camera and secured it A-OK. Buzz ticked seconds off on a stopwatch.

10, 9, 8, 7, 6, 5, 4, 3, 2, 1—*go*.

They ran up the stairs. They cut down hallways and found 311. Buzz opened the door. Crutch hoisted the camera. They followed love grunts to a doorway and let fly.

It was all Greek. The Mutant poured hubby the pork with his monster meat in plain view. Crutch tripped the shutter. *Pop pop pop pop*—the bedroom went flashbulb-white blind. Hubby wailed the fruit-gig standard How Could You? blues. The Mutant pulled on his pants and went out the fire escape. Buzz saw a bag of weed on the dresser and swiped it. Crutch thought, *This is the life*.

Buzz said, "It had to be a yard long."

Crutch said, "Under a foot. Remember, Chick Weiss gave us the measurement."

Clyde Duber said, "We could use him again. Did you get his number?"

Buzz said, "We can find him through the Screen Actors Guild. He's playing the sidekick on some TV show."

Clyde Duber's office, Beverly Hills. Knotty-pine walls, golf trophies and red leather. Dig the wall frieze:

It pertained to that big armored-car heist. Clyde grooved on it. The case was one big bug up his ass. There's an ink-stained bill behind glass. There's framed photos of blowtorched stiffs and loose emeralds. There's Sergeant Scotty Bennett. He's manhandling two male Negroes.

Clyde kept an amateur file on the case. It was his pet project. Scotty indulged him with knickknacks. Clyde loved Scotty's sweat-room tapes. They featured male Negroes screaming.

Crutch said, "Freddy Otash bought some hotel in Vegas."

Clyde poured a triple scotch. "Freddy's a dipshit. Rumors are circulating, and that's all I can say about that."

Buzz said, "Tell Dad about the Hughes deal."

Crutch scratched his balls. "*Life* magazine's offering a million bucks for a photo of Howard Hughes. I think we can do it."

Clyde made the jack-off sign. *Kids*—this white man's burden. Kid wheelmen, kid infiltrators, kid stakeout geeks.

Buzz nudged Crutch. "You got plans tonight?"

"I thought I'd drive around."

"Shit, you're going to peep Chrissie Lund."

Clyde said, "Who's Chrissie Lund?"

"She's USC frosh. She's got Crutch all wired."

Clyde sipped scotch. "Don't do anything I wouldn't do. Like 459 PC, breaking and entering."

Crutch blushed and checked the wall frieze. Memo: buy some tartan bow ties and get a Scotty Bennett crew cut.

Buzz seltzer-spritzed his scotch. "Get us a decoy job, Dad. Send us in to some Commie group."

"Nix that. You're too green and you look too square. You've got to be able to talk Commie lifestyle shit to make those gigs work. You kids don't know from social upheaval. All you kids know from is this college-girl gash you can't get."

Buzz laughed. Crutch blushed. Memo: study your file and prowl for Scotty's blow-job freaks.

"Who commissions those infiltration jobs?"

Clyde kicked his chair back. "Right-wing nuts with gelt. They're all doctors and kings. You've got Dr. Charles S. Toron, the Eugenics King. You've got Dr. Fred Hiltz, the Hate-Pamphlet King, and Dr. Wesley Swift, the Nazi-Bible King."

Buzz said, "Dr. Fred's a dentist. The other guys have mail-order degrees, like all those coon preachers."

Clyde said, "*Defrocked* dentist. He got strung out on anesthetic cocaine and started fucking peoples' teeth up."

Crutch thought of Dana Lund. Memo: bring a soft-focus lens. Buzz whipped out that bag of weed. Clyde rolled his eyes—*kids*.

"That reminds me. Dr. Fred's got a job for us. A woman stole some money from him and absconded."

Buzz looked at Clyde. Crutch looked at Clyde. Both looks said *Me*. Clyde flipped a coin. Buzz called tails. The coin hit the floor heads.

Crutch had a flop at the Vivian Apartments. It was a walk-up dive just south of Paramount. Grips and stagehands lived there. Bit players turned lunchtime tricks in a jumbo mop closet. Crutch crammed all his shit into two rooms.

His file shit, his camera shit, his car shit, his bug-and-tap shit. Clyde taught him surveillance. He had phone cords and wire mounts up the ying-yang. He had a full run of *Playboy* magazine. He had *Car Craft* back to '52. His wallpaper was forty-one Playboy Playmates.

He settled in for the night. He updated his notes on his mother's last known location. Christmas '67—Margaret Woodard Crutchfield writes from Des Moines. Every known records check—zero. Backtrack to '66—a Christmas card from Dubuque. Every in-between town, full records checks, zero.

Crutch got antsy. Buzz was who-knows-where, blitzed on who-knows-what. Buzz had this mean streak that he lacked. Buzz carried a fake cop's badge and coerced head out of hookers. Nix that. Holding it in was better.

It was warm out. A summer storm brewed. Crutch took a drive. He circled up to Hollywood Boulevard and out to the Strip. He looked at people. The longhaired girls jazzed him and the longhaired guys rubbed him wrong. He trawled for that '62 Bird and Scotty's blow-job bandits. He saw two fags in a '61 Bird and no more.

He drove east to Hancock Park. He cut his lights and perched at 2nd and Plymouth. That big Spanish house held him.

Window glow flickered, upstairs and down. He saw Chrissie in USC sweats—one glimpse and gone. He saw Dana tie her hair back in the kitchen.

Buzz didn't get it. Nobody got it. That's why he never told anyone. It wasn't Chrissie Lund. It was always Dana Lund, and she was fifty-three years old.

Dwight Holly

(Washington, D.C., 6/16/68)

SPOOKS:
The restaurant was thick with them. Mr. Hoover ran a head count. Dwight watched his eyes click. Colored waiters, colored lobbyist, colored baseball ace. The old poof was frail. He slurped his soup palsy-style. He'd lost some beats, his brain still sparked, his circuits cranked on *HATE*.

Harvey's Restaurant, midtown D.C., the big lunch rush. A big be-seen spot. Big eye-click action.

Mr. Hoover said, "Did Wayne Tedrow Jr. kill Wayne Tedrow Sr.?"

"Yes, Sir. He did."

"Extrapolate, please."

Dwight pushed his plate back. "Carlos Marcello bought off LVPD and the Clark County coroner. A blunt-force trauma homicide was ruled a heart attack."

Mr. Hoover smiled. "Stroke would have affirmed the golf aspect."

Dwight lit a cigarette. "I won't ask for more details, Sir. I'll commend your sources and move on."

"Captain Bob Gilstrap and Lieutenant Buddy Fritsch viewed the crime scene. They were aware of the animus between Tedrow *père* and *fils,* and both officers are beholden to Mr. Marcello."

"Mr. Marcello is a wonderful friend to the Nevada law-enforcement community, Sir. He sends lovely gift baskets at Christmas."

Mr. Hoover *beamed.* "Really?"

"Yes, Sir. The false bottoms cover casino chips and hundred-dollar bills."

Mr. Hoover *glowed*. "Did Junior take part in any recent Memphis operations that you might have heard about?"

Dwight winked. My lips are sealed. Mr. Hoover snagged a toast point and shooed off a waiter.

"You are an eloquent man, Dwight. You understand your audience and play to them inimitably."

"I rise to the occasion of you, Sir. There's no more to it than that."

Spook action stage left. A spook waiter sucked up to the spook baseball cat. Mr. Hoover tuned the banter out and tuned in to the spooks. He was seventy-three. His breath reeked. His cuticles bled. He lived off digitalis and skin-pop amphetamine. A Dr. Feelgood supplied daily injections.

Click—he's back again. Click—he's back to *you*.

"Our other homicides. The gaudier and more scrutinized ones likely to inspire loose talk."

Dwight stubbed out his cigarette. "Ray and Sirhan are psychopaths, Sir. Their statements confirm their paranoia, and the American public has come to expect grandstanding delusion in its assassins. There *will* be loose talk, but it will be replaced by public indifference over time."

"And the Tedrows? Are we exposed there? Reassure me in your most bluff-hearty manner."

Dwight said, "Senior's death is in no way suspect. Yes, he ran Klan ops for us, but it's never become public knowledge. Yes, he peddled hate pamphlets, but he was never as publicly voluble as our hate-pamphleteering chum, Fred Hiltz. Yes, he was slated to take over Ward Littell's job for Howard Hughes, which might have created speculation. Yes, I think Junior will get the job now. No, I don't think that any of it will serve to expose us in any significant way."

Mr. Hoover speared his last toast point. His hand trembled. Some table-hopping pols eyeballed him.

"Power. Was that Junior's motive?"

"I've known him all his life, Sir. I think 'fully justified hatred' describes it best."

A spook preacher braced the pols. Yuks and backslaps circulated. The guy wore cowboy boots with his clerical suit. Dwight recognized him. He hosted telethons for some spook disease and espoused leftist shit.

Mr. Hoover said, "Prince Bobby and Martin Lucifer King have departed, leaving the morally impaired disconsolate and providing the sane with dear relief. Operation Black Rabbit did not achieve the results we had hoped for, and toxic clouds of black nationalism are quite evidently aswirl. I would like you to assess the Black Panther Party and the United Slaves, also known as 'US,' as potential targets for a disruption program. I am thinking of a full-scale Cointelpro. There are also two lesser known cabals in Los Angeles that may also require scrutiny. Mark their lurid names: The Black Tribe Alliance and Mau-Mau Liberation Front."

Dwight got goose bumps. "I have an informant in L.A. I'll fly out and talk to her."

"*Her,* Dwight? Confidential Bureau informant number 4361?"

Dwight smiled. "Yes, Sir. We may be looking for an inside plant, and she knows every duplicitous left-winger in captivity."

"All left-wingers should reside in captivity."

"Yes, Sir."

"Stop by Las Vegas as well. Assess Wayne Tedrow Jr.'s mental health."

"Yes, Sir."

"The Mau-Maus were an African cannibal sect with no valid grievance. They diddled baboons and ate their own young."

"Yes, Sir. I know about them."

"Your knowledge does not surprise me. You're my obedient Yalie thug."

He lived in hotel suites. Roving agents had Bureau-vouchered digs nation-wide. He liked the Statler in L.A. and the Sheraton Chicago. The D.C. Mayflower was dud-ritz. The room service tanked, the pipes hissed, the bed creaked.

His study files and plane tickets were there on the desk. Mr. Hoover had them sent during lunch. Panthers/US/Mau-Mau/Tribe. *Mr. Hoover wanted this.* His L.A. flight left in two hours.

Dwight buffed his shoes, cleaned his gun and did doorway-bar chin-ups. Bullshit tasks quashed his nerves and kept him at one drink a night. *It was chilled.* RFK was all on Carlos. It was *his* wet dream. Sirhan Sirhan practically drooled. He'd never ID Otash credibly. Jimmy Ray got popped at the London airport. Extradition woe would extend. Jimmy would talk— that was certain. Otash ran him in circles. Jimmy's story would play as cracker fantasia.

Pete would hold. Otash would hold. The lone-nut consensus would kick in. Mr. Hoover would short-shrift all divergent queries. The one wild card was the kid.

"I've known him all my life, Sir."

And his daddy and my daddy and Indiana long gone.

His daddy was "Daddy" Holly, an upstart nativist and Klan huckster. Daddy Holly got rich selling Klan kitsch in the '20s Klan heyday. Daddy hatched his sons Dwight and Lyle out of wedlock and sent Louisa Dunn Chalfont back to Kentucky. Dwight and Lyle grew up in Klan kampgrounds. Daddy taught them to spell all hard "C" words with a "K." Daddy hated Jews, Papists and niggers and understood that the Klan was a shuck.

Daddy rose to Exalted Cyclops standing. Daddy sold kustom Klan robes, Klan kid's klothes and kanine kouture. Daddy got rich. The '20s boom sustained him. A rape-suicide scenario derailed him. His Grand Dragon mentor assaulted a young woman on a train. She drank mercury and killed herself. The story got massive ink. Rabid censure swept the Klan out of favor. Klan-backed politicians were ousted en masse. Daddy looked for new opportunities and invested heavily in stocks. His wealth grew straight up to Black Tuesday.

Dwight was twelve then. Lyle was nine. They lost their big house in Peru, Indiana, and moved to Shitsville. Daddy started ignoring them. Daddy found a protégé: a younger man named Wayne Tedrow. They dreamed up get-rich-quick schemes and hawked hate tracts. Dumb-fuck Hoosiers dug the kaptioned kartoon texts and katkalls at Franklin Double-Cross Rosenfeld. Wayne Tedrow hatched a son with a local girl, circa '34. Wayne Junior was a brilliant kid with a chemistry bent. Dwight dug him as a kid brother/son from the get-go.

Daddy Holly crapped out in '39. Cirrhosis took him down. Wayne Senior raised Wayne Junior in Peru. He ditched his first wife and married a fast skirt named Janice Lukens. Dwight and Lyle worked dead-dog jobs and put themselves through college. Dwight went on to Yale Law School. Lyle went on to Stanford Law School. Wayne Senior moved his family to Nevada and got rich off hate and real estate. Dwight joined the marines, got commissioned and killed Japs on Saipan. Lyle joined the navy, got commissioned and killed Japs on boats. Dwight joined the FBI in '46. Lyle joined the Chicago PD in '47. They both kept in touch with the Tedrows.

Wayne Junior grew up studious and wild. He served with the 82nd Airborne in the mid to late '50s and got a chemistry degree. Dwight worked hot-desk Bureau jobs and developed a rapport with Mr. Hoover. He almost bellied up in early '57. Mr. Hoover allotted him a brief rest reprieve. Lyle quit the Chicago PD. Mr. Hoover gave him a full-time assignment.

Get next to Martin Luther King. Infiltrate and subvert the Southern Christian Leadership Conference.

Lyle did his best. Lyle failed. Lyle failed because he rather liked Martin Luther King and because Martin Luther King was unstoppable.

Wayne Junior joined the Las Vegas PD. Dwight transferred to the Federal Bureau of Narcotics. He worked the Southern Nevada Office and spent time with Wayne Senior. Wayne Junior's life imploded in Dallas. A big coon hunt resulted. Wayne Junior waxed three shines that Dwight was set to prosecute. Yeah, he cared for the kid. But no passes for old friendships. You do not cross Agent Dwight C. Holly.

He went after Wayne Junior. Ward Littell and Pete Bondurant interceded. Wayne Junior waltzed on the spooks. Ward and Pete pulled strings *for* Dwight and forged a tenuous truce. Dwight was named chief investigator for the Southern Nevada Office. He didn't stay long. The job bored him. Mr. Hoover lured him back to the FBI.

Lyle killed himself in August '65. It was slightly hinky. Ward Littell was embroiled with Lyle then. Ward spread grief wherever he went and sometimes turned minor grief fatal. Lyle Dunn Holly, dead at forty-five. A boozer, a gambler and a womanizer. A sweet-natured hump spread too thin.

Dr. King had Mr. Hoover spread wafer-thin. It was a fucking grizzly bear versus a Chihuahua. Dr. King was a stone Commie. Mr. Hoover was a stone Tory. Dr. King fucked women with gusto. Mr. Hoover collected antiques and vintage pornography. History welcomed Dr. King. History withdrew the welcome mat and put Mr. Hoover flat on his ass. He concocted Operation Black Rabbit and tried *everything.*

Bug jobs, tap jobs, black-bag jobs, shakedowns, poison-pen campaigns. Tail jobs. Newspaper slander. Innuendo, coercion, plants, cutouts, propaganda, psych warfare. Black Rabbit went on for three years. The key personnel had rabbit names. Dr. King was Red Rabbit. Dwight was Blue Rabbit. Lyle was White Rabbit for a spell. Red Rabbit had a fag adviser code-named Pink Rabbit. Wayne Senior was Father Rabbit. The operation was a rabid rabbit hutch and a dead-end cluster fuck. Dr. King soared as Mr. Hoover withered. Dr. King had his nigger-florid "I have a dream" shtick. Mr. Hoover told Dwight that *he* had a dream without ever stating the words. He stayed out in the dream ether. Blue Rabbit made the dream cohere in Memphis. Blue Rabbit watched the resultant riots live on TV. Blue Rabbit saw a little colored girl dead from a stray bullet.

Dwight did fifty chin-ups total. He made himself all sweat and muscle ache. He showered, dressed and packed. He got out his anonymous check-writing kit.

One postal money order and one envelope. $300 to Mr. George Diskant in Nyack, New York.

Dwight wrote the check, sealed the envelope and wiped it fingerprint-free.

The flight left Dulles late. Dwight ate salted nuts and read black-militant memoranda.

The Black Panthers. Cool name, cool mascot. Founded in '66. Ex-convict and aggrieved-spook membership. Lots of meetings, lots of whoop-de-doo, exponential growth assured. Cop-haters. Celebrity "Brothers" Eldridge Cleaver, Huey Newton and Bobby Seale. "Off the Pigs!" rhetoric. Non-fatal cop snipings. A fatal shoot-out in Oakland, California—10/28/67.

Huey Newton wounded. One policeman dead. Criminal proceedings pending.

The Panthers hated the United Slaves. It was jig factional jive. US had a catchy motto: "Wherever you are, US is."

Fatal shootout—4/6/68—two days post-Memphis. Oakland again—this honky-hater hot spot. The Panthers called it an ambush. The cops called it "tactical surveillance." One Panther was killed. Eldridge Cleaver was wounded. Footnote: Brother Cleaver was a convicted rapist.

Dwight flipped pages. Most big-city PDs had files on the Panthers and Negro informants placed. Food drives, educational programs, black-culture rebop. Burgeoning numbers, hip cachet, minor newspaper clout.

An instinct: *the Panthers are too well-known to full-on operate.*

The Bureau ran a half-assed Cointelpro last summer. The goal: create Panther-versus-US dissension. Some San Diego agents circulated custom hate lit. The Panthers called US "chitlin chumps." US called the Panthers "pork-chop niggers."

An instinct: *US was too well-known to full-on operate.*

Note to Mr. Hoover: do not increase pressure on Panthers or US. Status-quo existing operations. Both groups will discredit themselves over time.

Dwight flipped pages. He hit sheets on the Black Tribe Alliance and Mau-Mau Liberation Front. They were garish, outlandish and distinctly criminal.

Darktown L.A. Rival storefront operations. Small membership stats in gradual ascent. Both groups: "Allegedly seeking to sell narcotics to finance their activities."

No known informants placed. Nomenclature out of *Amos 'n Andy.* "Lord High Commissioner," "Propaganda Minister," "Pan-African Ruler." Rat jackets on the key players:

A geek with four dope busts. A faggot carhop with two armed-robbery jolts. A bunco artist/voodoo priest. A card shark with ninety-one arrests and a phone book–size rap sheet. A "politically motivated" rape-o. Arrivistes, opportunists, Black Panther manqués. Buffoons prone to whimsy and carnage.

Dwight got goose bumps. Dwight fretted his law-school ring and read more pages.

More names, dates and locations. More details on BTA/MMLF brouhahas. A note from LAPD Sergeant Robert S. Bennett: "Per the armored-car robbery-homicides of 2/24/64, rumors of BTA & MMLF participation cannot be substantiated."

Street-corner agitation. Fistfights, drunk-driving beefs, Mickey Mouse rousts. The faggot carhop pimped drag queens. The card shark pimped his wife to cover his gambling debts. The Pan-African Ruler owned a porno bookstore and keestered his neighbor's pet goat.

His goose-bump count *zooooomed*. His nerves jumped. He ordered his one drink a night early. There, now—put your seat back and trip on Karen.

Confidential Bureau informant #4361—Karen (NMI) Sifakis. DOB 2/1/25, New York City. Fellow Yalie, history prof, Quaker-leftist subversive.

He brought her file with him. He loved the old surveillance pix and mug shots. There's Karen in '49, at a Paul Robeson bash. There's Karen outside Sing Sing—the Rosenbergs just got it. L.A., 3/12/61—Karen at a ban-the-bomb rally. His favorite: Karen composed in prayer as Berkeley cops bash heads all around her.

She taught history at UC Santa Barbara. Her husband was a lefty lawyer in Jew York. He rotated west two weeks per month. They quit fucking four million years ago. They stayed together for obscure Commie reasons and for the sake of their two-year-old daughter. Karen disdained violence. Karen built bombs, blew up monuments and always made sure that no human beings or watchdogs got hurt. She operated under the direct sanction of Special Agent Dwight C. Holly.

Quid pro quo. He let her destroy jingoist statuary. He pulled her activist chums out of the shit with some regularity. She ratted Reds who exceeded her low threshold for physical hurt. She was pregnant again now, at age forty-three. It was some kind of jack-off-in-a-jar/test-tube job that required hubby's assistance. Karen Sifakis—Jesus Fucking Christ.

They met at Yale. It was fall '48. He was a rookie Fed. She was a Smith College/Yale trial coed. They had a two-hour pub chat. They killed a bottle of scotch and a pack of cigarettes and made everlasting impressions. He dug her looks. She dug his looks. He didn't know it was mutual until three years back.

L.A., August '65. The Watts riot—crazy nigger shit ascendant. Mr. Hoover was aghast. He ordered file checks on all the college profs who signed pro-spook petitions. Dwight did a full week of file work. There's Karen's name. There's Karen's picture. Fuck—it's that tall, red-haired Greek girl from Yale.

He did some research. He learned that Karen wrote her doctoral thesis on the Indiana Klan. Prominently mentioned: Walter "Daddy" Holly him-self.

He conducted some interviews. He learned that some Indiana Klan klowns lynched Karen's Greek immigrant granddad. It was 1922. Daddy Holly ran a klavern two counties south of the lynch site.

He did more research. He pulled Karen's FBI file from the Central Records. He got her protest-march arrest records expunged in nine cities. He climbed a big limb to get her granddad some late justice.

One of the lynch guys had spawned a neo-Nazi grandson. Dwight tracked him to a county jail in Ohio. The guy was an evil sack of shit. Dwight got him moved to an all-nigger tier. The spooks gave him a come-to-God whipping.

He flew out to L.A. and knocked on Karen's door. She recognized him seventeen years later. He told her what he'd done and that his father was Daddy Holly. She asked him why he did it. He told her that he wanted to give her something that no one else ever could.

She invited him in.

They developed an arrangement.

He's black-bagged her house. He's read her journal. She describes her fascist-toady lover tenderly.

She always tells him, "We're too circumspect to self-immolate." He always tells her, "We're too tall and good-looking to lose." Sometimes he snaps out of nightmares and finds himself coiled in her arms.

The flight got bumpy. The seat-belt warning flashed. Dwight jotted notes on a file card:

"BTA & MMLF best bets. Check various police agcy files & hate-mail subscriber lists (left-wing, anti-white mailings) for leads on possible plant (Wayne Sr.'s stash/Dr. Fred Hiltz)."

The bumps leveled off. The plane descended. There's that big wide light. Jesus, L.A. looked good.

The bedroom was hot. The window unit went on the fritz and pushed stale air around. They'd sweated the sheets through to the mattress. Karen called it a "sauna fuck." Dwight kissed her wet hair, sheened up all the more red.

The husband was back east. He had a name, but Dwight never said it. Dina was out at nursery school. They had three hours.

Karen rolled on her back. She was three months pregnant. She showed a little. Her litheness was filling out into curves.

She stretched. She grabbed the bed rails and arched off her back.

Dwight put a hand on her belly and eased her down slow. She rolled into him. He hooked a leg over her and drew her in close.

"Are you sure it's not mine?"

"Yes. It was a procedure, and you were nowhere near the receptacle."

Dwight smiled. "It's a girl."

"Not necessarily."

"Girls are less trouble. Any male being you create will mean problems for me. I'll spend the rest of my career redacting his files and busting him out of jail."

Karen lit a cigarette. "Dina will blow up Mount Rushmore. She's starting to put out a vibe."

"Dina will marry a Republican. You know how I know it? She always wants me to show her my badge."

The window unit buckled. Icy air hit them. Karen shivered and nuzzled into him.

"A colleague of mine needs some help. He's being assessed for tenure, but he was blacklisted from '51 to '54. The chairman of the tenure committee hates him, and he's not above using that as a wedge."

Dwight laughed. "I thought all college professors were high-minded Commies above shit like that."

"I am, but they're not."

"I'll misplace his file or do some redactions. Let me know what you need."

Karen blew smoke rings. They hit the cold air and dispersed. Dwight took the cigarette and put it out.

"Smoking's bad for pregnant women."

"One a day, and only when we're together."

"I need some help."

"Tell me."

"I might be running a Cointelpro on some black-militant groups. I'll find the plant on my own, but I might need help finding an informant."

Karen kissed his neck and traced the knife scar on his shoulder.

"Why should I help you with something like that? Give me the rationale and explain how it conforms to our arrangement."

Dwight put his head up against hers. Their eyes were close. That odd blue all dark-flecked—some goddamn Greek.

"Because they're out to sell dope and cash in on social protest. Because they're shitbirds who abuse women. Because they'll get a lot of very impressionable young black men fired up to do crazy shit that will derail their fucking lives forever, and the overall social benefit that they'll create from being in business will be down around zero."

Karen kissed him. "All right. I'll think about it."

"I'm right on this one. You could help me out and do some good here."

Karen chewed her lips. Dwight kissed her and stopped it. They went telepathic. Karen said their credo.

"I will not further comment on the usurious nature of our relationship, lest I indict myself as a fascist collaborator and run from you screaming."

On cue, perfect timing, straight off a kiss. More than deadpan, less than droll.

Dwight went into a laugh fit. Karen clamped his mouth. He nipped her palm and made her stop it. She pointed to his clothes. His checkbook had dropped from his suit coat.

"Those anonymous checks. You've never told me *why*."

"I've told you I send them."

"You tell me just so much, and no more."

"You're the same way."

"It's how we stay safe together."

Their faces were close. Karen leaned in and got their eyes closer.

"You've done something terribly wrong. I won't ask, but you should know that I know."

Dwight shut his eyes. Karen kissed them. Dwight said, "Do you love me?" Karen said, "I'll think about it."

4

(Las Vegas, 6/17/68)

The Sheriff's blocked off Fremont. The low-roller casinos flew flags at half-mast. A lackluster motorcade slogged through.

Dig: a memorial parade for Wayne Tedrow Senior.

Noon in Vegas, 109° and climbing. City fathers in cowboy hats and broil-inducing suits. The mayor's last-second brainstorm. Senior was a heavyweight. Let's dispense respect.

The car procession crawled. The standing spectators sizzled and gaped, sun-stupefied. Some kitchen workers waved placards and booed. Wayne Senior ran their union and fucked them over with management side deals.

The LVPD sent an honor guard. Wayne stood on a platform with Buddy Fritsch and Bob Gilstrap. Buddy was *nervous*. He radiated *I need a drink*. He probably saw Wayne Senior's body.

Snail trail—the cars moved bumper-lock slow. Tourists capered and waved chip cups and beers. Negro protestors lugged anti-cop signs. A subgroup taunted Wayne. He heard muffled chants of "Honky killer!"

Sonny Liston bopped up to the platform. A dumb shit yelled, "Ali kicked your ass!" Sonny flipped him off. It got some laughs. Sonny sucked on a half-pint of Everclear. Buddy and Bob shied away from him. Wayne stepped off the platform.

Sonny said, "Did you kill him?"

Wayne said, "Yes."

Sonny said, "Good. He was a racist motherfucker. *You* a racist motherfucker, but you only kill niggers who deserve it."

That stupe yelled, "Ali kicked your ass!" again. Sonny chucked his jug at him and chased him. The crowd geared up for some fun. A Caddy rag-top inched by. The backseat was packed with showgirls. They smiled, waved and caught themselves—oops, we're supposed to look sad.

Wayne saw Carlos Marcello across the street. They exchanged smiles and waves. Wayne got jostled. The crowd swelled and pushed him into the platform. They looked pissed. Wayne saw why: Dwight Holly was shoving through with his badge out.

Wayne stepped over to a shady spot. It was semi-private. Dwight found him fast.

"Condolences for your father, but I'd have killed him, too, if I were you."

"I appreciate the comment, but I'd like to cut the topic off there."

"We go back, son. You shouldn't mind some ribbing."

"We share a history. You'd call it affectionate, I wouldn't."

Dwight lit a cigarette. "Tell me it's chilled."

"You mean tell Mr. Hoover."

Dwight rolled his eyes. "Don't nitpick me, Wayne. Tell me it's chilled and I'll pass the message along."

"It's chilled, Dwight. Tell me we're chilled on Memphis and we'll call it even."

Dwight stepped in close. "We've got a little seepage there. I'll tell you about it in a second, but you've got to hear the lecture first."

Wayne weaved a tad. A protestor spotted him and did the clenched-fist thing. Dwight pulled him behind the platform.

"You're juiced now. You're in with Uncle Carlos and you may get in with Hughes. I'd be a piss-poor friend if I didn't tell you to be careful."

Wayne stepped in close. " 'Friend'? You fucking coerced me into Memphis."

Dwight stepped closer. He bumped Wayne into a lightpost and pinned him there.

"Wendell Durfee came with a price, son. And don't tell me that you didn't want the job on some level."

Wayne pushed Dwight back. Easy hands, don't rile him. Dwight made nice and brushed off Wayne's coat.

"Give me an update on Carlos. Something to keep the old poof happy."

"It's stale news. The Boys want to sell Hughes the rest of their hotels and keep their skim guys inside. Hughes wants a peaceful town. Someone has to fill Ward Littell's shoes, and it's me."

"Senior was a racist! Junior is a killer!"—Wayne heard faint shouts.

"The envelope for Dick Nixon. Tell me about that."

"How did you—"

"We've got his pad in Key Biscayne bugged. Nixon mentioned it to Bebe Rebozo."

Wind blew bunting off the platform. The Senior/Junior chant grew.

"The Boys want to build some casinos in Central America or the Caribbean, and they want things slowed down at Justice. They'd like a pardon for Jimmy Hoffa by '71. They think Nixon will win the election and be amenable."

Dwight nodded. "I'll buy that, for now."

"The 'seepage'? *Memphis?* You were going to—"

"I'm trying to run down some hate-mail subscribers. I'd like to get a look at your father's lists."

Wayne shook his head. "*No.* I'm out of the hate business. Talk to Fred Hiltz."

"Shit, Wayne. I'm not asking you for the world, I'm just asking for—"

"*Seepage? Memphis?* Come on, don't string me out on that."

Dwight reached for a cigarette. The pack was empty. He threw it into the crowd.

"The St. Louis SAC called me this morning. There's talk coming out of the Grapevine Tavern."

"I don't follow you."

"It's a shitkicker joint. One of Jimmy Ray's brothers owns a piece. I had it bugged. A bullshit rumor was circulating there, and Jimmy bought into it. A fifty-grand bounty on King. Otash lured Ray in off the rumor and worked him behind it."

"Senior/racist, Junior/killer, Senior/rac—"

"Keep going. I didn't work that part of the job."

"Some rednecks found the bug. They figured out that it was FBI-issue, and now there's talk that the hit was Bureau-adjunct."

Wayne prickled. "Talk's talk, Dwight. Rumors are rumors."

"Yeah, but it's a little too close to Jimmy and these crazy stories he's telling."

"Which means?"

"Which means it might or might not go away, and if it doesn't, we'll have to do something about it."

" '*We*' or *you*?"

Dwight grabbed his necktie. "*Us,* son. Wendell Durfee wasn't for free."

The IV drip had run out. The nurse was on the couch, sleeping. Janice fell asleep watching TV.

Wayne checked her pulse. It ran weak-normal. The p.m. news was on, with the sound low. A reporter did the standard King/Bobby number and segued to Nixon and Humphrey.

Upcoming conventions: Miami and Chicago. Two first-ballot nods assured. Potential protests at both convention sites. The Nixon-Humphrey poll status—now a dead heat.

Wayne watched Tricky Dick and Hearty Hubert strut and mug. He had Farlan Brown on tap. The Grapevine news torqued him. "Talk" and "Rumors" might mean witness trouble. Dwight wanted to see Wayne Senior's mail lists. They were stashed in a bunker outside Vegas. Senior always called it his "Hate Hut." A shitload of hate lit was stored there.

Janice stirred and winced. Wayne rigged a fresh IV bag. Nixon and Humphrey talked blahblah. Janice opened her eyes.

Wayne said, "Hi."

Janice pointed to the TV. "They're homely men. If I'm alive, I won't know who to vote for."

Wayne smiled. "You've always erred on the side of looks."

"Yes. Which explains my bad luck with men."

The bag started draining. The juice hit the tube. Wayne flicked the dial and regulated the flow. Janice shuddered. The juice hit her arm and fed her a slight burst of color.

She said, "Buddy Fritsch called today."

"And?"

"And he's scared. He said there've been some rumors."

Wayne turned the TV off. "About that night?"

"Yes."

"And?"

"And Buddy said some neighbors have been talking. They said they saw a man and woman outside the house."

Wayne took her hands. "We're covered. You know who I know, and you know how these things get taken care of."

Janice shook her head and pulled her hands free. She got some strength up. The bed slid. Wayne clamped her arm to keep the needle in.

"I'll be gone soon, but I don't want people to know that we did it."

"Sweetheart . . ."

"We shouldn't have done it. It was hateful and vindictive. It was wrong."

Wayne flicked the dial. The bag puckered and fed the tube. Janice went out in an instant.

He took her pulse. It ran short of weak-normal.

Farlan Brown said, "I was sorry to hear about your father."

"These things happen, sir. He had a bum ticker and indulged bad habits."

" 'Bad habits'? A clean-living Mormon man like that?"

Wayne smiled. "Mormons drink and fuck more than the rest of the world combined, as I'm sure you know from personal experience."

Brown slapped his knees. He was tall and faux-hayseed friendly. His Michael Caine glasses magnified bad eyes. His suite was done up mock-Tudor. The Hughes group had the top six floors of the D.I. The big guy reposed in the penthouse.

Brown said, "You're a hot sketch, sir."

"Just think of me as my father's son. Give me the job, and I'll take it from there."

Brown lit a cigarette. "Tell me why I should give you the job, and convince me in under one minute."

Wayne said, "Collusion." Brown tapped his watch. Wayne shot his cuffs and displayed his gold Rolex. Wayne Senior taught him the trick.

"Howard Hughes is a delusional xenophobe addicted to pharmaceutical narcotics and vitamin-laced blood transfusions. His employees refer to him as 'Dracula.' Mr. Hughes relies upon lucid men like you to mediate the world for him and to facilitate his dealings with the venal politicians and organized-crime figures who run the state of Nevada and, arguably, the whole country. I am Carlos Marcello's liaison to the business community. I am a brilliant chemist who can cook up compounds that will zonk Dracula out of his fucking gourd. I will be Mr. Marcello's bagman to Richard Nixon and hopefully to the Nixon presidential administration. Dracula is bribing Mr. Nixon to the tune of five million dollars, and I will raid my late father's assets to match that amount. I will deliver it, along with Mr. Marcello's fifteen million, to Mr. Nixon personally, at the GOP Convention. I am charged with overseeing the upcoming grand design of Mr. Marcello and his organized-crime cohorts, which is the building of lavish hotel-casinos in a friendly, dictator-run banana republic somewhere south of here, and I will guarantee you that Hughes Airways will have the exclusive rights to fly the suckers in. You should carefully consider me for the job, because you know who I know and what I know, and because you have the utilitarian common sense to know that I will make *you* look good at all junctures."

Brown checked his watch. "Fifty-six seconds. You had the edge with Mr. Hughes going in, and now you've got the edge with me."

"Why did I have the edge with Mr. Hughes?"

"Because you shot some burrhead dope fiends in 1964, and Mr. Hughes thinks you'd be a good man to scare the coloreds out of his hotels."

Wayne said it *soft*. "I'm out of the hate business, sir. Please tell Mr. Hughes that I won't be willing to do that, and please tell him that I'll require an in-person meeting with him before you hire me."

Brown said it *soft.* "Sir, you are drastically impaired at this moment."
Wayne tossed four capsules in his lap and walked out of the room.

Two hours. Three tops.

He went back to his suite and stretched out. He pictured Dracula
twirling around the rings of Saturn and moon-hopping Jupiter. Maybe he's
flying or crashing airplanes. Maybe he's fucking Kate Hepburn on the back
lot at RKO.

The phone rang. Wayne picked up. Brown cut him off at "Hello."

"The job is yours. And Mr. Hughes *will* see you."

5

(Los Angeles, 6/18/68)

"Clyde tells me you like looking for women."

Bam—the Hate King's first words. *Bam*—at the door, no handshake or introduction.

Crutch said, "Yes, sir. That's true."

Dr. Fred Hiltz laughed. "He said, 'Looking *at* women,' but I won't press the point."

The Hiltz hate hacienda—a big Spanish manse. Beverly Hills, prime footage, Jew neighbors galore. A jumbo sunken living room festooned with hate art.

Fine oils. The masters reconsidered. A van Gogh lynching. A Rembrandt gas-chamber tableaux. Matisse does Congolese atrocities. Paul Klee does Martin Luther King charbroiled.

Crutch scoped the walls. Man Ray did Bobby Kennedy dead on a slab. Picasso did Lady Bird Johnson muff-diving Anne Frank.

Fuck—

Crutch fought off a dizzy spell. Hiltz said, "I met a cooze at Lawry's Prime Rib. Her name was Gretchen Farr. She shot me some trim and got me addicted. She stole fourteen grand from the bomb shelter in my backyard. You find her, you get me back my money."

Devil-horned kikes by Frederick Remington. Grant Wood does LBJ drawn and quartered.

"Description? Last known address? A photograph, if you've got one."

Hiltz fast-walked Crutch out back. The bum's rush: *Raus! Mach schnell!* They cut down long corridors. They dodged cats and cat boxes. JFK morgue pix were taped to the walls.

The yard featured a statue garden. A wetback hosed down a life-size Klan-klad Christ. Hiltz said, "I've got no pictures. Gretchen was photo-phobic. She's a tall, stacked cooze with a slight Latin tinge. She was stay-ing at the Beverly Hills Hotel, so I made her as kosher. I put Phil Irwin on her, but he went on a bender and blew me off. I tried to hire Freddy Otash, but he's not taking skip jobs these days."

The wetback hose-spritzed Hitler and Hermann Goering. Bird shit and dirt decomposed.

"What else can you tell me about her?"

"*You're not listening.* I know *buppkes.* I lead with my *schvantz* and it cost me fourteen big ones. *Get it? I'm* hiring *you,* because *you* know how to find people, and *I* don't."

A cat scaled Mussolini and sat poised for birds. Hiltz quick-marched Crutch over to some underground steps and shoved him down them. They hit a steel-reinforced door. Hiltz unlocked it and tapped a light switch. Fluorescent bulbs lit a twelve-by-twelve hate hive.

Hate-tract wallpaper. Hate-niggers, hate-Jews, hate-Papists, hate-Japs, hate-Chinks, hate-spics, hate-Commies, hate-the-muthafuckin' white oppressor. Hate placards stacked on the floor. Boxes full of Nazi arm-bands. Hate voodoo-doll pincushions: Jackie Kennedy Onassis, Pope Paul, Martin Luther Coon.

Hiltz grabbed a placard. A giant buck slave stabbed a cowering Jew merchant. The buck had a mammoth crotch bulge. The hebe had clawed feet and a rat tail. The banner read GENOCIDE IS THE SACRED MANDATE OF ALLAH!!!!!

"The *schvartzes* eat this shit up. You wouldn't believe the market all this black-militant *tsuris* has created. I've got a whole sideline going. It's *shvoogie* prison tracts, allegedly written by these radical shines in San Quentin. You know who really writes them? This kike nigger-lover guy I play golf with."

Crutch sneezed. The hate hive reeked of mildew and cat piss. That dizzy spell revived.

"Gretchen Farr. Tell me what you talked about. Tell me what she told you about herself. Tell me—"

"We didn't talk, we *shtupped.* We went *soixante-neuf* and did the beast with two backs. We did not waste appreciable time with discussion."

"Sir, can you give me *anything* I can—"

Hiltz pulled the lid off a king-size clothes hamper. The inside was crammed full of C-notes. The tally had to veer toward a half mil.

"Here's the enduring mystery, *schmendrick.* She only nailed me for fourteen G's. I know, because I count my gelt every night. You want my opinion? Gretchen was subtle. The cunt ganef nailed me for what she thought I wouldn't miss."

Crutch looked in the hamper. Hiltz grabbed a bill and stuffed it in his shirt pocket.

"Lunch is on me. Find her, and I'll get you a threesky with Brigitte Bardot and Julie Christie. Believe me, I've got that kind of clout."

Schvartzes, schvantz, shvoogies, the beast with two backs. A potential threesky. A time-clock gig for Clyde Duber Associates.

Crutch drove to the lot and braced Phil Irwin. Phil was huddled up with Chick Weiss, per some divorce job. Crutch took him aside and asked the standard skip-job questions. Phil was blurry on Gretchen Farr. No shit—Phil was blurry after 10:00 a.m. daily. Yeah, Dr. Fred hired him. Yeah, he called LAPD and Sheriff's R&I and learned that the Farr snatch had no rap sheet. He chatted up the desk guy at the Beverly Hills Hotel. The desk guy refused to check his guest file. He went on a bender in T.J. then. He took a Rotary group down to catch the mule show. Dr. Fred fired him.

Crutch asked the *big* question: Is Dr. Fred a Yid? Phil said, "No, but all his ex-wives are Jewish."

Scratch Phil. Next stop: the Beverly Hills Hotel.

Crutch drove there and got situated. He whipped his fake cop's badge on a fruit bellhop and made a sound impression. The fruit bellhop fetched the fruit desk guy. The fruit desk guy looked askance at Crutch's low-rent attire. Crutch told him he worked for Clyde Duber. The fruit desk guy dug on that. Clyde had panache and je ne sais quois. Okay, kid, let's talk.

Crutch asked the standard skip-job questions. The fruit desk guy responded. He called Gretch Farr "dicey." She rented bungalow #21 for three weeks. He wondered where she glommed the bread. She tricked with wealthy European and Latin guests of both genders. She paid cash for her flop and extra charges every morning. Gretch supplied one check-in referral: a phone drop called "Bev's Switchboard." It was a message pickup service for the fly-by-night crowd. Gretch was a quintessential fly-by-night chick.

That was it. The fruit desk guy sashayed off to fawn on some dowagers with poodles. Crutch hit the phone bank and called information. Bev's Switchboard: 8814 Fountain, West Hollywood.

He drove there and got situated. The address was a storefront adjoining a quick-script pharmacy. All the wheelmen copped uppers there.

He parked. He combed his hair. He pinned his bogus badge to his coat front and chewed some Clorets. He practiced winking à la Scotty Bennett. Memo: buy some tartan bow ties.

He walked in. An old girl was working a for-real switchboard. The place was claustrophobic—twelve by fourteen tops. Crutch caught a whiff of bug spray.

The old girl noticed him. He made her belatedly. Blow-job Bev Shoftel. An L.A. legend. She dispensed snout to all the big stars back in the '30s.

She said, "The badge is a fake. I eat my Rice Krispies every morning, so I know from giveaways."

Crutch said, "I'm a private investigator. I work for Clyde Duber."

Bev unhooked her headset and fluffed out her hair. Dandruff flakes flew.

"I blew Clyde Duber before you were born. I blew Buzz Duber on his twelfth birthday, so don't think you're intimidating me."

Crutch winked. His eyelid twitched and spasmed. Blow-job Bev whooped.

"The answer is no. Whatever you want, that's what you're getting."

"Gretchen Farr. I heard she's dicey, and I need a little peek at her caller file."

Bev said, "*Nyet.* And don't even think of asking for a header, 'cause I'm sixty-three years old and out of the biz."

"I could help you, babe. Believe me, I've got that kind of clout."

Bev whooped anew. "The comedy hour's over, *babe.* But you made me grin, so I'll shoot you a freebie. I overheard Gretchie speaking Spanish on the phone."

A call hit the switchboard. Bev popped on her headseat. Crutch said, "Please." Bev said, "Scram."

Blow jobs. Blow-job Bev blows Buzz and Clyde. Buzz coerces blow jobs now. Scotty's blow-job thieves.

It was too much. Crutch churned with it. He couldn't situate himself.

He hit the quick-script pharmacy and scored some Dexedrine. He popped four with coffee, de-churned and re-churned. He drove to his pad and skimmed a few *Playboy*s. He bopped up to the roof and eyeballed a girl sunbathing. The dexies coaxed memories. There's Dana Lund poolside, in a strapless one-piece. There's Dana playing chaperone at a prep school bash.

Dana. Gretchen Farr. Hotel assignations. Gretchen swings with men *and* women.

Crutch got that *oooooold* feeling and grabbed his *oooooold* tools.

The pharmacy was closed. Ditto Bev's Switchboard. A walkway led back to a rear parking lot. Clouds absorbed moonlight. The side door looked weak.

Crutch stuck a #4 pick in the keyhole. Two jiggles eased the main tumblers back. He pushed a #6 in. He twisted in unison. The lock button slid. The door snapped.

He let himself in and shut the door behind him. Bug-spray fumes made him sneeze. He got out his penlight and adjusted the beam to shine narrow. He saw a file cabinet up against the switchboard-outlet plugs.

Three drawers set on sliding runners. Marked: "A to G," "H to P," "Q to Z." He pulled the handles. All three were locked.

He zeroed in on the "A to G" lock. He punched a #5 pick in back to the drill point. One push and *pop*—

"A to G." Aaronson, Adams, Allworth. Some *B*'s, *C*'s and *D*'s. Echert, Ehrlich, Falmouth. There, Gretchen Farr.

Crutch held the penlight in his teeth and grabbed the folder two-handed. It was skinny. It held one page. He quick-skimmed it. The call log went back three weeks, to late May '68.

No address notes or personal stats on Gretch Farr herself. Just incoming calls listed.

Avco Jewelers, Santa Monica—four calls total. Six calls from foreign consulates: Panama, Nicaragua, the Dominican Republic. Huh? *Whazzat?*—this wild brew so far.

Three men first name–listed: "Lew," "Al," "Chuck." A bunch of call-me-back calls to Gretchen—L.A.-prefix numbers all.

Du-32758/"Wouldn't give name." Sal/No-52808. *He* knew that name and number: Clyde's actor pal.

Crutch got out his notepad and copied it all down. He got B&E sweaty. Bug-spray fumes tickled his nose. The fucking penlight hurt his teeth.

The Klondike Bar, 8th and La Brea. A Greek grail and a lavender lodestone for the limp-wristed set.

Crutch called Buzz from the outside pay phone. The sidewalk was a big K-Y cowboy cattle call. Crutch ran Du-32758 by Buzz and told him to check the reverse book. Buzz shagged the book, skimmed it and told Crutch "No sale." Crutch told him to call P.C. Bell and request a bootleg-number trace.

The sidewalk action got too gamy. Crutch sat in his car and scoped the door. Sal's Lincoln was back in the parking lot. Sal *lived* at the Klondike. He'd walk out sooner or later, with or sans the night's quiff.

Sal Mineo. Paid informant for Clyde and Fred Otash. Two Oscar nominations and Skidsville. One trouble-prone fruit fly.

Crutch got re-situated. The dexies had him head-tripping. The Toho Theatre was just south. Hip couples were lined up for a doofus art flick.

The girls had that long, straight hair. Every little head movement sent sparks aloft.

Someone drummed on his windshield. Crutch saw Sal Mineo—all spit-curled and tight-jeaned. He popped the door. Sal got in. He wore this look of wop-fruit enchantment.

Crutch pulled around the corner and re-parked. Sal said, "You could have come inside. You didn't have to lurk all night."

"I wasn't lurking."

"You always lurk."

"Shit, man. I was *waiting.*"

"You were *lurking.*"

Crutch laughed. "Okay, I was lurking."

Sal laughed. "Clyde wants something, right? You'd be lurking outside some chick's window if you were on your own dime."

Crutch gripped the wheel white-knuckled. Sal raised his hands—hey, no harm meant.

"Okay, I'll start over. What can I help you and Clyde out with?"

"Gretchen Farr. She took one of Clyde's clients for some money, and I know you know her."

Sal lit a cigarette. "Sure, I know her. I know that she fucks strings of men and rabbits with their money routinely, but I don't know how you traced her to me. If you explain that to me convincingly, I'll tell you what you need to know."

That pout, that greasy dago hair—Crutch balled his fists.

"I ran a phone check. You called her service two weeks ago."

Sal cracked the window and de-smoked the car. Sal tucked up his knees and went doe-eyed.

"I'd say Gretchen Farr is an alias. Don't ask me how I know, I just do. I don't have a line on her whereabouts, because she never tells people where she lives. As I said, she fucks strings of men, steals or borrows coin from them and disappears. I called her service because she called my service. We didn't actually speak. I've steered her to men before, but she usually develops her own prospects. She's *veeeery* careful, our Gretch. She always makes sure that her fuckees don't truck in the same circles."

Fuck gigs, fuck strings, fuckees—

"Photographs?"

Sal shook his head. "No. The most camera-shy girl this girl ever met."

"The 'fuckees.' Give me some names."

"*No.* I am *truly* drawing a blank, and Gretch *paid me* to steer her, and I promised I wouldn't tell on her, cross-my-heart, hope-to-die."

Crutch slapped the wheel. Crutch slapped the dashboard. Sal made with the doe eyes and never flinched.

"Feel better, sweetheart?"

Crutch flexed his hands. His fingers and palms stung. Sal twirled his spit curl and sighed.

Crutch said, "Why do you think Gretchen Farr is an alias?"

"She's too spic-looking to be a Farr. She's a Spanglo type if she's anything."

"And she doesn't *live* in L.A.?"

"No, she just passes through, causes travail and moves on."

"Known associates? Do you know *anyone* who knows her?"

Sal doe-eyed him. "You sound resigned, so I'll give you a nibble. I set Gretchie up with a realtor named Arnie Moffett, who is a *horrible* man who used to pimp for Howard Hughes. He bought a string of Hughes's old fuck-pad houses in the Hollywood Hills, so maybe Gretchie is staying in one of them."

Crutch cracked his knuckles. His head hurt. He couldn't get situated. His thoughts jumbled and veered.

Sal said, "I'm waiting for the day, sweetheart."

"What day?"

"The day that you figure out you're not at all tough."

Those caller-log names: "Al," "Lew" and "Chuck." They might be Gretchen fuckees. They might re-situate him. They might seed brainstorms.

Crutch de-torqued the dexies with red devils and Old Crow. He slept and called the three guys in the a.m. He dropped Gretchen's name. He spooked them. He set up meets at the Carolina Pines—three fuckee prospects one hour apart. He hit the Pines early and hogged a back booth. He scarfed pancakes and coffee and re-cleared his head.

Al showed on time. He was pissed. Shitbird, I'm married. You lured me here to grill me on some illicit snatch I promoted. Crutch badgered Al. Al revealed this:

He met Gretch at Trader Vic's. They had some nooners at his place and her place. She had a crib in Beachwood Canyon. Don't ask me where, I always went there half in the bag.

Gretchie said she had resources. She mentioned import-export gigs. She hit him up for five G's. He considered the request. He almost bounced. Something deterred him.

She emitted this stealth vibe. He snuck a look at her purse. He saw four different passports. He declined to front her the bread.

Passports for what countries? Jesus, I don't know. Known associates? People she talked about? Kid, we just *fucked.*

Crutch pledged silence and told Al to split. Al split. Lew showed up. He was pissed. Dickhead, I'm married. You lured me here to grill me on some illicit snatch I promoted. Crutch badgered Lew. Lew revealed this:

He met Gretchen at Stat's Char-Broil. They got a thing going. He drilled her at the Miramar Hotel and at some pad up by Beachwood Canyon. She tapped him for five grand. She splitsvilled. He tried to find the canyon pad. He failed. He was blotto every time he was there. He couldn't find the goddamn place.

Known associates? Passports? Topics of talk? Kid, you're not getting me—we hardly yakked.

Crutch pledged silence and told Lew to split. Lew split. Chuck showed up. He was pissed. Dipshit, I'm married. You lured me here to grill me on some illicit snatch I promoted. Crutch badgered Chuck. Chuck revealed this:

He met Gretchie at the Westward Ho Steak House. He boned her at a house a mile east of Beachwood Canyon. It was a rental deal. Price tags were still stuck to the furniture—I should have known.

He lent Gretchie five G's. She absconded on him. He called that Bev's Switchboard place and tried to find her. Old Bev was a sphinx. She rebuffed him. He got a gift in the mail the next day.

A Polaroid pic: Chuck and Gretchie Farr fucking. Chuck got the point: desist or your frau receives *this*.

Chuck desisted. Chuck knew goose egg about passports and known associates. What did you talk about? Kid, we just *screwed*.

Crutch pledged silence. Chuck split. Crutch bugged his waitress for a pencil and paper. She brought them. Crutch drew and re-drew Gretchen Farr.

The fuckees gave him slightly different descriptions. An Anglo with spic blood? Sure, maybe, maybe not. Bev heard her talk Spanish. She got calls from three consulates: Panama, Nicaragua, the Dominican Republic. Latin countries. Spicfest '68. She's wild, she's dark-haired, she's pale working on dark—go, pencil, go.

He drew Gretchie six ways. He gave her different hairstyles and made her smile and frown. He felt some wild spirit guiding him. His pencil broke. He got choked up and fucked-up when he saw where it all went.

He drew Gretchen Farr as Dana Lund, six times over. Gretchie was Dana writ dark.

Avco Jewelers was out at the beach. The window display featured highline watches laid out on velvet blocks. Crutch perched under a striped awning. He was amped up. He was running on greasy pancakes and dope residue.

He walked in. A fussbudget type stood behind the counter, messing with some pearls. He sized Crutch up. Navy blazer and gray slacks—okay, you'll do.

"Sir?"

"I had a few questions, if you'd be so kind."

"Certainly. Is there a piece you had in mind?"

"Piece" hit him weird. "Gretchen Farr"—he just blurted it.

The fussbudget fussed with his pearls. "And this pertains to?"

"It's an inquiry."

"I gathered that, but you seem too young to be a police detective."

"I'm a private investigator."

"Dubious, but I'll give you the benefit of the doubt."

Crutch got heat-prickly. "Look, someone called her answering service from your number. I'm just trying to—"

The door chime rang. An old lady waltzed in, swaddling a Chihuahua. She vibed hot-prospect-hot-for-some-pearls.

The fussbudget whispered. "Miss Farr came in two weeks or so ago, while I was out. She left a message for me to call her, which I did. We exchanged phone calls. She wanted advice on the recutting of a number of valuable emeralds she had in her possession. I asked about the provenance of the stones. She had no answer ready for me, which I found odd."

The old lady de-swaddled the Chihuahua. The cocksucker hit the ground yapping. The fussbudget stepped around the corner and swooned.

Buzz dubbed the Hiltz job "the case." Crutch dubbed it "*my* case" in his head. Dr. Fred had the bread to wind up Clyde's time clock. *Cherchez la femme*—the Hate King had the big bone for Gretchie. Buzz called P.C. Bell and bribed a drone to trace that bootleg number. So far, no make. Buzz tapped Clyde's cop contacts for dope on *la belle* Farr. So far, no make. Arnie Moffett was their one lead outstanding. Buzz called it "hot." Crutch called it "a scorcher."

They stood on the roof at the Vivian and hashed it all out. It was twilight. It was hot. A late sun fuzzed the sky moss green. Buzz smoked a joint and talked a blue streak, all cars and cooze. Crutch messed with his telescope.

He caught an extra call at Paramount—slick dance-hall girls. He caught Lonnie Ecklund working on a '53 Merc. He saw some drunks weaving out of the Nickodell. He saw Sandy Danner sneaking a cigarette on her mom's back porch. Lonnie/Sandy/Buzz/ Crutch—Hollywood High, '62.

Dana Lund was out of range. Crutch swiveled the telescope west. He caught Barb Cathcart grilling hot dogs. She wore a tie-dyed top and a peace medallion. Her freckly cleavage showed. Barb sang with a group called The Loveseekers. They lost every Battle of the Bands that they played. Barb beaver-flashed him at Le Conte Junior High, spring '58. His world de-centralized then. Barb's brother Bobby was a call boy. He allegedly possessed a fourteen-inch dick.

Emeralds, fuck pads, fuck lists, fuck logs, fuckees—

Buzz said, "You're a bigger freak than I am."

Crutch said, "Let's lean on Arnie."

Speedballs supplied oomph. Four dexies, two reds and firm jolts of Jim Beam. They *levitated* to the Miracle Mile. Crutch felt his eye sockets expand.

Moffett Realty was a hole-in-the-wall. It was right beside Ma Gordon's Deli, the "Home of the Hebrew Hero." The door was open. The lights were on. A skinny guy was kicked back at the one desk. He wore a red bowling shirt with a stitched-on ARNIE.

He was embroiled. He was staring into a swivel mirror, squeezing his blackheads. Crutch cleared his throat. Buzz cleared his throat. Arnie stayed transfixed.

Buzz said, "Uh, sir?" Crutch shushed him. Arnie said, "Frat boys, right? You want to rent one of my dumps for a kegger and lure in some gash."

The room de-situated. Funny lights swirled. Crutch said, "We're private detectives."

Arnie stood up. Arnie grabbed his crotch and said, "Detect this."

Crutch saw *RED. RED* room, *RED* room lights, *RED* world. He kicked Arnie in the balls. He jackknifed him. He rabbit-punched him. He threw him on the floor face-first. Arnie's nose cracked. Blood spattered. Arnie flopped and flailed for his desk phone. Crutch pulled the cord out of the wall and threw the fucking phone across the room.

Buzz trembled. His lips did funny things. Crutch saw the piss stain on his jeans and smelled the shit in his shorts.

Arnie flailed. Blood pooled off his nosedive. Crutch put a foot on his neck and de-flailed him. Crutch said, "Gretchen Farr."

Arnie gurgled. Buzz ran for the john, making like upchuck. Crutch threw down a handkerchief. Arnie rolled on his back, covered his nose and stanched the blood flow. Crutch pulled out his short dog. Arnie made a gimme sign and tilted his head. Crutch fed him little pops. Jim Beam,100 proof.

Arnie sucked, gasped and coughed. Arnie dredged up savoir faire. Arnie said, "You evil little shit."

Crutch squatted. He kept himself clear of the blood mess. He was all re-circuited while the room leaped and whirled.

"Gretchen Farr."

"She's a Commie. She's some kind of left-wing transient with more names than half the world."

"Keep going."

"She heard I used to score snatch for Howard Hughes."

Crutch said, "Keep going." Arnie made the gimme sign. Crutch fed him three pops. Arnie sucked down blood-laced bourbon and took a big breath.

"She rented one of my pads. The Hollywood Hills, a half-ass little house. Two-week rental, in and out."

"Keep going."

"They're skeeve pads. Fuck-film sets, keg-bust spots, short-term rentals."

"Keep going, Arnie. The quicker you tell me, the quicker I'm gone."

Blood soaked through the handkerchief. Arnie tossed it and wiped the excess spill on his pants. Buzz walked up, zipping his fly. He looked psychedelicized green.

Crutch said, "Give, Arnie."

"Give *what*? She's a Commie with some fucked-up agenda."

"Arnie . . ."

"Okay, okay. She pumped me for dope on the Howard Hughes organization. She said she wanted to get next to a guy named Farlan Brown. I said I knew him. He's this cunt man who plays Mormon to stay kosher with Hughes. When he passes through L.A., he always hits Dale's Secret Harbor."

TILT: Hughes, Gretchie, emeralds and that million-dollar—

"Dupe keys, Arnie. For the house Gretchen rented and all your other dives."

Arnie nodded and stood up. Crutch steadied him. Arnie weaved for a full minute. Crutch dug his legs in and steadied himself. His Red World veered and swerved.

Buzz split to change clothes and hit Dale's Secret Harbor. Crutch stayed swervy. He got the notion to re-brace Phil Irwin and run a driver's license check. He stopped at a pay phone and called the DMV police line. He dropped Clyde Duber's name and Gretchie's approximate stats. Zero— just one eighty-two-year-old Gretchen Farr, up in Visalia. He called Dale's Secret Harbor and paged Buzz. Buzz reported: Yeah, he asked around. He learned that Farlan Brown *was* a Hughes biggie. Hughes Airways was his main gig.

It was late. Crutch drove by the lot. Phil's 409 was gone. Crutch got re-situated. His swerve was mutating to bad nerves and yawns. He tried Canter's Deli, Linny's Deli and Art's Deli—Phil always late-nite noshed with Jew lawyer Chick Weiss.

Three stops, no Phil. He drove to Tommy Tucker's Playroom, Washington and La Brea. Phil was a mud shark. He craved colored trim. The Playroom fronted a coon whorehouse. Phil might be there.

Yeah, he was. There's his car by the back door. It's parked. It's rocking. There's his white ass exposed in the backseat. There's some fat dark legs spread wide.

It went on and on. Crutch parked and looked away. Phil and the spade chick supplied an "Oh, Baby" soundtrack. Crutch covered his ears at the crescendo. The spade chick climbed out of the car. She wore an Afro do and ran 220. She ambled back to the Playroom. Phil *fell* out of the car. He got up and homed in on Crutch's GTO. Hey, I know that sled.

Crutch got out and stretched. Phil teetered up. His Dodger sweatsuit was all disheveled.

"Have you been tailing me?"

"Well, looking for you."

"At 1:00 fucking a.m.?"

"Come on. Guys like us don't keep regular hours."

Phil lit a cigarette. It took four match swipes. He reeked of the spade chick's perfume.

"We've got a job, right? We've got some work, and you went looking for me."

Crutch shook his head. "No, it's just a re-interview. I wanted you to run the Gretchen Farr gig by me again."

Phil blew a weird-shaped smoke ring. "Okay, twenty bucks."

"Twenty bucks?"

"Right. I keestered Dr. Fred on the job, and I'll spill the straight dope for twenty."

Crutch pulled out his roll and forked over two tens. Phil flicked his cigarette at a '64 Olds. It smudged the nigger pink paint job.

"Okay, so I filed a couple of 'no lead' reports with Dr. Fred, chiefly because I didn't feel like chasing this fly-by-night Gretchen twist all over hell-and-gone and because I got bought off the job."

"By who? Who paid you?"

"It was a cash deal. Anonymous. A messenger service sent me the bread, and I ran a trace on the sender. Dig, it was the Hughes Tool Company. I thought, Jesus, *that's* interesting, then I lost interest myself and went on that bender."

Hughes again. Hughes man Farlan Brown. The Red World re-swerved.

Phil yawned. "That whole shot of time is fuzzy for me, but I've got this idea that I actually *saw* Gretchen Farr, somewhere up in the Hollywood Hills. She was with this older chick with a knife scar on her right arm. I'm also seeing a '66 Comet, maybe white . . . partial plate ADF2 . . . Fuck, what do I know? I was stinko."

The Hollywood DMV ran a records desk twenty-four hours. Cops could scoot by and do file checks at whim. Crutch dropped twenty clams and Clyde Duber's name on the night clerk. The guy let him into the file room.

He had the year and model, plus *partial*-plate stats. That meant no quickie ID. Phil was a dipso. His memory was suspect. The Comet might be non-California registered. The registration cards were stuffed in large boxes. They were marked by county of origin and filed by the registree's name. Start at L.A. County, *F* for Farr, *go*.

Crutch hauled boxes down and finger-walked through them. No Gretchen Farr/'66 Comet in L.A. County—let's go on from there.

He worked. He pulled cards all night. He went county-to-county. He started at *F* for Farr and worked backward and forward. Gretch probably employed false names. Farr could be name sixteen or name forty-two. Dope dregs drizzled out of his system. He felt like one big ache and yawn. Cobwebs stuck to his hands. Mildew clogged up his head.

He saw dawn out the window. He got to Kern County. No *F*-for-Farr listing, let's go to *G* and *H*. He hit a run of Hertz rent-a-cars, dispersed to offices statewide. He hit *paydirt.*

White '66 Comet, ADF-212. Registered out of Kern County and sent to L.A. County. Rented out of the Sunset-and-Vermont office.

Crutch pulled the card and ran outside to a pay phone. He called the Hertz number. He ID'd himself as Sergeant Robert S. Bennett, LAPD. The Hertz geek bought it. Scotty/Crutch laid out a spiel on the '66 Comet and Gretchen Farr—"What can you give me on that?"

The geek shuffled papers. The geek nixed Gretchen Farr—no surprise. Scotty/Crutch said, "Who's had the car lately and who's got the car now?" The geek said the Comet was due back at 10:00 tonight. Two-week rental. The rentee: a woman named Celia Reyes. Local address: the Beverly Hills Hotel. Driver's license from the Dominican Republic, the Caribbean hot spot, the Swingin' D.R.

Crutch parked outside the Hate Hacienda. Shrieky opera blasted from the backyard. He walked down the driveway. The gate was unlocked. Birds nested on the dictator statues. The music blared out the bomb-shelter door.

He walked over and popped down the steps. He made noise on purpose. Dr. Fred was at a draftsman's desk, drawing a cartoon. Dig that crazy jigaboo with the watermelon head.

Dr. Fred wore a Klan robe and sandals. A Luger on a gun belt bunched up his sheet. The music was earsplitting loud.

He saw Crutch. He hit a desk switch and killed an aria mid-shriek. He quick-drew the Luger and did some gunslinger shtick.

"You've got brown eyes. Are you Jewish?"

"You've got brown eyes, too."

"Yes, but I *know* I'm not Jewish."

Crutch rubbed his ears—the shriek reverb lingered. Dr. Fred said, "You've got blood on your pants."

"It was on your time card, sir."

"You're dying to tell me something. You want my opinion? I think you smell money."

The *shelter* smelled: must, mildew, money for sure.

"Gretchen, Arnie Moffett and Farlan Brown. Tell me what you haven't told me."

"Why should I do that, *schmendrick*? You know what *schmendrick* means? It's a synonym for *schlemiel.*"

"I'm trying to help you, sir. I'm just—"

"—a kid adventurer who fell into some shit with Clyde Duber. And now you've fallen into some shit with me. Clyde's paying you six dollars an hour, but I'm going to split a full million with you."

A squirrel sat on the steps. Dr. Fred aimed the Luger and plugged it. The shot sonic-boomed the shelter. The squirrel vaporized. Dr. Fred snagged the ejected shell in mid-twirl.

"I knew Gretchen was working me, but I didn't think she'd steal from me. A snatch is a snatch, but a ganef's a ganef."

Crutch rubbed his ears. "There's more to it than that."

"Why do you say that? You're a *schmendrick*. You're Phil Irwin minus the snootful of juice."

"Don't shit a shitter, sir. I'm putting some names together, and they're all going one place."

Dr. Fred said, "Dracula." Crutch went *huh*? Sonic-boom remnants banged his eardrums.

Dr. Fred re-holstered. "So, I got suspicious of Gretchie. So, I rifled her purse and found Arnie Moffett's number. So, I called Arnie. So, Arnie was pliable. So, I paid him for the scoop on Gretchie. So, he told me that

Gretchie was trying to get next to a Howard Hughes *macher* named Farlan Brown."

Crutch said, "So?" A last boom-warble faded.

"So, *I* wanted to get next to Hughes. We've got the same racial sensibility, and I've got a purification plan he can bankroll. I had a rival named Wayne Tedrow Senior. Between the two of us, we had the hate-tract biz dicked. He just died, and his numbnuts kid Wayne Junior may be Dracula's new point man. I want to get my hands on Senior's hate-mail stash and get next to Dracula, and I'm thinking this Mormon hump Farlan Brown is the key. I'm too controversial to make the approach, but a kid loser like you could breeze in innocuous. *Life* magazine is offering a million bucks for a snapshot of Hughes, and a kid opportunist like you could get close."

Tilt, swerve, veer and blood on his pants—Crutch said, "Yessir."

Another hotel suite. Another bum room-service meal.

Mr. Hoover told him to stay perched in Vegas. The Wayne Senior snuff vexed him. He wanted Wayne Junior mollified and assessed. Thus the bullshit layover. Thus the time at LVPD. Thus the limp salad and gristly steak.

Dwight pushed his plate away. Food taxed him. It slowed him down and sapped the jolt he got off nicotine and coffee. The Chicago guys owned the Stardust. The FBI was allegedly anti-mob. They kept a vouchered suite there anyway. Mr. Hoover had no beef with organized crime. That was strictly Bobby K.'s bête noire and downfall. Mr. Hoover hated Commies, jigs and lefty gadflies. Mr. Hoover probably *loved* limp salads and gristly steaks.

The fucking Stardust. Four thousand slot machines and velvet-flocked suites. The Chicago guys were hot to dump the joint on Howard Hughes. Count Dracula was hot to buy it. The guys would skim the Count blind.

And Wayne Tedrow *Junior* is facilitating it. Wayne's fucking his dying stepmom. They killed Wayne *Senior*. Dwight and Senior went *waaaaay* back. Dwight grooved Junior as a *wiiiiild* piece of work. Now he's out to get Junior a skate on Murder One.

Cluster fuck.

It was 114° outside. The wall vents spritzed ice. Dwight got that hotel-captive feeling and paced the suite.

Shit kept crisscrossing. Buddy Fritsch was *too* nervous. The Vegas SAC said Junior-killed-Senior rumors were fouling the desert air. Mr. Hoover was losing it. Mr. Hoover still *had* it to some degree. Sirhan Sirhan was foaming at the mouth in L.A. Jimmy Ray was foaming and fighting extradition. The Grapevine Tavern issue was percolating. He saw an ATF teletype this morning. Mr. Hoover telexed it in a tizzy. ATF might put the Grapevine under surveillance. Cracker habitués were moving dope and guns. Interagency grief. The Grapevine bug backfired and inspired conspiracy talk. Most conspiracy talk was dismissible. This might not be. It might require interdiction. Interdiction would *not* work with ATF hovering.

Proximity. Jimmy Ray's loose talk. Loose talk at the Grapevine. *Valid* loose talk—Jimmy Ray's brother owned a piece of the place.

Cluster fuck.

His nerves were frayed. His sleep was thin. Memphis spiked through at 3:00 a.m. nightly. Car noise sounded like gunshots. Little bed aches felt like someone hitting him.

Dwight walked to the bedroom window. Hotel suites made him miss Karen. Hotel suites got him torqued for real bedrooms. He'd black-bagged Karen's house a half dozen times. He wanted to stand still there with her absent. He wanted instinctive evidence that she had no other lovers. He found the quiet he was looking for and got his evidence confirmed. She tapped his D.C. suite once. He found some entry signs, rolled for prints and got two Karen Sifakis latents. She saw his anonymous check-writing kit. She read through his journal. He wrote "I fucking love her" just two days before.

They've told each other "I've prowled you" obliquely. He's read her journal. She probably hides the pages she doesn't want him to see. She's pestered him about the checks. He might tell her one day.

Dwight poured his one drink a night early. Twilight came and went. The dark sky pulsed and clashed with all the Vegas neon.

January '57. Icy roads on the Merritt Parkway. He was working the New York City office. He was driving a Bureau car, blitzed. He was en route to a Cape Cod weekend with his girlfriend. He plowed a divider and hit an oncoming car. He killed the two teenaged daughters of Mr. and Mrs. George Diskant.

He suffered minor injuries. Mr. Hoover chilled all inquiries with the Connecticut State Police. He checked into a sanitarium near New Caanan. He segued from sobbing fits to long stints of silence. He stayed at Silver Hill for one month and four days. He got his nerves back and returned to work. He stayed away from women until Karen.

Dwight sipped his one drink slowly. The sky show started chafing him. He got out his black-militant file and read through it.

The second read confirmed the first. The Panthers and US—too known and too infiltrated. The Black Tribe Alliance and Mau-Mau Liberation Front—obscure, with big exposure potential.

Karen could find him an informant. He or she could be white or Negro. He or she could rat out both groups politically. The infiltrator had to be a male Negro. He could rat out all criminal actions justified politically.

Maybe a cop. Maybe an ex-cop. Maybe a cop or ex-cop with a dicey past. Again, that notion: check hate-mail subscriber lists.

Wayne Junior had access to Wayne Senior's lists. Wayne Junior said he was out of the hate biz. Dr. Fred Hiltz was a Bureau informant. He was tight with that L.A. private eye Clyde Duber. Clyde was tight with the L.A. SAC.

A doorbell rang down the hallway. Dwight jumped out of his skin.

7

(Las Vegas, 6/20/68)

The Count chased pills with a red drink concoction. It looked like fruit juice and blood. He wore surgical scrubs and Kleenex-box shoes. His hair was long. His nails were claws. He wore a wool watch cap and a card dealer's shade.

Wayne made eye contact. It was rough. Farlan Brown made eye contact. He had more practice. He emceed the interview.

The Desert Inn penthouse. Chez Dracula. A hospital room with big wall-to-wall TV sets. Three screens of news chat. Martyred legends. Accused assassins. Nixon versus Humphrey and flashed-on poll stats.

The sound murmured low. Wayne tuned it out. His chair abutted Drac's bed. He smelled industrial-strength disinfectant.

Brown said, "Mr. Tedrow knows you have questions."

Drac slipped on a surgical mask. His voice eked through.

"Sir, do you believe that a lone gunman shot President John F. Kennedy?"

"Yes, sir. I do."

"Do you believe that a lone gunman shot Senator Robert F. Kennedy?"

"Yes, sir. I do."

"Do you believe that a lone gunman shot the Reverend Martin Luther King?"

"Yes, sir. I do."

Dracula sighed. "He's a realist, Farlan. He's a stout Mormon, and he's not prone to whimsy."

Brown folded his hands prayerlike. "You picked wisely, sir. Wayne has all the right skills and knows all the right people."

Drac coughed. His mask puffed. Phlegm dripped down his chin.

"You know our Italian friends. Is that true?"

"It is, sir. I know Mr. Marcello and Mr. Giancana quite well."

"They've sold me some wonderful hotel-casinos, and I intend to purchase several more."

"They'll be happy to sell them to you, sir. They welcome your presence in Las Vegas."

"Las Vegas is a breeding ground for Negro bacteria. Negroes have high white-cell counts. You should never shake hands with them. They emit pus particles through their fingertips."

Wayne deadpanned it. Seconds crawled. Brown smiled and stepped in.

"Wayne is matching your contribution to Mr. Nixon, sir."

Drac nodded. "Slippery Dick. I lent his brother some money in '56. It came back and bit Dick on the ass. It might have thrown the election to Jack Kennedy."

Wayne said, "I'll deliver the envelope at the convention. Mr. Marcello wants to be sure he has the nomination cinched."

Brown smiled. "I'm a delegate. Miami in August, my Lord."

Drac said, "The Negroes will riot and will require mass sedation. Animal tranquilizer might be the ticket. Mr. Tedrow could oversee the manufacture of the formula and test the dosage out on some Negro derelicts already in custody."

Wayne deadpanned it. Seconds slogged. Brown smiled and stepped in.

"Wayne has said that he'll monitor the convention for us. That's affirmative, isn't it, Wayne?"

"It is. I'd be happy to look around and do what I can to protect our interests."

Drac sipped his red drink. "It's Chicago that concerns me. Youth factions are mobilizing to create mass dissension that will discredit the Democrats. Would you be willing to help them play a few tricks?"

"With pleasure, sir."

"Hubert Humphrey is dough-faced and porcine. I would guess that he has a high white-cell count. He was born to lose presidential elections and die of leukemia."

Wayne nodded. Brown nodded. A male nurse entered the room. He placed a piping-hot pizza pie on Drac's bedside table. Brown shooed him off.

"Sir, did you read my memo? Our Italian friends are developing a hotel-casino plan for Central America or the Caribbean. Wayne will be overseeing it, and Hughes Air will have the exclusive charter rights."

Drac sniffed the pizza. "Which countries?"

Wayne said, "Panama, Nicaragua or the Dominican Republic."

"Good locations. Low cell-count zones all. Mr. Tedrow, will you confirm or refute a rumor I've been hearing? It's been troubling me."

Wayne smiled. The pizza pie bubbled. Drac said, "Was your father murdered?"

Brown squirmed a little. Wayne said, "Emphatically not, sir."

8

(Los Angeles, 6/20/68)

Stakeout:
The Hertz parking lot. 9:56 p.m.
Brisk drop-off biz running late.
The '66 Comet: due in four min-
utes or penalties would accrue.

Crutch sat in his GTO. He wore a tartan bow tie and a Scotty Bennett
hairdo. He bought the tie and got the crew cut today. They celebrated his
case and the Dr. Fred deal. They honored last night's ass-kicking.

He held his zoom-lens Rolleiflex. He had Arnie Moffett dupe-key fob.
The tie clashed with his polo shirt. The haircut clashed with current
trend. L.A. guys wore their hair long. Fuck that shit—he and Scotty were
avant-garde.

It was hot. He ran the AC and aimed the air at his balls. He talked to
Buzz an hour back. Bad news: no trace on that bootleg number yet. Memo:
Don't tell Buzz or Clyde about the Dr. Fred deal. Get the Hughes pic and
cut them in then.

Cars hit the lot: Buicks, Fords, Dodge Darts. People got out and
schlepped their keys into the office. Countdown: 9:57, 9:58, 9:59. On time
by seconds: that Comet, ADF-212.

It pulled in off Sunset eastbound. Steam whooshed out the hood slits.
The radiator probably blew.

Two women got out. Crutch zoomed his lens and got them up close.

Gretchen Farr/Celia Reyes—tall and Latin-tinged. It had to be her. She
was white, with that spic-pizzazz Something. She wore a tan shirt and
flared jeans. She was stunning and stacked-statuesque. About thirty-two.
Overmatched by her companion.

Maybe ten years older. More of *all* Somethings. Smaller, with a rolling-slouchy walk. Pale. Glasses. Near-black hair with gray streaks. Bare arms and a knife scar—Phil Irwin caught that.

They walked into the office. Crutch snapped photos. High-speed film—six frames walking in, six frames walking out.

They got into a '63 Fairlane. Crutch zoomed in *ultra*-close. Mud streaks on the license plate, no way to read numbers. *Why switch cars? They're vibing pros.*

The car pulled out on Sunset westbound. Crutch tailed it. He drove one-handed. He leapfrogged. He changed lanes and let a cab get between them. The car cut north on Berendo, west on Franklin, north on Cheremoya. Crutch hit the turn too close and double-clutched too fast. He stalled out. The Fairlane sped away, northbound.

He kicked the engine, tapped the gas too fast and flooded the carbs. *Easy now*—don't blow this. He waited a full minute. He checked out the addresses on Arnie's key fob. Gretchen Farr's ex–rental pad was one mile up the hill. Three more party pads were laced within a half-mile radius. The Gretchie pad was one of the four.

Easy now. Re-situate. Turn the key *slooooooow.*

He did it. The engine caught. He drove up into Beachwood Canyon and window-peeped en route. He saw loads of TV glare. He saw a pot party. He saw a flower-power chick doing the wah-watusi all by herself.

Snaky roads up the canyon. First address: 2250 Gladeview. There it is—a small Craftsman-style house.

Dark. No lights, no '63 Fairlane. Hit the other party pads—*they drove up here for a reason.*

The closest pad was six blocks southwest. Crutch drove there and idled at the curb. Shit—no lights, no Fairlane. He swung down to the next pad—four blocks due south. That's it—a small stucco house. There's window light and the sled in the driveway.

He parked curbside and walked over. The front window was curtained up. Dull light filtered through. He saw shapes moving. He cut down the driveway and eyeball-tracked them toward the back of the house. The side windows were cracked for air and uncurtained. He hunkered below the sills and followed shadows.

He heard muffled words. Word stew: "Tommy," "grapevine," "plant." Shadows hit the last window. The two women showed. They shared a look. They embraced and kissed.

Crutch blinked. It isn't real—yes it is. The image held and burned.

Gretchen/Celia ran her hands under the knife-scar woman's shirt. The knife-scar woman untied her hair and tossed it. Window light beamed off the gray streaks.

They stepped back toward the hallway. They became shadows again.

Crutch blinked and walked window-to-window. He ducked low. He saw shadows melded, but no flesh-and-blood *them*.

He walked back to his car and waited. He couldn't get re-situated. His breath and pulse kept re-circuiting.

They walked out a half hour later. They carried luggage to the Fairlane and placed it in the trunk. Moonlight gave him some detail. Gretchen/Celia looked dreamy. The knife-scar woman had kissed all her lipstick off.

They got in the car and drove away. It was late. There was no cover traffic. He couldn't tail them. He just sat there and watched their lights disappear.

There was nothing he could do.

They just left him.

He knew he'd never sleep. He decided to keep moving. He drove by the other party pads and saw keg bashes starting up. It was a mélange: hip kids, college kids and long hair all around. He drove back to the stucco place, picked a side-door lock and entered. He felt brazen. He turned the inside lights on.

The bedroom drew him first. The bed was warm. He touched the pillows and imagined their shapes on the sheets. He saw a single gray hair on the coverlet. He pressed his cheek to it and let it rest.

Something told him to go then. He left the house, got his car and just drove. He stayed up in the canyon. He did lazy figure eights all around the stucco pad. Time de-materialized. His beams hit a white Spanish house. The front door was wood-paneled and covered with strange markings. Something told him to get out and look.

He did it. He parked curbside and walked up. He ran his penlight over the door and studied the markings. Wild: geometric patterns etched in dark red.

Vertical lines down to the porch. A ripped-apart bird on the doormat.

You belong here. This could be yours.

Something told him the door would be open and to turn right inside. He did it. The living room was pitch-dark and musty. Plastic sheaths covered the furniture. He followed a metal-chalky smell to the kitchen. His breath went haywire. His hands shook. His penlight jerked. He steadied the beam with two hands and saw it.

The entrails in the sink. The severed arm/the missing hand/the brown skin, pure female. The geometric tattoo on the biceps. The deep gouge through and beside it. The crumbled green stones embedded bone-deep.

DOCUMENT INSERT: 6/21/68. *Los Angeles Herald Express* headline and subhead:

PRE-TRIAL MOTIONS IN KENNEDY CASE
ACCUSED ASSASSIN SIRHAN: "I'M A POLITICAL PRISONER"

DOCUMENT INSERT: 6/24/68. *Milwaukee Sentinel* headline and subhead:

BRITISH CUSTODY FOR KING SUSPECT RAY
FBI CALLS HIS CONSPIRACY TALK "FANCIFUL"

DOCUMENT INSERT: 6/27/68. *Los Angeles Times* subhead:

"ZIONIST GUARDS POISONED MY FOOD," ACCUSED ASSASSIN SAYS

DOCUMENT INSERT: 7/2/68. *Hartford Courant* headline and subhead:

RAY'S EXTRADITION LIKELY
ACCUSED KING ASSASSIN DESCRIBES "WIDESPREAD CONSPIRACY TO EXPLOIT ME"

DOCUMENT INSERT: 7/8/68. *San Francisco Chronicle* subhead:

FBI ASSURES PRESIDENT: KING ASSASSINATION WORK OF LONE GUNMAN

DOCUMENT INSERT: 7/12/68. *Nashville Tennessean* subhead:

HOOVER TO AMERICAN LEGION: "RAY WAS THE LONE GUNMAN, PURE AND SIMPLE"

DOCUMENT INSERT: 7/13/68. *Des Moines Register* headline and subhead:

NIXON-HUMPHREY RACE TIGHT
CONVENTION OFFICIALS PREDICT TROUBLE FROM "SUBVERSIVES AND HIPPIE YOUTH"

DOCUMENT INSERT: 7/16/68. *Seattle Post-Intelligencer* headline and subhead:

NIXON VS. HUMPHREY—IT'S TIGHT

MIAMI AND CHICAGO GEAR UP FOR "CONVENTION HIJINX"

DOCUMENT INSERT: 7/18/68. *Las Vegas Sun* article:

COLORFUL FREDDY O.

He's been a Los Angeles policeman and a celebrity private eye, as well as a World War II marine drill instructor. The plucky Lebanese-American kid from small-town Massachusetts has lived more than nine lives in his 46 years, and now he's starting out Life Number Ten as the owner-operator of the Golden Cavern Hotel-Casino.

Welcome to Las Vegas, Mr. Fred Otash!

He bought the Golden Cavern from "Big" Pete Bondurant, quite a colorful character himself, also a former L.A. cop, private eye and soldier of fortune. "Pete B. wanted to retire," Otash told this reporter. "I picked up the Golden Cavern for a song, and that song is 'Vegas Is My Lady.' "

Freddy O. has worn many hats in his lifetime. "That's true," he said. "And I've had a few hats knocked off my head." When asked to explain, he replied, "I was run out of the LAPD unjustifiably. I got my PI's license and verified scandal stories for *Confidential* magazine, but *Confidential* went down behind libel suits. That rumor that I doped a racehorse named Wonder Boy?—100% false. Yeah, I lost my license behind it, but when Hollywood celebs are in a jam, they still yell, "Get me Otash!," so I'm still the man to see in L.A."

Beverly Hills divorce lawyer Charles "Chick" Weiss confirms Freddy O.'s statement. "Freddy's the king of the L.A. private eyes, even though he lost his license and has gone into the hotel biz now. Listen, I do divorce work, and sometimes it's not pretty. Freddy's my liaison to the wheelman community, these hot-car guys who tail the cheating spouses to their extramarital rendezvous. He's a battle-trained urban warrior, just the kind of guy to make it big in a high-stress burb like Las Vegas."

"Howard Hughes can buy up all the big joints on the Strip and Glitter Gulch," Otash told this reporter. "I'm here to play to the junket crowd and the working Joe who wants to have fun without losing his shirt. Don't call my place a 'carpet joint' or a 'low-roller joint,' either. Call me the friend of the discerning gambler on a budget who appreciates a bang for his buck."

Los Angeles private investigator Clyde Duber offers a dissenting view of Fred Otash, which he claims is *not* the minority one. "Freddy is strictly shakedown," he said. "His only friend is the almighty dollar, so you might say that Vegas is the perfect place for him."

Ouch! Tell me, Fred O., what do you say to *that*?

"Clyde's just jealous," Otash said with a grin. "He always played second banana to me, and it's always rankled him. Yeah, I'm colorful, and I've got a few rough edges. You know my motto? 'I'll do anything short of murder, and I'll work for anyone but Communists.' How can you quibble with that?"

How indeed—and spoken like a true Las Vegan! So, once again, welcome to the Jewel of the Desert, Mr. Fred Otash!

DOCUMENT INSERT: 7/20/68. FBI telex communiqué. From: SAC Wilton J. Laird, St. Louis Office. To: Special Agent Dwight C. Holly. Marked: "Confidential 1-A: Recipient's Eyes Only."

SA Holly,

Per our phone conversation and your preceding memo (Confidential 1-A memorandum #8506) requesting an update on rumors pertaining to the M. L. King homicide circulating at the Grapevine Tavern, St. Louis, the following may warrant your attention:

1.—Electronic surveillance equipment, perhaps of Bureau manufacture, was discovered on the premises at the Grapevine Tavern in early to mid-June of this year. Confidential Bureau informants frequenting the tavern have reported that the apparatus was discovered by NORBERT DONALD KLING & ROWLAND MARK DE JOHN, convicted felons and tavern habitués and the acknowledged "leaders" of several other tavern habitués (CLARK DAVIS BRUNDAGE, LEAMAN RUSSELL CURRIE, THOMAS OGDEN PIERCE & GEORGE JAMES LUCE), all convicted felons active in numerous far-Right paramilitary organizations.

2.—The discovery of the apparatus has led to growing conjecture among the above mentioned. IE: that the apparatus was part of a monitoring process developed to lure accused King assassin JAMES EARL RAY into a "FBI-mandated" King assassination plot. While obviously preposterous, it should be noted that this rumor might prove to be damaging to the Bureau's prestige, given Mr. Hoover's many recent derogatory comments about King, and given that Ray's brother CHARLES ELDON RAY is a part owner of the tavern.

3.—This office had no part in installing electronic surveillance apparatus, if indeed it was Bureau-manufactured equipment that was discovered on the tavern premises. If some other Bureau field team installed the equipment, I did not know about it personally, nor was such equipment installed by any agent under my command.

4.—According to statements made by the above-referenced tavern habitués, there was frequent discussion of a $50,000 "bounty" on King, allegedly to be paid by a cabal of wealthy segregationists to any "White Race Warrior" who would "buck LBJ's liberal hegemony to off Martin Luther Coon." This preposterous line of talk was frequently indulged by numerous tavern habitués in the months preceding King's death.

5.—The "FBI hit plot" rumors are growing in both virulence and frequency. Alarmingly, confidential sources within the St. Louis Office of the Bureau of Alcohol, Tobacco and Firearms have informed me that the tavern will soon be placed under ATF surveillance, pertaining to evidence of gunrunning taking place on the tavern premises proper. The above-referenced tavern habitués are not gunrunning suspects, but I find ATF's proximity to the tavern disturbing, given the virulence and frequency of the anti-Bureau rumors & CHARLES ELDON RAY'S part ownership of the tavern.

Respectfully, SAC Wilton J. Laird, St. Louis Office/EYES ONLY/PLEASE DESTROY UPON READING.

DOCUMENT INSERT: 7/26/68. *Los Angeles Herald Express* article:

STILL A BAFFLER: "THE BIG HEIST"
AND THE COP STILL OBSESSED

Tuesday, February 24, 1964. It was chilly in Los Angeles, with storm clouds hovering. The early morning silence was shattered by the collision of a milk truck and a Wells Fargo armored car carrying a multimillion-dollar cargo of U.S. currency and priceless emeralds. The quiet corner of 84th and Budlong streets became the scene of a holocaust, and within minutes four armed guards and two members of a daring robbery gang were dead—the latter obviously betrayed and shot by a fellow gang member—and the robbery-murder case has remained unsolved for four and a half years now.

"Not exactly," Sergeant Robert S. "Scotty" Bennett stated at Piper's Coffee Shop. "It's been four years, five months and two days."

One does not quibble with Sergeant Bennett on anything pertaining to the case he has worked on so hard and for so long. He has been the lead investigator since that bloody morning, and his determination to crack the case has become legend within the Los Angeles Police Department. The man, all six-foot-five of him, is a legend himself. He has killed 18 armed robbers in the line of duty and commemorates the LAPD record with small 18's embroidered in the Scottish-plaid bow ties he always wears. When asked about those shootings, he replied, "When you let that buckshot go, there's no taking it back."

It's a funny line with a harrowing truth behind it: detectives working the LAPD's Headquarters Robbery Squad go up against armed-and-dangerous criminals routinely, and they are a determined breed of man proud to be wearing "211" tie bars, the number noting the California Penal Code designation for armed robbery. "The Heist," as it's known around the Robbery Division squadroom, is a near-constant topic of speculation, and Scotty Bennett addresses it with great relish. "It was planned down to a 'T,'" he said. "The fake milk-truck collision was very forceful and potentially fatal, which obviously convinced the guards that it was real. The robbery gang knew what the armored car would be transporting, and we've never determined exactly how they got that information. More importantly, we've never determined whether the heist gang was comprised of white men or Negroes."

Sergeant Bennett sipped coffee and continued. "The heist was conceived and executed boldly," he said. "And I believe that the leader of the gang decided beforehand to kill his underlings at the scene and obscure their identities, and their races, by burning their bodies past recognition. All fine and good, but obscuring racial identification requires more than burning the surface of the skin, and the man first dosed the bodies with a chemical accelerant that greatly enhanced the tissue damage of the burning. We've never been able to identify the chemical that he used, which is another reason why the heist has remained such a baffler."

Some other reasons?

"Well," Sergeant Bennett said, "we know that many of the cash stacks stolen from the armored car were wrapped with ink-exploding bands, and ink spill was found at the crime scene. Also, ink-stained bills have surfaced periodically in south Los Angeles, so I'm convinced that there was at least a partial Negro component to the gang. Also, the origin of the emeralds remains undetermined. It was a very valuable cargo, and intermediaries for the consigner and the consignee signed secrecy waivers with Wells Fargo, which has impeded the investigation."

And the persistent rumor that the emeralds hailed from Central America or the Caribbean?

Sergeant Bennett said, "Just that, a rumor. Entirely unsubstantiated."

And the rumor that black-militant organizations plotted and executed the heist?

Scotty Bennett laughed heartily. "Why mince words? Black militants are grandstanders who always claim credit for their deeds. The Panthers and US are informant-infiltrated, and we would have picked up leads by now. We've got two rowdy militant groups causing woo-woo in L.A. now, the Black Tribe Alliance and the Mau-Mau Liberation Front, but for the life of me I can't see them executing anything more complex than a liquor-store job or a purse snatch."

And the leader of the gang? The ruthless mastermind who killed his own men at the scene?

Scotty Bennett laughed even more heartily. "Tell him this," he said. "When I let that buckshot go, there's no taking it back."

DOCUMENT INSERT: 7/27/68. Internal FBI memorandum. Marked: "Stage-1 Covert"/"Director's Eyes Only"/"Destroy After Reading." To: Director Hoover. From: SA Dwight C. Holly.

Sir,

The following states the design and goals of our COINTELPRO aimed at discrediting and disrupting the black-militant movement at large and more circumscribed and localized black-nationalist groups in specific. Pending your approval, I have named the program OPERATION BAAAAD BROTHER. It is a nod to our less-than-successful OPERATION BLACK RABBIT and ironically celebrates the Negro verbal tic of using "bad" to mean "good." Male Negroes often address each other as "brother," which I thought you might appreciate. As I'm sure you know, a Negro extremist group called the "Black Nationalists of New Libya" precipitated racial violence in Cleveland, Ohio, this past week that left eleven dead, including three white policemen. This is the perfect time to initiate a physically small-scaled COINTELPRO that may well achieve large-scale national results.

It is my firm belief that both the BLACK PANTHER PARTY (BPP) and the UNITED SLAVES (US) are too well known and well infiltrated already. I believe that our goals would be better served by operating the Los Angeles–based BLACK TRIBE ALLIANCE (BTA) and MAU-MAU LIBERATION FRONT (MMLF). Our COINTELPRO could put them on the map and wholly discredit them concurrently. By controlling the public perception of two lesser-known groups at the outset, we would also discredit the black-militant movement as a whole. I have studied the initial Bureau intelligence reports on the BTA and MMLF that you sent me and have requested Intel Division dossiers on their members from LAPD. I firmly contend that they are perfect COINTELPRO targets and that their destruction should be the ultimate goal of OPERATION BAAAAD BROTHER. I believe our goal should be accomplished in this manner:

1.—Both groups are rumored to be considering the sale of narcotics as a means to finance their activities, which might provide us with avenues to exploit their inherent criminality and publically underscore the point that criminal activity and subversive political activity are one and the same thing.

2.—We must find a high-caliber confidential informant who will ingratiate him or herself with one or both groups and report back with assiduously detailed briefs on their political activities. I believe that a female informant would be the most effective. A woman schooled in left-wing-revolutionary jargon would have a greater chance of eliciting confidences and inspiring indiscreet conversation and would most likely be better able to maneuver between the two (male-dominated) groups without creating rancor. Toward the end of recruitment, I have confidential Bureau informant #4361 assisting me.

3.—The linchpin of the incursion should be the placement of a male Negro infiltrator, mandated to uncover and report the criminal activities of the BTA and MMLF. Ideally, the infiltrator should have had police experience. Also ideally (but much more unlikely), he should possess a past history of racial animus for whites. Toward that possibility, I have requested a wide array of police

agency personnel files and am currently seeking to secure a viewing of the hate-mail subscription lists of the late Wayne Tedrow Sr.
and Bureau confidential informant Dr. Fred Hiltz. Wayne Tedrow Jr. has refused to grant me access to his father's lists, but I
will persist with him.

   4.—Pending your consent, I would move to Los Angeles and
establish a full-time temporary residence there, along with a cosmetically obscured front office for OPERATION BAAAAD
BROTHER. Per initial operating expenses, I would request $60,000
in cold funds.

   In conclusion:

   I strongly believe that the BLACK TRIBE ALLIANCE and MAU-
MAU LIBERATION FRONT offer us an unparalleled opportunity to
disrupt and discredit the subversive designs of the black-militant
movement at large. I await your appraisal and response.

   Respectfully,

   SA Dwight C. Holly

DOCUMENT INSERT: 7/28/68. FBI telex communiqué. From: SAC
Marvin D. Waldrin, Las Vegas Office. To: Special Agent Dwight C.
Holly. Marked: "Confidential 1-A: Recipient's Eyes Only."

SA Holly,

   Per your preceding memo (Confidential 1-A memorandum
#8518) requesting information on rumors pertaining to the
6/9/68 death of MR. WAYNE TEDROW SR., I have developed the
following information:

   A.—Rumors that MR. TEDROW'S death was in fact a homicide,
all unsubstantiated, are circulating, according to Bureau informants within the Las Vegas Police Department and Clark County
Coroner's Office.

   B.—One source would seem to be an LVPD officer who allegedly
saw MR. TEDROW'S body on the night of his death.

   C.—A coroner's assistant told our informant, "It wasn't any
heart attack, not with his head caved in like that."

   D.—Eyewitness neighbors of MR. TEDROW allegedly told canvassing officers that Mr. Tedrow's son and ex-wife (former LVPD
SERGEANT WAYNE TEDROW JR. and JANICE LUKENS TEDROW)
were seen near MR. TEDROW'S home on the p.m. of 6/9/68.

Will forward all future data on this matter per Conf 1-A guidelines.

Marvin J. D. Waldrin, SAC, Las Vegas. Eyes Only/Please
Destroy Upon Reading.

DOCUMENT INSERT: 7/30/68. FBI telex communiqué. From: SAC
Wilton J. Laird, St. Louis Office. To: Special Agent Dwight C. Holly.
Marked "Confidential 1-A: Recipient's Eyes Only."

SA Holly,

Per Conf. 1-A memo #8506: rumors of the "FBI bugging" &
"FBI-mandated hit" on Rev. M. L. King are growing in both virulence and frequency, according to informally placed sources frequenting the Grapevine Tavern.

Respectfully,

Wilton J. Laird, SAC, St. Louis. EYES ONLY/PLEASE DESTROY
UPON READING.

DOCUMENT INSERT: 8/1/68. FBI telex communiqué. From: SAC
Marvin D. Waldrin, Las Vegas Office. To: Special Agent Dwight C.
Holly. Marked: "Confidential 1-A: Recipient's Eyes Only."

SA Holly,

Per #8518 & my 7/28/68 response, an addendum:

A—Sources outside LVPD & CCCO are now reporting "rife" &
"widespread" rumors of homicide per the death of WAYNE
TEDROW SR.

B—Confidential Bureau informants at the Las Vegas Sun report
that the newspaper may be considering an inquiry, chiefly because
of the "checkered past" of WAYNE TEDROW JR. and his alleged
current involvement with JANICE LUKENS TEDROW.

Will forward all future data per Conf. 1-A guidelines.

Marvin D. Waldrin, SAC, Las Vegas. EYES ONLY/PLEASE
DESTROY UPON READING.

DOCUMENT INSERT: 8/3/68. Verbatim FBI telephone call transcript. Marked: "Recorded at the Director's Request"/"Classified

Confidential 1-A: Director's Eyes Only." Speaking: Director Hoover, Special Agent Dwight C. Holly.

JEH: Good morning, Dwight.

DH: Good morning, Sir.

JEH: Before you ask, the answer is yes. Expedite OPERATION BAAAAD BROTHER in the manner you described in your memo.

DH: Thank you, Sir.

JEH: The title possesses a sublime jungle quality. As in "That brother John Edgar Hoover, he *baaad*."

DH: You are *baaad,* Sir. And I might add "inimitably so."

JEH: You might, and you should. And, on the topic of jungle artistry, I heard a very disquieting song on the radio this morning.

DH: Sir.

JEH: It was called "The Tighten Up." A Negro ensemble named Archie Bell and the Drells performed it. The song carried the air of insurrection and sex. I'm sure that white liberals will find it authentic. I told the Los Angeles SAC to open a file on Mr. Bell and to determine the identity of his Drells.

DH: Yes, Sir.

JEH: Enough bonhomie. Dwight, I am very disturbed by the Wayne Senior and Grapevine Tavern chatter. I've been reading the applicable communiqués, and I take this confluence of loose talk as both a personal insult and an affront to the Bureau. Wayne Senior was an FBI asset and James Earl Ray killed Martin Lucifer King without help from you, me, this agency, Wayne Senior, Wayne Junior, Fred Otash, the redneck sharpshooter Bob Relyea, or any other outside source. Do you understand me, Dwight?

DH: Yes, Sir. I do.

JEH: Make the rumors stop, Dwight.

DH: Yes, Sir.

JEH: Good day, Dwight.

DH: Good day, Sir.

9

(Miami, 8/5/68)

Collins Avenue was wall-to-wall elephants. They wore GOP banners and flailed their trunks in the heat. A carny crew herded them with switches. *They* wore top hats dotted with Nixon buttons. One guy fed the beasts peanuts. One guy urged gawkers to cheer.

The noise was big. Wayne dodged sign-wavers. Nixon signs bobbed upside his face. He lugged two big steamer trunks. Nixon was at the Fontainebleau. He had to walk. He couldn't drive. The elephant stampede shut traffic down.

The convention had just started. It was thick-aired and 94°. The air sealed an elephant-shit aroma. Wayne's suit wilted. Wayne's stomach queased.

More sign fools hit the sidewalk. Cuban chanters showed up—*"Cas-tro out! Cas-tro out! Cas-tro out now!"* They looked riot-ready. Wayne saw saps in their pockets. The Nixon chumps gave them some space.

The Fontainebleau loomed. Two big men spotted Wayne and cut through the crowd. They wore dark suits and earpieces. They carried walkie-talkies. The crowd caught the gist and let them through quick.

They made it over. They grabbed the trunks and whisked Wayne off in a VIP swirl. It was two minutes all topsy-turvy. They hit the hotel. A side door opened, kitchen help dispersed, an elevator appeared. They whooshed way up. They floated down a thick-carpet hallway and sent sparks off their shoes. The big guys bowed and vanished. A bigger guy opened a door and vanished double-time quick.

Wayne blinked. Zap—there's ex-Veep Dick Nixon.

In topsy-turvy Technicolor. In chinos and a Ban-Lon shirt. In need of a 1:00 p.m. shave.

He said, "Hello, Mr. Tedrow."

Wayne quashed a blink. Nixon walked up to him, hands in his pockets, no shake.

"I was sorry to hear about your father. He had become quite a good friend."

Wayne nodded. "I appreciate the sentiment, Sir."

"And the lovely Janice? How is she?"

"She's dying, Sir. She's quite ill with cancer."

Nixon made a sad face. It flopped. No sale for Mr. Sincere.

"I'm very sorry to hear that. Please extend my best wishes."

"Thank you, Sir. I will."

Noise boomed outside. Wayne heard *"Nix-on!"* and elephant bleats.

"I won't take up any more of your time, Sir."

"No, but I'm sure you'd like some form of acknowledgment."

"I'd like to pass it along, Sir. That's true."

"You want me to say that I'll sing for my supper."

Wayne looked away and scanned the suite. Presidential seals and knickknacks ran rampant. The ex-veep booked the Big Room pre-emptive.

Nixon said, "My Justice Department will not go proactive against your people. I understand that you have designs in Latin America or the Caribbean, and my policy for the country you pick will accommodate it. If the election appears tight, I'd appreciate some help at the polls."

Wayne bowed. Nixon wrinkled his nose.

"My wife went for a walk this morning. She said the beach was covered with elephant shit."

"It'll be donkey shit in Chicago, Sir."

"Hubert Humphrey is a dough-faced, appeasement-minded cock-sucker. He is unfit to lead this country."

"Yes, Sir."

"The hippies are mobilizing for Chicago."

"They are, Sir. And I'll be there to lend them a hand."

Carlos had a condo on Biscayne Bay. Wayne had time to kill. He rent-a-car-cruised Miami.

A street map got him west of the elephants. He couldn't dodge convention hoo-haw altogether. The city was infested.

Placard clowns everywhere. Pick your grievance: Vietnam, welfare,

Cuban policy. Longhaired kids defamed Tricky Dick and mourned Dr. King. Fiesty Latins wanted *"CASTRO OUT NOW!"*

Five- and ten-car motorcades. Floats with children and dressed-up dogs. Inflated elephants leashed to car antennas. Fools with bullhorns spouting gobbledygook.

Red, white and blue balloons. A Nixon banner epidemic. Favorite-son banners—low numbers beside the ex-veep. A twelve-wheelchair nursing-home motorcade—old girls sapped by the heat.

Twelve Nixonites. Balloons and wheelchair bunting. Four old girls with oxygen masks. Four old girls smoking.

Janice was dying. He watched her fight to live and wish to die in in-and-out blips. He cooked dope for her. She lived for the IV drip and fought her way out of stupors. He cooked dope for Dracula. He'd had three more meets with Drac and Farlan Brown. Farlan was due at the convention. They'd scheduled a meet.

Drac wanted to own Clark County, Nevada. The Boys wanted to sell him their share at usurious rates. Feed the cash funnel. Scour the Teamster Pension Fund books for loan defaulters. Usurp their businesses. Grab them, sell them and feed the cash funnel. Castro kicked the Boys out of Cuba. Find a new Latin hot spot, entrench and rebuild.

More banners. More motorcades. Another wheelchair brigade—crippled Vietnam vets.

Wayne looked away and cut down a side street. He cooked heroin in Saigon. He saw the war waste lives. The anti-Castro cause vexed him. His weekend in Dallas launched that distrust.

Dwight kept calling him. A persistent Dwight Holly was a fucking full-court press. His big-brother act doubled the grief. Dwight said the Grapevine was still brewing. Dwight said Vegas was brewing up evil chitchat on Wayne Senior's death. Dwight wanted to see Senior's subscription lists. He kept refusing. Dwight kept up the press.

Wayne crossed a long causeway and hit surface streets. He thought he saw—

A tail car. A leapfrogger. A blue sedan sticking close and dropping back.

He made three right turns. He lane-weaved. He hit a two-lane street and eliminated tail cover. The blue sedan fell back, stuck close, fell back. He got blips of the driver: a big, fat-neck type.

There's an alley—

Wayne cranked a left turn. The tail car braked, skidded and plowed some trash cans. Wayne crisscrossed two more alleyways and lost him.

. . .

It was a party. Sam Giancana called it a "buy Nixon" bash. Santo Traffi-cante laughed and shushed him. Carlos roasted a pig on the terrace. Droves of flunkies and call girls. Fools with noisemakers. Convention dele-gates with Italian surnames. Three bars and a mile-long buffet.

Wayne circulated. The condo was bigger than the Orange Bowl. He walked room-to-room and got lost twice. It was old home week. He saw a hood he popped for flimflam, circa '61. He saw a fruit actor he popped at a glory-hole stall. He saw a bevy of Vegas-transplant hookers.

Sam G. waltzed a woman by. Wayne caught "Celia" and *"hola"* instead of "hello." Carlos waltzed by and tapped his watch. Wayne caught "den" and "five minutes."

Wayne circulated. A commotion occurred. Flames shot off the terrace grill and ignited some curtains. A stooge put the blaze out with a seltzer spritzer and promoted a big round of applause.

A call girl walked Wayne to the den. Carlos, Sam and Santo were already ensconced. The walls were plywood-paneled. A photo frieze showed Carlos playing golf with Pope Pius.

The call girl split. Wayne sat down. Sam said, "Did he say 'Thank you'?"

Wayne smiled. "No, but he called Hubert Humphrey a 'dough-faced cocksucker.' "

Santo laughed. "He is absolutely correct there."

Carlos said, "Humphrey can't win. He takes the soft line on social chaos."

Sam said, "He's a pinko. He came out of the Farmer-Labor movement in Minnesota. They are 100% Red."

Santo sipped Galliano. "Howard Hughes. Tell us the latest and great-est."

Wayne said, "He wants to buy the Stardust and the Landmark. I assured him they're for sale. Farlan Brown thinks he may be breaching anti-trust laws, which might push the purchases off until next year."

Carlos sipped XO. "The cocksucking Justice Department."

Santo sipped Galliano. "Yeah, but lame duck. And I have to say that our boy Dick will not let shit like that impede us."

Sam sipped anisette. "The inside guys. That's what concerns me. We have to keep our people on the premises."

Wayne nodded. "Mr. Hughes agrees. I've convinced him that the tran-sition will run much smoother that way."

Carlos switched to Drambuie. "The Fund books. What's going on there?"

"I want to buy out banks and loan companies, so they can earn mar-ginal profits and double as laundry fronts. There's a Negro-owned bank in

Los Angeles that interests me. Hughes Air is in L.A., and we need a funnel close to the border."

Sam shook his head. "I don't like dealing with niggers."

Carlos shook his head. "They're impetuous and get agitated too easy."

Santo shook his head. "They've been demoralized by welfare."

Sam sipped anisette. "Which our boy Dick will put the skids to."

Wayne prickled. His skin itched. His ears throbbed.

Santo said, "Wayne's having an adverse reaction to this conversation."

Sam said, "Wayne's an open book in some ways."

Santo sipped Galliano. "What's the book? *Jungle Bunnies I Have Slain*?"

Carlos said, "Wayne's a coon hunter from way back."

Sam yukked. "So maybe therein lies the rub?"

Santo said, "What's the 'rub'? You sound like a faggot talking like that."

Carlos looked at Wayne. Carlos raised his hands and eased his palms down—*whoa, now, whoa, whoa.*

Santo coughed. "Okay, let's change the subject."

Sam coughed. "Okay, how about politics? Me, I'm voting for Dick."

Carlos coughed. "How about your scouting trip? Let's hear about that."

Sam switched to XO. "I been to all three places. To me, they're apples and oranges. Panama's got the fucking canal, Nicaragua's got the fucking jungle, and the D.R.'s got the fucking island breeze. They all got right-wing guys with their hands out pulling the strings, which is the most important thing. My friend Celia's from the D.R., so she's been lobbying for it."

Carlos made the jack-off sign. "Sam's pussy-whipped."

Santo made the jack-off sign. "Celia this, Celia that. Sam's got heat-stroke from that island pussy."

Sam flushed. Carlos raised his hands and eased his palms down—*whoa, now, whoa, whoa.*

Santo switched to Drambuie. "The front team. Let's talk about that. Once we pick our spot, we'll have to send some guys down."

Wayne coughed. "I want to bring in Jean-Philippe Mesplede."

Carlos gulped. Santo gulped. Sam gulped. Looks traveled three ways. Mesplede fucked Carlos on the Saigon "H" deal. He was a French-Corsican merc. He was an anti-Castro militant. He was in Dallas that weekend. He shot from the grassy knoll.

Sam sighed. "I'll admit he's a good choice, but we got problems with him."

Santo said, "I heard he's here in Miami. Wherever you got anti-Fidel shit, you got Jean-Philippe."

Sam said, "Is this where we all say 'Let bygones be bygones'?"

Carlos sipped Drambuie. "Three names keep popping into my head. A little birdie keeps telling me that Mesplede wants to clip them."

Bob Relyea. Gaspar Fuentes. Miguel Díaz Arredondo.

A redneck shooter and two Cuban exiles. Part of the Saigon cabal. Relyea sided with the Carlos faction and fucked over Wayne and Mesplede. Relyea joined the Memphis team and dropped Dr. King. Fuentes and Arredondo were anti-Wayne and anti-Mesplede. They plain disappeared last spring.

Santo sighed. "I'll concede he's a good choice."

Sam sighed. "I know he speaks Spanish. 'Let bygones by bygones'? I don't know, you tell me."

Wayne said, "I want him."

Santo sipped Drambuie. "He'll want to clip those guys."

Carlos said, "It's your call, Wayne."

Wayne cruised Little Havana. It was all-night, bug-brigade hot. Bug swarms, bug bombardments. Bugs bigger than Rodan and Godzilla. Bugs hit his windshield. He tapped his wiper blades and mulched them to bug juice. Little Havana was *HOT.*

He cruised. He eyeballed the sidewalk action. Bodegas, fruit stands, vendors selling shaved-ice treats. Leaflet distribution. Pamphlet-packing punks in "Kill Fidel" T-shirts. Political offices: Alpha 66, Venceremos, the Battalion for April 17. He turned off Flagler Street and scoped out rows of houses. He checked his rearview mirror every few seconds. Yes—there's that blue sedan again, leapfrogged two cars back.

He floored the gas, made four crazy turns and found a parking space on Flager. No blue sedan, okay.

Wayne went walking. His suit instantly rewilted. Street fools jostled him. He got weird looks—Joo ain't *Cubano,* joo white. The sky exploded. Dig those lights! Wayne made the source: fireworks from the convention.

People stood and gawked. Papas held their kids up. A street-corner fistfight froze in mid-blow.

Wayne watched. A leaflet-distribution guy waved a little flag. Wayne glanced in a coffee-bar window and saw Jean-Philippe Mesplede.

The glance flew two ways. Mesplede stood and bowed. *Le grenouille sauvage—habille tout en noir.* Black shirt, black coat, black pants—*le grand plus noir.*

Wayne walked in. Jean-Philippe hugged him. Wayne felt *at least* three handguns under his clothes.

They sat down. Mesplede was halfway through a fifth of Pernod. A waiter brought a fresh glass.

"*Ça va,* Wayne?"

"*Ça va bien,* Jean-Philippe."

"And your business in Miami?"

"Political."

"Par example, s'il vous plaît?"

"For instance, I was looking for you."

Mesplede flexed his hands. His tattooed pit bulls grew snarls and erections. He was an ex–French para. He went back to the Algerian War and Dien Bieu Phu. He pushed heroin wherever he went.

They switched to French. They sipped Pernod. Fireworks lit windows all around them. They rehashed Vietnam and their ops deal. Mesplede cursed Carlos, *le petit cochon.* Wayne did a riff on strange bedfellows. Bygones as bygones. Carlos had work for them. Let me tell you.

Ça va, Wayne. Okay.

Wayne described the casino plan and laid out the territorial options. Mesplede riffed on the geopolitics of Panama, Nicaragua and the D.R. Trade and agriculture. Current despots out to quash dissent and Red countermovements. Wayne sipped Pernod and got a liqueur-language buzz. Mesplede routed the riff to Cuba. He remained committed to the Cause. LBJ, Nixon, Humphrey—Castroite *cochons* all. The election meant *merde.* The hands-off Cuba policy would continue. They sparred on that, *un peu.* Mesplede knew *la Causa* vexed Wayne. He hated dope peddling. Their ops stint turned him against it. Strange bedfellows—*oui, oui.*

They got to the yes-or-no stage. Mesplede said maybe. He had pressing business first. Wayne raised three fingers. Mesplede nodded. Wayne said that he'd spoken to Carlos. It's *my* call now. I'll let you kill two out of three.

The fireworks went out with a flourish. *Wham*—high noon at midnight. The window light died. Mesplede switched to English.

"Who is allowed to live?"

"Bob Relyea."

"I know why, but please inform me precisely."

"He was in on a big job in April. He's too close to some people I'm with."

"Memphis."

"Yes."

"You were there, too."

Wayne prickled. "Yes, I was."

Mesplede spit on the floor. "Shameful. A horrible blow to the American Negro. I sympathize with them, because I revere their jazz artistry."

Prickles, heat bumps, heatstroke pend—

"You can take out Fuentes and Arredondo. That's as far as I can let it go."

Mesplede shrugged and bowed. "They may be here in Miami."

"Let's go find them."

They took Wayne's rent-a-car. Mesplede fouled it with French cigarettes. They drove. They got out and hit cocktail bars and all-nite bodegas. They dispensed cash tips and inquired about Fuentes and Arredondo. They got zero.

Wayne rode a buzz off the Pernod. He kept checking his rearview. He didn't see the blue sedan. He *thought* he saw a tan coupe leapfrogging. It got close, fell back, got close. The driver: a crew-cut kid, early twenties.

It schizzed him. He took evasive turns and made Mesplede carsick. The tan coupe vanished. They circled back to Flagler and rewalked it. The storefront offices stayed open late. Cuban Freedom Action Committee, Cuban Freedom Caucus, Cuban Freedom Council. Mesplede loved it. He spoke Spanish and captivated a slew of late-night loafers. They bummed cigarettes. Mesplede pressed his case. He logged three tips total.

Tip #1: Fuentes and Arredondo booked to the Midwest. Tip #2: They might be heisting department stores. Tip #3: They might be heisting gas stations in Chicago.

It was 4:00 a.m. Mesplede fell asleep in the car. Wayne woke him up and dropped him at his rooming house. He drove back to his hotel, near woozy. Elephants and Dick Nixon. Cuba, tail cars, mob ghouls, bugs like Rodan.

He unlocked the door. The room light was on. The blue-sedan man was sitting in the one chair. He was holding a .38 Smith. A Nevada AG's badge was pinned to his coat.

Wayne shut the door and leaned on it. The guy pointed to his gun bulge. Wayne tossed his .45 on the bed.

The guy said, "Chuck Woodrell."

Wayne *yawned.* "Tell me what this is. I know, but tell me anyway."

Woodrell *yawned.* "You and your stepmom killed your daddy. The AG knows it's a homicide, and he'd like to prosecute. He's aware that you work for Uncle Carlos and Mr. Hughes, and he *still* doesn't care, because he's a ballsy kind of guy. We've got a bloody print on Janice. Eight comparison points, so it's a clincher. We don't want to file on a dying woman, but business is business."

Wayne rubbed his eyes. "How much?"

Woodrell yawned and stretched. "Why don't you and Buddy Fritsch find me a suspect? That and fifty grand chills it."

10

(Los Angeles, 8/6/68)

The drop-front came furnished: three rooms in Naugahyde and scuffed chenille. The air conditioners worked. The couch folded out to a bed. It was ample space. Dwight figured he could live there full-time.

Silver Lake. A Bureau-vouchered office suite at Sunset and Mohawk. A barber college, fruit bar and porno bookstore downstairs.

Karen lived a mile northwest. It was a good spot for spontaneous nooners. He listed the office as "Cove Enterprises." It was fittingly bland. It winked at Karen's crib at Baxter and Cove.

Dwight moved in. He placed his clothes in the closet and set up a hot plate and coffee gizmo. He wired two standard phone lines and a secure scrambler line. He unloaded his surveillance equipment. He locked a box of throwdown guns in the safe.

He was fucking dog-tired. He'd caught the redeye in from D.C. His seat was midget-size. His legs were jammed to his chest. His one drink and one pill got him one hour's sleep full of nightmares.

Mr. Hoover okayed a wire transfer: sixty cold to a bank downtown. It was his six-month budget. Upkeep, informant fees and miscellaneous expenses. OPERATION BAAAAD BROTHER, on-go.

Dwight cranked the window units and produced that igloo effect. *Aaaah,* L.A. in August—hot, with no letup. He had three window views, all north-facing. Taco joints, cholos, smog in CinemaScope.

Mr. Hoover was riding him roughshod. The old poof was in a nitpicking frenzy. Rumors in stereo: the Grapevine and Wayne Junior. He told Mr.

Hoover they were chilled. It was a flat lie and a time-buyer. ATF was circling the Grapevine. He sent Fred Otash to St. Louis to check it out. The Wayne Junior deal could blow in an instant. Wayne refused to kick loose Wayne Senior's hate lists. Ditto Dr. Fred Hiltz.

Wayne said he was out of the hate biz. Dr. Fred wanted too much cash. Dwight stiffed a check-in call to the L.A. SAC last night. Jack Leahy ran mordant per Mr. Hoover, almost recklessly so. Jack called the old poof "Amphetamine Annie." Dwight yukked and recalled their last phone chat. Mr. Hoover raged, pouted and pranced. Mr. Hoover ran two beats short of normal now. Mr. Hoover listed the Memphis personnel just to say I KNOW.

Dwight got the heebie-jeebies. The igloo got *too* cold.

Let's check out Niggertown.

Malt-liquor signs marked the border. Menthol cigarettes followed. Schlitz, Colt .45, *Nig*ports and Kools. Coon consumerism. Afro pride. Slick spades with white features and negroid hair.

Dwight drove south. His Fed sled drew scared looks and sneers. It was hot. Smog hovered low. Lots of *baaaad* brothers be out. Jive sessions and parking-lot crap games. Lots of hair nets. Lots of stingy-brim porkpies atop gassed hair. Lots of LAPD street rousts.

He drove by the Panther HQ. The outdoor mural soared. Two black cats disemboweled a bleeding pink pig. The pig wore a badge marked FAScist oppressor. The backdrop was the Last Supper. Huey Newton played Jesus. Eldridge Cleaver and Bobby Seale played key disciples. The other disciples wore "Free Huey" T-shirts.

The US HQ was close. The door guards wore lacquered shades and black berets. They flanked a hi-fi plopped down on the sidewalk. Gibberish sputtered. Bongos banged the beat. Dwight heard "Instill the White Insect with Insecticide."

Enough. Dwight cut west. The Black Tribe Alliance had a storefront at 43rd and Vernon. Their door crest featured black fists, guns and white-pig cops with small peckers. The Mau-Mau Liberation Front—four blocks south. Cannibal wall art—white cops screaming in stew pots as black dudes seasoned and stirred.

Enough. It was Chairman Mao meets Minstrel Mike, spliced with Ramar of the Jungle. Dwight cut west. He passed the Peoples' Bank of South Los Angeles. He recalled his file notes. It was allegedly a money-wash joint.

Karen was guest-lecturing at USC. He cruised by on a timing hunch and caught her class filing out. The kids were longhaired and unkempt. They saw his gray suit and belt gun and went *eek*. The lecture hall was big. Karen lingered by the dais. Dwight jumped onstage and created sound waves. Karen looked up and smiled.

They kissed over the dais. A few students caught it and went *Huh?* Karen held a photo slide up to the light. Dwight looked at it. It was Mr. Hoover, circa '52.

"Don't tell me. You're teaching the blacklist again."

"Don't tell me you think it was justified."

"Don't tell me I haven't helped some of your Commie chums get their jobs back."

"Don't tell me I haven't reciprocated with favors."

Dwight smiled. "Is What's-His-Name in town?"

"Yes."

"When does he leave?"

"Tomorrow morning."

"Tomorrow night, then?"

"Yes, that sounds lovely."

They sat on the stage and let their legs dangle. They were tall. Their feet scraped the floor. Karen pulled his cigarettes out and lit up.

"One a day, right?"

"Yes, and only when we're together."

"I'm not sure I believe you."

"All right. Occasionally, after breakfast."

Dwight touched her belly. "You're showing more."

Karen touched herself. "That's Eleanora."

"Suppose it's a boy?"

"Then it's What's-His-Name or Dwight."

"And you're sure it's not mine?"

"Sweetie, it's not an immaculate conception, and you were nowhere near the receptacle."

Dwight pulled his legs up and stretched out on the stage. He yawned. He got half-second dizzy.

Karen said, "How's your sleep?"

"Shitty."

"Bad dreams?"

"Yes."

"Any horrible Bureau-sanctioned deeds that you'd like to confess?"

"Not right now."

Karen tossed her cigarette and stretched out beside him. He touched her hair. He counted the dark flecks in her eyes.

"Any new ones?"

"No."

"A person's eyes change as they age. It's perfectly normal, so you shouldn't fret over it."

"I fret over everything."

Karen touched his hair. "I wasn't accusing you. I was just commenting."

Dwight moved closer. Their heads touched. He smelled almond shampoo.

"Find me that informant. A woman. I'll operate her and my infiltrator, and I'll keep them separate."

"I'll think about it."

"You could do some good here. Both of these groups are uninfiltrated, which means they've got all kinds of latitude to pull bad shit."

Karen burrowed in a little. "Quid pro quo?"

"Sure."

"There's a rally here next week."

"Against the war?"

"Yes."

"Don't tell me. You'd like me to pull the photo-surveillance team."

"Would you?"

"Sure. I'll call Jack Leahy."

Karen rolled on her back and stretched. Dwight touched her belly. He thought he felt Eleanora kick.

He said, "Do you love me?"

Karen said, "I'll think about it."

They sat in the den. Dwight insisted. It was hate art–free. The rest of Hate House jangled him.

Dr. Fred said, "A hundred G's. That and a little favor gets you a thorough perusal of all of my lists."

Dwight yawned. "What's the favor?"

"Help me find this woman. She dinged me for fourteen G's and split-skied."

Dwight shrugged. "Call Clyde Duber. He'll set you up."

"He did. I got this numbnuts kid working for me. He's in Miami now, but I don't know if he's worth a shit. Come on, Dwight. The cash and one little favor."

Dwight shook his head. "Ten cold and a pound of cocaine I've been holding. It's superlative shit. You'll have the time of your life, until it kills you."

The phone rang. Dr. Fred picked up, mumbled and listened. Dwight heard *scree-scree* noise. It sounded like a Bureau patch call.

Dr. Fred nodded. Dwight grabbed the phone. The *scree-scree*s faded to an Okie twang. The caller said, "Dwight, it's Buddy Fritsch. I got me a cluster fuck here, and you better come."

A puddle jumper got him into McCarran. He cabbed downtown to LVPD. Buddy was holed up in his office. He was half-tanked. He was pacing. Three cigarettes burned in one ashtray.

Dwight shut the door and locked it. Buddy quit pacing and noticed him.

"I got this AG's man squeezing me. He's got a print on Janice, and he's rolling the dice. Okay, he offered me money, but I still can't see no way out, except to hand up Wayne and—"

Dwight grabbed him. Dwight threw him over the desk and dumped a file cabinet on him. Dwight pulled the air conditioner off the wall and dropped it on his back. Dwight kicked him in the balls three times.

"You get me a freak to hand up for Wayne Senior, and you do it now."

11

(Miami, 8/8/68)

Bug work:

The wires, the pliers, the screwdrivers. The drills, the mounts, the baseboard dust. Butterfingers: sweaty hands on gnat-size devices.

The Eden Roc Hotel. Drill job: suite 1206 into suite 1207. Crutch worked with Freddy Turentine. Freddy was the "Bug King." Freddy's bug résumé astounded. Freddy was on loan to Clyde Duber Associates. Freddy usually worked for "Shakedown King" Fred Otash.

They drilled. 1206 was their listening post. Farlan Brown was due in 1207 shortly. Time clock: the Find Gretchen Farr gig was moving way into five figures.

They drilled. They bored through to 1207 and pushed wires in. Crutch picked the door lock. They got full-suite access. They miked up the bedroom lamp shades. They tapped the two phones. They Spackle-covered the wall wires and applied touch-up paint. They stuffed baffling in the bore-through holes and sanded the rough spots down smooth. They swept up all the baseboard dust and zoomed back to 1206.

Finger-cramping drudge work—four full hours. Crutch was grit-encrusted. His fingers hurt. He had Spackle dust in his ears, eyes and nasal nooks. He took a shower and cleaned up. Freddy went to his room to snooze. Crutch turned the living room TV on and put the sound low. The screen faced the bug-tap receiver. He grabbed a chair, hooked on headphones and listened to dead air next door.

The TV half-ass absorbed him. Nixon got the nod, first ballot, yawn/snore/soporific. Nixon emitted stupe vibes. He did that V-for-victory thing and looked like a rube robot. The news cut to riot footage. The Miami Congo blazed. It derived from a spook housing-project brouhaha. Spooks were stoning and sniping white motorists. Nigger mobs, arson, looting. Hot-weather action. Groovy footage.

Crutch yawned. He was running on six-week sleep deficit, all per HIS CASE.

HIS case. Not Clyde or Buzz Duber's. *HIS* side deal with Dr. Fred. *HIS* shot at the million-dollar Hughes deal. *HIS* side deal side deal: Gretchen Farr as Celia Reyes. Add the knife-scar woman. Add the house with the door markings and the body parts in the kitchen.

HIS CASE.

Farlan Brown was Miami-bound. Wayne Tedrow Jr. was here already. Junior had Senior's hate-mail stash. Dr. Fred wanted it. Junior worked for Farlan Brown and Dracula Hughes. Dr. Fred wanted to sell Drac his racial-purity plan. Crazy shit—sure. But crazy shit with dollar signs attached.

$$$$$$$$$—

He's hoarded his secret knowledge. He's held it back from Clyde, Buzz and Dr. Fred. They don't know about Gretchen as Celia. They don't know about the knife-scar woman or the Horror House on North Tamarind.

HIS CASE—now six weeks in.

His pad was file-crammed already. His mother's file ate up most of his floor and shelf space. He rented a second file pad downtown. The Elm Hotel—twelve scoots a week. A piss-in-the-sink dive for rum-dum pensioners. He laid in some file boxes and reams of file paper. He's on the job full-time.

Filework: lead file, car file, forensic file, file on 2216 North Tamarind.

He researched the Horror House. It was *not* an Arnie Moffett party-rental crib. It was *near* the Gretchen/Celia–rented house and the other party cribs. Proximity did not equal connection. Yeah, but—the weird thrust of that night made *everything* seem connected. It was like a dream state. Gretchen/Celia and the knife-scar woman kiss—and his world re-situates.

House research. Paydirt: the Hollywood Chamber of Commerce owned Horror House and used it for fund-raisers. It stood unoccupied since mid-'67. He snuck in again and rolled every goddamn room for prints. He got nothing but smudges and bullshit partials. The Chamber let him look at their fund-raiser file. Groups were listed, guest lists were not. *There was no way to know who had been in the house.* The girl at the Chamber told him one blood-churning thing: sleazoid hippies broke in and squatted there sometimes. Question: what were Gretchen/Celia and the knife-scar woman *still* doing in the Moffett house? Easy answer: squatting rent-free after their real rent expired. Question: who bought Phil Irwin off the Find Gretchen gig? Possible answer: Farlan Brown, via Hughes Tool Co. Brown got wind of the gig. Brown wanted Gretchie un–fucked with. His motive? Who fucking knows?

House file to car file.

He bribed a clerk at Hertz Rent a Car. Gretchen/Celia returned the '66 Comet with the radiator blown. That mandated a no-rental stint. Thus, the Comet stayed untouched since the drop-off night. Crutch re-bribed the Hertz guy and got two hours alone with the Comet. He print-wiped and got one latent. He spent five weeks hand-checking female print cards at the L.A. County Sheriff's Department and LAPD. So far, no match.

Car file to forensic file.

Clyde had dirt on the county coroner, "Tojo" Tom Takahashi. Tojo Tom was a jailbait Johnny with a yen for young Jap cooze. Crutch leaned on him and told him to keep mum with Clyde on all this. Tojo Tom agreed. Crutch waltzed him into Horror House two nights after his first entry. They split a pint of Jim Beam and tamped down their nerves. They worked by Coleman lantern light. Crutch took photos. Tojo Tom examined and bagged the body parts and took blood and tissue samples. Crutch got pix of the tattoo on the arm and the geometric wall markings. Tojo Tom removed the crumbled green stones from the arm gouge and separately bagged them.

It took hours. The smell was foul. Crutch held the lantern while Tojo Tom brushed maggots off. Tojo Tom called it an "evisceration snuff." The victim was a young Latin woman. He had her blood analyzed and called Crutch with the results. It was type O+, very common, no outstanding characteristics. He found odd powder fragments in the gouged tissue and had them analyzed. Very odd: there was no toxicology make. Crutch had a gemologist analyze the green stone fragments. Emeralds? No, just green glass.

Forensic file to tattoo file. Canvassing from there.

Crutch hit a total of forty-seven tattoo parlors in and around L.A. He showed his photo of the partial tattoo to endless tattoo freaks. So far, no make. Tattoo file to lead file. He hit LAPD and Sheriff's R&I again. He checked mug books, teletypes and occurrence-field interrogation files for mentions of Gretchen/Celia and got zero. Cop files to INS files. He scanned photo sheets for every female immigrant from every Latin American country extant and got zero on Gretchen/Celia. He remembered Bev's Switchboard. Gretchen/Celia got calls from three foreign consulates: Panama, Nicaragua, the Dominican Republic. He called all three and got three more zeros: no records of calls to Gretchen/Celia. Her Dominican driver's license turned out to be a phony. The Dominican national DMV had no listing. That bootleg-number call to Bev's Switchboard? No make on it yet.

$$$ to ??? and back again—dollar signs, question marks and zeros.

The kiss. The shadows in and out of his vision. The knife-scar woman's gray-streaked hair. She didn't have a name. Gretchen/Celia had two. *He wanted to know that woman's name.* He drew pictures of her and papered his walls with them. He gave her her own real features, not Dana Lund's.

Their talk—"Grapevine," "Tommy," "plant"—what did it mean? He checked city directories nationwide. He found listings for 216 Grapevine restaurants, hotels, motels and bars. He didn't know where he should start checking or *if* he should start checking or if it meant anything.

So, Gretchen/Celia fucked men and stole their money. "Al," "Chuck," "Lew," Dr. Fred, Farlan Brown potentially. Sal Mineo spilled all that *he* knew. Gretchen/Celia was allegedly left-wing. What did *that* mean? She wanted to "get next to" Farlan Brown—say what? on that. The knife-scar woman—how did *she* play in? The dead woman in the Horror House—was *she* connected?

Crutch brain-looped and watched TV. He got nigger-riot visuals and headphone fuzz next door. *Dead* air—Farlan Brown's suite was still still.

Avco Jewelers. Gretchen/Celia gets advice on re-cutting emeralds. The green glass shards in the dead woman's arm.

Question marks, dollar signs—

He looped through Las Vegas six times. He spot-tailed Farlan Brown and Wayne Tedrow Jr. He saw them at the D.I. They took the private elevator up to Dracula's lair. Brown has *not* seen Gretchen/Celia in Vegas. He's sure of it. Maybe she never hooked up with him. Maybe she ripped him off in L.A. and split. He ran a Miami phone book/airline check on the names Gretchen Farr and Celia Reyes. He got zero Gretchens. He got nine Celias and ran driver's license checks on them all. None of them were *her.*

He ran a Miami-airline check on Wayne Tedrow Jr. and hit positive. He ran a hotel check and located him at the Doral. He tailed Wayne Junior three times. Wayne Junior might have tail-spotted him. The Clark County D.A. passed a Vegas rumor on to Clyde Duber: Wayne Junior might have offed Wayne Senior in June.

It was all dizzying. It was re-situating, re-wire-all-your-circuits shit.

The tails went A-OK. Wayne Junior met a black-clad, foreign-looking guy twice. Crutch hit his rooming house and records-checked him. Jean-Philippe Mesplede, French merc, age forty-five. Mesplede and Wayne Junior combed Little Havana twice. Crutch followed up. The deal: they were looking for two Cuban men named Gaspar Fuentes and Miguel Díaz Arredondo.

The nigger riot heated up. The TV screen almost throbbed. Spooks lobbed Molotov cocktails. Spooks chased honkies with two-by-fours. Crutch heard movement next door.

Yeah, it's Farlan Brown's voice. That's him tipping the bellman. There's the door again. The bellman's gone. There's phone-dial noise. Yawn—there's Brown on the horn with his wife.

Blah, blah—the kids are fine, the dog has fleas, I love you, too. Hang-up noise. Door-opening noise. A young woman's voice.

Yeah, dig it—

They negotiated—fifty for French, a yard for half and half. Brown took the latter. The bed was by the wall unit. Air hum drowned out most of the trick. The climax came in fuzzy.

Brown bragged post-coital: I'm a big cheese with Howard Hughes. The call girl said, "Is that so?" Brown blathered. I'm hip, I'm cool, I swing. I run Hughes Airways. I'll be running Hughes charter flights to some rocking new mob resorts.

The call girl stifles a yawn. The bedsprings creak. A zipper threads. Bye, bye, baby—she's out the door.

Brown got back on the horn. Crutch hit console buttons and activated the tap line. He got garbles and a dial tone. He heard a gruff "Hel-lo."

Brown said, "Freddy, it's Farlan." A man said, "What's happening, *paisan*?" Crutch made the voice: Shakedown Fred O.

He hit his tape feed. The spool turned. He got garbles and voices verbatim.

Brown: . . . Miami. You know, for the convention.
Otash: Nixon. Jesus, that fucking retread has got nine fucking
  lives.
Brown: This one's a keeper. He's going to win.
Otash: I've got a sports book at the Cavern. My guy's calling the
  race even money.
Brown: I'll take those odds.
Otash: Then place a bet, you cheap Mormon cocksucker.
Brown: A grand on Dick. For real, Freddy. I smell victory.
Otash: I smell you trying to Jew me down on a room rate. That's it,
  right? Your old buddy Freddy's an innkeeper now, so let's put
  the boots to him.
Laughter—six seconds' worth.
Brown: . . . Freddy, you're a pistol.
Otash: I've *got* a pistol. I'm a well-hung American of Lebanese
  descent.

Laughter—nine seconds' worth.

Brown: Okay. I need a big suite at the Cavern. It's a party for some Democratic delegates, right before the convention. Booze and girls, Freddy. You know my MO.

Otash: When?

Brown: August 23.

Otash: I'll give you 308. It's my private spot, so treat it nice or I'll sic Dracula on you.

Brown: Wooo! I don't want that!

Otash: You *got* that, you Mormon cocksucker.

Brown: Cocksuckee, you mean.

Otash: So, confirm or deny a rumor for me.

Brown: Sure.

Otash: Tell true. Is Wayne Junior working for the Count?

Brown: He is. And high up at that.

Otash: Fucking Junior always lands on his feet.

Brown: Care to elaborate?

Otash: No comment.

Brown: On that note . . .

Otash: Yeah. See you on the 23. Thank you, fuck you, and good-bye.

Two hang-up clicks—Miami and Vegas. Crutch switched to the bug line. There: yawns, bed creaks, silence and snores.

He hit switches and shut down the feed lines. It was 1:14 a.m. His stomach growled. He'd surveilled his way through dinnertime and then some. He called Freddy Turentine's room and roused Freddy. He said they had a bug job in Vegas—a hotel suite by August 22. Freddy said, "Remind me tomorrow," and hung up.

The TV was still on. Nixon did the V-for-victory thing. What a geek. He always needed a shave.

Crutch yawned and got antsy concurrent. He popped four dexies and snagged his rent-a-car keys.

Wrong turns and U-turns de-situated him. The Doral was near the Eden Roc. Wayne Junior's hotel—just two minutes out. One-way streets put him on a causeway. The bay water churned with confetti and floating Nixon signs. The exit markers confused him. Side streets sidetracked him. He smelled smoke. He heard gunfire. Neighborhoods devolved into shine shantytowns. He saw two spooks torch a '59 Plymouth.

The spooks saw him—Honky! Honky! Honky! Crutch gunned it and hung a Uey. The spooks chased his car. A tall spook lobbed a cinder block and hit his back window. The block decomposed. The window stayed intact. The spooks yelled spook-outrage slogans and spooked on back to the Plymouth.

Crutch got his bearings. He drove fast and steered clear of smoke stench and flames. The roving spook quotient upgraded to spook winos and porch loafers. He hit a spook-free zone and made it back to the causeway and Miami Beach proper. The detour got him finger-popping *alive*. He skimmed the radio and found a soul station. He grooved on Archie Bell and the Drells with "The Tighten Up."

He parked outside the Doral. He eyeballed the door and played the soul station. The DJ talked pro-riot Commie shit with cool spook music mixed in. Wayne Tedrow Jr. walked out at 2:49 a.m. He shagged *his* rent-a-car. Crutch tailed him.

Convention traffic was still steady. Tail cover was good. Crutch hovered two car lengths back. Wayne Junior stuck to spook-free zones and booked to Little Havana. He swooped by Jean-Philippe Mesplede's rooming house and picked up the Frogman. Crutch vibed it: another trawl for Gaspar Fuentes and Miguel Díaz Arredondo.

Flagler Street hopped. The coffee bars were open late. A radio guy did man-in-the-street interviews. Arson outside the Cuban Freedom Council— some beaners burning a straw Fidel.

Mesplede and Wayne Junior did their thing. Crutch knew it now. They ditched the car, walked storefront-to-storefront and asked questions. Crutch stayed mobile. He slow-trawled Flagler and *looked*. Mesplede and Wayne Junior did a one-hour loop and re-mobilized. Traffic was thin. Crutch hovered four car lengths back.

Wayne Junior pulled to the curb and walked to a pay phone. Mesplede stayed in the car. Crutch hit the brakes and pulled over *eight* car lengths back.

He got out his binoculars and zoomed in. Wayne Junior fed quarters to the phone slot—long-distance, for sure. Crutch got in *clooooose*. Wayne Junior's lips moved. Two seconds and *halt*—Wayne Junior just listened.

And trembled. And went pale. And hung up, walked back to the car and leaned in Mesplede's window.

More lip movement. Crutch zoomed in *très* close. The talk looked panicky. Mesplede slid behind the wheel and pulled out, peeling rubber. Wayne Junior walked to a parked taxi cab and got in the back.

The cab pulled out. Crutch tailed it. Traffic was too sparse to get close. Crutch killed his headlights and cued on the cab's taillights. They cut across this *biiiiiig* swath of Miami.

The terrain got rural. The roads got rough and swervy. The cab pulled ahead. Crutch turned his lights on just to *see*. Dirt roads swerved up to a rinky-dink airfield. Crutch saw a two-seater prop job on the runway.

He stopped the car. He couldn't see the cab. He got out and squinted in the dark. He was discombobulated. He couldn't see shit.

Floodlights snapped on. Crutch got glare-blinded. He blinked. He rubbed his eyes. He got some sight back. He saw Wayne Junior, standing by the airplane, looking straight at him.

12

Buddy Fritsch said, "I got us a suspect."

His den was polar-cold. He served highballs and Fritos. Chuck Woodrell had the flu and kept sniffling. Dwight kept tugging at his law-school ring. Wayne was frazzled—that bumpy flight and thirty-six sleepless hours.

It was 9:00 p.m. Miami felt like a fever dream. His time zones were stretched disproportionate.

Fritsch passed around a mug-shot strip: three views of a male Negro. Sylvester "Pappy" Dawkins, age forty-eight. A lean man with a fuck-you demeanor. Inked on the back: burglary raps from '42 up.

Woodrell said, "Woooo, boy."

Dwight said, "Hide the kiddies."

Fritsch said, "He's a residential burglar with rape-o tendencies. He was in custody near Barstow on the night Wayne Senior died, which don't make no difference to us. He's got no alibi for that night, and it's a little two-man PD. I can buy both them boys off."

The strip recirculated. Woodrell said, "Katy-bar-the-door." Dwight said, "Electric chair, sweetheart." Wayne shut his eyes and passed the strip back.

Fritsch slurped his highball. "Washoe County makes him for two burglary snuffs, so it ain't like he's a contributing member of society. He pulls B&Es all messed-up on goofballs, so he'll make a piss-poor witness."

Woodrell nibbled Fritos. "I like him. He's five seconds out of the trees."

Fritsch said, "I got a print transparency. We can roll it through a blood sample and pre-date it."

Dwight rubbed his neck. "How much?"

Woodrell said, "Fifty on my end."

Fritsch squirmed. "Uh . . . twenty for me? And I'll take care of the Barstow boys out of that?"

Dwight nodded. "I'll tap you-know-who. He wants to see this covered."

Wayne said, "No."

Fritsch froze mid-slurp. Woodrell froze mid-bite. Wayne said, "No more."

Woodrell sighed. "This is just about the biggest favor you'll ever get in this lifetime."

Fritsch sighed. "Don't be a Bolshevik, son."

Woodrell laughed. "Mr. Sensitive. With the niggers he's got on *his* résumé."

Wayne looked at him. "Stop right there. Don't make me take this any further."

Woodrell flushed and got shaky-kneed. Fritsch said, "Sweet Jesus." Dwight pointed to the two of them and the door. They caught the gist and walked out. Dwight stood up and hauled Wayne upright. Dwight grabbed his shirtfront and slapped him.

It stung. It raised blood dots. Wayne popped pain tears. It was a love tap by Dwight Holly standards.

"It's for Janice. It's for both of us and everything you've put your hands on. It's for this fucked-up hole we're both in."

Wayne wiped his nose. Blood pooled in his mouth. His tears dried quick.

"This has to happen, so you let it happen, *and you do not fold on me.* I need that from you, and I may need you for the Grapevine. Otash went to St. Louis, we'll need to talk to him about it, and we might have to go in at some point."

His blood tasted funny. Dwight held him up. His legs were gone.

"I need you to stand in. I need your father's mail lists, and if push comes to shove with the Grapevine, I want you there."

Wayne nodded. Dwight let his hands go. Wayne weaved and stayed up.

The sheets were moist. Her gown was damp. Her pulse ran weak-steady. Wayne flicked the dial and fed dope to the tube.

Heroin. His compound. A morphine-base synthetic.

Janice unclenched. Wayne wiped her brow and toweled the sheets half-dry. The night nurse was sleeping in the living room. Janice was all sweat and chills.

Wayne took her hands. "There's something that has to be done to give us some safety. When you hear about it, you'll know. It wasn't my idea, and there's no way around it."

Janice shut her eyes. Tears leaked. She pulled her hands free. They felt weightless, all veins and bone.

Wayne flicked the dial. Dope flowed bag to tube to vein. Janice went out, shuddering.

Her pulse was weak-normal. Wayne arranged her hair on the pillow. He grabbed the bedside phone and dialed Mesplede in Miami.

Three rings. A sleep-slapped *"Oui?"*

"It's Wayne."

"Yes, of course. My American friend in duress."

"Do something for me."

"Of course."

"There was a kid tailing me in Miami. I don't know what it's about, but it's trouble."

"Yes? And your wish?"

"Early twenties, medium-sized, crew cut. He's driving an Avis rent-a-car. The plate number is GQV-881."

"Yes? And your wish?"

"Find out his business and clip him."

The vault was twelve miles east of Vegas. Wayne Senior had dubbed it the "Führer bunker." It was a scrub-covered cement square sunk in a sand drift. It was straight out I-15.

Wayne brought a flashlight, a gas can and a Zippo lighter. The location was a mile off the interstate. The vault held copies of all Senior's hate tracts and his subscriber lists.

Wayne parked on a turnaround near a Chevron station and walked into the desert. It was 106° at midnight. Sand sucked at his feet and slowed his walk to a trudge. It was slow slow motion. He thought about Dallas the whole time.

He got there. He pulled off scrub branches, unlocked the door and hauled hate lit out. Titles jumped off covers. He saw *Miscegenation Generation* and *Jew Stew: A Recipe Book*. He saw *Pope Pontius: How Papists Rule the Jewnited Nations*. He saw doctored pix of Dr. King and little Negro kids. He saw facsimile editions of vintage Klan kodebooks.

He stripped the shelves. He lugged paper and ink-smudged his arms black. He saw hate headlines. He saw pornographic hate cartoons. He saw lynching photos with gag captions.

He built a big hate pile. It stood eight feet high. He doused it with gasoline. He sparked the Zippo and put the flame down.

The pile flared straight up and out. The big black sky went red.

13

(Las Vegas, 8/10/68)

The sky went red to orange. Dwight stood by the service pumps and watched.

The blaze backlit the desert floor and the highway. He saw Wayne's car on the turnaround. His tail-job-on-instinct got him *this*.

Two pump jockeys stood around, gawking. A hot wind blew smoke their way. Dwight walked to a pay phone, fed the slot quarters and dialed direct to L.A.

The smoke was thick with paper bits. Dwight felt the sting. Karen picked up immediately.

"Hello?"

"It's me."

"You're not supposed to call when he's in town, goddamnit."

Dwight said, "Talk slow to me. Just a minute, please."

Karen said something back. He didn't hear it. His eyes were all wet and fucked-up. He couldn't tell if it was the smoke or his crazy love for Wayne.

14

(Miami, 8/10/68)

Smoke and fire. The spooks refused to quit. Gunshots, sirens and a 4:00 a.m. light show.

Crutch pulled into the Avis lot. The clutch on his rent-a-car blew. The gears were stripped. The car lurched and lugged. He called ahead. The desk guy said, Screw the riot. You come right in.

Half-tracks rolled down Biscayne Boulevard. The governor called in the Guard. There's a string of cop cars and a six-seater Jeep. Fuck, the driver's smoking a joint.

Smoke and fire. Swamp heat. This orange sky edging toward mauve.

The car lurched and died by the gas pumps. Crutch got out and stretched. Heat and fumes smacked him. His head hurt. He'd been working the bug post full-time. He'd been up since God knows—

Someone/Something pushed him. He tumbled back in the car. His head hit the shift knob. His arms hit the dashboard. The Someone/Something pinned him down. He/It was all black.

Then the knee on his back. Then the gun in his face. With the silencer barrel-threaded and the hammer half-back.

"Why are you surveilling Wayne Tedrow? Be honest. Evasion will decree an even more horrible death."

The French accent. The Frogman. Frog couture all black.

"I repeat. Why were you surveilling Wayne Tedrow?"

Crutch tried to pray. The words hit his brain jumbled. His piss tubes swelled. He held it in. The weight on him helped. He remembered his lucky rabbit's foot and obscure Lutheran Church lore.

"I repeat."

His shit chute swelled. He held it in. The weight on him helped. He opened his mouth. He squeaked and got some sounds out. God or some unseen fucker fed him word soup. He saw his mother. He heard "Dr. Fred," "Howard Hughes," "Grapevine plant," "million dollars." He heard "Dead woman," "missing woman," "knife-scar woman," "green stones." He heard "Please don't kill me" six billion times in six seconds.

He shut his eyes. His tear ducts swelled. He held it in. Biting his tongue helped. Six billion years went by in six seconds. He saw his mother and Dana Lund six billion times. He tried for prayers and dredged up hymns.

The weight eased up. He clenched his tubes, chutes and ducts and stayed dry. He smelled brandy. The scent touched his lips strong. He opened his mouth. He dipped his head and took the pour. His throat constricted. He opened wider and let it roll in. He opened his eyes and saw the Frogman.

"I have been prone to sympathetic lapses before. You must affirm my perception of your youthful willfulness and capacity for acquiescence."

Crutch crawled into the passenger seat. His heartbeat kept multiplying. He was head-to-toe sweat. The Frogman stretched out in the driver's seat. He nipped off the flask and passed it back. Crutch chugged brandy and looked out the window. There's more smoke, sirens and riot cops—the spooks just won't quit.

Mesplede said, "I may ask you to report information to me."

Crutch nodded—yessir, yessir, yessir.

The flask went back and forth. A sync settled in. Their eyes stayed locked while the Frogman monologued. It was all CUBA. It was *le grand putain* Fidel Castro and the Cuban Freedom Cause. There was JFK's Bay of Pigs betrayal. There was LBJ's Commie appeasement. There was America's sissified accommodation and the Caribbean as a Spreading Red Lake. There were brave men willing to die to quash the Red Tide.

The flask went back and forth. The oration continued. Crutch rode the world's greatest buzz.

15

(Las Vegas, 8/10/68)

The night nurse took a break to play the slots downstairs. Wayne ran into her in the casino. She said, "You look ill—I'll bring you something."

He took the stairs up and burned off excess steam. He still smelled like charred paper. The suite was unlocked. He walked into Janice's bedroom.

The lights were on. The IV pole and drip bag were down on the floor. The tube was still attached to Janice's arm. The needle was half in, half out.

Two empty vials on the nightstand. Seconal and Dilaudid. A brief note: "Whatever your plan—please, not on my behalf."

Wayne sat with her. Her nightgown was still damp. The picture blurred with '64. He came home and found Lynette. Wendell Durfee had come and gone. A winter storm leveled Vegas. He sat with Lynette and listened to the rain.

Janice died clutching the bedsheets. Wayne pried her fingers loose and folded them on her chest.

West Vegas hopped at 2:00 a.m. The bars were air-cooled. The shacks weren't. Folks stayed out late to cool off.

Wayne cruised in. He passed the Wild Goose, the Colony Club and the Sugar Hill Lounge. Memory Lane. The ALLAH IS LORD signs. Night owls cooking bar-b-q in fifty-gallon drums. Streets named for presidents and designated by letters.

He had Pappy Dawkins' address. It should be off Monroe and J. He scanned faces. Everybody was black. Parked cars with running head-lights. Air-conditioned junkers. Beat the heat. Run the vents all night and sleep.

There's the place: a fuchsia-colored cinder-block dump on plywood struts.

Wayne parked and walked up. The lights were on. The door was open. The front room was furnished with scavenged car seats. A dozen fans pushed air around.

Two Negro men sat there. They were side by side on Chevy leather. Pappy looked older than his mug shots. The other man ran fifty-plus and wore a clerical suit.

They noticed him. They made him. Wayne made their little blinks. The fans churned up a stink: cat piss and stale marijuana.

Wayne shut the door. The smell compounded. Pappy said, "Sergeant Wayne Tedrow Jr."

Wayne coughed. "Not any longer."

"You mean you ain't with the po-lice or you the only Wayne Tedrow left?"

"Both of those."

The other man said, "He wants something. You should let him get to it."

Pappy twirled an ashtray. "Reverend Hazzard's trying to reform me. He visits me once a month, whether I asks him to or not. I say to him, 'This white motherfucker here killed three brothers awhile back,' he probably say, 'Turn the other cheek.' "

Wayne spoke to Hazzard. "This won't take but a minute."

Pappy hurled the ashtray. It knocked a fan over. The breeze went hay-wire. Some nesting moths stirred.

"Reverend Hazzard believes you turn the other cheek, but I most emphasizedly do not, unless you wants to bend down and kiss the cheeks of my coal black ass."

Hazzard touched Pappy's arm. Pappy grabbed a stray shoe off the floor and hurled it. A fan capsized. A breeze hit the back wall. A Scotch-taped pic of Malcolm X flew.

"Reverend Hazzard says, 'Forgiveness be next to godliness,' but I most emphasizedly do not, unless you wants to start by apologizing for killing Leroy Williams and the Swasey brothers and any other extraneous nig-gers that you also might have killed along the way."

Hazzard said, "Pappy, please."

Wayne said, "Sir, I apologize."

Pappy grabbed another shoe. "And that's all you got to say?"

"No, there's more."

"Which includes what?"

Wayne's legs fluttered. "Some cops are trying to hang a case on you. I don't want to see it happen. I'll get you some money, but you've got to get out of Vegas."

Pappy whooped. "Leave all *this*? On your white motherfucking say-so?"

Hazzard said, "Pappy, let him talk."

Pappy whooped falsetto. "Not until I've had my fun and extricated my pound of flesh, starting with, 'Hey, Junior, you apologize again.' "

Wayne said, "Sir, I apologize."

Whoop—"One more time now. I'm starting to enjoy this."

Wayne shook his head *no*. His legs almost caved. Pappy threw the shoe *at* him. He stepped aside. Pappy reached in his pocket. Wayne threw himself on the floor.

Metal flashed. Wayne ate rug grit and pulled his ankle piece. Pappy fumbled a snub automatic. Reverend Hazzard froze. Pappy rolled off the car seat and aimed down at Wayne.

They fired simultaneous. The floor exploded by Wayne's face. He aimed through plaster dust and *squeezed* the trigger *slow*. He hit Pappy mid-chest. Pappy spun and jerked the trigger. His hand spasmed. He sent shots every which way.

They hit the fans. Soft points—the blades diced and ricocheted them. Bullet shards became shrapnel pellets. They burst wide and tore out Hazzard's throat. He gasped and pitched off the car seat. Wayne aimed up and *squeezed slow*. The shot hit Pappy mid-face. He fell backward. His head hit a whirring fan and sent red up and out.

16

The squadroom was dead. LVPD ran a light crew from midnight on. Four detectives caught city-wide squeals. They got paid to doze at their desks or shag ass.

They slept. Dwight couldn't sleep. The desert fire still torqued him. He went by the Golden Cavern an hour back. Fred Otash was still up. They discussed his St. Louis trip. Freddy spent time at the Grapevine. The hit rumors: still escalating. The purveyors: six right-wing fucks. The ATF surveillance: intermittent, but sustained. The upshot: we can't go in with ATF hovering. We hold for now.

Dwight yawned. Late-night squadrooms consoled him. They were cop still-life tableaux. The St. Louis SAC pledged a late-night teletype. Dwight chair-perched by the machine.

The squadroom was quiet. The cops dozed. The detention-cage winos snored. The teletype machine rattled. Dwight pulled a sheet out.

Terse and shitty news. Be advised: ATF has Grapevine Tavern under lockstep surveillance.

Dwight tore the sheet up and trash-canned it. A patrol cop ran in. He was a beanpole rookie type in a lather. He yelled his good news and woke the crew up.

Body count! Somebody nailed that hump Pappy Dawkins and some shine preacher!

.   .   .

The street was sealed. Dwight badged the perimeter cop and pulled right up to the tape. Inside it: three patrol cars, one coroner's car and two dead jigs on gurneys.

Live jigs outside the tape: geeks in nightgowns, skivvies and pajamas. A fatso was snarfing chicken wings at 4 fucking a.m.

Two patrol cops by the house. Buddy Fritsch in civvies, looking justifiably freaked.

Dwight whistled long and shrill. Fritsch heard it and looked over. Dwight pointed to his Fed sled. Fritsch blew off the patrol cops and walked straight up.

Dwight opened the back door. Fritsch got in. He had the shakes. He pulled a hip flask and took two maintenance pops. Dwight got in and shut the door. Two tall men—their knees brushed.

"So?"

"So, who do you think? I got me four eyewits. White man walks in, shots fired, white man walks out. He's six-one, one eighty, pale, with dark hair. Sound like anyone we know?"

The flask booze smelled good—heavy-sweet bourbon. Fritsch took two more pops.

"Wayne blew his cork again. When that boy don't know what to do, he just goes out and hunts niggers."

Mumbo jumbo down the block. Dwight looked over. Fatso led some Zulus in a black-power cheer.

Fritsch sucked on his flask. "To boot, I got me a morgue call. Janice Tedrow took some pills and checked out."

Dwight said, "How much?"

"No, siree. I'm sorry, but there ain't no buyout on this one."

"How *much*, Buddy? You, Woodrell, the AG and anyone else we need to square this."

Fritsch shook his head. "Uh-*uh*. No sale. Your boy don't get no walk on this one."

Dwight tugged at his law-school ring. "Give me a figure. Be generous with yourself. I'll get you the money and let you grease everyone else."

Fritsch shook his head. "Uh-*uh*. No sale. Sorry, Wayne, but you killed two coons too many. This is 1968, son. 'The times, they are a-changin'.' "

Dwight laughed. Fritsch laughed. Dwight said, "Pick a figure."

"Uh-*uh*. No sale. This is one that you and Mr. Hoover can't buy Junior out of."

"Are you sure?"

"Sure I'm sure. I am absolutely, positively goddamn sure that there's no price tag on this one."

"One last time, then. For the record."

Fritsch jabbed Dwight's chest. "For the record, *no.* For the record, you put some hurt on me a little while back, and that's all the guff I'm taking from you. You may be Mr. Hoover's number-one goon, but I am a ranking police officer and a decorated World War II vet, and I am not eating any more shit dispensed by some Hoosier hard-on who thinks he's tough shit 'cause he went to Yale."

Dwight smiled and pointed to the flask. Fritsch smiled and passed it over. Dwight took a big pop and passed it back. Fritsch grinned and stretched. His suit coat gapped. Dwight pulled off his belt gun and stuffed it under the seat. Fritsch swallowed. His Adam's apple bob-bob-bobbed.

Dwight pulled his Magnum, popped the cylinder and dumped five shells. Fritsch rolled his eyes—don't shit a shitter. Dwight spun the cylinder and snapped it shut. Fritsch said, "You're bluffing."

Dwight put the gun to his head and pulled the trigger. The hammer hit an empty chamber.

"How much?"

"Fuck you. You bluff, I call. I am a ranking police officer, and this is my crime scene."

Dwight put the gun to his head and pulled the trigger. The hammer hit an empty chamber. Buddy Fritsch shit his britches. Dwight caught the stench.

"How much?"

"Fuck you."

Dwight put the gun to his head and pulled the trigger. The hammer hit an empty chamber. Buddy Fritsch pissed his pants. Dwight watched the stain spread.

"How much?"

"Fuck you fuck you fuck you fuck you."

Dwight put the gun to his head and pulled the trigger. The hammer hit an empty chamber. Buddy Fritsch sobbed.

Dwight said, "How much?" Fritsch kept sobbing. Dwight rolled down the window. He heard black-power chants and saw black fists raised.

Fritsch said, "Two hundred."

Dwight said, "It's yours."

It required a proactive phone call. It recalled January '57. He left two dead on the Merritt Parkway. Mr. Hoover rescued him.

Dwight called from his hotel suite. He got two rings and "Yes?"

"It's Dwight Holly, Sir."

"Yes? And the most pressing emergency that you wish to discuss?"

"Wayne Tedrow killed two Negro men. I need a good deal of money to cover it, and I'd be grateful for your help."

Mr. Hoover coughed. "And the amount?"

"Two hundred cold."

"Is Junior in custody?"

"No, Sir."

"And where would he be?"

"I would guess Wayne Senior's cabin in Lake Tahoe."

"Does he usually repose there after he kills male Negroes?"

"Yes, Sir."

"Does he watch the *Soul Train* TV show for upbeat entertainment and to expiate his guilt?"

"I would guess that he brews up narcotic compounds for the purposes of sedation and sleep."

Mr. Hoover worked for breath. "You haven't called me in a very long time, Dwight. It was January '58, I believe."

"You're close, Sir. It was '57."

"Are you questioning my memory, Dwight?"

"No, Sir."

"It was January of 1958. It was unseasonably warm that day on the Cross County Parkway."

That *night,* icy roads, the Merritt—

"That's right, Sir. I'd forgotten. It was so long ago."

"I'll wire the funds, Dwight. I'm as soft for you as you are for Junior."

"Thank you, Sir."

"The Grapevine Tavern, Dwight. Outlandish talk is circulating. ATF cannot lockstep the location forever. That outrageous chatter will have to be muffled at some point."

"I understand, Sir."

"Good night, Dwight."

He started to say "Good night, Sir." Coughs and a hang-up click stopped him.

The kid had lost weight. His hair had thinned. Some fresh gray was there with the brown. He went fit to gaunt in a week.

The funeral home smelled like spearmint. Dwight caught embalming fluid as the underscent. Wayne sat beside Janice's casket. The lid was closed. It was lustrous mahogany.

Dwight pulled a chair up. Wayne looked at him.

"Her golf clubs are in there."

Dwight smiled. "She'd appreciate the touch."

"I tried to warn him."

"I figured it was that."

"She was forty-six years, nine months and sixteen days old."

"You're a chemist. You'd know something like that."

"You're a lawyer. Tell me what this is about."

Dwight said, "It's chilled. I went to Mr. Hoover. If I went to Carlos, he'd have figured you'd lost it. Everyone will know sooner or later, so you'd better get back in the game."

Wayne stood up and flanked the casket. He hovered and ran his fingers over the grain.

Dwight said, "We've still got the Grapevine."

Wayne said, "I understand."

17

(Los Angeles, 8/19/68)

Scotty Bennett said, "I like your tie and your hair."

Crutch blushed. The tartan and the crew cut were his lucky charms. He got them the same day he saw Horror House. They prophesied all his magical shit.

Scotty loomed. They stood in the latent-prints room. Crutch was hand-checking print cards. He'd been at it two months.

"Run this by me again. You saw a girl at Woody's Smorgasburger. She drank a 7UP and left her prints on a glass, and you've been trying to ascertain her identity ever since."

Crutch blushed. "Right. I've been on a job for Clyde, and I've been ducking over here whenever I get a chance."

Scotty roared—kid, you slay me. He tucked a ten-spot in Crutch's pocket. He adjusted his tie and rubbed his crew cut.

"I'm forty-seven, you're twenty-three. I'm a policeman, you're not. Lose the tie and let your hair grow. You may get some."

The ten-spot dangled there. Scotty said, "Call Laurel. Webster-64882. Tell her I said to be kind."

Crutch re-blushed. Scotty winked and waltzed to the Robbery pen. Print cards jumped up and yelled *Study me!*

Back to work.

Lay out the photo blowup. Grab the magnifying glass. Lay out the next print card and notch comparison points. He had the rent-a-car print memorized. He knew every loop and whorl. He'd been through six zillion print cards since June 21.

He studied, he tossed cards, he yawned, he stretched, he blinked. Eye-strain goo pooled on his eyeballs. He hit a fast stretch—a card a minute and—

Then:

A fresh card. Familiar loops and whorls. 1, 2, 3, 4, 5, 6, 7, 8, 9, 10 comparison points—a courtroom-valid tally.

Crutch studied the card and the blowup. He wiped his eyes, he squinted, he *looked.* 11, 12, 13, 14—a perfect match.

He turned the card over. He read the stats:

"Klein, Joan Rosen/WF/DOB 10/31/26, New York City. 5'4", 120, brown eyes/dark brown & gray hair. Distinguishing marks: Knife scar on upper right arm."

Her, she, that woman. She had a name: JOAN.

She was forty-one. She was born on Halloween. Her rap sheet looked like a partial. Crutch saw arrests and no convictions. Commie beefs. Alien and Sedition Act violations, back to '44. Two armed robbery busts—'51, '53—no D.R. numbers for conviction.

Commie beefs. Heists. No attached mug shots. Crutch ran to the photo lab—

His new file room was cramped already. File boxes, file stacks, the big wall graph. He had two pads in one city. He slept in them both. He kept his mother's file at the Vivian Apartments. He kept his case file at the Elm Hotel. He kept hot-plate chow and shaving gear at both locations.

Crutch split to the Elm. The graph drew him first thing. He'd Scotch-taped masking paper up at eye level. He doodled on it. He drew lines and arrows and wrote daily progress and summary reports.

He got out his grease pen and found a fresh spot. He wrote "Joan" and circled it. He drew some arrows with black feathers and sharp little points, leading to:

"Farlan Brown leads going nowhere to (8/10/68) date. Brown meet at Golden Cavern (8/23/68). F.T. to wire suite."

"Gretchen Farr/Celia Reyes: all records checks negative to (8/10/68) date."

" 'Grapevine,' 'Tommy' & 'plant': what do they mean?"

"Tattoo ID, wall markings & powder on body parts: no make as of this (8/10/68) date."

"Bootleg phone #: phone co. trace in progress."

Crutch scanned the graph. Crutch drew arrows pointing to "Joan." Crutch circled the name with big question marks.

He flopped on the bed. He studied the photo-lab pix. A single mug-shot strip. One full-face shot, two profiles. Joan Rosen Klein wearing a neck board.

The board numbers supplied a date: 7/12/63. He knew the booking-number prefix. It meant "detained for suspicion." That probably meant a street roust or wrong-place-at-wrong-time grief. Joan was a Commie and a two-time robbery suspect—she'd attract heat.

She was thirty-six then. She looked the same now. She wore glasses. She smiled into flashbulb glare. That near-black hair with the gray streaks. That wide and harsh jawline. That composed set to her face.

Crutch shut his eyes, opened his eyes and studied the pictures again. He saw gray streaks that he'd missed the first bunch of times.

The bed was covered with library books. He'd checked them out post-Miami. They covered one topic: Cuba.

He kept in touch with Jean-Philippe Mesplede. The Frogman was his friend now. They talked long-distance, L.A. to Miami. The Frogman liked him. The Frogman thought he was a punk kid in over his head and refused to take his case seriously. Fuck him on that—let him think it. The Frogman thought it was just a thieving-girlfriend caper. Crutch held back the wild-ass dimensions.

Wayne Tedrow Jr. wanted Donald Linscott Crutchfield dead, but Jean-Philippe Mesplede relented. The Frogman called Wayne Junior "unstable and politically suspect." Wayne Junior sustained right-wing alliances and suppressed his left-wing tendencies. Froggy could not commit murder for such a compromised man.

So Crutch got to live and work his case and magnetize all his magical shit.

Their phone calls were all Cuba. A gorgeous island. A tourist mecca. A paradise raped by the Reds. Jack Kennedy betrayed the Bay of Pigs invasion. LBJ appeased Castro. The next prez would ditto his rat-fink policies. The Frogman raged to ravage Reds and reclaim the Caribbean cornucopia. White sands. Swank casinos "nationalized" and turned to Third World troughs. Brown women in pink bikinis.

Crutch skimmed library books and ripped out key photos. Dig it: Fulgencio Batista draped all over Jane Russell. Dig it: the roof pool at the Capri. Dig it: peons pulling fat cats in rickshaws.

He taped the pix to the wall. He ripped out a pic of Fidel Castro fomenting. The Frogman called Castro "The Beard." His facial hair harbored nests of Red lice.

Crutch taped the Castro pic to the wall and tossed his pocketknife at it. He nailed The Beard four times out of six. The picture started to shred.

The phone rang. Crutch jugged the receiver and caught it. He said, *"¿Hola? ¿Qué tal?"* The caller went, "Huh?"

The knife fell off the wall. Fidel was now *mucho* tattered. The caller said, "It's Larry from P.C. Bell. Buzz Duber said I should call you. I got a trace on that bootleg number."

Crutch grabbed his scratch pad. "Shoot."

"It's a house on Carmina Perdido in Santa Barbara. The renter's name is Sam Flood. That's all I've got."

It was plenty. "Sam Flood" was Sam Giancana's squarejohn name. Clyde told him that. *Sam G. called Gretchen/Celia at Bev's Switchboard.*

Larry blathered—Hey, fool, where's my bread? Crutch hung up and wrote "Bootleg #/Giancana" on his wall graph.

The words vibrated. Crutch drew little question marks around them. He got the urge to draw Joan. He taped her mug-shot strip to the graph paper and cut loose with paper and pen.

He got her hardness and her softness in alternating portraits. He never got the full her in one take. He gave her different hairdos. He de-swirled and re-swirled the lovely gray streaks every time.

18

(Las Vegas, 8/19/68)

The service was brief. The minister rushed. Storm clouds meant rain any second. The eulogy featured heaven–golf course metaphors.

Janice Hartnett Lukens Tedrow: 1921–1968.

Carlos Marcello and Dwight Holly attended. Farlan Brown was there. Dracula sent five grand in flowers. Half the caddy crews from the Dunes and the Sands showed up.

Wayne stood at the back. The dry air started seeping. The cemetery was segregated. A road bisected the white and Negro sections. White diggers worked the white side. Negro diggers worked the Negro side. The Tedrow-service diggers were off-duty blackjack dealers. They wore red vests, bow ties and eyeshades. The rain threat made them fidget.

The heaven–golf course shtick was protracted. Wayne looked across the road. A large service was beginning. Limousines, a hearse, a flatbed truck filled with roses. Scores of black people in black.

Wayne walked over. The people paid him no-nevermind. He saw a sign affixed to an easel. It stated the date and the name of the decedent: the Reverend Cedric D. Hazzard.

The hearse was parked nearby. Four men removed a casket. A minister walked up and opened the passenger door. A Negro woman got out. The minister fawned over her. She put him off with small smiles and gestures.

She wore a black crepe dress, a pillbox hat and no veil. She glanced at the road and saw Wayne. They shared a look for one second.

DOCUMENT INSERT: 8/20/68. *Seattle Post-Intelligencer* headline and subhead:

NIXON SURGES IN POST-CONVENTION POLLS
Ex-Veep Lengthens Lead Over Probable Dem Candidate Humphrey

DOCUMENT INSERT: 8/20/68. *Milwaukee Sentinel* headline and subhead:

1ST BALLOT NOD FOR HUMPHREY PREDICTED
"Expect Hippie Trouble at Convention," Top Chicago Cop Tells Rotary

DOCUMENT INSERT: 8/21/68. *Des Moines Register* subhead:

"Hippies," "Yippies," "Schmippies": Beat Cops Say They're Prepared

DOCUMENT INSERT: 8/21/68. *Las Vegas Sun* article:

GREAT GOLFER, GREAT LADY

Janice Tedrow was laid to rest at Wisteria Cemetery Monday morning. The flags at every country club in Las Vegas were lowered to half-staff in honor of the woman who was the Thunderbird ladies' club champion 9 times, the Sands ladies' club champion 6 times, the Riviera ladies' club champion 14 times and the winner of the Clark County Polio Drive Scramble every year from 1954 on.

"Janice Tedrow played near-scratch golf even as she suffered from terminal cancer," her physician, Dr. Steve Mandel, said. "That's talent and willpower." And when the mourning ranks at her funeral service swelled to the seams with local caddies, you know that they came because the woman was a true champion with the common touch.

Janice Lukens hailed from small-town Indiana. She married investor/real estate entrepreneur Wayne Tedrow in 1947 and soon made her way to the Queen City of the Desert, where she served on numerous charitable committees and played the meanest woman's golf game the state of Nevada has ever seen. 1968 has been a tragic year for the Tedrow clan. Wayne Tedrow died of a heart attack in June, and now the 46-year-old Janice's untimely death.

"God works in mysterious ways," the Reverend G. Davis Kaltenborn told this reporter after the funeral service. "That's why I chose golf as the central theme of my tribute. Life is an unpredictable trek toward an uncertain conclusion. I shared this insight with Mrs. Tedrow's stepson after the service, and he told me he understood that very well."

R.I.P., Janice. The starter at the Dunes told me you got six birdies the very last time you played golf on this earth. I see lots of sub-par rounds up there in the clouds for you, as well.

DOCUMENT INSERT: 8/21/68. *Las Vegas Sun* article

MURDER-SUICIDE SHOCKS NEGRO COMMUNITY

Sylvester "Pappy" Dawkins was 48 years old, a two-time convicted burglar and a reputed drug addict. The Reverend Cedric D. Hazzard was 52 years old and was the pastor of New Bethel Baptist Church in North Las Vegas. A stalwart of the Negro community in the Queen City of the Desert, he was as respected as Pappy Dawkins was disdained.

Yet the two men were friends of sorts. They would often meet at Dawkins' unkempt little house in West Las Vegas and talk until the wee hours about all manner of things. Now, in its grief, Las Vegas Negroes are wondering what the topic of conversation was right before it all went so terribly wrong on the night of August 10.

"We don't really know what precipitated this horrible tragedy," Lieutenant Byron Fritsch of the Las Vegas Police Department told reporters. "We only know that Pappy shot the Reverend Hazzard and then turned the gun on himself."

Horrible tragedy indeed. For many members of the Reverend Hazzard's congregation have movingly described their late pastor's diligent efforts to bring the word of God to Pappy Dawkins and to help him restore his moral equilibrium. "Ced was just that kind of a guy," Kenneth S. Wilson, a deacon at New Bethel Baptist Church, said. "Ask anyone who knew him."

"My late husband was a brave and true man who led with his

heart," the Reverend Hazzard's widow, Mary Beth, said. "He was committed to goodness and social justice." Mrs. Hazzard, 44, is the lead steward for the Las Vegas Hotel Workers' Union, and has spearheaded many charitable drives in the local Negro community. She is doubly bereft now. In December of 1963, her son Reginald, then 19, vanished and was never seen again. Reginald was a former straight-A student at Seminole High School and had won science-fair awards in chemistry. The trials of Job have visited themselves upon Mrs. Hazzard, but she remains optimistic. "Yes, my son is long missing and my husband is dead," she said. "I considered Cedric's mission to reform Pappy Dawkins to be rash and imprudent, however heartfelt, but he died in the act of dispensing compassion. I revere him for that. As for me, no, I will not succumb to defeat or despair. I have duties to discharge, and I will not be deterred."

The Reverend Hazzard's funeral drew over 300 mourners. An estimated $10,000 in floral tributes was received at Wisteria Cemetery. Mrs. Hazzard and members of the New Bethel congregation distributed them to patients at local hospitals.

The Reverend Cedric Douglass Hazzard: 1916–1968. Rest in peace.

DOCUMENT INSERT: 8/22/68. *Las Vegas Sun* headline and subhead:

HUGHES EYES STARDUST
WILL ANTI-TRUST LAWS THWART THE KING O' THE STRIP?

DOCUMENT INSERT: 8/23/68. *Las Vegas Sun* headline and subhead:

BILLIONNAIRE RECLUSE TO CLARK COUNTY: "I WANT TO BUY YOU!"
HUGHES SEEKS TO CONTINUE HOTEL-BUYING SPREE

DOCUMENT INSERT: 8/23/68. Telex communiqué. From: Supervisory Unit, St. Louis Office, Federal Bureau of Alcohol, Tobacco and

Firearms. To: Field Unit #112, all personnel. Topic: Grapevine Tavern surveillance.

Gentlemen,
    Continue 24-hour surveillance of location, per all precedingly filed directives.
    Thomas T. Wiltsie, Agent-in-Charge.

DOCUMENT INSERT: 8/24/68. Office-filed memorandum. From: Fred Turentine. To: Clyde Duber Associates (Attn: Clyde Duber, Buzz Duber, Don Crutchfield). Topic: Electronic surveillance of Suite 308, Golden Cavern Hotel-Casino, Las Vegas (Ref: Dr. F. Hiltz–Gretchen Farr investigation).

    C.D., B.D., D.C.,
    I got almost nil from yesterday's wire at the Cavern. I'll be frank: it was nothing but rich Mormons & hookers & chitchat about the Dem. conv. in Chicago. Farlan Brown was talking up his plans to be there (the Hughes org. is covering their pol. bets by sucking up to the Humphrey org). Nothing pert. to Dr. Hiltz & G Farr was discussed. I picked up a 1-way partial of Fred Otash talking on phone about a 8/30/68 meet with Wayne Tedrow & "perhaps others," but that was it. All in all, a bust. D.C. will be in Chi. for conv., so he can follow up there. The bug is now de-activated, but is still in place. I'll pull it when I get a shot at the suite vacated.
    Best,

    F.T.

DOCUMENT INSERT: 8/25/68. Verbatim FBI telephone call transcript. Marked: "Recorded at the Director's Request/Classified Confidential 1-A: Director's Eyes Only." Speaking: Director Hoover, Special Agent Dwight C. Holly.

    JEH: Good morning, Dwight.
    DH: Good morning, Sir.
    JEH: It's been too long.
    DH: I agree, Sir.

JEH: Wayne Tedrow Jr. Give me the upshot of his latest Congolese misadventure.

DH: It's covered, Sir. The coroner's inquest ruled homicide-suicide, and the papers have reported it as such.

JEH: I'm gratified. And the Grapevine Tavern? Is it still a Pandora's box of anti-Bureau chatter?

DH: Yes, Sir.

JEH: And ATF? Are they still perching?

DH: For now, Sir.

JEH: They cannot perch forever.

DH: I'm aware of that, Sir.

JEH: Let's discuss <u>OPERATION BAAAAD BROTHER</u>. Wayne Junior's dead Negroes have whet my appetite.

DH: I've secured a copy of Fred Hiltz's subscriber lists. I'm looking through them for leads on possible infiltrators.

JEH: And you paid him out of the cold funds I supplied you with to rescue Junior.

DH: Yes, Sir. Ten thousand cold and a pound of cocaine.

JEH: His poor sinuses. I shudder to think.

DH: Yes, Sir.

JEH: And you're still looking for an informant? Preferably a woman?

DH: Yes, Sir.

JEH: And informant number 4361 is pondering referrals?

DH: She is, Sir.

JEH: Aaah, Dwight. Your wistful inflection on the word *she* speaks puerile volumes.

DH: Some things can't be disguised, Sir.

JEH: The Klansman's son and the Quaker pacifist. God himself must marvel at your pillow talk.

DH: It's lively, Sir.

JEH: Am I ever discussed?

DH: Contentiously, Sir.

JEH: Does it perturb you that she might record your dubious liaison for posterity? Her curriculum vitae lists her as a daily journal keeper. She may well have jotted notes on her suppression-minded lover.

DH: I've black-bagged her, Sir. Her notes to date have been laudatory.

JEH: And rightly so, I'm sure.

DH: Thank you, Sir.

JEH: I'm slipping, Dwight. I know it, and I know that you know it. I am a boxer who has been in the ring for a very long time, but I remain dangerous because of and not in spite of it.

DH: I understand that fully, Sir.

JEH: Good day, Dwight.

DH: Good day, Sir.

DOCUMENT INSERT: 8/25/68. Extract from the privately held journal of Karen Sifakis.

Los Angeles,
August 25, 1968

I should be in Chicago. What's-His-Name is passing through en route to Philadelphia and will be calling me with reports. It's going to be bad; everyone knows it; everyone knows that Nixon v. Humphrey is no choice at all and that the war will continue regardless of the outcome in November. This entry and any other entries I may write during the convention will be ascribed here in my second journal, the one I hide at school and that Dwight must never see. It's the names I might record. Mr. Hoover (and Dwight by extension) is file-happy and thinks that everyone in the move- ment knows everyone else and has thus colluded across a wide spectrum of political activity. Of course, that's not true. Love affairs—usually brief and passionate and doomed by factional issues—may occur that pervasively, but not prosecutable political conspiracy. Paranoia defines the Right (although Dwight tends to eschew it and occasionally critiques it with sardonic humor) and the Left as well. Everyone knows everyone else and suspects everyone else and *needs* everyone else as well. Political agendas and personal agendas shift along those lines, which certainly defines the inimical worldviews, collusive agendas and deep com- radeship of Dwight and me.

God, Dwight Chalfont Holly and "comrade" in a single sentence!

Chicago is going to be bad. Danny T. and Sid F. have called with advance news. They are Marxist Nixonites in their determination to fuck up Hubert Humphrey and elect the man who will instill greater repression and provide a clearer shot at revolution at some ambiguously perceived later point. Of course, lives will be shattered and lost in the process and only utilitarians like me (and dare I say it, D.H.) understand that purely destructive folly.

Dwight can talk me into almost anything if he can convince me that it will divert destruction and death in the moment. Chicago feels like a widely willed moment of sincere outrage and horrible hatred that is politically and spiritually mandated beyond all utilitarian considerations, which is what scares me.

The convention-hall fence is topped with barbed wire and 5,000 riot troops have been flown in, with 5,000 more on call. W.H.N. (who secretly and ghoulishly loves weaponry) said that Maury W. saw boxes of rocket launchers being unloaded at O'Hare. There's a taxi-cab strike in progress; a large bus drivers' local stands ready to strike; the IBEW began striking on May 8 and thus telephone service within the city and environs is a complete mess. W.H.N. predicts a radical or radical-aligned (largely fool mischief-makers of the counterculture and fatuous Left) presence of 100,000 people. It is going to be bad because it's overdue to be bad and the statement needs to be made at a horrible and horribly attention-getting cost, which makes the whole thing all the more complexly deplorable to me.

So I will pray for peace and feel Eleanora grow within me and make love with Dwight, who knows many of the things I do but cannot confront them because the moment of moral explication would drive him insane.

As always, I will marvel in the aftermath of my prayers and ponder how much or how little quantifiable good our odd comradeship of conflicting ideology gives to the world. Mutual benefit. It sounds viciously capitalistic, but it is wholly egalitarian within that compromised context.

Dwight needs an informant to work the BTA and MMLF. He's got me half-convinced that both groups are viciously self-serving, ideologically unsound and destructive. Should I introduce him to Joan?

DOCUMENT INSERT: 8/25/68. *Los Angeles Times* headline and subhead:

DEMOCRATIC CONVENTION SET TO CONVENE
PROTEST TROUBLE LOOMS IN WINDY CITY

DOCUMENT INSERT: 8/25/68. *San Francisco Examiner* headline and subhead:

TROOPS ARRIVE IN CHITOWN
TENSION SIMMERS AS PROTEST YOUTH MOBILIZES

DOCUMENT INSERT: 8/25/68. Telex communiqué. From: Supervisory Unit, St. Louis Office, Federal Bureau of Alcohol, Tobacco and Firearms. To: Field Unit #112, all personnel. Topic: Grapevine Tavern surveillance.

Gentlemen,

Grapevine investigation to terminate 9/1/68. Discontinue all surveillance on that date. The U.S. attorney has deemed insufficient grounds to prosecute.

Thomas T. Wiltsie, Agent-in-Charge

19

(Los Angeles, 8/25/68)

ists:
 Hate-mail subscribers, hate-meeting attendees, hate-cartoon devotees.

Cross-referenced to:

Rap-sheet lists, DMV lists, subversive-group lists.

Cross-referenced to:

The hate lit itself. Sample copies. All hate-the-white-man shit. Negro mailees cross-referenced back to all the fucking lists.

Dwight worked in the drop-front. He built paper piles from Dr. Fred's stash and carbons from LAPD and the California DMV. Hate, hate, hate. Big paper piles—the Himalayas of Hate.

He'd been at it since his Vegas jaunt. He started with municipal PD intelligence files. He looked for male Negro cops with infiltration experience. He got no names. He went back to the subscriber lists then. He secured paper and culled paper and built shelves to rein paper in. It was a Negro name hunt. Find a male Negro hate bunny. Recruit him, coerce him, or entrap him—and teach him how to *re*-hate.

The glut of names was engulfing. The hate lit and hate pix supplied yuks. White men had small dicks, black men had big dicks, the dick-size diaspora defined black history. Jew doctors spread sickle-cell anemia. Audrey Hepburn had Jim Brown's black baby. Lawrence Welk was really black. Count Basie was really white. John Glenn was the world's first nigger astronaut.

Dwight name-hunted. *A* to *Z* and back again. Pebble-in-an-avalanche dreck. *U, V, W, X, Y, Z* and back to *A*.

Arthur Atkinson was a black Nazi. Willis Barrett subscribed to *Honky*

Hunter magazine. Ricky Tom Belforth subscribed to *Beg for It Black: White Wenches Wail for Real Men!* Bistrip, Blair, Blake, Bledsoe—stop, what's this?

Marshall E. Bowen/5652 South Denker, Los Angeles. Anti-Jew hate-tract subscriber, '65–'66.

The name hit familiar. Dwight hit the DMV lists and flipped to the *B*'s. There: Marshall *Edward* Bowen/male Negro/5'11", 175, DOB 5/18/44. CDL# 08466. Former address: 8418 South Budlong. DMV file note: background check for admittance to the LAPD Academy, 3/11/67. Current address, bingo: 5652 South Denker again.

Anomaly. Incongruity. Anti-white hate-tract subscriber, potential L.A. cop.

Yes, and the name *re*-hit familiar.

Dwight hit the subversive-group list. Bingo #2: There's Marshall E. Bowen again.

At Black Muslim meetings. At Black Snake Bund powwows. *Oooooh, Baaaaad Brother!*

Dwight called LAPD. He knew a guy in the Personnel Office. The guy kicked loose confidential stats on the QT. Dwight got him on the line and laid out Marshall Bowen. He applied to the Department in 3/67. Did he get on?

The guy said he'd check. Dwight held the line for six minutes. The guy came back on, all excited. Bingo #3: Marshall E. Bowen made it on LAPD.

Academy graduate, 6/67. Assigned to Wilshire Patrol. Still at Wilshire. Class-A fitness reports.

Marshall, you *baaad.*

Because:

You subscribed to hate lit. *You* went to Commie meetings. Brother, this be *baaad* behavior. They could kick yo black ass off LAPD.

Because:

Your background checkers fucked up and missed your hate history. Left-wing honky-haters are summarily excluded from LAPD.

You *baaaaaaad.* You exploitable, coercible and lose-yo-jobable. Yo black ass belongs to me.

Dwight called Freddy Otash in Vegas. Freddy was ex-LAPD. Freddy knew his LAPD shit.

The phone rang nine times. Otash picked up, brusque. "Who's this?"

"It's Dwight, Freddy."

Otash said, "Oh, shit. Don't tell me. The Grapevine."

Dwight laughed. "ATF's pulling out on the first. I think we'll have to go in then."

"And we're meeting with Wayne on the thirtieth?"

"Right, and I think you and I should get together before then."

Otash sighed. "Is Wayne ready for this?"

Dwight said, "I think so."

"Jesus, Wayne Junior. You can't count him in, you should *never* count him out."

Dwight lit a cigarette. "I had a question about LAPD."

"I'm listening."

"The background-check process. I'm looking at a colored kid named Marshall Bowen. He went to Commie meetings and got on LAPD last year. Tell me how that Commie shit could fall between the cracks."

Otash yawned. "I *know* the Bowen kid. He was a plant for Clyde Duber. Clyde sheep-dipped him and put him in with some Red groups."

Dwight said, "Freddy, you're a white man."

Otash said, "No, I'm not. I'm a fucking Lebanese."

Marshall Bowen, you *baaaaaad.*

Clyde pointed to his wall frieze. Dwight tracked the pictures. They show-cased that L.A. armored-car job. Burned bodies, inked bills, emeralds. A big cop mauling two Negroes.

Dwight sneezed. Clyde's office was sub-polar. The easy chair induced pangs for sleep.

Clyde said, "That case. It's a hobby of mine, and it's how I met Marsh."

"I know a little about it. Jack Leahy ran the Bureau's end for ten seconds."

"Right. It's still unsolved, and ink-stained bills have been turning up in the ghetto ever since. Sometimes LAPD leans on the people passing the bills, just to keep their hand in. That's what happened with Marsh. He innocently passes a double saw, and, oops, there's Scotty Bennett."

Dwight yawned. His ass was dragging. The goddamn chair was a sleep cloud.

"Don't stop there."

Clyde blew smoke rings. "So Scotty shagged Marsh and leaned on him, and Scotty B. leaning on you is a very unpretty sight. Marsh called a friend of his, who called me. I pulled Marsh out of the shit with Scotty, and I turned him out as an infiltrator. I put him into a half-dozen cockamamie pinko groups and colored groups, and Marsh was a damn good mole. He loves action, so he applies to LAPD, and he gets on over Scotty's protests."

Dwight yawned. "Tell me about his politics. He can't be a lefty or a hate-honky type, or LAPD wouldn't have taken him."

Clyde chained cigarettes. "What politics? He's a player. He lives for the game, and it's all a game, and the only fuckers who don't know it's a game are these rich right-wing nuts who pay me to dip the moles. *It's a gold mine.* I'm pulling in seventy-five G's a year off Fred Hiltz and Charlie Toron."

Dwight rubbed his eyes. "I just did some biz with Dr. Fred."

"My guy Don Crutchfield's tracking some Mormon hump for him in Chicago now."

"Left-wing Mormon?"

"Right-wing Mormon snatch hound who was dipping it to some snatch Fred was dipping it to. Jesus, don't ask. It's been going on all summer, and I'm thirty-two grand up on it alone."

Dwight picked up the desk phone. Clyde nodded go ahead. Dwight called his LAPD Personnel guy. The guy still had Marsh Bowen's file out. Dwight asked for his current duty schedule. The guy said Bowen was in Chicago, visiting his sick dad.

Clyde blew touch-the-sky smoke rings. Dwight put the phone down.

"He's in Chicago, and I can't get away. Can you have your guy Crutchfield put a spot tail on him? I want to get a handle on him before I make an approach."

"Sure, but I wouldn't mind knowing what all this is about."

"Mr. Hoover wants to stir up some shit with the niggers."

They ate dinner by the TV set. Pre-convention coverage covered the dial. It was a ghoul show. Mayor Daley looked cosmically pissed. Hubert Humphrey looked preemptively doomed. The camera cut to longhaired kids outside the hall. They looked malevolent. They catcalled flanks of riot cops. The cops looked like gargoyles perched.

Karen watched, all intent. Dwight picked at his food. Dina drew in a coloring book. She always drew choppers and police cars. It drove Karen batshit.

The footage droned. The ghoul chants sounded like Mixmasters on the fritz. The camera panned over boocoo Negroes. One woman wolfed french fries.

Wayne was in Tahoe, en route to Chicago. He was Mr. Trickster. Dracula and Farlan Brown were mischief-minded elves. Mr. Trickster was a trouper. The show must go on. He'd surmount his latest coon snafu and perform.

The footage droned. Dina colored in a smiling dog and drew fangs on him. Karen squeezed his knee and tried not to smoke.

A fat Negro eulogized Dr. King. The confab erupted. The lights went down for a slide show. King's picture hit the screen. Dwight shut his eyes.

His pulse raced. He took some deep breaths and tried to rewire. Karen leaned into him.

"You've been anxious lately."

"My sleep's in the shitter."

"When you're anxious, I'm anxious."

Dwight opened his eyes. "Don't be, all right?"

Karen smiled. "Tell me how I accomplish that."

Dwight hit the remote-control button. The TV bipped off. Dina didn't notice it. Karen ran her hand up his leg.

"I should be in Chicago."

"Jesus, babe."

"I feel like blowing up some fascist statues."

"Don't let me stop you."

"I may have an informant for you. There's this woman named Joan."

20

(Chicago, 8/25/68)

The Loop was hot. A choppy lake breeze goosed the thermometer. The cops wore helmets and short-sleeved shirts. They packed nightsticks and saps. The hippies wore deface-the-flag garb. They packed Coke bottles and rocks.

Potential fracas. Both groups spoiled for it. The night heat said GO— you know you want this.

Crutch watched. He clutched his grocery bag and stood out of range. His crew cut and square threads camouflaged him. The longhairs would ignore him. The fuzz would find him simpatico.

Shit fuck. Miami to *this*.

Face-off. The cops moved up two inches. The hippies moved up three. The gap shrank and got claustrophobic.

Crutch watched. Dexedrine and coffee had him psychedelicized. He'd been up thirty-six hours. He'd been running the listening post at the Ambassador East. Farlan Brown was hosting a party suite next door. Booze, girls and political rah-rah. Brown fucked the girls and greased the delegates. Brown promised them Hughes Air charters. Brown pressed them for details on Humphrey's campaign travel, so Wayne Tedrow and company could fuck Hubert up.

The cops moved two inches. The hippies moved three. The gap shrank. The hate intensified.

Crutch watched. The face-off got him antsy. Clyde overbooked him. He had the listening-post gig and an adjunct job: tail this L.A. cop in town. Buzz was on that gig now.

The cops moved up. The hippies moved up. A fat freak yelled,

"Pig!" The cops charged. The hippies faltered. A frizzy-haired guy chucked a rock. It bounced off a skinny cop's helmet. The cops hit the line, nightsticks first. The hippies had no turnaround or hurling range. Mow-down: the cops trampled and kicked and nightstick-knocked heads on the pavement.

A car pulled up to the fracas. Something flared red. Two spades lobbed a flaming-dogshit bomb at the cops. It fell short. The bag broke and dung-scorched some trample-assed kids. The spades did that clenched-fist thing and peeled out.

Crutch ran back to the hotel and bopped to the listening post. He had a southbound view of car fires and flame glow off the lake. The bug-tap console faced the north wall. He heard fuck-suck sounds through the speakers. He put on headphones. He heard the fuck-suck sounds louder. This part of the Dr. Fred job was pure bullshit.

It ran up Clyde Duber's time card. It yielded ziltch on Gretchen/Celia and Joan Rosen Klein. Clyde was juking that time card. Clyde told him not to brace Farlan Brown in person. All this jive was tangential to the women.

It was 1:00 a.m. Crutch noshed two cupcakes to downgrade his speed jolt. He placed Joan's mug-shot strip on the console. He kept looking at Joan and seeing new things.

His case was dead-stalled. Sam Giancana or someone close called Gretchen/Celia. That was a big lead and a dead-staller. You don't brace a heavy like Sam G.

He B&E'd Arnie Moffett's realty office on his way to the airport. He found no further notes on Gretchen/Celia. He checked LAPD and Sheriff's missing person files for notes on tattooed Latin chicks. He got zero there. He ran Joan Rosen Klein's name and stats by cop contacts nationwide. Fourteen PDs, fourteen cops. Robbery-unit cops, subversive-squad cops, intelligence-squad cops. Nobody knew shit per Red Joan.

She might have a Fed file. That approach was dicey. He'd have to tap Clyde to tap his Fed contacts. Joan was all his for now. He held the lead as his exclusive.

The fuck-suck noise died out. Pay me, pay me noise replaced it. Crutch skimmed a library book. It was all about Cuba. Rebel raids, burning cane fields, the Bay of Pigs rout. He kept reading books. He kept calling the Frogman long-distance. Mesplede was still looking for exile turncoats Fuentes and Arredondo. They betrayed *le sacré la Causa*. They were heist men. They might be clouting department stores in Des Moines or Duluth. The Frogman was his no-shit mentor. The Frogman worked with Wayne Tedrow, but stayed hinky on him. Froggy and Wayne were time-clocking for Count Dracula now. Their mandate: tricksterize at the convention and sodomize Hubert Humphrey's fall campaign.

Freddy Turentine filed a report on the Golden Cavern bug op. It was a bust—just whores and Mormons. *But,* Fred T. heard Fred O. mention an 8/30 meet with Wayne Tedrow and "perhaps others." That could be good. Wayne might say something or provide a lead on Dracula's lair. One photo/one million bucks—*Life* magazine's standing offer. The Frogman said *he* might request hot scoop on Wayne. Crutch said he'd provide it. Brainstorm: call Fred T. and tell him to keep the bug-tap gear in place.

The phone rang next door. Crutch switched to the tap-feed headphones. Static and voice garbles fuzzed up the line. He jiggled switches and got Farlan Brown.

" . . . Wayne, hi. Jesus, what time is it? I haven't opened the curtains since Coolidge was in office."

Wayne Tedrow: "It's 1:20."

Brown: "A.m. or p.m.?"

Tedrow: "Morning. I'm at O'Hare now. I'm waiting for that man I told you about. He's flying in from Sioux Falls."

Brown: "A French mercenary and Sioux Falls, South Dakota. That's a new one on me."

Tedrow: "He's trying to locate some long-lost chums."

Brown: "He won't find them in Chicago. All we've got here is class warfare."

Tedrow: "The airport's a mess. It's nothing but hopped-up kids and reporters. It's like one big staging ground."

Brown: "Hubert's fucked. Dick's going to make hay out of this one."

Buzz walked into the suite. Crutch waved to him.

Tedrow: "We'll need to get some sleep. We'll see you in five or six hours."

Brown said something. Static ditzed the line. Crutch dumped the headphones.

Buzz said, "Bowen's from hunger. He doesn't drink or chase pussy. He may be the world's most uptight jungle bunny. He goes to fucking museums and cheese shops."

Crutch snarfed a cupcake. "I'll take over now."

"Take over *what?* It's 1:30 a.m. Bowen's home with daddy, and the whole fucking city's going nuts."

"I'm restless."

"You're always restless."

Crutch snarfed cupcake #4. "I'll be back in five or six hours."

Buzz checked his notebook. "This fucker is uptight. 11:16 p.m. He bypasses two rib joints and a topless bar called the Honey Bunny. Where does he go? To Mr. Sid's All-Nite World of Books."

Crutch yukked. Buzz dropped his head on his chest and went ZZZ-ZZZ-

ZZZ. Something exploded outside. Crutch looked out the window and saw a cop car ablaze.

Late-night Chi-town hopped. Longhair legions roved. That lake breeze had their red flags swirling. Cops roved in flanking movements. It all looked synchronized. Mounted cops popped out of alleys. Their horses shit on the sidewalk. People threw things out of windows. Fruit and bric-a-brac rained down. It always missed the cops *and* the hippies. It felt like a general statement. You couldn't tell who the targets were.

Crutch rent-a-carred through it. The traffic was sub-snail-paced. Fender benders abounded. Marshall Bowen's daddy lived at 59th and Stony Island. It was middle-class colored—two-story houses up close to the street.

Clock in—2:41 a.m.

Crutch parked outside the house. One upstairs light was on. He put his Joan pix up on the dashboard and squinted at them.

He waited. He got a little squirrelly. His brain said *Go* while his body said *Sleep*. Marshall Bowen stepped out the door at 3:09.

He walked to the corner and hit a main drag. Crutch cut him ten seconds' slack. He U-turned the car and made the intersection. Bowen was three storefronts down on the left.

Crutch idled the car and watched. Foot traffic was brisk. Bowen poked his head in cocktail-lounge doors and kept walking. Some cops were out, smoking and lounging. Some longhairs turned the far corner and saw them. Crutch got a good view of it.

Bowen looked in windows and dawdle-strolled. A longhair held up a Coke bottle. A longhair stuffed a rag into it and lit it. All the longhairs tripped on the flame. A longhair hurled the bottle straight at the fuzz.

It broke short of them. The explosion was a dud. The longhairs yelled "Off the Pigs!" jive and ran away, laughing. Marshall Bowen turned around—Hey, now, what's this?

The cops charged him. He put his hands up—*no, please.* The cops hit him and pummeled him in one big blur.

21

(Chicago, 8/26/68)

Chemistry set.

Wayne stood in Farlan Brown's bathroom. Mirrored walls threw his own image back. He looked all wrong. You're too old, too thin, too trashed.

He grabbed a sink cup. He mixed airline scotch with opium chunks and a crumbled Valium. He stirred it with a toothbrush end and quick-guzzled it.

The effect hit him mid-body and worked its way up to his head. The required tingle occurred. He braced himself on the sink ledge and checked the mirrors. The required reversal occurred.

He walked into the living room. Drac's elves were all there. Head count: Brown and Mesplede. Six strongarm guys for Sam Giancana and eight off-duty cops. On the floor, dead center: a big steamer trunk full of hurt.

The goons and cops sat mingled. Brown and Mesplede stood behind the wet bar. They sipped breakfast Bloody Marys topped by celery sticks. Mesplede had passed out French cigarettes. The whole suite was smoke-swirled.

Brown nodded—your show, Wayne.

"Amphetamines, hallucinogens and hashish. Get it to the kids and make sure there's no reporters around when you do it. There's some plant evidence. You've got subversive literature and bomb-making diagrams. There's at least fifty Class-A felony pops in that trunk, every kid you pop will roll over on two dozen more, and you'll all get back at the Democrats for having their show in your city."

A few cops clapped. A few goons whistled. A cop passed Mesplede a file and mouthed the words "They're here." An obese goon cracked his knuckles.

Brown slapped his knees. Mesplede waved his celery stick.

Chemistry set—Wayne mixed a bedside cocktail. Nembutal and Jack Daniel's—a pro chemist's assuredly safe dose.

It went down warm and sat there. He stretched out to wait for the curtain. It was his sixteenth calculated dosage since West Las Vegas.

He'd stop soon. The compounds he cooked at Lake Tahoe would last him through next week. He was tapering his sleep jaunts off now. Tahoe topped out at twenty hours–plus. He kept up with Carlos and the Hughes group by scrambler phone. I'm recuperating in the woods. I've got a bum disk.

They bought it. They attributed his missing beats to illness. Dwight sealed the output on the killings. Word would seep over time. Two more dead shines—no one would care.

The curtain started spreading up. He saw the black woman dressed in black as the light slipped.

22

(Las Vegas, 8/26/68)

Freddy O. described the Grape-vine gestalt.

It was a shitkicker joint with a north-woods ambience suffused with far-Right detail. Glowing Hamm's beer signs. Polyester-flocked fir trees. Beaver pix taped above the urinals. Gun mags stacked everywhere. Racist-cartoon napkins—Sambo, stay out.

Dwight and Freddy floated in the Golden Cavern pool. The water was fjord-cold. They had the deep end to themselves. Freddy described the loose-talk gestalt.

It emanated from six lowlifes: Brundage, Kling, DeJohn, Currie, Pierce, Luce. They were stickup guys and pill pushers prone to right-wing hijinx. They were stone juicers and dope fiends. They stuck to themselves. They closed the Grapevine every night and stayed after hours to talk shit. They had keys to the joint. The proprietors trusted them to leave cash for their booze and lock up when they left. They were *not* ATF surveillance targets. That was good. ATF would not investigate their mass homicide.

A waiter brought Freddy a Cuba Libre and Dwight an iced tea. They floated and talked. Freddy said it's a three-man job. Dwight said no, four. Wayne knows a French-Corsican merc. The guy sounds perfect. Let's bring him in.

Freddy agreed. A zaftig blonde slinked by and provided diversion. Dwight slathered on more suntan oil. They discussed the meet on the thirtieth. We'll have Wayne and the merc then. We'll finalize.

Dwight said, "It has to be self-contained. Those six fools and nobody else. It's late, they're there alone, they're talking crazy political woo-woo and it all explodes."

Freddy said, "I agree. St. Louis PD comes in, works the crime scene, does the tests and says, 'That's that.' All the numbers match."

Dwight said, "We'll have to fire audibly. We want a barrage of overlapping shots to be heard and noted. We can't use silencers, because they'll leave tube fragments on the spent rounds."

Freddy said, "I agree. They all carry pieces routinely, but we won't have time to disarm them and kill them with their own guns. We'll need to bring in weapons with a traceable St. Louis origin."

Dwight said, "I agree, and that's your job. You're the St. Louis guy on this, so you 459 a few gun stores or pawnshops and steal some pieces the investigators can trace back. And revolvers, Freddy. I don't want any automatics jamming up on us."

Freddy sipped his Cuba Libre. "I agree. We pop them, we plant the guns they shot each other with, we pull their existing guns and move the bodies around to match the blood spill. That part of it is all crystal clear."

Dwight sipped iced tea. "We're in and out in under four minutes. You said they always blast the jukebox, right?"

"Right. The world's worst Okie music, and loud."

"That's good. It's partial cover on the shots, and the neighbors are used to racket at all hours. We goose the volume on our way out, which ups the chance that some local will stiff a noise-complaint call and some doofus patrol cops will respond and find the bodies."

Freddy hovered under the diving board. "We need one more key detail."

Dwight said, "Cocaine. They scored some pure shit and went nuts behind it. We leave some lines on the counter. We get Wayne to liquefy a portion of it. We get some small-gauge insulin needles and stryinges and boot them full of coke postmortem. We can inject them between their toes, and the marks will be too small to be noted at autopsy."

Freddy said, "It's tight and localized. It's a categorizable white-trash multiple homicide for all fucking time, and it's 'case closed' in twelve hours tops."

Dwight nodded. "We'll make it convincing. And don't worry about Wayne, he's solid."

Freddy laughed. "We're worried about him, but he's the stone killer."

Dwight laughed. "We're just lucky the dipshits are white."

A waiter walked a blinking phone up. Freddy got out of the pool and futzed with the cord and receiver. Dwight shut his eyes and tuned out the sun.

Freddy said, "It's for you. Your guy Bowen's in custody in Chicago."

23

The Frogman slipped Crutch a hash brownie. Their driver was an *on*-duty cop. The riot-zone Chicago tour boded all-time blast.

It was Mesplede's idea. He ran into Crutch in the lobby. Crutch was up for it. Bowen was in jail. Buzz was working the listening post. Observe History, sure.

Mesplede told him to steer clear of Wayne Tedrow—"You should be dead, *mon ami*." Crutch agreed. Mesplede reasserted: "I may ask you for bug-tap dirt on Wayne someday." Crutch *re*-agreed. History kept finding him: Miami, now *this*.

The red-flag boys. The no-bra girls. The cops with stubbed cigars. The nymph chicks tossing bouquets at National Guardsmen.

The cop driver swigged Old Crow. His cruiser was air-conditioned. They got the picture show devoid of night heat.

The street brawls. The hurled rock/nightstick action. The longhaired kids all bloodied. The kid minus one eye. The kid holding his teeth.

Mesplede said, "I will concede the war is unpopular. I will concede its protracted nature, but I will never concede its utter necessity."

Crutch looked out the window. A hippie boy flipped him off. A hippie girl flashed her tits.

Mesplede said, "Donald, do you believe in a free Cuba?"

"Yeah, Boss. I do."

"Do you believe that the perfidy of the Bay of Pigs demands a continued response?"

"Yeah, Boss. I do."

"Do you believe that Fidel Castro must be overthrown, and that the fifth columnists who have supported his regime must suffer the severest of penalties?"

"You know I do, Boss."

The cop driver brought a portable radio. Mesplede reached over the seat and hit the Play button. The cop-driver skimmed the dial and found a country station. A redneck tenor sang, "I love flags and corn liquor. Peaceniks and pot ain't for me."

Mesplede made an *ugh* face and flicked the dial. Discordant jazz— aaah, *oui*. Crutch made an *ugh* face. It sounded like a stripped-gear symphony. The hash brownie smacked his head. The outside colors shifted. Tendrils and double images appeared.

The cop driver turned onto a side street. The big-street action disappeared. Little one-story houses, all dark and sleepy.

Mesplede turned off the radio. The cop driver pulled over and stopped. Crutch was seeing single things as twos and threes. Mesplede got out and motioned Crutch to follow. Crutch got out and tested the sidewalk. The twos and threes returned to ones. The sidewalk firmed up his slack limbs.

He followed Mesplede. They walked up to the door of a dank little crib. Mesplede picked the lock. Crutch dug his prowess—two jiggles off a #4 pick.

They walked into the house. It was all dark. Air-cooler noise covered their footsteps. Crutch went straight to WOMEN in his head.

He followed Mesplede. The air-cooler hum increased. They hit a hall and walked down it. They stopped at a doorway. Mesplede hit a switch. Light hit two spic guys asleep in twin beds.

They stirred a little. One guy grumbled. Mesplede said, "Communists and Cuban traitors. Please kill them for me."

The gear music flared. Colors flared and receded. Crutch felt something cold in his hand. Crutch saw the spics all tendriled up as twos and threes.

The other spic grumbled. Both spics opened their eyes and looked at the doorway. Both spics fumbled at their nightstands.

Crutch raised the gun and aimed. Single images cohered. He fired with his eyes shut. The clip kicked off full automatic. He sprayed the bed. He heard silencer thunks. He smelled the blood with his eyes closed. He opened his eyes and saw two men with no faces trying to scream.

24

(Chicago, 8/27/68)

The lockup was SRO. Radicals and freaks crammed up the tank space. The jail usually ran all jig. The riot had the race quotas flip-flopped.

A jailer led Dwight down the catwalk. He inspired lots of clenched fists and "Off the Pigs!" chat. The interview room was two doors down a perpendicular hallway. Marshall Bowen was waiting for him.

Not bad. Fit, thoughtful-looking. A good pseudo-firebrand.

The jailer left them alone. Dwight tossed a pack of cigarettes on the table. Bowen shook his head and slid his chair back.

Dwight turned the spare chair around and straddled it. The pose backfired. Bowen pulled his chair closer in.

"You're not a lawyer. You're a policeman."

Dwight lit a cigarette. "I'm both."

"FBI?"

"That's correct. My name is Dwight Holly, by the way."

Bowen bowed mock-humble. "You're with the Chicago office?"

"No. I'm a national field agent."

"And you're concerned that a Los Angeles policeman got severely beaten for no justifiable reason?"

Dwight smiled. "I see no visible injuries. 'Severe' is an exaggeration, and you know it. You also know that you can't file suit against the Chicago PD and win, and if you do sue, you'll *severely* damage your reputation within LAPD."

Bowen smiled. "The booking officer saw my badge. If all this craziness hadn't messed things up, I'd be out by now."

Dwight tossed a bag of weed on the table. "Did he see this?"

Bowen balled his fists. Bowen smirked to say *I get it.* The reaction went levels deep.

"There's a threat. That means there's an offer coming."

Dwight put out his cigarette. "Clyde Duber says hello."

"So it's an infiltration job?"

Dwight shook his head. "Answer some questions."

"All right."

"Tell me your reaction to all this craziness."

"It inconvenienced me. I'm personally more than politically affronted."

"And the raw deal the Negro people in this country have received? Can you describe your take on that?"

"I don't think much about the Negro people. Do you?"

"I think about them more than I should."

Bowen laughed. "And why is that?"

Dwight shook his head. "Black militancy. You must have some opinions."

Bowen shrugged. "It's understandable, it's historically if not legally justified, it's ambiguously commendable, it provides opportunities for dubious ideologues and criminal entrepreneurs."

Dwight bowed. "Why did you become a policeman?"

"For the excitement."

"Are you enjoying your duties at Wilshire Patrol?"

"I'm a little bored."

"Who do you hate more? Hard-charging white cops like me or the worthless niggers who make up the bulk of your people and who you have always felt so fucking superior to?"

"It's a toss-up."

Dwight grabbed two chair slats and snapped them off clean. Bowen did not blink.

"I want to sheep-dip you. I want to create a scenario for your LAPD expulsion and put you into the Black Tribe Alliance and/or the Mau-Mau Liberation Front, in order to create political and criminal dissension. You will be required to work the assignment, under my direction, for any length of time that I choose. At the conclusion of the assignment, you will have the option of joining the FBI at a G-4 pay rate or of returning to the LAPD with a sergeantcy, in-grade pay status and a triple-A appraisal of promotability to lieutenant. A very wise Quaker woman once told me, 'Take note of what you are seeking, for it is seeking you.' If you are looking for excitement, this job will provide all you can stand."

Bowen said, "I'll do it."

Then he blinked, fluttered and flinched.

25

(Chicago, 8/28/68)

O'Hare was bad. Big arrival numbers, big departure numbers, big get-into-town/get-out-of-town volume. The terminals were refugee camps. The check-in lines and baggage lines were stay-all-day propositions. Tantrums flared. Epithets flew. Little shoves snowballed into fistfights.

News vendors made out. Everyone read the *Trib*. Dig the Lincoln Park riot. Dig the Grant Park riot upcoming. News pics captured mouths poised to scream.

Wayne read the *Trib*. Reporters and left-wing priests jostled him. They were baggage-line comrades. They'd spent two hours together. Let's talk outrage—we'll be here nine more.

The *Trib,* page six: "Radicals captured with bomb diagrams. Sedition charges discussed."

Wayne balled the paper up and tossed it. A dykey nun with a peace-dove button scowled at him. He was trashed. The Golden Cavern meet was two days out. The Grapevine felt imminent.

Cabs dumped outgoing passengers and snagged incoming meat. Wayne glanced around. This one kid looked familiar—the dumb bow tie and crew cut.

Wayne made him. The Miami tail kid, looking raw now. He told Mesplede to clip him.

He didn't see Wayne. The dykey nun got aggressive. She motioned two Negro nuns to cut in front of him.

Wayne let it go.

26

(Las Vegas, 8/29/68)

Butterfingers. The wires kept slipping and missing the holes. His hands were that trembly. His brain was that cooked.

Fred Turentine said, "You got the yips, son."

Crutch tried to re-concentrate. Bug work: suite 307 at the Golden Cavern Hotel. The Otash/Tedrow meet was tomorrow. This was their final spot check.

He pushed wires up the lamp base and crimped them. The pliers slipped. The lamp jiggled and almost toppled. Fred T. went whoa, son.

He killed two men. He wasn't quite straight with it. The Frogman was back in Miami now. He kept calling him. The phone just rang and rang. The dead spics were Commies and Cuban Cause traitors. They took lives and he took theirs, and that part didn't hurt. The picture replay hurt. He was zorched then. The replay ran in VistaVision and Cinerama. His world was double-imaged. The pictures re-ran with double clarity and at half the speed.

Fred caught a loose wire and re-taped it. Crutch fumbled the toolbox.

He couldn't sleep. He couldn't think about his case. He kept looking at the pictures of Joan.

27

(Los Angeles, 8/29/68)

The ceiling fan fluttered the sheets. The cool air gave them goose bumps. Dwight felt a contraction. He knew why— Eleanora just kicked.

Karen said, "I should be in Chicago. I shouldn't be in a folding bed in an FBI drop-front."

She was fuller now. Her nipples were bigger. Her hipbones had disappeared.

"It was bad. I'm glad you didn't go."

"What's-His-Name was at Lincoln Park. He called it a 'massacre.' "

Dwight grabbed his cigarettes. Karen looked tempted. Dwight put them back down.

"Don't make me jealous, or I'll hang a sedition case on him."

Karen laughed. "Did it feel inevitable to you?"

"If you mean preordained and mutually agreed upon, yes."

"You're very religious, you know. You understand your personal responsibility to God, but you're remiss and outright negligent in your secular practice."

Dwight smiled. "I rely on you for these perceptions. And I quoted you to a man in Chicago two days ago."

"How did you describe me?"

"As very wise."

"Not as duplicitous and compromised in my affections?"

"We didn't get that far."

Karen kissed his shoulder. "Did you find your infiltrator?"

"Yes."

"Then something's wrong."

"Why do you say that?"

"You're tense, but you're trying not to appear tense. You always do little things with your hands when you're trying to convince me that things are all right."

Dwight flexed his hands. His law-school ring fit loose. He was missing meals and running on coffee.

"Okay, you're right."

"Is it some bad thing you've done or some bad thing you're planning?"

Dwight gave Karen the look—case closed on that. She rolled onto her back and cupped his hands on the swell of Eleanora.

"I've got my infiltrator. He's brilliantly good, but that's all I can tell you right now."

"All right. And now you need an informant."

"Right. And you know that woman Joan."

Karen stretched. "I'll have to ask around. I don't know her personally. Someone will have to find her for me."

He felt a pulse on his hands. Soft—like Eleanora had moved more than kicked.

Karen reached for his cigarettes. Dwight grabbed them and threw them on the floor. Karen laughed and made her belly jiggle. *Then* Eleanora kicked.

Dwight said, "Do you love me?"

Karen said, "I'll think about it."

28

(Las Vegas, 8/29/68)

It was her. He knew it would be. He got the picture just to see her again.

It was a Nevada DMV photo. Mary Beth Hazzard sat posed for her driver's license shot. She was born 6/4/24. She was ten years, one month and fourteen days older than him.

Wayne sat in his car, outside the DMV. He'd bribed a clerk for a copy of the woman's driver file. License since 6/4/40. No moving violations. "Must wear corrective lenses to drive."

He read that newspaper piece. He saw her at the funeral. The widow Hazzard. The missing son. I got your husband—

She ran the Hotel Workers' Union. The union was fighting the Hotel Owners' Council. The issue was segregation. Dracula owned a score of union-targeted hotels. Picketing was going down at a dozen locations. The LVPD was monitoring it.

Wayne looked at the picture. He couldn't peel his eyes back. He liked the shape of her face and the flow of her hair.

29

(Las Vegas, 8/30/68)

The feed lines worked. The 307 to 308 wiring laid firm. Crutch bored a tiny spy hole through the wall yesterday. Sight and sound access, confirmed.

The console faced the connecting wall. Crutch settled in with his headphones. Fred T. was back in L.A. This gig was his solo.

The Frogman called him last night. Their talk calmed him down. Fuentes and Arredondo were rogue and Deep Red. The Chicago PD would short-shift their inquiry. The Frogman praised his balls and described a plan he was hatching.

Sabotage runs. Island hops with flamethrowers and C-4 explosives. Raids on Castro militia camps. Propaganda-leaflet runs. A heroin biz to finance the operation.

Froggy laid out the vile deeds of Fuentes and Arredondo. They were Red lice nesting in *putain* Fidel's beard. Crutch started grooving on his Commo kills. He went to a seamstress and got little 2's embroidered in his tartan bow tie.

The 308 door opened. *Click/thump*—that's the sound. Crutch checked the spy hole. On time: Fred Otash and Wayne Tedrow.

They sat down. They chitchatted. They sat away from the lamp feed. Their voices were dim.

Click/thump—the door again. This time: a tall, gray-suited man. Crutch heard garbles and read lips. Fred O. and Wayne called the man Dwight.

The console-to-spy-hole cord was stretched taut. Crutch pulled up a chair and got adjusted. Note: re-spackle the spy hole tomorrow.

The doorbell rang. Fred O. opened up. *Sacre Frog*—there's Jean-Philippe Mesplede.

Confluence. Clyde Duber's word. It's who you know and who you blow and how you're all linked.

Wayne introduced Fred O. to the Frogman. They spewed some staticky talk. Fred O. introduced Dwight to the Frogman and spieled his last name as Holly.

Confluence. Dwight Holly knew Clyde. Dwight Holly tapped Clyde to tail Marsh Bowen in Chicago.

Crutch got situated. His headphones fit tight and the spy hole was there at eye level. The 308 crew pulled chairs up close to the lamp feed. Fred O. bopped to the wet bar and came back with highballs and chips. Dwight Holly declined the drink. The other guys dug in. Crutch got a vibe: this had nothing to do with his case.

Clock it—3:18 p.m. Roll the tape, live.

The guys settled in. Sentence fragments overlapped. Dwight and the Frogman lit cigarettes. Fred O. looked plump and sassy, back to his normal bulk. Wayne looked raggedy-ass and too thin.

Fred O. said, "Enough bullshit," pitch-perfect headphone sound.

Dwight Holly said, "There'll be six men. They always stay after hours. It's always them and just them, and I don't think they'll vary the routine on the night we go in."

Wayne said, "When?"

Fred O. said, "We're set on my end. I've got the plant guns, Dwight's got the dope. I think we can be in and out in five minutes."

Dwight Holly said, "Four. The takedown will be easy. They'll be blitzed and they'll be surprised. It's all about rigging the forensic. St. Louis PD has a shit crime lab, but I still want the wound spill and trajectories to make some kind of sense."

Crutch started sweating. His earphones wetted up and produced crackle hiss. "Six men," "plant guns," "wound spill"—

Mesplede said, " 'Grapevine.' That is an American colloquialism, correct? It means 'a source of information.' So, it is idiomatic. And in that manner, it becomes the name of a hoodlum's meeting place."

Fred O. yukked. Ditto Dwight. Wayne flinched. Crutch caught it late.

June 20. THAT NIGHT. Talk fragments—grapevine/Tommy/plant—Joan and Gretchen/Celia.

The headphones *pooled* sweat. Crutch whipped them off, wiped them dry and put them back on. He got four-way garbles, fuzz, bips, pops, line hiss. Sweat-clogged feeder lines, *shit.*

More bips and line hiss. Food noise—Fred O. and the Frogman snarfed chips. Crutch took the headphones off, shook them dry and put them back on. He pressed up to the spy hole. He squinted. He tried to read lips and gestures and sync them to hiss. He got squeaks, he got crackle, he got words here and there in the mix.

He heard "Memphis." He saw Wayne twitch. He heard "patsy," "King," "Ray." Dwight Holly and Wayne shared queasy looks. He heard food noise. He squinted harder. He breathed harder. He fogged up the spy hole. He lost a full minute to *bip-bip-bips*.

He heard "witness."

He heard "grapevine" again.

HE STARTED TO GET IT.

Fred O. ran a monologue. His bass voice cut down line hiss. Crutch heard "Sirhan." Crutch heard "Bobby K." Fred O. mimed a shooting—bam, bam, you're dead. Wayne and Dwight H. shared a *très* queasy look.

HE GOT MORE OF IT. His bladder almost blew. He clenched up, sucked up and kept it in.

The spy hole was fogged. The bug line was clogged. Fucking potato chip–chomping noise fucked it up worse. Crutch took the headphones off, shook them and put them back on. Crutch spit on the spy-hole glass and shirt-wiped it clean.

He got more sight. He got more sound. He saw the Frogman's lips move. He heard incoherent yak-yak and "Dallas." He heard Frenchy word cuisine, "Cuba," "revenge."

The sound died altogether. Crutch shook his head. The phones cleared and the bug line re-fed. He got hiss, snap, crackle, pop, buzz, fuzz, bips. He heard "*Le grand putain* Jack." He saw Jean-Philippe Mesplede assume a rifleman's pose.

And he pissed in his pants.

And he shit in his pants.

And he vomited and gasped.

He pulled off his headphones. He ran to the console, pulled the main wire and ripped Spackle out of the wall. He made a small through hole. It fed into 308, all wire-free. The Spackle blew back into his suite. He squinted and put his ear to the hole—God, please please please.

The meeting was done. The men stood at the door. Dwight Holly said, "One last thing."

The other men nodded. Dwight Holly said, "No women. If there's women there, we pull out."

Fred O. nodded reluctant. Mesplede rolled his eyes. Wayne Tedrow clutched Dwight Holly's wrist.

30

(St. Louis, 9/3/68)

Throwdown guns—check. Insulin needles—check. Liquid cocaine—check. One last mug shot–memorization look.

Brundage, Currie, Pierce. Kling, DeJohn, Luce.

They were all inside. They were all armed. They were all blitzed. They entered between 10:41 and 12:49. Dwight played inside man and observed them. He chatted up Pierce and laid some groundwork. I'm a Schenley's sales rep. I do the deliveries. Sometimes they go late.

It was 3:10 now. They were still in there. Otash made a wax fit of the back-door lock yesterday. It was a clean walk-in. The Schenley's man and his pals with booze. Hey, Tommy Pierce—long time no see.

They parked behind the Grapevine. They wore jeans and duck-blind windbreakers—Okie hunter gear. They had four Schenley's boxes.

Dwight had a vented .45. Wayne had a .38 snub. Otash had a Colt Python. Mesplede had a long-barrel .32.

The van was stolen. Mesplede clouted it. They wore gloves for the ride over. Dwight felt calm. Otash and Mesplede looked calm. Wayne looked *too* calm—Dwight figured he was on something.

Music inside—hee-haw/hoedown shit. A country fiddle brayed and screeched.

Dwight tapped his watch. They got out of the van. Mesplede leaned in and dispensed the boxes. Otash walked over, unlocked the back door and left it ajar. A storeroom light was on. Dwight saw canned goods on shelves. High-pitched fiddle chords scraped.

Dwight tapped his watch—*now.*

They pulled out their guns and held them under the boxes. They clumped and made he-man grunts and nonchalantly walked in.

The storeroom led to the tavern proper. Their big-boot clomps and macho groans pre-announced them. The six fucks were sitting on two dumb leather sofas. They faced each other. A plank table was plopped down between them. It was covered with bottles, glasses and junk-food debris.

Dwight yelled, "Hey there, Tommy." Heads turned their way. Dwight head-counted and got seven, not six.

An extra man. Fortyish and curly-haired. Interloper/sorry, pal/it's just too late.

Looks traveled quick. Tommy Pierce cued the guys—this is okay. Dwight huffed and puffed over. Otash, Mesplede and Wayne were bunched behind him. It was a left-side, front-entry-wound, in-tight approach. *The seven fucks just sat there.* Dwight dropped the cue line: "Yeah, I know it's late."

Off that last syllab—

They dropped the boxes. They aimed and fired down. They emptied their guns at their pre-assigned targets, all body mass and face. *The fucks just sat there.* The shots swallowed them up. They pitched and jerked and bounced and stayed in their seats.

The noise was loud overlap and reverb. The cordite stink was bad and the barrel smoke was thick. The music went inaudible. Blood blew out their backs and pooled on the sofas in one continuous sweep.

Gurgles, belches, neck-wound coughs, shudders and gasps. Seven dead in one twitching sweep.

Dwight tapped his watch—*go.*

They put on rubber gloves.

They pulled belt-concealed guns off the dead men and paper-bagged them. Dwight checked out the seventh man. He was unarmed. Dwight went through his wallet. Fourteen bucks and a New York driver's license: Thomas Frank Narduno, almost forty-six.

He put the wallet back. Wayne got out the liquid coke and syringes. Blood leaked on the floor. They all looked down and stepped way clear of the spill.

Dwight knocked over the table. The booze and food debris blended in with the spill.

Otash arranged the bodies: three on the floor, four on the sofas.

Mesplede planted the throwdown guns. Three in their hands, three near their bodies.

The blood spill expanded. They all kept looking down and stepping clear of it.

Dwight pulled off their shoes and socks.

Wayne injected them between their toes and cotton-swabbed the blood drips.

Otash pulled their socks back on. Mesplede relaced their shoes.

Fiddle music brayed and screeched. The walls absorbed the gunshot noise—Dwight knew it.

They stepped waaaaay back from the blood spill. Dwight framed the scene. Sofa springs exposed. Kling's missing finger. Booze, cocaine, a group tantrum. Pierce's coughed-out dentures. DeJohn's shattered glasses.

Dwight tapped his watch—*out*. Wayne looked at him. Dwight couldn't detect anything.

Otash grinned. Wayne poured powdered cocaine on the bar.

Mesplede grabbed some blood-free potato chips.

31

(Las Vegas, 9/6/68)

You look *through* him.

It subsumes the shock and diverts the titillation. It deflects the insanity. It was his sixth face-to-face meet with Dracula. Wayne just discovered the trick.

"It's a pleasure to see you, sir."

Drac said, "Humphrey is very far behind in the polls. The hippies and yippies did him in."

Farlan Brown coughed. "Wayne and I were there, sir. We gave them quite an assist."

The trick worked with Drac himself. Castle Drac details remained. The condom-wrapped doorknobs, the Kleenex-box piles, the wall pix of Jane Russell's breasts.

Drac said, "On to November. Every Humphrey campaign stop must be a miniature Chicago. May I have your guarantee, Mr. Tedrow?"

"I'll try, sir."

Brown coughed. "Wayne's being modest, sir. When he says, 'I'll try,' he means 'I'll succeed.' "

Drac said, "Don't cough again, Mr. Brown. You're creating an unsanitary environment. If you cough again, I will terminate your employment and buy out your contract for five cents on the dollar."

Brown got up and left the room, waving a handkerchief. Wayne looked through Drac. Fresh details: plates covered with leftover food. Bugs scattered on pizza-pie crusts.

"You've lost weight, Mr. Tedrow. Have you been ill?"

"I had extensive dental surgery, sir. I've been unable to eat solid food for three weeks."

"Was the surgery performed under sanitary conditions?"

"Yes, sir."

"How old are you?"

"I'm thirty-four, sir."

"I'm sixty-one, sixty-two or sixty-three. I've sustained head injuries from my numerous airplane crashes and have lost some memories."

Wayne smiled. "You were born in 1905, sir. You're sixty-two years old."

Drac coughed. "Did you look me up in the *Farmer's Almanac*?"

"*Encyclopedia Britannica,* sir."

"Did it state how many women I have fucked?"

"It omitted that detail, sir."

"I have fucked countless women. Ava Gardner gave me both tertiary syphilis and the bubonic plague. Between my head injuries and those other maladies, I suffer constant pain. I am thus very grateful for your adroit skills as a chemist."

Wayne faux-beamed. "I'm very pleased that you feel that way, sir."

"Gain some weight, though. It pains me to look at a young man so gaunt."

"I'm going back on solid food tomorrow, sir."

"Good."

Wayne leaned in and stared *at* Drac. The filmy eyes and chancre sores got him this time.

"Mr. Hughes, may I ask a favor of you?"

"Yes. I rarely grant favors, but I'll permit you to ask."

"Sir, I'd like you to reinstate the Hotel Workers' Union at all your Las Vegas locations. I would also request that you brusquely tell the Hotel Owners' Council that they should drop the implicitly enforced employment color line that they have long adhered to."

Fresh details: tremors and puffs of dry spit.

"How firm a request is this?"

"It's a polite request, sir."

"Is it an ultimatum?"

"No, but it's a vouchsafe on my future as your business intermediary and chemist."

Drac shuddered. His jaw dropped. He had for-real fangs.

"Very well. I'll grant your request."

At least they were vicious. *At least they were white.*

It was his post-Grapevine mantra. He employed it along with opiate compounds. It got him through the flight back and the Hughes meet.

He was tapering off. He was sleeping better. Dwight called last night. St. Louis PD tagged the Grapevine their way.

Spontaneous combustion. Toxic booze/dope levels cited. A quickie coroner's inquest stamped it case closed.

He was feeling better. His appetite was returning. The throbs and kinks all over his body were starting to abate.

Wayne cruised the Strip. It was dusk and too hot to live. He saw heat-dazed picketers outside the Dunes and the Sands. He saw picketers waving their signs outside the Frontier. Most were black, some were white, all were plain thrilled.

He parked and walked to the picket line. He caught snippets of a joyous gobbledygook.

The Hotel Council caved. It was sudden—who knows why—it allegedly came from Howard Hughes.

Wayne stood there. The picketers ignored him. An LVPD goon squad lounged at the curb. They wore helmets and twirled their nightsticks. They plain seethed. Buddy Fritsch kicked at scattered cigarette butts and seethed the worst.

The picketers whooped and leaped and tore the tops off their signs. Wayne saw Mary Beth Hazzard raise one fist.

Buddy Fritsch saw him and teetered on over. He reeked of afternoon vodka and breath mints.

"Hey, killer. Want to smoke a few jungle bunnies while you're here?"

Wayne winked at him. Buddy winked back. The picketers looked over. They started nudging each other. Wayne smiled at Buddy and let the moment build.

"Times like this make me wish you were back on the 'ole LVPD. We could use a coon kill—"

Wayne gut-punched him. Buddy gasped and folded and went green in the face. The other cops froze. The picketers froze. Wayne grabbed Buddy's necktie, pulled him close and elbow-slammed his face. Wayne ripped his badge off his shirt and hurled it.

Buddy wobbled and stayed up. His face was all blood. Wayne let go of his tie. Buddy hit the pavement face-first. A bunch of the picketers cheered.

The cops stayed frozen. Wayne looked at the picketers. Mary Beth Hazzard stared dead at him. Wayne blew her a kiss.

32

(Los Angeles, 9/8/68)

Crutch Senior lived behind Santa Anita. He ruled a cardboard-box encampment. Winos and racetrack bums. Hooverville updated. Bet all day, booze all night. The California Lifestyle Supreme.

Crutch came with gifts: a good-bye C-note and a Reuben sandwich. Hey, Dad—I'm a dead man. I know all this top secret shit.

Fred Turentine called him yesterday. Fred Otash found some bug-tap debris in suite 307 and traced it back to him. Fred O. leaned on Fred T. Fred T. gave Crutch up for the bug job. Fred T. convinced Fred O. that *he* wasn't there, it was only doofus Crutchfield. Fred T. showed Crutch his broken fingers. "Kid, I don't know *what* you heard, but you better run."

He read the St. Louis papers. Seven dead at the Grapevine. Tavern "Hoodlum brawl escalates." He did some checking. James Earl Ray's brother was part owner. Killers. His Frogman pal on the grassy knoll. Bug talk: Sirhan & King, Memphis & Dallas.

The campground was behind the parking lot. The geezers lived in stereo boxes rain-treated with shellac. A big tarp covered twenty-odd Magnavox Mansions. Empty bottles covered the common yard.

Crutch knocked on Crutch Senior's box. Crutch Senior crawled out with a racing form and a short dog. Crutch gave him some room. Crutch Senior stood up, whipped it out and took a big piss. He aimed straight at Crutch's shoes.

"Hello, Dad."

Crutch Senior squinted. "Donald, right?"

"Right."

"The kid I had with Maggie Woodard."

"That's me."

"I remember Maggie. She was from Bumfuck, Wisconsin."

"Yeah, she's the one."

"She was a good lay."

"Come on, Dad. That's not nice."

Crutch Senior re-zipped. He was fifty-four. He wore a sweat-soaked Beatle suit and a Beatle wig. He was half-dead from open-sore cancers.

"You're in the shit and you need a touch. Sorry, but I'm tapped."

Crutch displayed the C-note and Reuben. Crutch Senior grabbed the bill and ignored the sandwich. He killed the short dog and tossed it on the empty pile. He swung the racing form and swatted Crutch in the face.

"You never found Maggie. You told me you would, and you didn't. I laid her the first time on Pearl Harbor day, and you never found her."

Bluff.

He worked out the plan yesterday. It predicted the knock on his door and the death sentence. Yeah, he put it all together. But, it was all instinct. Bug sputter, squelch, static and some words mixed in. He knew. They knew he knew. Fred O. would tell the others. Wayne would be pissed at the Frogman. Froggy let him live. It would blow up from there.

It was too big and played too preposterous. Clyde wouldn't believe him. Scotty Bennett wouldn't believe him. He could go on *The Joe Pyne Show* and air his inside scoop from the Beef Box. Joe Pyne would scoff at him. Some left-wing Jews and paranoid hippies *might* believe him. The hebes would turn on him in a hot tick. He was pro–Cuban Freedom Cause. The hippies would scoff at his crew cut and Scotty Bennett tie. No hippie girls would shoot him some trim.

Bluff.

He put the fail-safes in place yesterday. He devised the plan off his one ray of hope. *They didn't know his bug gear was defective. They knew they talked assassination. They would not recall exactly what they said. They did not know how credible his testimony would play.*

Crutch waited at the Vivian. The pad was near-empty. He moved his mother's file and his personal shit to the Elm Hotel yesterday. His case file was there. Buzz knew the location. He'd find the files and pursue or not pursue all relevant leads.

He waited. He skimmed old *Car Craft*s and *Playboy*s. He went to I. Magnin's yesterday. He bought Dana Lund a beautiful cashmere sweater. He had it gift-wrapped and placed a valentine card in the box. He didn't sign his name. He told Dana that he'd always loved her. He had to run now. He killed two men and knew some things that he shouldn't.

Magnin's delivered the gift. He parked across the street. He watched Dana open the box and read the card. The sweater delighted her. The note seemed to scare her. She looked around and slammed her door in a rush.

Joan Rosen Klein was out in the ether. He couldn't get her a good-bye gift. It broke his fucking heart.

Crutch skimmed the November '67 *Playboy*. Kaya Christian smiled from the foldout. She was his aptly named sweetheart. He knew her from Trinity Lutheran Church a million years back.

The southbound view beckoned. Crutch walked to the window and looked out. He saw Sandy Danner's house and Barb Cathcart's house and Gail Miller on Lon Ecklund's front porch.

All those shrubs that served as his perch spots. New shrubs blocking windows he'd peeped.

He leaned out the window. He caught smog in the air. He leaned too far. He started to drop. He heard noise behind him. A force slammed him down and pulled him back up.

He was on the floor. He was foot-pinned. He was blurry-eyed, half there and half not. He smelled oil on metal and knew they'd greased the door lock.

The half there expanded. The blur decreased. A full there came on. He saw Wayne Tedrow with a silencered gun and the Frogman holding a pillow. He clutched his Saint Christopher medal and prayed the Gloria Patria.

Their feet were dug in. The Frogman sweat-oozed nicotine. Wayne said, "You dipshit cocksucker."

Froggy dropped the pillow on his head. Crutch thrashed it off and gulped in air to say it.

"I've got four tape copies, plus depositions. Four bank safe-deposit boxes. I show up in person, six-month intervals. They verify me at the sites with photo and fingerprint checks. If I don't show, you know what."

Wayne looked at Mesplede. Mesplede looked at Wayne. Wayne picked up the pillow and foot-mashed it down on his head. He couldn't see. He couldn't hear. No voices, no gunshot, no pain or white clouds. Breath spurts and heartbeats—dear God, am I dead?

Then light and air and the model airplane dangling from his ceiling. Then some breath. Then Wayne's gun with the silencer untapped.

A red Fokker triplane. Historically cool. He built it and sniffed the glue the day JFK got whacked.

Crutch said, "I want in. I'll take whatever you've got."

33

(Los Angeles, 9/10/68)

"You were talking in your sleep."

"What was I saying?"

"I thought I heard 'at least' and 'vicious.'"

Dwight rubbed his neck. It always knotted at the same spot. He got a dream aftershock: Memphis and blood spray redux.

Karen sat up and leaned over him. She was sleep-puffed and lush. She crossed her legs and sat Indian-style. He scooted down and kissed her knees. He heard Dina one room over, talking to her stuffed frog.

"Tell me again, and convince me. My simple presence here is not screwing that little girl up forever."

Karen took his hands. "Only if she grows up and joins the FBI."

"There's some left-wing parenthood thing going on here that eludes me."

"She likes you more than she likes What's-His-Name. Let it go at that."

"I don't understand the fucking world you live in."

Karen kissed his fingers. "You understand it all too well. Your accommodations acknowledge my world and grant it an offhanded respect."

Dwight reached for his cigarettes. Karen grabbed the pack and tossed it on the dresser.

"Don't tempt me."

"All right."

"And explain yourself. Connect 'at least' and 'vicious.'"

That knot again—Dwight kneaded and rubbed.

"A friend said it. The full quote was 'At least they were vicious.'"

"Who was he referring to?"

"Babe, please."

"Mr. Hoover? The cops in Chicago?"

Dwight laughed. It made his neck throb. Karen tickled his legs and built on the laugh and made the hurt stop.

"All right, I'll tell you. He was referring to a dissolute band of right-wing thugs."

Karen grinned. "I like your friend. What's his name?"

"No comment."

"Is he a cop?"

"He used to be."

"Is he as tall and good-looking as you?"

Dwight grinned. "Emphatically not."

Dina said good night to the frog. It came through the wall plain. Dwight knew she wanted them to hear it. Karen bowed and put her hand on her heart.

"I think I've got a line on Joan."

"Quid pro quo, then. Blow up an extra monument and try not to get caught."

Karen curled around him. Dwight pulled off her barrette and let her hair go. He said, "Do you love me?" She said, "I'll think about it."

34

(Las Vegas, 8/11/68)

The union folks congregated at Sills Tip-Top. Wayne studied their MO. She'd show there sooner or later. It took him four cruise-bys.

Sills was crowded—the lunch trade and no empty booths. It was up in shitsville North Vegas. The color line was blurred there. The joint was quasi-segregated. Whites ate on one side, blacks on the other.

Wayne walked in. Mary Beth Hazzard was over on the black side. She was sitting with four union friends. They were all black. Wayne recognized them from his picket-line show.

Two people noticed him. A man nudged Mary Beth. She noticed him and whispered all around the booth. The people got up and walked out. They passed Wayne en route. They lowered their eyes.

Wayne walked over and put his hand out. Her hand was firm and dry. He said, "Mrs. Hazzard." She said, "Mr. Tedrow." Her eyes clicked to the opposite seat. Wayne took the cue and sat down.

They looked at each other. It was still. It made the restaurant noise subside. People started looking at them. *It* was still. Eyes just clicked their way.

Mary Beth touched her coffee cup. "I read about your father. You have my condolences for your loss."

The union folks had left their coffee cups and saucers behind. Wayne cleared a space for his hands.

"Thank you. My father treated union people horribly, so your condolences affirm your good manners very nicely."

"I wasn't fishing for compliments, Mr. Tedrow."

"I know. I'm just hoping you'll accept the one I gave you, and not consider it condescending."

Mary Beth smiled. Wayne felt a million eyes click.

"And my condolences for your husband."

"Condolences accepted. But in the spirit of candor, I'll add that Cedric was recklessly fervent and had no business being alone with Pappy Dawkins at 2:00 a.m."

Wayne glanced around for a waitress. Two waitresses caught it and looked away. A little black boy draped himself over his booth and stared at them. Two little white girls pointed.

"You're very nervous, Mr. Tedrow. If you're thinking of ordering coffee, you might want to reconsider."

Wayne smiled. "And besides, they won't serve me."

"They will if you make a big-enough fuss."

"Or put on a big-enough show."

Mary Beth smiled. "Your show at the picket line was memorable. It begs the question of what you were trying to say, but I won't press you on that."

Wayne fidgeted. Mary Beth pushed her coffee cup over. Wayne warmed his hands on it.

"I want to thank you for your part in settling the strike, Mr. Tedrow. The rumor is that you convinced Mr. Hughes."

Wayne said, "Yes, I did."

"And your motive?"

"You mean, my motive given my history?"

Mary Beth touched the coffee cup. "I don't judge your history as harshly as most black people around here would."

Wayne touched the coffee cup. His hands almost touched hers. She left her hands there. He pulled his back.

"And why is that?"

"You killed those men while you were looking for Wendell Durfee, so you get a pass from me on that one."

Peeple looked at them. A big fat black guy and a tall, skinny white guy flat-out fucking gawked.

"Why, Mrs. Hazzard?"

"Because Leroy Williams and the Swasey brothers supplied the dope that killed my sister. Because Wendell Durfee raped me on April 19, 1951, which makes me inclined to forgive your rash behavior and like you just fine."

Wayne looked at his hands. They jerked and spun the coffee cup. Some coffee spilled on Mary Beth's hands. She didn't seem to notice. She kept her hands there.

"I read about your son. The missing-person part, I mean."

"He was a brilliant boy. He knew a great deal about chemistry."

"I'm a chemist."

"Yes, I was told that."

"Were you inquiring about me?"

"Yes, I was."

"Why?"

Mary Beth pulled her hands back. "You're pushing me. Don't ask me to say things I'm not ready to."

Wayne looked around the diner. The whole goddamn room was looking their way.

"You described your son in the past tense. Do you think he's dead?"

Mary Beth shook her head. "There's times I do, there's times I don't. Sometimes dead's easier, sometimes it's not."

"Do you miss him?"

"Yes, I miss him terribly."

Wayne said, "I'll find him for you."

Part II

SHIT MAGNET

September 12, 1968–January 20, 1969

DOCUMENT INSERT: 9/12/68. Internal FBI memorandum. Marked: "Stage 1 Covert"/"Director's Eyes Only"/"Destroy After Reading." To: Director Hoover. From: SA Dwight C. Holly.

Sir,

OPERATION BAAAAD BROTHER now stands at the on-go stage, with the drop-front and preliminary operating funds secured, police agency paperwork on our target groups and their members assessed and our infiltrator selected and ready to be placed in an operational context both plausible and provocative. Bureau informant #4361 has supplied me with the name of a potential confidential informant (female), and I have requested her Bureau file from Central Records and will study it thoroughly before any attempt is made to facilitate a meeting. THE BLACK TRIBE ALLIANCE (BTA) and MAU-MAU LIBERATION FRONT (MMLF) occupy the identical political and criminal universe, which I will summarize, along with criminal/political summaries of the groups' "leaders." As previously stated, the groups are criminally inclined, staffed with career criminals and are determined to achieve their goals through criminal means. They are political rivals, and as such, our goal must remain fixed: to create inter-group dissension that will result in criminal charges and serve to discredit the entire black-nationalist apparatus.

1.—Both groups operate along near-identical lines. They employ storefront offices that serve as recruitment hubs, social clubs and gathering places for local Negroes and visiting radicals, thus photo surveillance may prove useful at some point. Both groups distrib-

ute anti-white, anti–Los Angeles Police Department literature and
hate literature besmirching rival black-militant groups, most often
vulgar pamphlets in the comic-book style. Both organizations
recruit on campus at local high schools and junior high schools.
Both organizations extort local merchants for food to deploy in
their Feed the Kiddies programs and liquor for their weekly pay-
to-attend "political mixers," in reality drunken parties that often
result in brawls. Both organizations have female followers—i.e.,
"groupies," who act as prostitutes and donate most of their earn-
ings to the "cause." Both organizations are rumored to have "safe
houses" where visiting radicals and members fleeing criminal
proceedings are allowed to hide out. Unlike the BLACK PANTHERS
and US, there have been no known instances of BTA and MMLF
violence directed at police officers. I will direct both our infiltrator
and informant to notify me immediately should they learn of any
such planned provocations. Both organizations are rumored to be
planning excursions into the narcotics trade, although I seriously
doubt that they possess the expertise required to be successful at
it. They are both, to date, small-time in their *organized* criminal
designs, although their individual "leaders" and followers quite
often possess major felony records. BTA members are suspected of
burglarizing a series of pornographic bookstores in the LAPD's
Wilshire Division; MMLF members are suspected of participation
in a series of employee-assisted faked robberies of all-night Jack
in the Box drive-in locations. The profits from these criminal
actions were allegedly donated to BTA and MMLF operating
accounts. A BTA member allegedly operates a still and produces
190-proof corn liquor; an MMLF member allegedly scalps counterfeit tickets to the local games of the Los Angeles Dodgers and Los
Angeles Rams. Again, these criminal enterprises create operating
expenses for the BTA and MMLF and spotlight the inherent criminality of their members. The exposure of endemic criminal activity is essential to our derogatory profile of the groups and will
provide a pithy courtroom commentary when our operation concludes and highly publicized legal proceedings begin.

2.—Per the "leaders," some key details:

A—EZZARD DONNELL JONES, male Negro, DOB 8/24/37. Two
convictions for possession of narcotics (1957, 1961). Has a mail-
order divinity degree and solicits funds at southside Los Angeles
churches. JONES is the "Exalted High Commissioner" of the BTA.

B.—CORNELIUS "BENNY" BOLES, male Negro, DOB 1/11/40.
One conviction for armed robbery (1964). Works as a carhop at

Delores's Drive-In in Beverly Hills. A purported homosexual and a suspect in the unsolved 1958 slaying of a male prostitute in West Los Angeles. BOLES is the "Assistant Lord High Commissioner" of the BTA.

C.—LEANDER JAMES JACKSON, male Negro, DOB 5/4/38. No discernible criminal record. Rumored to be Haiti-born and a practitioner of Haitian voodoo. Allegedly a bunco artist (selling fake magazine subscriptions, phony land deals, no-show construction contracts), a forger (welfare checks, money orders and basketball tickets), and an arms smuggler (unsubstantiated rumors of ties to violent leftist groups in the Caribbean). JACKSON is the "Armorer" of the BTA.

D.—JOSEPH TIDWELL McCARVER, male Negro, DOB 7/16/37. Alleged residential and pharmacy burglar, rumored to have committed over 100 burglaries since 1955. Inveterate gambler, with 26 arrests and no convictions for flimflam and bookmaking offenses. Runs a weekly dice game out of a black separatist church, with proceeds going to the MMLF. McCARVER is the "Pan-African Ruler" of the MMLF.

E.—JOMO KENYATTA CLARKSON, male Negro, DOB 3/4/29. No criminal record, but rumored to be a skilled, job-selective armed robber. A cartoonist and the author of the anti-white, anti-BTA hate comic books sold by the MMLF. Works as a dispatcher for the Black Cat Cab Company in South Los Angeles. Rumored to have committed numerous "politically motivated" rapes as an "expression of solidarity" for "Brother" Eldridge Cleaver of the BLACK PANTHER PARTY. CLARKSON is the "Propaganda Minister" of the MMLF.

F.—CLAUDE CANTRELL TORRANCE, male Negro, DOB 11/29/46. Numerous misdemeanor arrests: drunk driving, drunk and disorderly, petty theft, non-payment of child support, defrauding an innkeeper, vagrancy, impersonating a police officer and various gambling-related offenses. The principal player in MMLF's Feed the Kiddies program. TORRANCE is both the "Minister of Finance" and "Minister of Extortion" for the MMLF.

3.—Known haunts of the BTA and MMLF include the dispatch hut of the BLACK CAT CAB COMPANY, originally financed by a (allegedly in arrears) loan from the Teamster Central State Pension Fund, which marks it as a criminally defined enterprise; SULTAN SAM'S BARBER SHOP; SULTAN SAM'S SANDBOX (a cocktail lounge, Teamster loan–financed); SULTAN SAM'S PINBALL PARADISE (a game arcade/pornographic bookstore); CALVIN'S

ADULT EXTRAVAGANZA (a pornographic bookstore); and the
following bars and after-hour clubs: NAT'S NEST, MR. MITCH'S
ANOTHER WORLD, RAE'S RUGBURN ROOM a lesbian bar owned
by JOSEPH TIDWELL McCARVER'S sister RAE CHANTAY
McCARVER (Teamster Fund–financed), THE SNOOTY FOX, THE
SCORPIO LOUNGE, TOMMY TUCKER'S PLAYROOM and the CAR-
OLINA PINES COFFEE SHOP on Imperial Highway. It should be
prominently noted that the key BTA and MMLF personnel are
rumored to have ties to THE PEOPLES' BANK OF SOUTH LOS
ANGELES, rumored to have been initially seeded by a Teamster
Pension Fund loan (allegedly in arrears) and long suspected of
being a money-laundering front for Negro criminals. The bank's
longtime president, LIONEL DARIUS THORNTON, male Negro, DOB
12/8/19, has no criminal record, is a noted civic booster in the
Los Angeles Negro community and has long been suspected of
organized-crime ties.

4.—As I detailed in my previous confidential telex, our infiltrator will be LAPD OFFICER MARSHALL E. BOWEN, a gifted imper-
sonator with previous subversive-group penetrations financed by
CLYDE DUBER ASSOCIATES. I am currently creating a scenario
for OFFICER BOWEN'S cosmetically proffered expulsion from the
LAPD, perhaps to be shaped by OFFICER BOWEN'S hostile relationship with SERGEANT ROBERT S. BENNETT, an LAPD Robbery
Division detective much feared and despised in South Los Angeles.
I have researched SERGEANT BENNETT and consider him to be
the perfect foil for this scenario. I have set up a meeting with
LAPD CHIEF TOM REDDIN and LOS ANGELES SAC JACK LEAHY to
discuss OFFICER BOWEN'S expulsion/immersion. Along with us,
they will be the only law-enforcement personnel privy to this
information.

OPERATION BAAAD BROTHER now stands at on-go status. I
await your comments.

Respectfully,

SA Dwight C. Holly

35

(Los Angeles, 9/13/68)

Dwight read files. A radio spritzed the news. Nixon and Humphrey grubbed for votes and see-sawed poll-wise. Jimmy Ray and Sirhan Sirhan fomented in custody. Local grief: two ski-masked coons robbed a Brentwood home of cash and jewels.

The drop-front was file-full. It was file-saturated and file-fucked. He needed four more cabinets. He was file-fucked dick-deep.

He read carbons from the ATF and St. Louis PD. Confirmed anew: the "Grapevine Tavern Slaughter," case closed. One non sequitur: that surprise victim.

Thomas Frank Narduno, forty-five years old, out of New York. The odd man there. Bug devices found on his body.

Dwight checked Narduno's FBI file. It was sketchy. Narduno traveled in lefty circles. He was a two-time robbery suspect: Ohio and New York. No arrests, no convictions. He vibed fringe fool or Red recidivist. His Grapevine connection was superfluous now.

Relief.

He was relieved. Mr. Hoover was relieved. Mr. Hoover was still pissy underneath it. He kept rehashing Dwight's rest cure. Silver Hill, '57. The old poof was *three* beats off now. He called it "Happy Hills, '58." It didn't matter. The old poof had a file on it—stashed, indexed and extortion-ready.

He had a file coming: Joan Rosen Klein, potential informant. Central Records was telexing it. The pages were heavily redacted. Fat ink strokes blotted names, dates and locations. Karen implied that Joan might be difficult. Forewarned is forearmed: see the file before you meet her.

Dwight yawned. His sleep was shot, his nerves were thin, nightmares revived as daytime vignettes. He raided a Bureau evidence room and copped some sedatives. They goosed his one drink a night and one pill a night only. It fucking helped.

The chief was late. Dwight schmoozed with Jack Leahy. Jack did Mr. Hoover shtick. The old girl was buying antiques with lover boy Lance. Jack was spot-on. He had the mince and the wrist action. It was risky shit. Jack was a tough read. He was half G-man, half Mort Sahl.

Dwight laughed. "Guerrilla humor. Funny shit at the Improv, risky shit at the L.A. office."

Jack cleaned his glasses. "Twenty years and civil service. I'm snitch-proof."

"I saw you do Hoover as Oscar Wilde when you were a rookie."

"Then, I guess I'm just lucky."

Dwight smiled. "Or you've got an agenda, or you're just a fucking kamikaze."

The office was cop-blah: gray walls and flags up the ying-yang. Reddin pre-announced himself with Aqua Velva fumes. He was a big guy. He slapped backs and crashed behind his desk.

"Jack, it's been too long. Mr. Holly, I've been hearing about you for years."

Jack lit a cigarette. "Dwight 'the Enforcer' Holly. A blunt man with a politically dubious girlfriend."

Reddin yukked and waved faux wolfsbane. Jack winked. Dwight figured *el jefe* was good for five minutes.

"We want to sheep-dip one of your Negro officers, Chief. A young Wilshire Division patrolman named Marshall Bowen. My intention is to put him into the Black Tribe Alliance and/or the Mau-Mau Liberation Front. It's a long-term Cointelpro aimed at discrediting the black-militant movement. I'll be running it autonomously. Apologies in advance, but Mr. Hoover wants you bypassed on summary reports and memoranda."

Reddin flushed. "I like to know what's going on with my men."

Dwight lit a cigarette. "Mr. Hoover insists, sir."

Jack said, "He'll be working out of my jurisdiction. This is a bit of a slap in the face."

Reddin drummed his desk. "We've got plants in the Panthers and US. We share our intelligence with outside agencies when requested, which leads me to say I don't like the one-way aspect of this."

"Again, sir. Mr. Hoover insists."

Jack went limp-waisted. "If Mr. Hoover insists, Mr. Hoover insists."

Reddin smirked. "I've read Intel sheets on the BTA and MMLF. They're buffoons."

Dwight grinned. "We'll paint them with a broad brush. The Panthers and US will get tarred, as well."

Reddin lit a cigarette. "They're all tar babies."

Dwight laughed. Jack futzed with his ashtray. Reddin said, "All right. You're saying it's a publicized expulsion scenario, which will hopefully drench your boy in ghetto cachet."

Dwight nodded. "Right, and I'm thinking it will derive from a pre-existing personal feud between Officer Bowen and Sergeant Robert S. Bennett."

Reddin rolled his eyes. "Oh, Jesus, Scotty."

Jack said, "That psycho cocksucker."

Reddin slapped his knees. "Jack doesn't like Scotty. Scotty threw his weight around on that armored-car job we had a few years back, and it ruffled Jack's feathers."

Dwight put out his cigarette. "Give it up, Jack. You ran the Bureau's end for a week."

Reddin said, "With Scotty, a week can be an eternity."

Jack rubbed his eyes. "Why Bennett and this Officer Bowen? What sort of 'pre-existing feud'?"

Dwight rocked his chair back. "Some ink-stained bills from the armored-car job were circulating in the ghetto. Marsh Bowen innocently passed one, so Bennett leaned on him. Bowen got on LAPD over Bennett's objections."

Reddin said, "Jesus, Scotty and that case."

Jack said, "All right, I'll concede the viability of the context. The cast is great, and the script options are enticing."

Dwight smiled. "Here's the kicker. I don't want Bennett informed. The scenario has to play out without his knowledge."

The desk phone rang. Reddin took the call sotto voce. Jack said, "You'll copy me. Right, Dwight? For old time's sake?"

Dwight said, "No."

Tail job—all Niggertown.

Dwight drove a rent-a-car. Scotty Bennett drove an unmarked cruiser. It was a comb-the-Congo caper. Scotty threw his weight around. He exuded white-oppressor panache.

The fucker was huge. The bow tie and crew cut were a swinging caveman touch. Dwight frogged four car lengths back. Scotty canvassed liquor stores and scrounged free booze. Scotty waved to hookers and tossed Tootsie Rolls to little colored kids. Scotty drove by the Panther HQ and zoomed up on the sidewalk. A spear-chukker clique ran inside.

Scotty hit a parking-lot crap game and shuck-and-jived with the brothers. Scotty logged ghetto scuttlebutt. Scotty dispensed chump change to winos. Scotty greased his snitches with ten-spots and pistol-whipped a freaky nigger hassling an old lady. Scotty donated a case of gin to the Mighty Redeemer Church. Scotty frisked an informant, found a hypo kit and beat his black ass with a beaver-tail sap.

Darktown sizzled. It was mid-September hot. The shines wore warm-weather plumage. Lots of tank tops, porkpies and purple newsboy caps. Listless layabouts lapping up Schlitz Malt Liquor.

Scotty cruised by the Peoples' Bank of South Los Angeles. Dwight saw the prexy: Lionel Darius Thornton. Scotty drove by the BTA and MMLF fronts. The badass door guards wilted.

The hump sucked up fear and hate wholesale. He was a stone shit magnet.

The tour wound down at 4:00 p.m. Scotty hit the Harbor Freeway, the 101 and the Western Avenue exit. He double-parked outside a topless dive called the Rabbit's Foot Club. Dwight single-parked and foot-tailed him in.

A stacked redhead gyrated onstage. Pensioners and hippie boys leered at her. Scotty bowed and waved. The redhead walked backstage. A stacked blonde replaced her.

Scotty walked backstage. Dwight walked back and lingered by some curtains. He heard small talk and an unmistakable blow job. He walked back to his rent-a-car and waited. Scotty split the Rabbit's Foot Club nine minutes later. He shagged his cruiser and U-turned eastbound.

Dwight frogged him. Scotty took Hollywood Boulevard to Sunset to Alvarado south. Bam—east on 7th Street. Next stop—Vince & Paul's Steak House, 7th and Union.

Scotty parked and walked in. Dwight cut him eight minutes' slack. The bar was packed: wall-to-wall cops in civvies, juicing.

Dwight nursed a 7UP and tried to look un-coplike. Scotty glad-handed, raconteured and fondled a stacked brunette.

Scotty boozed. Scotty snarfed the free fried shrimp and rumaki. Scotty waltzed the brunette back to a storage room. Dwight lingered by the door. He heard small talk and an unmistakable blow job.

Enough.

Dwight walked back to his rent-a-car and waited. Scotty exited Vince & Paul's eighty-three minutes later. Dwight tailed him home to Pasadena. His family met him on the porch. Mrs. Scotty was a stacked blonde pushing fifty. Scotty had two teenaged sons and two teenaged daughters. The kids were *très* tall and looked just like Scotty.

"Do you hang out at Vince & Paul's?"

"Black cops aren't welcome there."

"What happened to 'Negro'?"

"It went out last year. 'Black' is more bold. It's got that tell-it-like-it-is quality that my people revere."

Dwight pushed his plate back. Ollie Hammond's Steak House out-classed Vince & Paul's. Their booth was secluded. Marsh Bowen picked at a salad.

"It's Scotty Bennett's hangout. Is that why you asked me?"

Dwight popped an antacid mint and lit a cigarette. His food had gone cold.

"I can read people, Mr. Holly. I know you've been mulling over Scotty."

"Don't fish for compliments. If I didn't consider you smart and percep-tive, you wouldn't be here."

"But you're wondering how adaptable I am."

"That's correct."

"I'll consider that a compliment and move on, then."

Dwight tugged at his law-school ring. "The inked-cash thing. How bru-tal was he?"

Marsh toyed with his fork. "He asked me questions with exaggerated courtesy and hit me with a phone book when he disapproved of my answers."

"Does he hate Negroes?"

"It's 'black,' Mr. Holly."

"Don't correct me, Officer."

No twitch or flinch. Spreading goose bumps and a forehead vein tapping.

"Does he hate Negroes?"

"More than you, but less volubly. And I'm sure he's killed a few more than you have."

Dwight flinched. "He seems to relish his time on the southside."

"He does, yes. He's 'Mr. Scotty' south of Washington Boulevard."

"This decorously expressed hatred of his. Is he well known for it?"

"Oh yes."

Dwight cracked his knuckles. "Scotty's the bait in your expulsion sce-nario. Tell me how you think we should play it."

Marsh did a pantomime. He squinted through a viewfinder. He framed the shot. He spoke through a megaphone.

"Vince & Paul's Steak House. The bar in full swing. Officer Marshall E. Bowen hits on Sergeant Robert S. Bennett's torrid waitress girlfriend with the man himself right there."

Dwight stuck his hand out. Marsh let it hang there. The moment built and fizzled. They both saw how dumb it looked. They laughed at the same time.

36

(Las Vegas, 9/14/68)

How *suite* it is.

His killer pals lived in hotel suites. Freddy O. had the Cavern. The Frogman had new Fontainebleau digs. Wayne Tedrow had this spread at the Stardust. Dwight Holly crashed in suites nationwide.

Crutch waited for Wayne T. *His* suite featured four rooms and a chemistry lab. His killer pals had college degrees. *He* got expelled from high school. He snapped that pic of Gail Miller's bush and blitzed his shot at a higher education.

Crutch waited. The foyer was velvet-flocked and gilt-mirrored. Caustic fumes wafted from the next room. The Vegas paper sat on a table. Wayne made the headline, secondhand.

The LVPD hung a posthumous beef on a shine named Pappy Dawkins. Said beef: the Wayne Senior snuff. "Heart attack"—bullshit. It was a sop to appease the family.

His killer pals made headlines. His killer pals *rigged* headlines. The inside rumor: *Wayne* offed his old man.

Crutch leaned against the wall. The flocking made him sneeze. Wayne and Froggy let him live. Yeah, he bluffed them. Yeah, he built the fail-safes. But, he had to *spill*.

He'd spilled *partial*. He spilled that Dr. Fred Hiltz hired him. Go, kid—goose Farlan Brown and Count Dracula. It's a thieving girlfriend gig. They grokked that part of it and believed him. He did not spill on Gretchen Farr as Celia Reyes or on Joan Rosen Klein. He did not reveal the foreign passports or Sam G.'s calls to Gretchen/Celia or the dead woman in Horror House.

Wayne opened the door and walked past him. No nod, fuck you, you're this bug I don't see. Crutch chased his shadow. A stink announced the chem lab. It was all vats and beakers on shelves.

Crutch hovered in the doorway. Wayne pressed a beaker up to his hairline. It was a *Shit, I've got a headache* thing.

"You wanted in. Okay, you're in. If you do what Mesplede and I tell you to do, you *may* survive. If you lie to us or steal from us or double-deal us or withhold information from us, we will kill you and bluff our way out of the jeopardy that you placed us in."

Crutch gulped. His Adam's apple popped. He stretched out his tie. Let those little 2's show.

"I've killed two men. I'm committed to the Cuban Freedom Cause."

Wayne gave him This Look. "The 'Cuban Freedom Cause' is right-wing bullshit. Mesplede is a deluded firebrand, I am not, and I would advise you not to become one. If indeed you did kill two men, it was out of your kid desire to suck up to Mesplede or your fear that *he* would kill *you* if you disobeyed him. Don't jerk my chain with your kid bullshit. Don't give *me* a reason to kill *you.*"

Crutch said, "Okay." He smirked like Scotty B. He willed his voice octaves deep.

Wayne said, "You work with Mesplede. Your job is to disrupt Hubert Humphrey's campaign rallies, for three hundred dollars a week. Humphrey's travel schedule is coming, so you talk to Clyde Duber, get a left-wing front list and find some politically motivated fools to help you out. You do not indulge your extracurricular kid activities on my time card. Do you understand me?"

Powder fumes swirled. The lab felt toxic. Crutch wiped his nose. Wayne laughed at him.

"I talked to Farlan Brown this morning. He's willing to forgive you for any kid shit you might have pulled while you were working for Fred Hiltz. He told me to tell you that Gretchen Farr took him for $25,000, and you can keep half if you find her and make restitution. He told me that at one point he bribed an alcoholic chum of yours off the case with an anonymous payment, because he feared unfavorable publicity, but now that you're working for me, you might as well stick with it, on a contingency basis."

Crutch grinned. Wayne revived This Look. Crutch *un*-grinned quick.

Wayne swallowed three aspirin. "Brown told me to forward this information to you. He said he got suspicious of Gretchen once and went through her closet. He saw an airline stewardess' uniform, with no airline designation and a name tag with the first name Janet. That's all he told me, and now I'll tell you. Do what you want with this, on your own time. Do not neglect your duties for me, and tell Dr. Fred and Clyde Duber that you're withdrawing from this idiot 'case' as of now."

Crutch held off a sneeze. Wayne said, "Get out of here. Common sense keeps telling me to kill you."

"Work F.B.'s stewardess lead."

"Giancana bootleg #—???"

"To date: no viable police paperwork on GF. Can't ask Scotty B. about JRK's ('51 & '53) armed-robbery arrsts (no #s to indicate convictions) without alerting Clyde. Likewise, can't request JRK Fed file. Per GF/CR: check nationwide birth recs or assume foreign parentage?"

"GF/CR & victim: check local PD Intelligence, Vice & missing person files while on campaign trip."

Crutch drew on his wall graph. His head bounced—L.A. to Vegas and back in four hours. His nose still itched. Wayne dismissed him with "Good-bye, Dipshit."

He needed more graph paper. He needed more file boxes. He might need a *third* file pad. Wayne warned him: do not withhold information. His case was high-risk now.

Crutch scanned the graph. Words swam. Through lines and clue nuggets cohered. He studied Joan's mug shots. He pulled a floor lamp up and made her gray streaks glow.

Brainstorm.

He got out his sketch pad. He drew a facial likeness of Gretchen Farr/Celia Reyes. He added an airline stew's outfit with the Janet name tag.

The Yellow Pages—there by the phone.

Airlines. Compile a list. Canvassing duty on tap.

Something was fucked. It was Beverly Hills, it was 2:00 p.m., it vibed major grief.

A bottleneck in Fat City. BHPD black & whites peeling out, lights and sirens. Two K-cars, two meat wagons, two news vans.

Crutch followed the cop cars. They peeled up through the biz district and hit the rare-air zone. The grief vibe intensified: more K-cars, choppers, cops with leashed bloodhounds. He cut west on Elevado. Traffic was dead-stalled. He saw a big bluesuit swarm outside Hate House.

He ditched his car and ran there. He dodged stalled cars and cut across front lawns. He sprinted down the neighbor's driveway and monkey-climbed the fence. The bluesuit swarm expanded. There's the statues and the bomb shelter and Dr. Fred. He's on a blood-soaked gurney. He's got shotgun pellets and scorched bone for a face.

The bluesuits saw him. He recognized some guys. Someone yelled, "Crutchfield, go to the station!"

Clyde was there. Ditto Phil Irwin. Ditto Phil and Clyde's Jew lawyer, Chick Weiss.

The Detective Bureau hall was packed. BHPD murders ran one per decade. It was a roundup. The fuzz were hauling in Dr. Fred's KAs.

Clyde said, "It's just routine. They saw my name, Phil's name and Crutch's name in Dr. Fred's appointment book."

Chick said, "It's got to be one of his ex-wives. He was married seven times. I did all his divorces. He was the biggest alimony defaulter on the planet."

Phil said, "Live by the sword, die by the sword. I think it's black militants. He wrote all these anti-coon tracts, so the coons waxed his hate-monger ass."

Crutch flashed on Gretchen/Celia. Crutch flashed on Joan. Crutch flashed on the cash-stuffed clothes bin.

Clyde said, "Nix on the militants, but it plays like a shine caper. I talked to the watch commander. He thinks it's that boogie heist team that robbed those people in Brentwood."

Chick said, "I'm a boogie art connoisseur. I dig Caribbean statuary. That doesn't mean I dig boogie 211 PC's."

Phil said, "Live by the sword, die by the sword."

Clyde rolled his eyes. Chick said, "As your lawyer, my advice is don't reveal shit. Dr. Fred was dirty in countless fucking ways. You don't want guilt by association."

The intercom buzzed: "Donald Crutchfield. Captain's office, please."

Crutch walked over. The door was ajar. He stepped inside. Dwight Holly was standing there.

"Hello, Dipshit."

Crutch shut the door. *Confluence,* Clyde's word, *it's who you know and who you blow and how you're all linked.*

"People keep calling me that. I keep trying to show them otherwise."

"It's the bow tie with the polo shirt. It's hard to see through to the real, dynamic you."

Crutch leaned on the door. His chest throbbed. Bile crept up. He felt like he looked green. Dwight Holly tossed him an antacid mint. He caught it and popped it. Dwight Holly winked.

"Wayne explained the stalemate you created. I said, 'Let's kill him anyway,' but softer minds prevailed. If you want to look for that woman who skimmed Farlan Brown, swell. Obey orders, you live. Disobey them, *c'est la guerre.*"

Crutch shut his eyes and saw Dr. Fred faceless. Triple-aught buckshot. Big game–stopping loads. He tasted blood in his mouth. He'd bit his gums raw.

Dwight Holly said, "Mr. Hoover wants this homicide short-shrifted. Some jigs pulled a robbery and it got out of hand. Dr. Fred was a Bureau informant, a hate peddler, a dope fiend and a compulsive pussy hound. It was a high-risk lifestyle, and the world will not mourn. Are you starting to see your role in this?"

Crutch opened his eyes. "He had a bomb shelter. There was a big hamper full of—"

"The shelter was ransacked and the money is gone. *Some jigs pulled a robbery and it got out of hand.* They'll blow the money on dope, Cadillacs and mink coats for their bitches, they'll continue pulling robberies until some white cops shoot and kill them. Now, are you starting to see your—"

"Don't tell BHPD about the Gretchen Farr gig. Don't mention Dracula or Farlan Brown. Lie. Dissemble. Prevaricate. Don't bring up you, Wayne, Freddy O., Mesplede, or any other dipshit-killer friends you might have. Don't embarrass your pansy boss, Mr. Hoover."

Dwight Holly grinned. "I thought I detected a brain there."

Crutch swallowed some blood. Dwight Holly tossed him another mint. It fell short and hit the floor.

"May I ask you a question about your tie and your haircut?"

"Sure."

"Do you have an unseemly crush on Sergeant Robert S. Bennett?"

Crutch said, "Fuck you."

Dwight Holly roared.

37

(Las Vegas, 9/15/68)

Files, graphs, lists. His suite was a chem lab/paper mill.

Teamster Fund book loan defaulters. Deadbeats and stiffs. Transaction files and credit sheets. Debit-projection files and cost-analysis studies.

Wayne read files and jotted figures. He worked with a scratch pad and three different pens. His back hurt from hunkering down and his fingers hurt from writing. His eyes hurt from file reads and column-figure scans.

Let's co-opt the Steve's Kingburger chain in Akron, Ohio. Let's buy a mall site in Leawood, Kansas. Let's co-opt the Pizza Pit chain and wash casino skim through it. Let's annex three low-life clubs in South L.A.: The Scorpio Lounge, Sultan Sam's Sandbox and a dyke den named Rae's Rug-burn Room. Let's grab the Peoples' Bank of South Los Angeles, for its laundry potential. Let's usurp Black Cat Cab. It's an all-cash biz, it's near the Peoples' Bank, it's close to the border and our foreign-casino sites.

Wayne put his pen down. He was wiped. He got off the dope that got him through West Vegas and the Grapevine. He got through his sobbing fits over Janice. He was getting fit again. He was getting impervious, because—

He was working.

He was mediating and colluding. He was working for Carlos Marcello and for and against Howard Hughes. Drac's hotel spree was forestalled by Justice Department edict. Tricky Dick would put the skids to that, should he prevail at the polls. His dirty-tricks squad would lend support.

He was dispatching. Jean-Philippe Mesplede was set to scout casino-site countries. Mesplede was a mixed-bag *grande plus*. He was tireless and competent and prone to sentimental gaffes. He let the numbnuts kid live. The kid's fail-safes were borderline sound. Borderlines were tenuous. He projected Dipshit's life span as roughly six months.

The kid was a shit magnet. So was he. So was Dwight Holly.

Dwight called him yesterday. His news: the Fred Hiltz homicide. Mr. Hoover wanted it entombed. That was good: Drac and Farlan Brown might get offshoot publicity. He told Dwight his Don Crutchfield story. Dwight said, "Should I kill him?" Wayne said, "Not yet."

He yawned and grabbed *The File*. It ran four pages. Dwight pulled strings and shagged it for him.

LVPD–Clark County Sheriff's: Missing Person Case #38992. Reginald James Hazzard/male Negro/DOB 10/17/44.

Scant and bleak. Pro forma: missing colored kids rated zilch.

Reginald Hazzard was a high school honors grad. He took college classes, worked in a car wash, kept his snout clean. The cops interviewed a few neighbors, learned zero, case closed.

The folder was unscuffed. The paper smelled new. It was an un-visited and un-mourned document.

He'd called Mary Beth three times. She never answered. He called at one-day intervals and let the phone ring twenty times.

He put the file down. He hesitated. He dialed her number again. He got four rings and her near-brusque hello.

"It's Wayne Tedrow, Mrs. Hazzard."

She near-laughed. "Well, it's good to hear from you, but I can't say I'm surprised."

"Can we get coffee?"

"All right, but I'll bring it."

"Where?"

"That first rest stop on I-15. I shouldn't be seen with you."

The then to now blurred. This rest stop and the rest stop near Dallas. Sand drifts and scrub balls then. Desert grit now. Wendell D. in pimp threads. Similar rest-room huts blurred seamless.

Wayne pulled in. Mary Beth sat in a '62 Valiant. It was midday and crowded. She'd parked away from the other cars. Wayne leaped in her car. She smiled and slapped the steering wheel. The horn beeped. Wayne banged his knees on the dashboard.

"We're not fugitives, you know."

Wayne said, "You could make a case for it."

She handed him a paper cup with a napkin attached. The bottom was seeping.

"I forgot to ask for cream and sugar."

"Any way's fine with me."

"Are you always so accommodating?"

"No, I tend to be a bit peremptory."

Mary Beth smiled. "I know. I saw Buddy Fritsch on Fremont Street yesterday. He was wearing a splint on his nose."

Wayne held the cup two-handed. The coffee was too hot. He sipped it slow. It was pure busywork.

"My friends think you're crazy."

"What do you say to them?"

"That men who want things from you usually give you things or show you things, which is the same as telling you things flat out. I say, 'Mr. Tedrow has something to tell me, and he doesn't have the words, but he sure knows a gesture.' "

Wayne put his cup on the dashboard. It rocked and sat still. He turned toward Mary Beth and laced his hands over one knee.

"Tell me about your son."

"He made me wish there were two or three more of him, which coming from a busy-making person like me says quite a bit."

"That describes your feeling for him. I was thinking of your assessment of him as a young man."

Mary Beth sipped coffee. "He was a reader and a chemistry dabbler. He went on binges with books and his chemistry sets. He was trying to figure out the world with his mind, which I respected."

A car pulled up next to them. A white couple gawked. Wayne said, "And the police investigation?"

"About what you'd expect. It came and went in about half a day, so Cedric and I hired a private detective. His name was Morty Sidwell, and I think he did an adequate job. He checked death records and police and hospital records all over the country and became convinced that Reginald was still alive. We ran out of money after a while, so we had to let the whole thing go."

The white people kept staring. Wayne kept looking over. Mary Beth said, "Let it go. I don't think I can take another gesture from you."

Wayne hitched his seat back. It freed up his legs. Mary Beth put her cup on the dashboard.

"President Kennedy was killed a few weeks before Reginald disappeared. He was very upset."

The white people drove off. Dad did some double-clutch thing and kicked gravel their way.

"Do you remember where you were that weekend?"

Wayne looked at her. "I was in Dallas."

"Why?"

"I was trying to find Wendell Durfee."

"And?"

"And I found him, and I let him go."

More cars pulled in. It got claustrophobic. Wayne jittered up and broke a sweat. Mary Beth put her hand on his knee.

DOCUMENT INSERT: 9/16/68. "SUBVERSIVE PERSONS" Summary
Report. Marked: "Chronology/Known Facts/Observations/Known
Associates/Memberships & Organizations." Subject: KLEIN, JOAN
ROSEN/Numerous Unknown Aliases/white female/DOB 10/31/26,
New York City. Compiled: 3/14/67.

1.—Summation: SUBJECT JOAN ROSEN KLEIN must be viewed
as a seditiously anti-American figure with pervasive connections to
dangerous radical organizations across a wide left-wing ideological
spectrum dating back over 20 years. She has been a "community
organizer," a planner of "protest marches" for numerous subversive causes, an instructor at dubious "Freedom Schools" that
espouse Communist Party–line doctrine, and, most pertinently, a
strong ally of radical-Left groups that have advocated the violent
overthrow of the United States government—i.e., THE SOCIALIST
WORKER'S PARTY, THE STUDENTS FOR A DEMOCRATIC SOCIETY
and THE REVOLUTIONARY ACTION MOVEMENT. These organizations have announced their solidarity with violent black-nationalist
organizations, the BLACK PANTHER PARTY and US, marking
them as Level-4 security risks. SUBJECT JOAN ROSEN KLEIN
has also been suspected (unproven) of participation in armed
robberies in Los Angeles in 1951 & 1953/no further information
available, and of two 1954 armed robberies in Ohio & New
York/no further information available.

SUBJECT JOAN ROSEN KLEIN'S grandfather, ISIDORE HER-
SCHEL KLEIN (1874–1937), was a wealthy emerald merchant and
left-wing polemicist who donated large amounts of money to anarchist groups, radical pro-labor groups & Communist Front causes.
His son JOSEPH LEON KLEIN (1902–1940) was a confirmed radical zealot, as was his wife HELEN HERSHFIELD ROSEN KLEIN
(1904–1940). Their 1940 deaths left SUBJECT JOAN ROSEN
KLEIN orphaned. She resurfaced during the war years and was
detained for Alien and Sedition Act violations, disorderly behavior
at Communist-organized protest rallies and was photo-surveilled at
nationwide meetings of the COMMUNIST PARTY USA, SOCIALIST
LABOR PARTY, STUDENTS PEACE UNION, LEAGUE FOR INDUS-
TRIAL DEMOCRACY, TRADE UNION UNITY LEAGUE, and at various rallies for exiled Communist sympathizer Paul Robeson.
SUBJECT JOAN ROSEN KLEIN is rumored to have authored the

most virulently anti-American literature distributed by the above-referenced organizations.

2.—SUBJECT JOAN ROSEN KLEIN considers herself to be an itinerant academic by trade and recently (1962) taught at a radically funded "Freedom School" adjunct of the University of Southern California, where she allegedly mentored Negro students in chemistry and physics. She has heavily cloaked relationships and mail-drop correspondences with numerous left-wing college professors who serve to facilitate her meetings with other like-minded subversives inhabiting the Communist/Socialist/Radical underground. SUBJECT JOAN ROSEN KLEIN travels extensively abroad (most likely under false passports), has allegedly spent time in Communist Cuba (in violation of travel-ban edicts) and allegedly has ties to the Communist-backed 6/14 Movement in the Dominican Republic and has written anti-American, anti-Dominican polemics excoriating the alleged mistreatment of Haitian peasants by "U.S.-backed fascist interests colluding with Dominican despots in the genocidal war against Haiti." These polemics were allegedly co-authored by a Dominican woman known only by the first name of "Celia."

3.—SUBJECT JOAN ROSEN KLEIN is known to have traveled extensively within the continental United States and is often flown (by wealthy fellow travelers) to insurrectionist hot spots to confer with radical leaders and advise them how to best achieve their ends. Her sub-specialty is the recruitment of the naïve college students who attend her "Freedom School" classes, and she has been rumored to have assisted many young people in "dropping out" and assuming "underground identities." Subversive-meeting-group index logs and photo-surveillance logs note SUBJECT JOAN ROSEN KLEIN'S attendance at loyalty-oath protest meetings in Los Angeles on 8/30/50; Free the Rosenbergs rallies in New York City in 6/52; rallies of the INDEPENDENT PROGRESSIVE PARTY in Boston in 11/51. SUBJECT JOAN ROSEN KLEIN was also spotted at Communist-backed rallies for the Stockholm Peace Petition in 14 U.S. cities in 1950.

4.—More recently, SUBJECT JOAN ROSEN KLEIN has mediated "peace pacts" between rancorous left-wing factions and (primarily white) groups allied with black-militant groups. She was allegedly the author of a 200-page pamphlet advising the YOUNG SOCIALIST ALLIANCE in their "Violent Workers War to Overthrow the State of Indiana." SUBJECT JOAN ROSEN KLEIN has (1966) worked as a "disk jockey" at the left-wing radio station Radio-Free Dixie and was recently spotted (photo-surveillance) with members of the violent radical group the <u>WEATHER UNDERGROUND</u>. Four issues of their Communist-influenced newsletter, "The Weather Report," bear her byline. <u>SUBJECT JOAN ROSEN KLEIN</u> is also rumored to be adept at maintaining "safe houses"—i.e., hideouts for violent fugitive radicals.

    5.—Known Associates: ████████████████████████

██
██
██
██
██
██
██
██
██
██
██
██
██

    6.—<u>SUBJECT JOAN ROSEN KLEIN</u> (current whereabouts unknown) must be considered a Level-4 security risk and should be put on the all-city alert for frequent mail intercepts, photo surveillance and possible regular stints of 48-hour detention. (Periodic updates to follow as new information accrues.) Routing #1499684/Central Records/Washington, D.C. SA Holly: please return by Inter-Bureau mail cover.

38

(Los Angeles, 9/19/68)

t's her hair.

The gray streaks. No conces-
sions for forty-one. Her bare arms
to spotlight the knife scar. She
vibed her age, she dressed mature, she eschewed kid aesthetics. The scar
was sufficient Fuck You.

They lit cigarettes. Their booth was big and wraparound. Ollie Hammond's was pre-lunch slow.

Joan Klein said, "You haven't mentioned the pay."

Dwight sipped coffee. "A thousand a month, cold. Spend a hundred a
week getting next to our targets. Buy food for the Feed the Kiddies scams,
so the brothers can allot more money for guns and dope."

"And my duties beyond that?"

"Report in full, be discreet, don't forward information that could only
have come from you. *Protect your informant status.* Warn me in advance of
potential violent crime and any specific talk of actions against police officers."

Joan smiled. "Beyond the usual 'kill the pigs' chatter?"

Dwight smiled. "Specific pigs, tell me. Nebulous, honky-pig-
motherfucker bullshit, I can do without."

It's her glasses.

The black frames, the loose fit, the dips down the bumps on her nose.

Dwight said, "You know Karen Sifakis."

"I know *of* a woman named 'Karen the Bombmaker.' She knows people
who know people who know me. *You* know all about cutouts, mail drops
and dead-letter fronts."

Heartburn—Dwight popped two mints. A persistent waiter hovered. Dwight glared him off.

"I've read your file."

"I figured you had."

"It's threadbare and full of inconsistencies. I can't tell if you're a red-diaper peacenik or an armed-robber manqué."

Joan blew smoke rings. "Assume both and there'll be fewer surprises."

Dwight stubbed out his cigarette. "No court filings, no paperwork. Four suspicion rousts, no DR numbers to indicate dispos—"

"Four robberies in cities undergoing labor strikes. Random roundups of Smith Act violators, names on Red Alert sheets, cops out for some fun."

Dwight poured them fresh coffee. "Did you roll over on any of your comrades?"

"No."

"How long were you detained?"

"It varied."

"Were you physically threatened?"

"A cop in Dayton, Ohio, hit me with a phone book."

"Your reaction?"

"An injudicious comment about his mother."

Dwight laughed. "And then?"

"They put me in a tank with some bull daggers. One girl was cute. I liked the kisses, but she moved a little too fast to suit me."

She spoke precisely. New York lurked in her vowels. She shifted her voice patterns—a skilled dissembler's trait.

Dwight said, "I've never rebuffed an amorous dyke in a holding tank."

Joan said, "I stabbed her with a fork. The tines cut through her cheek and lodged in her upper palate."

Dwight quashed a grin. Joan sipped coffee. She had a gaunt up-all-night look.

"How will we communicate?"

"Phone drops for now. Tuesdays at 10:00 a.m. The pay phone at Silver Lake and Effie."

"I have a teleph—"

"You're being disingenuous, Miss Klein. I don't want to know where you live, and I'll find you when I need you."

"Will you guarantee me no random detentions and no photo-surveillance hassles?"

Dwight shook his head. "No. If I ask that favor, the other L.A. agents will know you're working for me. I've already flagged your file with a false listing. As of last week, you were creating woo-woo with some militant fucks at UC Davis."

She didn't smile. He wanted her to. Her smiles leveled her harshness.

"May I tell you what I won't do?"

"I'm listening."

"I won't inform on young people who come in for a lark and get out when things get ugly."

"You're assuming they'll get ugly?"

"Yes, aren't you?"

Dwight said, "Not like you might wish. I don't foresee armed revolution in America, I don't see street-corner punks like the BTA and MMLF as the vanguard of anything more than a few fistfights and pimp rousts."

Joan smiled. Her harshness leveled *up*.

"Then why are you working so hard to suppress them?"

"Because they're driven by criminal design, because I despise disorder, because Mr. Hoover told me to."

"Because their antics will discredit the black-power movement at large. Because the better-known groups are more of a threat, but they've ingratiated themselves with the press. Because black militancy has achieved a degree of mainstream acceptance and you're trying to take it back to the gutter."

Dwight looked at her. She smiled for him. Her teeth were lipstick-smeared.

"I haven't asked you why you're doing this."

"For the money? Because suppression never works in the end? Because I'll find some people and shape their views in ways you'll never be able to assess, and Mr. Hoover will be paying me to create revolution on an undetectable level that will never make its way into any file he can gloat over at 3:00 a.m., when warm milk, cookies and Seconal don't work."

Dwight smiled. "You're very well informed."

Joan smiled. "One of Mr. Hoover's former housekeepers has a son in the Panthers. He's a gifted cartoonist. He did four panels on Mr. Hoover at bedtime. He peruses surveillance photos of well-oiled young black men sunbathing, and Aunt Jemima has to knock before she brings in her goodies."

Dwight slapped his knees. His elbows banged the table and dumped a glass. A waiter zoomed up and blotted the spill.

Joan said, "It wasn't that funny."

"I'll disagree there."

"You're very impolitic."

"Mr. Hoover and I share a history. Humor helps sometimes."

"Tell me about it."

Dwight shook his head. "Tell me about that scar on your arm and why you're so proud of it."

Joan shook her head. "I'm working on a new version. Something subtle and racist-inspired. Something the BTA and MMLF will groove on."

"You could tell me the truth."

"Utilitarian fictions are more my style."

His stomach churned. Dwight chased two mints with coffee.

"Who redacted your file? Your 'Known Associates' section has been inked, so you must have informed Federally."

Joan lit a cigarette. "I've informed, yes. I've never informed Federally, so there must be some names in there that some other Federal handler wanted deleted."

Dwight said, "I'm not sure I buy that."

"I don't care what you buy, Mr. Holly. We're both here to buy and sell, and I'm sure we'll create repression and revolution in a fucked-up, but somehow complementary fashion."

It was her smell. She was sweating. Her soap scent was gone. Her arm-holes were damp.

"I have a few specific questions, Miss Klein."

"All right."

"How will you get next to the BTA and MMLF?"

"I run a safe house. I've already made arrangements for the BTA to stash some guns there."

"And you won't tell me the address?"

"No."

Dwight said, "Here's your first test. You borrow the guns, fire them into acoustical baffling and bring me the spent shells. You replace the guns, so that I have the spents to run comparisons on."

Joan said, "No."

Dwight said, "Then there's no deal. Then I run a fifty-state detention sheet on you."

She squeezed the table ledge. Her fingers throbbed. The whole table shook.

"I won't reveal the location of the house, but I'll get you the shells."

"How do I know they'll be the right ones?"

Joan smiled. "Because you trust me?"

Dwight placed a plastic-wrapped block of cocaine on the table. Powder puffed out a stretch hole.

"Make some Commie spooks as happy as you've just made me."

Karen said, "I've never met her, but I've heard about the scar."

They were in bed. Karen was showing full-on. Dwight put a hand on her belly. Eleanora kicked twice.

"Tell me."

"It was that riot at the Paul Robeson concert in Peekskill. I think it was '49. Joan tangled with some Legionnaires."

Dwight turned on the desk fan. The bedroom air churned and stayed warm.

Karen said, "I saw a news spot on Dr. Hiltz. Remember, you told me you knew him."

Dwight nodded. "The Bureau bootjacked the investigation."

"Why?"

"He was a paid informant."

"Like me?"

"Less effective, more volatile and capricious, less politically astute."

Karen smiled. "That's one of the sweetest things you've ever said to me."

"You must love me, then."

"Well, I'll think about it."

They fell toward each other and found the fit. Dwight drifted with that smell, that harsh smile, that gray hair.

39

(Minneapolis, 9/22/68)

HHH in '68! HHH in '68! HHH in '68! The Twin Cities were Hubert turf. Scando types jammed the Berglund's Bazaar lot. Four hundred hayseeds. A good midday toll.

Fifty hippies stirred up shit. They were Clyde Duber recruits. They jabbed horror placards high. Dig it: gooks on fire, napalmed kids and U.S. jets trailing ooze.

Cheers and jeers: HHH! and hippie hate. Peace doves and slant kids with flame-flecked hairdos.

Crutch and the Frogman watched. They glommed the protest punks off Clyde's left-wing front list. They paid them with maryjane and tenspots. They hosted a poster party last night. Froggy served pizza, beer and weed. Crutch was the art director. He cut up magazines and found some swinging fascist pix.

The rally droned on. The roar accelerated: HHH! HHH! HHH!

Security guys plowed a path to the bandstand. Humphrey and some fatso pols wobbled between them. Crutch yukked. Froggy grinned. Dig it: we slipped THC in your breakfast coffee.

Humphrey charged up the steps and caught his foot on the platform. A security geek rescued him. The veep got his legs. He had blissed-out eyes. His fly was down. His BVDs showed. Chuckles circulated. Hubert addressed the crowd. He slurred his words. He said something like, "My fellow Abyssinians."

. . . .

They had a two-bedroom suite in St. Paul. It was full-boat on Howard Hughes. Room service ran twenty-four hours. They noshed New York strips, stuffed mushrooms and peppermint ice cream. The Frogman served Pernod and THC-laced cookies. They always got zorched and talked CUBA.

Mesplede was a broken record. Yeah, but that record *spun*.

LBJ, Nixon, Hubert—sissified sob sisters all. *Heroin.* We sell it, we buy guns, we depose Fidel. It worked in Vietnam. Betrayals deep-sixed Tiger Kadre. They'd run a tighter Krew now. Froggy was Wayne Tedrow's casino front man. He'd be cruising for the right right-wing country. Their sites would be Cuba-close.

We sell Big "H." We hook an island clientele. We make gun money and run speedboat missions. We rape the coast and kill Reds.

Crutch said, "I want in."

Froggy said, "My friend, I guarantee it."

Crutch pointed to his bow tie. Froggy said, "Your numbers will increase, once we determine our casino-site location."

Crutch swilled Pernod then. His peripheral vision fritzed. Froggy showed him his scalping knife. He'd scalped thirty-one Castroite fucks.

Travel lodging. He festooned the bedroom walls for his two-night stays. He kept his Joan Klein pix in his wallet. He taped up a big Cuba map and tossed darts at militia installations.

Crutch tossed and missed, tossed and hit. The surrounding walls got dart-dinged and pocked. He'd memorized most of the village names and all the roads into Havana. Memo: buy a scalping knife, just like Froggy's.

Crutch stared at the Joan pix. His Pernod/cookie buzz had him seeing new things. He'd talked to Clyde. Clyde's take: the Dr. Fred snuff did not play into the Gretchen Farr caper. The Feds usurped the inquiry. Jack Leahy was running it. Jack's take: it's that jig heist gang. They robbed that Brentwood house, they hit Dr. Fred next.

Crutch got panic pangs. Dwight Holly said, "Is there anything you're not telling me?" Crutch lied and said, "No." *Nobody knows about Horror House. Nobody knows about Gretchen Farr as Celia Reyes or about Joan Rosen Klein.* He clued Buzz Duber in to one lead: Farlan Brown's airline-stew revelation. Buzz was working that lead in L.A. now. He was checking airline offices with Crutch's sketch.

Pernod and THC. The bedroom walls wafting peach to magenta. Still no make on the dead woman's tattoo. Still no make on the wall markings. He broke into Arnie Moffett's office again, en route to the airport. He re-ransacked the house-rental files. He got more zero on Gretchen/Celia and Joan. He'd leaned on Arnie *baaaaaaad.* The cocksucker probably dumped their file post-beating.

His fuck-up-Hubert gig was now three cities in. He'd checked three local PD Intel and Robbery files. Zero—no mentions of Joan Rosen Klein.

Crutch dart-bombed the Bay of Pigs and Havana. His weird high got him all swelled up and misty. He taped the Joan pictures above his bed. The wall colors shifted—magenta to tropic sunrise.

Another shopping mall lot today. Last night's news: "Exhausted Humphrey makes policy gaffes." This gig was that gig re-psychedelicized. Froggy said he learned some shit in Chicago.

The crowd ran three hundred. They ran porky and Minnesota blond. They were noisy. They talked liberal rah-rah. HHH emoted on placard fronts. He tried to look studly. He failed. He looked like your pedophile coach.

Crutch and the Frogman stood beside the speaker's platform. A cheer went up: *He's coming! He's coming! He's coming!* Crutch saw Humphrey and some flunkies approaching, stage left. Four cops trailed them by four paces. Mesplede waved three fingers. Three moonlighting Teamsters waved back.

They opened canisters on the QT. They squatted on the QT. They poured liquid wax on the ground beside the platform. The shit was neutral-colored. It slithered and spread.

Four paces, three, two, one—

Humphrey and his flunkies slipped, slid and slalomed up the platform steps. Hubert did Frug and Wah-Watusi moves just to stay upright. The crowd yukked. Two cops pratfalled. The crowd re-yukked. A fat cat hugged Hubert. Hubert's look said "What's *this* shit?" The fat cat spoke into the microphone. More yuks leveled his spiel. Crutch signaled a guy by the platform. The guy toppled and mock-convulsed. The fucker was double-jointed. He kicked his arms and legs out at right angles. Alka-Seltzer foam dripped from his mouth.

Hubert fans yelled for help. Seizure Sid did his shtick. A fat babe jammed a frozen Mars bar over his tongue. Some chumps yelled, "Get a doctor!" and "Man down!" The crowd dispersed. Hubert fumed and tried to express compassion. The fat cat futzed with the platform mike. Reverb went *screeeee.*

Crutch signaled three groups in mid-crowd. Three fistfights broke out. The crowd *re*-dispersed. Two skinny nuns bopped the fighters with their PEACE NOW! signs.

Hubert stamped his feet. The cops flailed on liquid wax. Their fat jig-gled. They looked like honky pigs in nigger hate cartoons. Hubert did that V-for-victory thing.

Froggy signaled a blonde in go-go boots and tight jeans. Crutch handed her a Nixon sign and boosted her up onstage. Froggy waved to three groups of men. They started whistling and chanting, "Take it off!"

Hubert stood there. The fat cat dry-popped Digitalis. Some fresh cops charged the fistfighters. The peacenik nuns got trampled. Cops charged the platform. Liquid wax sent them sprawling. The blonde waved her Nixon sign. The crowd went nuts. "TAKE IT OFF!" went epidemic. The blonde pulled off her shirt and bra and did the Swim, the Fish and the Mashed Potato topless. Crutch kicked on a hi-fi gizmo under the stage. Dig it: Archie Bell and the Drells with "The Tighten Up."

A fuckload of cops charged the platform. Mesplede walked away. Crutch grabbed the discarded bra and sprinted.

Back to L.A.

Crutch killed time at the airport. The Frogman split to Miami on an ear-lier flight. The boarding gate featured a phone bank. Crutch called Clyde Duber Associates collect.

The secretary put Buzz on. Buzz said, "We got a lead."

"What are you—"

"That picture you drew. I got a make. PSA Airways, the fourth place I hit. The personnel director said, 'Bingo, that's Janet Joyce Sherbourne, and she was one all-time no-goodnik.' "

Crutch got out his notepad. "Slow, now. Tell me the story."

"It's some story, and it hooks in to the Dominican Republic. Remem-ber? Gretchen Farr got those answering-service calls from the Dominican consulate."

Buzz knew *that* part. Buzz knew shit per Gretchen as Celia or Celia's Dominican—

"Hey, are you there?"

"I'm here. Come on, tell—"

"Okay, the Sherbourne cooze was a bilingual stewardess. She worked the L.A. to Santo Domingo run exclusively, right up until that fucked-up lit-tle war in '65, when LBJ sent the marines in. Okay, so there's a layover in Mexico City, and the Sherbourne cooze gets caught with a gun and a half-dozen fake passports. Okay, she fucking wiggles out of custody, and nobody knows *how,* and *then* she vanishes off the face of the earth. *Now,* here's the good part, the part that is just so fucking perfectly Gretchie. It turns out that the cooze's job application was a complete fake, her fucking address was some kind of Commie safe house, and her personnel file got snatched from the PSA office."

Crutch let the phone drop. Buzz talked to dead air. Things went haywire. He saw Joan kiss Gretchen/Celia in slow motion.

The downtown library was near his file pad. The books were too big to steal. The Dominican Republic: maps, pix, history.

Memo: the D.R. was close to Cuba. Memo: the mob grooved the D.R. as a would-be gambling site.

Crutch lugged books over to a table. Dozing winos competed for space. He scoped out the map pages. He grokked the layout. The island of Hispaniola. The D.R. and Haiti on one slab of land. The Caribbean Sea, close to Cuba and Puerto Rico. Close to Jamaica and the Turks and Caicos Islands. *The Dominican connection: all over his fucking case.*

The D.R. bordered Haiti eastbound. The Massacre River formed the dividing line. Inlets dotted the coasts of both countries. All the city names were spooky spic and frog.

Crutch skimmed summary chapters. The race shit hit him quick. The Dominicans were light-skinned beaners. They grooved on their Spanish roots. Dark-skinned Dominicans were déclassé. It was like the U.S.: *white is all right!*

Rafael Trujillo had long political legs. He ruled from '30 to '61. He quashed dissent. He oppressed Haitians and slaughtered the fuckers en masse. He was pro-U.S. and anti-Red. He fucked lots of women and tortured and suppressed his political rivals. A Commie group called the 6/14 Movement tried to oust his ass in '59. Their "revolution" went *pfft.* Trujillo went schizo and veered out of line. He was sacking the country too overtly. JFK and the CIA thought he might go Red. The CIA whacked him in '61. The Frogman allegedly assisted. A less garish despot named Juan Bosch took over. "Free elections" and all the standard spic-reform bullshit. It looked like Bosch was veering Red. LBJ sent some marines in and nipped that shit in the bud. The current despot was a pint-size punk named Joaquín Balaguer. The D.R. was nothing but coups, revolts, plots, intrigue, slaughter.

Crutch hit a section on Haiti. *Woooo!—baaad nigger juju!* French-speaking spooks. Dictator "Papa Doc" Duvalier—Godzilla to Trujillo's Rodan. More oppression, coups, revolts, plots, intrigue, slaughter. Voodoo—oh, yeah!

Voodoo rites, voodoo rituals, voodoo curses, voodoo priests. Mind-blowing voodoo liquor and voodoo herbs. American spooks *ate* fried chicken. Haitian spooks fucked chickens and drank their hot blood.

Woooooo!

Crutch flipped pages. This voodoo shit was a gas. He hit a photo section. Spooks were capering and bopping around in chicken-feather hats. *Woooo, then there's this—*

This photo. This light-skinned Negro guy. This weird tattoo on his right arm.

Geometric patterns. Crosshatched. Like the tattoo on the dead woman in Horror House—

40

(Las Vegas, 9/26/68)

The Boys sported golf shorts with high black socks. They wore their cleated golf shoes indoors.

Carlos set the trend. It was *his* mock-Roman suite. He paced and punctured the carpets. Sam G. had dull cleats. He did minor damage. Santo T. had sharp cleats. His spikes raped the rugs.

Wayne stood by a covered easel. The Boys sat with 10:00 a.m. Kahlúas. Carlos twirled a five-iron. Wayne caught the Wayne Senior subtext.

Sam said, "We've got a 10:40 tee time."

Santo said, "Carlos, put the club down. Do not drag Wayne through memory lane in a way that might tend to torment him."

Carlos said, "I have no such intention. I'm just loosening up my fibular bones."

Sam said, "Have two more drinks. You'll leave your swing on the driving range and a grand a hole in my pocket."

Santo said, "Chop, chop, Wayne. You've got this tendency to perch, like there's a dark cloud over your head at all times."

Sam said, "There is. As much as I admire his rough edges, Wayne is a shit magnet."

Carlos twirled his club. "Go, Wayne. We came to listen."

Wayne cleared his throat. "The fall is going our way. Nixon's ahead in the polls, our dirty-tricks squad is doing good work, Mr. Hughes is pleased with his hotel purchases and is waiting for Mr. Nixon's Justice Department to loosen up a few anti-trust statutes, so that he can buy some more. Jean-Philippe Mesplede is ready to start scouting casino sites, so we're on-go there."

Sam said, "My friend Celia keeps lobbying for the D.R. She's relentless on the topic."

Carlos said, "Sam's relentless on the topic of that island-bred snatch."

Santo said, "Sam's relentlessly pussy-whipped. It's a disease of the weak mind and spirit."

Sam grabbed his crotch. "I got your disease hanging ten inches."

Wayne undraped the easel. The graph was cross-columned. It listed buyout businesses linked to profit projections.

"Three supermarket chains, all in the Midwest, all owned by the in-laws of made men and Teamster stewards. We purchase at five cents on the dollar and sell the land to mall developers. I think we'll realize fifteen million in profit."

Sam clapped. Santo clapped. Carlos twirled his golf club.

Wayne said, "The Peoples' Bank of South Los Angeles. They're way in arrears, but I think we should let them continue to operate, while we take a greatly enhanced profit percentage. One, it's a money-laundering front. Two, they can launder *our* money. Three, Lionel Thornton, the president, is mobbed up all over the map, and I think we can control him. Four, it's close to the hub for the Hughes flights to our casino sites, so we can fly cash straight in, unimpeded."

Carlos said, "I like it."

Santo said, "I like it, but I don't like the jungle-bunny aspect."

Sam said, "I like it, with a proviso. We keep Wayne off the premises, so he don't shoot all the customers."

Wayne flushed. Santo and Sam laughed. Carlos twirled his golf club.

Wayne tapped the easel. "Two more South L.A. businesses, with on-site illegal gambling that we can take *at least* 50% of, while resuming ownership of both enterprises. The first one is a nightclub named Sultan Sam's Sandbox. The second is a lesbian bar named Rae's Rugburn Room."

Sam yukked. Santo yukked with "nigger something" mixed in. Carlos poked him with the golf club. Santo shut up.

Wayne picked up a pointer and tapped the column lines. A toga fool brought in three fresh Kahlúas. The Boys imbibed. Carlos poked the toga fool with the golf club. The toga fool vamoosed.

The booze smell made Wayne queasy. Sweat pooled on his shirt.

"Black Cat Cab. South L.A., as well. Tiger Kab served us handsomely in Miami and Vegas, and Pete B. sold the Vegas end to Milt Chargin last summer. We'll use it for cash flow, cook the books and launder low-end skim through it. I think I can talk Milt into coming to L.A. to run the place. Beyond that, I've got a friend on the Feds who's running a Cointelpro in the area, and we'll have Milt log tips and feed them to him, which will keep Mr. Hoover on our side."

Sam said, "I know your friend."

Santo shuddered. "Dwight 'the Enforcer' Holly."

Carlos sipped Kahlúa. "A man with coon-hunter credentials of his own."

Sam said, "Yeah, which is not to say that he's in Wayne's league."

Santo sipped Kahlúa. "*Nobody's* in Wayne's league."

Carlos said, "Dwight's a white man."

Sam sipped Kahlúa. "So's Milt Chargin, for a fucking Jew."

Carlos sipped Kahlúa. "Milt's an amateur comedian. He'll be hobknobbing with the shines and having a high old time."

Sam said, "Milt told me a good one. 'What do you call a naked nigger sitting alone in a tree?' "

Santo sipped Kahlúa. "So tell us the punch line, dickhead."

Sam said, "The branch manager."

Santo howled.

Carlos twirled his golf club. "What's the matter, Wayne? You're not laughing."

Morty Sidwell had an office at 2nd and Fremont. He did bail bonds, divorce, missing persons. LVPD considered him kosher.

Wayne drove over. He was tracking Reginald Hazzard part-time now. A cop pal ran a fifty-state dead-body check. It hit negative. Ditto for arrest reports. Ditto for male Negro John Does, late '63.

Reginald was bookish. Mary Beth told him that. Wayne combed the checkout files of all the Vegas libraries. *Bam*—the kid checked out twenty-nine books in fall '63.

Advanced-chemistry texts. Books on left-wing political theory. Odd books on Haitian voodoo herbs.

Sidwell's office was above a topless joint. Wayne parked out back and took the exterior stairs. The club noise was brutal. Amplifier hum shook the walls. Bass thumps pulsed the floorboards.

Morty was sprawled on the couch. The office was hot. Morty wore a washcloth on his forehead. He saw Wayne and went *oy vey.* The walls featured Morty-and-friends art. There's Morty with Dino, Morty with Lawrence Welk, Morty with the late JFK.

Wayne straddled a chair. Reverb wobbled the slats. It was a social-protest song with a sexy dance beat.

Morty adjusted his washcloth. "Earplugs don't help, so I tried acoustical baffling. The owner and I settled on a compromise. Once a week, he sends one of the girls up. I get a sponge bath and a header. It's beneficial to my overall health."

Wayne said, "My name is—"

"I know who you are. Your daddy hired me to run a *schvartze* bongo player out of town in '58. He was a one-hit wonder. 'Bongo in the Congo' and no more. He was *shtupping* your stepmom, Janice, at the Golden Gorge Motel."

Wayne laughed. Morty said, "Condolences, though. I know they both passed away last summer."

Wayne shut his eyes and popped two aspirin. The chair slats rattled. The floorboards jumped.

Morty said, "Normally, I'd say 'How's tricks,' but with you I know they're always tricky. This tempts me to say, 'What do you want?' "

Wayne opened his eyes. "Reginald Hazzard. It was almost five years ago. The kid disappeared, the parents hired you to find him."

Morty yawned. "Yeah, I remember. Nice colored folks. Cedric and Mary Beth. Cedric got offed by a *shvoogie* hump named Pappy Dawkins. It's a real load of joy you're bringing me, I got to say."

"What happened with the investigation?"

"It went nowhere and my clients ran out of money. I ran some DB checks and told them that, to the best of my knowledge, the kid was still alive. That's it, over and out."

Tick, tick, tick—his old cop shit detector.

Wayne said, "There's more."

Morty said, "Nix."

"There's more, you know there's more, I know it, I'm not leaving until you tell me."

Morty pulled the washcloth over his eyes and held up three fingers. Wayne dropped three C-notes on his chest. The amplifier hum accelerated. The JFK picture shook.

Morty said, "The Hazzard kid hitchhiked out of Vegas. I'm talking like Christmas '63 or into the new year. He gets popped for vag at some little pissant shitkicker town on the California border, and don't ask me the name, because there's a zillion little bumfuck towns like that and I really can't remember. Sooo, Reggie's got a gun on him. Sooo, the cops book him for vag and a gun charge and beat the piss out of him. Soooo, this white woman shows up and bails him out, and Reggie and the white woman abscond, never to be seen again. It was a cash bail and a fake ID, and the case went cold and Cedric and Mary Beth ran out of coin. I told Cedric this, but he said, 'Don't you tell Mary Beth, 'cause all of this would just kill her.' "

Wayne said, "More details." Morty held up two fingers. Wayne dropped two yards on his chest.

Morty chewed a hangnail. "Soooo, it's a fucked-up little redneck PD.

They don't keep records. The cops come and go and run wetback fruit-picking crews on the side. They live to drink home brew and beat up bean-ers and coloreds, and whatever paperwork they had got lost, misplaced or stolen. Those cops comprised a grim experience for me, and that's all the news that's fit to print."

Wayne stood up. "Did you get a description of the white woman?"

"That I can give you. She was supposedly pale and in her late thirties, she wore glasses, had long dark hair with gray streaks, and a cop said something about a bad scar on one of her arms."

41

(Los Angeles, 10/1/68)

Minstrel Show.

Marsh Bowen worked. He *owned* Vince & Paul's. The white cops' bar done got BAAAAAAAAD BROTHERED.

Marsh was seven nights in. He spawned racial *tsuris* with soulful aplomb. The white cops knew *he* was a cop. That got him in. That did not excuse his black-power stud behavior.

Marsh with the muscle-man tank top. Marsh with the modest Afro. Marsh all over the white chicks—but no hard moves yet.

Dwight watched.

It was his seventh night. He perched near the bar and played tourist from Des Moines. No cops recognized him. Who's that big goofball? He sure likes this place. He wears sandals and high-water pants.

Hate was building. Dwight tracked it. *Who dat bell-bottomed Mandingo?* Scotty Bennett showed up every night. Scotty boozed, Scotty eyeballed Marsh, Scotty acted covetous and puerile. Scotty radar-tracked Marsh and his barmaid girlfriend every spare moment.

Dwight picked at a cheese puff. Marsh chatted up two cop-groupie stews. He shagged hors d'oeuvres off their plates and sipped their drinks uninvited. The girls *looooved* it.

Dwight watched. The Marsh Bowen gestalt intensified. Marsh was a preener and a player. Marsh might be duplicitous. Marsh should be pre-emptively spot-tailed. Tail-job prospect: that half-smart Crutchfield kid.

Dwight yawned. His stomach growled back. Food fucked with his mental momentum. Niggertown was seething. Jack Leahy fed him gossip. All this militant shit gored the LAPD's gonads. Off-duty cops were indulging klantics. Station-house tune-ups. Panthers waylaid and shit-kicked. Trumped-up dope busts, trumped-up drunk rousts, trumped-up warrant checks and—

A woman walked into the bar. Dwight saw gray streaks and glasses and clenched up. It kept happening. Wisps, blips—and it's never *Her*.

Marsh walked toward Scotty's girlfriend. He touched his chin—*the signal/it's now*. Scotty was eye-locked: back and forth, his babe/the buck slave.

Dwight got up and stood closer. Marsh swooped on the girlfriend. There, he's nuzzling her neck. There, he's licking her ear. There, he's tugging her earring with his too-bright teeth.

Scotty ran up behind him and grabbed his hair. Scotty kidney-punched him, two-handed. Marsh doubled over and spun around with an arm bar raised. He caught Scotty moving in. The jolt knocked him into the bar. Scotty grabbed his neck and sucked air in. He kicked out. He missed Marsh. He flailed at the bar top and grabbed a steak knife. Marsh stepped directly in front of him. Marsh smashed his nose with one flat palm and sent blood pluming. Dwight heard bones break. Scotty dropped the knife, wiped his eyes and came at Marsh biting. A dozen white cops got to him first.

DOCUMENT INSERT: 10/16/68. Extract from the journal of Marshall E. Bowen.

Los Angeles,
October 16, 1968

I've tasted Scotty Bennett's blood now. It was a much-belated revenge for the whipping Scotty put on me in April of 1966, a year before I joined the LAPD. I provoked that beating by passing several ink-stained bills from the robbery, and I provoked this beating of Scotty and my subsequent beating by his LAPD comrades under the flag of Special Agent Dwight C. Holly. On both occasions I assumed the dual roles of victim and provocateur. Two events, with two and a half years between them. The defining event of the robbery-murders, now four years and eight months in the past. Two confrontations fueled by one motive: I want to solve the robbery-murder case anonymously and keep the remaining cache of money and emeralds for myself.

I have never told a soul about my intention and have deliberately delayed the commitment of writing a journal. I was awaiting the fortuitous moment where my quest might appear truly feasible. That moment is now. I could have described my immersions in left-wing organizations for Clyde Duber, where I learned the acting skills, dissembling skills and poise that brought me to this point, but I'm pleased that I did not indulge that level of self-congratulation. I've always enjoyed being an underestimated black man, and now I'm a locally famous and somewhat over-praised and over-scrutinized black man. This is the adventure that I want to describe and dissect as I live it; this current confluence of events is surely the one story I have to tell.

I was severely beaten by somewhere between twelve and sixteen of my brother LAPD officers and spent four days at Central Receiving Hospital. My broken nose, facial lacerations and asymmetrically bent ears have enhanced my rather bland good looks and have added to my incipient black-militant cachet. I have Mr. Holly to thank for that. Mr. Holly sensed my gameness and willingness to play, and I will reward him with hard work and a very commanding performance as I pursue my own goals within the context of this operation.

The local newspapers, radio and television picked up the story of the horrible fracas between a black and a white policeman at a "convivial watering hole frequented by LAPD personnel." Mr. Holly served as the unseen publicity director for this event. The LAPD launched an internal investigation, and—of course—all the eyewitnesses lied, stating that I sexually accosted the barmaid and attacked Sergeant Robert S. Bennett proactively. Scotty got a broken nose and one week's "compassionate leave"; I was bound over for an interdepartmental trial board—i.e., a kangaroo court. Mr. Holly hired me a jabbery and flamboyant black lawyer reminiscent of Algonquin J. Calhoun of *Amos 'n Andy* fame. The lawyer spouted more racially charged malapropisms than the worst mail-order black preacher ever to bang a pulpit for power and profit. I was hosannaed as the "Black Jesus"; Scotty Bennett was excoriated as the "White Judas Iscariot." I was, of course, summarily fired from the Los Angeles Police Department. Mr. Holly later told me that the lawyer was a defrocked minister with a sinecure as a public defender in Visalia County. Gorgeous black-and-white collusion: white judges and prosecutors hire this man to assure the convictions of black clients they need to get off the streets.

I then became an oracle of racial bias, memorizing the blindingly articulate scripts that Mr. Holly wrote for me, withering critiques of institutional racism and the authoritarian mind-set—full of indignation, social rigor and righteous fury, all penned by a white lawyer cop with roots in the Ku Klux Klan. Mr. Holly read me through the scripts, well in advance of my speaking them. I was astonished and almost swoony. Mr. Holly is a big, handsome man and a powerful public speaker. I got the uncanny feeling that he actually believed the words he wrote as he was speaking them.

Mr. Holly is a very difficult man to decipher. He understands racial bias and says "jungle bunny" routinely.

I was invited to a fund-raising party for Senator Hubert H. Humphrey at a big home in Beverly Hills. Mr. Holly told me to go, so I did. I was quite the center of attention, until some movie stars arrived and eclipsed me. Natalie Wood made a fuss over my facial wounds and slipped me her phone number; Harry Belafonte shook my hand; numerous liberals boo-hooed the recent passing of Senator Kennedy and Dr. King. People looked to me for expressions of political outrage. I had none to give them, because I now require Mr. Holly's script-writing services in order to sound properly enraged. I will soon be a wonderfully apostatized black-militant convert, because a Klansman's son will fuel my anger with his radical perceptions, leaving me to wonder at their origins and marvel at the man himself all over again.

Mr. Holly gave me $8,000 in cold FBI funds and told me to move farther south into the "Congo." I should start frequenting the "jig joints" where my "soul brothers" congregate, to see what kind of "shine action" I draw.

Mr. Holly calls me a "shit magnet," and I think he's rather suspicious of me. I'd like to indulge "the Bent" right now, but I can't. Mr. Holly might be having me spot-tailed. I have to keep my personal pleasures on hold until I feel more secure in my role.

I have an entirely new life now. My mother is dead; my father is elderly and living in Chicago. I have no real friends and my relationship with Mr. Holly is mutually usurious. I now have a dauntless and implacable enemy in Scotty Bennett. I'm sure that I know more about Scotty than Scotty knows about me. I have read the sanitized official reports on the eighteen armed robbers Scotty has killed in the line of duty. They were all black men. They were all summarily executed, per the unspoken LAPD mandate that armed robbers must die. The policeman in me condones this sanction; there is a large body of empirical data that states that most armed robbers take innocent lives and must be preemptively interdicted. It is the ghoulishly cherry-picked "male Negro" armed robbers that makes Scotty so unique. Other hard-charging Robbery cops have a middling "equal-opportunity" mélange of white and Mexican kills. Not our Scotty. Oh no.

Last August 5, two University Division officers shot it out with four Black Panthers. The officers survived, but the Panthers did not. Two days later, Chief Reddin sent Scotty down to the Panther headquarters with pizza, beer and a pound of confiscated marijuana. Scotty was, by all accounts, courtly. The Panthers welcomed him with apprehension and seemed befuddled by his gifts. Scotty advised them not to shoot at Los Angeles policemen again. Should they do so, reprisals would be instantaneous and brutal. For every L.A. cop shot at, wounded or killed, LAPD would kill six Black Panthers.

Scotty walked out then. He did not take questions or linger for a slice of pizza and an ice-cold brew.

My admiration and hatred of Scotty Bennett run roughly equal. He was there on February 24, 1964. He has no idea that I was there, too.

I was nineteen. I had graduated Dorsey High School two years earlier and was living with my parents at 84th and Budlong. The sky was the first thing I saw. There were weird prisms of color and a gas stench in the air. I stood on the roof of my house and saw streams of police cars approaching. The siren noise was near deafening. I saw a crashed-up armored car and a milk truck and dark shapes emitting fumes on the ground. I saw a very tall man in a tweed suit and bow tie drive up and survey the scene.

My father made me abandon my perch. Three dozen policemen roped off the street. Rumors soon flooded the neighborhood: the dead robbers were white; the dead robbers were black; the bodies were scorched past recognition and were racially unidentifiable. The absence of the robbers' vehicle meant that at least one man got away.

Two men got away. I know this as fact. Scotty Bennett may know it, as well. I cannot prove Scotty's knowledge. I simply sense it.

LAPD was out in brutal force. Scotty was running viciously indiscriminate roundups of local "suspects" at 77th Street Station. The local citizenry was outraged. *I* was outraged. I went roaming the alleyways behind my house, a kid looking for adventure, coveting my proximity to history. That is when I saw the second man.

He was hiding behind a row of trash cans. He was young, in his teens or early twenties, and he was black. His face was chemically scalded, but extra precautionary gauzing, a mouthpiece and a bulletproof vest had saved his life. I took the man to an elderly doctor neighbor; he was in shock and refused to discuss the robbery-killings at all. The doctor treated the man's burns, fed him morphine and let him rest. Scotty continued to steamroll his investigation. Detained and released "suspects" came home bruised and pissing blood. The doctor decided not to turn the wounded man over. He had saved the man's life and could not now condone physical abuse that might well result in his death.

The man left the doctor's house after two days of care and never divulged his identity. He left the doctor with $20,000 in ink-stained cash. The doctor deposited it in the Peoples' Bank of South Los Angeles and told the manager, Lionel Thornton, to leak it back to the community in charity donations, if it could be done safely, with no harm to the recipients. Thornton somehow found a way to partially obscure the ink markings; the bills surfaced sporadically in southside Los Angeles. Scotty Bennett tracked that money assiduously. He detained and leaned on the innocent people passing the bills in his unique and uniquely persistent manner. The case remained unsolved. The racial identity of the heist gang's leader and the other dead heist men has never been determined. Scotty had become obsessed with the case, and so had I.

The doctor died in '65. The ink-stained bills continued to circulate through southside L.A. I maneuvered my way into a menial job at the Peoples' Bank, learned nothing substantive and quit. Scotty Bennett fascinated me. I wanted to test my courage by going up against him and to see if he would reveal information within the brutal context of a back-room interrogation. I had pilfered a stack of ink-stained twenties from the bank and began passing them. Scotty found me, toot sweet.

The room was ten by ten feet and walled with soundproof baffling to keep screams at a dull roar. I protested my innocence. Scotty was genial when he wasn't beating me. He deployed a phone book and a rubber hose; he loosened my teeth and decimated my kidneys. I stoically asserted my innocence. Scotty revealed no inside knowledge of the case. I refused to scream. After two hours, I got my pro forma phone call. I called a friend; the friend called his friend Clyde Duber; Clyde made some calls of his own and got me out.

Clyde liked me. Clyde had his own fixation on "the Case." It's a hobby for him, no more. It's a consuming quest for Scotty and me.

I entered Clyde's kid-private-eye world and began infiltrating left-wing groups for his rich and richly paranoiac right-wing clients. I became a fine actor, prevaricator, dissembler, spy and snitch. I learned how to improvise, extrapolate and work off of Clyde's rough scripts. I have never had a role as demanding as the one Dwight Holly has prepared for me, and I have never had a scriptwriter as brilliant as Mr. Holly.

I joined the Los Angeles Police Department in 1967. Scotty tried to quash my appointment and failed. "The Case" remains unsolved. I remain determined. I'm convinced that the answer resides in southside L.A. I choose to believe a persistent ghetto legend: here and there, black folks in trouble receive a single, very valuable emerald anonymously in the mail.

I think Scotty knows more about the events of 2/24/64 than the rest of the LAPD combined. I think he wants the money and the lovely green stones for himself. I view OPERATION BAAAAAD BROTHER as nothing but a godsend, despite Mr. Hoover's draconian intent. I have the perfect southside cover now. People will tell a radically reconfigured black militant things that they would never tell a cop. I must be very bold and very cautious, and work my way around Mr. Holly with the utmost circumspection.

42

(Los Angeles, 10/18/68)

Spot tail:

Marsh Bowen's pad, 54th and Denker, lace-curtain Niggertown.

It was Night #6. Dwight Holly hired him, through Clyde Duber. Clyde was unsure of Big Dwight's motive. Maybe Bowen vibed comsymp or security risk.

Bowen's sled was out front. He drove a '62 Dodge. Candy-ass wheels. Bowen was a nosebleed. He went to doofus parties and played Zulu chief. Bowen fucked with Scotty Bennett and got sacked off LAPD. It got him clout with loser liberals and showbiz Jews.

Crutch yawned. He'd clocked in at midnight. It was 2:06 now. He tilted the car seat back and scoped his dashboard frieze. He got the idea from Scotty.

Scotty had his heist pix all taped up. Crutch rigged his own version. There's Joan, there's a groovy D.R. beach, there's voodoo-vile spooks in Haiti.

The Bowen job torqued him and distracted him. It diverted work on his case and his dirty-tricks gig with Mesplede. Bowen was half-ass tail-savvy. It was like he sensed a car frogging him.

Crutch played the radio low. The tunes vexed him. It was all peacenik pap and jungle jive. Brainstorm: rig Bowen's car with a voice box and night-light.

He got out his toolbox, squatted down and ran over. He took a corkscrew and popped a hole in the left taillight. He taped a 9-volt battery voice box under the right wheel well and flipped the dial to Frequency 3. He ran back to his car and got out the receiver. Click—there's Channel 3 and current ambient sounds.

Crutch re-settled and re-zoned his head. He shined his penlight on the Joan pix. He had the knack now. He knew how to make those gray streaks glow.

Bowen walked out and got in his car. Night owl—2:42 a.m.

He pulled out. Crutch long-distance frogged him. That taillight hole supplied range and direction.

They drove. Crutch hovered six car lengths back. Coontown hopped. Bowen slow-cruised all-night rib cribs and bars locking up. LAPD was out BIG. Sidewalk dice games vaporized as The Man passed. Bowen drove by two black-power storefronts—BTA and MMLF. *You be window-shoppin'? What be wrong wid you?*

Street noise bopped off Channel 3. The jungle be late-nite loud. Bowen U-turned and shagged ass westbound on Slauson and northbound on Crenshaw.

Now, it's more white. Now, it's more civilized. Channel 3 is amping down. He's heading west on Pico, north on Queen Anne Place, right by the park.

Bowen bumped the curb and took the center walkway. Fuck—no way to frog close.

Crutch doused his lights and perched at the east curbside. The park was all wet grass, shrubs and trees. He eyeball-tracked the taillight hole and saw Bowen slow-weaving.

The light went off. The car sounds died. Crickets chirped on Channel 3.

Silence. Bowen's car door opening and closing. It's dark. It's all audio now.

More silence. Then two male voices. Then zippers snag and belt buckles rattle and all these scary moans.

DOCUMENT INSERT: 10/19/68. Verbatim FBI telephone call tran-
script. Marked: "Recorded at the Director's Request"/"Classified
Confidential 1-A: Director's Eyes Only." Speaking: Director Hoover,
Special Agent Dwight C. Holly.

> JEH: Good morning, Dwight.
>
> DH: Good morning, Sir.
>
> JEH: Do you feel like some campaign chat? The swing states
> appear close, but our boy Dick seems to be surging.
>
> DH: I think he'll win, Sir.
>
> JEH: He applied to the Bureau in 1939. I saw his application
> photo and thought, That young lawyer did not shave closely this
> morning.
>
> DH: And you altered the course of American history in the
> process, Sir.
>
> JEH: I alter the course of American history every day,
> Dwight.
>
> DH: You certainly do, Sir.
>
> JEH: Update me on the shenanigans of our murderous French
> bonbon J. P. Mesplede and Clyde Duber's upstart charge Crutch-
> field.
>
> DH: They're effective in a gadfly way, Sir. They're due in
> Miami next, and I'm sure Mesplede will not be able to resist the
> lure of that pissant island 90 miles offshore.
>
> JEH: You consider the Cuban Cause to be entirely moribund
> and existentially futile, don't you, Dwight?
>
> DH: Yes, Sir. I do.
>
> JEH: I most assuredly do not. Castro has been in power since
> 1926, and he is a worse tyrant than his predecessors Chaing Kai-
> shek and Cardinal Mindszenty.
>
> DH: Uh, yes, Sir.
>
> JEH: You sound dubious, Dwight. You do not normally falter
> during our snappy repartee.
>
> DH: I'm fine, Sir.
>
> JEH: You subsist on coffee and cigarettes. They have dulled
> your memory for established historical facts.
>
> DH: Yes, Sir.
>
> JEH: Would another rest cure at Silver Hill suit you? You

might recall the first one. I pulled you off the Dillinger case in '34. You were drunk and killed those Negro tourists from Indiana.

DH: Uh, yes, Sir.

JEH: "Uh" twice in one conversation? I think you do require a rest cure of some sort.

DH: I'm fine, Sir.

JEH: Moving along, then. Please update me on the Dr. Fred Hiltz case.

DH: It's covered, Sir. Jack Leahy is overseeing the investigation for the Beverly Hills PD. There's no way the Bureau will be embarrassed.

JEH: I think the robber-killers are black militants on a rampage. They may well be consorts of a criminal cartel called Archie Bell and the Drells.

DH: I don't think so, Sir. Archie Bell and the Drells are a musical ensemble, and Jack Leahy thinks—

JEH: Jack Leahy is a duplicitous agent with a seditious sense of humor reminiscent of the late heroin addict/comedian, Lenny Bruce. I track cocktail-party chitchat, you know. When I went in for my gallbladder operation, Jack Leahy told a Chicago agent that I was having a hysterectomy. This was in 1908, and I remember it well.

DH: So do I, Sir.

JEH: I know you do. You were working the Cleveland Office, then.

DH: Yes, Sir.

JEH: And OPERATION BAAAAAD BROTHER? Unwittingly facilitated by the fearsome Sergeant Robert S. Bennett?

DH: My infiltrator and informant are both in place, Sir. I'm sure they'll be approached soon. I don't think my infiltrator is entirely trustworthy, so I've had Don Crutchfield spot-tailing him. Bowen's done nothing irregular, so I'm pulling the tail as of tonight.

JEH: Ah, young Crutchfield. Clyde Duber's most persistently voyeuristic foundling.

DH: He is that, Sir.

JEH: And Wayne Junior? Persistently homicidal and racially unlucky? How is he faring?

DH: I'm seeing him tomorrow, Sir. I would guess that he's grappled with this most recent mishap and has moved on.

JEH: We must all move on. Persistence and tenacity cure all one's ills in the end.

DH: Yes, Sir.

JEH: Good day, Dwight.

DH: Good day, Sir.

43

(Las Vegas, 10/20/68)

*S*he looked through you and saw you anyway. She made you look back.

He told her his Morty Sidwell story. He stressed the redneck jail, the bailout, the scarred woman. Reginald's gun charge. Reginald's books. Her son's troika: chemistry, left-wing texts, Haitian voodoo herbs.

They perched at the rest stop. They sat in Wayne's car for more legroom. Mary Beth brought sandwiches and coffee. It was pouring. The rain covered them—nobody shot them cheap looks.

Mary Beth said, "What will you do now?"

"Keep going. Build a file. Learn what I can about this secondary life your son had."

"You wanted to say 'secret life.' "

"Yes, I did."

"Because you've got one yourself?"

Wayne sipped coffee. The cup burned his hands. Mary Beth got it fires-of-hell hot.

"I was reading you the whole time. The entire story was news to you."

"We've never discussed your occupation. You talked to Howard Hughes and broke the color line, but I don't know what you do the rest of the time."

A gust hit them. The car swayed. Mary Beth grabbed the dashboard bar.

Wayne said, "I facilitate things for Mr. Hughes and some gentlemen with similar interests. I spend a fair amount of my time with police officers and political operatives."

Mary Beth sighed. " 'Secret life' is a euphemism. I'm seeing a secret world here."

"I can't tell you much more than that."

"You deal with people I'd disapprove of. Let's leave it there."

Wayne messed with the defroster. It was a jumpy-hands task. The car got too cold or too hot. Mary Beth hit the Off slide and held his hand there.

"Last summer?"

"Yes."

"Three of our loved ones died. The man who killed my husband was posthumously indicted for killing your father."

Wayne slid his hand back. Mary Beth pinned it there.

"We never discuss it. You always bring up Reginald. You haven't allowed me to mourn, and you haven't done much mourning yourself."

Wayne coughed. Mary Beth laced their fingers up. His legs fluttered.

"I don't want us to live with all these dead people. We've had too much of that. I'll be spending some time in southside L.A. soon, and I'll be putting out some feelers on your son. He's nineteen, he's armed, he gets popped at a town on the Nevada-California border. My instincts are telling me L.A."

Hailstones hit the car. Wayne jumped. Mary Beth said, "Why are you so afraid of me?"

Dwight said, "Hoover's slipping. The old girl is in precipitous fucking decline. He'll be shacking up with Liberace by this time next year."

Wayne smiled. "You could retire and go into corporate law."

Dwight smiled. "You could retire and teach basic chem at BYU."

The Dunes lounge was mock-soothing. The mock-oasis look cohered. Mock sand drifts, mock camels at a chlorinated spring.

Wayne said, "The Dr. Fred job. What's the status on that?"

Dwight tiki-torched a cigarette. "The same jigs robbed a house in Newport Beach. No fatalities, but the same glove prints and identical fibers at the scene. I think they saw Dr. Fred's anti-spook shit. Things just escalated from there."

Wayne sipped club soda. "I could use some help on the L.A. end of my business. The Peoples' Bank and Black Cat Cab have defaulted their Teamster loans, so we're taking them over. I think Black Cat would be a good informant hub for you. I was thinking you could get Mr. Hoover to frost potential trouble there."

Dwight stood up. He was losing weight. His belt gun drooped to one side.

Wayne said, "No racial slurs around me, Dwight. I'd very much appreciate it."

"Sure, kid. I'm not out to hurt you."

Home was the Stardust. He had his living suite/chem lab upstairs. He'd need to rig a missing person file space soon. He ate in the downstairs coffee shop most evenings. It brought back Janice and his night-watch cop days.

Wayne worked on a cheeseburger. The coffee shop was integrated now. He coerced Dracula into compliance. Drac was devolving à la Mr. Hoover. Call it dope and longtime lunacy accruing. Farlan Brown confirmed the prognosis. LBJ thwarted Drac's Vegas designs. Tricky Dick would comply. Farlan passed along gossip: the Count just suborned some key Humphrey aides. It covered him, poll-wise.

The burger was overcooked. The black folks two booths over got rude service.

Mesplede and Crutchfield were tricksterizing in Miami. Sam G.'s lawyers were buying out the defaulting market chain. He called the boss at Black Cat Cab this morning. A buyout chat was set for next week.

A black family walked in. Two white waitresses vanished. The hostess pretended they weren't there.

Wayne walked up to his suite. The door was ajar. He pulled his ankle piece and eased the door open.

The living room lights were on. Mary Beth was on the couch. She wore a lovely beige dress.

"Ghetto skills and union connections. I bribed a chambermaid."

Wayne reholstered. Mary Beth said, "Your laboratory smells more toxic than Reginald's ever did."

Wayne shut the door and pulled a chair up. Their knees were close. He slid the chair back. Mary Beth moved closer in.

"Why do you carry a gun?"

"I wish I didn't have to."

Mary Beth opened her purse. "I got something very strange in the mail today. It was sent anonymously. The oddest thing. It was wrapped in a newspaper clipping about my husband and Pappy Dawkins."

The names burned for a second. Wayne held on her eyes. Mary Beth pulled out a wad of newspaper and unwrapped it. A green stone was tucked in the middle. It looked like an emerald.

It sparkled and glittered. Wayne stared at it. He leaned in to look closer. Mary Beth put her face up to his.

"We can't hold hands outside or do public things. I don't want to know about the bad things you do."

They were close. He lost her eyes getting closer. She touched his lids and shut them for him. Their noses bumped as she brought him in for the kiss.

44

(Los Angeles, 10/22/68)

NEGROFICATION:

The sartorial arm of <u>OPER-ATION BAAAAD BROTHER</u>. Marsh Bowen needed fashion tips. His colors clashed. He looked like a sepia lollipop. Evil niggers dressed all *Black*. It covered them by nightfall and offset their bright teeth.

Dwight slipped Marsh three C-notes. "New threads. I want to see you with that Eldridge Cleaver look. You be steppin' out o shadows like fuckin' Dracula to announce yo wicked intent."

Marsh palmed the money. They idled outside the observatory. A telescope bank looked south. L.A. was smoggy and harshly lit. Griffith Park broiled.

"You're a fine mimic, Mr. Holly."

"Your people make it easy."

"I'll take that as a personal complim—"

"Here's the compliment you've been so persistently anxious to receive. You have acquitted yourself brilliantly to this point, chiefly because your altercation with Scotty Bennett had mo muthafuckin' soul than I ever could have hoped for, and as such you are the heroic black man of the L.A. ghetto moment, which allots us a very short interval for you to be recruited by the BTA and/or the MMLF. You cannot join up, Officer. Your actions must draw them to you or you will arouse an undue level of suspicion. *You're an actor,* Officer. You have the actor's instinctive need to ingratiate, so you require stern direction to shape your performance. I doubt that you possess a moral core, so let me bypass the idea of that sort of compass to guide you. You must appear bold and exercise great caution. You must judiciously rat out your new friends and benefactors and make sure that there are other snitch suspects for the information you have proffered. Use your discretion pertaining to any lowdown you might have on major crime pending. No homicide, no armed robbery, no sex shit on women or children. And do not give your former brethren in the LAPD a context in which to kick yo black ass, because they most assuredly will."

Marsh swiveled a telescope and looked southbound. He always made his face blank and rode out confrontations. He always did offhand shit to hide his fear.

Dwight jerked the telescope. The eyepiece banged Marsh. He regrouped and went instant blank-faced.

"Here's your target list. Get next to Ezzard Donnell Jones, Benny Boles, Leander Jackson, J. T. McCarver, Jomo Kenyatta Clarkson and Claude Torrance. Call me every fourth day at the phone drop until I find you a cutout. Start hanging out at Black Cat Cab and Sultan Sam's Sandbox, start attending the Friday night crap game at the barbershop on 58th and Florence."

Marsh smiled. It verged on a simper. I'm above all this.

"Is there anything else?"

"Yes, there is."

"And that is?"

"It's this. You're undoubtedly the luckiest nigger on God's green earth."

"Because you're my director?"

"Because you're too publicly notable for Scotty Bennett to kill."

Joan handed him the shells. Six spents with baffling treads attached. She drove a '61 Karmann Ghia. The plates looked counterfeit. The headliner was trashed from poor upkeep or backseat fucking.

The Elysian Park cutoff. Near the LAPD Academy. A sweet view and an implied threat.

Dwight said, "How do I know they're the right shells?"

"Because you trust me?"

It was chilly now. Joan wore long sleeves. Her knife scar was covered. Dwight missed the stimuli.

"You were on it faster than I thought you'd be."

Joan lit a cigarette. "I thought you'd appreciate that."

"I do."

"I'm sleeping with Ezzard Jones' girlfriend. She's skeptical of the BTA. You'll hear all about it."

A spring-loaded sap was jammed between the front seats. The backseat was packed with leftist screeds. He smelled Joan's shampoo and stale marijuana.

Joan said, "I consigned the cocaine to Leander Jackson. He's a lovely Haitian man with an unseemly fixation on voodoo. He sold a few grams already. I gave my share to the MMLF's breakfast program. Claude Torrance was grateful. He's invited me to a series of fund-raising parties."

Dwight smiled. "There'll be brawls."

"I know."

"You'll be groped, in a demeaning fashion."

"I count on it."

"Why?"

"I'll stab the man who gropes me, with female witnesses present. They'll groove on me and tell me stories about the men. It's an MMLF party. Leander's beholden to me now. He'll be pissed when he hears I've been associating with the MMLF, but he won't cut me loose, because he'll dig the stabbing story and I'll be the only female hanger-on who can score dope."

Dwight grabbed his cigarettes. The pack was empty. Joan lit one of hers and passed it to him. Dwight smelled her hand cream.

She wore black boots. Her dress buttoned down to the hemline. The car was hot. Sweat pooled at the neckline.

Dwight said, "Who else have you informed for?"

Joan said, "I'm not telling you."

"Why is your file so heavily redacted?"

"I'm not telling you."

"Were those simply pro forma roundups, or were you at one time an armed-robbery suspect?"

"I'm not telling you."

"Give me the names of some known associates. I won't move on them. I'm just trying to get a handle on your history."

"Under no circumstances."

Dwight popped two aspirin. Joan pushed her seat back and rested her legs on the window ledge. An ankle bracelet rode up her calf, over the boot top. A little red flag on a gold chain.

Dwight smiled. Joan smiled. They blew lousy smoke rings and fumed up the car. Two LAPD sleds zoomed by. Black dudes were cuffed in the backseats.

Joan said, "There's a gym teacher at Manual Arts High School. His name is Berkowitz. He's a pedophile. I think you should reprimand him."

"Is this related to our operation?"

"Yes."

"I'd like more of an explanation."

"People tell me things that require me to respond. In part, that's why I'm working for you. I'm hoping you'll be amenable."

Dwight said, "I'll take care of it."

Joan said, "I'd like to see proof."

Dwight nodded. Joan drew her legs up and banged the horn by mistake. The noise was startling. They both laughed.

They met at a coffee cave on Hillhurst. It was near Karen's pad and the drop-front. It featured a kid's play alcove. Dwight dug it. It made him feel quasi-married.

Dina lounged in the alcove. Kids brought their stuffed animals. Karen kvetched her fate as the world's oldest mother. Dwight chewed gum. He quit smoking around Karen. It tempted her. He didn't want to mess up Eleanora.

Karen held her belly. She looked incongruous—this lean woman with this big bulge.

Dwight crumbled two aspirin and dropped them in his coffee. A new approach to stress headaches. Jack Leahy explained it. Vascular constriction, blah blah.

Karen said, "Nixon's going to win. He won't institute instant repression or do much of anything, which will infuriate my comrades fucking up the Humphrey campaign."

"It's all a little too convoluted for me."

Karen nibbled a sweet roll. "It's entirely understandable to you, which means that something's on your mind, or you wouldn't be making such blandly disingenuous comments."

Dwight laughed. "My infiltrator is running cocky. I'm going to have to knock him down a notch or two."

Karen crossed herself. Hybrid faith. The Greek Orthodox girl gone Quaker. A waiter brought fresh coffee. Dwight crumbled fresh aspirin.

"Why's Joan's file so heavily redacted?"

"I don't know. Have you asked her?"

"She won't tell me."

"Then let it go."

"Her entire KA section has been blacked out."

"Then some handler in her past did her a favor."

"She said she'd never informed Federally before. There's things she won't tell me, something about—"

Karen knocked over his coffee cup. His hands got doused. His aspirin tin went flying.

"You're tweaked on that woman. I know you. I've been reading you for months. Every instinct I have tells me that you've done some very bad shit lately, even by your fucked-up fascist stand—"

Dwight heard Dina crying. She'd heard Karen yell. Dina kicked at a mound of toys and ran from the other children. Karen chased after her.

45

(Miami, 10/23/68)

Hubert Humphrey deployed pidgin Spanish. Bilingual pols urged him on. The crowd was half white, half spic and all nonplussed. They were heat-wilted. The parking lot was sun-smacked and Hubert was a noon snooze. They craved cold beer and some yuks.

Mesplede stood mid-crowd. Crutch stood at the rear. They waved to the driver of a tarp-covered truck.

The truck pulled up to the edge of the parking lot. Crutch cued the driver. Three, two, one—the invasion force rolls out.

Two dozen out-of-work actors. More Clyde Duber plants. "Guerrilla Troupe" hambones done up as Fidel.

The beard, the boots, the green fatigues, the fat cigars—

"Fidel loves Hubert! Fidel loves Hubert! Hubert loves Fidel!"

Hubert stood there with his thumb up his ass. Eight Nixon-shirt guys jumped out of the truck and dispensed free beers. The Fidels circulated and passed out free cigars. The crowd went nuts. Crutch and Mesplede howled.

CUBA, CUBA, CUBA—Froggy talked it trilingual and *très grande* non-stop. Crutch kept thinking *D.R.* They rent-a-carred through Little Havana. They shared a reefer. Froggy kept saying "Cessna" and "coast run." Crutch kept seeing that photo in the library book.

The voodoo guy. The tattoo. The pattern like the dead chick in Horror House.

Mesplede passed the reefer back. Crutch took a last hit and ate the roach. They hit Flagler Street. The exile storefronts flew Cuban flags. Straw Castros hung from lightposts. Kids ran up and stuck pocket-knives in.

Crutch kept it zipped. He'd been talking D.R. like Froggy talked Cuba. "Keep it zipped." Dwight Holly told him that. He obeyed, so far. Marsh Bowen was a fruit. He kept *that* zipped. He bombed by Miami-Dade PD last night. He did file checks on Gretchen/Celia and Joan Rosen Klein. Froggy asked him where he went. He kept it zipped.

He was learning. His killer pals would respect that.

They drove to a rinky-dink airfield outside Miami. The crew was all Cuban. They were all diced and sliced from sugarcane work. Mesplede signed some papers and rented a two-seater plane. They took off and torched a joint at three thousand–plus feet.

Crutch got scared. The altitude cross-wired his high to acid-trip dimensions. He kept seeing people who weren't there. His mom did the Twist with Dana Lund. Blow-job Bev Shoftel blew Sal Mineo.

They flew low over Little Havana. Mesplede hit a lever and cut five thousand Nixon signs loose. Kids plucked them out of the air and flipped the plane off. Misplede dipsy-doodled south. They flew over a string of bridgeways and keys. Mesplede served Dexedrine chased with hash-spiked schnapps. Dig those brown cubes floating in white liquid.

Crutch imbibed. The cocktail re-cohered him. They flew out over the Caribbean. They passed two refugee rafts and dumped Nixon signs on them. The cocktail kept Crutch un-airsick. Mesplede pointed behind the seats. Crutch saw a Tommy gun with a hundred-round drum. He popped a bullet out. The tip had been dumdum-gouged and stuffed with rat poison.

Crutch got flutters. The cocktail had him anesthetized short of real fear. This big brown shape loomed. Froggy grinned at him. Crutch blinked. Now the shape's a pancake-flat island.

Froggy pushed the stick and brought them in low. They skimmed waves and water-bumped their wheels. Crutch saw the beach and some brownshirt spics ringed by sandbags. The spics were hunched over a .50-caliber machine gun. The thing had a vented barrel, feeder belts and a 360 swivel.

Froggy diversion-dipped and dove straight at them. The spics fired over, under and wide. Froggy came in ultra-low. The spics swiveled, re-swiveled and sent off panic shots. The noise was like typewriter clack meets the A-bomb.

Crutch rested the Tommy gun on his window ledge. Froggy got see-their-eyes low. Crutch head-counted eight. They were ducking and trying to swivel their machine gun in tight.

Crutch fired. He saw two heads explode. He saw one guy's ribs blow out of his chest and blood-blast a sandbag. Froggy cut through some low trees. Fronds buffeted the airplane and blocked their frontal view. Crutch fired behind him. Stitch shots, very precise. He got four guys standing together. He saw a tall guy's glasses shatter as his head pitched off.

Froggy pulled the stick back. Crutch saw Cuba upside down and held in his cookies. They flew backward over the ocean. He saw his eight new kills and that guy's head rolling toward the surf line.

Hangover.

Blackout.

He didn't remember the flight back or the ride to the hotel. He woke up in his bed. Mesplede was still asleep. He walked down to the restaurant and sat outside. He ordered pancakes and a Bloody Mary and kept it all down. He re-wired his head and grooved the awe of it. He killed two Cuban Reds in Chicago. He'd just killed eight more. Two plus eight was ten. He was moving toward Scotty Bennett's toll.

A shade tree loomed over his table. Lovers had carved initials and honeymoon dates on it. Crutch got out his pocketknife and stabbed in "D.C." and "10."

He walked back upstairs. His bedroom door was open. Mesplede was sitting on the bed. His briefcase had been pried open. The summary report on his case was out in plain view. Mesplede was on page 43.

Froggy had his gun out. Crutch gulped and brain-stalled for some lies. Froggy said, "You've withheld information twice. Your fixation on the Dominican Republic was a non sequitur that aroused my suspicion, so now you must tell me everything."

So he did.

He started with the Dr. Fred/thieving girlfriend caper. He layered in Farlan Brown, Gretchen/Celia and Joan. Add Horror House. Add all his futile cop work. Add Celia's Dominican roots and Haiti. Add the dead woman's tattoo and the tattoo on the voodoo guy in the picture book.

Mesplede pulled out Crutch's pocket atlas. It was open to the Caribbean page. He said, "Our agendas merge." He drew a straight line between the D.R. and Cuba.

46

(Los Angeles, 10/25/68)

Black Cat Cab featured black velvet walls and a black-history tribute. The time line spanned the Black Jesus to the Black LBJ. The flocked-on icons were peeling. The air conditioning ran twenty-four hours and messed with the motif. The boss weighed 428 pounds. The hut was stalactite-cold, per his orders.

Cordell "Junior" Jefferson: entrepreneur, Teamster-loan defaulter.

Wayne said, "The Boys are calling in their paper, Mr. Jefferson. There's some good news within that context."

Jefferson squirmed in his chair. It was triple-wide. The room ran 50°. He was sweating.

"You're tellin' me I'm about two months behind, so I gots to take this?"

Wayne shivered. "You're three years behind, sir. Three years, but my news is not all bad."

Jefferson spooned ice cream from a half-gallon drum. Some Panther types walked through the hut and evil-eyed Wayne. A big white man followed them. He radiated *Cop*. He wore a gray suit and a plaid bow tie.

Jefferson waved his spoon. "What's all this motherfuckin' good news you talkin' about, while you tryin' to pull the motherfuckin' rug out from under me?"

Wayne opened his briefcase and tossed ten grand in Jefferson's lap. Jefferson fondled it, smelled it and rubbed his face on it.

He snapped the rubber band holding it. He squeezed it into the world's fattest flash roll.

Wayne said, "You hold the deed on the biz. We bring in a white guy named Milt Chargin to help you run things, you help some cop friends of mine out with information and dry-clean some cash, for which you get 7% of the action."

"Suppose I says no?"

"Sir, you're smarter than that."

Jefferson ate ice cream and ruffled the roll. Wayne checked out the wall icons. He recognized the Black FDR and nobody else. A man with a triple-wide Afro walked in. He sneered at Wayne and went to the switchboard. Wayne pulled out a snapshot of Reginald Hazzard and flashed it at Fats. Fats shook his head no.

The Afro man tossed Fats a fresh tub of ice cream. Fats said, "Big Boy Cab is crowding *my* business. If *my* business is *our* business, then I could use some of *your* help."

Wayne smiled.

Mary Beth was asleep. The covers were up over her back. One leg was exposed.

Wayne watched her. She always fell asleep before he did. She kissed him and burrowed off by herself and gave him something to see.

He pulled a chair up to the bed and touched her knee. He waited. He liked to see her turn her head on the pillow.

The lab phone rang. Wayne got up and ran for it. He grabbed the call two rings in.

"Yes?"

"It's Dwight, Wayne."

"Yes, and at midnight."

"I've got a chemistry question."

"All right."

"Can redacted file paper be stripped to expose the typed words underneath?"

Wayne leaned on a shelf. It was crammed with heroin components.

"Maybe. I'll try, if you get me some C-4 explosive."

47

(Los Angeles, 10/26/68)

Darktown—85th and Central. An Afro-pride strip. A night club, a hair salon, a mosque. Street loafers at 2:14 a.m.

Among them: Jomo Kenyatta Clarkson.

Male negro, age thirty-nine. MMLF stalwart. Black Cat Cab dispatcher. "Propaganda Minister." Hate-lit scribe. Suspected rapist/armed robber.

Jomo's jiving with three male Negroes. They're slurping peach liqueur and smoking Kool cigarettes. They just had their hair frizzed at Sister Simba's shop.

Dwight was three stories up and directly across Central. The building was empty. He climbed the fire stairs and crouched behind a signboard. He held binoculars and a Poloroid pic.

The photo was Joan's proof. He waylaid the pedophile gym teacher and did some sap work. Joan's revenge or Joan's deterrent. He didn't care—it was the Joan Zone. Stray women were starting to look Joan-like. She was always Joan. She was never Confidential Informant #1189.

Dwight looked southbound. There's Marsh Bowen on his mandated late-night stroll. Dwight looked northbound. There's unit 4-Adam-29, slow-cruising.

Two white cops. Scotty Bennett idolaters. A C-note apiece.

On cue:

The cops sniff the Afro-pride strip. Jomo and the Jivehounds hide their jug. The cops cruise on. The jug reappears. Jomo and the Jigmeisters re-jungle-ize.

The cops see the lone male Negro. Shit, it's Marsh Bowen. *That's a good roust.*

The cops U-turn and pull over. The Afro-pride strip perks up. Party! Party! Let's groove social outrage and hate up The Man!

Sister Simba's empties out. Likewise the Scorpio Lounge. Jomo and the Junkyardogs electrify. Their Brillo-pad hairdos sizzle.

The cops exit their car. Marsh walks on by. One cop whistles, one cop yells, "Get back here." The spectators start making pig sounds.

Dwight's view was good. His soundtrack was bad. It was pig-snorted past comprehension.

Marsh walked back. Dwight saw the cops spread-search him and frisk him. He thought he heard "nigger" and "Scotty Bennett sends regards." He heard overlapping oinks, snorts and bleats. The cops emptied out Marsh's pockets. The cops goofed on his Afro comb. The spectators started chanting "Go, brother!" One cop shoved Marsh and jabbed at his chest. One cop yelled in his ear. The spectators cranked up their pig act. The verbal cop sprayed spit and goosed the volume. Dwight heard "nigger," "traitor," "nigger motherfucker" and "faggot."

Marsh lost it. He headlocked the verbal cop and ran him into a streetlight. The spectators clapped and Go, brothered. The pig noise went hi-fi. The verbal cop spun Marsh around and flipped him up on the patrol car. The other cop pulled his baton and started banging his head and his kneecaps. Marsh took a *BAAAAAD BROTHER* beating. Jomo and the Junglejivers saw the whole thing.

48

(Los Angeles, 10/28/68)

Two dozen cabs. All bumper-locked, in rows. All with the Big Boy logo: a dinge in a fez like that dictator dude Sukarno.

The dispatch hut was off-site. The lot was half a city block. An all-night guard patrolled the premises. He always drank his dinner at Sultan Sam's Sandbox. Froggy slipped two yellowjackets into his last scotch. The guy was snoozing in a Dumpster behind Sultan Sam's now.

Wayne and Froggy called the shots. Crutch did the shitwork and took orders.

Wayne molded the C-4 and placed it in the wheel wells. Froggy set up the detonator. Crutch rigged the cords cab-to-cab.

The setup took hours. They worked from midnight to 4:00 a.m. Crutch got cramps from squatting down and duck-walking. They all sweated bad and carried towels to get some dryness. The C-4 looked like Play-Doh and smelled like burned oil. The cords abraded your hands.

All done—4:11 a.m.

They walked out to the street and toweled off. Wayne looked grim, per always. The Frogman was smiling. Crutch felt prom-date swoony.

Wayne pushed the plunger. The fucking cabs exploded and jumped off the ground. The noise was immense. A dozen shades of red and pink erupted. Glass blew across the sky.

DOCUMENT INSERT: 10/29/68. *Los Angeles Herald Express* head-line and subhead:

NIXON-HUMPHREY RACE TIGHT

Ex-Veep Holds Lead in Key States

DOCUMENT INSERT: 10/30/68. *San Francisco Chronicle* headline and subhead:

NIXON VS. HUMPHREY: POTENTIAL SQUEAKER?

Pranksters Disrupt Humphrey Rallies;

Aides Accuse Nixon Campaign

DOCUMENT INSERT: 11/1/68. *Los Angeles Times* article:

MURDER OF HATE MERCHANT STILL UNSOLVED

The victim himself called his palatial Beverly Hills home "the House That Hate Built," so it's no surprise to many that Dr. Fred T. Hiltz, 53, former dentist, former golf professional and alleged FBI informant, should come to a horrible end in that very place itself.

On September 14 of this year, Dr. Hiltz was shotgunned in his backyard bomb shelter, and the crime has remained unsolved. There are suspects: a robbery gang who held wealthy families hostage in Brentwood and Newport Beach. But some local journalists and many assassination buffs take issue with that. Dr. Hiltz was a well-known purveyor of viciously worded hate pamphlets that attacked Caucasians as well as racial minorities, was rumored to have a backyard hidey-hole stuffed with cash, had been married numerous times and allegedly indulged in scores of liaisons with provocative women. Beverly Hills Police Captain Mike Gustodas told reporters, "Dr. Hiltz had volatile relationships, was in a dirty business and cut our work out for us, that's for sure."

Yet, it's the Los Angeles FBI Office that's doing the bulk of the work on the Hiltz investigation, and that fact is what so intrigues certain journalists and conspiracy theorists. Captain Gustodas had no answer to address that issue; he simply stated that the FBI had usurped BHPD's case for "national security reasons."

John Leahy, Special-Agent-in-Charge of the FBI's Los Angeles Office, told reporters, "Yes, it's a politically sensitive case, and there is a national security aspect, albeit a minor one. I'm not at liberty to divulge the details just yet, but there will be a full recounting when and if this agency makes an arrest."

An especially persistent rumor is that Dr. Hiltz was murdered by members of a black-militant group, as a political statement. SAC Leahy had no time for that theory. "I think it's ridiculous," he said. "No black-militant groups have claimed credit, and I also think that the danger of black militancy has been grossly overreported by the press."

Meanwhile, the Hiltz investigation continues.

DOCUMENT INSERT: 11/2/68. *Dallas Morning News* headline:

NIXON-HUMPHREY RACE DOWN TO WIRE

DOCUMENT INSERT: 11/3/68. *Hartford Courant* headline:

NIXON, HUMPHREY IN LAST BARNSTORMING EFFORT

DOCUMENT INSERT: 11/4/68. Extract from the privately held journal of Karen Sifakis.

Los Angeles,
November 4, 1968

Nixon's going to win. Humphrey is saddled with the attenuated onslaught of LBJ's war and the American people want a credible dialogue on the end of the war suffused with reactionary pap that will make them feel good about leaving (and, in fact, losing) the war, and Nixon is telling them exactly what they want to hear. Chicago was a disaster, not because it secured Nixon's victory, but because it made the Left appear rancorous, petty, vicious, divisive and buffoonish. *The sin of self-indulgence.* I must take note of my self-indulgent tendencies, and I should begin by classifying them as misconduct and thus drawing a clear moral line to interdict their practice.

Dina has started asking me the inevitable bright-little-girl questions about Dwight and W.H.N. and my relationship to the two men. Of course, I cannot tell her that W.H.N. and I are politically compatible, but not comrades, and we have never had a fully passionate relationship, but are friends in certain shared ideals and the business of parenthood. W.H.N. knows about Dwight, but never mentions him; the prescient and too-worldly Dina never mentions Dwight to W.H.N. because she knows it would hurt him and because she understands that it might adversely affect my relationship with Dwight. Dina will become a compartmentalizer (as I am) and may/will inherit my penchant for dramatic and dubious men. Dina likes Dwight more than she likes her father, because he is fierce with the world, but very soft with her, because he carries a gun, because I am demonstrative with Dwight in a way that I am not with her father and it makes her feel properly loved as a child and thus feel safe. And—brilliant girl—she understands something that I just figured out: that Dwight and I truly are comrades.

It's our lovers' passion and the tender barter of our antithetical roles and ideals. It's that we both want something (beyond each other) very deep and pure, and that I have a language for it, while he does not.

I keep thinking of troikas. Dwight, my largely absent husband and I are one. And, I now form the spark point of Dwight and Joan Klein. I'm not jealous, but Dwight is powerfully compelled by her. I have been less than truthful about my relationship with Joan, because I did not know how much of Joan's various real and rumored histories I should reveal to a man who is, at day's end, a police officer and a right-wing thug. Dwight told me early on: informants and operators withhold information to ensure their own safety and the safety of those close to them. That idea guides me in my lies by omission. Joan *was* an FBI informant at one time, but I don't know her operator's name or if he redacted her file. I have known Joan deeply for many years. Politically, I do not trust her any more than I trust Dwight.

I'm somewhat worried about Dwight. He's losing weight, is sleeping ever-more poorly and mumbles in his sleep. I keep jokingly asking him if I can blow up Mount Rushmore and he keeps *half*-jokingly telling me, "Yes." He's giving me too much latitude. Is it out of guilt? I keep thinking there must be some immeasurably horrible deed weighing on him that I must never know about, lest it destroy my love for him or make me love him that much more. I wonder how old Dina (and Ella inside me) will be when they discover that truth of women and men.

Dwight and I have our barters. I wonder what form Dwight's barters will take with Joan. Our shared world is humanly unquantifiable and ideologically confused. Which one of them is capable of implementing the most recognizable harm or good?

DOCUMENT INSERT: 11/5/68. Extract from the journal of Marshall E. Bowen.

South L.A.,
November 5, 1968

It was my second beating at the hands of my former—and future, once this operation has concluded—LAPD brethren. I fared better at my first one, for Mr. Holly's script had prepared me. Mr. Holly failed to witness this second encounter, and my wounds will have healed by the next time we meet face-to-face. I may or may not tell him of the incident, critique my spontaneous performance and request that he not discipline the officers involved. I may or may not tell him that the incident resulted in my making some wonderful new friends.

My unlikely rescuer was Jomo Kenyatta Clarkson, Propaganda Minister for the preposterously named Mau-Mau Liberation Front, along with his friends Shondell and Bobby. Jomo is garrulous and recognizably psychopathic and continues to break the world's land speed record for use of the word "motherfucker" in a single sentence. His arms bear self-inflicted machete scars as a tribute to the real Jomo Kenyatta's slaughter of British settlers in Kenya, circa 1947. Jomo and friends took me to Morningside Hospital, where a friendly white doctor, who treated Jomo for his most recent gunshot wound, treated my wounds and injected me with Demerol. The injection dulled my pain, lifted my spirits and allowed me to stop replaying the words "Scotty Bennett sends regards" in a near-continuous loop. I wanted to go home and rest then. Jomo wouldn't hear of it. He decided we should go pub-crawling.

We visited a series of after-hours clubs. I met numerous black males in the all-black attire that Mr. Holly has urged me to purchase, found it fetching on them, but decided that it wasn't really my style. I witnessed a live lesbian sex show at Rae's Rugburn Room and was generally shown off by Jomo at Sultan Sam's Sandbox, Mr. Mitch's Another World and Nat's Nest. I geared up and performed; Mr. Holly would have been proud of me. I repeatedly described my beating by the "LAPD pigs" and never had to mention my ex-pig status, because I am a local celebrity and my former occupation subtextually pre-exists in the ghetto *spiritus mundi*. I kept saying ridiculous things like "Tell it like it is" and "Right on, brother" and never once burst out laughing. The rest of the night, following day and night are blurry. Jomo took me by his place of employment, the Black Cat Cab Company, where I watched the very fat owner eat an entire gallon of ice cream. I started to fall asleep at one point. Jomo force-fed me several spoonfuls of cocaine, which got me talking. It felt like an out-of-body experience spawned by alcohol, drugs, sustained shock and many weeks of barely controlled stress, excitement and wonderment, all filtered through what Mr. Holly has described as my "innate actor's instinct and flair." I critiqued the institutional racism of the LAPD specifically and white racist America in general and was conscious that I was shucking Jomo and his friends as I did it, as I concurrently believed it and did not believe it, as yet another part of me was off at another level of bifurcation, directing the performance and goofing on the whole thing. I can't recall exactly what I said, but I do know that I was speaking at the limits of my mental capacity and powers of articulation. In retrospect, it felt like demagoguery, social analysis and apostalic fervor all rolled into one. And the amazing thing to me—that Mr. Holly would not find amazing at all—is that I don't know whether or not I believe a word of it.

Black Cat Cab was followed by a visit to Jomo's "crib" on East 89th Street. Many people, all black, were there. I heard six dozen hate-the-fuckin'-LAPD-pigs stories, told that many myself, and met two men whose armed-robber brothers were shot and killed by "King Pig" Scotty Bennett. Jomo tried to pass a shapely toffee-colored girl with a tinted Afro off on me, but I excused myself with something about my "main bitch." Jomo ensconced me in a room festooned with revolutionary wall posters and filled with stacks of fatuous polemics, and I fell asleep for a very long time.

My dreams were my standard ones and easily explained, given my life's overweening fixation. There were the shapeless waves of green representing the emeralds and the odd spatial doublings and triplings of prone shapes, my persistently unconscious urge to discover what truly happed on 84th and Budlong that day. At one point, I thought I saw a white woman with dark, gray-streaked hair looking in on me, but she/it was just a wisp.

Two dozen people were sitting in Jomo's living room when I stumbled out however many hours later. They gave me a standing ovation. It was a superlative reward for my performance.

I've moved to a dingy crib on the Watts border.

I've started spending time at Black Cat Cab.

My MMLF and/or BTA recruitment is imminent, but I am not rushing into anything.

I want this performance to last. It's my circuit back to February 24, 1964. Every disenfranchised part of me knows this to be true.

49

(Las Vegas, 11/5/68)

Tricky Dick won. Close, but no squeaker. More than a rat's-cunt-hair win.

Carlos threw a bash. His mock-Roman suite, mobsters and Mormons, election returns on TV. Call girls told I-blew-JFK stories. Farlan Brown said Dick was no headman. He was more like an S&M slave. He'd get stinko and bomb some Third World shit-hole. He'd fry some little kids and get all misty then. He'd bring in a sick chick with a whip to retool him.

Sober guests waved little flags. Drunk guests wore elephant hats. The Hughes hotels shot off fireworks: Viva Nixon! in red, white and blue.

Wayne circulated. Farlan Brown showed him Dracula's thanks note. Drac praised Wayne's hard work and chemical assistance. He mentioned the Hughes charter flights to the foreign casino sites—let's get started soon.

More fireworks. The Landmark scrolled a neon Nixon face on their marquee. Farlan said, "The cocksucker still needs a shave."

Sam G. said, "The casino sites. We've got to send Mesplede down soon."

Santo T. said, "Nicaragua has this tendency to go Red."

Carlos said, "Dick will put a pro-U.S. puppet in place. He knows you need a strongman to put the quietus on the Reds."

Sam said, "The D.R.'s the ticket. They've had a stable government since the '65 war. The new *jefe* is a fag midget. All he wants is some U.S. gelt and a nice pair of elevator shoes."

Santo said, "Sam's got this Dominican girlfriend leading him around by the *schvantz*. She's got him thinking Dominicans are white."

Carlos said, "Celia's a coal burner. She crosses over into Haiti and gets that black stick."

Sam grabbed his crotch. "Italians are built bigger than the moolies."

Carlos said, "Where'd you get that?"

Santo laughed. "Pope John the XXIII told him. They were hanging out at a cathouse with some nigger nuns."

Carlos handed Wayne a doughnut box. "Thanks for everything, *paisan*. Hughes, Nixon, the whole deal."

The ride back took forever. The hotels went Nixon-nuts and put dumb signs up. Traffic jams resulted. Tricky Dick was Mormoned-up and mobbed-up. He was good for biz. The Boys bought themselves four fat years.

The Stardust was Nixon-numb. Legislators told I-know-Dick stories and puked into slot-machine cups. Wayne took the stairs up. He heard the phone ringing in the hallway. 3:00 a.m. calls—oh, shit.

He ran and grabbed it. He heard Mary Beth in the bedroom.

"Wayne Tedrow. Who's this?"

"Long-distance, sir. Will you hold for President-elect Nixon?"

Wayne gulped. The line clicked twice. Wayne heard background hubbub and the Man's voice.

"Thank you for all your hard work. Be assured of my cooperation."
Click. What? Was it real?

Wayne walked into the bedroom. Mary Beth was watching TV. The Man did V-for-victory. A shirt button popped.

She killed the sound. "Who called so late?"

"You wouldn't believe me."

She smiled and pointed to the doughnut box. Wayne dumped it on the bed. Fifty grand fell out. Mary Beth whooped and covered her mouth.

"That's my find-your-son fund."

That lovely emerald was there on her pillow. Mary Beth threw it in with the cash.

50

(Los Angeles, Las Vegas, Washington, D.C., 11/6/68–12/24/68)

Nerves, brain loops, sleep on and off. Memphis kaleidoscopes mixed in.

One drink and one pill ran on-and-off insufficient. The Lorraine Motel shape-shifted. Hate cartoons transmogrified. Black gargoyles wearing Klan hoods.

Karen was concerned. She saw him running raw and couldn't stop it. What's-His-Name kept passing through and blitzing their time. Her pregnancy was advancing, she had more doctors' visits, she took her family back east for Christmas. She was tweaked on his tweak on Joan Klein.

Wayne was working on Joan's file redactions. The kid was a genius—maybe *he* could burn through black ink. He showed Joan the snapshot of the kicked-to-shit pedophile. Joan quid-pro-quo'd him à la Karen Sifakis. She gave up a Cleveland mail-bomb gang, a multi-indictment chart topper. He said, "Thank you, Miss Klein." She said, "You're welcome, Mr. Holly."

The snitch-out thrilled Mr. Hoover for six seconds. His attention span had shrunk to comic-strip dimensions. His monomania had grown to Russian novel–size. He hated black militants like he hated Reds in 1919. He talked black-militant woe real and largely imagined. He sent himself into coughing fits and fey tizzies. Dr. King was laughing his saintly black ass off in heaven. The boss nigger got resurrected as all niggers real and imagined and the old girl was powerless.

But he was still dangerous. But he still had dirt files on the whole fucking world—Dwight "the Enforcer" Holly included.

Mr. Hoover was pleased with OPERATION BAAAAAD BROTHER. Dwight told him that Marsh Bowen was being courted by BTA and MMLF. He did not tell Mr. Hoover that he paid two cops to kick Bowen's black ass. Bowen did not tell *him* about the beating and avoided face-to-face meetings until his injuries had healed. *Vanity* was the key to Brother Marshall E. Bowen. *Contempt* defined Brother Bowen secondarily. He was the diva with the abject need for an audience and the commensurate disregard. He was a brilliant and brilliantly complex actor. He would seduce, betray and entrap with insolence and show-must-go-on savoir faire.

The beating seemed to fracture his ego and instill a greater circumspection. The beating brought Brother Bowen some soulful southside strut. Now needed: a cutout to work Brother Bowen on a daily basis. He pulled Don Crutchfield's spot tails—Brother Bowen was toeing the line. The current boding question: will Brother Bowen cross paths with Comrade Joan Klein?

He called her "Miss Klein." He thought of her as "Joan." She possessed an eponymous quality. The gaps in her file and her reluctance to discuss her past enhanced his curiosity. She had traveled extensively. She facilitated left-wing woo-woo worldwide. Organizer, facilitator, armed-robbery suspect. Pamphleteer, informant, renegade academic.

Tell me what I want to know.

I don't know why I need it.

He gave Joan a scrambler phone. It let her call him untraced. She called him most nights. They observed informant-operator protocol while discussing their personal lives. He did not describe the full extent of his relationship with Karen Sifakis. Joan did not mention Karen at all. They did not talk business. They saved those discussions for their phone-drop chats. Joan told him that she had some money for him. He said, "What money?" She told him that Leander Jackson made a profit on Agent Holly's cocaine. Comrade Klein felt that she should return her percentage. He told her to keep the money. She thanked him. It was all so fucking gorgeously decorous.

They sparred and talked politics. He paved roundabout queries on her past life and associations. Joan rebuffed them with occasional brusqueness and a harsh humor. The cop part of him was all over her. The rest of him was a faltering half step behind. Joan had run safe houses. They had to have been upscale and well camouflaged. She had avoided prison time. There should be more police paperwork on her. He scoured for paperwork on her left-wing ancestors and found none.

Karen shared her scant Joan knowledge with a distancing resentment. He was certain that Joan knew more about him than he knew about her. The disparity had him running breathless.

He was making coontown inroads. Wayne brought Milt Chargin in to help Fatso run Black Cat Cab. The white shtickster and the black behemoth clicked as a business team. LAPD chilled out the Big Boy Cab bombing—the owner was a hot-car fence they wanted nullified. The Dr. Fred snuff faded to back-page status. Jack Leahy greased some reporters with Bureau cash and said, "Let this go, all right?" That *L.A. Times* piece was the last major mention. Wayne scheduled a meeting with the Peoples' Bank prez. It might get ugly. The Boys wanted their bank back. The Feds wanted information.

He cruised darktown some nights. It wired him up and induced exhaustion and occasional pre-dawn sleep. Late-night ghetto life was deadpan seductive. Vice cops donned rubber gloves to manhandle tranny whores. Record stores played Zulu music and sold LAPD pig dolls. Cops bought the bulk of them and stuck them on their car antennas. He listened to revolutionary radio. Bootleg-band stations were broadcasting out of bars and Muslim mosques. He told Joan that his favorite song was "Blue Genocide" by Muhammad Mao and the Pig Hunters. Joan said, "Comrade Dwight, *you're learning.*"

He saw Scotty Bennett out cruising sometimes. Scotty loved soul food. Sister Sylvia's Kitchen fed him for free. Scotty always tipped lavishly.

There must be a BTA and MMLF war. Marsh Bowen must facilitate it. Narcotics must figure prominently. It has to stay short of catastrophe, or Karen will not forgive him. It has to get fierce. It has to get him his mandated results and further Comrade Joan's agenda. It has to take them both to the identical place—so that she will tell him where she's been and what she knows.

51

(Los Angeles, 12/24/68)

Merry Christmas.

He got the standard card and five-spot from his mother. This one: postmarked Racine, Wisconsin. He brought his dad the standard C-note and Reuben sandwich. Dad did his fuck-off number and pissed on his shoes.

Memo: work on your mother's file. Query the Racine PD. Memo: your case file is updated. Your case is dead-stalled. Memo: get your ass to the rockin' D.R. and voodoo-vamped Haiti.

Christmas Eve, the wheelman lot, Clyde Duber's yule bash. Deli food and keg beer. Cocktails by the gas pumps, free uppers from the quick-script pharmacy.

Crutch circulated. He was amphetamized and holiday-lonely. Wayne sent Froggy to Panama. Fuck that place. All roads led to the D.R. All front-man reports would point there.

Phil Irwin was poking a spade chick on the service lift. Scotty Bennett brought some go-go girls in to give snout. Buzz Duber's car was Santa's Blow Job Zone. Fred Otash dispensed free play chips for his Vegas dive. Bobby Gallard shot craps with Clyde and Chick Weiss. They used Scotty's pissed-on Vietcong flag as a blanket.

Crutch re-circulated and got re-blue. He was bored. Dwight Holly pulled him off the Marsh Bowen gig. He kept mum on Bowen's fruitness and held it as a hole card. He kept up the spot tails anyway—they might go somewhere. Clyde had him working divorce gigs full-time. Buzz gave up on "the case." He never had full-scale knowledge or full-on balls for the job. Buzz was a yuks & fucks guy. Donald Linscott Crutchfield killed ten Communists. Arland "Buzz" Duber extorted hookers for skull.

Scotty drifted by. Bobby Gallard schmoozed him up. Hey, boss—that Bowen chump got famous off that shit he pulled with you.

Scotty smiled and winked.

Scotty pointed to the 18's stitched on his tie.

Scotty scrawled 19 in the air.

Peeper Christmas.

Crutch drove by Julie's house, Peggy's house and Kay's house. The girls were his age. They always exchanged gifts after dinner. Dad rigged the same outside lights every year. Crutch knew the routine.

Julie's window view was better than last year. Julie's folks gave her geek boyfriend some geek reindeer socks. He got that "Oh shit" look. Julie nudged him—be nice, now.

The family knocked back eggnog. Dad got sclerotic-flushed. The geek shuffled his feet and displayed a wedding ring. Mom and Dad boo-hooed. Everybody hugged. Julie's brother Kenny died at 1st and Arden. Two-car wipe-out, late '62. Kenny was a glue-sniffer and a whip-out artiste. He whipped it out on Buzz's girlfriend, Jane Hayes. Buzz and Crutch kicked his ass, circa '61.

The Julie Show bombed. You'll be so happy, boo-hoo. Crutch drove by Peggy's house and Kay's house. The window curtains were drawn. Next stop: 2nd and Plymouth.

Bright windows. No lawn manger—Dana Lund had taste. He killed his lights and waited. He shined his penlight on the dashboard and Christmas-lit Joan. He brain-tripped: Joan's face and Dana's story.

Her husband, Bob, died in Korea. Chrissie was four then. Dana went back to nursing and sold real estate part-time. She was born in 1915. She'd be fifty-four in March. She dated rich stiffs intermittently. She started touching up her gray hair in mid-'64. Crutch noted it then.

Chrissie walked through the living room. Dana followed her. Crutch choked tears back. Dana was wearing the sweater he bought her on the day he thought he would die.

Options: Trinity Lutheran Church or Marsh Bowen's new pad. Midnight services de-blued him sometimes. Nix that: the pastor knew his peeper rep and hated him. He was still wired. That meant Niggertown by default.

Marsh Bowen was racially regressing. His pad on Denker was jig-upscale. His pad on East 86th was a coon cave. Cinder-block struts, window bars, spookedelic paint.

Clock in: 12:51 a.m.

Crutch parked and waited. The radio supplied distraction. He got Christmas carols and Brother Bobby X, live at Rae's Rugburn Room. Brother Bobby ragged on the Jews and wished black folk an off-the-pigs New Year. Marsh Bowen walked out at 1:14 a.m. New vines: trim-cut and all *blaaaaack.*

Bowen walked past his car and schlepped it down to Imperial Highway. Bright lights there: all-night gas stations and coffee shops.

Cut him slack, he's too close, he'll see you.

Crutch waited two minutes and jammed southbound. He hit the corner and looked both ways. No pedestrians. He slow-cruised Goody-Goody's and the Carolina Pines, big windows at both locations. There's Bowen in the Pines, drinking coffee solo.

The place was semi-deserted. Crutch parked and ambled in slow. Fruit Alert: Bowen eyeball-trolled all the single men.

Walk in, get close, within eavesdrop range.

Crutch shagged a table two over. It provided a back view of Bowen. A waitress brought coffee. *Aaaahhh,* good—re-fuel those jets.

Bowen fidgeted and checked his watch. Fruit Alert: a fat Mex smirky-eyed him. Bowen shuddered and looked down.

Crutch checked the door. It popped open. He blinked. It can't be. He rubbed his eyes—yes, no, *yes.*

Joan Klein walked in and sat down with Bowen. She removed her overcoat. She smiled. She took off her beret and shook out her hair.

She cleaned her glasses on a napkin. She looked older without them. She wore a black knit dress. Her knife scar was covered. Crutch went hot/cold/hot/cold/hot/cold.

Joan and Bowen talked. It was sotto voce. Crutch peeled and re-peeled his ears and couldn't hear shit. Bowen sipped coffee. Joan sipped coffee and smoked. A white couple gave them a pissy mixed-couple look. Joan touched Bowen's arm—one time, two times, three. Bowen three-time flinched. Crutch picked up sound waves. He got Joan's husky voice. It burned straight through him.

He kept his head down. Their eyes never clicked. Joan's talking more, Joan's on the make, Bowen's homo-reluctant. Joan kissed Gretchen/Celia at the rental house that night.

Crutch leaned closer. His ears throbbed. He couldn't read Joan's lips. Bowen coughed and said, "Weird dream of you." Joan spoke a little louder. She said, "Safe house."

That's it, no more, back to soft talk and—

Crutch got *un*-wired and *re*-circuited and *re*-wired.

Safe house, rent house, fake stewardess Gretchen/Celia. Fake address: *"Some Commie safe house."*

Crutch put a dollar down and walked out *sloooooow.*
Safe house, rent house, death house. Confluence, proximity—

His tools got him in. Horror House: the third tour.

No hippies or winos residing. Unchanged since last time. More dampness, new winter stench, accelerating decay. The floorboards creaked louder, the cold air stung more.

His last tour. He had to do visible damage. He couldn't come back. Her presence here was a long shot. He had to try.

Lock picks, pry bar, crowbar, flashlight, penlight. Burglar's jerry-rigged stethoscope, three hours to dawn.

He walked the house top-to-bottom. He opened every drawer and scanned every shelf. He cut open every piece of upholstered furniture. He looked behind every framed picture and pulled up every rug.

The house was cold. Cold sweat drenched him. He dropped his tools, wiped his hands dry and kept going.

He climbed ladders and checked every wall and ceiling beam. He beat rats to death with a shovel in the attic and combed every inch. He pried off the downstairs floorboards and poked through cobwebs, insect nests and dirt.

It was raining. Dawn was breaking slow. That gave him more time. He was dirt-caked. His sweat turned it to a thin mud.

He tapped every wall panel. He put his ear to the stethoscope and listened for hollow thunks.

It was Christmas morning, he heard church bells, he almost cried.

Clouds passed outside. Some daylight streaked in. He saw a loose step near the top of the staircase.

He walked over. It was the upper part of the step. The nails were loose. The two pieces wobbled.

A one-inch gap showed. He pried the piece of wood off and saw a hidey-hole. It was two feet long and half a foot high. Inside it:

A rusted-out .38 snubnose. Rusty pistol ammo. Four mildewed pro-Castro pamphlets. Nine pro-wetback flyers. A U.S. OUT OF VIETNAM poster. A small notebook—stapled pages, smudged ink and eroded text throughout. One visible date: 12/6/62.

Crutch held his penlight up to the pages and squinted. He couldn't discern words. He saw numbers and got an instinct: foreign cash-exchange rates. He got the general format: meeting minutes for some Commie pow-wow.

The page-by-page text devolved into blurs. The last page held three clear signatures at the bottom.

Terry Bergeron, Thomas F. Narduno, Joan R. Klein.

HER.

Crutch touched her name. He was sweating and dripping mud. The page fell apart in his hand.

Something else tweaked him. "Thomas F. Narduno," brain tease.

It took some time just standing there. It came in a burst.

The St. Louis papers. The piece on the Grapevine killings. The odd left-wing victim: Thomas F. Narduno.

He cleaned out the hidey-hole. He put everything in his toolbox. He heard the church bells again. He walked outside and stood gasping in the rain.

52

(Los Angeles, 12/26/68)

ayne said, "You have options within the ultimatum, sir. We're allotting you considerable autonomy."

Dwight rolled his eyes. "You're a stalwart of the local Negro community and a Democratic Party bagman, I'll grant you that. *Beyond that?* You're a mobbed-up money washer in hock to the Boys, and all we're asking you for is more of the same."

The office was oak-paneled. The chairs were green leather. The MLK oil portrait overruled the room. Wayne willed his eyes away.

Dwight said, "The brothers around here call you 'Lionel the Laundryman.' You're like that guy on the detergent box. They call you 'Mr. Clean.'"

Lionel Thornton smirked. He was five-three. His desk was seven-three. Wayne and Dwight had small chairs. He had a throne. Wayne and Dwight were big white men. He was a small black man. He wore the world's sharpest chalk-stripe suit.

Wayne said, "You wash some foreign-bound construction money and casino skim. You stay on as the bank's president. You help Mr. Hoover and Agent Holly out with information as requested, which allows you to personally keep 3% of every dime you wash."

Thornton smiled. Dwight hummed the Mr. Clean jingle. Wayne peeled his eyes off Dr. King.

Dwight pulled out his cigarettes. Thornton shook his head. Dwight started to light up. Wayne stopped him.

"I'll go to 3½%, a 5% pay raise for your employees and a 15% salary raise for you. There's twenty thousand dollars in my briefcase. That's your bonus for cooperating."

Thornton lit a cigarette and blew smoke Dwight's way. Dwight stood up. Wayne nudged his foot. Dwight sat back and folded his hands.

Dr. King in burnished oils—more handsome than in real life.

Thornton said, "Give me the briefcase, too."

Wayne bowed. Dwight smiled. A gunshot popped outside. Dwight jerked and touched his belt gun. That goddamn portrait. Oak panels in a black slum.

Thornton said, "Mr. Hoover has an operation going. Mr. Holly's presence today attests to that. My guess is that you're hassling some deluded black militants. I'll wish you well and leave you to it, but I cannot inform for you or offer you on-premises oversight, or keep separate books for you."

Wayne nodded. Dwight's chest was pounding—Wayne saw his shirt move. Thornton stood up and teetered on platform shoes.

"One last favor. For Mr. Holly, I think. I noticed the sap in his waistband."

Gunshots overlapped—closer this time.

"My wife's ex-husband is bothering her. I'd like him to desist."

An intercom buzzed. Wayne and Dwight stood up. Thornton pointed to the portrait.

"Vicious white motherfuckers like you killed him, but his voice will prevail in the end."

Wayne said, "Sir, I hope so."

He refurbished the lab. He dumped the heroin makings and added a collage. Reginald Hazzard photos four-walled him.

Partitions set off a file space. He brought in file boxes and reams of paper. He'd worked LVPD Intelligence. He knew how to build case files and log information. Mary Beth bought him a cashmere sweater for Christmas. He told her he *really* wanted a Teletype machine.

Mary Beth said, "You've got all these pictures of my son but no pictures of me." He told her he wanted to find her son because he'd already found her. She told him to keep going. He said she looked different every time he saw her, so pictures would spoil the surprise. She told him to keep going. He said they never met outside his hotel suite. He enjoyed imagining the ways she looked in the world.

The file space had potential. The lab was small and well equipped. He had a spectroscope, a fluoroscope and the proper chemicals to work on Dwight's pages.

Wayne unplugged the telephone and sat down to work. He talked to Carlos and Farlan Brown earlier. His news: Lionel Thornton folded. Farlan's news: the prez-elect was sending permission letters for the casino-site team. Also included: passes to the inaugural hoo-haw. Funny, but: Mesplede wanted Dipshit Crutchfield on the team. Wayne relented. Dipshit worked cheap and might mandate a nuisance hit at some point. Keep the punk short-leased.

Dwight's chem job was improbable and exacting. The file pages were carbon acid–based and burned under caustic applications. He'd been at it part-time for two months. He'd destroyed two-thirds of the Joan Rosen Klein file and failed to peel through a single line of redaction. A notion hit him this morning. Throw spectroscope and fluoroscope light on the typewriter marks. Bombard the ink lines with contrasting rays. Dab high-pH hydroxic acid on the perceived letter shapes and see what forms and what erodes.

He rigged his light bars, documents, acid base and swabs. He wore tinted magnifying goggles. He slid a redacted sheet on an absorbent blotter. He let the lights fly. He squinted and *thought* he saw a capital *S, J, R* and *K* near-microscopically outlined. He realized that he'd extrapolated. He knew FBI file parlance. He'd *thought* his way through to "SUBJECT JOAN ROSEN KLEIN" and no more.

BUT:

He could sacrifice that ink line. He could look for the other logically following boldface letters. He could refine his light and application technique that way.

More light now. Different angles. More hydroxic acid, more/less/more/less—

He burned through the possible "JOAN ROSEN KL"—fizz straight onto the blotter.

The acid pooled and bubbled.

An ink line blurred and faded.

The typewriter marks for "EIN" showed up faint on the page.

Wayne trembled. He pulled out the test page and slid in the page marked "Known Associates." He counted fourteen black-inked lines and brought down the lights. He dabbed hydroxic acid. He burned ink lines, he faded ink lines, he blurred ink lines and got typewriter marks pure unreadable. He squinted. He refocused his lights and singed paper. He refocused and got blots. He refocused and redabbed and got the visible numbers "7412." More burns, more blurs, a *U,* an *L,* a *T.* He refocused and dabbed again. He got the blur-faded, typewritten-marked "Thomas Frank Narduno."

53

(Los Angeles, 12/27/68)

Sap gloves broke bones and spared your hands. They maximized hurt and minimized self-damage.

Dwight beat on a bantamweight Negro named Durward Johnson. Lionel Thornton watched. Johnson looked like Billy Eckstine, minus the mustache. The gig went down behind Johnson's house. Baldwin Hills was high-end colored. The alley was paved. Christmas lights lined the fence tops.

Dwight pulled his punches, went in light and broke bones regardless. Thornton stipulated face work. Johnson grasped a fence link and kept himself upright. Thornton stood out of spray range.

Jabs and right crosses. The cheeks and the jaw—don't fuck with his eyes or his brain.

His nose broke audibly. His teeth dribbled off his split tongue. Dwight's glove seams popped and leaked ball bearings. Johnson's toupee flew off his head.

He stayed upright. He spit out cracked bridgework and hit Thornton's shoes. Thornton smirked. Johnson said, "I fucked your wife, nigger."

Dwight threw a big right. Johnson grasped the fence two-handed. Dwight stumbled and fell into the punch. It landed full force. It took Johnson and a stretch of fence links down. Dwight fell along with them.

The world went upended. Christmas lights blinked *above* him. He got up and helped Johnson up. Thornton was gone. Johnson weaved into a neighbor's backyard and crashed in a pool chair.

Dwight pulled the gloves off and walked back to his car. A business card was stuck under the wiper blades.

Sergeant Robert S. Bennett/Robbery Division/LAPD. Below that: "Vince & Paul's, 1 hour."

That pedophile was nothing. The guy fucked with kids and Joan wanted him hurt. He showed Joan the Polaroid. The perv was beat to shit. She touched his arm then. He leaned into her and let their hands brush. They held the pose to tell each other something.

Durward Johnson was shitwork. Thornton was a maladroit dwarf. It was ugly. His hands ached. It gave him that hide-out-and-drink-yourself-well-again thirst.

Dwight flexed his hands. He had two sprained fingers. His cuticles bled. Ball bearings were jammed under his nails.

He called Joan before the Johnson job. They discussed Nixon's inaugural. She said some rogue Reds were flying to D.C. They had guns traceable to a Florida bank job. They planned to wear Nixon masks and clout three banks on inauguration eve. Joan provided their names and addresses.

He called the Miami Office. The bank team nailed the fucks at the airport. They were en route to Austin, Texas. They planned to clout three banks dressed as LBJ.

He called Karen then. He offered her a monument bombing to celebrate the bust. Karen was headed to the hospital. Eleanora wanted out *now*. Dwight heard What's-His-Name in the background.

Vince & Paul's was slow. The waitresses wore Santa's wench garb. Dwight squeezed three ball bearings out of his hands and bloodied the tablecloth. He ordered just-this-one-drink-and-no-more.

The waitress brought him a double scotch. The first sip warmed him, the second sip blared an alarm. He felt his legs return. Scotty Bennett slid into the booth.

"You should have told me."

Dwight stirred his drink. "Who, in fact, did tell you?"

"Those cops you paid to whip on Bowen."

"I'll apologize in advance, then. It's Mr. Hoover's operation. He wanted you bypassed."

Scotty sipped his bourbon-rocks. "You're sheep-dipping Bowen. The Panthers and US are too well infiltrated, so you're sending Bowen in to work the BTA and MMLF."

Dwight said, "Off the record, yes. On the record, our greatest chance at success stems from Bowen's altercation with you."

Scotty chewed an ice cube. "Let's get this back on the right footing. I want to see all Bowen's reports and all the filed Bureau paperwork."

Dwight said, "No." Scotty killed his drink. His barmaid girlfriend brought him a refill.

"The BTA and MMFL are clowns. They're not worth working. They couldn't find their ass on a toilet seat."

Dwight shook his head. "I disagree."

"Why?"

"They're career criminals with a valid grievance. A fair segment of this society condones their actions. There's a rule of thumb to organizations like these. The most forceful psychopath assumes leadership and creates the agenda, and the BTA and MMLF have some doozies."

Scotty smiled. "You talk like a lawyer."

"I am a lawyer."

"And you know about psychopaths, because you've spent twenty years doing strongarm jobs for Mr. Hoover."

Dwight raised his drink—touché.

"It's that 'valid grievance' line I'm not buying."

"Come on, Sergeant. We're both white cops. We didn't create the world, but we both know how it works and we both know you can't let pissed-off coloreds cash in and fuck up the world because their people got a raw deal and some hopped-up white kids think they're cool."

Scotty cracked his knuckles. "If Bowen goes bad, on his own or in a context you placed him in, I will not hesitate to take him down for it. That means any and all criminal actions. That means I'll go in unilaterally, without fear of you, Mr. Hoover, Chief Reddin or anyone else involved in this operation."

Dwight cracked his knuckles. His shirt cuffs were exposed. They were blood-soaked.

"Will you keep quiet about this operation?"

"Yes."

"Will you refrain from entrapping Marsh Bowen or going after him proactively?"

"Yes."

"Will you inform me of any tips you may have picked up on the BTA or MMFL?"

"No."

"Will you maintain a hands-off policy on the BTA and MMLF during this operation?"

"No."

"Suppose I go over your head and talk to Chief Reddin?"

Scotty smiled. "You won't do that. We both know where it would take us."

Dwight smiled. "Let's step back and give each other one concession."

Scotty said, "I'll go first. Will you inform me of any pending armed robberies to be performed by BTA or MMLF members?"

"Yes. My operating parameters are very strict on that. Bowen will inform me of pending robberies, and I will inform you."

"And if Bowen has no knowledge and I learn of pending robberies on my own?"

Dwight raised his glass. "Then embellish your reputation and kill the motherfuckers with my best wishes."

Scotty raised his glass. "What's my concession?"

"Talk up your hatred of Bowen to cops, your informants, anyone who'll listen to you. The more you hate him, the more clout he'll have with the brothers."

Scotty shrugged. "That's not much of a concession. I'm doing it anyway."

The jukebox snapped on. The music went *LOUD*. Dwight pulled the cord out. The music swooped and died. Dwight got a range of schizzed looks.

Scotty stretched. His shit got exposed: belt gun, shoulder gun, toad-stabber, knucks.

"It's Christmas. Ask Santa for another concession."

"Try not to kill Marsh Bowen. It goes against your nature, but it's the white thing to do."

Scotty said, "Deal." His barmaid girlfriend walked over. Scotty motioned her away.

"You know, I have quite a few southside informants."

"Yes, you do."

"I picked up a nice tip today."

"I'm listening."

"Marsh Bowen is a faggot."

The hospital sent a telegram to the drop-front. Eleanora Sifakis, seven pounds and four ounces, healthy. "Mother will call soon."

Dwight poured himself just-one-more-drink and ice-packed his hands. His head swerved—Karen/Joan, Karen/Joan, Karen/Joan.

He sipped his drink. He salved his fingers. He swerved with Eleanora on earth and Marsh Bowen as a queer. The phone rang at 11:14 p.m.

He picked up. Wayne said, "I burned through most of the file pages, but all I got was one KA name. Thomas Frank Narduno. It sounded familiar to me, but I couldn't place it. Ring any bells?"

Big bells:

The lefty Grapevine vic. Heist suspect: New York and Ohio. Bug devices found on his body.

Wayne said something about fluoroscopes and hydroxic acid. Dwight hung up and poured just-one-more-drink.

It burned and brought up shudders. Dwight dialed the scrambler-phone number.

No rings on scramblers. Just faint hiss and "Hello, Mr. Holly."

"May I sleep with you tonight?"

Joan said, "Yes."

54

(Cuban Waters, 12/27/68)

Fins and churned waves. Mesplede tossed chum. Sharks hovered and snapped high for it. Bright moonlight made them glow. The speedboat launched from Boca Chico Key. Destination: Varadero Beach, Cuba.

Mesplede had called him in L.A. Wayne approved him for the Nicaragua and D.R. trips next month. Froggy filed a negative Panama report. Panama was out. Nicaragua would get nixed. The D.R. would get the nod. Cuba was close. His case was all there.

Crutch ate Dramamine. He was seasick green. He wanted to fortify: booze, pills, hash. Froggy said *nyet*.

"This will be intimate, Donald. I want to see how you perform."

They were forty miles out. They wore lampblack and frayed fatigues. They carried combat knives and silencer-tapped Magnums wrapped in plastic.

The shark escort bobbed and snapped. Mesplede baby-talked them. The chum was all cat innards. Mesplede had a pal with a cat-killing pit bull named Batista. Batista was a Bay of Pigs K-9 Korps vet. He raged to kill cats in a free Cuba.

The speedboat zoomed and crunched waves. Crutch fought flashbacks: Horror House, the meeting list, Joan Klein and Thomas Frank Narduno.

A shark brushed the boat. Mesplede *petted* him. The chum smelled ten times worse than cat shit. They hit the ten-mile point. The chum ran out. Mesplede cut the motor and let waves push them in.

Swells rode them toward shore. It was bumps and chop and water knee-high in the boat. Crutch ate more Dramamine and took deep breaths.

They saw the shore. They dropped anchor by some shoals sixty yards from the beach. They had infrared binoculars. They saw five militia guys playing cards at a picnic table.

Exile intelligence. A guy in the Cuban Freedom Council tipped Froggy. The cardplayers: all torturers at La Cabana prison. They castrated rightist insurgents. They walked from their barracks and played cards Tuesday nights.

The boat was moored. Gull noise killed the scrape-against-rock sound. Crutch put on goggles. Mesplede wore a mask. Their weapons were triple-plastic-wrapped.

They rolled into the water. It was freezing cold. They swam diagonally. A beachfront tree line covered the moon. The cardplayers smoked. Cigarette tips glowed—little sighting devices.

They reached the beach and *rolled.* Dark sand and white sand dusted them. They dumped their headware. They got more breath. Crutch ate sand and willed back stomach cramps.

Ten feet to the table. Two shapes sand-drift *rolling.* Five targets, twelve bullets, close range.

Mesplede gave the signal. They positioned themselves prone, two-hand aimed and fired. Their muzzles flashed, their silencers thunked, they heard body impact. Table chunks shattered. They saw cigarettes drop. They heard skull-crack impact and saw two men pitch forward.

Three men stood up—big body-mass targets. Three men jabbering and unsnapping holsters.

Mesplede fired. Crutch fired. They took their legs out, knocked them down and gut-shot them. Crutch buried his head and sucked sand.

Silencer echo and wave noise. Gulls squawking and no return fire.

Crutch pulled his head up. Mesplede was standing by the table. His flashlight was out. Crutch weaved over.

Five dead men. Three cigarette tips still glowing.

Froggy said, "Scalp them."

Crutch shook his head. Froggy grabbed his hair and yanked him into the table. Crutch banged his knees and went down in the sand. He was kiss-close to a faceless man. The man's hairline was powder-scorched. A flap of skin dangled.

Froggy watched. Crutch pulled his knife. He said some kind of dumb-kid prayer and jammed the blade down. He missed the flap and yanked up from the eye socket.

55

(Las Vegas, 12/27/68)

Mary Beth wore his Christmas-gift sweater to bed. It was way too big. She tucked her chin under the turtleneck and goofed on him. She pulled the cuffs over her hands.

"There's no guarantee that you'll find my son, but you're determined to spend all that time and money anyway."

The bedroom drapes were open. The Nixon signs were down. The hotels were hawking yuletide cheer now. The green bulbs reminded him of that emerald. It was like a dream revived.

"There's no guarantee that I'll find him, but my instincts keep telling me L.A. I'm building an informant network there, so there's always the chance that something will pan out."

"Have you done something like this before?"

Wayne rolled away from her. He smelled her shampoo on the pillow. He took a breath of it.

She said, "You found Wendell Durfee, didn't you?"

Wayne looked at her. "Yes, I did."

"And you killed him?"

"Yes."

She pulled the pillow over and got their eyes close. She did that a lot. She said they both had these green flecks.

"Sweetie, I already figured that out."

56

(Los Angeles, 12/27/68)

The Bureau kept a suite at the downtown Statler. Karen's baby was just born four blocks away. Joan wore a red dress. Dwight wore his most-Fed gray suit.

Christmas lights blinked on Wilshire. The prior tenant left a bottle of Ten High. Joan saw Dwight's ratched hands and dosed them with bourbon on a washcloth. It stung. Dwight held tears back. He thought of Thomas F. Narduno and wondered what Joan knew about everything. He thought of Karen and Eleanora.

Joan said, "Save your hands. You're fifty-two years old."

"How do you know that?"

"I'm not telling you."

"What do you want from all this?"

"Tell me what 'all this' means."

"The job. The oper—"

Joan touched his lips. "I'm here because I want to be. I would have asked you if you hadn't asked me."

His hands burned. Some tears leaked. Joan stood on her tiptoes and kissed them off his cheeks. The outside lights shaded them weird colors.

They fell on the bed. Joan held his head and kissed him. Her breath tasted like cigarettes and dry wine. She wiped off his tears with her thumbs.

He held her in with his arms. His hands were useless. He wanted to grab her hair. He knew it would kill his hands. He couldn't stand this wet-eyed thing. If he touched her hair, he'd hurt himself and never want it to stop.

She pushed his head back. She kissed him. She leaned over him and pinned his wrists and let her hair fall on him. He nuzzled the dark parts and bit at the gray streaks and forced her legs apart with his knees. She pulled his arms up and pinned his wrists above his head. Lights played over her underarm stubble and her knife scar. She saw that he wanted it. She let his wrists go and let him roll into her sideways. She held her arms up and let him kiss her there. He heard himself gasping and saw them both naked and knew he'd lost track of the time. She said things. They weren't quite words. She might have said his name. She held him softly. She took his hands softly and let them brush here, here and here. He kissed all the places his hands touched. She held his hands and held his head there every moment. She spread her legs for him to touch and taste and be held there. She gasped as he gasped and his eyes burned from all the tears and his hands didn't hurt at all.

DOCUMENT INSERT: 1/12/69. Extract from the journal of Marshall E. Bowen.

January 12, 1969

I'm being courted. The pace is slower than Mr. Holly would like. Both the BTA and MMLF have found me, along with the Panthers and US. Eldridge Cleaver invited me to lunch. He brought with him a dubious literary agent, who wanted me to write a memoir entitled *Brother Pig: An Ex-Cop Tells It Like It Is Within the Genocidal LAPD*. I declined. Mr. Cleaver looked at me suspiciously. The ghetto rumor is that Mr. Cleaver is a very well-placed informant himself and reports to cutouts at various Federal crime commissions that no longer trust Mr. Hoover to rationally assess information. Brother Cleaver had the look of informant/arriviste, and I think he may have seen it in me.

I've nixed the Panthers and US. My relationship with Jomo Clarkson has me leaning toward the MMLF. Jomo is rumored to be heisting liquor stores; if I come across anything more specific on that, I'll report it to Mr. Holly.

The southside clubs are the chief recruiting arms of both organizations. If one spends time at Sultan Sam's Sandbox, Rae's Rugburn Room, Nat's Nest, Mr. Mitch's Another World, the Snooty Fox, Tommy Tucker's Playroom and the Carolina Pines on Imperial Highway, one will be approached by BTA/MMLF brothers, who will speak injudiciously, suck up a bit and urge you to attend rallies and other planned activities. These men love to talk and describe their criminal actions. I have met pimps, ticket scalpers, the burglars of pornographic bookstores. A BTA member fed me 190-proof liquor from his basement still and took me to a Lakers game with counterfeit tickets. BTA kingpin Ezzard Jones—replete with bogus divinity degree—solicits funds with limited success at southside churches and complains that his girlfriend is getting it on with that persistent white woman, Joan. Benny Boles cruised me at a BTA bar-b-q and pushed all my danger buttons. He has an armed robbery conviction ('64) and alledgedly killed a male-prostitute lover in '58. Leander Jackson is charming with his Haitian lilt, vexing with his voodoo talk and hard to picture as an arms dealer, former member of the Tonton Macoute Haitian secret police and heavy conduit to leftist groups in the Caribbean. J. T. McCarver runs dice games for the MMLF, is a reputed pharmacy burglar and deals goofballs to Jordan High School students while Claude Cantrell Torrance, the MMLF's Minister of Finance and Minister of Extortion, deals to the Manual Arts student body. (Note: The MMLF are Manual Arts football fans; the BTA are Jordan High fans, and both groups push hate-whitey and kill-the-pigs pamphlets on and off the two campuses.)

Both groups front programs to feed wholesome breakfasts to impoverished ghetto children. White liberals find this fetching and donate money that the MMLF and BTA spends on hate-lit supplies, guns and dope. The breakfasts are homey affairs, often written up and photographed by a doting media. The breakfast food is extorted from local merchants and the children are fed sugar-packed concoctions like Fruit Loops, Cocoa Puffs, Trix, Crispy Critters and Puff-and-Stuff Pals. Sunday breakfasts are often followed by "media mixers," featuring Bloody Marys, soul food and reefer. These are hilarious, mixed-message, mixed-race moments. Yeah, we wants to kill all de pigs and destroy de white power structure, but we thinks *you* cool.

And these dumb white motherfuckers think they *are* cool. And these dumb white motherfuckers feel exalted in the presence of swinging black militants.

So, the BTA and MMLF are rivals, and I bop between both groups and keep my eyes open. Individuals are viciously bad within both groups, but I do not see a percolating or slowly assertive group viciousness in ascent. Both groups have guns stashed in safe houses (Joan Klein allegedly holds guns for BTA members), but both groups are primarily in love with guns for their implied statement of masculinity and rarely carry them, for fear of LAPD street rousts. There is much talk of dealing heroin to finance revolution, but "revolution" is a comic-book, racist-polemic pipe dream to these people, and I doubt if they could put together the seed money necessary to buy heroin in significant quantity.

So it's pamphlet sales, parties, pub crawls, rallies and big talk in great quantity. Both groups peddle bootleg editions of Mao's *Little Red Book* and Franz Fanon's *The Wretched of the Earth.* I've read both books. They both contain wisdom. Given my life in Los Angeles, my parents' horrible tales of life in the South, my own LAPD experience and my two auspicious beatings by LAPD, I empathize as much as my compartmentalized psyche and soul will let me. But *revolution? Accomplishing anything other than a glancingly ephemeral social good?* These people are lost in the overall puerile, selfish, ride-the-zeitgeist game of it, things will go wrong in the end, and my efforts of suppression and interdiction may provide my own brand of glancingly ephemeral social good.

I can only allot "social good" a smidgen of ink. I'm here for the adventure and to solve the armored-car heist case and accrue all financial benefit.

I'm being courted. I'm listening, I'm learning. I think I'll be specifically recruited for criminal enterprises—based on misreadings of my ex-cop status—before too long.

I see Scotty Bennett out cruising sometimes. We always wink and wave at each other, because we're both addled by the notion of stoicism and acting cool while you harbor big emotion and hate. Scotty bought me the key to the ghetto, and I'm grateful to him for that.

I've got both beatings in perspective now, I think. I sense that they are bringing me closer to the money, the emeralds and the secrets of 2/24/64.

Mr. Holly and I continue to talk via phone drop every third or fourth day. He's looking for a cutout to work me on a more regular basis, while he continues to run the operation. I've indulged the Bent at Queen Anne Park a few times since Christmas, and I must remind myself to be more cautious and discreet. I had coffee with Joan on Christmas Eve. She seemed to be coming on to me— sorry, no sale—and working me on some level. I either dreamt of her or saw her that night I slept at Jomo's crib, which is odd in itself. Women are, by and large, difficult for me, and I find Joan unsettling and a little frightening. I may write up my perceptions and get them to Mr. Holly.

Mr. Holly continues to trouble me. I find myself thinking about him much more than I should.

DOCUMENT INSERT: 1/16/69. Extract from the privately held journal of Karen Sifakis.

January 16, 1969

Eleanora is squalling and keeping me up all night and I'm realizing that the joy of Dina as a full-fledged child and a developing moral being had blunted me to the debilitating regime of new motherhood, this time at age forty-three. I'm not sleeping, W.H.N.

is staying in L.A. full-time to help, his constant presence hinders my internal life and in no way compensates for the assistance he's giving me with Ella. I haven't seen Dwight since Ella was born; W.H.N.'s presence has effectively quashed that. Dina misses Dwight and asks about him when W.H.N. is out of earshot; I assure her that he'll be back soon, to tell her wonderfully sanitized tales of his adventures with the FBI.

She was asking me questions about J. Edgar Hoover last night. Her father had told her (too vividly) stories of Hoover's cowardly actions during the 1919–1920 Red Scare. Dina asked me (again, out of earshot of What's-His-Name) why her father hated Hoover so much, while Dwight held him in such high regard. I did not tell her that Dwight and Hoover share a complex moral history, that her father is an intractably aggrieved ideologue and that Dwight is punch-drunk behind all his conflicting notions of authority and considers it best to tell little children comforting tales. Dina wouldn't get it, and I wouldn't blame her. I keep wondering just how far Dwight has gone to appease Mr. Hoover in repayment of the debt he carries for the man.

I have brought Eleanora into a chaste and duplicitous marriage and into a troubled world, with Richard Nixon poised to assume the White House. Dwight will be buying her odd stuffed animals soon, like the alligators he bought Dina, and she will grow up thinking that predators (like Dwight!) are soft and cuddly. At some point she will point to me for confirmation of this. If I am the least bit candid, I will concede my great love for the man, which will in some small way explain why the teddy bears her father bought her hold no great emotional sway.

I miss Dwight. I'm going to boot What's-His-Name out of town soon, so we can spend time together and Dwight can meet Ella. He's fixated on Joan Klein—I can sense it. As always, I pray that my maneuverings and the connections that I facilitate cause more good than harm.

57

(Washington, D.C., 1/20/69)

"We have endured a long night of the American spirit. But as our eyes catch the dimness of the first rays of dawn, let us not curse the remaining dark. Let us gather the light."

They had boxed seats for the big speech. They had preferred parade-route passes. They had tickets for six inaugural balls.

The new prez soaked up applause. Froggy said, "He is a bland man. We must circumvent his lack of commitment to the Cuban Cause."

Crutch touched his lapel pin—a solid gold 15. He took the scalps and kept his lunch down. Froggy bought him the pin. It honored his close-range-killer status. He still had nightmares per that eye socket.

"Our destiny offers, not the cup of despair, but the chalice of opportunity. So let us seize it, not in fear, but in gladness—"

There's LBJ—exhausted and vicious. There's Earl Warren, there's Dick's frau, Pat, there's ex-Veep Humphrey. Hey, Baldy—Froggy and I keestered you!

Nixon shut it down to cheers and a standing ovation. Froggy mimicked snores. Senator Charles H. Percy scowled at him.

Everybody stayed standing and milked the moment. Crutch memorized details. LBJ's heifer daughters. Some stray Kennedys. Hey, fuckers—Froggy shot your Uncle Jack!

Crutch stood there, clapping. People walked by him. He thought of his mother and Dana Lund. He touched his lapel pin. He thought of Joan. He thought of his case and the D.R. upcoming. The Nixster walked past. He'd shaved close this morning. Nixey sat out World War II on some Jap-free atoll. *He* killed Commies close range. Jack the K. killed Japs on PT-109. It was a shuck. Boats didn't count. Jack was no close-range killer.

The crowd thinned out. Crutch re-memorized. Mesplede said, "Enjoy your extremely minor role in this, Donald. But remember that our destiny lies south of here."

"Tell me again, Froggy. I dig the repetition of it."

"What is that?"

"Tell me how we're going to make the money to buy the guns to kill the Castro guys."

"We are going to sell heroin."

They ball-hopped. D.C. was all limos and floodlit monuments. The air was gunpowdered. Fireworks caused most of it. The rest was coons shooting guns off in coontown.

Yippies in Nixon masks weaved in and out of traffic. Crutch saw a mugging by the Lincoln Monument. They shared a limo with some GOP stiffs and Ronald Reagan. Crutch told Reagan he dug *Hellcats of the Navy*. Governor Ronnie grooved on Crutch and called him "young fellow."

The ball-to-ball action was blurry. Crutch saw a million famous faces. Mickey Mantle, Floyd Patterson, some TV-show babes. Mummylike J. Edgar Hoover.

They got a tip on a bash at the Hay-Adams. They flagged down a gypsy cab and spent two hours driving six blocks. The driver was a Jamaican dinge with braided hair and a crocheted beanie. He said he was Pat Nixon's lover. He had some homegrown *ganga*. They toked up and listened to a long travelogue. The dinge extolled the fine Dominican gash and warned them about Haiti. Voodoo be real. You got to bring good *gre-gre*. You put a virgin's snatch hair in a locket and dangle it on your dick. You swear fealty to Baron Samedi.

They got to the Hay-Adams. The bill was two C-notes. The hotel looked familiar. Crutch got the gist: the dinge drove them in circles.

The lobby was plush. Mesplede saluted General Curtis LeMay. LeMay waved his cigar back. Crutch *re*-re-memorized. Open doorways/loud music/Lucy Baines Johnson and a stone swish actor doing the dirty-dog Twist.

The bash was in 1014. The doorway was open, the noise was big, the census was mob guys and pols. Crutch looked left and saw Bill Scranton and Carlos Marcello. Crutch looked right and saw Sam Giancana, snaked up with a tall brunette.

She turned their way. It was oh-my-fucking-God Gretchen Farr/Celia Reyes.

Part III

ZOMBIE ZONE

January 24, 1969–December 4, 1970

58

(Los Angeles, 1/24/69)

Black Cat bopped. It was redecorated and biracial now. Black personnel, white co-boss Milt Chargin. Scratch the velvet walls. Dig the orange-and-black striping.

It was Sam G.'s idea: let's revive Tiger Kab. Miami and Vegas, the anti-Castro days. Wayne, it's your job. Tigrify those cabs and make the shines like it.

Junior Jefferson noshed ice cream. "Tigers are okay, but panthers got more soul."

Milt Chargin said, "I detect a political statement there."

"It ain't politics. I'm just seeing two more white dudes than I usually see, which is contributing to the headache I gots from that strippedy-ass wallpaper."

The hut was SRO. The co-bosses sat in scuffed BarcaLoungers. Wayne perched on the window unit. Two men stood by the switchboard. Wayne ID'd them from file pix: Marshall Bowen and Jomo Kenyatta Clarkson.

Milt said, "The car painters are coming in today. You'll groove the new look. They're attaching tiger tails to the rear bumpers."

Jomo said, "This is jive honky bullshit. You're appropriating the racial identity of this business. Tigers are faggoty animals that punks dig on. Panthers are deadlier, but they got a distinction that makes you white fuckers squirm."

Wayne yawned. He was sleep-shot. Two calls rocked him last night. Sam said, "You're the Tiger Kab overseer." Dwight said, "I've got a job for you."

"Racial identity is one thing, Mr. Clarkson. Comfort's another. I've ordered air-conditioning units for the whole fleet."

Jomo picked at his machete scars. Political, self-inflicted. Marsh Bowen wore an all-black ensemble. He failed to look sinister. He looked like a male model slumming.

Junior said, "I likes that. Fat folks tend to sweat."

Milt lit a cigarette. "You've got to lose weight, schmuck. Obesity comes back to haunt you later in life."

"Ain't gonna be no 'later in life' for me. A race war's coming, and I just hope I ain't too plump to run."

Milt sighed. "If a race war is coming, why are you having such a good time with me?"

"'Cause you a funny old kike motherfucker, and you makes me laugh."

Jomo glared at Wayne. Junior passed him a full-page cartoon. It was a mimeo sheet, all reprint-blurred. LAPD pigs butt-fucked Black Panther leaders while Richard Nixon watched and jacked off.

Junior slurped ice cream. "Maybe the brothers in US are putting that shit out to discredit the Panthers."

Milt said, "The world does not need more hatred. The world needs more love. Inter-racial fucking and sucking would revitalize our great nation and spare us all lots of grief."

Junior yukked, Wayne laughed, Marsh Bowen grinned. Jomo *glaaaared* anew. A switchboard call came in. Jomo ignored it. Tires screeched outside. A shotgun blast and glass explosion followed. Wayne pegged the distance: one half block.

"New ownership means new rules. That doesn't mean I'm here to put the skids to everything you've got going on the side. Minor crime, fine. Politics, sure. Dealing weed and pills, fine by me. No heroin, no violent crime, no armed robbery. The Boys don't want it and I won't tolerate it. I'm ex–law enforcement, so you'll just have to get used to the way things are being run now."

Junior shrugged. Milt gulped. Marsh went blank-faced. Jomo pulled out a knife and carved "MMLF" on the wall.

The blade cut down to the baseboard. Plaster crumbled. Tiger-striped flocking peeled.

Wayne smiled at Jomo. "I'm glad you brought it up. From this point on, 2% of the Tiger Kab profits will go to the MMLF's Feed the Kiddies program."

Milt and Junior split outside. Marsh stepped aside. The knife was stuck in the wall. The handle wobbled from the thrust. Jomo picked his teeth with a diamond stickpin.

Wayne walked up and pulled the knife out. He wiped the blade on his pants leg and placed it on the switchboard.

Jomo picked his teeth. The stickpin jumped and drew blood. He slow-pivoted and walked off.

Wayne passed Marsh a note. It read: "I'm your cutout. France's Drive-In in one hour."

Dwight laid it out: Bowen was an FBI entrapper. His job: take down the BTA and MMLF. Dwight provided the case file and described the incursion to date. Dwight's specific plan: *heroin.*

Wayne was appalled. He cooked "H" and ran "H." He saw it fuck up the Vegas ghetto and the U.S. troops in Saigon. Dwight used the phrase "non-lethal dope war." It was Fed triplespeak. Passive FBI sanction of a local-ized narcotics trade. Interdiction and prosecution for a media effect.

Dwight said, "Sure, you hate narcotics. But this settles all your old debts." Dwight said, "You're a badass ex-cop. I'm betting the brothers will get their rocks off on you. Tell Bowen to spread the word on your Vegas shit. I want to create an ambivalent reaction."

"And by the way—Bowen is queer."

Wayne looped through the southside. It was smoggy. Street billboards magnetized him. Black models hucksterized. Be black and smoke ciga-rettes, be black and drive garish cars, be black and drink top-shelf booze. He drove slow. Pedestrians eyed him. He tried to read faces in split-second views.

He belonged here. He had business here. Reginald might have passed through here. He was building a file. He requeried the Clark County Sher-iff's and found more paperwork. They'd be sending him report carbons soon.

He had L.A. work and Vegas work. The Boys kept suites in the Count's hotels. Nixon was prez now. He overturned LBJ's anti-trust injunctions fast. The Boys sold Drac the Landmark Hotel and two thousand prime Vegas acres. Drac's new fixation was atomic waste. Underground tests scared him shitless. He called Wayne in to explain nuclear fission. Drac believed that A-bomb rays enhanced the black sex drive.

Work was delegation. He sent Mesplede and Dipshit south. Mesplede nixed Panama as a casino-site location. Next stop: Nicaragua. Work was vexing. Mary Beth kept pressing him for details. He put her off and pressed on *her* work. She described paltry pay rates, management hassles and fly-by-night health-plans. He listened for short bursts of time and got all bollixed up. It was his world versus her world. It got his head racing.

He met with Lionel Thornton again. They discussed money transfers and the final wash of assets. It was tense. Thornton sat him face-to-face with the Dr. King portrait. Some world-clash thing resulted.

Thornton was pissy and treated his workers like shit. Wayne told him to bring in a union maintenance crew and toss the scab crew out. Thornton fumed. Wayne told him to square the debt to his employees' credit union. Thornton pounded his desk. Wayne told him the mail room pipes were leaking asbestos. That constituted a health risk. Please address the issue now. Thornton kicked his desk and ratched his shoes. Wayne saluted the portrait.

"What do you know about me?"

"I know you killed three black junkies under dubious circumstances when you worked LVPD."

"Beyond that?"

"Beyond that, I know that you were looking for a man named Wendell Durfee, who had raped and murdered your wife."

"You're correct so far. Do you know what happened to Wendell Durfee?"

"He was murdered here about a year ago. It's a Central Division unsolved. I wouldn't be surprised if you told me you did it."

The drive-in was an Oreo spot on the race border. A jazz hut stood at the rear. The carhops were black *and* white—pretty girls on skates.

They sat in Wayne's rental car. The bolt-on trays cramped them and made them sit sideways.

"I did it."

"I figured you had. Is there anything you'd like me to do with the information?"

Wayne stirred his coffee. "Spread the word judiciously. You were on LAPD then. Describe your presence at the crime scene. It was brutal beyond words. The investigators made me for it, but my father had too much clout."

Marsh stirred his coffee. "What do you know about me?"

"Dwight Holly briefed me and telexed me the master file. I know about Scotty Bennett, your work with Clyde Duber and the operation to date."

"And your assessment?"

"I disapprove of the heroin aspect, but it's viable within the overall context."

"*Dramatically* viable? Like your racial baggage in plain view for the brothers to see?"

Wayne smiled. "Tell me some things. Rumors, perceptions, how you see it so far."

Marsh tried to cross his legs. The car tray stopped him. He almost looked un-cool.

"Both groups are courting me. I doubt that they can score narcotics, so that strategy may prove problematic. There's been a series of southside liquor-store robberies with attendant rumors of black-militant suspects, but nothing more substantive than that. You know about those hate cartoons. It's either the Panthers versus US or vice versa, although my more conspiracy-minded brothers think it's the FBI. Mr. Holly has assured me that it is not."

A carhop skated by and waved at Marsh. She looked like a younger Mary Beth.

Wayne said, "There's an outing tonight. Let's call it a get-acquainted party for the Tiger Kab crew. I want you there. You convince Jomo and at least one BTA man to come. There's some after-hours clubs I want to buy. I wouldn't mind stirring up some political shit with witnesses around."

That carhop skated by again. Marsh threw her a faux-lusty grin. Wayne pulled out his show pic of Reginald Hazzard. Marsh studied it and blinked.

"Have you seen him?"

"No. Who is he?"

"A young man I'm trying to find. He's seventeen in the picture, but he'd be twenty-four now."

Marsh smirked. Actor's gaffe, red flag—Wayne caught it.

"Tell me what you were thinking. Be candid, or this deal of ours won't work."

"I was wondering if you planned to kill him."

Wayne looked at the carhop. She had Mary Beth's eyes.

"I'm out of that line of work now."

"I'm glad to hear it."

"Have you ever heard of black people recently in the news getting emeralds anonymously in the mail?"

Marsh blinked and said, "No."

The painters striped a '63 Lincoln limo. The JFK Deathmobile as jungle barge. Southside L.A. as the River Styx.

The backseats faced each other. The guys sat knee-to-knee. Wayne, Marsh, Junior, Milt. Jomo and BTA armorer Leander James Jackson.

Smoked windows. Backseat stereo. Archie Bell and the Drells on six speakers. 151 rum and hash-spiked Kool filters.

The barge embarked from the Tiger Kab lot. Junior's skinny brother Roscoe X drove. Wayne stayed sober. The other guys indulged. Milt did shtick. Nixon pimps his plain-Jane daughters to cover his campaign nut. Gay Edgar Hoover craves black schlong. Junior snarfed Eskimo pies and chocolate-dipped bananas. Jomo and Leander worked up an I-hates-you glare. Marsh checked out Wayne sidelong.

They drove by LAPD rousts. Jomo rolled down his window and made pig noise. They hit the Snooty Fox. A Moms Mabley type did ridicule patter and insulted the audience. She singled out Milt and Wayne. They were ofay mud-shark motherfuckers out to muff-dive black chicks on the rag. This vampire cat beat them to it. He done cunnilingized the southside dry and be snoozin' in his coffin as we speaks.

Wayne checked out Marsh sidelong. Marsh emitted ghetto laughs convincingly. File faces popped to life. There's Benny Boles. He's a fruit. He's trolling. He's checking out Roscoe X. There's Joseph Tidwell McCarver. He's the MMLF's "Pan-African Ruler." He's with three whores. He's trading clenched-fist greetings with Jomo.

A junkie combo replaced the comic. The piano man nodded out and banged his face on the keys. The crew split. The barge dropped them at Rae's Rugburn Room. The floor show featured hooded women with dildos. Strobe lights played over insertion points. The soundtrack featured the Beatles with "All You Need Is Love."

Milt and Jomo dug it. Leander and Junior looked away. Wayne decided to buy the place. It was packed. It had money-wash potential.

Next stop: the Scorpio Lounge. A soul-food buffet and a low-stakes dice game. The croupier was a topless chick with a two-foot Afro. Afro-heads bobbed in back booths. Blow jobs went for ten dollars per.

Jomo and Leander fueled up That Glare. Marsh and Wayne watched. They exchanged little nods. They exchanged telepathic waves—Marsh, it's on you.

Let's buy the place. It's a cash cave. Mr. Clean will make that green glow.

The crew rolled to Sultan Sam's Sandbox. Wayne got a contact buzz from the hash smoke. Buy the place—easy call—it's 1:00 a.m. packed. The joint had a Far East motif. The waitresses wore turbans and see-through saris. The walls were studded with big colored stones. The green ones reminded Wayne of that emerald. It was like a dream revived.

He trolled for file faces. He snagged one close by. Ezzard Donnell Jones, BTA bossman. He was with a white woman. Wayne caught a back view. She had dark, gray-streaked hair. Perfect smoke rings dispersed above her.

The crew sat at three tables. Wayne watched Marsh cup his hands and work quick. He crumbled two Benzedrine rolls into powder. He scooped it up, table-hopped and did some buddy-buddy drapes. He dropped powder in Leander's scotch and milk. He jiggled the glass and sidled over to Jomo. Jomo worked on bourbon with a malt-liquor chaser. Marsh distracted him and powdered up both drinks.

Wayne nodded. Marsh nodded back. Wayne touched his wristwatch. Marsh flashed ten fingers.

It was 2:00 a.m. The crew was yawning. Milt mentioned food. Junior said, "I hear *that.*" The gestalt circulated: the Pines on Imperial Highway.

The chow consensus built. They booked to the barge. Milt and Junior plopped in first. Wayne and Marsh hovered. Jomo and Leander got squished in together. They bristled at the contact.

The barge pulled out. Jomo and Leander got jostled in tight. They squirmed apart. They shoulder-rolled and got themselves a few inches. Wayne and Marsh sat facing them. Milt and Junior dozed. Jomo looked sulky and blurry. Leander started to get bennie-bipped.

His mouth twitched. His hands talked. Little plucks at his trousers, little puckers and grins. He bumped Jomo. Jomo pulled away. Their feet bumped. They scuffed each other's shoes. Fucker, don't invade my space.

Jomo started to get big-eyed. Say now, what's *this*? He scratched, he stretched, he bumped Leander's foot. Wayne nudged Marsh—*that's it.*

Marsh said, "Hey, Leander. I'm not sure I buy all that Tonton and voodoo shit you've been talking. Run that by me again."

Jomo said, "That shit don't fly with me. All forms of mystical jive keep the black man enslaved. Haiti is a sissified, punk-ass place. Voodoo was invented by the French white man to keep the black man shackled up and fucking dead chickens."

Leander lit a Kool king-size. He inhaled and torched it all the way down in one breath. He exhaled through his nostrils. The whole backseat smoked up.

"Voodoo give me the power to do that. Dragon breath. Papa Doc can do that, so could half my friends on the Tonton. You think 151 is strong? You try klerin liquor. You try herbs and blowfish toxin. You want to fuck with the white man? You get a *bokur* to zombify him. *Bokur* put a spell on that Dominican fuck Trujillo. CIA hit, bullshit. You slaughter Haitian people, zombies come for you. That is the pure truth, baby boy."

Jomo lit a Kool king-size. He inhaled and coughed and dropped the cigarette in his lap. It burned his pants. He went *shitfuck* and swatted out the flame.

Leander laughed.

Leander said, "MMLF fucks dead chickens. BTA fucks beautiful black sisters."

Jomo pulled his knife. Leander pulled his knife. They both reared back for more stab room. Their arms hit. They twisted clear. They stabbed simultaneous, chest-high, full-force.

Fabric ripped. The blades cut through overcoats and suitcoats and hit blunt. Jomo's blade snapped off. Leander's blade twisted sideways. It gouged Jomo's arm and stuck in the seat back.

They both went in clawing and gouging. Leander showed his teeth and snapped at Jomo's neck. Wayne gave it two more seconds. Marsh jumped in telepathic. Milt and Junior dozed on. Roscoe X ran the barge off the road.

59

(Los Angeles, 1/26/69)

Picture spray:

Wayne Tedrow kissing a black woman. An ad-libbed FBI shot. A Vegas agent snapped it outside Wayne's hotel suite.

Photo #2: one-month-old Eleanora Sifakis. A future bomb maker in swaddle cloth. She looks like Karen—not her cashew-dick hubby.

Mr. Hoover *loved* the Wayne photo. Insane Wayne: the woman and cutout ascendance. An inter-group knife fight his first day.

Dwight kicked his chair back. The drop-front was musty. L.A. was rainy and warm. The air was thick. He was smoking more. His desk was cluttered. The Thomas Frank Narduno file was all over it.

The file was innocuous. Suspicion rousts, lefty leanings, no "Known Associates" list. Narduno—dead at the Grapevine. Narduno—the one *visible* name on Joan's KA list.

Thomas Frank Narduno: robbery suspect in New York and Ohio. No convictions, no Ohio or New York paperwork extant. Joan Klein: robbery suspect in New York and Ohio. No convictions, no Ohio or New York paperwork extant. No dates listed in Narduno's file. Ohio dates listed in Joan's file: both 1954. Also listed: two L.A. robbery rousts, '51 and '53. No DR numbers or other paperwork extant.

Dwight placed Joan's file by Narduno's file and read both files again. Nothing went *Boo!* He'd telexed every big-city and mid-city PD in New York and Ohio. He got zero on Joan Rosen Klein and Thomas Frank Narduno. Joan told him a cop beat on her in Dayton, Ohio. He'd queried Dayton PD on their unsolved heists, circa '54. There were two payroll jobs, netting sixty grand total. Masked men, no women, case closed. He'd had the file telexed. There was no mention of Narduno, Joan or left-wing suspects. Joan's "random roundups" statement? Maybe true.

Dwight lit a cigarette and cracked the window. Wind and rain messed with his pages. He propped Eleanora up on his desk lamp.

Fuck—Joan Rosen Klein and Dwight Chalfont Holly.

A month now. The Statler, the Ambassador, the Hollywood Roosevelt. Neutral spots. The drop-front was Karen's.

They talk and make love. They discuss the operation and avoid *What Do You Want?* It's informant protocol and implicit lovers' pact.

Joan was getting tight with the BTA. Marsh was BTA- *and* MMLF-friendly. They were both torqued on those cartoons flooding the Congo. Joan made the FBI for it, *BAAAAAD BROTHER*–adjunct. She was wrong. Most of the cartoons defamed the Panthers and US. Some defamed BTA and MMLF. He made it as amateur street art. It didn't play as planned provocation.

Hate.

The Dr. Fred snuff—still unsolved and stonewalled by Jack Leahy. Hate and *dope*—the jungle was "H"-dry. Marsh Bowen *dryly* credited black-power consciousness.

Wind toppled Eleanora. Dwight shut the window and put her picture back up. He missed Karen. Eleanora devoured her time. What's-His-Name was back in L.A. to assist. Karen didn't know the whole Joan story. She might sense it. He didn't feel guilty. He felt stretched. It was one more seeping compartment.

He grabbed the wastebasket and pulled out the Wayne photo. He did some DMV research and ID'd the woman last week. Mary Beth Hazzard. Wayne's West Vegas snafu. The widow of the dead preacher.

He got her DMV file. He compared her driver's license photo to the kiss shot. It was a drop-dead all-time moment. It brought him back to Joan in a rush.

"What are you thinking about?"

"A friend of mine and the woman he's with."

"Tell me about him."

"He's in The Life reluctantly. He's brilliantly skilled and competent and prone to catastrophe."

"Where is he now?"

"I don't know."

"Are you comfortable with telling me more?"

"No."

"You're usually the one asking me all the questions."

"I know, that's true."

A trade show full-booked the Statler. Doors slammed down the corridor. Loud revelry persisted.

It was raining hard. They kept the windows open for the breeze. The room heat kicked in at odd intervals. They pulled the sheets on and off.

"Leander Jackson and Jomo Clarkson had an altercation."

"I know. I picked Leander up at the hospital."

"He called you?"

"Yes."

"You're strictly BTA now."

"Not entirely."

"Tell me about it."

"I'm not going to."

"Yet?"

"Yes, yet. I need a moment to work something out. I'll let you know when it's settled."

Dwight yawned. His pill/drink quota hit him early. Joan said, "You should try to sleep."

He turned off the lights. He kicked his feet out of the sheets for some coolness. Joan tossed her hair and draped a leg over him. Her head fit snug on his shoulder. He reached around and cupped her knife scar.

Four hours, dreamless. A record these days.

Joan was gone. She never left good-bye notes—just lipstick prints. This one: on their spare pillow.

He picked up the nightstand phone. He needed room-service coffee and a line to D.C.

He heard receiver clicks. He pushed the disconnect button and got three more, faint.

Dwight smiled. Bug-and-tap skills. Her curriculum vitae expanded.

He walked to the window and looked down. The porte cochere was busy. He saw a shadow dissolve. He saw smoke rings drift above the awning.

60

(Managua, 1/28/69)

This beaner bin on a lake. Statues of notable führers. Peasants, urban spics and cops with Sten guns. Threadbare overall.

No Hughes flights in. They took La Nica Air to Xolotlán Airport. It was winter muggy. Kids swarmed the cab and hawked baseball cards. Parrots swerved and shit-bombed monuments.

Traffic was slow. Exhaust fumes were thick. The cars ran to pre-'60s belchers. Most street names noted dates: Calle 27 de Mayo to Calle 15 de Septiembre. Froggy said it all pertained to quashed revolution.

Side show, getaway, breather. Nicaragua was a no-sale deal and a sterile stopover. The D.R. was next.

One bright spot loomed. Froggy had a line on an ex–marine colonel. The guy was here now. He lived in the D.R full-time. He'd been in Santo Domingo since the '65 war. Froggy's merc network set up a meeting later.

The guy's name was Ivar Smith. He agreed to write the pro-D.R. report to Wayne and the wops. Smith called the Frogman yesterday. He said he knew four anti-Castro Cubans. They were *eeeeevil*. They'd *looooove* to do wet work out of the D.R.

The cab swerved around a peon with an oxcart. Froggy picked his nose and tossed chump change at beggars. Crutch fingered his lapel pin and re-ran some recent head tapes.

D.C., inauguration night, the Hay-Adams. There's Sam G. and Gretchen/Celia. Mesplede knows Sam. Mesplede does *not* know her. Two-second intros, *auf wiedersehen*.

He told Froggy later: *it's that thieving babe.* Froggy shrugged and said the one word: "Cuba."

A parrot zoomed down and landed on the window ledge. Crutch fed him Fritos out of the bag. He re-punched his replay button and spooled back to Christmas Eve.

Horror House, the hidey-hole, the Commie meeting ledger. The date: 12/6/62. The names: Bergeron, Narduno, *Joan.*

The Hollywood Chamber of Commerce owned the house then. Three Commies got access. He went by the Chamber and chatted up a clerk. Bum news: the house went unrented in fall/winter '62.

The parrot ate all the Fritos and squawked for more. Crutch tried to pet him. The cocksucker bit his hand and flew off.

He foot-tailed Sam and Gretchen/Celia to the Willard Hotel. They had separate suites there. He burgled Gretchen/Celia's suite the next day. He located her address book. He brought an evidence kit and dusted the cover right there. He got one Joan Rosen Klein latent.

The book pages were coded: weird letters, numbers and symbols. He Minox-photographed every page and put the book back where he found it. He took a *biiiiig* risk and told Froggy what he'd done. Froggy called a CIA pal in Virginia. A code-breaking manual should arrive in Managua this week. He checked outbound D.C. flights. Sam went back to Vegas. Celia Reyes: Santo Domingo–bound.

"Donald, your hand is bleeding."

"A parrot bit me."

"Was it red?"

"Yes."

"Then you should have killed it."

The Hotel Lido Palace was lake-close. United Fruit guys hogged the bar and talked golf and oppression. The jukebox played the Chiquita banana song non-stop. UF ran Nicaragua and deployed their Somoza-family puppets. Dissent was a persistent woe akin to parrot shit. UF had a snitch network and a police force. Their mandate: rebuff Red revolt.

Crutch and Froggy settled in and moseyed down to the bar. The waitresses wore hoop skirts and banana-bunch hairdos. Froggy said the country was on Red Alert. Commies were bug-bombing fruit fields. Puppet Man Somoza had pledged reprisals soon.

They glommed an outside booth by a koi pond. Cats perched and drooled for fish dinners. They pawed and snapped and never got close. The koi had sonar and radar.

Ivar Smith was a tall guy in golf togs. He was a gasbag right-winger fueled on pre-noon Singapore Slings. He was the D.R.'s boastmaster general and welcome wagon. He ran a security firm. It assisted Bossman Balaguer's goon squads. Balaguer craved those U.S. casinos and ached for a fat tourist trade. Yeah, I'll write that report. The D.R. is ripe fruit. *Yanqui, sí, Commie, no.* We want your biz.

Pay me. I'm the conduit. I'll grease Balaguer. The CIA contingent—all boozed-up snatch hounds. Balaguer was a subtle *fascisto.* He raped pubescent tots in private and evinced public decorum. He was anti-Trujillo that way. The D.R. boded tourist bonanza. Smith's boys and the La Banda thugs ran pesky jigs back to Haiti routinely. Balaguer had a dual agenda: circumvent due process and eugenically bleach the country three shades lighter. The casinos would attract the swells. Smith's boys and La Banda would serve as street cleaners and dump trucks.

Yeah, Haiti was close. The Massacre River formed the aptly named dividing line. Smith riffed off Haiti and voodoo. Papa Doc Duvalier raped Haiti like Trujillo raped the D.R. They called Trujillo "the Goat." He blitzkrieged Haitian settlements within the D.R. It was race shit. Pale-skinned Dominicans have Spanish roots. They hate ink-black Haitians, with their chicken-fucking religion and French affect. The Haitians have leftist allies. There's a Commie group called the 6/14 Movement. Smith and La Banda suppress it for kicks and grins.

Wooooo—six Singapore Slings and still on!

There's a small town on the north D.R.-Haiti shore. A corrupt Tonton Macoute man runs it. It's a good Cuban-ops staging point. Secluded inlets up the wazoo.

Smith segued to those *eeeeevil* Cubans. They were in Managua now. They were all stone killers. They've got a boocoo heroin CV. They conduit stolen pharmacy dope through a group of UF stockholders in Miami. There's some ex-CIA in the group. A big member: Dick Nixon's pal, Bebe Rebozo.

Bad apples. They target pharmacies owned by comsymps. They pulled jobs in Guatemala and Honduras. They're allegedly ripping off a pharmacy here tonight.

Smith faded out talk-wise. His face went rumdum red. Mesplede took over.

I want to meet the Cubans. I can get them construction-boss jobs. I have heroin credentials. I want to stage anti-Castro ops.

Smith staggered out of the bar. He pulled a banana off a waitress's head and bit in, peel and all.

.   .   .

The phone book was *en español*. Crutch pulled out the page listing *farmacias*. Managua was Podunk-size. Six drugstores, *no más*. The city was laid out grid-style. *Calles* and *avenidas* crossed. He'd never seen a pharmacy rip-off. Froggy was snoozing. Let's check out the Cubans at work.

The desk clerk gave him a street map. Downtown Managua was small and walkable quicksville. It was peon-packed. *Mamacitas* cooked meat pies on bar-b-q's built from chain links and trash cans. It was pigeon meat. Pigeons perched everywhere. Kids shot them with BB guns and tossed them in paper sacks.

Some nice trees, a lake breeze, garish-colored buildings. Jackbooted cops with barbed wire–wrapped saps.

The grid made it easy. Crutch found four pharmacies fast. They looked innocuous: bright walls, narrow aisles, white-coat spics at back counters. Big cardboard ads for Listerine and Pepsodent. No rob-me vibes.

Crutch schlepped down Calle Central to Avenida Bolívar. Little spic-lets waved dead pigeons. Crutch tossed them American dimes and watched the brawls that ensued.

Número 5: a joint with a big red cross and a jumbo Coke machine. No vibe. It was pushing 6:00, closing time—*trabajo, finito.*

Crutch turned down an alley. Eye magnet: Gonzalvo Farmacia. A quiet little place with a big, loud poster.

Diseased kids begging. Nixon with fangs. Bright red Commie slogans. *Mucho* exclamation points.

Four *cholos* across the street, in a '55 Merc. Yeah, they look *eeeevil.* Their sled looks *satanic.* Lake pipes, fender skirts, car-antenna scalps.

The *reeeeall* thing. Dark Latin hair, rawhide-cured, stitching on the skin flaps.

Crutch cut back to the main drag. He reconnoitered and found a walk path behind the building row. Four down to the pharmacy, maybe a side window loose.

He got low and crouch-walked. He hit the rear of the pharmacy and peeped windows. The back ones were barred. He saw the dope shelves and three pharmacists working. The side windows were un-barred. One was air-cracked. A big cardboard sign on an easel covered it.

Crawl space, hiding place.

Crutch cracked the window two more inches and vaulted in. His knees banged the sign. He grabbed the easel part and kept it upright.

He peered around it. The sign was for Noxzema skin cream. A good-looking chiquita salved her bare arms and went ooh-la-la. A boss type shooed out two customers. The three pharmacists stood at the counter and tallied receipts.

Prime view. There's the clock, it's 5:58, the four *bandidos* walk in.

The boss type looks pissed. The guys fan out. One guy scopes the Bryl-creem, three guys walk to the rear. The boss type turns his back and tidies the candy shelf. The Brylcreem guy pulls a silencered revolver and walks straight up. The boss type turns around and goes "Oh." The Bryl-creem guy sticks the barrel in his mouth and blows off the top of his head. Silencer thud, brain and skull spray. No crash—the boss type just slides down the shelf row and dies.

The pharmacists keep working. One guy walks up with Ipana tooth-paste. One guy walks up with Clearasil. One guy walks up with Vick's VapoRub. The pharmacists catch the drift. One man starts weeping. One man clutches his saint's medal. One man tries to run.

The Ipana guy pulled his piece and shot them all twice. They fell in a clump. Their shrieks and gurgles got jumbled up. The Clearasil guy jumped the counter and made for the heavy-dope vault.

Blood dripped off a shelf of asthma products. The VapoRub guy dipped his finger in. He found a white wall space. He wrote *"MATAR TODOS PUTOS ROJOS."*

Crutch walked back to the Lido Palace. Wobble legs got him there. The heist guys were in and out quick. He left his hiding spot shaky and sob-bing. He stole a Coke and some Bromo and chugged it to keep his bile down. He wobble-walked to the bar, had three scotches and weaved up to his room.

Someone had placed a brown-wrapped box on the bed. The postmark was Langley, Virginia. He unwrapped it. Froggy delivered—here's the code-breaking book.

He got out his pix of Gretchen/Celia's address book. He arrayed them on the desk. He skimmed the codebook and turned to the table of con-tents. He saw a "Symbol Index" listed. He turned to it. Lots of fucking sym-bols, alphabetically described. The geographic and political distinction in bracketed text.

Crutch scanned his Minox pix. Gretchen/Celia's symbols: stick fig-ures circled with X marks and artful slashing backgrounds. He skimmed the codebook. No numbers or letters corresponded to Gretchen/Celia's numbers and letters. He went back to the "Symbol Index" and started at A.

He hit the H listings. He saw "Hexes" and "Haitian Voodoo." He saw numbers linked to drawings linked to letters. A few of the numbers and letters matched Gretchen/Celia's shit. He saw variants of her stick figures and *X* marks. He read the text: "The voodoo priest's depiction of spiritual chaos while a subject/victim is hexed."

Horror House, last summer. The markings there, the symbols here, the derivation expressed.

Call it: Gretchen/Celia's pages were a paper curse and a voodoo book of the dead.

DOCUMENT INSERT: 1/29/69–2/8/69. Extract from the journal of
Marshall E. Bowen.

Los Angeles

It was a minor knife fight with major political implications for
two extremely minor political groups. But, I facilitated it and it
occurred on Wayne Tedrow's first day as my cutout.

Jomo suffered minor lacerations and Leander received chest
bruises when Jomo's knife blade snapped off. Wayne got Jomo to
Daniel Freeman Hospital; he was stitched up and released within a
few hours. I got Leander to Morningside Hospital. He confounded
the doctors by swallowing several Haitian herb pills in the emergency room. The placebos calmed him down somewhat. Jomo is
MMLF; Leander is BTA. Which way do I jump? My personal
dilemma, certainly. As always, I abut that maddening disjuncture:
the viable construction of black identity and the dubious construction of revolution, as implemented by criminal scum seeking to
cash in on legitimate social grievance and cultural trend.

I now sense this: Mr. Holly knew I would succeed as his infiltrator because I am too smart to accede to the rhetoric of revolution
and too hip to buy the simpleminded reactionary response. Mr.
Holly understands that ambivalence shapes performance and that
actors are, in the end, self-centered and solely concerned with
their performing context. He'll let me walk a thin ideological line
and actually risk a black-militant conversion, because he knows
how selfishly motivated I am. Brilliant Mr. Holly. A nonpareil
talent scout with a superb eye for acting ensembles. Casting
Wayne Tedrow as my cutout plays to my strengths and Wayne's
strengths and has paid off immediately. An ex-cop with enormous
racial baggage is overseeing Tiger Kab; the brothers think he's
rogue and rather dig him. And nobody suspects that he's FBI-
adjunct.

Both men are pressuring me: Wayne wants me to align myself
unilaterally with either the BTA or the MMLF; Mr. Holly wants me
to somehow facilitate the dope-pushing arm of OPERATION
BAAAAAD BROTHER, an aspect of my duties that Wayne disap-
proves of with almost Calvinistic fervor. Heroin is scarce around
here; I credit some form of black consciousness for its relative

scarcity, if not black militancy itself. Thus, I cannot rat out BTA or MMLF members for the procurement or sale of it anytime soon. There have been more southside liquor-store robberies, replete with rumors of black-militant suspects, but my subtle queries on that topic have yet to turn up names. I'm hoping the Jomo-Leander fracas will fester among the BTA/MMLF leadership and produce some exploitable discontent. In the meantime, I'm making the scene.

I have party-crashed a mélange of political poseurs. They are recreating a dank form of New York café society, circa 1930. El Morocco, the Stork Club and '21' then; Sultan Sam's Sandbox, the Scorpio Lounge and Rae's Rugburn Room now. The skin tone has darkened, the fashions have changed, the cultural bar has been vulgarized and revitalized. These people love to see and be seen. Ezzard Donnell Jones, Joan Klein, Benny Boles, Joe McCarver and Claude Torrance club-hop most evenings. I always rate a "Right on" or "Hey, brother," because I am a celebrity, martyr and prized commodity in one package. They sense that I want to be one of them, and I think they see my lack of one-group allegiance as a sign of coyness and of understandable reluctance. *We gots to let the brother choose. Sheeeeit, brother was a motherfuckin' pig just a few months ago.*

There has been an unsettling barrage of hate cartoons flooding the southside for the past several weeks. The chief targets have been the Panthers and US, along with street-art salvos directed at BTA and MMLF. My cartoonist and hate-tract writing friend Jomo ridicules the artistry and has convinced me it did not spring from his hand—"Not my style, brother. This is Mr. Hoover's work for goddamn sure." Mr. Holly disputes that—convincingly—because he's given to blunt confirmations or denials, sees me as a brother cop on his side and would not try to disingenuously assert that the Bureau is above such tactics. Dwight Chalfont Holly, social realist, a man who calls a spade a spade and sometimes a spook, shine, dinge, coon, jungle bunny or smoke. The master of the mixed message. A critic of the LAPD's vilely abusive conduct on the southside. A man who sadly admits that suppression never works, expresses a rather haunted respect for Martin Luther King and enjoys making me the straight man in impromptu *Amos 'n Andy* routines. I despise the hackneyed expression "a piece of work," but that is Mr. Holly defined. The same phrase applies to his tortured aide-de-camp and quasi–kid brother, Wayne Tedrow—perhaps even more so. How odd that Wayne is the true killer of the two; how odd that he seems to be much less driven by racial animus and appears to be more capable of sustaining equitable relationships with blacks. I like Wayne; I've enjoyed the several cutout/operatee meetings that we've had. I've spread the word on how he killed the three black junkies and psycho rapist Wendell Durfee. Of course, the brothers *loved* it. Wayne has become the stuff of ambiguous ghetto lore already. Ooooh, that Wayne T.—he *baaaaad.*

And something else.

I arrived early for one of our meetings. Wayne was caught unprepared. I saw him looking at a photograph of a black woman. Wayne was quite obviously embarrassed. He put the photo down and gave me a look that brusquely stated *Don't Ask.* I didn't ask Wayne; I asked Mr. Holly, who replied, "Wayne goes deep with you dark motherfuckers," and cut the topic off there.

I did some Las Vegas newspaper research and identified the woman as a union steward named Mary Beth Hazzard. She's a decade older than Wayne and is the mother of a long-missing son named Reginald. Reginald Hazzard is the young man in the photograph that Wayne showed me on the day we met; Wayne has been showing the photograph to almost everyone he encounters on the southside and seems determined to find the young man, come hell or high water. My newspaper research also revealed this: a West Las Vegas dope addict killed Mrs. Hazzard's minister husband last year, then killed himself. Astonishingly, the dope addict was posthumously indicted for the murder of Wayne's father in June of '68. More astonishingly: the Vegas rumor is that Wayne and his late stepmother/lover killed Wayne Senior themselves.

Wayne and Mr. Holly absorb me on several levels. They are not rogue cops à la Scotty Bennett—they are rogue authoritarians. And Wayne miraculously entered my life just as all my subtle queries on the armored-car heist had panned out fruitlessly and I found myself once again at the start-over point. In that moment, I meet Wayne. He casually asks me if I've heard stories of black folks receiving emeralds anonymously. He shows me a photograph of the young black man he's looking for. The young man vaguely resembles the burned-faced man I met on 2/24/64. I feel like I'm entering a serendipitous dream state. What does all of this mean?

DOCUMENT INSERT: 2/11/69. Verbatim FBI telephone call transcript. Marked: <u>"Recorded at the Director's Request"</u>/<u>"Classified</u>

Confidential 1-A: Director's Eyes Only." Speaking: Director Hoover, Special Agent Dwight C. Holly.

JEH: Good morning, Dwight.

DH: Good morning, Sir.

JEH: Wayne Tedrow and the sullen Negress Mary Beth Hazzard. I would be remiss in not expressing my horror and delight.

DH: Yes, Sir.

JEH: Guilt assumes many forms. Mrs. Hazzard is not a comely Negress in the Lena Horne mode. She is undoubtedly given to phrases like "power to the people" and predisposed to the music of Archie Bell and the Drells.

DH: Yes, Sir.

JEH: You are being deliberately obtuse this morning, Dwight. You went through a spell like that when I deported Emma Goldman in 1919.

DH: Yes, Sir.

JEH: Sirhan Sirhan is on trial and the formal James Earl Ray proceedings should begin in April. Would you say the Bureau is covered there?

DH: Yes, Sir.

JEH: And the Dr. Fred Hiltz homicide?

DH: Again, Sir. We're covered. Jack Leahy has the case buried.

JEH: Jack Leahy is the Alger Hiss to my HUAC and the Costello to my Abbott. He is a traitor and an unfunny nightclub comedian who has ridiculed my penchant for antiques.

DH: Yes, Sir. No one has ever quite figured Jack out.

JEH: He was your partner in '23. You worked the Milwaukee Office with him.

DH: Yes, Sir. I remember.

JEH: I'm appalled by those hate cartoons circulating in South Los Angeles. I want you to determine their origin immediately and send me copies of all such works of filth extant.

DH: I'll get on it, Sir.

JEH: Wayne Tedrow as Marshall Bowen's cutout. Do you still defend the choice?

DH: Vehemently, Sir.

JEH: Why, pray tell? Because the dusky widow of the preacher he killed has imbued young Wayne with a surfeit of soul?

DH: Yes, Sir. In part.

JEH: And our Congolese cuties the BTA and MMLF? Will they cooperate with our agenda and push heroin sooner or later?

DH: I think they will, Sir.

JEH: And the infant daughter of informant 4361?

DH: Lively and healthy, Sir.

JEH: And your newer informant/inamorata?

DH: She's in my thoughts, Sir.

JEH: As you are in mine, Dwight.

DH: Thank you, Sir.

JEH: Good day, Dwight.

DH: Good day, Sir.

DOCUMENT INSERT: 2/13/69. Pouch communiqué. To: Wayne Tedrow. From: Colonel Ivar S. Smith, USMC (Retired). President, ISS Security Limited, Santo Domingo, Dominican Republic. Marked: "Hand Pouch Deliver Only"/"Destroy Upon Reading."

Dear Mr. Tedrow,

This letter follows up your colleague Jean-Philippe Mesplede's recent trip to the D.R. to view casino-site locations and to discuss the possibility of building said hotel-casinos in this country. I am pleased to tell you that President Joaquín Balaguer is very anxious to have your businesses here and has pledged considerable resources in an effort to convince you to come. A brief history will give you a sense of the D.R. and our island neighbor Haiti and will, above all, convince you that this is a safe place for American tourists and your overseers and their hotel-casino personnel.

The D.R. comprises the eastern two-thirds of the island of Hispaniola, and Santo Domingo, discovered by Columbus in 1492, is considered to be the oldest city in the Western world. Innumerable coups involving Spain, France and Holland led to the current Dominican secession from Spain; numerous battles between indigenous Negroes and the French resulted in independence for Haiti. Relations have remained strained between the D.R. and Haiti; this stands as the case today. Haiti, however, exists in a state of dire poverty, while the D.R. is developing into the very model of a safe and sane, pro-U.S., anti-Communist republic. The Haitian border is heavily patrolled by Dominican forces, assisted by agents of President Balaguer's personal intelligence unit La Banda, in collaboration with my security firm. Informant networks have been recruited by the above agencies; the Haitian population of the D.R. and illegal Haitian immigration into the D.R. has been well interdicted and suppressed. The Haitians are a primitive race of people, heavily reliant on their practice of voodoo and made tractable by their addictive use of klerin liquor and mind-altering herbs. The president of Haiti, François "Papa Doc" Duvalier, came to power as a voodoo proponent and keeps his people suppressed by allowing voodoo to flourish. His private police force, the Tonton Macoute, are recruited from voodoo societies and enforce voodoo as President Duvalier's chief means to retain the societal status quo and keep himself in power. Under Dominican President Trujillo's rule (1930–1961), there were several Dominican army slaughters of unruly Haitian émigrés; on June 14, 1959, a Castroite group called the 6/14 Movement staged a failed invasion of the D.R.'s shores. The brief 1965 Civil War was, in fact, a farce, sternly resolved when President Johnson sent in a marine contingent to restore order to a nation seeking to establish free elections. A leftist named Juan Bosch was fraudulently elected and held power briefly. A truly free election was held in 1966. Bosch was deposed and pro-U.S. President Balaguer was honorably elected. The last official marine unit withdrew from the D.R. on 8/19/68.

President Balaguer is no flamboyant Rafael Trujillo, but President Balaguer knows how to keep dissent at a low roar and understands the importance of maintaining a tidy nation that American and European tourists will want to visit. He is on superbly good terms with the military, should crack-downs or clean-ups of Haitians or left-wing insurgents be required. And President Balaguer is willing to proactively invest in your hotel-casino foray by pledging land free of charge for casino sites in Santo Domingo proper and outside of it (see addendum report for structural studies and soil-composition studies). He will grant Hughes Air the exclusive flight rights to reserved VIP landing strips at the Santo Domingo Airport, will build extra runways for the increased air travel free of charge and will supply un-skilled Haitian and Dominican peasant workers for the casino build. A construction company that he is part owner of will supply building materials at a reduced cost and my security firm and La Banda stand ready to provide 24-hour security for the building sites. I am recommending four Cuban men—WILTON MORALES, FELIPE GÓMEZ-SLOAN, CHIC CANESTEL and CRUZ SALDÍVAR—as casino-site work bosses. They are Cuban mercenaries, Spanish- and English-fluent, and have pre-existing work relationships with the operatives in my security firm and the agents in La Banda. Again, I will stress: the threat of revolt or the shenanigans of left-wing gadfly groups will pose no threat to the casino build, and the presence of unruly

Haitian émigrés and Dominican peasants will be curtailed before it
can reach the point where it might upset visiting tourists. As of
this writing, President Balaguer is preparing an addendum incentive package as his way to say *"¡Bienvenidos!"* to you and your
investors' group.

In summation, I can only state that you and your people would
be well advised to say *"¡Sí!"* to our proposal. You will be welcomed
to a country with a stable political climate, a solid economy and a
leadership anxious to lend a helping hand.

Sincerely,

Ivar S. Smith, USMC (Retired)

61

The Clark County Sheriff's sent more paperwork. Wayne went through the folder and pinned documents to the wall.

Interview notes—LVPD file repeats. Repeat dispo reports, smudged file carbons.

The file alcove was overpacked—let's move chem bins for more shelf space. Stop, here's something—

Wayne pinned it up. A parking ticket, 11/29/63. Fire-hydrant obstruction. 2082 Monroe Street, North Vegas. Reginald Hazzard got tagged the week before he disappeared.

It was tri-racial turf. Nellis AFB decreed that. The commercial strip was all slot joints and one-buck buffets. They were one-race-only deals. Whites had the Shamrock, blacks had Monty's Mosque, the Mexicans had Al's Alamo.

The residential streets were mixed and cut through diagonally. Wayne parked on Monroe and went walking. He'd read Ivar Smith's report and summarized it for the Boys. The soil and structural stats were superb. Balaguer wanted their biz. He was *paying* them to come and build. The Boys said let's go. Wayne called Smith in Santo Domingo. Smith said Balaguer wanted fifty grand a month personal. Wayne said okay. The Boys said okay. Wayne proposed a hands-off chit from Dick Nixon. Farlan Brown said we need a phone-chat liaison. Wayne's candidate: Dwight Holly.

The prez was a cop buff and an FBI washout. He loved to schmooze with tough-guy Feds. Dwight "the Enforcer"?—none better.

The houses were all ant-sized and eroded cinder block. Windows were foil-crimped to beat the heat. Wayne started at 2082 and knock-knocked. It was 4:10 p.m. He got tri-racial residents off shift at Nellis. He smiled, he said hello, he showed Reginald's picture. He got four no answers and fourteen straight nos.

He kept walking. A North Vegas PD car cruised by. A cop recognized him and went Pow!

He got three more no answers and nine more nos. He walked by a house with an open garage adjacent. He saw a black man vat-boiling on a hot plate. He smelled tropical plants and ammonia base.

The man waved to him. Wayne walked up. The vat fumes knocked him back. The man laughed and laughed.

They shook hands. The man squeezed words out between chuckles. He had a French island lilt. Wayne scoped the garage. It was *his* lab unkempt—cheap gear and tape-marked bottles.

Urera baccifera. Diodon holacantheus. Crapaud blanc. Theraphosidae E., *Anolis colestinus, Zanthroxyllum matinicense.*

Spiny plant powders, topical irritants, ground tarantulas, lizards and toads.

The man smiled. Wayne said, "Tetrodoxin posioning."

The man bowed. "You are a chemist?"

"Yes."

"Have you other things to tell me?"

Wayne scanned labels. *Tremblador, Desmembres,* puffer fish, stinging nettle. *Diffenbachia seguine*—a prime spiny plant.

"I hope you're using these compounds for a beneficial purpose."

"Oh yes. If eliminating an infestation of rabid gophers in my backyard can be considered that."

Wayne smiled. "Then my best advice is to add more ammonia and cook the powder into an emulsion paste."

The man grabbed a pen and wrote French on a scratch pad. Wayne ID'd scents: alkalines mixed with herb residue.

He pulled out his show picture. The man put on glasses and bent down a gooseneck lamp.

"Yes, I have met this young man."

"When?"

"I vividly recall it. It was right after the president was shot."

"And the circumstances?"

The man dabbed ointment on a finger cut. The skin puckered and closed in an instant. Wayne smelled caustic hydroxide and something all new. The effect stunned him flat.

"He was a pleasant young man and a knowledgeable amateur chemist. He had heard of me. He was curious about the anesthetic qualities of Haitian herbs, particularly their pain-killing and flame-retardant potential."

62

(Los Angeles, 2/18/69)

Emma Goldman, Moscow, Archie Bell and the Drells. Clogged veins abet Looney Tunes.

The old girl was gonesville. How long could he last? How much shitwork could he assign?

Race shit abets hate shit. Dr. King had a dream. Mr. Hoover had a comic-book jones.

Hate cartoons and hate sonnets. "This little piggie went to market. This little piggie stayed home. This little piggie got offed by a Panther, after he sucked his big bone."

Dwight drove print shop to print shop. He worked off a phone-book list. A pro printed this shit. It was print-shop quality.

It was raining. He'd hit sixteen print shops. He displayed his hate shit and ruined moods en masse. His badge and nerves induced freakouts. Numbnuts clerks flashed the peace sign.

Mr. Hoover dug the peace sign. It was the "footprint of the American chicken."

Dwight drove northeast. He was five hours in. The southside and the Miracle Mile were kaput. Hollywood was next.

He hit a print shop on Fountain and a print shop on Cahuenga. He played his police radio between stops. The LAPD band hopped. A Stop the War march downtown. A fruit-picker march in Boyle Heights. Lots of monkeyshines due south.

He got "No" and "No, sir." He headed east. He hit a print shop on Vine and a print shop on Wilton. A zit-faced kid yukked at the hate shit. A hippie chick went, "Om."

He hit a print shop on Vermont. He smelled maryjane and incense. Two counter kids weaved and goof-grinned. They saw him and grokked his occupation. A joint passed girl to boy. The boy ate the roach.

Dwight flashed his hate spray. The boy said, "So? It's not illegal." The girl tee-heed.

They perused the shit. Dwight spread it out for a better look-see. The girl focused on the heavy-hung buck. The boy said, "It's a free country."

"Did you print this material?"

"Yeah, sure. It's a free country."

The girl tee-heed. "Well, sort of."

"Who brought it in? What did they look like? Who picked it up? How did they pay and/or where was it sent?"

The girl said, "This is censorship." The boy said, "It's a free country."

Dwight walked to the door, threw the bolt and walked back to the counter. The girl chewed her lip. Dwight flexed his hands.

The boy wilted. "It was a cash sale and a delivery to a place in Eagle Rock. This woman, strong-looking, you know, like a ball-buster chick you don't want no part of."

Dwight smiled. "Early forties, dark, gray-streaked hair, glasses. A knife scar on one arm."

The kids slack-jawed him. Dwight said, "Tell me her name." The girl said, "Joan."

The neighborhood was hilly and semi-low-rent. You got some big vistas and snaked freeway views. White stiffs and beaners co-existed. WALLACE FOR PRESIDENT bumper stickers and taco wagons chopped low.

The address was a bungalow court with a mottled paint job. Some hun-yuck had raped white stucco for a tie-dye effect. Eight apartments with built-in mail slots. Snooze-quiet at 3:00 p.m.

Dwight rang the door buzzer. It was wake-the-dead shrill. He put his ear to the hinge crack and heard empty-room air. He waited thirty sec-onds and wedged his pocket shim in the lock jamb. The door popped easy.

Too easy, un-Joan.

He walked in and chain-locked the door. He turned on the ceiling light and got the whole pad in a glance. A living room–bedroom, a bathroom-kitchenette. A pop-up wall bed unfolded.

A runner's roost—not a safe house. A short-term place—a fugitive's stopgap.

Dwight walked through. He knew he'd find canned goods in the kitchen. He knew he'd find cheapo toilet gear in the can. He knew he'd find clothes he'd never seen her in. He saved the dresser for last.

Faded jeans, boots, summer dresses styled to offset her bare arms.

He touched everything. He'd black-bagged Karen's place a dozen times. He never touched her softer things.

Dwight sat on the bed. Two pillows were placed against the railing. The rain kicked up again. The roof leaked a few feet from him. He tossed the pillows. Of course: a Magnum and a diary underneath.

The gun had rubber-band grips. They were non-print-sustaining and steadied your aim. The diary was black leather and almost weightless. That implied new pages.

He opened it. A Polaroid snapshot fell out. It was him, sleeping. The backdrop was their Statler room. He was curled toward Joan's side of the bed.

He put the photo down. His hand trembled. He gripped it calm again on the bedrail. He pulled the one page out. It was handwritten—Joan Rosen Klein's slashing block print.

WE ARE DETERMINED TO ACHIEVE THE SAME RESULTS AND ARE DRIVEN BY A NEAR-IDENTICAL UTILITY. OUR SHARED GOAL IS TO PERPETRATE A CONTAINABLE CHAOS. DWIGHT IS COMMITTED TO FURTHERING THE FBI'S SHORT-TERM ENDS. I WANT TO CREATE THE ILLUSION THAT THE OPERATION HAS REACHED ITS LOGICAL AND SUCCESSFUL POINT OF TERMINATION. DWIGHT BELIEVES THAT THIS CONCLUSION WILL DERAIL THE BLACK-NATIONALIST MOVEMENT. I BELIEVE THAT THE BLACK-NATIONALIST MOVEMENT WILL BE ONLY MOMENTARILY DISCREDITED. DWIGHT WILL HAVE DONE HIS JOB AND WILL HAVE SEEN HIS ASSIGNMENT THROUGH TO A COSMETICALLY VOUCHED END. THE REBUTTAL TO THAT NON-END WILL BE A CONTINUOUS AND CONTINUOUSLY GROWING LEVEL OF DISBELIEF, MORAL HORROR AND UNOFFICIAL CENSURE THAT WILL LEAD IN TIME TO AN AS-YET-UNIMAGINABLE PLANE OF LIBERATION. THE FBI WANTS THE BTA AND MMFL TO MOVE HEROIN. THEY BELIEVE THAT IT WILL EXPOSE BLACK NATIONALISM AS INHERENTLY CRIMINAL AND REVEAL BLACK PEOPLE AT LARGE TO BE INHERENTLY DEPRAVED. THE FBI'S SHORT-TERM GOAL IS A SEDATED BLACK POPULACE; ITS LONG-TERM GOAL IS THE PERPETUATION OF RACIAL SERVITUDE. I WANT THE BTA AND MMFL TO MOVE HEROIN. I WILL RISK THE SHORT-TERM PROBABILITY OF SQUALOR IN FERVENT HOPE THAT THE SUSTAINED DEPRAVITY OF HEROIN WILL LEAD TO A RICH EXPRESSION OF RACIAL IDENTITY AND ULTIMATELY TO POLITICAL REVELATION AND REVOLT. IN THAT SENSE, I SEE HONOR, HOPE AND BEAUTY

WHERE DWIGHT DOES NOT. OUR GOALS ARE BOTH INIMICAL AND FULLY SYNCHRONOUS. WE DIVERGE AND COHERE IN EQUAL MEASURE. WE ARE DEVOUT UNION AND MISALLIANCE. I HAVE BEGUN A POWERFUL PATH WITH A RACIST PROVOCATEUR WHO HAS GIVEN ME SOMETHING UNFATHOMABLE AND PRECIOUS. I WILL PUT MY GOALS ABOVE HIS AT ALL TIMES AND WILL CONCEDE THAT I CANNOT FORESEE THE SPECIFIC DETAILS OF OUR JOURNEY.

A gust hit the window screen. The pages blew out of his hand. The word *comrade* roared through his head.

63

(Santo Domingo, 2/26/69)

Drac flew them down. El Jefe sent a stretch. The runways were fresh-poured blacktop. Peons toiled up through the landing.

Aeropuerto de las Américas—strictly bush league. *Bienvenidos:* cardboard cutouts of Joaquin Balaguer beside the customs hut.

Crutch and Froggy de-planed. It was smack-your-head hot. Two Policía Nacional cops lugged their luggage to the limo. Four Harleys rumbled over. The stretch was '56-vintage. The choppers pre-dated it. The cops wore puffed jodhpurs and stormtrooper boots. The D.R., Take 1: We're low-rent, but we try. Don't fuck with us. We'll kill you or suck up to you, according to whim.

The escort pulled out. The backseat was pre-cooled. Flags snapped off giant whip antennas. Crosses, ribbons, *"Dios Patria Libertad."* Canned cocktails poked out of an ice chest. Crutch and Froggy popped daiquiris and worked up a buzz. Balaguer was throwing a lunch bash in their honor. The Presidential Palace, upcoming.

Crutch looked out his window. Some fucking island. The beach was no beach. Bare rocks dropped off at the surf line. The Malecón was a down-market palisades. The bluffs were rocky and brown-grassed. The boulevard was half pavement, half gravel. Froggy said, "We are needed here. We will further our personal agenda and revitalize the economy."

Slums. Lots of spooks and spook-spic hybrids. Tin-roof buildings: ancient and cracker box–new. Boing-your-eyes paint jobs: hot pink, lime green, canary yellow.

They de-limo'd at the El Embajador. It was a cut-rate Fontainebleau upside a cut-rate Miami. A polo field adjoined it. Light-toned beaners rode white horses and banged around white balls. Light-toned women scoped the action from golf carts. They wore summer dresses and slathered on suntan oil.

Hotel slaves fawned and whooshed them up to their rooms. They were full bar– and goody basket–equipped. Crutch had a view: pastel pads, sludgy rivers, dilapidation. Statues and droopy power lines.

Pinch me—I'm here.

He changed into a seersucker suit. He was going for that Ivy League/white kahuna effect. He walked back down. Mesplede was black-suit spiffy. Ivar Smith met them in the lobby. He was slurping a liquor-laced sno-cone. It smelled like crème de menthe.

They re-limo'd and took off. Crutch and Mesplede switched to canned martinis. The streets were narrow and ground down to soil. Foot traffic was two-thirds light spic and mulatto. The real darkies had a voodoo vibe. Crutch re-spun his head tape to Managua.

That codebook, that address book, the voodoo symbols crisscrossed. Twenty-odd days of code work. No make on Gretchen/Celia's numbers and letters.

Tin-roof shantytowns and heat-wilted lowlifes. *Calles* and *avenidas* named for sugarcane kings. Streets named for dates, à la Managua.

Mucho vacant lots. Potential casino sites all. Two on Avenida Máximo Gómez, two on Calle 27 de Febrero. The escort was an onslaught of muscle. The choppers were un-mufflered. Their motors revved loud.

Smith said, "I'm lining up the work crews. They'll sleep in tents on the sites and work twelve-hour shifts. The Cubans will meet you at the hotel tonight. They want to drive up to the north shore and look at staging points for your other business."

They cut down Avenida San Carlos. The street was full-paved. The Palacio Nacional loomed. It was high-domed and built from roseate marble. It was a mini–White House, peach ice cream–colored.

Some ragtag kids loitered across the street. They held placards topped with red flags. They were mostly spook-spic crossbreeds, à la Harry Belafonte.

The palace gates opened. The limo braked and slowed. Smith cracked his window and pointed. It unleashed a rout.

There's a parked van near the kids. On cue—four hard boys roll out. They're all light-skinners. They've got piano-wire saps.

They charged. The kids ran. They caught them and trampled them and truncheoned their legs raw. The kids were too wire-whipped and bloody to stand up. They knee-walked and crawled to an alleyway. It took ten seconds tops.

Smith slurped his sno-cone. "The good guys are La Banda. They're

Jefe's personal guys who work with my guys. The bad guys are 6/14. They have yet to figure out that dissent comes with a price."

El Jefe was a midget. He ran five-one maximum. He *mi casa es su casa*'d them with no sincerity.

Balaguer knew their names in advance. He called them Señor Mesplede and Señor Crutchfield. He sent his regards to Señor Tedrow and his investors' group. He did not say "the Boys," "the mob," "the Outfit." Smith called Balaguer "Jefe." Balaguer *scaaaared* him. Jefe sniffed his breath and smirked. Smith popped Clorets on the sly.

A palace tour followed. Smith slipped a Jefe stooge a satchel. Crutch knew the contents: fifty G's U.S. The tour was all statues and jingoist oils. Recent Führer Trujillo was omitted. Froggy was in on the Trujillo hit. The Midget was clueless. Crutch dug on that.

Lunch was seafood salad and paella. Three light-skinned women and the local CIA boss showed up. The chiquitas were courtesans brought in to un-stag things. Crutch sat down in eyeball range. The CIA guy and the Midget flanked him.

He kept it zipped and peeped cleavage. Mesplede amused the women with his pit-bull tattoos. The CIA guy's name was Terry Brundage. He boozed and talked at Ivar Smith's gasbag pace. He was a kidder. He joked at Mesplede's expense. Your buddy wants to buy a PT boat. Did he serve with JFK? Has he ever been to Dallas? You're not dope-peddlers and anti-Castro brigands, are you?

Crutch kept it zipped. The term *open secret* bonked him. A woman nailed his peeper act. She waved her napkin—shoo, you.

The Midget bloviated in English. He announced his spiels with little coughs that amounted to *ACHTUNG!* He talked up his Rural Development Plan. He told a joke about Papa Doc Duvalier and a chicken. He extolled his Urban Development Plan. Let's build some pre-fab shacks to house the poor and lower the crime rate. Let's build high rises to shield them from view.

Dessert was rainbow sorbet. The Midget spoke straight at Crutch.

"What is the intended meaning of your lapel pin?"

"I've killed fifteen Cuban Communists, sir."

The Midget weaved a hand—*comme ci, comme ça*. Crutch froze with his spoon raised. Sorbet dripped on his suit.

"There is a term for young men like you, Mr. Crutchfield. It is *pariguayo*. The literal meaning is 'party-watcher.' It derives from the time the United States Marines interdicted the spread of communism in my country. It describes the young marines' reluctance to ask our girls to dance."

THE EYE.

He hears "Scalp them." He can't do it. He's hurled in the sand. The dead man's face is powder-burned. A skin flap is loose. His knife slips into the eye socket. His grip falters. The blade severs the eyeball. He shuts *his* eyes. He can't look. A two-handed thrust cracks ocular bones. He puts a foot on the dead man's neck and steadies his work plane. His knife blade is serrated. He saws through to the scalp flap. Foot pressure forces blood from a neck wound. It soaks his boots. He's a pump station now. The scalp removal takes ten minutes. Foot pressure re-routes the blood through the nostrils, eye sockets and ears.

Then crackle sounds and smoke and—

That's wrong. I always get the scalp and wave it. Froggy always applauds me.

Crutch woke up. He was steam-room wet. Smoke poured from the air conditioner. He grabbed a soda siphon and spritzed out the fire. Sparks crackled and fizzed. The smoke dissipated and left a muck residue.

The room was broiling. He opened the windows and let air in. He stripped the bed and soaked the sheets in cold bathtub water. He rigged a wall-to-wall clothesline with some mason's cord from his suitcase. He hung the sheets up and turned on a desk fan. It created a cool breeze.

The Eye, The Dream. His sixth or seventh re-run.

He got out his codebook and work sheets. He got out Gretchen/Celia's address book. He started counting letters, numbers and the spaces between assumed words. A month's work. Substitution code. The letters *K* and *S* identified. Gobbledygook. No make on full-length words.

Crutch studied and drew theoretical lines. The sheets puffed. The fan rearranged grit in the air.

The phone rang. Crutch picked up. Mesplede said, "The Cubans are here."

Partners now—the drugstore killers.

The Brylcreem guy was Wilton Morales. The Ipana guy was Chic Canestel. The Clearasil guy—Cruz Saldívar. Vick's VapoRub—Felipe Gómez-Sloan.

Everybody swapped handshakes and backslaps. The guys looked similar and blurred into one spic. Four mid-sized men. All fortyish, all fit. All bulged up from concealed weaponry.

It was 8:00. The mandate was night ride. Mesplede mentioned coffee. Canestel proposed speed.

Saldívar pulled out six vials. Morales said they'd clouted a Rexall in Miami. Look: Mollencroft liquid methedrine, a potion for narcolepsy.

They fueled up in the parking lot. The dope was acidic. Pepsi chasers kept it down. Gómez-Sloan had a '62 Impala. It had Jeep tires and an off-road transaxle. They piled in and drove north.

They hit the Autopista Duarte. It was two lanes, undivided. The city dissolved into scrubland and cane fields fast. Darkies cut cane under arc lights. Pale-skinned guys on horseback bossed them around. The lights made whole rural sweeps glow.

Signs announced the Plaine du Massacre. The river divided the D.R. and Haiti in the northwest. "Massacre" meant more than carnage in pure French. Froggy dug the irony. Trujillo massacred boocoo Haitians up to '60.

The meth hit home. Crutch went head-to-toe orgasmic. It hit the other guys. They talked blue streaks verging on purple. It was all French and Spanish. Crutch tuned it out and brain-screened womens' faces. Closed loop: Dana Lund, Gretchen/Celia, Joan.

There was no other traffic. It was jungle-dark. Gómez-Sloan ran his brights full-time. The terrain shifted. They went up over hills. Mountain ranges hemmed them in—the Cordillera Central and the Cordillera Oriental. They climbed steady and strong. The Chevy had a giant tank full of high-test gas. They cut through towns: Bonao, Abajo, Jarabacoa. They saw scroungers combing garbage dumps. They were all black. Mesplede called them "Haitian arrivisites." They had voodoo amulets around their necks. One guy wore a bird-wing headdress. One guy had a blood-painted face. Froggy switched to English and laid out his Trujillo hit tale.

It was early '61. The Goat was drinking at the Red Trough and nipping at Russia's Red Tit. JFK said enough. Likewise the Dominican army boss and the D.R. gentry. Terry Brundage hired the crew. Two crash cars, one escape car, four shooters. It was a pincer movement/auto wreck outside Santo Domingo. The Goat and his bodyguards came out blazing. The in-close shooters killed the bodyguards. Mesplede sniped the Goat from an off-road perch.

The Chevy climbed. The air got thin. They cut west at Moca. The Río Yaque del Norte was due west. Haitian wetbacks ran across the road with squishy tennis shoes and soaked trousers. One guy was handcuffed. A cop on horseback chased him. More horse cops popped out of the brush. The darky weaved and ran straight into a dog pack trailing leashes. The dogs leaped and went at his face. The Chevy topped a hill. Crutch heard howls and screams and no more.

They cut back north. Dawn came up. They hit the shoreline outside Puerto Plata. Still: no fucking beaches, just rocks to the surf. Mesplede said they needed a safe inlet. We stash our boat there. It must be Haiti-close and thus Cuba-accessible. The Windward Passage separates Cuba from Haiti. The Mona Passage separates Puerto Rico from the D.R. We score heroin in Puerto Rico and sell it in Haiti. We stage Cuban coastal runs off the north shore. We are south of U.S. Coast Guard patrols. The Haitian and Dominican navies are moored on the Caribbean. We have the north-shore Atlantic to roam.

They got out, stood on the rocks and pissed in the ocean. They were speeding at six thousand rpm. The tri-lingual chatter was parrot squawk. Crutch kept it zipped.

Morales said, "The Crutchfield boy never speaks."

Mesplede said, "No, but he is competent and persistent."

Canestel zipped his fly. "He is a *pariguayo*."

Crutch laughed. The other guys laughed. They stood on the rocks and bullshitted. The Cubans told Bay of Pigs stories. Crutch talked up his wayward-spouse gigs. Mesplede riffed on the Tiger Mystique.

The origin: Tiger Kab in Miami. Garishly painted taxis and anti-Castro ops. The mob's Saigon-to-Vegas dope funnel. Tiger Kadre/Tiger Krew, *arriba*! Cuban runs off the Florida Keys in the vessel *Tiger Klaw*.

Tiger Kab was in L.A. now. It washed casino-build money. Tigers were fierce and beautiful creatures. We must honor their impeccable dignity and our symbiosis with them.

Saldívar tiger-growled and batted Gómez-Sloan. Morales and Canestel tiger-hissed.

Mesplede said, "We are the new Tiger Krew. Our PT boat will be the new *Tiger Klaw*. We will paint tiger stripes on the hull and fly Castroite scalps from the radio antenna. The numerical designation will be PT-109, to ironically defame the man I killed in Dallas."

64

(Las Vegas, 3/3/69)

Wayne cooked herbs. Tree-frog glands and alkaline solutions. *Ocimum basilicum.* Tetrodoxin poisons—all Haitian strains. Lizard powder and a polychaete worm.

He juggled vats and boiled powder into paste. The Haitian man gave him herb packets. He trapped some lizards in the desert and dissected them. He removed their gallbladders and salivary glands.

He was retracing Reginald Hazzard. Reginald braced the Haitian man, late '63. He had minor knowledge of Haitian herbs. He had queries on their pain-killing and flame-retardant potential. The man gave Wayne the same advice he gave Reginald. Wayne followed the man's instructions, with nil results.

He created the paste. It *enhanced* pain and *jump-started* small fires. It burned through treated fabric quickly. That might mean flawed advice and overall specious knowledge. Reginald might have worked to the same chemical end or might have fully succeeded. The Haitian man might be a loony. He was a mystic. He believed in zombificaton. He held that voodoo enhanced chemical efficacy.

Wayne poured the paste in a jar and went back to reading. He borrowed the library books that Reginald borrowed, fall '63.

Haitian chemistry: klerin liquor, herbs, blowfish toxin. Left-wing theory: Marx, Franz Fanon, Herbert Marcuse. The science felt unsound. There were no controlled results. The described results read like a form of religious lunacy. The left-wing thinkers went long on theory and fell short on precedents. Their case was revolution. Every theory looped back to its sure necessity. Reginald was nineteen and looking for answers. He found politics and magical chemistry.

A Haitian fixation. An odd coincidence. The advance team was in the D.R. now.

Wayne walked to his file space and skimmed odd note sheets. His time line was incomplete and ended abruptly.

"White woman bails RH out of jail, not seen since."

He stared at the time line. He scrawled question marks beside it. He wrote, *"Did Marsh Bowen blink at RH photo? Very unlikely."*

He got up and washed his hands in the lab sink. Toad particles stung his skin.

"You're shitting me."

"No, I'm not. Farlan Brown set it up."

"Jesus Fucking Christ."

"No, Richard Milhous Nixon."

Dwight dined on Bromo-Seltzer and aspirin. The Dunes Lounge was a tomb. Jody and the Misfits played stale oldies. Patrons shagged back to the slots.

Wayne said, "It's a pro forma deal. You reassure the president, I'll reassure the Boys. The D.R.'s a sweet spot, we're all A-OK."

"Mr. Hoover will want me to report back. I'll keep things light and tell him what he wants to hear."

"Which is?"

Dwight lit a cigarette. "That Nixon's as absorbed with black militants as he is. That he understands the national security threat of Archie Bell and the Drells."

A drunk careened by their table. Wayne pulled his chair closer in.

"The knife fight. Did you get feedback from your informant?"

Dwight shrugged. "She said the BTA brothers hate the MMLF brothers a whole lot more now. She didn't mention our boy Marsh in the middle."

"I know Clarkson, but I've hardly met Jackson. He's Haitian, right?"

"Right. He's got no rap sheet, but he was allegedly a Tonton Macoute cop in Haiti. He emigrated, changed his name and became a black-militant asshole. Why are you asking? He's not as bad as most of those fucks."

Wayne shrugged. "Coincidence. Idle curiosity."

Dwight cracked his knuckles. " 'Idle,' shit. The guy who's idle is Marsh. I want you to jerk his leash. Tell him he has to join the BTA or MMLF and hand up some snitches on collateral groups to keep the old girl wetting her panties."

Wayne smiled. "I'll tell him."

"And tell him to score some heroin while he's at it."

Wayne squeezed his water glass. The edges almost snapped. Dwight said, "Get off your high horse, son. It's not like you haven't cooked it, run it and sold it to black folks yourself."

He needed air. He walked the Strip in a rainstorm.

Dwight had his shit pegged. Dwight knew how to make him work and how to wet down his fuse.

It was cold. The rain carried ice chips. The hotel marquees fritzed and lost letters.

The Boys overbooked him. The Teamster loan buyouts devoured his time. He'd purchased thirty-four busted businesses since New Year's. The L.A. money wash was all systems go. The Peoples' Bank was the main laundry chute. Tiger Kab and the low-life clubs washed residual green. Mesplede and Dipshit were in the D.R. Hughes Air took them down.

Drac was tailspinning at Gay Edgar's rate. Wayne met him in private hospital rooms and assuaged his fear of the Bomb. Drac wanted to curb black breeding. His solution: put fallout in the collard greens at soul-food restaurants. Drac got two blood transfusions daily. Drac bought eight gold mines, two silver mines and a golf course since New Year's. His lawyers were filing injunctions against the state of Nevada. Drac wanted to ban all A-bomb testing. Farlan Brown said his legal bills ran fifty grand a month. Farlan asked about Dipshit—is he still looking for that cooze rip-off chick? Wayne said probably. Dipshit follows women around when he doesn't know what else to do.

The rain turned to hail. Wayne ducked into the Top O' the Strip. Art and Dottie Todd sang "Chanson d'Amour" for the twelve thousandth time. The bar revolved and gave revelers a 360 view. Ice came down in sheets.

Sonny Liston was defacing publicity pix of Muhammad Ali. The going rate was ten scoots apiece. White losers bought them and displayed them in their dens. Sonny wrote "Draft Dodger" and drew devil's horns on Ali. Drac had a half-dozen. Farlan Brown sent the prez a Liston special: Ali sucking LBJ's dick.

Wayne waved. Sonny ditched the losers and came over. A waiter brought Wayne a Coke and Sonny a scotch-rocks. They schmoozed up the old days.

Sonny was a Tiger Kab alumnus. Wayne told him the biz had just moved to southside L.A. Sonny said he'd beat feet and lend support to the brothers. Wayne said he'd appreciate it. Sonny said he'd heard a rumor—you and this black woman.

Wayne admitted it. Sonny brought up Wendell Durfee. Wayne said he was looking for the woman's missing son. Sonny laughed for two minutes straight. It galvanized the whole room. People looked over. Wayne glared them off. Sonny caught his breath and drained his cocktail.

Wayne said, "Are you finished?"

Sonny said, "You and your nigger quests."

Graph boxes, arrows. Connecting lines to and from.

A box marked "Library Books." Connection points: the boxes marked "Political Texts" and "Haitian Herbs." A box marked "Parking Ticket." Connection point: the box marked "Haitian Herb Man." A box marked "Jail." Connection point: the box marked "White Woman/Bail."

The graph helped him think. The wall placement let him think sitting and standing. It supplanted and reduced his file work.

Wayne scanned boxes. The LVPD summary sheet said *Read Me.* He sat down and skimmed it again. It summarized Reginald's loneliness. High school, J.C., the car-wash job. Nobody really knew the boy. Piss-poor acquaintances and no friends.

"Before you ask me for the dozenth time. No, we never discussed Haitian herbs or left-wing political texts."

Wayne swiveled his chair. Mary Beth put her hands on his shoulders and straddled his lap.

"I wouldn't have given you a key if I knew you'd use it to torment me."

"You're prone to torment, so I'm only checking in as usual."

Wayne pulled her shirttail out. "We could lie down for a while."

She touched his lips. "We could and we should, given that you've got that policeman-with-routine-questions look on your face."

"They're not routine."

"I know that, sweetie. I'm just teasing you. It's just my way of curbing my tendency for brusqueness."

"Which means?"

"Which means I'm here at this moment, and Reginald's not."

He kissed her. She traced his jawline. There's her eyes. As always, those green flecks.

"The emerald. Remember, you said you'd—"

She covered his mouth. It always meant *You hush.*

"Yes, I asked around. I learned nothing of specific value, which didn't surprise me. What I *did* learn was that there is a persistent and persistently amorphous myth that black people in dire need get emeralds anonymously in the mail."

Wayne stood up. Mary Beth held on and stayed in his lap. She laughed. He carried her into the bedroom and dropped her on the bed.

She bounced a little. She kicked off her shoes and pulled off her socks.

"I don't want to spoil the mood, but I remembered something."

Wayne took his shirt off. "About Reginald?"

"Yes."

"Tell me. Don't spoil the mood, but—"

"I found some of his old school clothes, so it jogged my memory. It was the spring of '62. Reginald took a field trip to Los Angeles. It was a science fair at USC. He told me he went to a few classes at a 'Freedom School.' They had a little makeshift office on the campus."

Something went *click*. He couldn't place it. He went blank in dead sync. Mary Beth threw a shoe at him.

"I'm here. My son is not."

65

(Washington, D.C., 3/17/69)

Nixon said, "Look at the rug. It's the details that get me. The goddamn bird has all those arrows and leaves in his claws."

Dwight looked at the rug. Likewise Bebe Rebozo. The Oval Office, 6:00 p.m. drinks. Nixon on his third old-fashioned.

Bebe said, "Mr. Hoover had a radio show back in the '30s. I was a youngster in Havana then. There was a 200,000-watt station that broadcast it out of Miami."

Nixon pulled the cherry out of his glass. "Agent Holly doesn't give a shit about rugs or Mr. Hoover's salad days. He wants to put the quietus on all this goddamned black-militant nonsense that's been going around."

Dwight said, "That's correct, Mr. President."

"And he'd like my word that I'm not plotting any upheaval in the Dominican Republic."

Dwight nodded. Bebe went ooh-la-la. The prez and the First Friend looked fraternal. They were swarthy. They wore mauve alpaca sweaters with the presidential seal. The Rotary meets the Rat Pack.

Bebe lit a cigarette. "The D.R. and I go way back. I owned some cane fields there in the '40s. There's this exile group I toss a couple of shekels at. They're operating out of there now."

Nixon coughed. Bebe snuffed out his cigarette and fanned the air. It was snowing. Windows showed off a portico and a huge lawn.

Bebe said, "My guys used to sell heroin. It's a quick turnaround on your investment. If you want to fight communism, you've got to get down to the nitty-gritty."

Nixon stirred his drink. "Tell it like it is. Heroin has financed every Third World coup since God was a pup. Right, Mr. Holly?"

"That's correct, Mr. President."

"Farlan Brown said you went to Yale. How come you're the one with the badge and I'm the one with all the headaches and this goddamned silly sweater?"

Dwight smiled. "It's the vicissitudes of fate, Sir."

" 'Vicissitudes,' shit. That Irish cocksucker Jack Kennedy stole the '60 election from me. *That's* a 'vicissitude.' What I've got now is the god-damned last laugh."

Bebe ate his cherry. "I like Dwight, Mr. President. You should appoint him attorney general."

Nixon chortled. "Hoover's got too much dirt on me. He'd never go for a hatchet man like Dwight calling the shots."

Bebe said, "Are you a hatchet man, Dwight?"

"Yes, sir. I am."

Nixon picked at a hangnail. "Where does Hoover stash his secret files? I had an aide who said he kept a vault at the Willard."

"The basement of his house, Mr. President. It's moisture-sealed and fireproof."

Bebe snorted. "He's got nothing on the president that the man himself has not volunteered to the public."

Nixon rolled his eyes. Bebe stammered. Dwight examined his drink coaster. It featured the same pissed-off bird.

Bebe said, "The D.R.'s a toilet. Your investors will have to upgrade the appearance of the place if you want to lure tourists down. I just visited my exile group and took a little look-see. Balaguer's solidly pro-U.S., but the CIA guys are all drunks and gash men. There's a retired marine colonel named Smith who buffers Balaguer on most of the dirty work."

Nixon said, "Accountability. You put a straw man out in front of you. When the shit hits the fan, you're out of range. *Me?* I was at a Red Sox game or grinding the old lady."

Dwight laughed. Bebe futzed with the emerald ring above his wedding band.

"My group's got two new hard-ons. This French merc and his kid buddy. They may not oust Fidel, but they'll die trying."

Nixon yawned. "Castro's got legs. The American electorate has had it up to here with Cuba. I'll let the exiles pull their stunts as long as it doesn't come back to haunt me at the polls."

Bebe acted hurt. Darling, how could you? Dwight looked away.

Nixon said, "Dwight, let's talk turkey."

"I'm all ears, Sir."

"Describe Hoover's mental state. Assume that I'm an insider with some previous knowledge and that nothing leaves this room, be assured that candor will serve you in the long run and tell it like it is."

Dwight shot his cuffs. "He's in exceedingly poor physical and mental health. He's obsessed with black crime, black mating habits, black political activity and black hygiene. His judgment is questionable at all levels. He is very obviously impaired. He is hemorrhaging prestige in the law-enforcement community. He's prone to embarrassing gaffes. He makes intemperate and highly impolitic remarks routinely. He's vituperative in the extreme. He's hanging on with brute will, hatred and daily injections of amphetamine in the keester. Despite this great wealth of infirmity, he remains tenuously lucid and must be considered a deadly adversary and thus a significant and utterly essential friend."

Bebe whistled. "Tell it like it is, baby."

Nixon whistled. "Amen, brother."

Dwight felt his pulse race. Nixon winked. It flopped as a you-my-man ploy.

"Keep me updated on that. Will you, Dwight?"

"Yes, Sir. I will."

Bebe flashed his emerald ring. "Nice, huh? I got it in the D.R."

Echo Park was flooded. The rent-a-boats were moored and tarp-covered. The rain was incessant. The ducks were off hiding. He bought popcorn for nothing.

He was dead. He took the D.C.-to-L.A. red-eye, squashed between Buddhist priests. They saw his gun and om-cleansed his aura. His pills and drinks uncleansed him. He got an hour's sleep.

He called Mr. Hoover and reported the Nixon meet. He described it as "perfunctory." The old girl was enraged. Dwight mollified him. Hoover launched a fourteen-minute anti-Nixon rant. He wanted news on the hate cartoons. Dwight said his leads dead-ended.

Two nights, three hours' sleep. Back-to-back MLK nightmares. Dr. King sermonized. Dwight watched from a back pew.

Karen walked up. She had Eleanora swaddled. They stood under the boathouse awning. The baby was triple-wrapped, warm and safe.

Dwight said, "She looks like me."

Karen smiled. "It was a procedure, and you were nowhere near the receptacle."

Eleanora had Karen's hair and bone set. She slept through the storm noise.

Dwight said, "It's been a while."

"It has. I've had Ella and you've had the operation."

"What's-His-Name is leaving soon, right?"

"Yes."

"We can log some time in then. I got you a key to the drop-front."

Karen stepped away. "That's an I've-got-nothing-to-hide gesture."

"Point taken, but it's true."

"You're ducking the issue."

"Say her name, then. Accuse me of something. Give me the chance to confirm or deny."

Karen lit a cigarette. Her hand trembled. Dwight held Eleanora while she smoked.

"Mr. Hoover called Bayard Rustin a 'prehensile-tailed night creature' at the American Legion."

Dwight said, "I know."

"His remarks regressed from there."

"I know. Jack Leahy showed me a copy of the speech."

Eleanora kicked. Dwight rocked her back to sleep. The awning leaked. Water dripped near their feet.

Karen said, "There's a safe house near Cal Riverside. I've been in it. There's a closet with four pump shotguns and a box of hand grenades. A man with a Mao Tse-tung mask and a shotgun has robbed four markets in San Bernardino."

Dwight studied Eleanora. Her feet kicked while she slept.

"I'll always take armed robbery. What can I do for—"

"The Philadelphia Office has my husband's file under review. Agents have been pestering the dean. One man got quite bold and risqué. 'You college folks get around a lot. I heard the wife's been playing footsie with Mr. Hoover's number-one hard boy.' "

Dwight kicked the wall. The impact disturbed Eleanora. Karen tossed her cigarette and took the bundle back. Ella cooed and shut her eyes.

"Mr. Hoover told that agent about us, Dwight. It violates the agreement we've had from the beginning."

"I know."

"Mr. Hoover called Coretta Scott King 'a diseased go-go girl' on national TV."

"I know."

"Can you please say something more than that?"

"Mr. Hoover is losing his mind. He's old and he's sick. No one has the balls to pull the plug on him, because he's got dirt files on the whole fucking world."

"Including you?"

"Yes."

Karen rocked Eleanora. The clouds went double dark and kicked loose a downpour.

"There's times I can't run from it, Dwight."

"Run from *what*?"

"From the things you never talk about. From how far you've gone for that man. From every horrible thing that you've done."

Dwight reached for Eleanora. Karen pulled her back. Dwight walked out into the rain.

Three pills and drinks failed him. His circuits sparked and kept him awake. Adrenaline ate through the sedation. He got dressed and drove to Eagle Rock.

It was midnight. The courtyard was quiet. The rain brought red flashes and thunder peals. Dwight picked the lock and let himself in.

He hit the lights. The pad looked identical. He walked to the bed and tossed the pillows. He found the same gun and diary. He opened it and found new sheets.

MY SHORT-TERM AIMS AND DWIGHT'S SHORT-TERM AIMS HAVE BLURRED. I HAVE COME TO SHARE DWIGHT'S VIEW OF THE BTA AND MMLF. THEY ARE CRIMINALS DRIVEN BY PERSONAL ANIMUS AT THE EXPENSE OF POLITICAL CONSCIOUSNESS. DWIGHT CREDITS THEM WITH NO CONSCIOUSNESS; I CREDIT THEM WITH DAWNING CONSCIOUSNESS BLUNTED BY THE SELF-SERVING PATHOLOGY OF ANGRY MALES IN GROUPS. THESE MEN MUST PUSH HEROIN AND FACILITATE A DEFINABLE SQUALOR. IT MUST BE THE CONTAINED CHAOS THAT DWIGHT AND I BOTH DESIRE. THE DAWNING OF CONSCIOUSNESS MUST BE PROVOKED THROUGH THE APPLICATION OF MORAL TERROR. DWIGHT AND MR. HOOVER BELIEVE THAT THE STIMULUS OF HEROIN WILL PROVE OVERPOWERING TO BLACK MILITANTS, THEIR FOLLOWERS AND THE UNCOUNTABLE BLACK PEOPLE MOVED BY THEIR RHETORIC. THEIR MASS CAPITULATION WILL CONFIRM VILE RACIST CARICATURE, DISCREDIT BLACK RADICALISM AND SUPPRESS ITS EMERGING MAINSTREAM APPEAL. I BELIEVE THAT THE DAWNING OF POLITICAL CONSCIOUSNESS WILL SERVE TO CONFRONT AND TRANSCEND THIS OBSTACLE, REINVENT THE FORMERLY CRIMINAL AND CAST THEM IN THE HERO ROLES THEY NOW SO SELFISHLY AND FATUOUSLY SEEK. THIS CONTROLLED CHAOS WILL NOT CONCLUDE IN POLITICAL DISSOLUTION. THE CHAOS IS TOO STEEPED IN THE HORRIFYING CONTEXT OF WHITE NEGLECT AND INJUSTICE TO BE ANYTHING BUT LIBERATING. I HAVE SEEN AND DONE HORRIFYING

THINGS IN MY LONG REVOLUTIONARY STRUGGLE; MY DEPLOYMENT
OF HEROIN IN ALGERIA IN '56 PROVED AMBIGUOUS. I STERNLY TRUST
THAT ANY AND ALL CONFLICTS IN THIS JOURNEY WILL RESOLVE IN MY
FAVOR, NOT DWIGHT'S, AND THAT NO HUMAN BEINGS WILL DIE.

Dwight reread the pages. He skimmed and jumped and hopscotched the text. The printing blurred. The booze and pills kicked in late. He saw spots and ink wisps. The floor rolled. He lay down and shut his eyes.

The bed rolled. The floor dipped. He didn't know if he was awake or asleep or someplace in between. He drifted. It was scary and peaceful. His head and limbs felt funny. He went blank for a while. He opened his eyes and saw Joan.

She sat on the bed. One leg was cocked. Her knee brushed his hip. She wore boots over black nylon stockings full of runs. Her hair was tied back.

"How did you find it?"

"The cartoons you had printed. You left an easy trail."

"The cartoons were a bust. It won't happen again."

"Who drew them?"

"An old Freedom School student of mine."

Dwight sat up. Dizziness slammed him down. Joan squeezed his knee. Dwight traced her stocking runs and found some bare leg to touch.

She said, "Heroin."

"They can't score it. They won't be able to deal it for ten seconds without getting popped."

"I could help them."

"I'll consider it."

Joan laced up their fingers. Dwight tore out a stocking run and cupped her whole leg.

"How many of these places do you have?"

"I'm not telling you."

"You left the diary out for me to find. Did you get the idea from Karen Sifakis?"

"Karen's a mail-drop friend. I don't actually know her."

"Did you leave the diary out for me to find?"

Joan nodded. Dwight said, "Nobody dies." Joan took his face in her hands.

The dizziness faded out. He felt his body again. Her hands steadied him.

Joan said, "What do you want?"

Dwight said, "I want to fall. And I want you to catch me on the way down."

66

(Santo Domingo, 3/20/69)

His eyes hurt. He kept seeing word prisms. His fingers were paper-cut.

A month of code work. Maybe some progress. Making words out of numbers, letters and spaces.

Tiger Krew bombed up Autopisa Duarte. Ivar Smith sold them a Dominican army half-track. Saldívar and Canestel tiger-striped it. Morales painted on a big tiger paw. They headed for Piedra Blanca and Jarabacoa. Slave crews were breaking ground on their sites. The Midget sold them the two rural lots and two lots in Santo Domingo. La Banda recruited work crews from La Victoria prison. The jailbirds got sentence reductions if building deadlines were met.

Balaguer's construction firm stood ready. La Banda evicted paupers from the out-of-town sites. The casino build was *on*. The PT boat was ordered. They were meeting a Tonton Macoute guy to discuss the dope biz later.

Crutch Murine-dosed his eyes. The half-track treads chewed up pavement. Froggy drove. The Cubans perched above the wheel wells. Crutch sat in the machine-gun nest. They passed through cane fields and glades. Crutch blasted tree stumps for kicks.

Wetback Haitians ducked across the road. Morales fired at their feet. Crutch yawned and stretched. The code work induced a boocoo sleep deficit.

Voodoo. The probable book of the dead. Letters, numbers, symbols and mathematics. It's a Horror House murder lead. Book symbols match the Horror House symbols. It's Gretchen/Celia's book. Fuck—he *still* can't see Joan and Gretchen/Celia as killers.

He's giddy with it. He thinks Gretchen/Celia is in-country. He's combed every records-check resource and can't find her. Mesplede told him not to brace Sam G. "Your 'case' is all frivolity. We are here to move heroin and depose Fidel Castro."

The terrain was steep. The half-track mulched fallen tree bark. Crutch practiced stitch shots. He aimed at trees and severed limbs with .30-caliber fire.

Wayne Tedrow was coming soon. The Boys told him to cinch the deal with the Midget. Geologists bagged soil at all four sites. They said it would sustain heavy building. Mesplede found a shore spot on the D.R.-Haiti border. It was near Cap-Haïtien. Their Tonton guy was Mr. Big around there.

Tiger Kart rolled into Piedra Blanca. Local peons saw the beast and hightailed it. The site rocked. Bulldozers plowed shacks. Policia Nacional guys detained the dispossessed. They spoke Spanish. Morales translated for Crutch. It was eminent domain. Jefe needs your house. You get forty bucks and a food chit.

Some evictees wept and glared. La Banda guys flanked the bulldozers. They stood at parade rest and carried carbines at port arms.

The construction boss moseyed over. He told Gómez-Sloan the land was sound. La Banda would bring some prisoners up to clear brush. His crew would build a pre-fab bunkhouse. The prisoners would sleep shackled. Cop crews with bullwhips would oversee their work.

On to Jarabacoa.

Crutch got road-sick. Tiger Kart tread-crunched everything in its path. It was 2:00 p.m. and hell-hot. Suntan oil dripped down his neck. His head was back in Santo Domingo. His torch for Joan and Gretchen/Celia burned strong. He saw them as Commies. He didn't see them as killers. The matching symbols might not mean Murder One.

Santo Domingo was on-the-whole shitsville. The Gazcue section was Hancock Park for spics. It was a light-skin zone. He started peeping there last week. He looked for Joan and Gretchen/Celia. He settled for random women. He followed them from parks to restaurants. He followed them home. He peeped bathroom and bedroom windows.

Tiger Kart rolled into Jarabacoa. The town was full of tin-roof huts and jungle plumage. The site was two roads down. Crutch heard bulldozer crunch. Three kids ran out of the brush. They wore masks and Uncle Ho shirts and carried flame-topped bottles. Get it? *Molotov cocktails.*

They hurled them. The bombs hit Tiger Kart and made pissant explosions. Crutch swiveled his machine gun and fired their way. He cut down some cane stalks and missed the fuckers.

The kids got away. Jungle brush covered them. Tiger Kart rolled to the site. Shackled-up workers lugged debris. Bulldozers blitzed foundations. A four-jailbird crew hauled discarded-roof sections and cut up their hands. A cop on horseback whipped a slow guy.

The straw boss waved. The Krew tiger-growled back. Crutch heard three gunshots on the Autopista.

Tiger Kart cut back and rolled northbound. They saw the Molotov kids, dead in a ditch. They were head-shot point-blank. Their Uncle Ho shirts were slashed. Their hands and feet were severed.

A La Banda guy stepped out of the brush and waved.

Ivar Smith stashed a Jeep for them. Tiger Kart was too big for the border river crossings. The Plaine du Massacre was close by. Morales sniffed the air. He said he smelled the Goat and the soul husks of slaughtered Haitians. Crutch saw blood drawings on tree trunks. He got a vile voodoo vibe.

The Jeep was full-gassed. A canvas top beat the sun out. Dirt roads got them to the river. Tonton guys perched by the bridge. They wore stovepipe suits, wraparound shades and straw porkpies. They waved the Jeep across. They exuded French savoir faire and black hipster cool.

The river was muddy and eighty yards wide. Spades popped out of the water holding crawfish. They crossed and took dirt roads to the Cordillera Central. The ride was all swerves and plows through fallen brush. Morales puked in a paper bag. Froggy cranked it in low gear, forty mph–plus.

Pauper pads whizzed by. Tin-roof shacks plaster-laced with giant rhinestones. Wood shacks with pix of voodoo priests on the doors. Tree branches hung over the roadway. Lynched chickens dangled from them. A few leaked fresh blood.

They hit the peak and descended. Flat roads led to the north shore. A spook in a dead-bird hat hexed them from the roadside. Gómez-Sloan shot at him and missed.

The terrain was tropical forest. The air smelled like salt water and dirt. Every half-ass tree was blood-marked. Beware the Zombie Zone.

They hit the shore. The salt air heated up. Froggy consulted a map and slalomed on rock-strewn sand. Crutch saw an inlet. A wild-ass jigaboo popped out of nowhere and stepped in front of the Jeep.

He was six-eight. He ran 140. He had a Fu Manchu stash. He wore a purple porkpie and a madras suit. Two .45's, two emerald rings, a crystal neck pendant filled with blood.

Froggy braked. The jig beamed and tossed rose petals in the Jeep. They were scented. They drifted down and perfumed up the Krew.

"I am Luc Duhamel. Welcome to my kingdom, baby boys."

His palace was a stone hut with a BAR placement and a barbed-wire fence. A speedboat was moored in the water. A golf cart was tethered to a flag-pole. Three voodoo-sect flags flew. The yard was strewn with dead rodents. Carnivore birds swooped and gorged.

Luc sat them down inside. The walls were sequined. Everyone got their own faux-mink chair. Luc served klerin liquor in rhinestone goblets. Everyone sipped hesitant and swallowed it intact.

Luc took his coat off. His skinny arms were needle-tracked. Crutch got big-eyed. Mesplede and the Cubans deadpanned it.

Mesplede said, *"En français?"*

Luc shook his head. "English, baby boy. There is no challenge in speaking one's native tongue."

Saldívar said, "Heroin." Gómez-Sloan said, "Smack." Morales said, "The beast from the East."

Canestel rubbed a fake beard—the kill-Castro code. Luc said, "Yes, Colonel Smith informed me. He said these men will become your *bons frères.*"

Froggy sipped klerin liquor. "We are purchasing a PT boat. It can do forty knots."

Saldívar sipped klerin liquor. "Colonel Smith said you have a heroin source in Puerto Rico."

Morales gagged on klerin. "It is a U.S. protectorate, but *Tiger Klaw* will be very fast."

Gómez-Sloan said, "We understand that President Duvalier must be compensated."

Canestel *sniffed* his klerin. "It is a three-island parlay. We will profit and Cuban Communists will die."

Luc looked at Crutch and pointed to his goblet. Crutch guzzled the whole thing and saw stars.

"And you, baby boy? Have you anything to say?"

"Sir, I'm just happy to be here."

The Krew ate dinner in Gazcue. Ivar Smith and Terry Brundage joined them. Dominicans dined late. It was pushing midnight. Crutch was achy from the ride back. He was amphetamized. He kept brain-screening the dead kids. Three gunshots, no hands and feet.

The restaurant was open-air and right off the Malecón. Salt air had the wallpaper withered down to strips. The other guys talked death shit and chowed with gusto. Crutch poked at a squid and eyed women.

They were dining upscale. It was light-skin turf. He had a good range of Spanish land-grant types. His daily rev was incessant. Late-night uppers weirdly re-volted him and put certain women in slow motion. His brain camera clicked for stills and panned for sensuous movement. Women ate, talked, laughed and touched their friends or escorts. He knew when to look and how to go with the swirl.

A La Banda dude dropped by the table. Ivar Smith palmed an envelope. The dude said, "From Bebe Rebozo." Smith rubbed his fake beard. Crutch zoned them out. Morales nudged Gómez-Sloan. They said, *"Pariguayo"* in sync.

Crutch smiled and played with his food. The swirl re-adjusted peripherally. A woman crushed out a cigarette, tossed her head and exhaled. Her hair flew. A ceiling fan churned her smoke. She wore buckled high-heel shoes and a pale green dress. She raised her arms and tied her hair up. Dark stubble, beaded sweat. She was pale, with brown freckles. She wore a man's wristwatch.

Crutch walked to the john. The woman adios'd her friends and went out the front door. Crutch ducked through the kitchen, cut down an alley and hit the street ten yards behind her.

She took Calle Pasteur to Avenida Independencia. She took Máximo Gómez to the Malecón bluffs. A sea breeze tossed her dress up. She pushed it down like it was funny. Crutch fell back to twenty yards and re-framed his shot. She walked *fast*. His head processed it *slow*.

She turned back on a no-name street. The sea breeze evaporated. The turf went residential. She smoked. Window light caught her plumes on the updraft.

Crutch fell back five yards. The neighborhood was swank—ancient houses, eggshell white, no loud colors. She cut left on Avenida Bolívar. She unlocked the door of a slick two-story pad.

Crutch stood across the street and framed window lights. A blond woman tidied books on a shelf. His woman walked up behind her. The blond woman turned around. They smiled at the same moment and fell into a kiss.

The moment went fluid and held. Crutch watched. Their bodies merged and filled the window frame. Their hands went here and there and enhanced the embrace. The kiss *held*. They made it go *faster*, he made it go *slow*.

The light went off. His woman hit a switch. He strained to hear voices and heard none.

. . .

He called in sick. Froggy said, *"Ça va"* and "bad timing." *"Tiger Klaw* is in dry dock at St. Ann's Bay, Jamaica. You will miss her arrival."

He laid in supplies: uppers, coffee, scratch pads and pens. He brought in three auxiliary fans. He attacked the code.

He started with the letters *S* and *K.* He gleaned them from CIA substitution-code study. Three-number designations announced each *S* and *K.* Each number required subtraction and multiplication tolls. Sums designated letters of the alphabet. It was arbitrary. The sum stages varied at different tabulation points. The code-breaker's job: form words and letters from number gibberish.

Numbers, letters, *symbols.* Let's assault the symbols first.

They were squiggles, stick figures and *X* marks. They dotted Gretchen/Celia's address book at irregular intervals. The CIA codebook listed them as voodoo-derived. "The voodoo priest's depiction of spiritual chaos while a victim is hexed."

Symbols—go. Do not move on to letter numbers until you know.

He ate uppers, he drank coffee, he ran three fans plus the AC. He stared at the forty-nine symbols in Gretchen/Celia's book. He poured sweat in an igloo.

Three symbols repeated: squiggle, stick figure, *X* mark. They had to have the same *repeated* meaning. He stared at the book for nine straight hours. His brain jumped to this:

Repetition meant banality. It meant boredom on Gretchen/Celia's part. She spiced her narrative up to amuse herself and to confuse potential readers. The symbols did not bode portent. They were innocuous.

His second jump: they were abbreviations. His third jump: the explicated text would be coherent, but shorthanded. Gretchen/Celia's cursive writing was fevered. She was anxious, she composed in haste, the code work absorbed her energy. His fourth jump: the symbols were substitutes for *and, the* and *to.*

He crossed the symbols out and added those words on his copy sheet. It felt coherent. The placement felt correct.

His chest hurt. His heart banged blood to his rib cage. He heard voices in his head. He saw *THE EYE* and the *SEVERED HANDS AND FEET* without conjuring them. He hemorrhaged weight and felt his trousers go slack.

Two days in. Additions, subtractions and multiplications brain-broiling. He passed out, despite the uppers. He woke up seeing numbers. He developed a tremor in his writing hand. He wasn't sure of what he had. He decided to call repeated sums vowels. He thought he got *L* and *T.* He kept getting the sum 14. His world went tilt.

The Fourteenth of June Movement, aka 6/14. Castro-backed Reds invade the D.R.

And:

The preceded each 14. His code break was valid so far.

That gave him the *O* and the *F.* That gave him the *J,* the *U* and the *N.* Re-tilt: the vowel *E* was always in the right place.

He ate more uppers, he drank more coffee, his piss turned near brown. His skin hugged his bones like a junkie's. He got six more number-letter sums that felt right on. He passed out for five hours. He woke up woozy and *prayed.* He forced himself to eat an apple. He chased it with a handful of ups. He got re-re-re-re-re-re-vitalized and started building words on code work and instinct.

It took eleven hours. It confirmed Managua. Yes, it's a paper curse and a book of the dead. No, it's much more.

Abbreviations, omitted words, fractured text. Fully coherent despite it. The story of 6/14/59 inside out.

It's 6/13/59. The movement is Castro-backed and based in the Beard's captive Cuba. Two converted yachts sail the Windward Passage to the north D.R. shore. Two hundred rebels are aboard. They've got M1 Garands, bazookas and machine guns. It's all men minus two: Joan Klein and Celia Reyes.

The force lands at Estero Hondo and Maimón. Dominican Army sharp-shooters are waiting. All the rebels are captured or killed.

It's 6/14/59. A DC-3 departs from Cuba's Red Shore. Eighty armed men are poised. They wear the armbands of the Unión Patriótica Dominicana. The plane flies under-radar low and lands outside Constanza. The rebels kill soldiers guarding the airfield and steal their vehicles. They race into town, kill more soldiers, run to nearby mountain ravines and hide.

Army patrols scoured the hills and captured or killed the rebels. Seaborne and airborne rebels were held at the San Isidro Air Force Base and at Trujillo's torture chamber, La Cuarenta. Trujillo's personal goon squad hacked them with machetes and fried them in electric chairs. The Goat ordered huge roundups of suspected 6/14 sympathizers. Simpatico government figures were assassinated. Comsymps were tor-tured, killed, reluctantly released. The 6/14 Movement was truly born in the Goat's prisons. The Beard brooded over the gone-bust invasion. Anti-Fidel sentiment swept the D.R. Right. The Goat was offed in '61. The Beard staged a second invasion on 11/29/63. This group was formally called the Agrupación Política Catorce de Junio. The rebels numbered 125 this time. They landed at six north-shore locations, shot some sol-diers and fled to the hills. Interim prez Juan Bosch ordered a "rabbit hunt." Soldiers combed the hills and wiped out the rebels. A few survived. They infiltrated the D.R. Left and made revolutionary woo-woo anonymously.

Crutch read Gretchen/Celia's pages. He kept jumping ahead of the decoded text. He was voodoo-vexed and amphetamized. His head banged blood to his rib cage.

The base narrative stopped. An "Expression of Solidarity" with slaughtered Haitians followed. The Goat and the Midget were accused of genocide.

Lists: the Trujillo Haitian dead, the Balaguer Haitian dead, 6/14 sympathizers abducted and killed by La Banda. List: "Excommunicated" 6/14 traitors killed by the members themselves. Lists: names, dates and death locations.

There's a single name at the bottom: María Rodríguez Fontonette.

Her monicker/nickname/political alias is "Tattoo."

Her date of *disappearance* is June '68. She *vanished* in Los Angeles.

The tattoo, the skin color, the location/date.

It's that night.

It's Horror House.

It's the night he saw Joan and Gretchen/Celia kiss.

DOCUMENT INSERT: 3/29/69. Extract from the privately held journal of Karen Sifakis.

March 29, 1969

Eleanora rules my days. She is a mighty empress and imperious ruler of my heart, as well as an exhausting bundle of ceaseless energy and need. She focuses me and deflects my actions and thoughts not directly related to her. My husband is back in Philadelphia now; his months-long presence here amounted to indentured servitude, as well as assisted me in the prosaic tasks of new motherhood and kept me away from Dwight. Now, I am alone with Eleanora—and, in fact, besieged by her—and Dwight is back with a besieging force.

Our fight at Echo Park was horrible; I have no right to question his actions with Joan, for our very union is duplicitous and a grave misdeed in and of itself. One difference between Dwight and me: adultery is hardly as onerous as spawning political chaos. Another difference: I wish to skate by with my misdeeds, while Dwight harbors the buried urge to be punished for his. That is a succinct primer on my love for him.

I see political misdeeds escalating and find myself reflexively attributing them to the FBI, Mr. Hoover and, by extension, Dwight. Two Panthers were shot and killed at UCLA in January. The killings allegedly derived from a long-standing Panther-US grievance and came to a head over the creation of an Afro-American Studies Center on campus. I know that the Bureau has double agents in both organizations and is committed to spawning inter-group discord. A Panther spokesman called the killings "political assassinations carried out by US on orders by the pig power structure." I have come to hate the word *pig* as much as I hate the word *nigger* and find myself damning Dwight for his perception of ingrained criminality in the black-nationalist movement. Indictments are pending against numerous Panthers in New York City for an alleged plot to dynamite-bomb the Penn Central tracks at rush hour. Are they insane? Don't they know *black people* would have been killed? I bomb monuments and have never physically damaged a human being. Am *I* insane to be doing this under Dwight Holly's sanction? What horrible price will I pay for my role in assuaging this man's guilt, and where does that guilt specifically come from?

Mr. Hoover seems determined to go out in a psychotically hateful blaze of glory, and he has found an unrelenting minion in Dwight, who now has Joan Klein to aid and abet and perhaps comfort him. I am afraid that Dwight will passively permit or actively suborn the BTA and MMLF in the sale of narcotics and that he has found a willing accomplice in Joan. Joan understands the concept of narcotics as a tool of revolution and has deployed it before. I fear that Joan and Dwight seek the same physical end for antithetical political motives. They want to bring the BTA and MMLF to a point of public censure and blithely underestimate the human cost.

I've told Joan intimate things about Dwight. She knows that Dwight has burgled my home on occasion and that I leave a much less candid and controversial journal out for him to peruse. I'm afraid that expressions of my troubled love for Dwight have pushed Joan toward him in the effort to further her own political goals.

Joan has been to dauntingly dangerous places of revolution and has committed deeds—and, yes, misdeeds—that I am both thankful and regretful I am incapable of. I do not doubt her sincerity or utter commitment and have seen her in moments of frank goodness—our shared teaching duties at the Freedom School in '62 was one instance—but I utterly fear her fury and will. She and Dwight possess a blindsiding like-mindedness and emotional hunger. I pray that it will not supersede their utilitarian instincts and cause dire harm.

DOCUMENT INSERT: 4/2/69. Extract from the journal of Marshall E. Bowen.

Los Angeles,
4/2/69

I'm in trouble. The incident last night may get back to Scotty Bennett. The consequences may fuck up the balance of my personal life and the operation and thus my search for the armored-car money and emeralds. Mr. Holly has been pressing me for snitch-outs and Wayne has been pressing me to fall in with either the BTA or MMLF exclusively. When pressed, I vacillate and consider my options. Rarely do I vacillate to the point of stunned inaction. Last night I did.

Wayne has become a southside regular. He's been buying cocktail lounges and after-hours clubs and has been making the scene at Tiger Kab. Of all people, Wayne has brought ex–heavyweight champ and self-described "chump" Sonny Liston into the Tiger Kab fold. Sonny is a boozing, pill-popping, whore-chasing fool. The brothers are afraid of him and afraid to admit that they dig him. Sonny is very right-wing. He hates Muslims and militants and grooves Richard Nixon and the Vietnam War. His two losses to Muhammad Ali, combined with his chemical intake, have stretched his brain cells thin. He is, however, funny, unlike Tiger Kab kokaptain Milt Chargin, who will go to any and all degraded lengths to make black people laugh and to appear cool. Tiger Kab is now *très* au kourant. The Krew is picaresque working on combustible. We are riding the black-nationalist zeitgeist. The Panthers get the headlines while the BTA and MMLF make the scene with the fervor of Stork Club nobodies seeking out Walter Winchell. Please notice us: we're black, we're violent, we're trying to score dope and we're *cool*.

I vacillate and visit both the BTA and MMLF headquarters; I endure constant LAPD surveillance and three or four street rousts a week. My ex-LAPD status enrages southside bluesuits. They've taken to calling me "boy" and detaining me for twenty-minute spells while they run radio warrant checks. I always turn up clean; they always release me with jabs in the chest and parting epithets. I am quietly enraged and say nothing.

I can't exercise the Bent. I'm afraid to, I'm speciously famous now, any assignation might result in a roust or a phone call to LAPD. I have to put my intimate urges on hold while I assess, while Mr. Holly and Wayne press me, while the BTA and MMLF brothers tap their black-booted feet impatiently and urge me to choose sides.

I have subtly pumped every southside acquaintance, fool and boon companion I know and spontaneously meet for information on the heist and have learned nothing. I see Scotty Bennett around the southside constantly. He always doffs his black-style-conscious porkpie hat and *winks* at me.

Scotty knows a great deal about the heist. I know that. He's the brilliant lead detective with five years of knowledge stored. I strongly sense that he's hoarding knowledge from the LAPD at large.

It's as if Scotty is taunting me and pressing me as Mr. Holly
and Wayne taunt me and press me with their powerfully masculine and obdurately circumscribed wills. I keep thinking of Mr.
Holly with women and what it would look like, until the images
begin to vex me and hurt. Wayne is guilt-tripping with a black
woman and providing me with a similarly erotic picture show.
He's looking for the woman's missing son, who bears a minor
resemblance to the surviving robber from the heist. I don't consider it a true lead; the robber's face was badly burned and Reginald Hazzard was a mere nineteen then. It's more like an
affirmation of the dream-state aspect of my life now, with all the
new figures weaving through and beckoning.

Benny Boles has been cruising me quite boldly; he's as out as I
am euphemized and will probably pounce if I go with the BTA.
He's a murderer and recognizably psychopathic, which may
account for his confidence in his masculinity. I see Joan Klein at
the clubs regularly. She quite consciously beckons. She's a vora-
ciously sensuous dancer, concurrently in and out of sync with her
male and female partners. She glimpses me in the shadows,
bestows eye contact and acknowledges me without ever losing the
music's beat. It's as if she's telling me things about myself that
she's gleaned from her dream state. I've found myself bringing
fantasies of Joan and Mr. Holly to bed with me. They don't know
each other in the real world, but I know them both there and
they've converged within my psyche.

And Jomo.

He's certainly scum, but I have been charged to fraternize with
and entrap scum, and I like him anyway. We've been spending
time together at Tiger Kab, MMLF and the clubs; Jomo has gotten
more at ease with me since his knife fight with Leander Jackson.
He's been talking up a significant roll that he's accrued, and I've
been very cautiously grinding him for details to give to Mr. Holly.
I was at that task up to moments before the incident last night.

We had been on a grocery-store extortion run. It was
connivance and implied threat: we wanted boxes of Cocoa Puffs
for the children attending the MMLF's Feed the Kiddies soirees.
From there we went to an MMLF-sponsored bar-b-q and pamphlet
giveaway at Foshay Junior High. Jomo was decorous with the
kids. It was both ghastly and heartwarming, given the man's
nature. I'm sure his dope balance had something to do with it: he
had been snorting coke/Seconal speedballs all day.

We left Foshay, drove toward Jomo's pad and stopped at a

liquor store on Florence Boulevard to buy cigarettes. Jomo staggered and bumped a potato-chip rack. The proprietor was black and took offense. He said, "Nigger, what's wrong with you?"

Jomo vaulted the counter and pistol-whipped the man, as I froze and did nothing. Jomo then stole two bottles of J&B scotch and three cartons of Kool cigarettes.

I did nothing. Jomo kicked the man and shouted anti-BTA epithets. I'm sure the proprietor recognized me. I'm an ex-policeman, a celebrity brother and a notable southside cat-about-town.

67

(Los Angeles, 4/3/69)

Milt C. had a puppet named Junkie Monkey. He did dreary shtick with him. It regaled the brothers. Sonny and Jomo howled on cue.

The switchboard was flooded. Jomo juggled calls. Jordan High was battling Washington. All-city cager—folks needed kabs.

Junkie Monkey wore a pimp hat and a checkerboard suit. A dope spike dangled from one arm. Milt moved his ape lips.

"Dese LAPD pigs hassle me. I be smack-back on ma fron' porch, an' it be a muthafuckin' humbug roust. Dey say, 'What you doin' wid dat hypodermic needle?' An' I say, 'You white muthafuckas got de needle *dicks,* an' I gots dat tar paper throbbin' a hard fuckin' yard.' "

Junior yukked. Jomo plugged calls and yukked. Sonny said, "Junkie Monkey's a jallhouse sissy and a draft dodger. Muhammad Ali fucked his simian ass."

Wayne checked his watch. Marsh was due *now.* He just got a phone-drop message. Another brain *click* clicked him. More memory loss and tug.

A month ago. The fight with Mary Beth. Reginald, the "Freedom School," why that soft *click*?

He was swamped. Drac and the Boys overbooked him. His cutout job added to it. He couldn't work on the *click* just yet.

Junkie Monkey said, "The Beatles bop down to da muthafuckin' ghetto to score some black trim. Dey meets dese two unhealthy-lookin' sistahs name of Carcinoma an' Melanoma an'—"

Wayne looked out the window. Marsh walked by outside. Wayne got up and followed him back to the fleet lot. Sixteen Tiger kabs glowed.

Marsh was cool-day sweaty. Wayne gave him his handkerchief.

"Tell me."

"I was with Jomo two nights ago. He beat up the counterman at a liquor store and 211'd him. I'm fairly sure the man recognized me."

"Why'd you wait this long to tell me?"

"It's my tendency. I tend to wait things out."

"What were you waiting for?"

"Scotty. Every liquor-store proprietor on God's green earth knows him and owes him."

Motown blared. Some fool goosed the dispatch-hut hi-fi. Wayne steered Marsh over to the alley fence.

"He hasn't called Scotty. You'd have heard by now."

"Yes. That's what I'm thinking."

Wayne said, "Give me something."

Marsh wiped his forehead. "What do you mean?"

"Give me a lead for Dwight. Tell me something to convince him you're working."

Marsh sighed. "Liquor-store heists. There's been a bunch of them."

Wayne mimicked the sigh. "We're back to liquor stores?"

"That's not what I mean. I'm saying I may have something."

Wayne sighed harder. "Liquor-store jobs in South L.A. with *black suspects*? Can you give me something more original than that?"

Marsh wiped his forehead. "Jomo's been talking up this big coin he's got, but he won't reveal the source."

Wayne shook his head. "That's insufficient. I'll frost your deal two nights ago, but you're going to start working harder."

"Jesus, Wayne."

Wayne pushed him into the fence. "You're going with BTA. You're going to suck up to Leander Jackson and pick a public fight with Jomo. I'm going to the Dominican Republic. We'll stage it when I get back. You're going to level Jomo over the liquor-store deal. You're going to call him a 'punk-ass, evil, no-account nigger,' and I'll be there to watch you do it."

"Jesus. Just give me—"

A kab pulled in and up. Wayne stepped back and cleared a space.

"You'll do it. I'll tell the world that you're a faggot if you don't."

The liquor store was close by. The counterman was bandaged from the eyebrows up. Wayne walked in and bought a bag of potato chips. The man sniffed fuzz.

"LAPD?"

"Ex-LVPD. I retired."

The man rang the sale. "Why'd you retire?"

"I shot some unarmed black guys and it got out of hand."

"Did they deserve it?"

Wayne gave him a dollar. "Yes."

The man gave him change. "Did you feel bad about it?"

"Yes, I did."

The man smiled. Wayne pointed to his bandage and tossed him a cash roll. Two grand in fifties, rubber band–wrapped.

"Did you call Scotty?"

"I was thinking about it."

"That Scotty's a pisser."

"He's all of that. These same brothers robbed me on six different occasions, so I called up Scotty, independent. I told him the regular LAPD wasn't doing their job. Scotty said he'd take care of it, which he did."

"That must have been some sight."

"It was. They came in with ski masks and went out under sheets. Scotty shoots double-aught with little spiky things attached. Wasn't much left of them."

Wayne ate a potato chip. "You've got a certain loyalty to Scotty."

"Yeah, like I suspect you got for that Marshall Bowen guy."

Wayne tossed cash roll #2. The man fanned it.

"Bowen must be jungled up with some money guys. 'High-level informant.' Does that sound right?"

"Your mortgage is way in arrears. I'm prepared to cover it."

"My electric bill's behind, too."

"Anything else?"

"Yeah, one more thing. I want one of those tiger limousines for my daughter's sweet sixteen."

USC was close by. His schedule was tight. Drac had requested a phone chat. Yes, sir. Nuclear fallout will kill you. No, sir—no time soon. Yes, we should ban the Bomb. No, the world powers will not accede on your say-so.

Wayne parked and strolled the campus. The student body was half square kids, half longhairs all aggrieved. Left- and right-wing flyers covered signboards. YAF vs SDS, VIVA vs SNCC. Kids with guitars, kids in letter sweaters, a few black kids in dashikis.

Wayne walked and braced passersby. The "Freedom School"? Beats me. He checked the campus directory. No, no listing.

He kept at it. He pay-phoned Farlan and postponed the Drac chat. He saw some custodians on a smoke break and walked over.

They were black. They sniffed cop. Wayne sniffed ex-con labor. He laid out ten-spots and pitched them, smiling.

"There was something called the 'Freedom School.' It was here on campus six or seven years ago."

Three guys blank-faced it. One guy said, "Defunct, man. Tapped out before the Watts uprising." One guy said, "There's some bungalows catty-corner from the rec center. Nobody uses them. Look for this dusty old door with this faded-out poster."

Wayne said thanks and strolled. The walkways were tree-lined. Clandestine pot fumes swirled here and there. He found the rec center and the bungalows. He saw the postered door.

Fall, '64. *SAVE THE RUMFORD FAIR-HOUSING ACT! "PROPERTY RIGHTS" MEANS "RACISM"!!!!*

The door looked flimsy. Wayne shoulder-popped it easy. He stepped in. A back window provided light. The room was wall-to-wall boxes.

He went through them. They held stacks of flyers and polemics. *¡Huelga!,* Hands Off Cuba!, fruit-picker strikes. Support Al Fatah, the PLF, the 6/14 Movement. Remember Leo Frank, Emmett Till and the Scottsboro Boys. Civil-rights rants, black-power screeds. Malcolm X, Franz Fanon, Free the Rosenbergs. Free Algeria! Free Palestine! Down with the evil Goat Trujillo, Uncle Sam's insect. United Fruit: *Do you know what that banana on your plate just cost?*

He hit a group photograph. It was dated 9/22/62. It looked like a faculty shot.

Seven men and women outside the bungalow. Three are white, four are black. Two white women off to the side. One woman is tall and red-haired. The other woman is shorter. She's mid-to-late thiryish. She has dark, gray-streaked hair and black-framed glasses.

Click. Blip. Maybe, probably, not quite.

The *click* clicked on and clicked off short of *Eureka!* The *blip* took a weird form. Sultan Sam's Sandbox, three months ago. Smoke rings and a back view of streaked hair just like that.

Wayne squinted at the photo. The woman wore long sleeves. No scars stood out. Reginald went to this school. Reginald got popped in the redneck town. *Maybe, not quite probably*—the woman bailed him out.

Drac Air flew him in. The plane landed on the private Hughes runway. Cops with bullwhips supervised the VIP lounge build.

Joaquín Balaguer sent a limousine and four flanking motorbikes. The vehicles were mid-Trujillo vintage. All five were jackhammer-loud.

They drove into Santo Domingo. The windows were smoked. Bright colors filtered in monochromatically. The limo lurched through traffic. The pictures were sepia-soaked. It was a pauper-nation newsreel. Kids pulled rickshaws, beggars begged, goons chased sign-waving youths. It was a quick-shutter slide show. Blink and you see oppression. Blink and it's gone.

Wayne was bleary-eyed. Slide show: he kept seeing that woman's face. The glasses, the streaked hair—the slide jammed and re-ran her image. He read the 6/14 tract on the airplane. It decried Dominican despots and innocent Haitians slaughtered. It prophesied future despots more savvy than the Goat. It predicted U.S.-Dominican collusion in the interest of a Yankee tourist trade.

Reginald meets the Haitian man. They discuss voodoo herbs. *Click*— memory tug and loss. The woman, the "Freedom School," mental gears stripped short of connection.

Wayne rolled down his window. The monochrome newsreel went eye-burning bright. The colors assaulted. The salt air burned. Cops chased protestors down a dead-end alley and pinned them to a wall. Wayne saw a single nightstick raised and heard a single scream.

The limo dropped him at the El Embajador. A toady ensconced him in a plush suite. He had a wide view. The Río Ozama was due west. Black kids dove and fought each other for fishing-boat chum. The skin tone shifted district to district. He saw occasional red flags on sticks.

He walked down to Mesplede's suite, knocked and got no answer. He walked to Dipshit's suite and saw the door ajar.

He breezed in. It was a kid's crib. Magazines were tossed pell-mell. Dipshit dug *Playboy* and *Guns & Ammo*. Dipshit was a picture punk. He had a Polaroid camera. He had ad-lib pix of women up the ying-yang.

Brown bottles on a nightstand. White-labeled, what's—

Sulfur oxide precipitant, ammonia, acetic anhydride.

"Hi, Wayne. What's shaking?"

Dipshit wore a Colt Python with Bermuda shorts. Dipshit licked an ice-cream cone. Dipshit had acne.

Wayne smiled and walked up. Dipshit stuck his hand out. Wayne bent his fingers, proned him out and kicked him in the balls. Dipshit dropped his ice-cream cone and went blue.

"No heroin. You don't make it, you don't buy it, you don't sell it. I'll kill anyone who does."

Dipshit puked butter brickle and cone shreds. A shadow hit the wall.

"*Ça va,* Wayne. *C'est fini, l'héroïne.*"

Balaguer negotiated. The payouts and contingency plans favored the Führer. The overall deal favored the Boys. Balaguer haggled and conceded. Wayne took the same tack. They chatted in a parlor at the Palacio Nacional and worked from scratch sheets. Mesplede and Dipshit were off boozing. Smith and Brundage were off golfing. The Cubans were off whoring.

Building costs, labor costs, airport kickbacks. Reduced fares for U.S.-D.R. flights. Incentive payments. No-customs-interference chits. Stateside money-wash details. Inspection tours by Dwight Holly, President Nixon's liaison.

The last point bugged Balaguer. Wayne mollified him. Sir, the tours would be by and large cosmetic.

Der Führer liked that. Wayne bait-and-switched behind it. Tourism only works in peaceful settings. Too much evidence of poverty will turn tourists off. President Nixon understands that, sir. He is your typical tourist writ more politically astute. Visitors will find your enforcement efforts confusing. Goon squads and roving dissidents are greek to them. They cannot extrapolate. They will be shocked by what they see.

Balaguer bristled through the discourse. Wayne forfeited three money points to cut him slack. The chat took six hours. Balaguer stood up to bid adios.

Wayne said, "No whips, sir. I'm afraid I have to insist."

Cosmetic.

He saw it fast: food giveaways and less hurt from La Banda. The slide show felt marginalized. His shutter popped quicker. He saw or didn't see at an accelerated rate. The monochrome view helped: Mesplede's car had smoked windows.

The Santo Domingo sites were plowed and construction-ready. They were police-guarded. They were in half-decent areas. Airport shuttles could take tours through good neighborhoods. Tour packages would be all-inclusive. Guests would be urged to stay inside and spend.

Santo Domingo was Jim Crow. Light-skinned people, dark-skinned people and a stratified mix. Wayne remembered Little Rock, '57. The 82nd Airborne and forced desegregation.

Mesplede drove and chain-smoked. Dipshit sat in the backseat and worried his dipshit lapel pin. Radio music stifled conversation. Caribbean jazz, brassy and repetitive.

The Autopista ran them north. The road was bad. The cane fields and glades de-saturated the existing monochrome. Black people ran across the road. Mesplede swerved around them.

The Piedra Blanca site was construction-vetted and guarded. The high-rise view would take in a few shacks and encompass wide greenery.

The site felt rapidly vacated. Wayne saw bloodstains on a discarded two-by-four.

They stayed a few minutes and split for Jarabacoa. *C'est fini, l'héroïne*—nobody talked.

The ride took three hours. Wayne rolled down his window and de-smoked and jazzed the car. The bright colors hurt his eyes. He smelled jungle rot and gunpowder.

Jarabacoa was identical. The guards were servile and offered them *cervezas*. Wayne saw a bullwhip stashed behind a bush.

A black man sprinted past a cane field. His face was all open-sored ooze.

Wayne said, "Jean-Philippe, you go back. Crutchfield, you're driving me into Haiti."

Mesplede tossed his cigarette. "We have only the one car, Wayne."

"There's a bus station a mile back. We'll drop you."

The air conditioner tanked. They climbed the Cordillera Central in a mobile sauna. The open windows got them hot air and bugs like Godzilla. They crossed south of Dajabón. A wobbly pylon bridge spanned the Plaine du Massacre. *Fascisto* border guards waved good-bye and hello. Gators sunned on the Haitian banks, surrounded by leg bones.

Skin tone darkened. The bright colors held as the poverty index spiked. Rusted tin-roof shacks and mud huts. Blood-marked trees and lynched roosters dripping entrails.

Dipshit drove. His hand trembled on the shifter. Wayne shut his eyes and put his seat back full supine. The upholstery was sweat-slick. Moisture pooled at the piping.

"No more fuckups. I'll kill you next time."

Dipshit said, "Okay."

"Your fail-safes are bullshit. Nobody would believe you. You're a jerkoff. You eat ice-cream cones and perv on women. Mesplede's soft for you, but I'm not."

Dipshit said, "Okay." His voice squeaked and broke.

"I'll say this once. You don't get out of The Life unmaimed or alive. Killing Communists and working for guys like me gets you nothing but your next nightmare."

Dipshit said, "Sure"—this whisper-squeak.

Wayne opened his eyes. The road was dirt now. Jalopies, oxcarts and a village: thatched huts and pastel cubes flying voodoo-sect flags.

Rhinestone-rock walls. Murals on easeled signboards. A tavern called Port Afrique.

Wayne said, "Stop the car."

Dipshit pulled over. Wayne got out. Black folks milling about got magnetized.

"Go back to Santo Domingo. I'll get back on my own."

Dipshit shrugged and screeched off. Wayne walked into Port Afrique. He smelled ammonia base, semi-toxics and untreated alcohol. The place was rectangular. There was a stand-up bar with bottle shelves behind it and no more. French slogans covered the side walls: "By the power of the saint star, walk and find." "Sleep without knowing or sleeping."

The barman looked at him. Three other men followed his eyes. They held sequined goblets. Fumes rose out of them. High acidity, low alkaline content. Klerin liquor, certainly. Odds on semi-poisonous reptile-gland compounds.

Wayne walked to the bar and bowed to show respect. The three men walked away. The shelf bottles were transparent and tape-marked in French. Colored talc, tree bark, pharmacologically active snake powder.

The barman bowed. Wayne pointed to an empty goblet. The barman's look said *Are you sure?*

"*S'il vous plaît, monsieur. Je suis chimiste, et voudrais essayer votre plus potion.*"

The barman bowed. "*Comme vous voulez, monsieur. Mais vous comprenez q'il y a des risques.*"

Wayne said, "*Oui.*" The barman opened bottles and dipped a spoon. Fungible plants, bark, puffer-fish liver. *Bufo marinus:* a sea snake's porotoid gland. Klerin liquor from a siphon. An unknown liquid that made it all foam.

The fizz increased. It smelled like a volatile component bond. The barman served the goblet with blessing gestures. Wayne bowed and placed U.S. cash on the bar.

The three men walked over. One toasted him, one blessed him, one handed him a sect card. The foam burned the air all around them. Wayne drank the potion in one gulp.

It scorched his throat and shuddered through him. The barman said, "*De rien, monsieur. Bonne chance.*"

He found a shady spot outside the village. He stood there and turned off external noise. He heard the air breathe and knew he brought belief to the moment. He felt the soil under him swirl.

His pulse beat and wired his limbs to the trees surrounding him. His peripheral vision expanded and allowed him to see from the back of his head. His eyes watered. He saw Dr. King and the Reverend Hazzard swimming. Dr. King had Mary Beth's coloring. The pastor had Marsh Bowen's eyes. Birds perched inside him. Their chirps resounded as those mind clicks he kept hearing back in the world. The sun turned into the moon and dropped into his pocket. He kept seeing the woman with the dark, gray-streaked hair.

68

(Los Angeles, 4/10/69)

S cotty said, "Marsh fucked up. He witnessed a 211 and didn't report it."

Dwight lit a cigarette. "I know."

"Marsh copped to it?"

"He told his cutout."

"You mean Wayne Tedrow?"

"That's right."

Scotty laughed. "Inspired casting. The spooks are afraid of him, so they adore him. Nobody suspects that he's FBI-adjunct, because he's working for the Boys."

Piper's Coffee Shop on Western. The 1:00 a.m. clientele: cops and Schaeffer's Ambulance ghouls.

Dwight said, "Who told you about Wayne?"

"One of my numerous southside informants."

"The liquor-store guy?"

"My lips are sealed."

Dwight rubbed his eyes. "Let's talk about Jomo."

"Give me a concession first."

"All right. I'll let Jomo go if you let Marsh slide."

"Meaning?"

"Meaning, you can have Jomo independent of my operation. Meaning, he's my best black-militant psycho, but I can live without prosecuting him. Meaning, you've got something going that you won't talk about, because you didn't call me at midnight for a nigger-strongarm roust."

Scotty cream-dosed his coffee. "Correct on all counts. Jomo's got a lot of bread, and I think I know where he got it."

"And if you need Marsh as a witness, you'll call him in."

"That's correct."

Dwight chained cigarettes. "Will you promise not to reveal Marsh's Bureau status?"

Scotty bummed a cigarette. Dwight lit it for him.

"Yes. Will you promise not to pop Jomo for any and all Federal offenses while I build my case?"

"Yes."

Scotty took one drag and stubbed out his cigarette. Two cops walked by and saluted. Scotty winked at them.

"Thanks for coming out. I realize it was short notice."

Dwight stretched. "It's all right. I couldn't sleep, anyway."

"There's always booze."

"It quit working for me."

"There's always women."

Dwight said, "I'm stretched a bit thin there."

69

(Mona Passage, 4/10/69)

"*C'est fini, l'héroïne.*"
"You're a jerkoff."
"*Allons-y, l'héroïne—oui!*"
Tiger Klaw pushed waves. Destination: Point Higuero, Puerto Rico. Saldívar manned the turbines. Froggy manned the bridge. Gómez-Sloan and Canestel manned the torpedo drops. Morales read the owner's manual.

Crutch manned the fore machine-gun placement. Luc Duhamel manned the aft. They launched from Luc's private inlet. They skirted the north coast to the passage unobstructed. It was death-defying shit.

That bankroll clique bought the boat. Bebe Rebozo supplied the bulk of the bread. Luc knew a dope cadre in Point Higuero. *Tiger Klaw* sidled the night side. Their *baaaad* baby made four sabotage runs to date.

Luc's inlet to the Windward Passage and Cuba's Red Reefs. Two militia launch docks destroyed and thirty Fidelistos *mort.* "You eat ice-cream cones and perv on women." Yeah, but nineteen Commies rot dead.

Tiger Klaw: wood-hulled and World War II vintage. Tiger-striped, tiger-pawed, christened "109." *L'hommage à le grand putain Jack.*

Crutch ate Dramamine. *Tiger Klaw* wah-watusi'd in choppy waves. Dusk doused the sun and freon froze the water. Land approached starboard. Saldívar spotted semaphore blinks. Froggy steered *Tiger Klaw* toward a cove. Shoals hemmed them in. Lantern light strafed the bow. Crutch saw four spics with Tommy guns.

The spics grapple-hooked the bow and tied *Tiger Klaw* tight. The fit held: machine-gun mounts cinched to rock fissures. The Krew hopped off. Sand sucked at their socks. The P.R. spics looked like the Cubans. They all had that macho-maimed visage. Names went around. Crutch kept it zipped. The spics bowed to Luc. It was his pedigree. Six-foot-eight voodoo priest and Tonton cop. Luc was an all-time rare turd.

The Krew followed the spics. Jungle brush pressed up to the beach. Night bugs swarmed. The lantern light killed most of them dead in the air. Crutch saw a fishing shack. Two spics door-guarded it. The inside was eight by eight. Powder bricks sat on a table.

Saldívar brought the money in a knapsack. Luc brought sucrose filler, a razor blade and a hypodermic syringe. The spics crossed themselves and blessed his test flight.

Gómez-Sloan slit the bricks. Saldívar spooned powder into a purple solution. It turned yellow. Froggy went *voilà!* The spics went *¡arriba!* Luc swabbed his spike, stretched a tourniquet and geezed up.

All eyes on Luc. He's at Cape *Coon*averal. He's heading for liftoff.

Luc tapped the plunger. Blood hit the syringe. Luc listed, lulled, levitated and left them for Cloud 9.

The water was cold. Waves banged the hull and sudsed the foredeck. Crutch had watch duty. He had to get wet. He brain-tripped. The Dominican women kiss. It takes him back to Joan and Gretchen/Celia and their kiss last summer.

The voodoo death book. Tattoo vanishes that summer. She's a 6/14 traitor. Joan and Gretchen/Celia *want* her dead. Slasher homicide—or maybe something else.

"You perv on women."

The Cubans didn't scare him. Luc didn't scare him. Froggy, Scotty and Dwight Holly—nix. Wayne *scared* him. Wayne didn't scare the other guys. Froggy defied Wayne. Froggy said they could keep the dope biz clandestine. Wayne killed Martin Luther King and several lesser-known niggers. Wayne had a black girlfriend. Wayne was scary because he processed evil shit and fed it back to you, uninvited.

He dropped Wayne off in hellhole Haiti. Wayne came back three days later, gaunt and head-tripped. He okayed a transfer: bucks from the Boys to the Midget. The jail crew and slave crew were working now. The Cubans and La Banda cracked the whip. Tiger Krew's work ran non-stop. They supervised the sites. They maintained *Tiger Klaw.* They strawbossed the build on a full-mooring berth. Luc's voodoo slaves were gouging an inlet space. Froggy called it "Tiger Kove." Luc had dope *coon*ections in Port-au-Prince. Tonton spooks would lay the smack on the dealers. Boss spook Papa Doc would glom a big cut.

Wayne said no smack. The Krew contradicted. Wayne *scared* him. He *hated* Wayne. He had a picture of Wayne shaking hands with the Midget.

Luc taught him a voodoo hex. He cursed Wayne with it. He stuck pins in a dead chicken. He drew his blood and stuck the pin in Wayne's picture face.

A wave doused him. It fucked with his brain pix. Crutch fired tracer rounds at the sky.

The CIA guys were golf nuts. Terry Brundage shot scratch. His flunkies had low handicaps. Their office was the ex–caddy shack on the Midget's private golf course. La Banda ran a torture bunker under the ninth hole.

Crutch walked in. The floor was synthetic grass. Cocktail glasses served as golf holes. Terry and his flunkies wore T-shirts and nubby-silk knickers.

Terry said, *"Hola, pariguayo."*

Crutch laughed. One flunky blew a putt. One flunky sunk a *loooong* one. The place was messy. Three desks, short-wave radio, teletype machine. A file bank with drawers overstuffed.

The watercooler held a cup dispenser and pre-mixed daiquiris. Crutch grabbed a cup and pulled a short slurp.

Terry twirled his putter. "Did Mesplede send you?"

"No, it was my idea. I thought I'd check your dissident file. I think there's been some Commies nosing around the sites."

The flunkies packed their golf bags. They shoved shotguns in with their sticks.

Terry filled a thermos with rum goo. "There's some skin mags in the john. If you're looking for chicks, you'll be better off there."

The file bank was chaos. Four cabinets, sixteen drawers, no system. Dumped folders, loose snapshots. No tracking or routing numbers. Nothing alphabetized.

Crutch worked drawer-to-drawer. He locked himself in the office. He had four hours. Golf and boozy hoo-haw took that long. He dumped drawers and skimmed documents. He scanned for *anything* Joan Klein/Celia Reyes/6-14–related. He got name lists, membership lists, suspect lists, interrogation lists and assumed-dead lists. He saw a shitload of Commie acronyms and lists in Spanish. He saw a *fourteen-thousand-name* enemy list for Rafael "the Goat" Trujillo. He saw a list of suspected safe houses in Santo Domingo and half-ass memorized it. He saw *fragments* of a 6/14/59 time line. The narrative was fractured. Half the pages were missing.

He knew the basic facts already. The new shit was horrific. The Goat machete-murdered 6/14 sympathizers en masse. He wiped out border villages. He fed children to the gators in the Plaine du Massacre. A list followed: 6/14 members captured. No Joan, no Gretchen/Celia, no María Rodríguez Fontonette.

The narrative ended. Non sequitur pages followed. Crutch dumped three more drawers and got this:

A fractured string of paragraphs on an un-numbered page. The name María Rodríguez Fontonette. Her moniker, "Tattoo."

She's 6/14. She's a turncoat. She ratted out the invasion. La Banda knew. Countermeasures were swiftly prepared and effected. A Tonton Macoute traitor assisted the rebels and escaped to parts unknown. His name: Laurent-Jean Jacqueau.

Crutch re-read the page. He read the pages following it and behind it and re-skimmed every page he'd read already. Nothing revised or enhanced the fractured narrative. Three and a half hours to *this*.

He dumped four more drawers. He got more names, names and names. He dumped two more drawers. He saw a file folder. "Reyes, Celia" was typed on the front. The folder was empty.

He slurped rum goo straight from the spout. He dumped another drawer. He saw a million photos of Commie-looking spics. He saw a pic marked 6/14/59. He heard screams somewhere under the golf course. The room light dimmed for two seconds and came back on strong.

He turned the photo over. It's an aerial shot. There's a rocky beach. Soldiers hold guns on scruffy rebels.

He blinked and squinted. He looked very close. He saw one woman in with thirty-odd men. It was Joan Rosen Klein. Her right fist was raised.

Smoke whiffed out a cooling shaft. A stink followed. The invasion was ten years ago. Joan's hair was all dark.

More smoke and stink. Another scream—pure Kreole French. More stink—pure scalded flesh.

70

(Los Angeles, 4/13/69)

Junkie Monkey ragged Sonny Liston. It pushed Sonny's buttons. Sonny shot his wad on drag queens and had no oomph for Ali. His manhood got de-jizzified.

Jomo plugged calls. Junior snarfed cognac-dipped moon pies. Milt's shtick was protracted. Wayne and Marsh watched Sonny seethe.

It was raining. The roof leaked. The stripedy wallpaper peeled. A Dr. Feelgood owed Tiger Kab 350. He paid off in Desoxyn and Dilaudid. Sonny and Jomo were speedbally pissed.

Junkie Monkey was fey today. Junkie Monkey preened his Afro and pursed his lips.

"Ali be so *pretty*. That young man can rhyme and play the dozens like no one else this girl has ever seen. 'Liston's gonna flee. He'll go down in three.' 'This ain't no jive. He be out by round five.' 'He can't last to four, 'cause he be out fuckin' whores.' 'He ain't got no hope with his arm full of dope.'"

Sonny sipped rocket fuel—liquid meth and Everclear. Sonny lit a Kool filter king.

"It ain't funny. Do the one where Lady Bird Johnson sucks my dick."

Junkie Monkey pouted. "This simian sister is *soooooooo* tired of your reluctance to acknowledge that pretty young man who has brought colored folk into the Age of Aquarius, while you be actin' as the organ-grinder's monkey for the pig power structure and the mob."

Sonny balled his fists. His cigarette crumbled. Marsh looked at Jomo. Wayne looked at Marsh. Junior waddled to the john. Milt taped a plastic cigarette to Junkie Monkey's lips.

" 'He'll be seein' heaven when he goes down in seven.' 'If he last to nine, his punk ass is mine.' "

Jomo said, "That's enough. That shit is wearing me thin."

Wayne nodded. Marsh caught it—*we're close.*

Junkie Monkey preened. "And this girl is *soooooo* tired of you poseurs who don't know Eldridge Cleaver from Beaver Cleaver and Franz Fanon from my fat fanny, you silly—"

Jomo said, "Shut up, pops. That's the last time I'm saying it."

Wayne signaled Marsh—now.

Marsh said, "Easy, brother. Let the monkey do his thing."

Jomo popped his knuckles. All eight—slow and loud.

Wayne signaled Marsh—more.

Marsh walked to the switchboard. Jomo was close. Marsh leaned on a chair.

"What gives you the right to push old men around? I'm talking about you, nigger. I'm talking about that poor liquor-store man you whupped on, who did you no motherfucking—"

Jomo stood up. Marsh moved close. They both grabbed chairs. Jomo swung wide and missed. Marsh ducked. The chair hit the switchboard.

The legs snapped. The console shattered. Call plugs dropped to the floor. Marsh swung tight. He caught Jomo's back, he caught Jomo's legs, he grazed Jomo's head and carved half an ear off. Jomo stumbled and hit the console. Marsh uppercut him. He aimed crotch-high and jammed a chair leg into his balls.

Jomo screamed. Marsh ran outside and screamed in the rain. It sounded like one word repeated. Wayne jammed up a window to hear.

It was *BTA! BTA! BTA!* Marsh jabbed the chair in the air and kept shouting it. People poured out of storefronts. Some people cheered.

He went trolling. It was trolling with intent. It pertained to that recurring *click.*

He'd argued with Mary Beth. She told him about the "Freedom School." He went there and saw the faculty photo. The woman with the gray-streaked hair. The *click* he couldn't place. The semi-*click* back to that pub crawl.

Three months ago. The first Tiger Kab bash. The back view of a woman with that same hair.

His mindscape in Haiti. The herbs and her shape-shifting picture.

Wayne cruised the southside. His phone fight with Mary Beth echoed. She pressed him on his trip. He lied—the D.R. and Haiti aren't that bad. My investors will boost the economy. Balaguer isn't Trujillo. Please believe that things will improve. Mary Beth scoffed. I know better, babe.

Wayne turned down Central Avenue. The clubs were zooming. He saw that woman at Sultan Sam's Sandbox. She might be there now. It was a slim-chance long shot.

He'd spent three days in Haiti. He dope-tripped non-stop. He kaliedoscoped his whole life. Faces grew out of trees and stream water. The herbs burned through his system. It was a zombie state. He had to sit still and listen. He didn't have the will to create thought or run. He fell asleep after a million hours tripping. The real world returned to him, changed.

Wayne cut east on Slauson. He saw dope buys outside a gumbo stand. Tiger Krew wanted to push heroin. He quashed it. They wouldn't betray him. They feared his clout with the Boys. The Krew would probably make Cuban runs. Cuba: the nut Right's idée fixe.

Some BTA poseurs walked by. They wore cossack hats and slim-cut black suits. Marsh delivered. He was Mister BTA now.

A crowd stood outside Sultan Sam's. Wayne double-parked and walked to the head of the line. The bouncers called him "boss." The Boys owned the place now. The black people behind the rope cold-eyed him.

He opened the door and looked inside. Everybody was black. No white woman with gray-streaked hair.

He drove to Rae's Rugburn Room and played big white bwana. He got more cold eyes and heard some pig noise. She wasn't there. He hit the Snooty Fox, Nat's Nest and the Klover Klub. The pig noise escalated throughout.

Cherchez la femme. La femme n'est pas là.

Wayne drove to Mr. Mitch's. He didn't own the place. He greased two bouncers for a VIP entry. A black man flamboyantly oinked him.

The interior was cave-dark. The hostess seated patrons with a flashlight. She walked Wayne to a table. He saw Sonny ensconced with Junior Jefferson. Two booths up: Ezzard Donnell Jones and the woman.

Wayne joined Sonny and Junior. They were bombed on Mr. Mitch's jet fuel. The bottle radiated.

Sonny said, "Jomo's gonna be carrying his balls around in a wheelbarrow."

Junior snarfed lychee nuts. "Marsh be best advised to keep himself scarce the next few days."

Sonny sipped brew. "You too fat and Wayne too skinny. Every time you reach for a moon pie, hand one to him."

The woman smoked. The woman tossed her hair. The woman swayed to a canned-music beat.

Wayne pointed over. "Who is she?"

Sonny said, "She hangs out with the BTA and she dances up a storm. I don't like them glasses, though."

Junior said, "I think her name is Joan."

Wayne watched Joan. Sonny and Junior ignored him. He built himself a head space. The club went quiet. Wayne synced the music to her movements. He thought he tasted voodoo herbs and klerin booze. Sensory wisps—a flashback for sure.

Joan cleaned her glasses on her shirttail. Her eyes went soft without them. A shiv extended out from one boot.

She slouched a little. Her movements were fluid. She blew artful smoke rings.

The music tone shifted. Joan stopped swaying. She put money on the table, got up and split.

Wayne got up. Darkness covered him. He followed Joan out to the rear parking lot. She got into a '59 Chevy. The plates were mud-streaked. She was a tail-savvy pro.

She pulled out and hit Manchester westbound. Wayne shagged his rental car and idled forty yards back. Joan drove middle-lane slow. She deployed her signal lights and played good citizen. She turned onto the Harbor Freeway northbound. Wayne zoomed up and dawdled back.

It was late. Traffic was scarce. Wayne leapfrogged to look innocuous. They passed through downtown and Chinatown. The Pasadena Freeway ran them north. Joan cut onto the Golden State westbound. Wayne caught up and fell back. Joan bombed through Atwater and skirted the Glendale off-ramps. She veered right and hit an Eagle Rock exit. Wayne laid back and watched her taillights. She stopped outside a bungalow court on a hill.

Wayne stayed put. Joan parked the Chevy at the curb and unlocked the Dodge next to it. The lights went on. She U-turned and headed straight at him. He saw her face in the windshield. The front plate was mud-smeared.

Her turn signal flashed. She cut east on Colorado Boulevard. Wayne lagged slow, caught up and fell back. They drove through Pasadena. Joan turned north on Lake Avenue. Pasadena bled into Altadena. They ran up toward the San Gabriel Hills. Wayne let two cars buffer-zone them. He stuck his head out the window and fixed on Joan's taillights.

She turned left on a side street. Wayne floored it, turned and braked back. Joan parked and walked up to a small shingle house. Someone opened the door and let her in. The Eagle Rock location vibed *safe house*. Ditto this pad.

Wayne parked and ran over. The house lights were on. He squatted and ducked around to the driveway. He caught shadows inside. The window shades were half up. He stood and looked in.

A small living room. Stacks of rifles and handguns piled on furniture. Blankets draped over them.

Carbines, M14's, scope-mounted Rugers. Automatics and revolvers in a box.

Jomo Clarkson walked in. His head was sutured and gauzed. Joan followed him. They talked soundless. He looked agitated. She looked calm. The closed window killed audio.

Joan took off her coat. Wayne saw the knife scar on her right arm. *CLICK:*

That file Dwight sent him. No picture attached. He burned through redacted type. He found one KA name and told Dwight. He shredded the file. He couldn't recall the KA name. The *CLICK* felt solid and *INCOMPLETE*.

Joan and Jomo talked. Wayne pressed up to the window. He caught audio hum, no words formed, he couldn't read lips.

He saw a gas station down the block. He ran for the phone booth—

Dwight sipped coffee. "The late-night call-out. I'm starting to get used to it."

Canter's Deli on Fairfax. The 3:00 a.m. clientele: cops and ultra-soiled hippies.

Wayne said, "Who's Joan?"

Dwight raised his hands—beats me—disingenuous, unconvincing.

"Is she Joan Rosen Klein? I treated the redactions on her file last year, but I never saw her picture."

Dwight reprised beats me. Wayne slapped the table. Their coffee sloshed and spilled.

"Tell me about her."

Dwight shook his head. Wayne slapped the table. The bread basket flew.

"She's got a knife scar on her right arm."

Dwight fucking smiled. Wayne balled his fists. Dwight touched his hands—son, don't do this.

"I saw her with Jomo Clarkson. 1864 Avondale in Altadena. It's a safe house. There's a fuckload of guns."

Dwight fretted his law-school ring. It dropped off and fell in his lap.

"Keep going."

"Jomo's been talking up a roll he's got. He's a heist man and an anti-white-tract writer. Fred Hiltz, remember? The hate-tract king gets offed, and BHPD tags it 'unknown black suspects.'"

Dwight got up and ran. Wayne grabbed his ring off the floor.

71

(Beverly Hills, 4/14/69)

BHPD let him read the file. Hoover's pet thug at 4:00 a.m.? The watch commander complied.

Dwight sat in the muster room. The file was abbreviated. Mr. Hoover short-shifted the case. Jack Leahy had shitcanned it, per his dictate.

One folder, nine pages, a four-page lead sheet. Numerous male Negroes listed. Mostly rat-outs by police informants and pissed-off loved ones. A general tally of male Negro heist men. No Jomo Kenyatta Clarkson, no black-militant fucks et al.

Dwight read the crime-scene report and autopsy protocol. Eyewits reported two masked Negroes. Cause of death: massive shotgun wounds. Also listed: four .38-caliber slugs lodged in the head.

Hold it—

The protocol included bullet pix. The lab tech said all four shots blew from one gun. Soft-points, six lands, eight grooves, semi-flat projectiles.

Hold it right—

Joan fired safe-house rounds into baffling. *He* told her to. Spent shells—right there in his briefcase.

Dwight popped it open. The bullet pile was plastic-wrapped. He found one dented .38. He grabbed the photos and ran down the hall to the crime lab.

The door was open. Nobody was there. Candy-ass PDs were like that. Dwight looked around. By the back wall: a ballistics microscope.

He walked over and put his shell in the holder. He laid the photos on the counter. He tweaked the dial and squinted. He got in close. He got a

six-land, eight-groove spread and a near-identical flathead. He checked
the photos. The same gun fired both bullets, dead cert.

He heard sirens outside. He heard a radio call one room over: *Code 3,
all K-cars, Altad—*

Mob scene:

The L.A. Sheriff's, BHPD, twenty black & white and plainclothes units.
Bluesuits hauling out blanket-wrapped guns.

Dwight pulled up to the barricades. The street was arc-lit pink-white.
Squares milled around in their pj's. Cops poured in and out of the target
pad. Safe house, no shit.

The barricade guard walked up. He was a Sheriff's geek with post-
teenage acne. Dwight stepped out of the car and badged him.

"Come on, give."

"Uh . . . sir?"

"Tell me what we've got here."

The geek snapped to. "Well, we got a tip on a gun stash and that homicide of that hate guy last year. It's BHPD's case, so we called—"

"Jomo Clarkson. *Where is he?*"

The geek stepped back. "Well, LAPD shagged him out from under us.
This Robbery bull showed up with a peremptory warrant. He took the guy
to 77th Street Station."

Dwight got light-headed. "Is there anyone else in custody? A white
woman? Did LAPD pop a woman with the black guy?"

"No, sir. This detective just hustled the colored man off real quick.
We've sure got the guns, but I don't know anything about a woman."

Dwight got in his car and burned tread in reverse. He banged the curb
off a U-turn and looped side streets to the Pasadena Freeway. He attached
his gumball light and hit 120. The run downtown took six minutes. The
Harbor Freeway got him to the Congo. The station was a quick jump off
the exit.

He parked in the patrol lot and pinned his badge to his coat. He walked
past the front desk. The duty sergeant was snoozing. He heard inebriated
jigs howling back in the jail.

The squadroom was upstairs. Dwight jumped the steps three at a time.
The bullpen was wall-to-wall desks and walk spaces. The morning-watch
cops read teletypes and hunt-and-peck typed. They looked bored. One
guy waved. Dwight cut down a bisecting hallway. Sweat rooms lined the
right wall.

There's Scotty.

He's eating an apple. He's wearing a brown suit and a plaid bow tie. He's looking in a double-front window.

Dwight walked over. Scotty winked. Dwight looked in the window. There's Jomo, cuffed to a chair.

Scotty said, "Don't tell me. Mr. Hoover wants the Hiltz thing chilled."

"Why tell you? It wouldn't do me any good."

Scotty laughed. "Would you like to watch?"

"Yes. Will you give me a concession first?"

"Yes."

Dwight pulled out his cigarettes. Scotty took two and lit them both up.

"What happened? Tell me why we're standing here."

Scotty tossed the apple in a trash can. "Your boy Marsh called me and snitched Jomo for some liquor-store 211's. I grabbed him before BHPD could glom him for the Hiltz job, which I think he's good for. Funny thing, though. I talked to Marsh on the phone, and it sure didn't sound like him. More-fucking-over, it sounded like a woman was whispering in the guy's ear and telling him what to say."

Dwight touched his ring. It was gone. Scotty stubbed his cigarette out on the wall. Jomo spat at the mirror space. The glob hit a bolted-down table. Jomo squirmed in his bolted-down chair.

Scotty opened the door. Dwight followed him in. They pulled chairs up and loomed over Jomo. The fucker was floor-bolted and chair-cuffed in tight.

"I want to talk to a lawyer. Get me one of them frizzy-haired Jewish guys that work for the Panthers."

Scotty said, "Mr. Holly's a lawyer. He'll advise you of your rights."

Dwight said, "You have the right to confess and avoid physical punishment. You have the right to tell Sergeant Bennett exactly what he wants to know. I'll require prompt answers to my questions, as well. If you cooperate, we'll give you a pack of cigarettes and a candy bar. If you resist, we'll kick the shit out of you and dump you in the queen's tank."

"This is fucking humbug shit! I know the law! *Miranda-Escobedo* passed in 1962!"

Scotty said, "*Miranda-Escobedo* doesn't apply here. This is a kangaroo court, and you're the kangaroo."

Jomo spat on the table. Scotty pulled a rubber-hose chunk from his waistband. It was ten inches long and friction tape–gripped.

"Over the past seven months fourteen liquor stores have been robbed in southside Los Angeles. You match the general description of the suspect. A confidential police informant called me today. He gave you up for the crimes, and I found him credible. I would advise you to confess. If you require legal counsel, you may address your attorney."

Dwight said, "Confess."

Jomo said, "Marsh Bowen snitched me. First, he whups me, then he snitches me. You see the stitches on my head? That ex-pig motherfucker did that. You think I'm not gonna get no get-back when I get out of here?"

Scotty flexed the hose chunk. "Son, I would love to see that happen. Marsh put some hurt on me as well, and I would love to see him get his comeuppance."

Jomo squirmed. His cuff chain rattled. The cuffs were tight-ratcheted. His wrists bled.

"Marsh snitched me, right?"

Scotty said, "That's correct."

"So let me out of here. Give me a skate on them chump-change 211's and I'll get us both some get-back."

Dwight said, "Confess first. We'll get you a day pass to get your shit in order. I've got a Jew lawyer buddy. He'll plead you out. You'll do a year at the honor farm, tops."

Jomo spat on the table. "Fuck your mother. You a fascist cockroach and a minion of the pig power structure. Your mama sucked my big black dick."

Scotty winked at Dwight. Scotty circled the table and stood behind Jomo. Scotty stroked Jomo's Afro with the hose chunk.

"Confess, son. It's in your best interest to do so."

Jomo said, "Fuck you."

Scotty swung the hose chunk. Jomo screamed. Perfect kidney shot.

Dwight said, "Confess." Jomo spat on the table. Scotty swung the hose chunk. Jomo screamed louder. Perfect kidney shot.

Dwight said, "Confess." Jomo retched for air. Scotty placed a sheet of paper on the table. Dwight skimmed it. The fourteen 211's were listed.

Scotty said, "Look at the list and nod your head. We'll consider it a confession."

Jomo spat on the table. Jomo said, "Fuck you."

Scotty swung the hose chunk. Jomo screamed. Perfect kidney shot.

Dwight said, "He looked at the list. As his lawyer, I'm calling it a confession."

Scotty bowed. "I agree. I'll write it up later, and Mr. Clarkson can sign it when he's capable of holding a pen."

Jomo dripped bile. Blood was laced in. His head lolled. His cuffs cut deep. His eyes did funny things.

Scotty said, "I have a good deed in mind."

Dwight said, "Tell me."

Scotty fondled the hose chunk. "We could get BHPD a clearance on an old case of theirs. We could get you a clearance on that safe house and those guns."

Dwight thought of Joan. "Forget the safe house. My people might get compromised. Let's concentrate on the Hiltz job."

"Hiltz job" tweaked Jomo. *Say what? Whazzat? Don't know no Hiltz job.*

Scotty said, "Last September 14, two male Negroes pulled a string of residential robberies and in the process killed a wealthy hate pamphleteer named Dr. Fred Hiltz. I believe that you were Male Negro #1. I think you should confess to those crimes and reveal the identity of Male Negro #2. Mr. Holly, how would you advise your client?"

Dwight said, "Confess."

Jomo spat blood on the table. Jomo said, "Fuck you."

Scotty swung the hose chunk. Jomo screamed. Perfect kidney shot.

Dwight said, "Confess."

Scotty said, "Confess."

Jomo spat blood on the table. Jomo *gasped,* "Fuck you."

Scotty swung the hose chunk. Jomo screamed.

Dwight said, "Confess."

Scotty said, "Confess."

Jomo spat blood on the table. Jomo *sobbed,* "Fuck you."

Scotty swung the hose chunk. Jomo screamed.

Dwight said, "Confess."

Scotty said, "Confess."

Jomo spat blood on the table. Tissue chunks were laced in. Jomo rolled his head upright and took a big breath.

"Okay, I did them jobs. Me and a nigger named Leotis Waddrell. Leotis ripped me off. Went to Vegas and blew our stash on coke and roulette. I snuffed him. He's out in the desert. You let me cop to Homicide-Two, I give you the fucking body."

Scotty said, "He confessed."

Dwight said, "I'll verify it."

Scotty said, "I've got a few more questions."

Dwight shook his head. "Get him an ambulance. He tried to escape and you nailed him. You can post-date the confession."

Scotty shook his head. Scotty tickled Jomo's chin with the hose chunk.

"February 24, '64. The armored-car heist on 84th and Budlong. I'm sure you've heard about it. Dead guards, dead robbers, a very large take in cash and emeralds. The lead robber killed his own men and burned their bodies past recognition. He got away, and I'm halfway convinced that a second man may have gotten away, as well. While I have you here, may I ask if you know anything about that?"

Dwight blinked. It didn't track, it didn't play, it didn't pertain—

Jomo blinked. Blood dripped down his chin.

"Man, why you askin' me this? That case is age-old stale bread."

Scotty swung the hose chunk. Jomo screamed. Perfect kidney shot.

Dwight stood up. Jomo lolled his head on the table. Scotty grabbed his hair and jerked it. The tabletop was blood-smeared.

"Rumors, scuttlebutt, anything you might have heard. I asked a civil question and I expect a civil answer."

Jomo pulled his head away. His Afro came loose. It was a paste-on wig. Scotty laughed and threw it on the floor.

"One last time. The events of February 24, 1964. Tell me what you know about—"

"Man, I don't know shit! Rumors is rumors! Maybe it's BTA before they was BTA, maybe it's white guys! Man, I don't fucking know!"

Scotty stroked Jomo's scalp with the hose chunk. Dwight said, "Enough."

Scotty stuck the hose chunk in his waistband. Scotty said, "As you wish."

"Call an ambulance. Get him to Morningside."

Scotty winked. "Sure, Dwight. I'll call an ambulance, and we'll say good night now."

Dwight walked to the door. His ring was gone. His feet were numb. He smelled bile and blood.

Scotty said, "I still owe Marsh Bowen one."

Dwight got out the door and downstairs. His feet were gone. He hit the parking lot shaking. Joan was leaning against his car.

Dawn at the fascist cop shop. Black & whites parked all around her. The Red Goddess in a pea coat and scuffed boots.

"I'm as good as you are. Are you convinced now?"

Dwight said, "Yes."

It was cold. Joan shivered and jammed her hands in her pockets.

"Word will spread. Marsh handed up Jomo. We certified Marsh and got Jomo off the street in one go. It's why I let the MMLF store guns in a BTA safe house. The BTA and MMLF will take it from there."

"You knew Marsh was my infiltrator."

Joan nodded. "*Off a fight with Scotty Bennett?* It was so fucking bold that it had to be you."

Dwight shivered. " 'Nobody dies.' Remember?"

"There's some guns that won't hurt anyone."

"It might not be that simple."

"Which should not impede our actions."

Two cops walked by. Dwight stepped toward Joan. He took her hands with his cop world in view.

"Why this? And why now?"

"We both have blood on our hands. Maybe I've got more than you."

"What do you mean?"

Joan said, "There's things I know about you."

DOCUMENT INSERT: 4/21/69. Extract from the privately held
journal of Karen Sifakis.

Los Angeles,
April 21, 1969

The outside world infringes on the quiet home life I've tried to
create for my children. The newspaper lands on my door every
morning, and I can't help but look. Then Dwight knocks on my
door and tells me what the newspapers have omitted.

Two Panthers were charged with non-fatal assaults on two
police officers in Brooklyn; legal actions against the Panthers are
proceeding in a dozen cities. Dwight thinks the Panthers are self-
destructing. They are riddled with FBI and municipal police informants, who are creating internal discord, which leads to
intra-group violence, which gets large-scale publicity, which leads
to large-scale public censure, which leads to more publicity-seeking
violence. The Panthers, and occasionally US, get the headlines,
while Dwight continues to hammer at the lowly BTA and MMLF,
because he considers their antics to bode as a fully contained
media event that he can orchestrate at whim. In that sense, he is
the quintessential "Man with a Job," and "the Job" appears to be
getting to him.

The newspapers tell me that "black-militant firebrand" Jomo
Kenyatta Clarkson, "who admitted to a daring series of liquor-
store holdups," committed suicide while in custody at the Los
Angeles County Jail. The incident has sparked a revitalized hatred
between the BTA and MMLF. I've heard street talk about this. It's
considered gospel: ex-policeman Marshall Bowen, now an avid BTA
supporter, ratted off Clarkson for the robberies. I came to a real-
ization belatedly: Bowen must be Dwight's infiltrator.

Dwight has never named the man. He protects the identities of
his cutouts, infiltrators and informants. He has done that with me,
although Mr. Hoover, in his declining state, has spoken injudiciously about my relationship with Dwight. Mr. Hoover is a celi-
bate homosexual prone to crushes on rugged and assertive men.
My intimate accord with Dwight, suffused with conflicting ideology, must confuse and appall the old man no end.

The Clarkson matter weighs on Dwight. The machination—

whatever went down with Clarkson and Bowen—had to have been at Dwight's instigation, perhaps with Joan Klein's involvement. I've seen Dwight twice recently. We made love, but he seemed to want the consolation more than the sex. He kept bringing up the topic of heroin and how leftist radicals view it as a political tool. I smelled Joan all over that construction.

Dwight sleeps even more fitfully now. I can feel him twitching his way through nightmares. When he awakens, he peers at me almost suspiciously. It's as if he's wondering what I know about him and what I've told other people. We've burgled each other's homes. He's read my much less candid journal. I've seen his check-writing kit, and have mentioned it to him elliptically. My black-bag jobs are a subtext of our relationship, one that Dwight accepts. I've often wondered about the specific nature of Dwight's debt to Mr. Hoover. Last week, I did some checking and came up with an answer of sorts.

I recalled the starting date of Dwight's check ledger: spring 1957. I knew the check recipient's names: Mr. and Mrs. George Diskant of Nyack, New York. I did some newspaper microfilm research then, and learned the story.

It was January '57. A man traveling north on the Merritt Parkway hit a center divider. He was drunk. The collision killed Mr. and Mrs. Diskant's two teenaged daughters. The man was not named, nor was he ever criminally charged.

I can only assume that Mr. Hoover pulled strings. I would also be foolish to assume that Dwight's horrible bond with that man was shaped by a single incident and no more.

Joan has told me that she knows things about Dwight. She leaves it at that. I wonder if she knows more about him than I do, despite their shorter-term dealings. I may be granting Joan a prescient quality that she does not really possess. Still, I swear that I can smell her on Dwight.

DOCUMENT INSERT: 5/1/69. Extract from the journal of Marshall E. Bowen.

Los Angeles,
5/1/69

It's May Day. I'm standing on the roof of my building, observing traffic jams on the San Diego and Harbor freeways and an anti-war march downtown. The BTA and MMLF are passing out leaflets along the march route. I declined to participate. I expect that there will be skirmishes and that I will be viewed as the cause.

I'm very frightened. It's an escalating feeling that has me coming out of my skin. It started last month, when Wayne told me to confront Jomo—"I'll tell the world that you're a faggot if you don't." Oh, yes, the threat worked. I confronted Jomo and Jomo is dead, and I'm a direct link in the cause and effect.

If Wayne knows, who else knows and how did they find out? Does Mr. Holly know? Do Scotty Bennett or the LAPD at large know? Does the FBI know? Do men within the BTA and MMLF know?

How did I reveal myself? Was it the absence of women in my life that led Wayne to an informed supposition? *I am not in the least effeminate and have always gone to great lengths to rid myself of the affect that men with the Bent generally possess. Do I swish? Do I assume hands-on-hips poses unconsciously? Do I lisp? Are my shit-kicking/black male mannerisms butch queer in some codified manner? Has some two-second anonymous trick out of my very circumspect past come forth to recognize me as a local celebrity and rat me off for police favors? Do people simply sense auras in the sexually charged/dream-state world I inhabit?*

All of this frightens me. The upshot of the Jomo situation is much more perilous.

Scotty Bennett popped Jomo for that liquor-store spree that I suspected him of. Mr. Holly, who appeared oddly shocked by the incident, told me that Scotty beat Jomo half-dead at 77th Street Station and sent him to Morningside Hospital with severe kidney damage. Jomo hung himself in his cell several days later. That latter part of the story made the papers and got brief coverage on TV. Mr. Holly told me the story that never received public exposure: that Jomo confessed to a series of high-stakes residential robberies and the Dr. Fred Hiltz murder of last year.

The crimes netted an estimated $750,000 and were committed with a partner in no way aligned with the BTA or MMLF. The man blew all of the money on cocaine, gambling and prostitutes in Las Vegas. Jomo learned of this, killed the man and body-dumped him in the desert. Mr. Holly interviewed Jomo in the L.A. County Jail the day before he killed himself. Jomo told Mr. Holly that his half of the robbery take was earmarked for a "buy heroin" fund for the MMLF. Vicious and hapless criminal fools: Jomo pulls daring high-line jobs *and* clouts liquor stores. Jomo trusts his whore-chasing, dope-fiend partner. The MMLF's dope seed money is squandered. I beat up Jomo, Jomo gets popped tangentially and offs himself. I should be grateful that Scotty busted Jomo—because Jomo would have come after me sooner or later. Jomo's *dead*? All the better. Unfortunately, it's playing out much differently.

The word is out: I gave Jomo up to Scotty.

It isn't true.

Everyone who counts believes it anyway.

My new BTA brothers are glad. Right on, Brother Marsh: that nigger Jomo was stone-*baaaad* and stone-anti-BTA. I'm covered with them and uncovered everywhere else.

I told Wayne I didn't snitch Jomo. He said he believed me, but I'm not sure he does. I told Mr. Holly I didn't do it. Mr. Holly said he *didn't* believe me, but his disbelief was not fully convincing. Scotty knows I'm not the informant, but he came by Tiger Kab yesterday and *hugged me* in full view of the crew.

Scotty wants people to think it. I've lost all sane track of what Wayne and Mr. Holly want people to think.

I've been hung out to dry. I don't know who did it. I don't think Scotty simply attributed the snitch-out to me as a means to avenge Mr. Holly's staged beating. Somebody did this to me. I don't know who, but it has to be politically motivated. Nobody knows I'm a plant, except Wayne, Mr. Holly and a very few people in the FBI and on LAPD.

It could be any black-militant street fool or fool ideologue. It could be some marginalized or factionalized BTA or MMLF fool with a fool's gut instinct.

I've started wearing a bulletproof vest. The MMLF allegedly has a "bounty" out on me. Some MMLF fools saw me on Central Avenue and tossed brim-full malt-liquor cans at me.

I'm frightened. I wear that vest and spend hours standing in front of my bedroom mirror, perfecting mannerisms. *Have I betrayed the Bent unconsciously? I am not in the least effeminate. Did someone prescient within my overall dream state simply discern the Bent in me?*

I've stopped making queries on the armored-car heist. My lust for the money and emeralds has been subsumed by a survivor's instinct. I'm sitting still for now, but Wayne and Mr. Holly are demanding results. Mr. Holly has been talking up the BTA as a heroin conduit. He wants me to proffer the notion to my BTA brothers, who are too motherfucking dumb to score heroin at a yard sale at a poppy farm in Thailand, which Mr. Holly can't quite grasp.

I'm scared. I'm sitting still. I'm waiting. I'm wearing that vest. I'm studying dead-straight men and practicing their moves and masculine craft in my mirror.

Per dead-straight, there's one bright spot in my life right now: my crazy Haitian friend, Leander James Jackson. Leander loves me, but he's *stone* straight, so tough luck there. He had that knife fight with Jomo—which Wayne and I provoked—so he *loves* me for my alleged snitch-out, which resulted in Jomo's death. I told Leander that I didn't do it. Leander laughed and said, "Baby boy, I don't believe you."

Leander loves 151 rum and reefer and enjoys recounting his days in *la belle* Haiti. He tortured dissidents for the Tonton Macoute, practiced voodoo and took a sharp left turn. He assisted a group of rebel invaders and fled the island one step ahead of the noose. I wish I could tell him, "Baby boy, I'm frightened, so I'm sitting still these days."

I have one friend, many nameless enemies and two enemy friends hovering close. Wayne knows that I have the Bent. I don't want Mr. Holly to know it, or to know that pictures of him and that strange woman Joan haunt my dream state. It would kill me if Mr. Holly knew.

72

(Santo Domingo, 5/3/69)

ELECTRIC CHAIR.

He couldn't shake the picture. Shit kept reminding him. He found that golf-course bunker. La Banda left a black guy strapped in. His palms had melted on the electrodes. The restraints burned him bone-deep.

Crutch waited at the airport. Sam G.'s flight was due. The VIP lounge was up and going. The seats were thronelike. They had that *ELECTRIC CHAIR* look.

The flight was late. Drac Air always ran tardy. The lounge featured Führer art. Oil paintings of the Midget hogged wall space.

Crutch fretted. Wayne was due back soon. He had skim money for the casino build. Wayne laid down that no-dope law. Tiger Krew defied it four times. Four runs to Puerto Rico. Four layoffs to Luc's guys in Port-au-Prince. Subsequent sales to Haitian hopheads.

Sam's flight was late. Sam might have Gretchen/Celia in tow. Crutch volunteered for the chauffeur gig. Froggy found that hinky.

His case was popping. He ID'd his murder vic: María Rodríguez Fontonette, aka "Tattoo." He saw that list of massacred Haitians. He memorized the names. It might supply leads. He gave Froggy an update. Froggy scoffed at him. "This is simply your voyeur fixation run amok. Kill more Communists and obsess on fewer women."

The Drac Air flight descended. Little kids ran up and tossed leis. It was the Midget's idea. He went to Hawaii once.

A baggage cart whizzed by. It looked like a mobile *ELECTRIC CHAIR*. The electrodes *liquefied* the guy's skin. Rich beaners played golf overhead.

His case was all voodoo. That be *baaaad* juju. Beware the Zombie Zone.

Sam G. said, "For all his crazy nigger shit, Wayne is a fucking white man. He's got the stateside funnel running like a charm. We're pushing skim from our Vegas hotels through this nigger-owned bank in L.A. We've got Tiger Kab and the jig clubs for the residual wash. Wayne's been keestering Hughes and running our Teamster buyout gig like a fucking virtuoso."

No Gretchen/Celia—that was a bust. The caffeinated Sambo was an equal drag. They toured the Santo Domingo sites. Sam was impressed. The foundations were poured. The first two floors were erected. La Banda bullwhipped the slaves and fed them bennie-laced Kool-Aid. Work proceeded *faaaast*.

They drove up to Jarabacoa. The Autopista was rife with rickshaws and Haitian refugees. Sammy got spooked. The shines were machete-mauled and wore chicken-head hats. Luc and the Cubans waited in Jarabacoa. Crutch pre-warned them: Don't mention Big "H" to Big G.

Sam said, "I'm having dinner with Balaguer, and I'm going to have to castigate him about all these evil boogies in plain view of the tourist trade. Batista was excellent in that regard. The downtrodden knew not to fuck with the white visiting class and the light-skinned beaners who ran the show. I am going to make that precise comment to El Jefe."

Headless hens impaled on cane stalks. Blood-marked trees. D.R. cops with leashed mastiffs. Wetback spooks sprinting.

Sam said, "This needs to be curtailed. If folks want a scary thrill, they can take the Mr. Toad ride at Disneyland."

A shine in a chicken hat hitchhiking. He's got zombie eyes. He's jacking off. He's got a two-foot dick.

Sam pulled Crutch's sidearm and fired at him. The shot blew wide and nailed a tree-lynched bird.

Crutch kept it zipped. Sam said, "This country needs a Billy Graham Crusade. You bring the Reverend Graham in to create a sanctified mood, then all the converts backslide at the crap tables. Shit like that can flourish in a properly suppressed climate."

Jarabacoa was a-go-go. Three floors were up. The slaves worked *rápidamente*. The Midget's contractors pushed them. The Cubans dispensed discipline. The whole group swigged Kool-Aid. It created conviviality. Luc brought his three pit bulls. They wore sequined collars and pointy voodoo hats attached with strings.

Crutch slurped Kool-Aid. The buzz hit him quick. The Krew lounged at a picnic table. Luc nuzzled his dogs. Sam pointed to Luc's emerald ring.

"What is it about emeralds?"

Luc said, "Say what, baby man? Please tell me what you mean."

Sam yawned. "I mean, there's people who dig gemstones in general, and people who only dig emeralds, and when they dig emeralds, they dig emeralds in a big way."

Luc smiled. "I understand this. There is a tradition of emerald worship both in Haiti and the D.R. Emeralds represent 'Green Fire' in voodoo text. They shine light on a dark history."

Sam yawned wide. "My girlfriend Celia's Dominican. She can talk emerald lore up the ying-yang."

Crutch volted off "Celia." Luc bristled weird.

"And what is Celia's surname? *Je m'appelle* Celia who?"

Sam said, "Celia Reyes. She's meeting me at the hotel later, which means I should scram."

Luc *re*-bristled. Crutch *re*-volted. A pit bull went aaaa-oooo!

THE EYE, THE HANDS AND FEET.

The melted skin, the bloody stumps, the knife blade. The Cuban beach and the dead kids' faces. The wires crack. The lights go out. The black guy screams.

He woke up in a new locale. Sweat pooled in his headphones. It was dark outside. He checked his watch—8:14 p.m.

Bug job—quick and ad lib.

He got Sam back to Santo Domingo. He had booked him at the El Embajador. Sam got suite 810. Sam popped a Seconal and hit the bedroom. Crutch booked suite 809, high-risk.

He bored a hole through to the 810 living room. He ran a wiggle wire in. He bored a second hole and wall-clamped it. He attached a mini-mike. The baseboard dust blew back into *his* suite. The wire/mike was minuscule. It looked like spic maintenance on the fritz.

Celia was due soon. Luc hinked on her name. Emeralds. Green glass on the body of María Rodríguez Fontonette.

Crutch yawned. He was whip-whoozy. He did his work and Seconaled off the Kool-Aid for a nap. Note to Sam and Celia: if you talk in the bedroom, I'm fucked.

He fucked with his amplifier. He got next-door static and ten minutes of zilch. There—*click*—the bedroom door opens.

Sam yawned. Sam did that *oh my cabeza/I'm jet-lagged* thing. Click—the TV's on. Spanish jabber, fuck that, he turns it off.

Crutch adjusted his headphones. Sam yawned—*oh my cabeza, sleeping pills come with a cost.*

Pop—a door opens. Squeals, baby-baby's and huggy-kissy sounds. Spanish words—the bellman bows and scrapes. *Pop*—he's out the door. Voice garbles—Sam and Celia. *Fizz/pop*—someone opened champagne.

Glasses clink. Plop-on-couch sounds. Two minutes of oh-baby garbles and smooches. Celia's *looooong* breath of it.

Crutch readjusted his headphones. He got static, squelch and Sam: "Emerald," "colored guy," "called it 'Green Fi—'"

The feed fritzed. Shit—all undertones. Crutch perked his ears and got half-audibles. He started to get a subtext.

Sam's pussy-addled. He's thirty years older, he's a wop doofus, Celia's playing him.

Glasses clink. A match scrapes. Celia coughs and exhales. Sam puts out half-audibles. Sam says, "Your silly emerald thing." His tone's patronizing. Celia puts out *third*-audibles. She says something garbled and "emerald intrigue."

Crutch pulled off the headphones and stuck the wire points in his ears. He got a volt charge and more volume. Celia said, "The construction sites. How's the work going?" Sam bragged and monologued. No full words formed. His tone said it plain.

Celia's tone ditto. She's probing, she's mollifying, she's leading him. Three words in six minutes: "footage," "access," "security."

The audio died. Crutch eyeballed the wire hole. He had to *see.*

Tiger Klaw lolled in Luc's inlet. The voodoo slaves built a nice berth for her. Luc lounged on the foredeck. His dogs snoozed under the bridge. Scalps drooped from the front antenna. They bore the Tiger Krew paw brand.

Crutch hopped on board. Luc was effusive. He was snorting smack and voodoo-herb speedballs. Crutch perched by the machine-gun nest. Luc flexed his nostrils and fed his head.

Crutch said he couldn't sleep. He was in the neighborhood, blah blah. Luc said, "You are *pariguayo*. You are always looking and thinking. This means you think of questions to ask. You are a very young man out of his depth in a horrifying region, where your questions will often be met with unpleasant answers. I do not begrudge you a very long drive at a very late hour to talk to me, baby boy."

A dog ambled over. Crutch ruffled his coat. The dog nuzzled him.

"I'm a bit of a history buff, and I know you've been here quite a while."

Luc wiped his nose. "I have been here since time began. I have carried

the visage of dogs, chickens and men. I know the histories of both countries on this island and would be happy to share my knowledge with you.
Was there some knowledge you specifically require?"

"I was thinking of the 6/14 invasion. I know there's a story there."

"I know the story. Take a drive with me and I'll tell it to you."

Luc owned a '61 Lin*coon*. The paint job was a Haitian history show. Black
demons impaled white Frenchmen. Luc's dogs raped their wives. Baron
Samedi's cloak covered the hood and wheel wells. Papa Doc Duvalier
smiled on the trunk.

It was hot. Luc put the *coon*vertible top down and ran the air *coon*di-
tioning. Bugs bombed the car. Luc offed them with voodoo-herb bug
spray. One puff killed the cocksuckers. Two puffs vaporized them.

They drove through inner Haiti. Villages blipped and vanished. Darkies in whiteface blipped out of the haze.

Luc ran his brights. The Lin*coon* had heavy-duty tires. They kicked big
rocks out of their way.

Crutch shut his eyes. He kept seeing demon wisps in the shadows. Luc
motor-mouthed.

"The 6/14 insurgents were skilled in Haitian voodoo and had voodoo-
chemistry skills. A Marxist ideologue named María Rodríguez Fontonette
was supposed to dose the water supply near the invasion sites along the
D.R. coast, in hopes that it would induce a mass spiritual awareness in the
Dominican peasantry. Herbs and blowfish toxins in non-lethal quantities,
baby boy. She wanted to bring ecstasy to the peasants and create spiritual chaos with the police and army contingents. Alas, she betrayed the
rebels to the Tonton and the Policía Nacional. Thus, we were able to
quash the invasion. Most of the insurgents were killed. Some were captured, imprisoned and executed, a very few escaped."

Crutch opened his eyes. A whiteface ghoul capered in their headlights.
Crutch shut his eyes quick.

"There was a woman named Celia Reyes, right? I saw how you reacted
when Sam mentioned her. She had a friend. An American woman with
dark, gray-streaked hair."

Luc lit a cigarette. "Oh, they escaped, baby boy. They were among the
few."

"Emeralds. Sam said Celia loves emeralds, and you said emeralds have
this significance."

Luc turned on the radio. A low chant in French built. Luc said, "Emeralds do as emeralds do, baby boy. They are a power unto themselves."

Crutch opened his eyes. They bombed south. The coast air evaporated. The bugs got bigger. Luc drove with his knees and bug-bombed them two-handed. The bugs dropped dead all over Crutch. He went *eek* and tossed them out of the car.

They entered a village. It was small: two mud huts, six graveyards, two taverns. Luc said, "We should visit a friend of mine. He is a *bokur*. He would enjoy meeting you, baby boy."

Crutch said, "Groovy." Luc slowed down and idled up to a tavern. A light was on. A voodoo-sect flag flew out front. It matched the flag on Luc's Lin*coon*. Luc parked and ushered Crutch inside.

A fat darky stood at a tonic bar. He had two Mixmasters churning goo and four hot plates stewing shit in saucepans. Luc bowed to the darky. The darky bowed to Luc. They spoke in French. They touched emerald rings. Luc said, *"Il est 'pariguayo.' "*

The darky poured steaming brew in a goblet. Crutch grabbed it and chugalugged.

It burned. It tasted like dead leaves and fungus. His vision blurred and came back 20-20. He burped odors from his last ten meals and stumbled over to a chair.

The room went round, square and rectangled. Fun-house mirrors warped out of the walls. They rolled pictures at him. He couldn't discern details. Luc laughed. The darky said, *"Pariguayo, oui."*

Crutch squinted. His eyes framed a back wall. It was plastered with anatomy charts. Internal organs were highlighted. Pins extended from them.

Crutch re-squinted. A skull morphed into Wayne Tedrow's face. He got up to jab pins in Wayne's eyes. His arms and legs wouldn't move.

Luc laughed. The darky laughed. Luc said, *"Le pauvre pariguayo."*

He saw his mother's face and Dana Lund's face. He saw Dana naked with Chrissie Lund's eyes. He saw THE ELECTRIC CHAIR, THE HANDS AND FEET AND THE EYE. He tried to talk. His vocal chords froze. He tried to stand. His legs walked away from his body and ran outside. He tried to move his hands. His fingers melted. He saw ten thousand snapshots of Joan.

Luc said, *"Pariguayo."*

The darky said, *"La poudre zombie."*

Crutch tried to scream. His mouth dissolved into the 3rd Street tunnel under Bunker Hill. Luc and the darky grabbed him and dragged him into a back room. He tried to resist. His arms turned into bird's wings. They dumped him. They locked the door behind him. Rats roamed the floor. He tried to roll away from them. They crawled on his back and pinned him prone. He saw Joan. He started crying. His tears turned different colors.

The rats scurried to his face and started licking. He saw their fleas and the open sores on their bodies. Their tails coiled and flicked saw teeth at him.

He couldn't move. *La poudre zombie.* He saw Joan. He heard mumbles next door. Words in French formed. He saw the girls in his high school French class. His teacher said, "Donald, you're a bright boy. Learn to listen, learn to speak."

The rats nibbled at him. He saw printed French words and heard Miss Boudreau translate. He heard "emeralds," "suspects," "kill him." He heard "Laurent-Jean Jacqueau," "America," "changed name."

"Trujillo and Duvalier." "Emeralds." "Lost in America." "Celia." "1964." "The boy wants the stones."

The words stopped, the mumbles re-started, black-and-white pictures appeared. Clyde Duber's office, Scotty Bennett's dashboard frieze. Crime pix—*THE ARMORED-CAR HEIST.*

Crutch heard footsteps. Crutch heard a gun hammer cock. A rat walked over his face. Crutch willed his mouth open. The rat looked inside. Crutch pressed down and bit its head off.

The rat thrashed. Crutch kept biting. The blood and fur taste did something to him. The door opened. Luc and the darky walked in. Luc's .38 was pressed to his leg.

Crutch laid there. The rat squirmed and died in his mouth. Luc and the darky got close. Crutch reached up and grabbed the gun. Rats skittered all around them. Luc and the darky froze. Crutch aimed and blew their nigger brains out.

73

(Santo Domingo, 5/6/69)

J*oan.*
    The plane taxied in.
    Backdraft toppled the Midget's welcome signs. Wayne woke up. He still had his satchel—four hundred grand cuffed to his wrist.

The dream was fragmented. He saw Joan three weeks back. The dream played most nights since. Factual club noise and music. Fictive knife-scar imagery.

He returned Dwight's ring. Dwight refused to discuss Joan. His guess: she was his informant. Joan taught at the "Freedom School." Reginald Hazzard attended. Wayne went back to the Freedom School and re-checked the records. There was nothing on Reginald. His little *click* clicked in, finally.

The Freedom School was listed in Joan's Fed file. He'd shredded the file. Dwight refused to get him a new copy. Another *click* clicked. There was something else he'd forgotten or missed.

Wayne deplaned. His limo was waiting. The smoked windows shut out Tijuana-by-the-Sea. He ran a national records check on Joan Rosen Klein and got nothing. He laid out southside queries. The consensus: she's a BTA hanger-on and a boss chick with a past.

The limo crawled. Balaguer's "Urban Renewal Plan" flatlined traffic. The ditchdiggers wore jail denims. They took mincing steps. Their shackled ankles bled.

Mary Beth was problematic now. His workload kept them parted. His search for Reginald torqued her. She was up front. You work for the Boys. You run bag to dictators. He cajoled and mollified her. He euphemized and lied. She just plain seethed.

Dwight was problematic. Jomo Clarkson suicided in custody. Marsh was terrified and denied that he ratted Jomo out. The snitch-out bored Dwight. The stance was weirdly un-Dwight.

The limo cut down the Malecón. Signs announced the Midget's food giveaway. A flatbed was parked. Dark- and light-skinned paupers lined up. Two La Bandaites tossed paper bags at them. The bags broke. A mini–race riot ignited. The bags contained meat scraps and dented dog-food cans.

Marsh was scared. Wayne and Dwight agreed: he's volatile and might double-deal. Let's have Dipshit rotate stateside and hot-wire his crib.

Haiti sideswiped him. The herb trip recircuited his memory. He saw through the ground and tracked tree roots. He saw magic creatures at play.

Horn blare doubled and tripled. A foot chase stopped traffic flow. Kids with leaflets. Sprints down the street and end-run zigzags. La Banda goons peeled out. One kid group, two goon flanks. Pincer movements, no exit/dead end. The kids ran straight toward a cop line: Policía Nacional guys with plastic shields and clubs.

The pincers pressed. The brownshirts absorbed the kids. Their clubs were spike-pointed. Light blows tore flesh.

The kids tried to run into buildings. Foyer guards saw them and locked their doors up. A kid ran beside the limo. He was shirtless. One eye gushed blood.

Wayne opened his door. The kid tried to hurdle it. He hit the sill and went flying. Wayne grabbed him and threw him in the backseat. The kid resisted. Wayne pinned him and yelled at the driver. The kid caught the gist and yelled in Spanish. Wayne heard numbers and "Calle Bolívar." The driver U-turned and bombed down an alley.

Wayne popped his suitcase and pulled out a shirt. The kid held his eye socket. Blood poured through his fingers. Wayne tilted his head and reversed the flow.

The limo hit a clear stretch. The driver gunned it and rode his horn. Their antenna flags got them through bottlenecks and red lights. Calle Bolívar popped up. The driver downshifted and brodied to a small house mid-block. The kid was passed out. Wayne picked him up and carried him inside.

The office was small. The furniture was scuffed and mismatched. It looked like a sub-rosa Commie medical source. A nurse and doctor grabbed the kid. They seemed to know him. They ran him straight into a back room and shut the door.

Wayne sat in the waiting room. The satchel cuff gouged his wrist. The phone rang every ten seconds. The walls closed in a little. He thought of Haiti and Mary Beth.

The phone kept ringing. An hour ticked off. The doctor walked out. His gown was bloody. His hands were rubber-gloved.

"I saved the boy's eye."

"I'm glad."

"You are?"

"My name's Wayne Tedrow."

"I would guess that you are at the El Embajador."

"That's right."

"You have my thanks. You performed a brave deed."

He went by the Santo Domingo sites. They were cosmeticized.

Two more floors were up. It was too fast. The workers greeted Jefe Tedrow. They were ringers. They looked like actors from a plucky peasant script. No whips or guns visible. Leg chains haphazardly stashed.

The limo ran him north. The rural sites were identical. The Jarabacoa site included a lunch buffet. The fat and sassy workers dined with the bosses. Wayne shimmied up a tree and scoped the area. Forty yards off: La Banda fucks and the real workers chained.

Wayne dozed en route to the Tiger Krew inlet. The smoked windows provided a shut-out-squalor view. He woke up and saw Dipshit outside the encampment. The punk Commie hunter looked halfway distraught.

The driver slowed. Wayne tapped him and motioned him to stop. Dipshit looked up. Wayne said, "You're flying back to L.A. with me. Dwight and I want you to hot-wire Marsh Bowen's place."

Dipshit nodded. It was half eager, half numb. Wayne tapped the driver. The limo pulled into a clearing. Mesplede and the Cubans were there. The Cubans were interchangeable. He never got their names straight. One litter, four mean cubs.

They saw the limo and waved. Wayne got out and walked up. They were hanging things on a line strung between two tree trunks. Wayne smelled decomposition.

Mesplede walked up. Wayne pushed him aside. There: five scalps, Tiger-paw marked.

The Cubans posed—feet dug in, smirks, bandoliers and gun belts. Mesplede hovered. He wore his scalping knife on a thong.

Wayne said, "No more runs. No political bullshit while you're working for me. One more infraction and *muerto*."

The Cubans readjusted: smirks, thumbs in their belt loops, feet dug in wiiiiide. Mesplede knife-scratched his neck.

Wayne plucked the scalps off the clothesline. Wayne walked merc to merc. Wayne mashed the scalps in their faces.

"Viva Fidel, you fucking lowlifes."

The suite phone rang at midnight. It jolted him up. He fell asleep with the lights on. Santo Domingo was a window blur. He thought about the gashed-eye kid straight off.

"Hello."

"Did I wake you?"

"Yes and no."

Mary Beth said, "I hope you weren't dreaming."

"Well, yes and no."

"I'd ask you how things are going, but I'm not sure I want to know."

Wayne rubbed his eyes. "I got a lead on the woman who bailed your son out of jail."

"Sweetie, I wasn't talking about Reginald."

Wayne looked at his briefcase. "I know you weren't. I told you because it's about you and me, and not about what I do for a living."

"Or about the people you work for?"

Wayne sighed. "Babe, please don't do this. Not on the telephone."

Mary Beth sighed. "It'll be worse in person."

"Then let's be fucking civil and not do it at all."

"We should say good night now."

"Yes, I think we should."

The line clicked and disconnected. Wayne looked out the window. The sky was neon-free. The Midget told Sam G. he wanted *mucho* neon. Sam said they'd provide some.

The buzzer rang. Wayne got up and opened the door. It was Celia Reyes. He met her in convention-time Miami. She was Sam's consort then.

She said, "Hello, Mr. Tedrow." She wore a white dress and a linen blazer. She extended her hand. He stepped aside and held the door open. Celia sat on the couch.

"I wanted to thank you for my friend Ramón. The doctor said you gave generously of your time."

Wayne pulled a chair up. "I'm glad he'll be all right."

"The doctor said it was quite a sight. You carrying Ramón, with a briefcase attached to your wrist."

The briefcase sat between them. Wayne pointed to it.

"It was unwieldy, yes."

Celia smiled. "You're not questioning my presence here."

"I half-expected some sort of approach."

"Why is that?"

"You could make the point that I wanted it."

"I have a friend. We think you may be sympathetic to our work."

Wayne smiled. "Yes, that may be true."

"Would it upset you if I told you that we knew some things about you prior to your actions today?"

"People tend to know things about me. It tends to do me more harm than good."

"May I inquire about your beliefs?"

Wayne said, "I'm following signs. I'm beginning to think that I may have a purpose that exists beyond my will to comprehend it."

Celia pointed to the briefcase. "The contents?"

"$400,000."

"May I have it?"

"Yes."

"Will there be more?"

"Yes."

Celia picked up the briefcase and walked to the door. Wayne opened it. A shadow flicked down the hallway. A smoke ring evaporated. Wayne knew it was *her*.

"Celia said you were quite gracious."

"She caught me at the right moment."

"I won't press you about that."

"You could. I'd be candid. I'd press you on a few topics and hope you'd be candid in return."

"You can ask me anything. I'll give you answers or I won't."

"I was going to ask you about your relationship with Dwight Holly and about a young man you knew at the Freedom School and almost certainly rescued from harm a year later."

"I'm not telling you."

"That's a direct answer."

"I told you it would be."

"Yes, you did."

"I hope my bluntness won't terminate our working together."

"I won't permit it. I'm a very blunt ex-policeman, and I tend to get the answers I want."

"You haven't asked me what Celia and I know about you, which is a more pressing question to ask."

"I'll assume you know everything, and let it go at that."

"I've enjoyed talking to you, Mr. Tedrow."
"Thank you for calling, Miss Klein."

Wayne woke up over Texas. Airplane scotch and voodoo herbs put him out from takeoff.

Dipshit was reading *Playboy*. The little hump looked haggard and scared.

Deep-gouged bluffs loomed below them. Trees stuck out sideways. Storm clouds made them vanish.

Wayne thought, *This Is All Magic.*

Wayne thought, *I've Gone Red.*

DOCUMENT INSERT: 5/13/69. Verbatim FBI telephone call transcript. Marked: "Recorded at the Director's Request/Classified Confidential 1-A: Director's Eyes Only." Speaking: Director Hoover, Special Agent Dwight C. Holly.

JEH: Good morning, Dwight.

DH: Good morning, Sir.

JEH: Your telex implied that you have bad news. "Tell it like it is," as President Nixon often states in his fawning efforts to sound au courant with longhairs and insurrection-seeking Negroes.

DH: Yes, Sir.

JEH: There's also "Can you dig it?" and "Are you cool with it?" which are new favorites of the white radio personalities who have taken up the chant that I am too old for this job.

DH: Yes, Sir.

JEH: "Right on, brother" is an expression that is considered "in the groove" these days. I addressed Vice President Agnew in that manner last week. He gave me a clenched-fist salute. I was deeply gratified. It was akin to receiving the French Legion of Honor.

DH: Yes, Sir.

JEH: You're stalling, Dwight.

DH: Chief Reddin called me, Sir. He told me that he had taken Marsh Bowen off roster. He's been fired from LAPD, so LAPD is in no way accountable for his actions. The firing was clandestine, which protects us at least so—

JEH: OPERATION BAAAAAAD BROTHER must not be derailed or in any way diverted. Bowen must not know that he's been fired. Why did this occur? Tell it like it is.

DH: I think Scotty Bennett went to Reddin and offered a rationale for the firing. I believe that Bennett's personal animus precipitated this action.

JEH: Bennett has favored us in at least one regard. He did not expose the late Jomo Kenyatta Clarkson and his late crime partner as the killers of the late hate merchant Dr. Fred Hiltz, which has spared the Bureau a great deal of ape-inspired scrutiny.

DH: Yes, Sir.

JEH: Jomo Kenyatta Clarkson has fucked Pat Nixon on numerous occasions. A confidential informant in the Hollywood commu-

nity informed me of this fact. They were under the influence of
the drug Quaaludes, commonly known as "ludes."

DH: Yes, Sir. I was think—

JEH: There will be Bureau raids on Black Panther offices in
Denver, Chicago and Salt Lake City during the first week of June. I
am grateful for it, but it lacks the illuminating pizzazz of our
operation, which is a fully formed explication of Negro criminality
and indigenous moral sloth. I want the BTA and/or the MMLF to
sell heroin. The public has been numbed to death and charmed to
sleep by the Panthers. They need evil apes they can sink their
teeth into. I assure you that I am telling it like it is.

DH: Yes, Sir.

JEH: The honorary Negro Wayne Tedrow. Lay it on me,
brother.

DH: He's status quo, Sir. He was in the Dominican Republic
nec--

JEH: Dick Nixon is peeved at Wayne, once removed. Wayne
pulled the plug on a plucky little group of anti-Castro brigands that
Bebe Rebozo was bankrolling. Bebe is determinedly anti-
Communist. I respect him for that.

DH: I'll be speaking to the president tomorrow night, Sir. I'll
advise him on the Wayne matter as you advise me.

JEH: Do what you like. Tell it like it is, because I'm cool with it.

DH: Yes, Sir.

JEH: Nixey boy has never learned the rudiments of achieving a
close shave. I use Wilkinson Sword blades. My personal file on
Nixon would ruin him. The files in my basement would create
Armageddon instantaneously.

DH: Yes, Sir.

JEH: The BTA and/or the MMLF must push heroin. We must
create a properly controlled chaos.

DH: Yes, Sir.

JEH: I dream of Martin Lucifer King quite often. He invariably
wears a red-devil costume and carries a pitchfork.

DH: Yes, Sir.

JEH: Do you dream of him?

DH: Frequently, Sir.

JEH: And how is he attired?

DH: He always wears a halo and wings.

JEH: (Abrupt and muffled comment/phone transcript terminates here.)

DOCUMENT INSERT: 5/14/69. <u>VERBATIM STAGE-1/CLOSED CON-
TACT/TOP-ACCESS ROUTING telephone-call transcript</u>. Closed file
#48297. Speaking: President Richard M. Nixon and Special Agent
Dwight C. Holly, FBI.

RMN: Dwight, good evening.

DH: Good evening, Mr. President.

RMN: You're not taping this, are you, Dwight?

DH: No, Sir. Are you?

RMN: Yes, I am. I've got a device that records my calls auto-
matically, but one of my slaves comes by and dumps the tapes in
a vault. They'll never see the light of day, and we'll be pushing up
daisies if they do.

DH: I'm cool with it, Sir.

RMN: I can dig it. Did you vote for me, Dwight?

DH: I'm not registered to vote, Sir.

RMN: You're a bad citizen. You're like your friend Tedrow, who
messed with my friend Bebe. He's the First Friend, Dwight. I enjoy
these talks of ours, and Wayne has been instrumental in facilitating our arrangement with the Italians, but Bebe is Bebe and
Wayne fucked with him.

DH: May I make a few blunt comments, Mr. President?

RMN: Tell it like it is.

DH: Wayne Tedrow is a very competent man given to the occasional extravagant gesture. The foolishness that he interdicted
may have proven detrimental to the casino build in the D.R. Mr.
Rebozo's pet exile group is composed of dubious far-Right ideologues with a giant oozing hard-on to depose Fidel Castro, and as
you once told me, Sir, the fucker is here to stay. I would describe
Mr. Rebozo's exile comrades as heedless and whimsical at best,
gratuitously psychopathic at worst. Wayne did the prudent thing,
Sir.

RMN: You're absolutely correct, Dwight. Moreover, the D.R. is
a shithole, the Boys may take a bath on their hotels, and Joaquín
Balaguer is solidly anti-Red and a good deal more tractable than
Rafael Trujillo. That cocksucker was a nightmare. You wouldn't
believe the CIA file on him. The shit he pulled with his so-called
bitter rival Papa Doc Duvalier was horrific. They looted land,
smuggled emeralds, and foreclosed banks and split the profits.
While they're doing this, the Goat is slaughtering Haitian refugees
and Papa Doc is fucking half of his girlfriends.

DH: Strange bedfellows, Sir.

RMN: On that note, let's talk about you-know-who. I was listening to the radio today. A disc jockey called him "Gay Edgar."

DH: The media has been unkind lately, Sir.

RMN: Do you think he takes it up the keester?

DH: I think he finds the closet too confining for that, Sir.

RMN: A little schlong would make him less uptight.

DH: Yes, Sir.

RMN: He's losing it. Right, Dwight?

DH: Yes, Sir. But, again, he's utterly dangerous and should be handled delicately.

RMN: And he's got those goddamn files.

DH: He does, Sir.

RMN: And they're wildly revealing and impolitic.

DH: Not as much as this conversation, Sir.

RMN: Dwight, you're a pisser. It's fun to belt a couple and jaw with salty guys like you.

DH: Sir, I enjoy our chats very much.

RMN: That Irish cocksucker Jack Kennedy stole the 1960 election from me.

DH: Yes, Sir.

RMN: The cocksucker is dead and I'm the president of the United States.

DH: Yes, Sir.

RMN: Keep tabs on you-know-who for me. Will you do that, Dwight?

DH: Yes, Sir. I will.

RMN: Good night, Dwight.

DH: Good night, Mr. President.

74

(Los Angeles, 5/16/69)

D wight said, "You're afraid of something. Your hands are shaking."

Dipshit slid a wire through a bore slot. His pliers jumped. Marsh Bowen's pad was bug-tap-amenable. The phones were big and old-fashioned. The wall molding was soft.

"Don't mess with me. I can't concentrate."

Dwight smiled. "It's a periodic. Wayne will rotate through and check the listening post. He'll tally the calls."

The job entailed drill work. Dipshit was good. He laid down a drop cloth and kept his space tight. Marsh was at a BTA gig. They had three hours.

"How many Communists have you killed now?"

"More than you."

"Are you still peeping?"

"I peeped your mother. She was turning tricks on skid row."

Dwight laughed and checked out the living room. Marsh employed the Stanislavski Method. The crib was in character. Black-power posters, pix of foxy black chicks with guns.

"I was talking to President Nixon about you."

Dipshit spackled a drill hole. His hand shook and held firm. He wore a tool belt and magnifier. The loser kid as bug pro.

"Don't mess with me. We're running late."

"You and Bowen are soul brothers. You're scaredy-cats, but you damn well persist."

"Bowen's your coon daddy. Come on, let me work."

"How many Communists have you killed?"

"Jesus, man."

Dwight checked his watch. It was midnight. Jig soirees ran to the wee small hours. Reefer and speeches, gasbags and demagogues.

Dipshit finished up. Hot-wired: two lamps, three wall panels, two phones. Dipshit was sweaty and dust-caked. Dwight tossed him a towel.

"How's tricks in the D.R.? Are you peeping down there?"

Dipshit toweled off. "Quit riding me."

Dwight walked the pad—final look-see, no loose ends. Marsh breathed the Method. Commie books, ribs in the fridge, no telltale cop or queer shit.

The job was good. No dust sprays, no mounts or wires loose.

Dipshit was nerve-knocked. His breath spurted. His legs fluttered. The tool belt jiggled on his hips.

Dwight said, "Don't fuck up. Wayne's looking to kill some fool right-winger."

"He did not call JFK a cocksucker."

Dwight did the hands-on-heart thing. "I'm not lying to you."

Norm's on Vermont. The 1:00 a.m. clientele: pot-smacked kids noshing budget steak meals.

Karen brought Eleanora. She snoozed in her car seat. Dwight kept staring at her.

"She looks like me."

"No, she doesn't. It was a procedure, and you were nowhere near the receptacle."

Dwight yukked and sipped coffee. Karen lit a cigarette. Dwight propped up a menu and shielded Ella from the smoke.

"You like Richard Nixon. I can't believe what it says about you."

Dwight smiled. "You love me. What does that say about you?"

Karen twirled her ashtray. "I have some friends in the San Mateo County Jail. They're being denied habeas."

"I'll take care of it."

"How's Mr. Hoover?"

"A little uptight."

"Is Marshall Bowen your infiltrator?"

"No comment."

"Is Joan as good an informant as I am?"

"Time will tell."

Ella stirred. Dwight rocked the car seat. Karen peeked over the menu. Ella grinned and went back to sleep.

"You're too thin, Dwight."

"I've heard that before."

Karen smiled. "Bad dreams?"

"You know the answer to that one."

"I'll qualify it, then. 'Bad dreams born of a guilty conscience?' "

Ella kicked her leg out of the car seat. Dwight tucked it back in.

"I love her, you know."

"Yes, I know that."

They laced up their fingers. Dwight said, "Do you love me?" Karen said, "I'll think about it."

He dawdled at Norm's. The geek show was a riot, the drop-front was musty, he wouldn't sleep anyway.

Cops and peaceniks. Late-night film buffs. Stragglers from the porno book bin next door.

The waitress kept bringing coffee. Dwight smoked in sync with her. Time metastasized.

Wayne walked in and sat down. He was too thin. He had new gray hair.

Dwight said, "You're the bad penny."

"You know why I'm here."

"We've been through this. I'll admit that she works for me, but that's as far as I'll go."

Wayne brushed off the waitress. "I saw a tall red-haired woman with a baby walk out of here an hour ago. I ran her plates and got her name, and I'm assuming that she was here with you."

Dwight lit a cigarette. "Why did you assume that?"

"Because I don't believe in coincidences."

Dwight worried his law-school ring. It rolled across the table. Wayne rolled it back to him.

"I saw a photo of the faculty at a left-wing 'Freedom School.' Karen Sifakis and the woman we're discussing were standing together."

Karen said she never met Joan in person. She said they were mail-drop comrades. Joan said the same thing.

Dwight shrugged. Wayne said, "Tell me." Dwight said, "I'm not going to."

A gaggle of drunks walked in. Two cops at the counter bristled.

"Say her name, Wayne. I want to hear you say it."

Wayne said, "Joan."

Dwight did the hands-on-heart thing.

75

(The Dominican Republic, Haiti, Caribbean Waters, Los Angeles,
5/16/69–3/8/70)

R*otations:*
The D.R. to L.A. and back.
The casino build, the smack biz,
Cuban coastal runs. His case
wedged in.

He offed Luc Duhamel and the *bokur* and kept it all zipped. He torched
the shack and Luc's Lin*coon* and night-walked back to the D.R. Luc
plain vanished. Some Tonton ghouls braced Tiger Krew with routine
questions. Crutch toughed it out. Word surfaced: Luc got snuffed in a
voodoo-sect war. Reprisals followed: spells, machete massacres and
zombifications. Crutch laid low and rode it out. His nerves had him
noggin-nudged and gored out of his gourd. He had nightmares in Voodoo
VistaVision.

He found good homes for Luc's dogs. Froggy found some Tonton guys
to run the Haitian end of the biz. Luc's inlet remained Tiger Kove. *Tiger
Klaw* was moored there. The Puerto Rican and Cuban jaunts launched
from Luc's old turf.

Work was full-time. His case was part-time. There's the voodoo-shack
epiphany. He's zombified. His brain broils as his body is *bokur*-bound and
immobile. Emeralds/1964/Celia. Laurent-Jean Jacqueau/America/changed
name. His mind melts and morphs to the *ARMORED-CAR HEIST*.

He tracked the epiphany and validated it. He B&E'd the La Banda ops
office and found some paperwork. It was cryptic and written in Spanish.
He took Minox pix, developed the film and pidgin English–translated. An
emerald shipment left Santo Domingo, 2/10/64. Destination: L.A. The
sender and recipient—not listed. No mode of transport listed. No names
to latch on to. The paper trail dead-ended there.

He tried to track Tonton turncoat Laurent-Jean Jacqueau. He took 6/14/59 as his disappearance date and extrapolated. He checked outbound emigration records. He got nothing. He checked incoming U.S. émigrés and got nothing. He started with Jacqueau's real name. That didn't work. He tried his initials. That didn't work. He expanded from there. He checked intake sheets on all Negro Caribbean males and got nothing.

All he got was scuttlebutt and oral history. The Goat and Papa Doc were emerald fiends. He got that and no more. Likewise emeralds and Laurent-Jean Jacqueau. Likewise emeralds, Celia Reyes and Joan Rosen Klein. He raided three file troves: the CIA, La Banda and Ivar Smith's group. He saw no target names listed. He got no Green Fire leads.

Rotation.

He made sixteen Cuban runs and eight dope runs, all top secret. All accomplished in defiance of Wayne T. Wayne paid Ivar Smith to surveil Tiger Krew and report back to him. Ivar told Froggy this. Froggy and Ivar countermanded Wayne. Ivar double-dealt Wayne for a cut of the dope biz. They developed a warning system. Ivar pre-announced Wayne's visits. The dope biz and Cuban runs were curtailed then. Tiger Krew anti-Castroized and dope-dealt while Wayne was gone. *Tiger Klaw* launched from seclusion. The Puerto Rican runs were clandestine. The Tonton spooks ran the conduit to Port-au-Prince.

His dead-Commie count stood at twenty-four now. The coastal runs entailed torpedo lobs. *Tiger Klaw* slipped in and bomb-slathered the coast. Moored boats went down with scorched Reds on board. The scalp runs got to him more. The body counts were lower and high nightmare quotients resulted. All the runs were nerve-knocking. He fueled up on voodoo herbs. Froggy and the Cubans never suspected.

Le poudre zombie almost killed him. The heist revelation issued from that altered state. He trusted the moment and kept trying to re-capture it. Most voodoo herbs were brain-bracing and benign. He logicked that one out. He snuck into Haiti and scored herbs to rev him *and* calm him. The shit worked. It buttressed his balls and got him to Cuba and back. It never revived revelations per his case. It helped with his nightmares.

ELECTRIC CHAIR, THE HANDS AND FEET, THE EYE.

Bad dreams kept him up. He dosed himself with voodoo herbs and went peeping. It wore him out. Woman imagery subsumed his dreams most nights.

He dug on voodoo. He didn't believe in it. He hexed Wayne a million times, anyway. He grooved the ritual. Wayne was too big to fuck with. Voodoo had a power beyond his volition. He grokked that aspect of it.

His life was work. The casino build was go, go, go. Twelve floors were up at all four locations. Heavy rains slowed things down. Slaves died from overwork and required replacement. Froggy and the Cubans bossed the work crews. La Banda goons assisted. Ivar Smith warned them of Wayne's visits. Froggy brought ringer work crews in. Wayne brought bribe and construction cash. Crutch steered clear of him and hate-hexed him. Froggy and the Cubans oozed mock innocence. They hated Wayne. Wayne required big-time connivance and kid gloves.

Rotation.

Crutch worked in the D.R. and L.A. His case was bifurcated: the María Rodríguez Fontonette snuff and the armored-car heist. Celia blew in and out of Santo Domingo. He couldn't track her down. He ran more paper checks. He surveilled the known safe houses on the La Banda list. He tailed Commie punks from CIA dissident lists in the dumb hope that they knew her. It was futile. He got diverted by random women. Window glimpses swerved him for days at a pop. He had to find Celia. She was his spark point to Joan.

Rotation.

Crutch lied to Froggy. He laid out "Clyde Duber needs me in L.A." tales. Froggy said sure. He flew to L.A. and prowled. He read Clyde's heist file a dozen times, got the gist and no more. He called Wells Fargo. He tried to track the emerald shipment and got rebuffed. He went back to Clyde's file. Scotty Bennett's obsession with the case was confirmed. That was old news. The *new* news: Scotty's filed reports were threadbare.

Omissions. A paper dearth. He *knew* Scotty. They bullshitted at the wheelman lot. Scotty showed him reports on minor heists—always detail-packed. His reports on 2/24/64—slight by comparison.

He tried to pump Scotty. He came on *suuuubtle,* but Scotty did not reveal shit. He didn't tell Scotty that he'd hot-wired Marsh Bowen. Scotty would slam Bowen at the proper time.

A ripe rumor rippled: Bowen snitched a spade named Jomo for some liquor-store jobs. Jomo offed himself in jail. Scotty told Crutch that he was spreading the rumor. Safe bet: Bowen's queer ass was cooked.

Rotation.

The island was a Zombie Zone. L.A. was a safe zone. He dropped by the wheelman lot and brought beer and pizza. He went by his pad at the Vivian and his downtown file pad. He read his mother's missing person file. It helped smother his nightmares.

His mother sent him five bucks and a Christmas card. This one was postmarked Kansas City. She split in 1955. She sent her first card that year. She sent a card for Christmas '69. It was 1970 now.

She was still alive. Like Celia and Joan. Like Dana Lund and all the

Hancock Park girls in windows. His case was stalled. Scotty had to have more paperwork. Dana Lund had new gray hair. She wore the cashmere sweater he'd bought her at Christmas.

Dana's gray streaks looked like Joan's. It was all a fucking knife to the heart.

76

(Las Vegas, Los Angeles, the Dominican Republic, Haiti, 5/16/69–3/8/70)

D*ream State.*
It was Bowen's stated concept. It was his life now. It was unquantifiable. It reminded him of his early chemistry studies. Some experiments brought assured results. Many did not. He took greater risks and became more attuned to uncertainty. A world existed beyond his comprehension. The notion drove him and consoled him, then and now.

His herb trips clarified his dream state. They brought him an unforeseeable hope. They dulled his sense of risk more.

He flies to the D.R. and detours into Haiti. He hires Tonton thugs to protect him as he chemically dallies. He brings money for Celia and Joan. He tells Celia to deploy the money and spare him the details. She has pledged to leave the building sites alone. He has donated $1,649,000. The results are unquantifiable.

Dream State.

He liquidated his father's estate and reimbursed Balaguer's construction firm. That covered his first impromptu tithe. He became an embezzler then.

The Boys trusted him with quickly tallied and un-vouchered cash. They knew he loved power and gave little thought to financial remuneration. He skimmed skim off Drac's hotels. He diverted payments from Teamster-book buyouts. He cooked the books at Tiger Kab and the southside clubs. He quick-wash-and-dried funds through the Peoples' Bank. He delivered monthly stipends to Balaguer and near-equal funds to Celia.

He asked to speak to Joan. It pertained to a young man she knew at one time. Celia said, "Under no circumstances" and "Please don't ask me again." He refrained from further requests. He chased Joan and the ghost of Reginald Hazzard back to L.A.

Dwight refused to discuss Joan. Wayne submitted a Federal file request through a friend on LVPD. Joan's file was missing from Central Records. The Bureau had no file on Joan's colleague Karen Sifakis. Dwight pulled both files. He was sure of that. He ran a nationwide PD check on both women and got nothing. That second little *click* kept *clicking* him. He did anti-redaction work on Joan's file. His memory *clicked* and stalled out there.

He scoured South L.A. He couldn't find Joan. He built a partial Joan-Reginald time line. The Freedom School, '62. The jail bailout, '63. He scoured files in the D.R. Joan: tied to Celia Reyes and embroiled in Dominican revolt. Joan: one file photo. The 6/14 invasion and a younger woman with a fist raised.

Late '63: Reginald studies Haitian herbs and hard-Left politics. Joan's a renegade professor. It's a wild tutelage. The Haitian connection—jump then to now.

Joan is BTA-tight. The BTA "Armorer": Haitian hellion Leander James Jackson. Brother Jackson had a knife fight with the late Jomo Clarkson. Wayne and Marsh Bowen provoked it. Jackson was allegedly ex–Tonton Macoute. Wayne tried to run a Tonton records check on him. The Tonton kept no written records.

More file checks, more dead ends.

No file on Leander James Jackson. No immigration files on men with those three initials. No Fed or muni-PD files extant.

Jackson: most likely unrelated to Reginald and Joan. He considered bracing Bowen on Jackson and decided against it. Bowen would probably double-deal confidential information.

Dream State.

He cruises southside L.A. He looks for people who aren't there. He's got Tiger Kab and the clubs as information hubs. Nobody knew Reginald then or knows Reginald now. He's hand-checking LAPD and Sheriff's station files. He's looking for one name in millions of words.

I will find Reginald Hazzard just as I found Wendell Durfee. I will impart mercy as I once imparted death.

His dream state imposed clarity. It seamlessly bridged L.A. and the D.R. The hotel-casinos were going up. It was a controlled experiment with quantifiable results. He was tithing revolution at a consistently opposing rate. Ivar Smith was watchdogging Tiger Krew. The fucks were abstaining from Cuban runs and had scotched their dope biz. *That* was quantifiable. *That* controlled experiment worked. He visited Tiger Krew. He soaked up their hatred and fear. The RED borders of his U.S.-Caribbean junkets blurred.

The Boys loved him. He hated them and sucked up to them and bilked them. The Boys knew he was with a black woman. They kept quiet because they needed his skills. He spends time with them. He fraternizes with queer black militants. He's riding his dreamscape through a zeitgeist with an off-RED flag aswirl.

Marsh Bowen was full-time wired. Wayne checked the listening post every third day. Marsh and his pals talked revolutionary shit and never *did* shit to create revolution. They can't score heroin. Half of them don't *want* to score heroin. A few have tenuous moral qualms. Most just fear the fuzz. Chicago cops killed two Panthers in December. The Panthers shot it out with LAPD the same month. It was a non-fatal/let-off-steam/could-have-been-us moment. *Whew! Heroin?* Brother, I'm not sure.

It frustrated Dwight. It delighted Wayne. He smoked weed with Marsh once. They again discussed the dream-state concept. Marsh didn't know he was wired. Marsh didn't know that LAPD bagged his ass. They stood in the Tiger Kab lot. Wayne got this nutty idea: *I'll tell him I killed Martin Luther King and see how he takes it.*

Dwight didn't trust Marsh. Dwight was right—he's a time-buyer and a favor-doer lost in compliant calculation. Marsh bailed Ezzard Donnell Jones out of lockup twice—77th Street and University stations. Marsh was afraid of MMLF reprisal and BTA whiplash. Marsh's mindscape was all stasis and circumspection.

Dwight's brainscape was all machination. He was losing weight. He was boozing to suppress his nerves and notch some sleep. Dwight said Mr. Hoover was reaming him for results. Wayne said, "How?" Dwight mimicked a junkie shooting up.

The pantomime was spooky. Wayne got chills. Dwight said, "Son, you cannot fuck with me on this."

Dream State.

He did not tell Mary Beth about his tithing. She would consider it stealing. She would critique his guilty conscience. She would disapprove of his herb trips. She would view his experiment theory as a fatuous riff of the times. Her resentment was an indictment. She brought it to bed with them. He brought images of Joan for fire and consolation. She considers his quest to find her son grandiose and self-serving. She cannot comprehend the scope of his debt.

77

(Los Angeles, the Dominican Republic, 5/16/69–3/8/70)

She's gone.
    She left him with nineteen file cards and no good-bye note. She left a lipstick smear on her pillow.

The cards listed snitch-outs gleaned from the BTA. Joan gave up six armed-robbery teams, two kidnap gangs and eleven mail-bombing leftists. Dwight attributed the work to Marsh Bowen. It bought the time-buyer more time and wowed Mr. Hoover. The old girl ordered the Federal raids herself.

A brief return to form, followed by more slippage.

"Dwight, those prehensile-tailed creatures must sell heroin. I fear that they will not accomplish this in my flickering-out lifetime."

He mollified the old girl. The old girl responded with a daily telex barrage. Racist doggerel and hate cartoons, sent through the FBI mail flow.

Pat Nixon pulls a train for Archie Bell and the Drells. Slippage verging on breakdown.

He walked away from it. He tried to find Joan.

Phone checks, records checks—nothing. Subtle probings with Karen—no go. Wayne nailed that "Freedom School" lead. It proved that Joan and Karen lied to him. Wayne redacted Joan's file. He told Dwight that a little *click* kept eluding him. Dwight knew what it was. Wayne stripped inked paper and got the name Thomas Frank Narduno. The man knew Joan. They were comrades. Dwight and Wayne's gang killed Narduno at the Grapevine Tavern. It begged the biggest questions of their lives:

What does she want? What does she know? Why have we let her in?

Dwight print-dusted the Eagle Rock and Altadena pads. No prints, no diary notes, no guns under pillows.

She's gone.

His nerves are stripped gears. He stares at the drop-front walls and lets time evaporate. He takes more pills with more booze and sleeps worse commensurately.

He filled the Joan void with Karen. Joan gave him nineteen snitches. He gave Karen the quid pro quo benefit. He bailed her friends out of jail in record numbers. Karen pulled more Quaker woo-woo than ever before. He has Dr. King nightmares. Karen gets a monument-bombing chit the next day. He keeps thinking of Silver Hill. The doctors told him not to think. He stared at the walls and thought anyway.

She's gone.

He's got more time to think and stare at walls and wait for the walls to speak back. OPERATION BAAAAD BROTHER was in a soul coma. The BTA and MMFL brothers were losing their fire *fast.* October 18, '69. The Panthers ambush two L.A. cops. One cop is wounded, one Panther is wounded, one Panther is dead.

December 8, '69: The big pig-Panther shoot-out at Panther HQ. Woundings, no deaths. LAPD reprisals?—probably. Most likely implemented by Scotty B.

Marsh Bowen was useless. The wire was useless. The talk was Revolution 101 for burrheads and dupes. His new Marsh vibe: the fuck had an agenda. The fuck was lying in wait. He should have produced more or plain rabbited from the Jomo thing.

Scotty weighed on him. Scotty had an agenda. Scotty got LAPD to fire Marsh. Scotty put out the word: no reprisals on Marsh. He snitched Jomo, I don't care, don't fuck with him or I'll fuck with you.

The sweat-box room, the hose shots, the Q&A. *Why the grilling on that armored-car heist?*

Suspicion.

It kept aging cops up nights. Their brain compartments seeped. They saw shit that wasn't there and missed the shit that was. He had phone chats with President Nixon and Mr. Hoover. President Nixon feared Mr. Hoover's file stash. Mr. Hoover feared President Nixon's soft line on black militants and Commies. Mr. Hoover was obsessed with Wayne's black girlfriend and feared that coon-killer Wayne had gone Red. Nixon sent Dwight on a scouting trip to the D.R. He wanted Dwight's take on the Midget. He wanted to make sure his mob deal wouldn't boomerang. Dwight dipped down to Santo Domingo. The casino build was going strong. The Midget gave good lunch. La Banda gave good oppression. He called the prez and told him the D.R. looked kosher.

Suspicion.

He called Mr. Hoover and reported the trip. Mr. Hoover was *suspicious*—"Dwight, did Nixon talk about *me*?"

Dwight said, "No, Sir. He didn't." Mr. Hoover was aghast and relieved. He told a *fourteen-minute* joke about Dr. King and Lassie. He told a *sixteen-minute* joke about the prez and Liberace.

Suspicion.

He had downtime in Santo Domingo. He hobknobbed with Tiger Krew and felt shit percolating. His hunch: they were moving smack behind Wayne's back. He didn't tell Wayne. Why promote chaos?

The D.R. felt creepy-crawly. L.A. felt good on the rebound.

She's gone.

His birthday was last week. He turned fifty-three. The prez called and requested a D.R. backup trip. Karen bought him dinner at Perino's. He got a plain white envelope in the mail.

It came to the drop-front. His name and address were typed on. There was no return address.

He opened the envelope. Inside: a little red flag on a stick.

DOCUMENT INSERT: 3/8/70. Extract from the privately held journal of Karen Sifakis.

Los Angeles,
3/8/70

My daughters are playing in the next room. Four-year-old Dina is watching fifteen-month-old Eleanora steady herself on a large rubber beach ball and teach herself to walk. At some point, she'll become jealous of Ella's rapid progress and push her to the floor; Ella will cry, get up and keep going. It will be the third or fourth time this has happened. I reprimanded Dina the first time. She blamed Dwight for her actions. She had overheard Dwight telling me that Ella was quickly becoming the dominant little girl, and Dina had better "log some payback while she's able."

I should have reprimanded Dwight for the statement. He said those words some months ago, and it's too late for reprimands now. I'm looking back at the past year's journal pages and feeling disparate events cohere. Dwight has been affording me greater and greater latitude in my political actions and has been bailing out my politically jailed friends at an ever-accelerating pace. The matchup of dates makes it all the more evident: Dwight's remarkable generosity begins the moment he tells me that Joan has disappeared.

Of course, they are lovers. Of course I could not tell Dwight that Joan's vanishing acts are very well established, because I have lied to him about the breadth of my friendship with Joan. Dwight asked me about Joan and the USC Freedom School several months ago. Of course I lied about it; of course Dwight knew I was lying. We are in far too deeply with each other to issue reprimands or otherwise revise the rules of a duplicitous, usurious and compartmentalized union. The odd thing? I find myself approving of Dwight and Joan as lovers. I love Dwight more than I ever have, because Joan has served to instill doubt in him. Dwight is beginning to erode. I pray that the process will extend and change him gently, and not take him to grief and madness. A very real fear attends this prayer offering. I am more fully realizing that Joan manipulated me into a meeting with Dwight. Toward what end? This prayer must include all other persons who inhabit their hellishly self-willed orbit.

I had lunch with Joan shortly before she went away. She hinted at a tropical destination and told me she had left Dwight some paperwork. She said that she hoped it wouldn't go bad, like '51, '56 and '61. I did not ask Joan to embellish her statement. I mentioned Dwight and his penance money and hinted at his personal catastrophe in 1957. Joan told me that she knew the story, but refused to tell me how she knew. And in that moment, I knew that Joan loved Dwight sans all political agendas.

I cried a little. Joan hugged me and gave me a beautiful emerald.

DOCUMENT INSERT: 3/8/70. Extract from the journal of Marshall E. Bowen.

Los Angeles,
3/8/70

Fear time.

It's fear time now, and it's been fear time for a while. I've been fearful for so long that it's become almost banal. I'm now hyperalert to the signs of panic expressed by my body. Months of general fear have made me more sensitive to acute and justified fear. I've been surviving and buying advantage moment to moment.

An anonymous informant bought me time with Mr. Hoover and Mr. Holly. A nineteen-snitch package, graciously attributed to me. It bought Mr. Holly time with Mr. Hoover, I'm sure of that. It validates OPERATION BAAAAAD BROTHER, which buys me more time to pursue armored-car heist leads. The MMLF has lost interest in me over time. MMLF members see me at the clubs, alone or with my BTA brothers. They avert their eyes, spit on the floor or make obscene gestures. There are shoving matches as both groups co-opt space at peace marches. I'm apprehensive more than fearful in those contexts. I monitor my body for signs of panic and realize that I've been granted time.

Time liberates me and constrains me. A friend on LAPD told me that LAPD had secretly terminated my employment. Mr. Holly and Wayne obviously knew this and never told me. This makes me a Federal operative with no police sanction and no assured position within law enforcement once my assignment concludes. Last week,

I found bug wires in my apartment. I did the prudent thing: I let them sit. It had to have been instigated by Wayne and Mr. Holly. They do not trust me. Their distrust is fully justified. I have been very careful in whom I talk to in my home and what I talk about, in person and on the telephone. The discovery of the bug-tap apparatus vouched my justified paranoia and confirmed me in my role of apostatized ex-cop black militant. I assumed that role the moment I rented this apartment and have embellished it with greater and greater flair every moment since. Men with the Bent have to be cautious. I behave as if I do not have the Bent and have done so since Wayne made his "faggot" remark. In my heart, I feel like a radicalized ex-cop, weighing his options in all arenas. My actor's sense of time and identity has proven invaluable here.

Wayne and I have smoked dope a few times. We discussed the oddly different and oddly similar metaphysical states of our lives. It was in many ways the most beguiling interchange of my life.

Time has been bestowed on me. I am probably ghetto-safe because Scotty Bennett wants me ghetto-safe. The revised ghetto word is that I may be a police informant. This is Scotty's protracted vengeance on me, I'm sure. The worrisome thing is that I see no vindictive punch line or conclusion in sight. Scotty greatly enhanced his ghetto-legend status late last year. In the process, he dealt a severe blow to black nationalism in Los Angeles and bought me more time on the score-heroin front. There were Panther-pig dustups in October and December. Both incidents received wide publicity. A full dozen Panthers have now disappeared, six per incident. Scotty fulfilled his promise of August '68. Reprisal, deterrent, vengeance enacted and time purchased for me. The upshot? More BTA bewilderment, fear and indecisiveness. The growing notion that smack is heat we don't need. I've got the sense that MMLF is reacting similarly. And, nuggets of gold in with the dirt: more and more rank-and-file brothers think that dealing smack is *wrong*.

With gifts of time handed me, I stepped up my queries on the heist. I must have said, "Say, man, you remember that armored-car job back in '64?" a million times and received a million dumbstruck looks and bullshit answers. I have mentioned Reginald Hazzard and described his tenuous resemblance to the burned-face robber an equal number of times, with the same results. Then two things clicked, independently.

I was engaged in a routine phone-drop talk with Mr. Holly. He casually mentioned Scotty's brutal grilling of Jomo Clarkson.

Scotty asked Jomo a string of pointedly non sequitur questions pertaining to the heist. Mr. Holly found this confusing.

It sat with me for weeks. Aaah, Scotty—what do you know and what aren't you telling us? Shortly after that, I bailed Ezzard Jones out of jail twice. The first time was a drunk-driving beef. I pulled Ezz out of 77th Street Station and took him out drinking from there. A week later, Ezz was popped for drunk-and-disorderly. I filled out paperwork in the University Station squadroom, was left alone briefly and took advantage of it.

I checked the Unsolved 211 file cabinet and found a routing sheet for the heist. I memorized the divisional record number, called LAPD R&I and impersonated a cop. The clerk consulted the master file and came back on the line. She said, "I'm sorry, Officer. No such DR number exists."

And I knew then:

Scotty had a private file stash. He was pulling filed reports in from throughout the LAPD's geographical divisions and was hoarding the information for himself.

I am certain of it. There can be no other explanation.

78

(Jarabacoa, 3/12/70)

Heavy rain stalled out work. The thirteenth-floor framing dragged. All four sites dipped behind schedule. A few slaves escaped.

La Banda reacted. They combed the crews and drew torture lots. "Hate-ins": lashings and slaves screaming in the rain.

Crutch watched the latest. A monsoon just passed over. The ground was ankle-deep mud. The site was packed with sodden lumber and equipment. It was all miasma and muck.

The La Banda guy used a tassel whip. Little bulbs supplied extra pain. Crutch bopped behind voodoo herbs. It focused him and zoned the ugly shit out.

The slave was strapped to a bulldozer. His shrieks boomeranged. The lash-to-lash echoes overlapped.

The whip man was good. The tassels cut down to the rib bone. The slave crew watched. Crutch shut his eyes.

The slave collapsed. A La Banda guy bug-sprayed his wounds for added hurt and disinfection. The slave ate mud. It muffled his screams.

A horn honked. Crutch looked over. Froggy had a new '59 Cadi*black*. It was de rigueur striped. Froggy called it "Tiger Kar."

The Cubans were crammed in with Tommy guns. Canestel pointed north—*Tiger Kove now.*

Crutch got queasy. Tiger Kar ran rough roads on soft suspension. He was squished between Morales and Saldívar. His brainpan popped. He kept checking the rearview mirrors. He'd had this surveillance vibe. He couldn't validate it. *Hell hound on my trail.*

They hit Tiger Kove at dusk. *Tiger Klaw* was gassed to go. The storm had passed over. Residual chop pushed them east. The north shore and the Mona Passage—one big whitecap. They made Point Higuero early. They smoked weed to kill time. The Puerto Rican spics trusted them now. Froggy called them their "Tiger *Kompañeros.*"

Crutch heard onshore movement. The spics popped out of the brush. They lobbed the dope suitcase on board. Gómez-Sloan lobbed the cash suitcase at them. It was kwick and kompanionable.

The Krew unmoored the *Klaw* and sailed away, kove-bound. White-caps bucked them. Crutch launched a torpedo for kicks. It hit a shit-flecked atoll and exploded.

They moored and draped *Tiger Klaw* with camouflage netting. They took Tiger Kar back to Santo Domingo. Crutch dozed off his dope jolt. Mosquitoes buzzed into his mouth and woke him up periodic.

It was dawn. The Krew decamped at the El Embajador. Froggy told Crutch to hold the suitcase. The Tonton guys would shag it to Port-au-Prince tomorrow. Crutch yawned and elevatored up to his suite.

He opened the door. He re-caught the vibe. He smelled cigarette smoke. He saw a tip glowing.

The light snapped on. There's Dwight Holly on the couch. There's some shit on the coffee table.

A paint can and a paintbrush. A syringe and a morphine Syrette.

Crutch shut the door and dropped the suitcase. Dwight pulled out a pocketknife.

"How much are you holding?"

"Three pounds."

"That'll do."

His mouth dried up. His bladder swelled. The walls loop-de-looped.

Dwight said, "Take your shirt off."

"Man, you can't—"

"*I'm not saying it again.* You're taking your shirt off, I'm taking the suit-case. I won't stop you from running out the door. I'll call Wayne and rat out your dope business the moment you do."

Crutch pulled his shirt off. His sphincter almost blew. Dwight opened the paint can and dipped in the brush. The paint was bright red.

He walked the walls and pulled off the artwork. He painted "6/14" above the couch. He re-dipped his brush. He painted "6/14!!!!" above the wet bar. He re-dipped his brush. He painted "Death to Yanqui Dope Ped-dlers" beside the door.

Crutch prayed and tried not to cry. Dwight popped the Syrette and plungered the syringe. Crutch held his arm out. Dwight clamped his biceps and brought up a vein.

Crutch squeezed his Saint Chris medal. It snapped off his neck. Dwight poked the vein and geezed him up.

He went loosey-goosey. His bladder blew. He didn't care. His eyes rolled back.

Dwight flicked his lighter and warmed up his knife. Crutch braced his hands on the door. Dwight carved "6/14" on his back.

79

(Las Vegas, 3/14/70)

Wayne linked boxes. His wall graph was Op Art. Boxes and arrows off at odd angles. Boxes and arrows. Reginald to Joan to the Haitian herb man.

Graph boxes and boxed carbons—LAPD and the L.A. County Sheriff's. His LVPD contact secured them. Call it a dim long shot. Occurrence reports, field-interrogation cards. The L.A. cops hard-rousted black kids routinely. Reginald's name might be there.

Wayne checked his watch. He had an hour, tops. His bags were packed. He had skim cash for Celia. He booked a red-eye to the D.R.

Arrows and boxes. "Library Books" to "Bailed Out of Jail." A new box: "Leander James Jackson/BTA/Tonton Macoute."

The hallway door creaked. He heard Mary Beth in the living room. Her keys jiggled. She dropped bags on a chair. She exhaled like she was pissed.

He stared at the graph. He locked his satchel and attached the handcuff chain. He check-marked "Leander James Jackson."

"I want you to stop all this."

Wayne turned around. Mary Beth stared at the satchel.

"I don't want you to find my son. He doesn't want to be found. If he's alive, he made that decision of his own free will, and I will not dishonor him by forcing a reunion."

Wayne jammed his hands in his pockets. Voodoo-herb residue made his eyes run.

Mary Beth stepped close. "Whatever you've done in the past, I'll forgive you. Whatever you're doing now, I'll forgive you. I'll forgive you for not trusting me, because you don't want to be forgiven, you just want to create more risk and intrigue and buy yourself more punishment."

Wayne left-hooked the wall. He dented the molding, his knuckles bled, his wristwatch face shattered.

Mary Beth said, *"Who have you hurt? What have you done?"*

He walked to the safe house. Santo Domingo looked different. The visit was ad-libbed. He didn't call Ivar Smith or the Boys. He just wanted to *see*.

It felt like wide-screen hi-fi. He usually limousined. It bought him eye-ball relief and less volume. This was the shit. The sewers reeked, the noise peaked, the cops perched and pounced.

It was winter-warm/night-air sticky. Wayne wore a sport coat over his cuff chain. The address was in Borojol. The district was all go-go bars and low-peso hotels. Haitian vendors sold klerin-laced ice cream.

Wayne found the address: a pink cube off the main drag. His free hand ached from the wall punch. He banged his bracelet on the door. Celia opened up.

She wore a bloody smock. The space behind her was crammed with cots and fluid-drip stands. Four boys and two girls were head-sutured. Barbed-wire sap wounds—Wayne saw the stitch cuts oozing.

He saw the doctor he met last year. Two nurses changed bedpans. One boy had a foot stump. One girl had a bullet crease down to her cheekbone.

A back window framed an alley space. Wayne saw Joan outside, smoking. Scalpels poked out of her boot tops.

Celia pointed to the satchel. Wayne unlocked it. His hand throbbed. Celia scooped out the money.

"How much?"

"One forty-eight."

"I spoke to Sam. He told me that Balaguer has agreed to four more casinos. They'll have to burn or flood Haitian villages before the building can begin."

Wayne shut his eyes. His senses reloaded. He smelled the skin rot there in the room.

He opened his eyes. Celia repacked the satchel and slid it under a cot. A boy screamed in Spanish. A girl moaned in Kreole French. Joan turned around and saw him. Wayne sidestepped cots and walked out to her.

Her hair was tied back. Her glasses fit crooked. She had small, rough hands.

"Did you bring a donation?"

"Yes, but not quite as much as last time."

"I'm confident that there'll be a next time."

"Yes, there will be."

Joan lit a cigarette. Her fingernails were blood-caked.

"How real is all of this to you?"

"Tell me what you know about me. Tell me how you know."

"I'm not going to."

A gunshot cracked somewhere. A man dog-bayed. Joan said, "The doctor should look at your hand."

Wayne shook his head. "I tried to find you in L.A."

"Yes."

"I wasn't the only one looking for you."

"I'll find the man we're discussing when it becomes necessary."

The dog man bayed. Two more dog men piped in. A dog woman bayed from the opposite direction.

Wayne said, "There's some things you could tell me."

"I'm not going to."

The dog pack bayed and threw bottles at walls. Glass shattered in stereo.

"You haven't answered my question."

Wayne flexed his hand. "Some people you wait your whole life for. They send you someplace you'd be a fool not to go."

Joan reached in her pocket. Wayne noticed tremors. She pulled out a small red flag on a stick.

Wayne said, "Get me a silencer threaded for a .357 Magnum revolver."

The Santo Domingo sites were back from the street and one-man-guarded. The guards knew him. The crews slept in tents thirty yards adjacent. The demolition shacks abutted the foundation struts. The interior walls were baffle-wrapped and unleaded. Dynamite, C-4, nitro. All pure flammables.

The surrounding ground was rain-damp. The work bosses talked site-to-site via pay telephone. Soak a tight synthetic cord and plastic-sheath it. Allow enough circumference to air-feed the flame. Rig the phones and call the phones and pray for a simple ignition.

The rural sites would be harder. They were sixty miles apart. That might mean a bomb-toss gambit.

Wayne found an all-night auto-parts store. He bought the tools and two acrylic-pad car seats. He bought a thick plastic hose at a hardware store and went back to his hotel.

He cut the seats down to fabric strands and gasoline-soaked them. He memory-measured. He cut the hose sections down to an approximate length. He perforated them and created flame-feeders. The pay phones stood on loose dirt. The wire rigs should be easy. The phone-call currents might or might not ignite.

A boy delivered the silencer. Wayne worked all night. He turned his suite into a workshop. He called the desk and rented a car for tomorrow night. He dosed himself with voodoo herbs and slept through the day.

His dreams were mostly peaceful. Dr. King, sermonizing and laughing.

He got up and made himself eat. He packed his rental Chevy and drove to the first site. His hand didn't hurt. He couldn't hear external sounds or feel his feet on the pedals. He was way-inside-his-head calm.

11:26 p.m.

He parked across the street. The guard was pacing and smoking. The slave tent was dark.

Wayne jammed a pair of tin snips down his waistband. The guard walked to the gate and came on nosy. Wayne rolled down his window and yelled *"Hola."* The guard recognized him and unlocked the gate.

Wayne got out and walked over. The guard did *You el jefe* shtick. Wayne pointed to the moon. The guard turned his back. Wayne put the Magnum to his head and fired once.

The silencer worked. The soft-point bullet pierced and spread. The guard fell dead with no exit spray.

Wayne walked to the car and got out the tubing. He walked back and dug the dirt trench with his hands. He pulled keys off the guard's belt and unlocked the explosives shack. He unscrewed the back of the pay phone, unfurled the wires and clamped them to the edge of the tube.

Sixteen minutes.

He unrolled the tubing, end to end. He filled the trench with it, phone to shack. He ran to the slave tent and tapped the floodlight by the entrance.

The slaves stirred. They were shackled cot-to-cot. Most were black, some were light, most looked Haitian. They stared at him. They saw the gun in his belt and genuflected. The postures got them caught up in their chains. Wayne pulled out his tin snips. They started screaming. Wayne grabbed the nearest man and cut his wrists free.

The man just looked at him. Wayne stepped back. The man jumped up and down and waved his free hands. The other men stared at Wayne and *Got It.*

They raised their hands in unison. Shackle chains linked them together. Wayne walked man to man and cut them free. They swarmed him and lifted him high. He memorized their faces as they ran.

.   .   .

The second site was two miles off. The gate was unlocked. The guard snored in a sleeping bag by the pay phone. Wayne shot him in the head and lugged up his tools.

The ground was soft, the trench laid flat, the work went fast. The job ran nine and change.

The slave tent was made from near-transparent gauzing. It was rain-soaked and heat-absorbent. Four all-night floodlights baked it.

The slaves were awake. Their cots were sweat-soaked and dipped to the ground. They saw Wayne and just lay there. Murmurs built and stayed short of shouts. Wayne walked cot to cot. The first slave pulled his hands back. Wayne grabbed his wrists and cut his chain off. The other slaves got the picture. They held their wrists up.

Wayne worked man to man. They got up slowly. They stumbled and hobbled. Nobody looked at Wayne. A man did a voodoo benediction. Two men tore through the gauzing and ran.

Wayne watched them. They sprinted to a small hut and kicked and shouldered the door. It fell off its hinges. They grabbed the rifles and Sten guns inside.

The Autopista ran straight north. He needed a view. Elevated and within his sight range.

A gas station popped up at Reparado. Foothills and a downslope horizon. A single phone booth. A big nightscape frame.

The calls would be short of long-distance. No operator patch-through. It might or might not work.

Wayne double-dipped the coin slot and dialed the first site phone. He got sixteen rings and nothing. Ring seventeen echoed and brought a pink glow. Ring eighteen whooshed a big red-streaked sky.

He dropped coins and dialed the second number. The flame burst on the second ring. The red patches merged.

The rural sites troubled him. The phones and shacks were badly spaced. The slave tents were foundation-flush. That meant casualties.

The Midget knew by now. La Banda knew. The rural sites would get fast reinforcement.

Wayne parked in a thicket outside Jarabacoa. He ate herbs and willed himself not to think. Tree branches lifted his car. He saw ten million stars. Constellations moved at his fingertips. He heard sounds that could have been gunfire and could have been drums.

Coins dropped from the sky. He opened his mouth to taste them. Dial tones rang and sparked light shows. The colors lulled him someplace safe.

The sun woke him up. Windshield glare hit him. His eyes blurred. He saw flames and smelled smoke.

He started the car and took back roads. He passed a fire truck and two Policía Nacional cars. The flames shot up over a tree line. He saw the Jarabacoa site burn.

Show me more—

He stopped the car. He got up and stood on the roof. He saw two site guards lynched from tree limbs. He saw "6/14" smeared on a foundation block and a discarded Sten gun.

Show me—

He jumped onto a tree branch and climbed to a summit perch. The world expanded. Foliage swirled somewhere close. He saw light-skinned kids and black men running with guns.

Show—

He looked south. The world re-expanded. He did spontaneous math and geometry. Coins dropped. The sky exploded where the other site should be.

80

(Los Angeles, 3/19/70)

Stragglers left Sultan Sam's. Sambo locked up. Dwight perched in the rear lot.

Afro music pulsed inside. A copmobile cruised Central. The stragglers oink-oinked. The cops let it slide. The spooks outnumbered them.

Dwight checked his watch. Joan phone-dropped him. The lot at 2:00 a.m. That made her eight minutes late.

The music downshifted to bebop. Dwight laid his piece on the briefcase. He got the shit through customs. He split the D.R. in short-hair sync.

His White House contact called. Nixon was agitated, verging on pissed. Some Commies sabotaged the casino sites. La Banda tagged it 6/14.

Dipshit got out in pre-sync. Dwight carved him and robbed him and told him how to lie. Get to L.A. and work the Bowen wire. Let Mesplede mourn the dope. Tell him Clyde Duber needs you.

Dwight rolled up his window and earplugged the bop. He hit L.A. and put out feelers. Tell her we're on, she'll get it, she'll know. He braced every left-wing denizen on Planet Earth. It took six full days.

Headlights strafed him. A '63 Dodge pulled into the lot. Dwight blinked his brights. The Dodge blinked back. Dwight grabbed his shit and got out of the car.

Joan pulled up beside him. She doused her lights and kept the motor running. An alley lamp backlit her. She looked done in, verging on fraught.

"You never said good-bye."

"It didn't seem necessary. I knew we were incomplete."

"Where were you?"

"I'm not telling you."

"Tell me what's wrong."

"No. I'm not going to."

Dwight touched her hair. Joan leaned into his hand for a heartbeat. "We're on?"

Dwight passed her the briefcase. "Get it to BTA through a cutout. Keep your name out of it if you can. We want Bowen to think it's a windfall. Kid, we got lucky, it just dropped on your head."

A horn honked. Dwight aimed at the sound. Joan reached out and eased down his gun hand.

"I need you to say it."

Dwight leaned into the car. Joan pressed his hand to the doorsill.

"We should say it. Belief works that way."

Dwight said, "Nobody dies."

81

(Los Angeles, 3/19/70)

Dead air. Dawn air and insomnia—the shits.

The bug post was a shine shack on Marsh Bowen's block. The feed lines ran through overhead phone wires. Extraneous calls popped in. You heard a coon cacophony.

Funny and diverting. Non-lethal. Lots of pimp talk and holy roller spiel.

Crutch yawned. He was jet-lagged four days on. Big Dwight scripted him. Froggy saw his carved-up back and fucked-up room and bought it. Clyde needs me, Boss. Go, my son. You will be avenged.

Convergence: a faux-Commie dope rip-off and real sabotage.

Froggy called and broke the news. The 6/14ers torched the sites. The Midget was prepping a Big Red Roundup.

Crutch shifted his headphones. A call hit the air: the asthmatic biddy next door.

Mama wheezed and ragged Governor Ray-gun. Crutch rode out a nerve jolt. He bugged Sam G.'s suite. He heard Sam and Celia talking. She pumped him on the casino sites. He remembered high school Latin. *Post hoc, propter ergo hoc.* After this, because of this.

Yeah, but:

It felt dumb, it felt wrong, it felt un-Celia and un-Joan.

Mama wheezed—Ray-gun cut my welfare check. Crutch got antsy. He dumped the headphones and pulled off his shirt.

A wall mirror faced the console. Crutch stood up and craned for a look. The wound was scabbed over and peeling. Scar lines extended. The numbers were visible, the branding might stick.

He kept looking. He glanced at the console. His Joan pix were there on the ledge.

The math came to him. One year, eight months and twenty-seven days. He had tracked her that long.

The red light blinked. Bowen—incoming call.

Crutch slipped on his headphones. He heard Bowen, yawn-voiced. He heard "Marsh, it is Leander James Jackson."

A happy cat. Cheery. Big Haitian lilt.

Greetings ping-ponged and devolved into off-the-pigs chat. That Haitian sound. "Baby boy"—the late Luc's verbal tic.

Wait—

Leander James Jackson. Laurent-Jean Jacqueau. The same initials.

Haitian men. Jacqueau, the Tonton traitor. Jacqueau, the 6/14 convert. Jacqueau, unfindable in the U.S.

Line static, feeder fuzz, reverb and squelch.

Bowen: inaudible/"Have to score smack."

Jackson: squelch/"In my country, it is known as the 'beast from the East.' "

Squelch/fuzz/static. A stray call cuts in. Wheezy Mama's back. Ooooh, that Ray-gun.

Big Dwight. The bootjacked dope. The black-militant gig—

File work.

Read files when tweaked. Read files when bored. Read files when up all night, hammered. "Read files" was his mantra. It consoled his ass and work-supplied him.

It was 7:10. Crutch bombed to Clyde Duber Associates and let himself in. Clyde and Buzz showed up nineish. That gave him file time.

Clyde's hobbyhorse—the armored-car job. Four file cabinets.

Crutch pulled up a chair and pulled folders. They were *re*-pulls. He knew the file sideways and backward. Old facts hit him: names, dates, locations. Forensic stats, scorched bodies. Did a second heist man *ex*-cape? Photos: Scotty B. scowling. Scotty hard-nosing male Negroes.

A loose sheet fell out. Crutch unfolded it. A hand-drawn street map. 84th and Budlong, 2/24/64. *X* marks for the slaughter. Little houses street-numbered and sketched to scale.

Crutch studied the map. Something skimmed his skull. Some other file, some other fact, some complementary numb—

Oh, yes. That's it. Safe guess: Clyde doesn't know.

Marsh Bowen lived on that block then. He was nineteen. He was fresh out of Dorsey High. He lived with his mom and dad.

File work.

Read files when bugged. Read files when buzzed. Read different files when other files scorch you.

Crutch holed up at the Vivian. He studied his mother's file. He picked at his 6/14 scabs and grooved on the scarring. Zombie Zone outtakes zapped him.

THE ELECTRIC CHAIR, THE EYES, THE HANDS AND FEET. La Banda stunts and the black guy's hands melted.

He got scared. He popped two red devils with an Old Crow chaser. It un-scared him. He grabbed his binoculars and aerial-peeped.

Barb Cathcart watered her front lawn. She wore a shift dress. A cool wind gave her goose bumps. Gail Miller's mom breezed with the mailman. Old lady Miller hated him. He picture-peeped Gail and snapped a shot of her bush. He got kicked out of Hollywood High.

The phone rang. Crutch jumped on it.

"It's Crutchfield."

"Donald, I am outraged."

Cool it—*he doesn't know/he can't know.*

"What happened, Froggy? Tell me."

"Wayne performed the sabotage. He was seen purchasing explosive material. He desecrated the northern sites in order to blame 6/14. He very obviously enlisted Communists to assist him. I think his *putain Rouge* comrades are the ones who robbed you."

"Froggy, tell me—"

"Balaguer has made an expediently reasoned decision. He has decreed no reprisals on Wayne. He has decided that 6/14 should pay and that future dissidents should be taught a lesson. Tiger Krew will be part of this, which mandates your immediate return."

He got sweaty hands. The phone slipped. It hit the floor. The receiver cracked.

The red devils hit full-on. He hated-hexed Wayne, pins to eyeballs. He got this voodoo-vile idea.

He knew her name and her job stats. He wrote the note at the Barstow rest stop. He used the hood of his car as a desk.

Dear Mrs. Hazzard,

I work for your friend Wayne Tedrow in numerous illegal capacities. He routinely underestimates me and refers to me as "Dipshit." I suspect that Wayne has been less than candid about events in his recent past and that you may have doubts about his stability and moral character.

Your doubts are fully justified. Wayne was involved in the murder of Rev. Martin Luther King in April 1968, and was a suspect in the murder of his own father two months later. It is highly probable that he was involved in the tragic shooting deaths of your husband and a West Las Vegas criminal later that summer. You deserve to know these things. I intend you no harm; I only want to set you straight.

Yours truly,
A Friend

Hot potato.

The union was just off Fremont. His buzz was waning. Drop it, hex him, don't candy-ass.

The office crew was filing out. People fast-walked to their cars. Crutch double-parked and scanned faces. He saw the woman approach an Olds 88.

He got out and sprinted at her. People ducked and went *What?* She turned around and saw him. He quick-read her eyes. *Who's this crazy young man?*

He dropped it on her and ran around the corner. He ducked into a carpet joint and had three quick belts. It glued his shit together. He got this devil-may-care rush.

Fremont ran one way. The window overlooked the street. She had to drive by. Where's that Rocket 88?

He waited twenty minutes and walked back to his sled. He gave the parking lot a look-see.

She was braced up against the Olds, sobbing. Her fingers were bloody. She was grabbing at the doorsill to hold herself up.

DOCUMENT INSERT: 3/21/70. Extract from the journal of Marshall E. Bowen.

Los Angeles,
3/21/70

It happened just this morning. It was the single most shocking event of my life, both eclipsing and enhancing that day six years and one month ago. I have memorized it instant to instant and will extend the process of mindscaping it, so that I never forget.

I woke up later than usual; late fragments of a dream were passing through my head. The backdrop was an amalgam of the clubs on Central Avenue, replete with posing black militants and white hangers-ons. Benny Boles, Joan Klein and the late Jomo were in the mix; I cannot specifically recall anyone else. Music was playing—hard bop—and it faded into police-band radio crackle. I sat up in bed and realized that the pigs were parked in the driveway outside my apartment door.

I put on a robe, walked to the door and opened it. Scotty Bennett was standing there. He was wearing a tan poplin suit, a plaid bow tie and a straw porkpie hat. He handed me a bottle of Seagram's Crown Royal with a red ribbon tied around the neck. He said precisely this: "Don't say I never gave you anything but trouble."

It wasn't horrifying or intimidating or in any way erotic. Scotty smiled and said, "Let's talk about the heist. There's what you know and what I know. Let's make up and make some money. Let's get you back on LAPD."

The doorjamb kept me upright as I went light-headed. Scotty said, "I picked up a tip. Some Commie woman wants to unload three pounds of junk on the BTA. Let's see if we can make you a hero on that one."

The word *hero* was transformative; the most vicious killer pig of his era grew a halo and angel's wings. Scotty winked at me. I faltered at winking back and stuck out my hand. Scotty hugged me instead.

82

(Las Vegas, 3/22/70)

The Boys kept calling. Ivar Smith backstopped them. It was all anti-Red rage.

6/14 torched the sites. Prescient—the Midget just okayed four more builds. Wayne took the calls: Carlos, Santo, Sam. Terry Brundage called. Mesplede called. The rage level built. The calls stopped dead two days back.

He played along. He expressed his own faux rage.

Dream State.

Wayne studied his wall graph. The Leander James Jackson box grabbed him. He stared at it. He drew connecting lines. He recalled his trip out.

The roundups were starting. He called Celia. She said his work inspired their work. Safe houses were hiding their people. La Banda would find people to interrogate and maim. There would be a fearful cost. We have to say it—belief works that way.

Airport security was threadbare. The customs crew got pulled for the Red raids. He flew out easy.

Wayne drew lines. The re-*click* clicked. Memory tug and loss. It clicked to Joan's redacted file. It was a brain tweak. He got that tug and no more.

He stepped back and reframed the wall. He took in broad data. He saw a tacked-on note slip off to one side. He knew it wasn't his.

"Dear Mrs. Hazzard." Dipshit's indictment. Mary Beth's response scrawled below.

"I find this fully credible. If you had told me yourself, I might have forgiven you."

. . .

He signed papers at his lawyer's office. He went by the Hughes Tool Company and cashed out a bank draft. He flew to L.A. and drove to the Peoples' Bank. Lionel Thornton let him into the vault. He bagged $1.4 million in casino skim, Tiger Kab receipts and after-hours club profits. He filled three briefcases. He called Hughes Charter and booked a Santo Domingo flight.

Trees grew upside down. Joan tossed emeralds and seeded clouds. Each raindrop was a mirror.

He saw his childhood in Peru, Indiana. He saw Dwight and Wayne Senior and the Klan in disarray. His mother walked into a raindrop. He learned chemistry at BYU. Molecular charts etched themselves green. Tree roots reversed their growth. They held his eyes and let him look in. He saw Little Rock '57 and Dallas '63. JFK waved good-bye. Wendell Durfee laughed. He apologized to Reginald Hazzard for not finding him.

The air melted. Moist particles produced snow. Dr. King whispered chemical equations. The world made sense for an instant. Joan rubbed emerald dust on her knife scar and watched it heal. Janice told him not to worry. The planets realigned themselves and explained physics as whim. He heard "belief works that way" and let his eyes rest on the sun.

A cab ran him to Borojol. The driver was spooked. Red alert—you could see it.

The door knocks, the traffic stops, the street roust/shakedowns. The cops on rooftops with binoculars. The cops scanning crowds and mugshot sheets.

The cab dropped Wayne at the safe house. A window was half-cracked. He smelled blood and disinfectant and heard half a scream.

Joan appeared in the window. They looked at each other. She saw his suitcases and gestured to someone inside. The door opened. Wayne turned that way. A young man grabbed the suitcases and ran back in.

Wayne looked in the window. Joan placed her hand on the glass inside. Wayne placed his hand over hers. The glass was warm. Their eyes held. Joan walked away first.

A cab dropped him at the river. He crossed the bridge into Haiti at dusk. A Tonton man recognized him—ça va, boss.

Wayne walked into a village. Masked revelers danced through a grave-yard. Men sat propped up on tombstones. They were motionless. *Le poudre zombi*—goblets rolled off their laps.

The revelers wore machetes in scabbards. Their masks were blood-smeared. The air was scent-thick: reptile powder and poultry musk.

Wayne walked into a tavern. Bizango-sect banners created a mood. He attracted a range of looks. He pointed to bottles and created a concoction he'd never tried before. The barman built his drink. A green foam burned his eyes as he drank it. He left much too much money on the bar.

Two graveyards bisected the next tavern stretch. Wayne walked across them and read headstones in French. His ancestors reburied them-selves under his feet. He saw a zombified man convulse. He tasted the gunpowder and tree-frog liver in his drink.

Masked revelers followed him. A dog wearing a pointed hat bit him and ran off. He eyeball-tracked constellations. He fluttered his lids and made meteors arc.

The *click* revealed itself. Thomas Frank Narduno, dead at the Grape-vine. Joan's known associate. A Joan-to-Dwight motive yet to play out.

He entered a tavern and ordered a potion. Six *bokurs* watched him drink it. Two men offered blessings. Four men waved amulets and hexed him. He left much too much money on the bar.

He walked outside. The sky breathed. He felt the moon's texture. Craters became emerald mines.

An alleyway appeared. A breeze carried him down it. Leaves stirred and sent rainbows twirling. Three men stepped out of a moonbeam. They wore cross-draw scabbards. They had bird wings where their right arms used to be.

Wayne said, "Peace."

They pulled their machetes and cut him dead right there.

83

(Los Angeles, 3/25/70)

"BTA scored some smack. It was an old-prison-buddy deal. Ezzard Jones put it together."

Dwight said, "Keep going."

"It came out of nowhere. A bunch of Panthers turned tail to Oakland after the December thing. A big connection got stiffed. His guys are willing to lay the stuff off on consignment."

The Carolina Pines on Sunset. The 8:00 a.m. clientele: drowsy whores and Hollywood High teachers.

Dwight lit a cigarette. "Keep going."

Marsh twirled his fork. "BTA's got a pound and a half. The funny thing is that the lay-off guy dumped an equal amount on MMLF. I don't know how it went down, but it was some kind of consensus. 'Let's have a pow-wow so our shit don't go bad, brother.' I'm supposed to mediate a 'summit meeting' next week."

Fucking Joan. Stone-brilliant. She spread the wealth and doubled the indictments.

Dwight blew a Joan-style smoke ring. It came out blurry and dispersed too quick.

"Do it. Make it happen as fast as you can."

Dwight went back to the drop-front. It was musty. He opened the shades and cracked the windows. He pulled a telex out of the tray.

D.H.,

The Dominican embassy contacted me a few moments ago. Regretfully, I must inform you that Wayne Tedrow was murdered in

Haiti sometime within this past week. The crime appears to have been motivated by political and racial grievance. The body was disposed of on the Dominican side of the Plaine du Massacre. Pieces of paper scrawled with garish symbols and anti-American slogans were found in the victim's pockets. Please assess this situation per the victim's dealings with RMN, Mr. Hughes and our Italian friends, et al. Call me upon receipt of this communiqué.

JEH

The dark room helped. The walls enclosed him. Street noise was steady. He ran the window unit and leveled out the hum.

He pressed himself into small spaces. His desk cubbyhole and the closet felt safe. He tucked up his legs and rode out the cramps. He covered his head for more darkness. He threw his gun down a heating shaft so he wouldn't shoot himself. His shirt was soaked from sobbing all wrapped up.

Time drilled a hole someplace. He dumped his booze and pills down the shaft so he wouldn't run to sleep. The phone rang and rang. It was all gunshots. He covered his ears. The phone kept ringing. He crawled out of his nest and threw the phone on the floor. The receiver was close, the line crackled, he heard her voice.

The hole expanded. He grabbed the phone. He got out "Yes?" and "You never called me here before." His voice was Wayne's.

The line fuzzed. He lost her voice. The line cleared. He got her again.

"Balaguer's rounding up and torturing people. Wayne bombed the sites. Balaguer's making a statement."

Dwight coughed. The line fritzed and died. He cracked the shades and got sight back. His eyes swirled. He called his L.A. patch-call guy. A recorded message rolled. He asked for a callback: one minute with The Man.

The light hurt. He pulled the shades back tight. Blackout curtains and time travel: Wayne with his first chemistry set and his Scottish immigrant grandfather.

Peru, Indiana. Spring '48. Wayne mixes powders and builds a rainbow.

The phone rang. He grabbed the receiver. A flunky said something. Dwight wiped his eyes. The line clicked. Richard Nixon said, "You've got balls to call me out of the blue."

"Wayne Tedrow's dead. Balaguer's going nuts and rounding up people for some shit that Wayne pulled. We all go back with Wayne, Sir. With all due respect, this has to stop now."

Nixon whistled. "Sure, Dwight. I'll call the little prick. Jesus, those fucking Nevada Mormons are crazy."

84

Street view, mirror view. He couldn't stop looking.

His suite was penthouse-high. The vista was wide. The fuzz kicked Red ass across a *biiiiig* plane. The show was a week running. Roundups, hassles, brawls. Skirmishes up the ying-yang.

The window show got to him. His carved-up back, ditto. The 6/14 brand was a keeper. The scar was permanent. He *sort of* dug it. It astonished him and made him *look*.

Crutch walked mirror to window. He was shirtless, he was sweaty. Heart pings—*bip, bip, bip.*

Ivar Smith just called him. The Crutchfield hex worked. Some voodoo niggers whacked Wayne Tedrow's nigger-lover ass.

His head hurt. His vessels vibrated. It was a top-ten Richter-scale migraine. L.A. scared him back here. L.A. was *worse.* He read the signs: Dwight Holly and Marsh Bowen had some fucked-up dope thing going.

Tiger Krew dope. *His* dope. One fucking obvious conclusion.

Crutch stared out the window. Shit perked far and near. It was an ant show. The street was an ant farm. Cops and Commies skittered.

Sirens blared. It was earache-loud and stereophonic. The sound felt citywide. Spic ant groups froze.

He walked to the mirror. His scar was pink and creased. 6/14, *por vida.*

That heist lead torqued him: Leander James Jackson as Laurent-Jean Jacqueau. He located Jackson in coontown and spot-tailed him. He learned *buppkes.* He spot-tailed Marsh Bowen. Paydirt: Marsh meets Scotty Bennett at Tommy Tucker's Playroom.

Hated rivals—*très* chummy. *Say what?*

Crutch walked to the window. His head hurt. He sweated. He panted and fogged up the glass.

He wiped it clear. He blinked and squinted. The ant show was gone.

Coffee sounded good. Bop to Gazcue and slurp java. Re-calibrate and re-cogitate. Groove on the hex. Recap and reconsider the case.

Crutch strolled. He cut across the polo field. He scoped women at the paddock. He hit Calle Bolívar and made for the Malecón.

No fuzz, no ant farm. That siren blare was some kind of all-clear.

His head still hurt. The pain re-circulated and stung. He heard a car idling behind him. He heard foot slaps on pavement. He saw shadows up ahead.

Pile drive:

Two guys behind him, two guys up front. They've got bandanna masks, one's slipping off, it's Felipe Gómez-Sloan.

They slammed him. He flailed. He got clotheslined, he got rabbit-punched, he got tape slapped on his mouth. He got an arm free and ripped Canestel's mask off. The street flipped, the sky hit him, he saw Tiger Kar.

They dumped him in the trunk and threw the lid down. He pulled the tape off. He kicked at the latch point and gagged on stale air. Tiger Kar peeled out. He heard backseat banging. The trunk lining ripped and let air and light in. A knife blade stabbed and carved space.

There's more light. There's a hand. There's Froggy's pit-bull tattoos.

Froggy yelled. It was word bouillabaisse. *Cochon, pédé, putain Rouge.* *"L'héroïne" en français,* "cocksucker" in English.

The blade kept stabbing. Crutch squirmed away from it and kicked out. He hit Froggy's hand. The blade ripped his tennis shoe. He contorted and pulled his feet back.

Fumes filled the trunk—five fuckers smoking. Crutch saw Froggy's eyes in the trunk hole.

"It was not 6/14. It was Dwight Holly. There was a security camera in the lobby at the hotel. The camera was equipped with a timer. It cannot be anything else."

The Cubans tiger-hissed. Saldívar blew smoke in the trunk. Crutch gagged and kicked at his face.

Froggy laughed. Crutch squirmed against the truck latch. Cigarettes bombarded him. He swatted out the coals.

He prayed. His headache lodged behind his eyes and white-bordered things. Froggy said, "The bombings have greatly upset Sam and Carlos. Sam and Carlos do not know of your part in this, although I have told them you may well be soft on Communists. I doubt that President Balaguer will risk another round of construction and potential sabotage. Sam and Carlos think you should embellish your anti-Communist credentials."

Tiger Kar zoomed. It felt like the full-bore Autopista. Crutch prayed. He zoomed through the psalms and the Gloria Patria. His head pounded. His eyes burned. He saw Jesus and Martin Luther at Wittenberg. Smoke filled the trunk. Cigarette butts followed. Tiger hisses, tiger growls, mugging faces at the hole.

Pariguayo, pariguayo, pariguayo.

Crutch vomited and gasped. Road bumps sent Tiger Kar swerving. Crutch pressed his face to the trunk hole and sucked air in. Gómez-Sloan jabbed a cigarette at his nose.

He screamed and rolled away from the hole. He heard *pariguayo, pariguayo, pariguayo.* Tiger Kar braked and brodied. The doors slammed. The trunk lid popped and let I-see-Jesus light in. Hands grabbed him and placed his feet on the ground.

It's a shit-ass place. It's a garbage dump with six shacks adjacent.

Paper refuse and mulch. Fifty tons of ground *something.* Bones poking out of an ash mound. Wiggles inside it—gator tails snapping through.

Pariguayo, pariguayo, pariguayo.

The sun burned his headache out through his eyes. The grabbing hands held him and walked him. Somebody strapped a big weighty thing on his back. The thing had a hose, a nozzle and a trigger. Somebody put a spout thing in his hands.

Pariguayo, pariguayo, pariguayo.

It was L.A. or the D.R. It was the Boyle Heights dump or Watts swampland or some 6/14 deal. The sun melted the spout thing into his hands. Other hands pushed him to an open-front shack. Two dozen people were bound and tape-gagged.

Black people. Men, women and kids—bone-thin and squirming. Pus-packed sores. Yellow eyes jumping and glazing.

The spout thing smelled like gasoline. The yellow eyes talked to him. It was L.A. or Haiti. The people were darktown riffraff or voodoo lords. The psalms kept replaying.

Hands steadied him. Hands flexed his hands on the spout thing. Clouds doused the sun for a moment.

He stepped forward and turned around. He saw all five of them and got their names straight for the first time. The sun re-eclipsed and winked at him. He tapped the trigger.

The flame tore up and out. They screamed and went spastic on fire.

The ammo on their belts blew up. Pieces of them exploded.

DOCUMENT INSERT: 3/30/70. Extract from the journal of Marshall E. Bowen.

Los Angeles,
3/30/70

"Black-militant summit": savor the concept.

I was to be the facilitating agent. Leander James Jackson would represent the BTA and Joseph Tidwell McCarver and Claude Cantrell Torrance would negotiate on the MMFL's behalf. This august event was couched as an afternoon bar-b-q at Joe McCarver's crib. There would be ribs, chicken, greens, booze, reefer and sweet-potato pie. Joe's backyard would be festively decorated. His four-year-old daughter and six-year-old son would provide diversion and perhaps serve to squelch overuse of the word *motherfucker.*

I had possession of the dope. I would be in charge of negotiating the BTA/MMLF percentage cut and the ultimate splitting of profits. Most importantly, this was where I would shift my allegiance from Mr. Holly to Scotty.

The plan resulted from Bowen-Bennett summitry at Tommy Tucker's Playroom. We determined that immediate action would be required. The dope split would be accomplished; the BTA and MMLF fools would leave the pad holding big poundage; Scotty would swoop down for the bust. It meant betraying my FBI-infiltrator status prematurely, thus shafting Mr. Holly and Mr. Hoover, with hopes of getting back on LAPD in a flash. If the plan meshed, both the BTA and MMLF would be fully discredited, the Feds would get their indictments and I would be reinstated to LAPD. Mr. Hoover and Mr. Holly would be furious. I had unilaterally terminated the operation, with Scotty's assistance. Resentment would simmer and then dissipate. Scotty and I would then be free to pool our information on the heist. We would form a powerful two-man team to go after the money and emeralds; OPERATION BAAAAAD BROTHER would be considered a success. This wild swath of my young life, with all its attendant mindscapes, would assume an entirely new dimension.

I asked Scotty how he knew of my fixation with the heist, enough so to brace me on it. Scotty told me he had picked up tips that I had been making subtle queries, going back months. On instinct, he did a background check on me. Bingo: my 84th and Budlong address showed up on an old driver's license.

Joe McCarver owned a small stucco house off 68th and Slauson. The day was warm. The backyard was comfortably strewn with lounge chairs; the kids splashed around in a wading pool. Scotty was parked in an unmarked unit, two blocks away. He had a two-way radio with dial-in capacity. All I needed was four seconds with Joe's bedroom phone.

"This be good like a *motherfuuuuucker*," Claude Torrance said as we sat down. The dope sat in the middle of a long picnic table, as if it were an altarpiece. Intergroup tension needed to be brooked before we began the negotiation, so 151 rum and spike-laced grass was served. I partook sparingly. The other three men consumed a full bottle of the rum and smoked several reefers. Joe attacked the food; I prepared the opening remarks of my mediation. Then Claude started fucking with my head.

"Brother, an' I calls you 'brother' with a big muthafuckin' grain of salt, let me ask you, *brother*, why'd you rat out Brother Jomo Kenyatta Clarkson to the muthafuckin' pigs last year?"

I said something neutral. I did my conciliatory "Hey, brother, be cool" thing.

Leander stepped in; I'm sure he considered my response sissified. He said, "Listen to me, baby boy. I put a knife in Jomo and saw him bleed weak blood. He was anemic from weak thoughts and a strong appetite for evil. I put a hex on his nigger soul, and he die the next day. I have connections to Bizango-sect *bokurs* and the ghost of Baron Samedi. They *make* Jomo off himself. They send legions of red ants up the hole in his dick to eat out his eyes and his brain. That is the pure truth, baby boy."

I held my breath.

Joe put down a chicken wing and cracked his knuckles.

Claude said, "Baron Samedi sucked my big black dick," and spit on Leander's shoes.

Then:

Leander pulled a gun. Joe pulled a gun. Claude pulled a gun. There was the briefest of pauses where they might have stepped back. A strong wind whipped through the backyard. A bottle toppled. The noise rang loud. That did it.

All three men had fat-clip automatics. They all fired at once, as I ducked under the table.

It was very close range. The noise was horrible. Leander shot and killed Claude. Joe shot and killed Leander. Leander shot and killed Joe as he was going down. The three men were on the ground by the table. They were technically dead, but still twitching. They kept firing and sending shots out. The children screamed and tried to run. Stray shots and ricochets hit them. I saw the little girl's brains blow back into the wading pool.

I curled up, covered my head and waited for more shots or death-throe noise. There was none. I looked around and saw the three dead men and two dead children. It was over in less than ten seconds. I had an epiphany. It was instantaneously realized mind-scaping. I immediately prepared a tableau for my heroic, trial-by-fire redemption.

The house and backyard were flanked by vacant lots on three sides, which gave me both privacy and time to work. Calmly, I pulled my gun and shot the dead Claude Cantrell Torrance in the head. Just as calmly, I shot the late Joseph Tidwell McCarver and Leander James Jackson. Finishing up, I took the three guns out of their hands and fired off random shots. I smudged the grips, then calmly placed the guns back in their hands.

Sure—they fired on each other. But I assumed control and took them all out. Too bad about the kids. I tried to sweep them to safety, but ricochets caught them first.

I walked through the yard and stretched the bodies out in convincing cross-fire positions. I wiped up the drag marks with paper towels and checked out the scene. I ran into the house and stiffed a faux-panicked call to Scotty.

His siren kicked on instantly; I heard it from two blocks away. I walked slowly back to the yard.

DOCUMENT INSERT: 4/1/70. Los Angeles *Herald Express* article.

BLACK-MILITANT BLASTOUT

Two days ago, a backyard barbecue in South Los Angeles erupted into violence and three men and two children lay dead. Initial news reports attributed the killings to a high-stakes narcotics deal gone bad. It now appears to be much more than that.

The three adult victims—Leander James Jackson, age 31, Joseph Tidwell McCarver, age 32, and Claude Cantrell Torrance, age 23—were rabid black-militant activists, LAPD Sergeant Robert S. Bennett told reporters at a press conference. The two murdered children—Theodore and Darleen McCarver, ages six and four, were McCarver's two offspring with his common-law wife. Sergeant Bennett went on to reveal that there was a sixth person in Joe McCarver's backyard: former LAPD Officer Marshall E. Bowen.

"You may recall Officer Bowen from an encounter he had with me on October 1, 1968," Sergeant Bennett said. "Officer Bowen's actions resulted in his being fired from LAPD. In reality, the encounter and the subsequent firing were just a ruse to allow Officer Bowen to convincingly infiltrate the Black Tribe Alliance and Mau-Mau Liberation Front, two deadly black-nationalist groups intent on selling heroin to finance their subversive activities."

Officer Bowen assumed the microphone. "Jackson, McCarver and Torrance had extensive criminal records and Communist ties," he said. "I had been gathering evidence against them since my fake firing from LAPD a year and a half ago. The purpose of the barbecue was a 'dope summit meeting' and the culmination of my work as an FBI infiltrator. Regrettably, a verbal argument escalated into a gunfight. I ran in and attempted to lead the two children to safety, but stray bullets got to them first. At that point, I entered into gunfire with Jackson, McCarver and Torrance, as they were firing at one another."

FBI Director J. Edgar Hoover praised Officer Bowen's "brilliant work in throwing a monkey wrench into the activities of two Communist-aligned organizations." Newly installed LAPD Chief Ed Davis announced that Officer Bowen will return to the Los Angeles Police Department as a sergeant and will receive the LAPD's highest award: the Medal of Valor.

DOCUMENT INSERT: 4/2/70. Milwaukee *Sentinel* article.

ODD RUMORS FROM DOMINICAN REPUBLIC

The Dominican Republic has been comparatively peaceful since the 1965 civil war, a brief military engagement that ended nearly five years ago. The U.S. Marines, satisfied at the quashing of potential Communist revolt on the island, had left. An interim leftist dictator had been deposed, and centrist-reformer Joaquín Balaguer has been in power since 1966. But for the past several weeks, dire rumors have resounded from within the "D.R.," as it is popularly known.

None of the rumors have been factually substantiated, but they have been persistently similar, leading some American journalists to wonder if the events are connected.

There has been a rash of demonstrations by left-wing groups in Santo Domingo, most particularly the Castroite "6/14 Movement." Government sources have said that this is not unusual; free speech is encouraged within the D.R. and thus the demonstrations are in no way anomalous. The sites of four hotel-casino buildings financed by U.S. interests were rumored to have been sabotaged two weeks ago, which government sources also denied. Add on the murder of an American man by members of an anti-Dominican voodoo sect and the discovery of the charred bodies of one French man with radical right-wing ties and four Cuban exiles allegedly backed by wealthy Americans in the Miami-based exile community, and you have the stuff of great conspiracy talk.

CIA Station Chief Terence Brundage told correspondents: "It's just that. Talk, and nothing else. You've got a bunch of unrelated rumors and no more."

This assessment was seconded by a spokesman for President Balaguer. "All poppycock," he said. "The casino sites were not sabotaged. Structural flaws brought them down, and we are back in discussion with our American investment group, which is anxious to start rebuilding soon."

DOCUMENT INSERT: 4/3/70. Verbatim FBI telephone call transcript. Marked: "Recorded at the Director's Request/Classified Confidential 1-A: Director's Eyes Only." Speaking: Director Hoover, Special Agent Dwight C. Holly.

JEH: Good morning, Dwight.

DH: Good morning, Sir.

JEH: You sound glum, while I am elated. I have not been in such a mood since 1919. You were there at the dock with me, Dwight. We waved bye-bye to a truculent Emma Goldman.

DH: Yes, Sir.

JEH: Young Bowen soared in the end. And I do not condemn him for his "end run" with the LAPD and the outsized Sergeant Robert S. Bennett. Our sepia seducer wanted his job back, and who can blame him for that?

DH: Yes, Sir.

JEH: The BTA and MMLF have momentarily eclipsed the Panthers. The Bureau has gotten a million vats of good ink. Both groups are headed toward mass indictment. It is a vivid explication of Negro moral turpitude, replete with dead pickaninnies to tug at your heartstrings.

DH: Yes, Sir.

JEH: You sound glum and screechily high-strung, Dwight. You should—

DH: I need to foist a bluff under your name and President Nixon's, Sir. If it comes back to you, I'd very much appreciate it if you'd offer confirmation. And I will never ask you for another favor.

JEH: Glum and impertinent. A Dwight Chalfont Holly that I have never heard before.

DH: Yes, Sir.

JEH: I'm flying high, Dwight. My answer is resultantly yes. We put the BTA and MMLF down like foaming-mouth dogs. I'm telling it like it is.

DH: Thank you, Sir.

JEH: Good day, Dwight.

DH: Good day, Sir.

85

(New Orleans, 4/4/70)

U-turns and wrong turns. Mis-marked cul-de-sacs. The road map was ten years outdated.

Signs sent him down exits and back to cloverleafs. He dodged road debris and loafing hard hats. It was hot. Things looked florid. The world moved slow as he ran breathless.

Dwight cut down an access road. Finally—signs to the Town & Country.

He was full-fucked shot. He stayed alone with it. Karen was back east and Joan vanished. It was full-time overtime. He saw the crime-scene pix. They looked bogus. LAPD bought or went along with Marsh Bowen's version. Dipshit sent him a note.

"Dwight—I saw Marsh with Scotty B., two nights before the shootings. They looked friendly. It surprised me, so I thought you should know."

The road was potholed. Wetlands pressed up on both sides. Dwight pulled into a clearing. The motel was L-shaped and sandblasted pink. Three golf carts sat outside the office.

Dwight parked beside them. The office door was open. A golf ball dribbled out and rolled down the steps. It was a stop frame. It ran heat-sapped slow. Everything he saw looked scary.

He locked up the car and walked over. His suit wilted. He saw Santo, Sam and Carlos in golf duds.

The office was knotty pine. The Boys sat in beanbag chairs and poured liqueurs from cut-glass decanters. Carlos pointed to a chair and the door. Dwight complied. Santo slapped a wall unit and roused cold air.

Sam said, "Dwight's too thin."

Santo said, "This is not a man bearing glad tidings."

Carlos said, "We've got good news. Let's hope his bad news don't intervene."

Dwight sank into his chair. Air swooshed out of it. He felt weightless.

Santo sipped anisette. "Dwight H. at a loss for words. What's this I'm seeing?"

Sam sipped Galliano. "He's been eating crow. He's lost weight on the all-crow diet."

Carlos sipped XO. "He's a man who's suffered a loss. Wayne T. torched the building sites and robbed us blind for God knows what reason. He's coming to grips with all the grief caused by that Mormon cocksucker."

Dwight said, "I know you have plans. I only need a few minutes of your time."

Santo sipped anisette. "You're right in that regard. Time is a commodity we are currently short of."

Sam sipped Galliano. "I'm writing a book about Wayne. It's called *Death of a Coon Hunter.*"

Carlos sipped XO. "Some Reds fried Tiger Krew. I'm betting they went out shooting."

Santo switched to Drambuie. "They were too zealous for my taste. Tell it like it is. They were right-wing nuts."

Sam switched to schnapps. "Dipshit is the last man standing. He was off peeping windows when the Krew got barbecued."

Carlos sipped XO. "Why mourn recent history? Balaguer's back in the fold and picking our pockets anew. This time we won't hire nigger-lovers or neo-Nazi mercs with sidebar agendas."

Santo sipped Drambuie. "White stiffs love to lose money in lush tropical locales. It's the Age of Aquarius, baby."

Sam said, "Let the sun shine in."

Carlos said, "Right on, brother. Let it all hang out."

Dwight shook his head. "No foreign casinos. That's straight from President Nixon. The D.R. was a goddamn big fuckup. It's not going to happen again. The president is emphatic. You'll find him cooperative in every other way, but your casino plan is dead as of now."

They stared at him. They did double takes. It went stop frame and triple time.

Carlos threw his glass at him. It hit the wall and cracked. Santo and Sam threw their glasses. They fell short of the chair. Too-sweet booze splashed him.

Dwight got up and walked out. His legs caved. He fell into the car. He saw a bed and a lawn at the end of a tunnel.

86

(Los Angeles, 4/5/70)

The lot.
Old home week.
Back in the fold.
Dipshit, pariguayo. You killed the guy who killed JFK. You offed umpteen Reds and had boocoo adventures. You're twenty-five. You've got gray-flecked hair and lines on your face. Your back is all sliced up.

Crutch sat in his sled. The old crew circulated. Clyde and Buzz Duber, Phil Irwin and Chick Weiss. Bobby Gallard and Fred Otash.

He got more are-you-all-rights and you-don't-look-so-goods. Fred O. evil-eyed him. Freddy was in on the King-Bobby hits. Freddy knew he knew. It was all stale bread now.

Biz circulated. Chick sent Bobby and Phil out on a rope job. That producer at the Ravenswood was priapic. Wife #3 craved Splitsville while hubby craved Greek meat.

Hey, man. Weren't you embroiled in some cool shit in the Caribbean?
Not so cool. I should have stayed home.

He cut the villagers loose. They did a big-white-bwana number and ran into the brush. He torched Tiger Kar and walked back to Santo Domingo. He packed up and got the fuck out of Dodge.

The Boys never braced him. He got to L.A. and dismantled the fail-safes. He re-clicked with Clyde and Buzz and went back to tail jobs. Buzz buzz-bombed him with questions. He downplayed everything. Buzz asked him about his case. He said he gave it up.

A rainstorm came on. The guys perched in their cars. He was eight days back. Clyde saw that he was fucked-up and ladled work on him. He deployed that heavy-hung Filipino across all gender lines. He kicked in doors and snapped *mucho* pictures. Sal Mineo needed gelt and consented to pork a woman. The deal died with Sal's soft dick. It felt wrong. It should have jazzed him. It scared him, instead.

Everything scared him.

Nothing clicked in *safe*. He had his pad at the Vivian and his file pad downtown. They felt unsafe. He picked at his mother's file and his case file. That felt unsafe. He peeped Hancock Park. Julie Smith was married, pregnant and out of the house. Dana Lund had a dimwit boyfriend. She'd aged as much as he had.

Crutch tapped the ignition and ran the radio. He heard a song burst: "Faces come out of the rain." It spooked him. It was voodoo-derived. The song was aimed *at* him. It was raining now. He squinted out the windshield and tried to read faces. Zilch—just pedestrians with umbrellas.

He sees signs everywhere. He stays up all night or sleeps too long. He has these kid crying jags—*Dipshit, pariguayo.* He sees shit involuntarily. They're Zombie Zone re-takes with L.A. backdrops.

His case was deactivated somewhere in his head. It was there, back burner boiling. Leander James Jackson was Laurent-Jean Jacqueau, but both guys were dead. Gretchen/Celia was somewhere. It hurt to think about Joan.

The rain came down zigzagged. Crutch saw two fender benders. Radio news blah-blah'd: Hanoi Jane Fonda and James Earl Ray.

Crutch doused it. A black chick walked down Beverly. The hex backfired—he thought about Wayne.

You tried to tell me, I didn't listen, I ratted you out. You're dead inside days and I'm here. Fucker, you re-hexed me. I can't keep food down. I'm afraid to be alone and I schiz around people. I went to church this morning. I wanted to revoke the hex. The pastor kicked my peeper ass off the pew.

Pariguayo in English: "party-watcher."

Clyde took him to a big LAPD bash. Jack Webb served as emcee. Marsh Bowen got the Medal of Valor.

Marsh was a fruit. Who knew and who didn't? Who did and didn't care? Marsh posed for pix with Scotty Bennett. They were salt-and-pepper pals now. The "Black-Militant Blastout"?—a righteous Fed snafu. Big Dwight's operation backfires and the fuzz make hay. Dwight was off somewhere. He called the drop-front a bunch of times and got no answer.

Thunder and lightning cracked. The sky went flamethrower red. Crutch got a fear jolt. He ran to the service bay and stood under the roof.

Two mechanics worked on a '62 Olds. Crutch watched them pull the flywheel and re-fit the clutch. A newspaper was creased flat on the workbench. Crutch checked it out.

The *Vegas Sun.* A piece on Wayne's funeral. A photo of Mary Beth Hazzard, black-veiled.

She wept. *She believed what he told her and grieved nonetheless.*

The Stardust was mid-Strip. Wayne's suite had an easy-shim door. He'd read a book on voodoo. Hex removal was a snap. You touched the victim's belongings and retrieved your thoughts. He didn't believe it. It was Lutheran text removed a million heartbeats. He figured he owed Wayne.

The drive took six hours. The rain never let up. Faces came and went with the radio music. He parked underground and elevatored to Wayne's floor. Nobody answered his door knock. He shimmed the door and got in.

The suite looked the same. The same furniture, the same caustic stink. The place looked preserved.

He walked back to the lab. A file space was built right beside it. Paper stacks, boxes, wall graph. A replay of *his* file nooks.

The arrows, the connecting lines. The neat handwritten notes.

He followed lines and arrows. Facts, logic, conjecture. It all made perfect sense.

Mary Beth's missing son. Emeralds. Haiti and Leander James Jackson. The woman with the dark, gray-streaked hair.

Celia, leftist firebrand. A hint of Joan and Dwight Holly in love.

His case and Wayne's—indivisible.

Dear God, that little red flag.

87

(Silver Hill, 4/5/70–12/4/70)

The bed, the lawn. The white buildings, the injected sleep.

Coercion got him in. He spent thirty days then. He stayed eight months now. Thirteen years of penance tithes formed his time between stays. His first visit was happenstance. The context was drunken neglect. The issues raised were guilt payments and abstinence. This stay resulted from reckless intent and cruel political thinking. The death toll was uncountable. The mind-set that created the actions mandated a conscious address.

He was here. She was wherever she went when she vanished. She knew she was complicit. Her heedlessness had spawned chaos on other occasions. She went away to build the will to return.

Silver Hill was beautiful. His stay covered three seasons. He got spring blaze, summer glow and snow.

He sent Mr. Hoover a telex. It stated his need for a long rest and did not state his location. Mr. Hoover knew he'd be here. A card arrived a month later.

Take as much time as you need. I have a new job for you. It's in Los Angeles. You'd start in January.

"File superintendent." "Dirt-digger," euphemized. Hoard gossip and scandal skank. Feed the old girl's private stash.

Low-risk work. A non-death-causing assignment.

L.A. was L.A. He might feel safe north of the southside. Karen was there. Joan might surface and find him.

He collapsed in New Orleans. He chartered a Bureau plane and flew straight here. Doctors examined him and found him physically sound.

They force-fed him big meals and put proper weight on his frame. They sedated him. He slept eighteen hours a day for six weeks running. He woke up startled. He saw his lost ones the moment he opened his eyes. He sobbed. He segued into panic jolts and threw himself at walls. Male nurses shot him up. He went back to sleep and did it all over again.

His bedroom walls were padded. The throws didn't hurt. He wanted to cause pain. He thought it would blur the dead people's faces.

He got through that part of it. Repetition burned it out. The docs decreased his sedation. He avoided the head-shrinkers and the other patients. He spent time with a flock of tame goats. They lived protected on the grounds. They were there to console the burnouts.

He fed them and petted them. He mail-ordered stuffed animals and sent them to Karen's kids. He pretended that the kids were his kids and that he had a life where nobody got fucked over and hurt. Those thoughts killed him. He'd lose it and weep and get afraid that he could never go out in the world again.

His lost ones came at him. He'd sit still with them. He spent weeks listening to them and weeks talking to them. He got to where they could co-exist.

They came and went. He started to see what they wanted and what he owed them. They gave him his mind back on a consignment basis.

Karen sent him notes full of Quaker prayers for peace. The girls sent thank-you cards for the stuffed animals. Karen sent a photo of all three of them. Their address and phone number were scrawled on the back. Dina wrote above it: "If this man is lost, please return him."

He carried the photo. He spent hours with his goats. He thought all of it through and began to see it.

A detailed operation. A multicontext design. An explicative scenario. Tell it like it was then and how it is now.

Mr. Hoover's racial lunacy. The FBI's war on the civil rights movement. Its calamitous faux pas with black-militant groups.

A huge feat of exposition. A densely packed indictment. A treatise on the collusive mind-set. JFK, RFK and MLK are dead. Let me tell you how.

A big social document, with key players brightly lit. Marsh Bowen: a duplicitous homosexual and merciless provocateur. Mob figures with vile ghetto ties. Mr. Hoover's orbit of hired guns. Special Agent Dwight C. Holly—called forth to confess.

An event of gravely stern measure. A grand idea culled from Mr. Hoover's file mania. An epic of malign paperwork rendered banal by the staggering weight of its emptiness. A text so deep that it would defy all easy reading and inspire contentious study for all motherfucking time.

He saw it all. He wrote nothing down. He rested and nuzzled his goats.

Karen sent him a peach pie for Thanksgiving. He shared it with his goats. He got fretful about them. He braced an administrator.

The man said, "They'll never be hurt, Mr. Holly. They'll be here for life. They're here for people like you."

He rested. He slept. He had some peaceful dreams about Wayne. He revised and embellished his idea. He could tell her soon. He knew he couldn't find her. He sensed that she'd find him in L.A.

He was wrong. It happened abruptly. She found him there with his goats.

He heard footsteps. He turned around and saw her. She looked more fierce and breathtaking than he had ever seen her. She had carried every bit of her weight.

He said, "Hello, comrade." He pulled out the little red flag.

She said, "What are we going to do?"

He said, "Let me tell you."

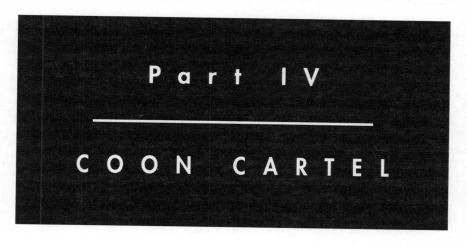

Part IV

COON CARTEL

December 5, 1970–November 18, 1971

DOCUMENT INSERT: 12/5/70. Verbatim FBI telephone call tran-
script. Marked: "Recorded at the Director's Request/Classified
Confidential 1-A: Director's Eyes Only." Speaking: Director Hoover,
President Richard M. Nixon.

RMN: Good morning, Edgar.

JEH: Good morning, Mr. President.

RMN: How are you feeling? You looked a little under the
weather at the American Legion brunch.

JEH: I assure you that I am fit as a fiddle, Mr. President. And,
as you know, I am always "ready to sing."

RMN: "Sing for your supper." You understand that old saw
when you run the goddamn country.

JEH: Yes, Sir. And, while we're on the topic, let me state that I
would devoutly hope that I would be able to sing well into your
second term.

RMN: Edgar, you're a rare old turd. Anyone who underestimates you should have their head examined.

JEH: Thank you, Mr. President. I would also add that we have
been friends since 1914.

RMN: I was born in 1913, Edgar. We must have met at a party
in my bassinet.

JEH: (Six seconds' silence.) Well . . . er . . . yes, Sir.

RMN: You've probably got a file on it. You open a file every
time some left-winger cuts a fart.

JEH: If I consider the person subversive, then, yes.

RMN: What's shaking in the black-militant universe? My guys at Justice are saying that that foolishness is on the wane.

JEH: Perhaps so, Sir. The Panthers and US are heavily infiltrated and caught up in litigation, and the admittedly minor BTA and MMLF are kaput. Sixteen felony indictments, Sir. A small FBI operation, but a gem.

RMN: That "Blastout" was a home run.

JEH: Yes, Sir. And I would have called it a grand slam.

RMN: Hmmm.

JEH: (Coughing spell/eight seconds.)

RMN: Are you all right, Edgar?

JEH: I'm getting over a cold, Sir.

RMN: I wasn't exactly thrilled with the congressionals last month. You lose a seat here, a seat there, and before you know it, they add up. I might ask you for a little help before the '72 general rolls around. The Democrats will field a good team. I'd like to get some derogatory poop on them in a timely fashion.

JEH: Uh . . . what type of—

RMN: "Black-bag job," Edgar. Don't go coy on me. Don't pretend you didn't pull that shit with Lyndon Johnson.

JEH: Uh . . . yes, Sir.

RMN: Dwight Holly would be a good man for that.

JEH: Dwight proffered a bluff in our names, Sir. He advanced a no-foreign-casinos edict to our Italian friends. The notion is sound, but the very act itself was quite cheeky.

RMN: Dwight's my main man. We jaw on the phone sometimes. You're right, the plan is A-OK. I keep the Boys at arm's length and pardon their guys out of jail at the proper intervals. It'll all look kosher that way.

JEH: Yes, Sir. I agree.

RMN: Big Dwight's a pisser. You said he's taking some kind of rest cure, right?

JEH: That's correct, Mr. President. He'll be returning to the Los Angeles Office next month.

RMN: Dwight's salty. I like that about him.

JEH: (Coughing spell/fourteen seconds.)

RMN: Are you all right?

JEH: Yes, Sir. I'm fine.

JEH: (Coughing spell/twelve seconds.)

RMN: Jesus, Edgar.

JEH: I assure you, Mr. President. I'm in the pink.

RMN: If you say so.

JEH: I should be run—

RMN: Bebe Rebozo told me a pisser of a story the other day. He was hobknobbing with some pols in Paraguay. They told it to him.

JEH: Uh, yes, Sir.

RMN: It's some kind of myth. This secret stash of emeralds has been financing right-wing coups since God was a pup. Have you ever heard—

JEH: (Coughing spell and muffled comment/transcript ends here.)

88

Scotty Bennett

(Los Angeles, 12/7/70)

"Among the many things I learned during my time under-cover is that inherent criminal-ity is inherent criminality, re-gardless of the racial or political grievance that serves as its justification, regardless of the soundness or unsoundness of the ideology expressed."

The spiel got applause. Mayor Yorty and Chief Davis clapped. Scotty clapped along. Marsh looked good. Sergeant's stripes on new blues. A close-cut Afro.

Full house: the Academy gym, cops and politicians. No Feds—big surprise there.

"The LAPD has superbly interdicted the criminal aspects of black nationalism as it has honored the legal right of black-nationalist civil address, while concurrently opening its arms to a new generation of minority police officers."

Scotty yukked internal. He hit up Marsh back in March. He let time simmer. Today was the day: the big heist summit.

The fucker could speak. He chose his words and rocked with the rhythm. He eschewed a homo aesthetic.

The chief dug him. Rank and filers resented him. Sam Yorty grooved his Uncle Tom act.

Marsh cranked it. *Woooo,* some crescendo! He stabbed the air like JFK. He hit the MLK note of redemption. He got a standing ovation.

The audience swarmed the lectern. Marsh was Mr. Gracious. Scotty winked on his way out.

. . .

Armed Robbery—211 PC. His den treasure-troved it.

Eighteen wall pix. Eighteen kills documented. The twelve Panthers went unsung. You can't photograph the dead-and-buried.

Liquor-store jobs and market rips. Sitting-duck ambushes and shoot-outs. Eighteen dead male Negroes.

Marsh thought he hated black folks. Marsh was wrong. He never said the word *nigger*. He hated killers, dope-pushers and heisters. Black militants were up there. His all-black kill sheet was luck and demographic. Shit played out that way.

Ann and the kids were in Fresno. The house was a stag-party zone. Scotty laid out booze, dip and Fritos. Scotty pulled all his files out.

Marsh Bowen tweaked him from the get-go. Marsh passed that ink-stained cash. Marsh worked at the Peoples' Bank briefly. Marsh got on LAPD. All tweakers, but inconclusive.

Then Marsh goes Fed and fucks him. Then Marsh starts making heist queries. Then he runs a DMV check and gets 84th and Budlong.

Scotty snarfed Fritos and bean dip. The wall photos spoke.

Rydell Tyner said, "Jesus, Scotty." He said, "Son, I warned you."

Bobby Fisk bled out at All-American Liquor. He gave Bobby's flash roll to his grandma.

Lamar Brown had a pencil neck. Triple-aught buck severed his head.

The basement bell rang. Scotty opened up. Marsh was back in civvies.

"Hello, partner."

"Hello, Scotty."

"Make yourself at home. If you show me yours, I'll show you mine."

Then to now: six years and ten months. Marsh kicked it off. He was there that day.

There *was* a third robber. He was black. The lead guy shot him, chemically scalded him and left him for dead. The third man crawled to an alley and hid. Marsh lived on that block then. He saw the third man. He saw his bulletproof vest and extra precautionary gauzing. He figured it saved the man's life. LAPD was out *bruuutal*. Marsh was outraged. He took the man to a doctor neighbor's house and hid him there. The doctor treated the man's wounds and burns. The man refused to discuss the heist-killings and never revealed his identity. He left two days later. He gave the doctor twenty thousand dollars in ink-stained cash. The doctor deposited it in the Peoples' Bank of South Los Angeles. He told Lionel Thornton to leak the cash back to the community. Charity donations: do it prudently. Small amounts of cash surfaced in the black community. Scotty leaned on the passers. The doctor died in '65. Marsh got obsessed with the case. He got a job at the bank, learned zero and quit.

Scotty took over. *He* was there that day. He sensed the case as The Case from Jump Street. He beat the bluesuits to the crime scene. He found nicked shells from a jammed automatic and pocketed them. The armored-car guards fired revolvers. Likewise the milk-truck driver, the lead guy and the two dead heist men. Thus: a third man had come and gone. *He* fired with the jammed automatic.

A third man—logic now physically confirmed.

Scotty walked the crime scene. He saw a blood trail leading away from it. The trail stopped near that alley. He blotted up a blood sample and got enough to type. He found some chemical-scalding pellets a few feet away. They were saliva-coated. He figured the third man spat them out.

They both knew that day: a third man escaped.

Scotty had the blood tested, covertly. The type: rare AB–. The other dead men had different blood types. The nicked shells: no go, brother. He jam-tested and test-fired every automatic in LAPD custody. Then to now: every booked-in mid-size auto. The results: all negative. He had the pellets tested. Shit—no chemical make.

Marsh jumped ahead. I've got a new lead. I'll tell you at the wrap-up. I'll drop some confirmation now. I checked the files at University and 77th. I discovered bogus routing numbers. I know you've got a private paper stash.

Scotty pointed to his file trove. Scotty refueled their drinks and took off.

He tracked the emerald shipment and made some progress. It started in the Dominican Republic, all government-vouched. The government stonewalled LAPD. Scotty tried everything. Other cops tried with less gusto. Nobody could track the stones' provenance. Scotty's take: the origin was dirty, the jewels were rogue. The senders decided against diplomatic-courier shipping. They chose Wells Fargo instead.

And:

The shipment records vanished from the Wells Fargo office a week after the heist. It was a pro B&E. The Wells Fargo execs went stonewall. They refused to talk to LAPD at all.

Marsh cut in. He'd heard rumors—black folks in need receive emeralds, anonymously. Scotty knew the rumors. Ghetto legend, who knows, I can't verify it.

Scotty revved up to the good part. This is the glue. It all sticks together here.

He glommed a partial eyeball witness six months after the heist. The guy said the lead robber was *white*. Okay, he's Caucasoid. Okay, there's the black robber rumors. Oreo teams in '64—*veeeeery* rare indeed. The witness had no further description. Scotty got frustrated there. You win, you lose. He built a lead sheet on a Wells Fargo exec. It never bloomed past speculation.

The guy's name was Richard Farr. He disappeared after the heist and the Wells Fargo B&E. Farr was half Anglo, half Dominican. Scotty culled paper on him. No lead tweakers resulted. The D.R. connection was a tweaker. Sub-tweaker: Farr might be some kind of Commie.

Scotty poured refills. Marsh took on a schoolboy look—sir, please teach me.

The investigation sandbagged. Nothing popped. Leads melted to sludge. Scotty worked the ID angle. It took years. He brought in his coroner pal, Tojo Tom Takahashi.

Tojo Tom froze flesh grafts from the scorched bodies. He isolated skin cells off one guy and lab-tested them. He found diseased leukocytes. The disease was indigenous to white men only.

Scotty did a fifty-state paper check. It took years. Paydirt, late '69. The place: Dogdick, Alabama. The man: Douglas Frank Claverly.

Dougie had that skin disease. Dougie was a Klanned-up ex–armed robber. Exhaustive background check—zero. Yeah, but: Dougie disappeared in 1/64—one month pre-heist.

Scotty redeployed Tojo Tom. Tojo ID'd the bogus milk-truck driver. A melted good-luck ring did it. The ring was embedded in a skin cavity.

Tojo extracted the ring and lab-tested the skin cells attached. Okay, it's a black guy. Tojo brought in chemicals and microscopes and raised words off the ring: JJL & CV.

Scotty traced the ring to Modesto. It took fucking weeks. Jerome James Wilkinson ordered the ring. He was a male Negro. He had no criminal record and no family. He worked as a strikebreaker. He vanished 1/64, one month pre-heist.

Enter Dr. Fred Hiltz. Punch line: the emeralds were going to *him.*

Marsh drop-jawed that one. He used to work lefty groups for Dr. Fred and Clyde Duber. Scotty said he knew that. Scotty contradicted long-held heist text.

The stones were allegedly headed to a Wells Fargo vault. The cash was a bank-deposit load. The stones were *really* being sent to Dr. Fred himself. A dummy corporation would hold them. A Dr. Fred stooge would play courier. Dr. Fred *craaaaved* the stones. There was some nutso right-wing emerald myth he creamed for.

Dr. Fred was offed in '68. Marsh said he knew the basic facts. Scotty laid out the inside scoop.

He popped Jomo C. for that liquor-store spree. Someone pretended to be Marsh himself. The fake Marsh offered up the liquor-store snitch and a snitch on a major gun stash. That shit brought Marsh ghetto peril. Marsh knew that all too well. Marsh knew that Jomo confessed to the Dr. Fred snuff and to whacking his crime partner. Here's the shit Marsh didn't know.

Scotty Q&A'd Jomo with Dwight Holly present. Big Dwight heard Jomo's Hiltz-case confession. He did not see Scotty's second go-round.

The L.A. County Jail. The isolation cell block. Jomo's one-man cell.

Jomo feared him now. Jomo called him "Mr. Scotty." Jomo folded from two kidney shots.

He said a "cutout" fed him the Hiltz heist. You'll find a bomb shelter. Steal the cash. Don't kill Dr. Fred. *Warn Dr. Fred.* Tell him not to reveal shit per February '64. He'll know what you mean.

Jomo had no heist knowledge. Scotty determined that. Jomo clammed up. Jomo refused to state the cutout's name. *Cutout:* an intelligence-agency term.

Scotty pressed. Scotty rubber-hosed Jomo. Jomo screamed and held his mud. Scotty hit Jomo too hard and killed him. Scotty rigged a toilet water–soaked bedsheet and faked a suicide.

Marsh got the shakes. Son, did I scare you? Scotty built him a highball and dumped fresh chips on his plate.

It fortified him. He spilled the rest of his tale.

Guilt-tripper Wayne Tedrow. His Find Reginald Hazzard quest. The boy looked like the third man. Marsh just checked an LVPD file. The kid had chemistry knowledge. Marsh thought about it. An old vibe resurfaced: the deep-burned bodies meant chemical skills. The pellets and chemical scaldings—Scotty agreed.

He dipped a Frito. "We have to make the Hazzard kid's blood type."

Marsh air-drew dollar signs. Scotty air-drew 50-50. Marsh said, "This should be fun."

89

(Los Angeles, 12/8/70)

Chick Weiss dug Negro art. Afro stuff and island stuff. Virility statues and armless spirit guards with wings.

They cluttered up his office. Doorstops and desk knickknacks. Carved wood with deep eyes sunk in.

Crutch and Phil Irwin pulled chairs up. A Zulu god stood between them. He was half life-size. His dick was three-headed. His rhinestone eyes looked cheap.

Chick prepped a panatela. He had a black-goddess cigar prop. He spread her legs, stuck the cigar in and severed the tip. He pushed a button. Her mouth wooshed out a flame.

Phil dug it. Crutch looked away. Chick cleared space and dumped his feet on the desk.

"Camera job. Papa's a billboard mogul and mama's a flower-power chick. Papa's tight with LAPD. One of his guys showed him a surveillance tape of that Griffith Park love-in. Mama's blowing a guy by the merry-go-round. Papa hired Clyde to get the goods on him. They're shacking at the Sunset Breeze Motel on alternate Tuesdays. I want you to get in subtle. Live film, *bubbies.* No hit-and-run snapshots on this one."

Crutch stood up. Phil stood and hangover-weaved. He bumped the Zulu god. Some sequins dropped off his dick.

Chick said, "Go, you fucking heathens. This is priceless art you're so frivolous to."

. . .

The day was hot. Phil bribed the desk guy. Crutch B&E'd the tryst room and fucked up the AC. They air-cracked the window. The camera lens would fit in. Phil said Chick was perved on surveillance film. He had a full library. He loved to watch plain-Jane chicks and chump Charlies fucking. It was illegal and unethical. Chick didn't care. He had clout. He threw perv-film parties for the L.A. elite.

They car-staked the lot. Phil pressed Crutch on his recent shit. He kept it zipped. Unit 6 was their target. The flanking units were hippie hives. The geeks blasted loud rock all day. That meant air cover.

Crutch sipped coffee. Phil sipped 151. They schmoozed gossip and Mando Ramos at the Olympic. Freddy O. bought Tiger Kab—what a fucking hoot.

Phil loaded the camera. The target car pulled up. The wife and the hippie stud entered Room 6.

Crutch flash-shot them. His camera date-scrolled the arrival time. Phil lugged the film camera up to the window crack.

He poked the lens in. He hit the On switches. The film cans were full. Roll it, C.B.

The camera ran soundless. It was cool. Visuals sufficed for California divorce. The wife and the hippie were *loud.* Crutch heard it over the rock noise. Cameraman Phil popped in earplugs.

Crutch tried to doze. Fuck me, fuck me's killed it. Chick's goddamn statues. Red rhinestone eyes. Wings where arms should be.

The love-nest door opened. Phil pulled out the camera and crouched. The wife and hippie shagged their sled and split. Phil carried the camera over.

"They went sixty-nine. I got the setup shot and the whole thing in one take. Chick will groove it."

Crutch said, "You're a loser."

Phil grabbed his crotch and grinned.

She sent her card early. Christmas was weeks off. This one: postmarked Amarillo, Texas.

Crutch pocketed the five-spot. Crutch placed the card in his file box. '55 to '70—sixteen cards total. Margaret Woodard Crutchfield covers half the U.S.

His closet was file-stuffed. He hung his clothes in the bathroom. His case file ran six boxes here. He had nine boxes stashed downtown.

He looked out the window. Christmas lights were up. Yeah, it's a ritual. Yeah, you should go.

. . .

He stole the red flag from Wayne's file cove. He taped it to his dashboard. He'd ripped up his Joan pictures. It was a de-hexing move. Hancock Park was dead without the Joan pix. He needed her for juxtaposition.

Eight months home. Residual shell shock. He still can't sleep. He can't work his case. His nightmares are banal now. Barbiturates subsume them. He works for Clyde and chauffeurs part-time. Freddy Otash bought Tiger Kab. Wayne Tedrow had cash-drained it. Freddy got it cheap.

It's a black lifestyle hub. It panders to hepcats, militants, and Motown fools slumming. Sonny Liston makes the scene. Rock Hudson trolls for dark dick in tigrified limos. Redd Foxx brings cocaine and moon pies. The white drivers wear tiger-stripe tuxes. The spades dig the slave roles reversed.

His case, Wayne's case, the heist. Three cases united. He saw Wayne's trove in April. He's been immobilized since then. He thinks about it. He follows the loop.

L.A. to the D.R. and Haiti. Back here again. He's tracking Gretchen Farr. She ripped off Fred Hiltz. She's aka Celia Reyes. She kisses Joan. He sees Horror House. Body parts, voodoo powder, green glass. Celia's linked to the D.R. Celia's got a codebook. Months of code work. Success. Book symbols match the death-house signs. He ID's the victim: María Rodríguez "Tattoo" Fontonette.

Joan and Celia are deep Red. Tattoo betrays the Cause. She ends up dead at Horror House. Celia's embroiled with Sam G. She wants to fuck up the casino sites. Crazy Wayne gets there first. *He* gets mobbed up. He bugs Sam's hotel room. He's pushing dope with Luc Duhamel. Luc zombifies him. He hears "loose emeralds," "1964," "Laurent-Jean Jacqueau." *It's all connected.*

He's back in L.A. He's adjunct to Dwight Holly's Fed gig. He's bugging Marsh Bowen. "Marsh, it is Leander James Jackson." That means it's Laurent-Jean Jacqueau.

It's all connected. Marsh lived at 84th and Budlong *Then.* Marsh is tight with Scotty B. *Now.* Their peace pact preceded "the Black-Militant Blastout."

Wayne's file. Weird emerald giveaways. Reginald H., long missing. Reggie splits Vegas *two months* pre-heist. The kid knows chemistry. The kid studied *Haitian* herbs. Joan taught Reginald at the Freedom School. Joan bailed him out of jail. It's December '63. The heist bodes.

Joan's omnipresent. She's Dwight Holly's snitch and probable lover. Dwight's rubber room–resting. *Where's Joan and why can't I find her?*

. . .

Crutch drove to 2nd and Plymouth. Dana's Christmas lights were up. Her tree filled the front window. Gift boxes were stacked branch-high.

Corny music—Ray Conniff—her usual yule slush.

He bought her a cashmere sweater at Bullock's. It was black and cable-knit. Elk horns fit through little toggles.

It was Christmas-wrapped. He walked up and placed it on the welcome mat. He rang the bell and vamoosed.

Radical chic:

Four Tiger kabs peeled out of the lot. Crutch saw François Truffaut, some black dudes and Hanoi Jane herself. A Tiger stretch rumbled up. Phil Irwin drove it. His tiger tux shed faux fur all over the seat. His passengers: Chick Weiss, César Chávez and Leonard Bernstein.

The stretch bombed southbound. Crutch walked into the hut. Fred O. worked the switchboard. Redd Foxx sniffed coke. Milt C. had Junkie Monkey up on his lap. Sonny Liston was toking maryjane.

Junkie Monkey said, "March 8, Jew York City. Muhammad Ali versus Smokin' Joe Frazier. See it on closed-circuit TV at Tiger Kab, the home of the Coon Cartel."

Sonny blew smoke in Junkie Monkey's face. Milt made the Junkster gag and cough.

"Ali is a sissified draft dodger. Islam is a gutter religion. Ali takes it up the shit chute from Gamal Abdel Nasser and the *Dish*onorable Elijah Muhammad."

Redd Foxx howled. White powder and snot flew. Fred O. yukked. Crutch haw-hawed.

Sonny unwrapped a morphine suppository. Quick hands: he dug into his pants and popped it up his ass.

"Come on, kid. You're driving me to Vegas."

The champ nodded out at San Berdoo and passed out at Barstow. Crutch Dexedrine-all-nightered. I-15 was dead. Crutch drove 105. The desert was dead cold. Six zillion stars burned.

The radio hummed low. Mountain ranges broke up reception. Crutch caught an oldie string. Circa '60 prom songs. The Peeper Magical Mystery Tour.

The music re-sputtered. Crutch flicked off the dial. Sonny yipped like a dog in a dream.

Crutch checked the rearview. Sonny was prone, with his feet out the window. Sand blew into the car. Sonny said, "Shit."

"Are you okay, champ?"

"Don't call me 'champ.' 'Champ's' what you call all them stumblebum sparring partners you see on skid row."

"Okay, boss."

Sonny lit a cigarette. He torched the filter, dropped the match and tried again. Six more swipes got him combustion.

Crutch said, "I saw you fight Wayne Bethea. You kicked his fucking ass."

Sonny dog-yawned. "I knew a cat named Wayne. He kept killing black guys he didn't want to. That boy just didn't have no hate for anybody, but shit kept finding him. He kept trying to find niggers to kill and niggers to save, and this woman of his thought it was all the same goddamn thing."

They hit a rise. The Vegas Strip emanated. Colored lights compressed by darkness.

Sonny said, "Drop me at the Sands. I'm meeting some people."

Crutch goosed the gas. He felt re-hexed and *de*-hexed. Sonny dropped three RDs in his tux pocket. His tiger koat was all pilled—fur balls up the wazoo.

"Don't deadhead back. Park somewhere and rest up."

It was 4:00 a.m. The Strip was a-go-go. Lots of cabs and golf-cart travel. The carts were wet bar–fitted. The passengers quaffed cocktails, the drivers swerved.

Crutch pulled up to the Sands. Sonny laid a C-note on him and ruffled his hair. The coffee shop was glass-fronted. People saw the crazy limo and howled.

Sonny got out. People waved. He weaved into the coffee shop. Mary Beth Hazzard walked over and hugged him.

The dexies fought off the RDs. He parked the limo under the Stardust and thrashed until noon. His tiger tux shed. Fur threads tickled his snout. He felt full-force-fucked in the soul.

He gave up on sleep and opted for pancakes. A short stack and coffee re-vivified him. Do it, fucker. You'll get re-zombified if you don't.

He drove to the Hotel Workers' Union. The limo took up two parking slots. He got some pissy looks. They turned to yuks quick. His tiger tux was a roar.

A janitor gave him directions. He was all pins and needles. Her office door was open. She looked up from her desk.

He said, "I'm sorry about Wayne."

She put down her pen.

He said, "He tried to warn me about some things."

She straightened her desk blotter.

He said, "I see things that other people don't see. I know how to find people."

She opened her purse and pulled out a key ring.

90

The girls chased a neighbor's dog. He watched from two houses down.

Dina had speed. Ella had a toddler's gait. The dog ran in elusive circles. Ella charged, fell and got back up. The front yard contained them. His stuffed animals were there on the porch.

Dwight pushed his seat back. The car was packed: tinctures, solvents and brushes. Notepaper of varied stock.

He left Silver Hill early. He started his Bureau work next month. Joan understood his plan. She signed on with blood-deep support—belief works that way.

Nixon called him yesterday. How was your rest? Welcome back—and, by the way . . .

The prez was building an ops squad—four black-bag men. Dwight declined. The prez acted hurt. Dwight recommended Howard Hunt at CIA.

Ella caught the dog. He pushed her down with his paws and licked her. Ella grinned and laughed.

Karen got in the car. They knocked up their arms embracing sideways. They kept banging their legs.

They found a fit and stayed with it. The girls looked over and waved.

Karen held his face. "You look the same."

"You look better."

"I thought you'd be fat from all that pie I sent you."

"My goats ate most of it."

Karen tucked her knees up. "My husband's in the backyard. I'll have to go in a minute."

"Later this week?"

"Yes."

"The Beverly Wilshire?"

"I'll never say no to that."

They laced hands on the steering wheel. Karen said, "Mr. Hoover's new dirt-hoarder. I'll be begging you to delete files inside of ten minutes."

"What's wrong with five? You know I'll do it."

Karen laughed. "You want something. This impromptu visit after so many months just isn't you."

Dwight rubbed her knees. "I think you should put together a team. There's a Bureau Records Center in Media, Pennsylvania. I think you should tap it in early March. There's at least ten thousand surveillance files there. You could steal them and expose the Bureau's harassment policies in one go."

Karen lit a cigarette. "I don't believe what I'm hearing."

"You should."

"And this is *your* idea? It didn't come from—"

"Not now, please."

"No weapons, in and out."

"That's right."

"And you'll tell me more. 'Need-to-know' basis?"

Dwight nodded. "Yes, and soon."

Ella fell and scuffed her knees. She started crying. Karen said, "I have to go."

Dwight said, "Do you love me?"

Karen said, "I'll think about it."

Files:

The file room was back lot–size. High shelves, deep shelves, rolling-ladder access. Political files, criminal files, civil files. Informant files. Surveillance files, gossip files and general-sleaze files. 600,000 files total.

All indexed. Chained index binders at every shelf front.

Dwight walked the shelf banks. The ladders ran on greased casters. Twelve-foot-high, floor-bolted structures. Twelve shelves per bank. Twenty-four banks total.

"You're early. Almost a month, in fact."

Dwight turned around. Jack Leahy leaned on a ladder.

"You'll hate the job. These files do not represent Mr. Hoover at his best."

"The Bureau's most impolitic SAC. How have you lasted this long?"

"Lawyer's luck. And civil law compared to *this*? Come on."

They shook hands. Jack sat on a ladder rung.

"I haven't seen you since the Hiltz case and the start-up of BAAAAD BROTHER."

"Well, two times lucky, and two times unexposed."

"Yeah, but at some goddamn price."

Dwight shook his head. "I'd rather not talk about it."

"I don't blame you. The old girl, third-rate militants and Scotty Bennett in one go? I'd have called in a rest break before you did."

"Can it, Jack. It's old news now."

Jack coughed. "Well, shit, you know the drill. You monitor the general dirt files and supplant them with informant pieces. You've got cops, criminals who want favors, newsmen, bug men, waiters, doormen, wheelmen, repo men, hotel clerks, barflies and the aggrieved great unwashed of the universe. Try to *underpay* for your dirt. The old girl wants the shit, but she wants it at bargain-basement prices."

Dwight sneezed. The file room was overcooled. Dry air fought off paper rot.

"Are you running standing bug posts?"

Jack rolled his eyes. "We've got bugged fuck pads and hotel suites. Duke Wayne blows into Chicago. The doorman at the Drake calls the Chicago SAC. Before you know it, the Duke's upgraded to the penthouse. Too bad it's hot-wired. The Duke's a cross-dresser, by the way. He wears a size-fifty-six extra-long muumuu."

Dwight laughed. "Anything else I should know?"

"Half the fruit bathhouses in L.A. are wired. The old girl caught a city councilman at a joint on La Cienega once, so she's running nine listening posts full-time."

Dwight plucked a file and skimmed it. Johnnie Ray sucks dick in Ferndell Park. The suckee is an FBI informant. Lana Turner dives dark sisters, circa '54. A snitch calls from Sultan Sam's Sandbox.

Jack said, "How's the old girl's health? I saw her in D.C. last month. She looked positively spectral. I had an informant once named 'Jean the Mean Queen.' She had to be the old girl's long-lost sister."

Liberace's all-boy cathouse. Scopophile Danny Thomas, nympho Peggy Lee. Muff-diver Sol Hurok. Masochist James Dean—the "Human Ashtray."

Dwight replaced the file. Margin notes lingered. Ava Gardner and Redd Foxx. Jean Seberg and half the Black Panthers.

"Have fun, Dwight. I told the old girl it's a swinging new world, but she didn't believe me."

· · ·

He rented a fallback. It was a work space/crash pad. It was close to the drop-front and Karen's place. He and Joan had keys. They kept their gear there. The bungalow overlooked Karen's street. He could watch the girls play.

Baxter and Cove was close. Two blocks and binocular range.

Dwight parked and lugged in boxes. He had brooding time. He was meeting Joan at the Statler later. The fallback was a plotter's den. Living room, kitchen, bathroom, mattress for naps.

He pulled a chair out to the terrace. He pointed his Bausch & Lombs south. Karen walked across her yard. Dina and Ella chased cats.

Karen looked haggard. His offer stunned her. She knows it's an adjunct op. She knows the main op is big. He can't tell her the gist. We're going to kill Mr. Hoover and frame Marsh Bowen for it.

They'll manipulate a convergence. Marsh will be pre-indicted by forged document trails. They will lead back to the year zero and extend beyond 2000. They'll recruit a pro shooter. Bob Relyea shot MLK. He should shoot again. The assassin is a homosexual black policeman. He kills the era's prime symbol of white authority and ends his own life immediately. Planted paperwork reveals public policy gone bad. Marsh Bowen has been consumed by a politically incubated madness. The FBI suborns him and sends him undercover. He undergoes a radical transformation. He concurrently attempts to exploit his situation. He's beset by sexual demons that induce a harrowing shame. The "Black-Militant Blastout" leaves two children dead. Marsh Bowen resumes his police career with honors derived from innocence slaughtered. Mr. Hoover created the overall context. Special Agent Dwight C. Holly implemented it.

They will create a Marsh Bowen diary. It will detail a brilliant black man's rising tide of conversation and psychic disjuncture. Entries will describe his odd friendship with Special Agent Holly. Agent Holly unburdened himself to Marsh Bowen. He laid out the FBI's war on the civil rights movement and described Mr. Hoover's rabid racial animus.

The King hit plot would not be mentioned. It would eclipse the shock of Mr. Hoover's death and spawn apocalypse. The fictional Holly-Bowen friendship would be deeply etched. It would encompass a world of guilt and hope. The diary would form a syllabus. It would bring readers to a copious glut of pre-existent FBI paper. The paper would form a narrative of banal minutae that would attenuate into horror. Grand juries would indict Marsh postmortem. Conspiracy talk would engulf the body politic. Every real and concocted trail would lead back to Mr. Hoover and his legacy of hate.

Mr. Hoover was partially discredited now. His anti-King salvos had become public fare. They were negligible compared to this. They lacked hardcore shock value. This would be a huge event. It would spawn waves of disbelief and tragically resigned acceptance.

He would be the trigger man. He would sit in committee rooms and grand-jury chambers. He would stand on the U.S. Senate floor. He would describe his exploitation of Marsh Bowen. He would detail his own lifetime of racial rancor, minutely outline his black-militant faux pas and chart the human cost. He would reveal his friendship with Marsh and paint a vivid picture of a white man and a black man as mirror-twinned souls in duress. He would embrace Marsh with forgiveness and the distanced love you feel for those you refract. He would tell the story of his crack-up. He would resign himself to an invasively scrutinized life.

Karen's house was a stone's throw. Dwight trained his binoculars. Ella threw building blocks at Dina. Big sister laughed and ran.

He told Joan the plan. They were in bed. They rented a guest house near Silver Hill. She trembled the way he trembled routinely. He struck the awe in her that she had always struck in him.

He'd go to prison. Four to six felt right. Protective custody, tennis courts, Fed-informant perks. There might be some animals he could care for.

Joan said, "Take these. They'll help you sleep." Two brown herb capsules.

They didn't put him out. They put him in between. Joan guided him places. She put her hands on his chest and made him breathe in sync. She started out in French and Spanish. He caught most of it. *Cap-Haïtien, Cotuí, Pico Duarte. Puerto Plata, Saint-Raphaël, El Guyabo.*

Breathe through, I'm here, you're safe now. I'll tell you what we did with Wayne's gifts.

It was the Statler. He knew that. They had Bureau-vouchered digs. Joan covered his eyes and told him to go where she said.

Every dime went to the struggle. We refurbished four safe houses and bought black-market medicine. Celia painted the walls. Balaguer planned to turn Tiger Klaw into a pleasure yacht. Four comrades dynamited the hull in dry dock.

We airlifted food and medicinal herbs to the slums outside Dajabón. A small sect there has canonized Wayne Tedrow. They wear newspaper photos of him, attached to pointed hats. A dream myth exists about Wayne now. People believe that winged men murdered and martyred him.

Be still now, I know you see it, I know you loved him. We honor the dead through imagery. Belief works that way.

Celia ran an arms funnel. We purchased weapons in Cuba and shipped them to Port-au-Prince. I bought inmates out of La Victoria prison and got them forged ID cards and guns. Money went to converts in La Banda. They left jail doors open and shredded documents. A young man whom Wayne rescued from harm repaid his debt in full. He killed six La Banda torturers at a whorehouse in Borojol. Celia blew up the torture chamber under El Presidente's golf course.

We lost some of ours. Random reprisals were inevitable and cost us dearly. El Jefe muzzled published and broadcast accounts of our actions. Word spread through printed leaflets and secret-band radio.

Many of the slaves Wayne freed have joined us. Some of them wear his picture around their necks. There have been skirmishes on the north D.R. coastline. A 6/14 demolition team blew up Tiger Kove. Many voodoo sects hold the building sites to be sacred ground. Many people refuse to walk across them. We shotgunned two Tonton Macoute leaders and three vicious bokurs on a golf course near Ville-Bonheur. Celia is lost somewhere in the D.R. or Haiti. She has been unreachable for months. I cannot find her and cannot conscionably continue my search with our work still to do. If you have seen some of this or all of this and my pictures have guided you, you should now try to sleep.

The Statler supplied guest robes. One size fits all. His fit too small, Joan's engulfed her.

She was up first. Room service had come and gone. Dwight poured coffee. Joan examined paper stock. The room-service cart was a workbench. The couch was a study perch.

"How do we age the documents?"

"Two runs in a convection oven. You chemically treat the paper and cook it. You add the ink or type the text on later."

"How do we differentiate the printing and cursive styles?"

"We cut stencils and print or write longhand within the boundaries."

Joan lit a cigarette. Her eyes were red—late nights and heavy smoking.

"The diary is the big thing. It's our basic text, so it has to be found."

Dwight sat on the couch. "We have to be sure that he doesn't already have a diary. We've got to locate it, so that we can snatch it and replace it, right before the convergence."

"Typed, right? We don't want to hand-forge a document of that length."

Dwight sipped coffee. "Right. If he has a typewriter, we'll purchase an identical one and go from there. I'll get a typeface sample on my first B&E."

Joan took his hands. "Scotty Bennett? He's tight with Marsh now."

Dwight shrugged. "Scotty's a wild card. He's a decorated cop on the one hand, a brutal fuck on the other. The important thing is that he densifies the overall text. He's killed eighteen armed robbers and at least a dozen Panthers, and it will either come out or be stonewalled to the extent that it looks very goddamn bad for LAPD."

Joan smiled. "How were your dreams?"

Dwight smiled. "Vivid, while you were talking. A little raw after that."

Joan pointed to a matchbook pile. Fruit joints all. The Tradesman, the Jaguar, the Falcon's Lair. Marsh cruises Hollywood. Marsh keeps amyl-nitrate poppers in a hidey-hole.

"He might have a lover who would contradict our profile."

Dwight shook his head. "He's a loner, he's discreet, he's especially circumspect now that he's celebrated. He's on the cover of *Ebony* magazine this month."

Joan stubbed out her cigarette. "Who shoots?"

"A Klansman I've dealt with before."

"Competent?"

"Yes."

"The hard part will be putting them together."

Dwight sipped coffee. It killed a headache tapping in.

"Marsh has to be secluded. It won't work unless he fires from a distance. The shooter can fire, kill Marsh and plant the throwdown. It's all about manipulating a proper convergence and rigging a workable line of sight."

Joan nodded. "It's all pretext. It's giving Marsh a reason to be there."

Dwight said, "Yes, and L.A. would be the best location. One, Marsh is here. Two, LAPD would be working the case full-tilt, as it tries to bury anything that might embarrass them. Jack Leahy would roll out for the Bureau, and Jack's a mordant piece of work with a weird take on Mr. Hoover."

Joan rubbed his temples. She kneaded a bulging vein flat.

"It's going to take months."

"It's all about creating the levels of subtext. We have to layer in misinformation at the start."

"Incoherence will inspire a more rigorous scrutiny."

"And a greater degree of paranoia and a more desperate mass desire to make it all fit."

Joan said, "That precipitating event. Have you thought about it?"

Dwight cracked his knuckles. "I've gone ahead. The Bureau has a Records Center in Media, Pennsylvania. There's 10,000 surveillance files stored there. It's an easy black-bagger."

Joan smiled. "A publicized B&E?"

"Yes, a pre-announcement. Hopefully, it creates a public expression of outrage and becomes a primer on file work that will serve to make our event that much more accessible."

"The more people go to the files, the more they'll see and won't see. They won't really know what they're looking for, so they'll study harder and the process will fracture and attenuate."

Dwight stretched. His neck hurt. He'd slept curled into Joan.

"Karen."

Dwight said, "Yes. She's taking the team in."

Joan pulled her hair back. "Well, she's very good."

"Yes."

"You cannot tell her what we're doing."

"I know that."

"There's two sets of ethics at work here."

"I know."

Joan lit a cigarette. Dwight studied her face. More stress lines. More gray hair than dark now.

"Who redacted your file?"

"I'm not telling you."

"Tell me how things have gone wrong for you. Tell me how you got through it and how you got it up for all this."

"I'm not telling you."

Dwight cracked his thumbs. "You knew Tommy Narduno. He was killed at the Grapevine Tavern."

Joan stared at him. "Yes, he was. I'm sure that you and your colleagues killed him, just as he was sure that you ran the King operation."

Dwight stared back. "Tell me how he knew."

"He saw you in Memphis two days before. He knew what you were to Mr. Hoover. He saw you distributing envelopes to some Memphis cops."

Dwight blinked. Smitty's Bar-B-Q. A cop spits tobacco juice, a cop fans C-notes, a cop wolfs burnt ends.

"What else?"

"Karen said you were in bad shape that whole spring."

"The 'Freedom School.' You and Karen go back."

Joan leaned into him. He was sweating. His robe was full wet.

"Karen and I go back further than you know."

"And you manipulated her in order to meet me."

"Yes."

"Why?"

"Because I just knew."

"That's not an answer."

"Because I sensed a shared agenda. Because I thought you might help me kill Mr. Hoover."

Dwight stared at her. She touched his leg. Wayne smiled from somewhere. *Look, Ma. No fear.*

Joan said, "We came up with the same idea independently. I've wanted to kill him since I was a child, and I won't tell you why."

DOCUMENT INSERT: 12/16/70. Extract from the privately held
journal of Karen Sifakis.

Los Angeles,
December 16, 1970

Of course, I'm going to do it. I'll entrust the job to my closest
and most prudent comrades; no one will be hurt in the performance of the act. Dwight has gotten me a schematic drawing of
the Records Center and has convinced me that the building will be
unguarded. The alarm system is outmoded and the building itself
is fairly secluded. Bill K., Saul M. and Anna B.-W. have agreed to
take part. Dwight calls it a "feat of explication, in and of itself." Of
course he's being disingenuous; of course, he knows that an opportunity to fully expose the FBI's illegal surveillance practices is too
great for me to resist. He's set the date of March 8. The Muhammad Ali–Joe Frazier boxing match takes place that night. Dwight
thinks the local cops will be popping into taverns to listen to it on
the radio and watch it on bootleg TV, so their powers of concentra-
tion and will to proactively seek out unusual occurrences will be
diverted.

My comrades are committedly non-violent. I cannot say that
wholeheartedly about Dwight. He suffered a nervous collapse in
the wake of the black-militant madness and feels complicit. I see it
in his ever-more-tender regard for my children. Should I reveal a
certain secret there? Two children died in the course of that drug
deal. That particular shock seems to drive him. I see him doing
what I do. I compartmentalize my children and work assiduously
to assure their safety as I comport myself with considerable recklessness in the world. I exemplify hubris in a manner that Dwight
does not; his recklessness is traumatically defined, while mine is
cloaked in spiritual trappings and may even be considered a
puerile lifestyle choice.

Ella is almost two now. She carries the stuffed animals that
Dwight bought her everywhere she goes. Like Dina, she now
knows that she has two part-time fathers and has hit the jackpot
in the delighted dad department. When they're older, they'll ask
me to explain it. I'll say, "It was a wild time," and feel like a fool.

This is my first journal entry since last March. In it, I described my lunch with Joan and her gift of the beautiful emerald. I've been more and more frequently recalling our conversation of that day. Joan spoke of dreams as an interconnected state of consciousness, a virus that passes between like-minded people who cannot concede their like-mindedness for fear of the forfeiture of self. It made sense to me, although the mystical aspects seemed very un-Joan. Many strange and strangely surreal things make sense these days, because "It's a wild time." In that regard, both Joan and I are Dwight's dream guides. I attempt to bring him the dream of peace and I am jealous that Joan may have brought him the dream of a fiery conversion of thought.

And thought to Dwight always results in action.

My husband left town four days ago. Dwight has been coming over on alternating nights. I'm sure he's sleeping with Joan on the nights we're not together. And he's calling up to talk politics at least once a day. He tries to sound utilitarian, but idealistic perceptions keep creeping in.

I've been noticing binocular glint at all hours, coming from a high summit on Baxter Street. I back-tailed it to a small bungalow and snuck in. I recognized the clothing in the closet. It was Dwight's and Joan's, of course.

I noticed document-forging tools on a table and boxes full of chemicals and paper. I pray that my dreams of peace may intersect with their dreams and keep them from creating more harm.

DOCUMENT INSERT: 12/18/70. Extract from the journal of Marshall E. Bowen.

Los Angeles,
December 18, 1970

I rousted a black street fool for vagrancy last week. He had misdemeanor warrants in the system and possessed no visible means of support. I was about to arrest him, when he screwed his face up in recognition. He smiled and stated quite flatly: "You The Man."

He was right: I am The Man. I am a highly decorated ranking officer on LAPD; I am, according to *Ebony* magazine, "an icon of the new black masculinity," and "odds-on for chief of police one day." Political office should not be ruled out, nor should a career in television journalism. I am a magazine cover boy; *Ebony* and

Jet, with *Sepia* soon to follow. I am permitted to be magnanimous, given the new bounty of my life. So I told that street fool, "You're right, brother. I *am* The Man," and cut him loose.

I'm working the Hollywood Division Detective Bureau. I drive a nightwatch K-car and coordinate felony-level investigations at their inception. I get awed looks and resentful looks from criminals of all stripes and awed and resentful looks from my brother officers. I'm twenty-six years old, with three years on LAPD. I'm a sergeant working a prestigious detective-division assignment. I'm the heroic black man who went undercover and broke the backs of two vicious, dope-dealing black-militant groups who were really *anti*-black at their core. I am no longer a downscale brother slumming for cosmetic effect. I've moved from a dingy crib in Watts to a nice house in Baldwin Hills. Allow me to say it again: I am most assuredly THE MAN.

I cashed in on the black-militant zeitgeist, the biggest and the best. The black-nationalist movement is in disarray. It's a nationwide cavalcade of indictments, trials, convictions and sundry legal hassles, the result of years of police infiltration and inter-group squabbles. Eldridge Cleaver is hiding in Algeria. The Panthers and US have exploded behind petty turf wars, general ineptitude and native fractiousness. The BTA and MMLF are kaput. My testimony put my dope-smoking, booze-guzzling, whore-chasing comrades in prison. Wayne Tedrow sought death by grandiose gesture and found it in Haiti. Mr. Holly had a nervous breakdown. I'm *feared* in the ghetto now. I'm a known snitch, a celebrated turncoat and a hard-charging cop.

"You The Man." Yes, I certainly am.

I've been hanging out at Tiger Kab. The new owner is a man named Fred Otash. "Freddy O." is ex-LAPD, an ex–private eye, a mobbed-up soldier of fortune and a magnet for unsubstantiated rumors. Freddy pulls shakedowns, Freddy dopes racehorses, Freddy was in on the MLK and RFK hits. I believe none of it and all of it. I'm *The Man*. I've got the recent verifiable history and much more current cachet.

Sonny Liston remains a Tiger Kab regular. We spend time together. He loves authority and loves it that I was a fink the entire time that he's known me. Sonny has quite a bad heroin habit and misses his friend Wayne very much. He speaks wistfully of Wayne; I often commiserate with him, for I cared for Wayne, as well. Sonny knows that I knew Wayne at Tiger Kab; Sonny does not know that we were collusive partners. I miss my conversations with Wayne more than anything. Our dream states meshed for a few sweet moments, and we tried to decipher what it all meant.

I don't miss Mr. Holly. We haven't spoken since that last time before the "Blastout." He knows the sanitized version of events that day, and that I've profited from them. He doesn't want to see me, nor do I want to see him. Mr. Holly reminds me of the football coach I had a crush on at Dorsey High. I feared him and craved his respect and affection. I entered an arc of self-recognition and outgrew him over time. Mr. Holly, adieu. You taught me things. Thank you for the ride.

I exercise the Bent discreetly and only well out of town. Ventura and Santa Barbara are cool for that. I roust fags on Selma Avenue and Hollywood Boulevard, and carry weighted sap gloves for the task. I have a rule: any fag who lisps or swishes too persistently in my presence receives a beating.

I'm a cop. I attract a range of enmity in my white cop brothers. It doesn't matter. I'm tight with the only white cop who counts.

Scotty asked me if the dead children got to me. I said, "Not much." We'll never truly trust each other, but we like each other just fine. We've pooled our heist information and have agreed: we must find Reginald Hazzard. I called Mary Beth Hazzard in Las Vegas yesterday. I laid on my noble black man charm, cited my friendship with Wayne Tedrow and explained that I knew about Wayne's search for her missing son. I cited my LAPD connections and volunteered my help. Did Wayne keep a file on the matter? Did he discuss the case with her?

Mrs. Hazzard was polite. No, they did not discuss Reginald's disappearance. She threw out the file after Wayne's death. She didn't read it. She didn't want to know.

I called Scotty. We wrote the file avenue off. I checked Vegas hospital records and learned Reginald Hazzard's blood type. Yes, it was AB−. Yes, it matched the escaped robber's blood.

Scotty ran a nationwide records check on Reginald and learned nothing. We agreed: he might be dead or he might have left the country. Scotty is running a passport check now.

We've scheduled a second strategy meet. Scotty told me the prophetic last words of a cocktail-lounge heister he shotgunned in 1963. The man stuck up the Silver Star Bar on Oakwood and Western. Scotty shot him in the back going in. The man had a very few moments to live. He said, "Scotty, you The Man."

That makes two of us.

91

(Los Angeles, 12/19/70)

Customs kicked loose. Rejected passport app. #1189, 3/14/64.

It's two and a half weeks post-heist. Reggie's in New Orleans. He applies for a passport, under his own name. He's got bogus ID and gets nixed. The New Orleans office: *known* to be lax. The ID: forged, for sure.

Scotty put the phone down. The squadroom was quiet. His cubicle was clutter-free. He took two drags off a cigarette and stubbed it out. He started brain-jamming.

Reggie's the linchpin. Reggie tries to split the country. He gets rebuffed in New Orleans. Did he try again? Did he *get* the passport and split successfully?

Jomo Clarkson, *baaaad* Negro. Jomo's fed dope on Dr. Fred Hiltz. You heist that racist mofo. You *scare* him per 2/64.

Jomo said a "cutout" fed him the dope. "Cutout": pure intelligencese. Jomo died abruptly, but try all this:

A *woman* prompted the fake Marsh Bowen. She told him to snitch Jomo. A *woman* phone-ratted Marsh as a queer. Dwight Holly observed his first Jomo grilling. The word *woman* quasi-torqued him.

Scotty lit another cigarette and took two more hits. His brain jam accelerated.

Junkie Monkey said, "I smells pig. I sees me a giant pork roast on two feet. Why dat porcine motherfucker wearing dat funny little tie?"

The loafing brothers chortled. Scotty doffed his hat and bowed.

Sonny Liston froze, snorting. The dispatch table was all powdered up.

Fred O. plugged switchboard calls. Scotty pointed him out back. They worked Central nightwatch in '52. Freddy could carve a buck. Freddy had secret skills.

The lot needed a sweep-up. The discarded rubbers and malt-liquor cans offended him. Fred O. said, "Get my interest. It's costing me money to talk to you."

Scotty popped a Tums. "Fruit squeeze. There's a homo I *do not* trust."

Fred O. poked his ears with a Q-tip. "It's an expensive proposition. You'll need the bait, a bug man and a watchdog."

"I can get you five grand."

Fred O. pointed upward. Scotty said, "Ten."

"Fifteen. Final call. Since we're old-soldier buddies, I'll get going on it and give you time to rouse the bread."

Scotty said, "Okay."

Fred O. said, "I worked a fruit squeeze with Pete Bondurant back in '67. We put the boots to a civil-rights cat. It was Fed-adjunct. A guy named Dwight Holly financed it."

Scotty rolled his eyes. "I know Holly. I don't want him privy to this."

"Fine by me."

"Give me the personnel."

"Pete and I had a homicide wedge on Sal Mineo. He got miffed at his pansy boyfriend and sliced him. Fags dig his action. We could use him again."

Scotty chewed his Tums. "I've met Sal. If it's male, he'll fuck it. He was a movie star for six seconds. My mark might go for that."

Freddy lit a cigarette. "Fred Turentine for bug man and Phil Irwin for watchdog. Fred T.'s the best in the West. Phil's a damn good wheelman, and he's driving part-time for me."

Scotty shook his head. "Phil's an alky and a mud shark. Every gin joint and black girl he sees distracts his attention."

Freddy shrugged. "Okay, the Crutchfield kid. He knows Sal, via Clyde Duber. He's got balls in his own pervert way."

Scotty bummed a cigarette, took two hits and tossed it.

"All right, I'm in. There's three caveats at the start, though. One, this is an ace-in-the-hole gig for me. Two, I want to hold all the film and the snapshots. Three, I control the threat of exposure."

"Sure. I'm cool with that. It's your money, it's your call."

A Tiger kab peeled out. Wilt Chamberlain rode shotgun. The headliner smooshed his Afro.

"The mark's a cop. We've got to be very careful. He's not some silly faggot you can ride roughshod."

. . .

"So Reggie files out of New Orleans and gets rejected. Let's assume he files out of other offices with better ID or fake-name ID and gets rejected or accepted then. Another run of phone calls won't cut it. We need to see the fucking reject files, because they've always got pictures. I've done some research. The most lax customs offices are Milwaukee, St. Pete and Lynn, Mass. Fucks with bum IDs or forged IDs hit those places first. You've got leave time accrued. You go there, you get badge-heavy, you check out the files."

Pipers on Western. The 4:00 p.m. clientele: ambulance fools slurping coffee.

Marsh said, I'll do it."

Scotty said, "Right on, brother."

"What about the Peoples' Bank? I'm thinking we could brace Lionel Thornton."

Scotty shook his head. "It's too dicey. One, he's up the ass of every L.A. politician worth half a shit. Two, you had a job there and learned nothing. Three, I put kid-cop plants in the bank in '66 and '67, and *they* learned nothing."

Marsh picked at his food. He was finicky. He *alllllllllmost* vibed swish.

Scotty ketchup-doused his french fries. "Okay, it's '64. Dr. Fred's looking to glom those emeralds. Now, it's '68, and Dr. Fred gets 211'd and offed. Now, it's '69. Jomo tells me that a 'cutout'—his fucking term—told him to warn Dr. Fred about February '64."

Marsh nodded. "Keep going."

"Okay, *you* snitch Jomo, but it's not really you. It's spring '64. The Fed gig is hopping and you're Dwight Holly's plant. Wayne Tedrow's *your* cutout, he's looking for Reggie, too bad Reggie's mama tossed his file, it's water under the bridge and I'm betting Wayne was stretched too thin work-wise to make much progress on the search front. It's the term *cutout* that keeps coming back to me. *It's stone intelligence-cop slang.* I'm thinking there's some kind of left-wing/right-wing/cop-confluence thing going on here."

Marsh nodded. Scotty said, *"Cherchez la femme."* Marsh shrugged. Brother, what you mean?

"There was a *woman* whispering to the fake you. Big Dwight hinks when I mention it. Let's go to last March now. I get a tip that some Commie *woman* wants to unload three pounds of junk."

Marsh scrunched his face up. Marsh *smooooothed* his face out. Instant reversal. Brother, dat vibes wrong.

92

B*lak-O-Rama:* "the New Afrodesi-essence."

Crutch skimmed the debut issue. Phil Irwin and Chick Weiss laid it on him. Phil dug the spade babes with wide-wing hair and crocheted bikinis. The lead piece ballyhooed Tiger Kab. It was "the hip hub of the New Black Masculinity." It was a "social laboratory that shows that integration can work."

Biz was slow. Crutch perched in a Tiger limo. His tiger tux had dandruff. The tiger seats had the mange. He had *baaaaad* eye strain. He'd read Wayne Tedrow's file six times.

He stashed the file at his downtown pad. The new boxes engulfed the place. The read-throughs taught him this:

Wayne did not connect Reggie Hazzard to the armored-car heist. Wayne did not know that the heist linchpinned the whole thing. Wayne did not heist-connect Joan Rosen Klein. Wayne did not *fully* connect Laurent-Jean Jacqueau/Leander James Jackson. Wayne did not determine *which* tank-town jail Joan bailed Reggie out of. Wayne died before the "Black-Militant Blastout." Wayne did not know that Scotty B. and Marsh B. were now partners. *Wayne did not make the heist connection at all.*

Crutch skimmed *Blak-O-Rama.* Key clients offered quotes. Wilt Chamberlain said, "Finest rides in L.A., baby." Archie Bell said, "Tiger Kab sticks it to The Man." Allen Ginsberg said, "Tiger Kab is multiracial avant-garde."

Phil Irwin brodied into the lot. He kabbed Chick Weiss and a Cuban whore. Chick was wild-eyed off ludes. Buzz Duber brodied out of the lot. He kabbed Lenny Bernstein and a he-she mulatto.

It's the hip new hub. Moonlighting wheelmen and dexie-drenched coffee. Tiger Kab rocks round the clock.

Crutch de-limo'd and walked the lot. Lenny the B. checked out his basket. Chick and Phil popped ludes and went *aaaah*.

Chick said, " 'No-fault.' You heard it here first. It spells the death knell for you loafing cocksukers."

Phil said, "It's coming in. It's part and parcel to all this permissive hippie shit that's sweeping the country. You don't have to show cause for divorce no more."

Chick said, "That means shysters like me don't pay perverts like you to kick in doors and peep windows."

Phil said, "*Perverts?* That's the pot calling the kettle black." Chick shushed him. Lenny the B. popped a lude and went *aaaah*.

Crutch flipped them off and hopped into the hut. The Coon Cartel was up and at it. Milt C., Fred O., stray Panthers and cops. Sonny Liston, on a toot.

He held up the *Vegas Sun*. He quoted it *loud*.

"Ex-champ on skids. Former heavyweight kingpin residing in Brokesville. Numerous confidential sources have told this reporter that local resident Sonny Liston, onetime world heavyweight boss and fierce fistic fountainhead, may be filing for food stamps or looking for a Joe Louis–like casino-greeter job soon. His coin is rumored to be going, going, gone, the result of hellacious habits, and talk of a third fight with Muhammad Ali, should he survive his March 8 title tiff with Smokin' Joe Frazier, is considered by fight pros to be no more than a passing pipe dream."

Redd Foxx said, "Sounds true to me." Junkie Monkey said, "I turn your sweet ass *out*. You *never* be broke if you peddlin' that big black booty for *me*."

Sonny said, "This is fucking bullshit. I got fourteen G's in Kellogg's Rice Krispies stock and six G's in my pocket."

Freddy signaled Crutch. They walked into the can. Freddy bolted the door.

"How'd you like to work a fruit shake? I'll pay you two grand."

Crutch swooned. "Shit, yeah. I'll do it."

"We want Sal Mineo for the bait. You know him, so you recruit him. He gets three and a half and no right of refusal. Mention my name, which should quell any protests."

Crutch gulped. "Who's it for?"

"Scotty Bennett."

Crutch re-gulped. "Who's the mark?"

Freddy laughed. "That cop Marshall Bowen. Badass spade's a rump ranger."

.   .   .

Sonny geezed in the backseat. They were halfway to Vegas. Christmas was five days hence. The Tiger Krew wore Santa Claus caps.

Crutch took his off. It clashed with his tiger tux. Midnight evaporated—another deadhead.

Fruit shake. Trouble in paradise. It's got to be heist-derived.

Sonny untied his arm. "I gots the word on you, Peeper. You tattled Wayne's shit to Mary Beth. Santa's elves told me *alllllll* about it. That means I be watching you."

Crutch palpitated. A coyote ran across the road. He lost the wheel and almost plowed it.

The radio re-kicked. Mountains killed the signal forty miles back. Brenda Lee with "Jingle Bell Rock."

Crutch checked the rearview. His pulse topped two hundred. Sonny was smack-back. His dentures had slipped halfway out.

Yule songs consoled him to Stateline. Diversion therapy meets memory lane.

Christmas, '54. Granny Woodard's in from Ortonville, Minnesota. She strokes out in March. His mother splits in June.

Christmas, '62. Paul McEachern kicks his ass. Christmas, '66. He steals Dana Lund's boyfriend's car and cherry-bombs the gas tank.

Sonny stirred. What dat needle doin' dere? Crutch kept it zipped. Vegas loomed thirty miles up.

Sonny said, "I ain't broke and I ain't no charity case. *Vegas Sun* runs some jive piece and some anonymous fucking fool sends me a green-ass emerald in the mail. Wraps the fucking thing up in the fucking newspaper, so's I get the fucking point."

Body shot—Crutch went airless and double-visioned. The road dipped. He clipped a fence post. The moon did a hop, skip and jump.

Sonny gripped the door ledge. Crutch steadied the wheel. The moon halfway re-settled.

"Can I see the envelope and the emerald?"

"No, Peeper. You can't. You can get me to Vegas in one motherfucking piece and leave me the fuck alone."

Emeralds, fruit squeeze, the Coon Cartel connection. It is all one.

He dosed himself asleep in the Sands parking lot. He woke up and re-dosed with waffles and Bloody Marys. Redd Foxx sold Sonny four bags in

L.A. Sonny geezed one bag in the limo. Sonny should be comatose as we speaks.

Crutch staked his crib out. The Tiger stretch drew riveted looks. The crib was upscale by colored standards. The neighborhood was half ofay.

Now or never.

He had a wiggle shim and his lock picks. Sonny's road-hog Buick was parked out front. The door knocker was a brass boxing glove.

Raise the dead. You don't want errors here.

Crutch banged the knocker, rang the bell and kicked the door. He got no response and re-did the sequence. The dead air intensified. He wiggle-shimmed the door and walked straight in.

Snores hit him. Sonny was gaga on a Naugahyde couch. He used a bungee cord as a tourniquet. The spike was loose in his fist.

"Champ on skids?" Yeah. The crib was over-soiled and under-furnished. The ceiling leaked sawdust and freon juice. Dog dishes collected it.

Quick toss—no fuckups here.

He pre-walked the pad. Living room, kitchen, two bedrooms. No bookshelves, no dressers, clothes paper-sacked. Hit the kitchen built-ins first.

He went through the trash. He found scorched TV-dinner tins and pint-vodka empties. He went through the kitchen drawers—eureka, that's it.

Plain white envelope, standard size, no return address. Sonny's name and address block-printed. L.A. postmark, the clipping inside, no green-ass emerald.

Crutch grabbed the envelope by the edges. He dropped it in a plastic bag and put a scrawled envelope down in its place.

Sonny dog-yipped in his sleep.

Clyde wired him three grand, c/o the Dunes. He ran it up to five at the wheel. He had his Reggie Hazzard pic. He bought a Nevada-California road map. He called in sick at Tiger Kab. He tucked the Tiger stretch in a day garage so he wouldn't look like a geek.

He rented a Ford sedan. He dumped his tiger tux and bought a sport coat. He went out to grease shitkicker cops. Wayne should have done it at the get-go.

Tank towns. Border burgs and agri-dumps. Desert dots with six-, eight- and twelve-man PDs.

Rainbow Hill, Crescent Peak, Dyer, Daylight Peak. Woodford, Minden, Pahrump, Salisbury, Mid-Lockie. Fourteen towns with "Cal-Nev" in the mix.

He drove tank town to tank town. He flashed his photo attached to a

C-note. He lubed redneck cops, straw-boss cops and wetback smuggling freaks. He stressed December '63. He described Joan. He mentioned the bail jump—may I check your records, please?

Some cops blew him off. Most cops took the cash. Some cops said they shitcanned their skip sheets. Most cops cited turnovers and plain stonewalled him.

He worked it for three days. He went through $3,400. He slept in cheap motels and had Joan dreams. He hit nine-tenths of the road-map towns. He worked his way back to L.A.

He hooked off I-15 at McKendrick. The PD was a Quonset hut upside a lettuce field. Jail trustees did stoop labor. The motor pool was four old Fords and sixteen horses. The lettuce pickers wore stenciled denims. The cops drove golf carts and quaffed brews.

Crutch parked beside a tethered roan. A sunburned cop walked up. He had malignant sores like Crutch Senior.

"Help you, young man?"

"I had a few questions, if you'd be so kind."

The cop stuck his hand out. "Kindness costs money. Let's not pretend that it don't."

Crutch threw him fifty. "A vag and gun-possession bust. December '63. A black kid got popped and a white woman with dark, gray-streaked hair bailed him."

The cop stuck his hand out. Crutch shook his head. The cop said, "I was there that day. Kindness ain't for free."

Crutch forked over two fifties. The cop snapped his fingers. Crutch re-forked two more.

The cop picked a nose scab. "Nigger boy and a Jew broad. Absconders. Don't ask to see records, because there ain't any. The kid left some Commie books and chemistry books in his cell, might still be in Property."

Tools:

Print powders and brushes. Print-transparency tape. A magnifying glass and Joan Rosen Klein's print card.

Targets:

Sonny Liston's envelope. Magruder's *Basic Chemistry*. Franz Fanon's *The Wretched of the Earth*.

He worked at the Vivian. He set aside desk space and laid it all out. His big gooseneck lamp supplied light.

The book pages were porous. They wouldn't sustain prints. The dust jackets were glossy and would. The envelope was slick and smooth-surfaced. The print-lift odds were good.

Crutch dipped a brush in red powder. The dust jackets were white and light beige.

He put on rubber gloves. He folded the books open with the jackets in place. He got near-flat planes: front covers, back covers, spines. He placed the envelope to one side.

Deep breath now.

He light-dusted the books and the envelope. He got smudges, swirls and smears. He added a second dust coat. He got two viable prints on the Commie book. He got two viable prints on the envelope.

Deep breath now.

He grabbed the magnifying glass. He studied the book prints and Joan's print card. One print looked good straight off.

Whorls, swirls and inversions. Comparison points: 4, 5, 6, 7, 8, 9—

Match.

Joan touched the Fanon book with her right-hand forefinger. It occurred 12/63 or before. The book was held by McKendrick PD since then.

Crutch studied the second book print. Do it—brain-stamp every bit.

He memorized it. He studied Joan's print card and ran the magnifying glass back and forth. No—no second print match.

He laid down the transparency tape. He lifted the unknown print clean. He reinforced it with a black plastic strip. The print showed in exact detail, white on black.

Deep breath—one to go.

He switched to the envelope. He studied the two prints. He memorized them. He re-studied Joan's print card. He squinted through the magnifying glass. No—no match.

He laid down two strips of transparency tape. He lifted the unknown prints clean. He reinforced them with black plastic strips. The prints showed in exact detail, white on black.

He laid the two envelope strips beside the one book strip. He ran the magnifying glass back and forth. One print strip was markedly different. One print strip matched perfectly.

That meant this:

Joan touched the Commie book in 1963. A second person touched the book then. The same person touched Sonny's envelope, late 1970.

It couldn't be the McKendrick cops. Wild guess: Reggie Hazzard.

Reggie had no rap sheet. That meant no print file extant. Reggie had a Nevada driver's license. The Nevada DMV did not require fingerprints.

The envelope was L.A.-postmarked. Was the emerald sent from there? Was it *sent* to L.A. to send?

It's not a *real* print make. It's all suppositional. There's still that second envelope print.

Deep breath now—more fucking work.

Christmas came and went. New Year's blurred by in rainstorms. Sonny Liston OD'd a week later. The Tiger Kab wake was a happening.

Redd Foxx and Milt C. performed. *Blak-O-Rama* gave it feature ink. Fred O. supplied booze. Chick Weiss supplied dope and island-bred hookers. The Duber boys showed up. The drivers formed a kab kortege and bombed through darktown. Panthers and pigs noshed "Q" in perfect peace. Lenny Bernstein quoted Krishnamurti. Scotty Bennett sparred with Jerry Quarry. They traded for real. It almost got ugly.

The fruit squeeze was on hold. Freddy wanted fifteen grand. Scotty tried to Jew him down to ten and got nowhere. Scotty was hustling the gelt. Freddy told Crutch not to brace Sassy Sal just yet.

He did divorce jobs for Clyde. He sent Mary Beth Hazzard queries: did Wayne leave more paperwork? He part-time Tiger-kabbed. He studied print cards every night at the downtown DMV.

Insomnia and eye strain. Vials of Nembutal and vats of Visine. Hand-check print cards. Compare them to the two plastic strips.

He kept a head tally. He lost count at ten thousand. He kept a card-per-night tally. He lost track on January 6.

He showed up late on the seventh. He bribed the night clerk, SOP. He brought his print strips, his magnifying glass and his Visine.

He opened a new box. He went through eleven no-gos. He hit print card #12. The swirls talked to him.

Deep breath now. The second envelope print. No, yes, no—maybe.

Points: 1, 2, 3, 4, 7, 8, 9—up to 14—good measure.

Perfect matchup. *Fuck—a name he knew.*

Lionel Darius Thornton, male Negro. Born 12/18/19.

The Peoples' Bank dude. Lionel the Laundryman. The Coon Cartel *consigliere.*

93

(Los Angeles, 1/9/71)

Chez Marsh: cultured and non-militant.

He got in with tungsten bolt-tappers. Infrared shades induced night sight. Leave the lights off to de-saturate.

Baldwin Hills. A one-level ranch off Stocker. Black bourgeoisie. Tubular furnishings. A *coooooool*-school aesthetic.

Dwight moseyed through. It was 9:49 p.m. Marsh had a keynote-speech engagement. GOP heavies dug him. He was up-by-his-bootstraps. Governor Reagan got him the gigs.

It's a first walk-through. Let's learn the spread.

Dwight snapped pictures. His Minox shot bright-light flashless. The fallback had a darkroom. Joan could develop film there.

Rauschenberg and Rothko in brushed-steel frames. A severe space, overall. A metal womb.

He tapped wall panels. He went through shelves and file drawers. He saw art books, tax records and blank stationery. Marsh was a paper-hoarder. He thought that. Joan called him a "clandestine diarist."

Dwight walked through the bedroom. The tube motif extended. Marsh loved brushed metal. It was functional and harsh. It exuded male odor and excluded feminine scent. Marsh was all refined obduracy.

Marsh was the all-new malcontent assassin. This was his psychopath's lair. It was cold and prim. It must go to *horrifying* from there.

Dwight examined the nightstand drawers. He went through Marsh's address book and snapped every page. He saw first-name-only men listed. He saw numbers for the Klondike, the 4-Star, the Tradesman, the Spike.

Marsh felt safe now. His ops pad was Actors Studio. This pad was fag reference–rich.

They needed plant spaces. Marsh, the queer pack rat with the chaste art-school taste. The house was a beautiful picture. Let's supply an eroding frame.

Plant fruit-bar matchbooks here. Plant sodomy pix there. Semen-streak the sheets pre–hit day. Hide shit-caked dildos in the bathroom.

The house would attract astounding scrutiny. The façade had to crumble slowly. The terror had to slowly accrete.

Dwight tapped wall panels. No telltale thunks perked yet. *Plant spaces.* Subversive lit and poli-sci porno. Joan's instinct: he keeps a diary, locate it, we'll pull it and insert ours pre-hit.

An Underwood electric. Typewriter paper stacked beside it.

Dwight rolled in a sheet and typed out all the letters, numbers and symbols. They looked naked eye–correct. He photo-snapped the keyboard and the strike pads. There might be strike-pad flaws. They would have to tool mark–duplicate them. Forensic teams would examine the machine. They had to create a sound verisimilitude.

He tapped more wall panels. He got no hollow sounds. It was a first prowl. He didn't trust his ears yet.

Hiding spots. The forensic teams would tear up the place. Marsh must be pungently revealed postmortem. He was wildly ingenious and resourceful. The pad should explode with late-breaking finds.

Plant paper here. Plant paper there. It's *his* life refracted. He hoards paper for Mr. Hoover. He looks for paper-plant slots on the job.

He was a month in. Mr. Hoover gave him a pay-level raise. The file section was all scandal skank. Most of it was L.A.-based. Marsh was an L.A. native. Every L.A. Office file would be combed for mention after his death.

He skimmed files and looked for data-insert points. It was operational subtext. You hide age-yellowed data. It implies an emerging political imbalance and closet-queer pathology. The FBI's file mania indicts Marshall Bowen. Non sequitur files are combed diligently. Mr. Hoover is postmortem-indicted. The file compilation is prissy tedium and officially sanctioned scatology. Moral horror and titillation will war in the public arena. Special Agent D. C. Holly will state what it all means.

He spent hours in the file-storage unit. Jack Leahy found it odd. He found Jack odd. Jack was always cracking wise about the old girl's health. Jack didn't know that she was still more lucid than not.

Files:

Joan disdained the Records Center raid in Pennsylvania. She thought it would exposit file mania too soon. She thought he was exploiting Karen. She was making a Quaker pacifist a death accessory.

They stopped discussing it. It just sat there, unsaid.

Dwight went through hall closets. He saw Marsh's pressed uniforms and a gun belt rolled up on a shelf.

Find some actors. Cop-dress one up. Grab a patrol car. Rig a Griffith Park backdrop. There's a fake Marsh in uniform. His head is averted. A handcuffed suspect is blowing him. Marsh has a gun to his head.

Age-fade the snapshot. Drop it in a frayed uniform. It's a forgotten knickknack.

Score some street uppers. Tuck them behind his underwear. Marsh is jacked-up on duty and cruising for sport.

Dwight walked out the back door. Marsh had a lovely view. The location was sweet. Marsh was twenty-six. He had a year to live, tops.

Room service brought New York steaks and a too-fat Bordeaux. He was drinking less. Joan was drinking more. Their sleep stints had reversed.

They ate in their robes. Fat rain drummed the windows. They burned a synthetic log in the fireplace.

Joan said, "I don't like the break-in. It's precipitous."

"You're worried about the convergence."

"Yes, I am."

"It's the one thing we can't force."

"They have to be voluntarily in the same place at the same time."

Dwight slouched in his chair. "The same *city,* with the perch pre-established. It should be in L.A. He's stayed at the Beverly Wilshire the last six times he's been here. He always requests a suite with a north-window view. You've got seven two- and three-story buildings directly across the street. Two have office-rental signs up. The other buildings are boutiques and restaurants. They have second- and third-floor storage rooms facing the hotel."

Joan lit a cigarette. "Keep going. Tell me what you're thinking."

"I'm thinking we should find a black kid about Marsh's age. A close resemblance is crucial. He should rent an office and we should decorate it. It's where he goes to fuck boys, use drugs and hoard guns. I'll steal semen tubes from a hospital. We'll lay in the fluids gradually. Marsh is cracking up. His drug use is escalating. I'll have the shooter skin-pop him full of coke on his way out. I'll show him how to boot toxins into his liver to approximate long-term drug abuse."

Joan blew a smoke ring. "You are so astonishingly gifted, comrade."

Dwight took her hands. "You're worried about Celia."

"I don't want to talk about it. She's always understood the risks."

"I could make a few phone calls."

"I don't want you to."

Dwight smiled. "When I connected you to Tommy Narduno, I thought you were coming after me."

Joan smiled. "I considered it. Tommy thought he could reveal the Grapevine aspect of your operation and create a media ruckus. He was always naïve that way. He was a muckraking journalist at heart. He was wearing a wire on the night you killed him."

Dwight trembled. Joan pointed to the wine. Dwight shook his head.

"What convinced you to pass on it?"

"Karen convinced me. She implied that you were ready. She quoted Goethe at one point. The phrase she used was 'the fall upward.' "

Dwight opened a window. Hailstones brushed his face.

"Jomo and the thing with Marsh. What was your reasoning?"

A gust shook the panes. Joan turned her chair and let the wet hit her.

"There were your ends and my ends. They were both synchronous and inimical. I knew that Marsh had to be your plant. Your pathology showed itself in your choice. It was bold, grandiose and self-destructive. I spent time with Marsh and found him to be weak and almost fawningly self-serving. He cruised men when he thought I wasn't looking, which was true actor's faux pas, dramatically unsound and narcissistic. So, I called Scotty Bennett and revealed his inclination. So, I called Scotty again and mediated Marsh's betrayal of Jomo Clarkson. It was a two-fold strategy. I wanted to put Marsh in jeopardy and force him into allegiance with the BTA. I considered Jomo to be evil, and I was fairly sure that Scotty wouldn't be able to resist killing him."

Wind tossed the tablecloth and dumped the Bordeaux. Dwight pulled Joan out of her chair.

Puckett, Mississippi. Six trailer parks and nine Klan kampgrounds.

Bob Relyea ran the Exalted Knights Klavern. He pandered to the local cops and snitched to ATF. He sold magic mushrooms and hate tracts. He robbed gas stations. Bob was ex–Tiger Krew. He pushed heroin in Saigon and worked with Wayne Tedrow. He shot Martin Luther King.

It was kool and klear. The kampground konsisted of a korrugated bunkhouse and a K-9 kennel. Four fucks stood around the shooting range. The targets were department-store dummies. They wore Eldridge Cleaver masks.

Bob saw the car pull up. Dwight braked and stopped short of the kampground. Bob jogged the rest of the way.

Dwight popped the passenger door and the glove box. A C-note roll rolled out. Bob caught it and tucked it under his sheet.

"And that's just for talking?"

"That's right."

"Don't tell me. If I shoot somebody, there's lots more where that came from."

Dwight said, "That's right."

Bob said, "Wooo, boy."

Dwight lit a cigarette. "You get fifty thousand. You take out the target and the fall guy right there. It's two easy shots. That part doesn't worry me at all. It's bringing the two together. I'll abduct the fall guy and position him if I have to, but I'd rather not."

Bob picked his nose. "The target guy's a big deal?"

Dwight winked. Bob said, "Talk's gonna bubble."

"I want it to. There's a subtext here."

"Who's the target?"

Dwight laughed. "You'll know him when you see him."

DOCUMENT INSERT: 2/6/71. Extract from the privately held
journal of Karen Sifakis.

Los Angeles,
February 6, 1971

I'm going through with it, whatever it abuts, facilitates or
foreshadows on Joan's and Dwight's end. I am taking the risk of
implementing violence. I feel loyal to Joan and am grateful to her
for the change she has created in Dwight. We have traveled a long
road together. It would not be bragging for me to assert that my
pacifism has mitigated Joan's violent actions over the years. It is
surely true that her brash being has sporadically brought me
closer to God and non-violent confrontation. She is *of* me and I am
of her and Dwight is *of* both of us. There is deep alchemy in where
we connect and where we diverge. I continue to trust in our dialogue as much as I fear potential outcomes. My horrible fight with
Dwight has forced me to admit the arrogance and speciousness at
the core of my moral logic. The fire of his conversion has convinced me of the necessity of this risk.

Dwight now knows the length and breadth of my relationship
with Joan, if not the specific details. Joan has laid hints, or has
revealed the friendship in looks and asides that the brilliant and
brilliantly paranoid Dwight has seized upon and brought to mental
certainty. I have lied to Dwight by omission; I am now certain that
Joan used me in order to get to him; now Dwight and Joan lie to
me by withholding the details of their "Operation." I am fully
culpable for the creation of the Dwight-Joan bond. I should have
told Dwight that Joan has deployed fake identities and that they
have cloaked much of her subversion. I should have told Dwight
that Joan had planned a series of armed robberies back east. I
should have told him that we were in Algeria together and that I
held a prayer vigil for the French paratroopers that Joan and her
comrades ambushed outside Béchar. I should have told him that I
was part of the 6/14 invasion, in a non-violent planning role. I did
not tell him these things, because I ghoulishly desired the confla-
gration of *Them*, because I wanted to unleash *Them* to fulfill some
buried rage in *Me*, to inflict *Them* on the circumspect, ideologically

compromised, radically chic and ever-so-careful world I live in with the unique fury I knew *They* would evolve.

Now I must live out my creator's role in this, play my support-ing part, damn the vicissitudes of radical lifestyle as I pray for peace. I will break and enter, steal files, explicate the file-hoarding practices of an oppressive bureaucracy and hope that a much-anticipated boxing match between two gifted black fighters does not push my actions to back-page status. Irony: Dwight has called the break-in a "media event." The Records Center is in Media, Pennsylvania.

The fight with Dwight took place here in my home; Dina and Ella heard the flare-up and storming-out conclusion. It was an altercation I spawned from my own hubris. I overestimated my influence on Dwight and belittled Joan's influence. I was shrill, petty, jealous and philosophically unsound. Dwight came at me with a convert's and converted lover's fury. "You blow up things, you destroy symbols, you attack sympathetic portrayals of institu-tions forty fucking times removed," he said to me. "It allows you to feel smug while people suffer and die, you'll continue to do it until a chunk of exploding plaster from a Confederate monument puts out a black kid's eye, then you'll come back here and mope and pray and figure out something spectacular and Quaker-correct to do to put yourself back in the game you so dearly love, which is violent by its own basic nature."

And he was right.

And then he said, "And do not ever patronize Joan Rosen Klein, because you gave her to me."

And he was right. And so I will go forth with the task that he and Joan have assigned.

DOCUMENT INSERT: 2/21/71. Extract from the journal of Mar-shall E. Bowen.

En route to Boston,
2/21/71

I have been traveling and tracking potential leads since my last meeting with Scotty. My accumulated work-leave time has served as a cover. I have allegedly been on a cross-country auto trip. I have now laboriously hand-checked the passport acceptance files and reject files in New Orleans, St. Petersburg and Milwaukee, with Lynn, Massachusetts, upcoming. These are the cities that Scotty has deemed to be the most lax, permissive and incompetent in their passport-issuing practices. I have indulged the Bent in those cities and have reveled in the freedom of cavorting in non-local-celeb locales. Reginald Hazzard was not issued a passport in those cities and was not to be found in the reject files. His photograph—with and without medically addressed burn scars—was not attached to any of the thousands of application cards I have scanned.

So, I've been traveling and enjoying my time outside of L.A. I've been calling Scotty every few days, to report "no luck." I've been mindscaping, having very vivid dreams and pondering Scotty's "*Cherchez la femme*" remark a great deal.

It was a woman who ratted me out to Scotty. Dwight Holly reacted strangely when Scotty mentioned that fact to him. I'm becoming convinced that the woman is Joan Rosen Klein.

Joan cultivated me in late '68 and early '69. I was Dwight Holly's infiltrator, and I knew that Mr. Holly had an informant in play. Joan was very worldly and seemed overqualified for the low-rent black-militant world. She was very persistent in her approach of me, she may have been trying to seduce me, but her finely tuned predator's sense told her she'd have no luck there. It all felt mindscapingly right to me, up until the moment I ran into Junior Jefferson, shortly before I left on this trip.

Junior was gobbling chicken and waffles at Tommy Tucker's Playroom and was grousing about the fate of Tiger Kab. First, the Boys buy Black Cat Cab away from him and rename it after that faggoty animal. Then the late Wayne Tedrow embezzled all the Tiger Kab cash and the Boys sold the biz to Freddy Otash. So, Freddy fires him and 86's him from the premises. Now, Tiger Kab is the swingingest place on Planet Earth, they're showing the Ali-Frazier fight on closed-circuit TV—and he can't come.

We continued to commiserate. We talked up the "Blastout" with a certain wonderment. Junior said, "You was a fuckin' FBI pig-snitch the whole time." I admitted that was true. Junior said he was cool with it and very casually mentioned that he saw Dwight Holly and that "Joan Jew-Commie babe" holding hands at a chink joint on Pico last week.

Cherchez la femme.

Lynn is a dingy shoe-factory town amid scores of dingy towns of the same size, and I found the customs office to be dingy as I walked in. A florid Irishman was working the desk. He almost shit when a well-dressed black man flashed an LAPD sergeant's badge. I'll credit him with wit, though. After I explained the purpose of my visit, he said, "You don't look like Jack Webb, Sergeant," and led me back to the file stacks.

It was the sixth card in the fourth box I went through. The photo was of Reginald Hazzard, with a severely burn-scarred face. The name beside it was ink-smudged and unreadable. The routing stamp on the back was crystal-clear.

Reginald was granted a visa to travel to Haiti, 6/11/64.

It came to me instantly: I will not tell Scotty this.

94

Scotty said, "I got the bread."

Fred O. said, "He robbed a liquor store. He's got expertise in that regard."

Fred Turentine said, "I hate fruit bugs. The audio tracks are unsavory."

Barone's Pizza on Ventura. A noted Valley grease spill. They had a private room. It featured photos of notable wops.

The beer was scald-your-teeth cold. The pizza was burn-your-mouth hot. Scotty tossed the envelope on the table. The Crutchfield kid had ants in his pants. He kept scratching his balls.

Scotty poured brews. "Let's talk about results. I second-mortgaged my house, so I'm not looking for big delays or fuckups."

Fred O. knife-shaved the foam off his glass. Suds flew on the floor.

"I ran a fruit shake for Dwight Holly a while back. He's a white man. We could use him for some added oomph."

Scotty said, "*No.* Dwight and I clashed on his Fed thing. I don't want him to know about this."

Fred T. shagged a slice with anchovies. *Ooooh,* that's hot.

"I'd just as soon avoid the guy. I heard he's working the file slot at the L.A. Office. He had some kind of crack-up."

Scotty sipped beer. "I want vivid shit. Snapshots, film, varied sex acts. The kid brings Sal in. Sal and Marsh get a hot thing going. I want fuck-and-suck action with different backdrops."

The kid said, "I'll locate Sal."

Fred T. said, "Hey, he speaks."

Fred O. said, "Draw your shades. The peeping panther is loose."

Scotty panther-growled and winked. Canned music hit the room. Dino warbled, "That's amore."

"*Vivid shit.* Remember, it's not a cash shakedown. It's a threat if push comes to shove."

The crew was good. The pizza was shitty. His beer-burned teeth still stung.

Marsh was back. His customs-office tour went poof. The passport angle was dead. Reggie Hazzard: back to square one.

The gas gauge hit empty. Scotty eased off the freeway. There's a Richfield with a phone booth up ahead.

He pulled in. He told the pump jockey full service. He dumped his chump change in the phone slots and called Marsh.

"Hello?"

"The Reggie bit is dead for now. I'm getting frustrated."

"That's two of us."

"I'm thinking we should brace Lionel Thornton."

"I don't disagree."

Scotty rubbed his teeth. "Be less equivocal. You won the fucking Medal of Valor. You're Ramar of the Jungle now."

Marsh laughed. "You're right. We should do it."

"When?"

"March 8. Thornton launders the Tiger Kab money. They're showing the Ali fight. Thornton will be there and take the money back to the bank."

Scotty said, "I dig it. We'll grab him en route."

95

(Los Angeles, 3/4/71)

Fruit loop:

He'd hit the Manhole, the Cockpit, the Anvil, the Tradesman, the Forge. It was Creepsville. Sicko Sids ogled his booty. Amyl-nitrate poppers, leather, bare chests in chain mail.

Sal was never home. Sal habituated homo hives and all-nite coffee shops. Pancake loop: the Pines, Arthur J.'s, Biff's Char-Broil.

Crutch drove back to the Klondike. It was Sal's home base. The barman cashed his residual checks. Sal got his regular schlong there. He was banging the owner, two busboys and the fry cook.

Crutch double-parked out front. Lounging fags swooned for his kab. Lenny Bernstein walked out with two sailors. Fags called sailors "sea food."

Lenny waved to Crutch. Crutch waved to Lenny. Crutch thought, It all started here.

Summer '68. Dr. Fred hires him. Find me Gretchen Farr. His case is almost three years old. It might be breaking.

Fingerprints. Joan touched one of Reggie Hazzard's books. That's validated. A second person touched the book and Sonny's envelope. Good guess: Reggie H. A third person touched the envelope. Print confirmed: Lionel Thornton.

Question:

Does Reggie forward the emeralds to the black folks in need?

Answer:

Probably, yes.

Reggie survived the heist. Reggie had a portion of the cash and the emeralds. Reggie doesn't live in L.A. Reggie's elsewhere or Wayne would have found him. Reggie's secretive. L.A. postmarks might attract heat. Reggie's long gone.

A *biiiiig* lead—now cluster-fucked by the fruit squeeze.

Crutch watched the door. Rock Hudson walked out with Arthur-Arlene Johannsson. Arthur-Arlene pushed Dilaudid and maryjane brownies. Chick Weiss did all his divorces. The *wives* paid alimony. You married a *drag queen*? Fuck you.

Rock waved to Crutch. Crutch waved to Rock. A Tiger kab pulled up. Phil Irwin drove. Chick Weiss rode shotgun. Arthur-Arlene pushed Rock in the back. His pressed-hair wig was askew.

Crutch twirled his red flag. Joan was gone. He couldn't find her. He got a she's-in-L.A. gestalt anyway. L.A. was L.A. L.A. was the Joan Zone. He tailed Dwight Holly twice. Dwight might be Joan's lover. Dwight was tail-savvy and lost him.

There's Sal. He's got Natalie Wood and a butch bitch in tow. Natalie was a show lez. She muff-munched at Hollywood parties. Clyde rescued her from a dyke slave den, circa '60.

Crutch whistled. Sal caught it and walked over. Natalie and the dom dyke French-kissed. Two limp-wristed lover boys clapped.

Sal leaned in the kab. "Don't tell me. Clyde's got a rope job."

"Not exactly."

"No girls. We tried that once, remember?"

Crutch said, "Freddy Otash. I know he's got something on you, so it's not like you can say no."

Sal sighed. His spit curl wiggled. Crutch popped the door. Sal got in and lit a Kool menthol. Crutch smelled the hash/mint blend.

He pulled around the corner and parked. Sal said, "I hope he's hung."

"You get three and a half."

Sal toked his quasi-joint down to the filter. Sal did his doe-eyed thing.

"We've been here before. I've parked with lots of men, but with you it wasn't the least romantic."

Crutch said, "Don't start with me."

"Believe me, I'm not."

"The mark's a guy named Marshall Bowen. He's that cop who's half-assed famous."

Sal groaned. "Another spade. With Freddy, it's always a spade. I like dark meat, but not as a steady diet."

Crutch popped the glove box and pulled out his flask. Sal grabbed it and snatched a quick hit.

"So, sweetie. Did you ever find the erstwhile Gretchen Farr?"

Crutch re-grabbed the flask. "No. Close, but no cigar."

Sal grabbed it back. He took a hit and re-passed it. Crutch took a hit. Sal re-grabbed it and held it in his lap.

"I haven't seen her, either. Gretchie was strictly fly-by-night, in her own unique way."

Crutch grabbed the flask. Sal relinquished it, reluctant.

"You told me everything you knew, right?"

"Well . . ."

"Come on, man."

"Well . . ."

Crutch balled his fists. Sal went *oooo, I'm scared.* Crutch drained the flask. Sal rubbed his thumbs and forefingers. Crutch laid out a yard. Sal held up two fingers. Crutch re-dipped his wallet and re-laid him.

Sal cranked the seat back and stared at the headliner. He snuggled and futzed with his spit curl.

"Well . . . you know our Gretchie's MO. She fucked strings of men, borrowed bread from them and disappeared. Are we up-to-date now, sweetie?"

Crutch nodded. "Yeah. You introduced her to guys, but you can't remember their names. She was always careful not to bang guys in the same social circle, so they couldn't compare notes."

Sal nodded. "That's *riiiiiight.*"

Crutch punched his seat bolster. Sal jiggled. It made him *laaaaaugh.*

"You don't *scaaaare* me, Crutchy. And, frankly, I don't believe all those silly rumors about those Communists you killed."

A headache freight-trained him. Behind the eyes, a beaut. He dug out his aspirin and dry-popped three. *Keep it zipped/do not fucking blow this.*

Sal kicked off his sandals and toe-curled the dash. Miss Froufrou had big, smelly feet.

"So, right before we talked about her the first time, I saw Gretchie at a party. I didn't tell you about it because it all seemed so unreal."

"And?"

"Well . . . Gretchie said there was this chick named María, also known as 'Tattoo.' She bought her way out of the 'book of the dead,' she betrayed 'the Cause," but she 'did penance.' Believe me, none of it made the *leeeeast* bit of sense to *this* girl, until Gretchie told me that María was coming to L.A., she was 'wild,' could I set her up with some movie-biz guys? That was more my language, so I said I'd ask around, which I did *not* do, because Gretchie owed me money for some referrals I gave her, but she never paid me, so where was the incentive if she was just going to rip me off again? *Soooo,* it all just went away. Gretchie never mentioned María again, but she *sort of* paid me for the referrals. She gave me this teeny little emerald and this herb stash. It was Haitian dope, and it was a bummer."

Deep breath now.

Sal said, "*Really,* dear heart. Have you ever heard such fantasia?"

96

(Los Angeles, 3/6/71)

Print work and ink work. Get the details.

Homo napkin notes. Fake diary excerpts. Print transfers to fag porn novels and propaganda texts.

The fallback was quiet. Dwight worked alone. He bar-hopped last night. He hit the Jaguar, the Tradesman and the Falcon's Lair. He laid down dollar bills and snatched the napkins. The fruits smelled fuzz en masse.

He printed herky-jerky. "Love your hair!" "Anytime, sweet" and a phone-number smudge. "I saw you on TV!!!! Can't believe I saw you here!"

Varied print styles. Crinkly paper. Pocket debris, lifestyle minutae.

"The Hard and the Hung" by Lance Greekman. "AmeriKKKan Gestapo" by Richard T. Saltzman, Ph.D. "Blow the Man Down" and "Semen Demon." Dissertations on Mr. Hoover's war on Dr. King.

Dwight applied print strips. Marsh mock-touched book covers. Dwight wrote queer crush notes. Smeared phone numbers, napkin rips, words half-obscured. Marsh: "I've got 9 inches. How about you?"

He kept his desk neat. He worked with rubber gloves. He plastic-bagged his piecework. He brainstormed a fake diary entry.

Think it through. Type it in. You've got an identical Underwood. Remember: tool-gouge the small *C* and *J*.

You'll be there at the convergence. Joan will insert the fake diary.

That means more B&E runs. He might have a real diary.

Dwight cleared desk space. He bagged the books and notes and got out a scratch pad. The Silver Hill photo was up against a lamp. Karen, Dina, Ella. Their address/phone number. "If this man is lost, please return him."

He covered it with a handkerchief. He mock-Marsh-ascribed:

"My process of radicalization truly began when I realized I could not control my perceptions. Physical symptoms manifested in direct proportion to my attempts to keep them suppressed. It was as if a virus had swept through me. It was significantly more discomfiting than the panic I endured when I became fully aware of my homosexuality a decade ago. A self-hatred took hold then and a politically defined and outwardly directed hatred has taken hold now. My hatred has lingered on immediate targets—the brutish Scotty Bennett, the imperviously exploitative Agent Holly and my racist alma mater, the LAPD—and it has gradually and inexorably ascended to an ineluctable plane. I cannot halt the spread of the virus until I dose myself with the anti-toxin that only JEH's death will create."

He read it through again. He covered the desk with a drop cloth and walked out to the terrace.

Clouds top-framed Silver Lake. A haze covered Karen's house. Their fight rescrolled. It scared Dina. Ella seemed to study it. He kicked around a notion. Ella knew things that he didn't. Ella got them from Joan.

Shit stirs in the *spiritus mundi*. Karen tells Joan about him. Comrade Tommy's in Memphis hit day. Karen read his dreams and held him through his nightmares. *Joan just understood.*

A squirrel perched on the terrace ledge. Dwight soft-lobbed him acorns. He shagged them with his paws and skedaddled.

The door gizmo buzzed. Dwight looked through the side window. Eleanora hopped on the porch.

Dwight ran through the front room and opened the door. Ella stormed his legs. He scooped her up with one arm. Ella play-bit his neck.

Karen leaned on a porch post. Dwight said, "You could have broken in."

"I was saving it for Media."

"Thank you."

"Don't mention it."

Ella wriggled. Dwight put her down. She ran into the front room.

"How'd you find it?"

Karen stepped inside. "I tracked the binocular glint. I thought, I detect a voyeuristic presence, and applied spatial geometry."

Dwight laughed. Karen draped an arm around him. He walked her away from the desk. Ella peeked in a cardboard box. Dwight grabbed her and whisked her off.

She broke free and pointed. She made a *What?* face.

Dwight said, "They're throwdown guns, sweetie."

Karen dropped her purse and kicked it. Dwight said, "Do you love me?" Karen said, "Yes, goddamn you."

Inserts:

He worked in the file section. He kept loose inside. He was nonchalant and late-night-clandestine.

He pulled Vice files and tattle files. He found field interrogation cards and inked in Marsh Bowen's name. Marsh at three fruit-bar sweeps, Marsh at a drag ball, Marsh at a hate-whitey bash.

He walked to the subversive-file bank. He dropped in a chemically aged file.

Joan created it. He supplied the perspective. A now-dead agent wrote the file, late '66. Marsh worked for Clyde Duber then. Marsh worked against Clyde for the Black Muslims. The agent had suspicions. Clyde never knew.

He cashed in stock. He secured Bob Relyea's down payment. He needed Mr. Hoover's travel schedule. Tomorrow a.m.: he flies to Media.

He skimmed the snitch-file index. Names sideswiped him. Bill Buckley snitched neocons. Chuck Heston snitched potheads. Sal Mineo snitched rump rascals wholesale. Salacious Sal: botched bait for the Bayard Rustin squeeze.

He found more F.I. cards. He blue-inked one in cursive. He block-printed two in black. Busy bee Marsh—'66 and '67. Fistfights at the Klondike. Lewd shit with hippie boys at Griffith Park love-ins.

Dwight packed up his briefcase and walked out. He saw Jack Leahy at the elevator.

"Don't tell me. You can't sleep, and you're starting to dig on the files."

Dwight smiled. "You're the only Fed on earth who has ever said the words *dig on*."

"True enough, but you haven't answered my question."

Dwight pushed the down button. "Dirt files are addictive. Ask you-know-who about that."

Jack laughed. "I haven't spoken to the old girl in a dog's age. I outrank you, but she talks to you much more than to me."

"You're being impolitic, Jack. You're forgetting who you're talking about and who you're talking to."

The doors opened. They stepped inside. The doors jerked and shut.

"Is there a spot tail on me, Jack? As long as we're being insubordinate, I'd appreciate an answer."

Jack shook his head. "Dwight 'the Enforcer' Holly. Buzzed on coffee and cigarettes for the twenty years I've known him, and finally starting to see things."

He walked into the drop-front. The phone was ringing, persistent. He dumped his briefcase and fumble-caught the receiver in the dark.

Karen said, "Nobody dies," and hung up.

97

(Los Angeles, 3/8/71)

Ali! Ali! Ali!

The Congo coursed with it. Bootleg broadcasts beamed from liquor stores and pool halls. They got the full TV monte. Sidewalk gangs got portable-radio squelch. Jugs and joints circulated. The groups ran ten to one hundred. Central Avenue was *coon*caphony.

Cathode light bounced out windows. Pirate hookups: Mosque 19, Sultan Sam's, Cedric's Hair Process. The scene ran inside and outside. Parking-lot action boomed. Stacked-heel pimps laid down round-by-round bets.

Scotty cruised by Tiger Kab. The hut was SRO and boob tube–bright. The Krew was rapt. Fred O., Milt C., Peeper Crutchfield. Countless southside Zulus. Junkie Monkey in boxing mitts, atop the TV set.

And Lionel D. Thornton—with a zippered cash sack.

Scotty idled by the lot. Marsh got in. He wore crepe-soled shoes and gloves. Scotty grabbed his gloves off the dashboard. They eyeballed the hut.

The radio fluttered. The signal cut in and out. Marsh tweaked the dial. Static and verdict—Frazier gets the nod.

Marsh turned it off. Scotty said, "He's got a piece."

"I know. Small revolver, back waistband."

"He'll walk. I don't see his car."

"It's six blocks to the bank."

Scotty passed his flask. Marsh took a nip.

"I lost a hundred."

Scotty said, "I'll underwrite you. I won three bills."

"You bet against Ali?"

"I was at Saipan. Draft dodgers fuck with my head."

Marsh passed the flask. "Give me the count. Jap infantry or 211 guys. Who gets the nod?"

Scotty took a nip. "I torched an ammunition bunker. I fried a hundred Japs in their sleep."

"Did you win a medal?"

"The Navy Cross. Nice, but not as big as your deal."

Marsh smiled. The flask moved contrapuntal. Lionel Thornton walked out.

He hoofed it southbound. The bank doors were side-street/south-facing. Scotty said, "We'll take him there."

Hut action exploded. Fuckers screamed, "Frazier." Fuckers screamed, "Ali." Two brothers traded blows. Fred O. broke it up. The TV set toppled. Junkie Monkey hit the deck.

Scotty hauled westbound and cut south on Stanford. He cut east on 63rd Street and parked across the street.

Marsh said, "That storage door just west of the main doors. He won't see us there."

Scotty put his gloves on. "He's four minutes out."

Marsh gulped. He was racy and a tad damp. Scotty sensed his pulse.

"How's your wig, brother?"

"It be tight, brother. *You knows I wants this.*"

Scotty winked. "Let's go, then."

They walked across the street. The door well concealed them. Marsh checked his watch. Scotty heard footsteps.

Closer now. Louder. There's his breath, there's his shadow, there's the jangle of keys.

There's the key in the lock, there's the click, there's the door sweep.

They jumped.

They smothered him. They dog-piled him. They pushed him inside. The cash sack flew. Scotty hand-muzzled him. Marsh grabbed his piece. Thornton kicked and wriggled. Marsh caught a shoe in the face.

Thornton tried to bite. His mouth couldn't move. Marsh rabbit-punched him. Thornton lost all breath. Marsh grabbed the keys and inside-locked the doors. Thornton kept thrashing. Scotty swooped him over his head and threw him twenty feet.

The cocksucker flew. His whole body cartwheeled. His feet brushed the ceiling. He landed by the front teller's cage.

He screamed. Marsh pulled a standing lamp over and tossed light on his face.

The floor was dark. The lamp was a funnel spotlight. You got Thornton's face, that's it.

He screamed. Scotty stepped on his neck. He stopped screaming. His mouth was bloody. The crash landing took out his front teeth.

Scotty nodded. Marsh said, "We're interested in the ink-and non-ink-stained cash and the emeralds. You know what we mean. We think you have information that might assist us."

Thornton thrashed. Scotty stepped down harder. Thornton stopped thrashing. Scotty pulled out his reserve flask. Pastor Bennett's confession brew: bourbon and Valium chips.

Marsh palmed it. Marsh grabbed Thornton's hair and jerked. Thornton's mouth went wide. Marsh poured him a jolt. Thornton almost tossed it. Marsh stepped on his face and kept it in.

Scotty nodded. Marsh withdrew his foot. Thornton gulped air. Thornton said, "No."

Marsh slapped him. Thornton bit at his hand. Scotty grabbed his hair and pulled him behind the teller's cage. Marsh unfurled the cord and carried the lamp over.

The teller's cage was dark. The lamp was a funnel spotlight. Marsh framed Thornton's face. The cage row got backlit.

Scotty said, "You can't win here. You can make this easy or hard."

Thornton dribbled blood on the floor. A bug skittered over. Marsh stepped on it. Thornton sucked in a breath.

"White-trash cracker. Uncle Tom piece of shit."

Scotty nodded. Marsh pulled a sap and whipped Thornton's knees. Thornton bit through his bottom lip and stifled a scream.

Marsh said, "Sergeant Bennett and I have pooled our information on this matter. We *know* that you've laundered at least a small portion of the heist money. Would you care to comment?"

Thornton spat blood and loose tissue. Thornton crawled to a wall post and propped himself up. Thornton shook his head—no, ixnay, fuck you.

Scotty pulled the lamp closer. Marsh tilted it for more glare. Thornton was mouth flap–bloody. Marsh grabbed the flask and poured in a jolt.

Thornton tried to retch. Scotty grabbed his hair and pulled his head back. Marsh relubed him.

Gargles now—blood, bile and blend. It started to seep out. Marsh mouth-clamped Thornton and forced it back in.

He shook his head—*nyet, nein, no.* Marsh removed his mouth clamp and sap-whipped his legs.

"Sergeant Bennett and I have developed separate information that we've decided to share. We were both there that morning. It would be foolish for us not to cooperate."

Thornton shook his head. A loose tooth flew. Scotty unclamped his hair. Thornton proned out and back-swallowed blood. He shook his head—*nein, nyet, nyet.*

Marsh said, "I had a neighbor. He was an elderly black physician. He attended to a heist-gang member who had been left for dead by the leader of the gang. The doctor received twenty thousand dollars in ink-stained cash as a payment for his services. He gave the money to you and told you to leak it prudently out to the community. The surviving gang member recovered and has not been seen since. Would you care to comment?"

Thornton wide-eyed it. His brain pulse went visible. Fucking brilliant Marsh. Scotty thought, *Oh, you kid.*

The cage was hot. Scotty was wet. Marsh was wet. Scotty saw a wall unit and hit the switch.

Cold air whooshed. Thornton sucked it up. Marsh sapped his knees. Thornton screamed. The wall-unit rattle blended in.

Marsh raised the sap. Scotty shook his head. Thornton blinked lamp glare out of his eyes. Scotty moved and provided shade. Marsh squatted by Thornton and sap-tickled his chin.

"Sergeant Bennett and I believe that the surviving gang member was a young chemist named Reginald Hazzard. I have a theory that I have not yet shared with Sergeant Bennett. I think that perhaps young Hazzard found a way to partially or fully obscure the ink markings and that perhaps *you*—a seasoned money launderer—ended up with the laundry list for *all* of the cash. Would you care to comment?"

Thornton *wiiiiiide*-eyed it. It was truth serum–valid. Marsh, you genius cocksucker. *The gang leader braced the Laundryman independently.*

Thornton pissed his pants and shit his pants. Fey Marsh stood up and went *phew.*

Scotty winked. The wall-unit blew ice chips. A cockroach dipsey-doodled through the blood spill.

Marsh said, "Reginald Hazzard."

Thornton sobbed and spit blood.

Marsh said, "Who sends the emeralds to the black people in need?"

Thornton rolled out of the lamplight. Marsh kicked him in the back. Scotty shook his head. Marsh went *What now?* Scotty pulled his penlight and wide-dialed the beam.

Marsh pulled out a roll of duct tape and sealed Thornton's mouth. Scotty cuffed his right wrist to a wall pipe. It went telepathic: let's toss the place.

They worked with two penlights and Thornton's master keys. They sifted, dug, pored, overturned and upended. They *triple*-tossed the place.

They opened every office drawer and cash drawer.

They checked every cupboard.

They scanned every shelf.

They pulled up every rug.

They cut open every padded chair.

They went through every closet.

They broke every light fixture.

They scanned every surface, plane and cubbyhole for vault-combo stats.

They did it once, twice, three times. They mini-checked all the fucked-up debris.

Marsh said, "There's nothing here."

Scotty said, "Yes, there is."

"Man, he's not that stupid. He's got a spot at his house or a stash hole someplace."

Scotty shook his head. "He's complacent. He launders out of here. He's got to have records he can tap into. He's got a vault somewhere."

Marsh ran back to Thornton. He *was* Mr. Clean and the Laundryman. *Now* he's all shit, blood and piss.

Marsh slipped on sap gloves. Twelve ounces per—lead palm and finger strips.

Marsh said, "You tell me now." Marsh flexed his hands. Marsh punched Mr. Clean in the back.

Thornton sobbed and curled up tight. Scotty ran over and eased Marsh back.

"No. Don't. Be calm now, brother. We hit the walls first."

Marsh went limp. Yes, brother—okay—yes, yes.

Scotty let him go. Marsh crashed into the wall unit. Scotty ran to the storage closet and grabbed a crowbar. Marsh goofy-grinned.

They banged the walls.

They ripped and gouged the walls.

They took turns swinging.

They threw sweat. They got drenched. They took turns to catch their breath and kept swinging.

They hit Thornton's office walls and the break-room walls and the teller's cage walls. They hit the bank proper walls and kept swinging. They ripped out baseboard and timber. They ate plaster dust and chips. They heard Thornton moaning and coughing. They swung and ripped and traded shots and weaved on their feet.

They hit the rear hallway. Scotty leaned back, dead limp. Marsh took the first swing. A wall chunk fell out. A cloth ledger dropped in his hands.

It was plastic-wrapped and tape-sealed. It was twelve-by-eight and paper-packed. Scotty tore the cover off. Marsh scanned the first page. It was all bisecting columns and numbers. Dates on the far left. The first one: 4/64.

They wiped their eyes. They turned the pages. They saw dates, figures and number-coded designations. They saw the day-by-day/held-at-bank sums. Final figure: seven mil plus.

Marsh said, "The heist cash was seed money. He launders it and lends it. They started with two, and it stands at seven now. That's what they've got here. It's an on-the-premises tally."

Scotty said, "There's a vault."

The ledger was leather-lined. Marsh knife-slashed the edges and reached in and around. A piece of paper slid out.

Schematic drawing. A black box. Numbers noting size and placement. A tuck-away. Maybe here, maybe not. A secret vault. *Not the main vault.*

They walked back to Thornton. He was sitting up. His blood was sticky-thick and crusting. He made a little tooth pile. Plaster dust covered him. His sweat made it mud.

Scotty said, "Where's the vault?"

Thornton shook his head.

Marsh held up the drawing. "The vault. The combination."

Thornton said, "No."

Scotty kicked him in the leg. Thornton flipped him the bird. Marsh bent the finger back and broke it. Thornton mouth-muzzled a scream.

Marsh grabbed the crowbar and ran to the hallway. Scotty checked his watch—three hours inside. Thornton spit a tooth in his lap. Scotty winked at him.

"I'm always amazed when bright guys like you go the hard way. We should all be celebrating now."

Thornton said, "Fuck your mother. White-trash, peckerwood scum."

Wall knocks started up. Marsh swung hard and fast. More dust and mortar shards blew. More mulch fallout settled.

Marsh kept it up. Thornton spat dust-thick blood. Scotty sat down and shut his eyes. He was all-over ache.

The banging stopped. Marsh went, *"Woooooooooo!"* He ran over. Scotty kept his eyes shut. The lids weighed ten thousand pounds apiece.

"It's a clip file, brother. It goes back to spring '64. You've got the clips on the beneficiaries and a list of their names and addresses. It's History, man. There's the families of some guys who got lynched in Mississippi, the church girls from Birmingham, this woman who lost her son in the Watts riot."

Scotty opened his eyes. Marsh was cradling paper scrolls and news clips. Thornton gritted his mouth. His teeth were gone. It was a gum-to-gum grit.

Marsh dropped the paper load. It fell short of a blood spill. The chilled air fluttered it.

"Hundreds, partner. Police-shooting victims, sick people, protesters shot down south. You've got Mary Beth Hazzard and her dead husband all the way up to 'Ex-Champ Liston on Skids.' "

Scotty love-tapped the Laundryman. "Tell me the combination."

Thornton shook his head.

Scotty said, "Are the emeralds on the premises?"

Thornton said, "Fuck you." Marsh grabbed his right thumb and broke it.

THAT'S a scream—ten seconds long.

Scotty said, "Tell me how well you know Reginald Hazzard." Thornton said, "Fuck you." Marsh grabbed his right pinkie and broke it.

THAT'S a shriek—twelve seconds long.

Scotty said, "Are the emeralds on the premises? Do you send them out? Are they sent to you to send? Is Reginald overseas somewhere? Who else is involved in all of this?"

Thornton said, "Fuck you."

Marsh grabbed his left thumb and broke it.

Screams and shrieks. Earsplitting shit—a full minute.

Scotty pulled out his confession flask. Marsh grabbed Thornton's hair and jerked. Thornton opened up wide. Thornton sucked like he wanted it. His eyes said Refill.

Sure, Boss. It's on the house.

Thornton retched and kept it down. Scotty checked his watch. One minute to let it seeeeeep.

Thornton flushed and flexed his hands. Thornton kneaded fucked-up body kinks. Liftoff at forty-three seconds.

"I don't know where Reggie is. I get mail drops from overseas. They're sent under mail cover from different locations. I forward the emeralds, but they come to me through a cutout."

"Cutout"—woooo—mother dog!

Scotty said, "Name the 'cutout.' "

Thornton coughed. "I don't know her name."

Scotty said, "Her?"

Marsh said, "Describe her."

Thornton dry-coughed. "White, in her forties, glasses. Dark hair with gray patches."

Marsh did a double take. Scotty read it. Brother, I knows you.

Thornton wet-coughed. Blood dripped down his chin.

"Where's the vault?"

"I'm not telling you."

"Give me the combination?"

"I'm not going to."

"Put this thing together for us. We've got time to listen."

"I'm not going to."

"Explain the business code in the ledger."

"I'm not going to."

Marsh flexed his sap gloves. Scotty jerked his arms back.

"Go in his office and get his address book. It's in the top right-hand drawer."

Thornton leaned back and trembled. Marsh ran off, scanning his penlight. Scotty checked Thornton's handcuffs. His wrists were ratchet-gouged deep.

Marsh ran back. Scotty skimmed the book name by name. They read by penlight. Marsh hovered over him. "A" to "K"—two women. Janice Altschuler, April Kostritch. A tweaker at "L"—SAC John Leahy/FBI #48770.

Two more women: Helen Rugert and Sharon Zielinski. Cutouts? Basic vibe: *no.*

Scotty tossed the book. Marsh said, "Altschuler, Kostritch, Rugert, Zielinski."

Thornton hack-coughed. "Those women are city council staffers and lawyers. I told you, I don't know the cutout's name."

Scotty cracked his knuckles. "Where do you call her?"

"I *don't.* She calls me."

Marsh picked the book up and thumbed through it. Scotty cracked his knuckles loud, upside Thornton's face.

"Why is Jack Leahy's name in your book?"

"We're friends. We play golf."

"Are you an FBI informant? Is 48770 your confidential Bureau number?"

"No, we play golf!"

Scotty slapped him. Thornton thrashed his head. Scotty wiped blood and snot on his pant leg.

"Are you a confidential Bureau informant?"

"Yes."

"Did you ever know or work with the late Dr. Fred Hiltz?"

"The fucking 'Hate King'? Why would I?"

Truth serum—I'll buy it.

"Who do you snitch to Jack?"

"Ghetto scum, man. Dope-pushers and Panther-type fools."

Marsh dropped the address book. Scotty penlight-signaled him. Marsh signaled him back. They got each other's eyes. They telepathized.

Scotty said, "Where's the vault, Mr. Thornton?"

"I'm not telling you."

Marsh said, "What haven't you told us that you should have told us in the name of full disclosure?"

Thornton laughed. "Man, you are nothing but a nigger full of four-dollar words."

Scotty said, "Please take us to the vault."

"I'm not going to."

Marsh said, "Where are the emeralds?"

"If I knew, I wouldn't tell you."

Scotty shrugged.

Marsh shrugged.

They penlight-drilled Thornton's face. They got a big funnel target. Marsh pulled a throwdown piece and capped him.

98

(Los Angeles, 3/8/71)

Sassy Sal loved soul food. He dive-bombed the post-fight buffet and out-snarfed the brothers. He was reefer-ripped. He was libido-lashed. He wolfed chicken wings and grooved low-life maleness. Marsh Bowen was missing. Crutch wanted Sal to see him. Sal's job: kick-start their vibe.

The party poked on. The re-hash ran sans pithy perception. Panther pedantry. Fractious Frazierites and mongoloid Muslims.

Fools milked the moment. The cover price included chow and a dope smorgasbord. Big Mama's Kitchen catered. Fred O. supplied pharmaceuticals. On-site consumption raged. Geeks crawled into Tiger kabs and passed out.

Where's Marsh?

Crutch yawned. He was nerve-numb. *His* re-hash ran rampant. Tattoo wants to meet movie men. She's been de-hexed. The envelope prints: possibly Reggie Hazzard's, for sure Lionel Thornton's.

Sal noshed collard greens. Crutch yawned anew. He'd been reading. His new kick: chemistry and left-wing dialectic.

He was in his Reggie Hazzard head. He sent Mary Beth another file-request letter and got no answer. He was reading Reggie's books. He performed some simple experiments, per instructions. He liquefied two powders and blew up a trash can. He learned about United Fruit in Guatemala. He went with the narrative. Good guy/bad guy roles got reversed. He got eyestrain. He started seeing *RED*.

Marsh walked into the hut. He looked shivery-shaky. What's that trouser stain?

Sal noticed him. Sal made an ooo-la-la face. Marsh walked back to the can. Crutch tailed him. Marsh left the door cracked.

Marsh washed his hands. Dark smudges went light red and pink. He doused his shirt cuffs and wrung the fabric. Crutch smelled blood.

Marsh wiped his face. Marsh pulled out a pen and wrote on his left arm. Crutch squinted and caught it.

FBI/48770.

99

(Media, 3/8/71)

Resident Agency. A two-room records drop. One office in a four-story building.

Media was Snoresville. A trolley ran twelve miles to Philly. The front door was made for thin-head pry bars.

It's 11:49 p.m. The world's abuzz: Frazier takes Ali.

Dwight parked on a side street. He had a near-diagonal view. He saw the front door and the office windows.

Karen ran him through it yesterday. They discussed outcomes.

His take: Mr. Hoover will stonewall it. That meant newspaper leaks. Go to the *biiiiiiig* dailies. Include documents. Tweak some muckraking journos. Let it build on its own. Leak the file pages through cutouts. Invent a name for a lefty group. Claim the B&E under their flag.

Joan disagreed. Her take: we're robbing the big revelation. His take: this is the prelude and primer. The Media files are *bland.* They detail prosaic hassles and routine surveillance. The juicy shit is elsewhere. *Our* operation will reveal it. The post-Hoover FBI cannot stonewall it. Media will have exposited the term COINTELPRO. Fed-speak will distort the truth. *I* will tell the world what it really means. The Bureau cannot regroup post-hit. Media will have created a file hue and cry. Obfuscation will not work post-hit. *I* will be found. *I* will break ranks. *I* will step forth to testify.

Dwight held up binoculars. A van entered his sight line.

Four people got out: two men, two women. They dressed like middle-aged squares. The women carried bulging purses stuffed with laundry bags. Karen wore a suburban-mom pantsuit.

They had his dupe key. They slow-walked to the front door and unlocked it. Karen pick-gouged the lock housing to simulate a B&E.

They shut the door. It stayed dark. Penlight bips reflected. Take the back stairs. Don't risk the lift.

Dwight checked his watch. It hit midnight. He watched the four windows. A half minute elapsed. Penlight beams strafed.

A car passed the building. Late-model Merc, dud mom and dad, the country club set. Pops ran the radio. Dwight heard "Ali."

The beams kept strafing. The windowpanes flickered. A black & white passed the building. Two fat cops yawned.

Dwight counted watch minutes. The second hand crawled. The windows stayed dark for a forty-eight-count. Okay, that's it.

He watched the lobby. There they are. The laundry bags are bulging. Go out the door. Get the van and take off.

The other three walked ahead. Karen stood on the sidewalk and faced him. He kissed his fingers and touched the windshield. Karen raised a clenched fist.

DOCUMENT INSERT: 3/12/71. Los Angeles *Herald Express* article.

SHOCK WAVES FROM SOUTHSIDE ROBBERY-MURDER
Complex Portrait of Victim Emerges from Investigation

Lionel D. Thornton, 51, the president of the Peoples' Bank of
South Los Angeles, died a horrible death Monday night. Returning
from a viewing of the Ali-Frazier boxing match at a popular local
taxicab stand, he was waylaid outside the bank and forced inside.
He was subsequently robbed of his cab-stand receipts, tortured
and killed. Preliminary investigation by the Los Angeles Police
Department has revealed that the robber-killer or killers went
through the bank in a fit of rage, perhaps looking for a hidden
vault or perhaps currency secreted by Mr. Thornton on the
premises. Sadly, the crime may have derived from never-
substantiated rumors pertaining to Mr. Thornton himself.

"I've got nothing but good things to say about Mr. Thornton,"
the lead investigator, Sergeant Robert S. Bennett, told reporters at
a hastily called press conference Tuesday afternoon. "He's been
a mainstay of the local black community for many years, as one
can feel in the outpouring of grief over his death and in the number
of glowing tributes we have heard since the news broke this
morning."

Sergeant Bennett, 49, is overseeing six full-time detectives
charged with solving the case and bringing the suspect or suspects
to justice. "I personally believe Mr. Thornton to have been a
blameless individual," he told reporters. "That stated, I believe
that this crime stems from the long-held southside rumor that
perhaps Mr. Thornton had organized-crime ties and was hoarding
laundered money on the bank's premises. I do not believe the
rumors. I believe that the crime stemmed from persistently held
misinformation. The tragedy is that Mr. Thornton gave his life for
$2,000 in cab receipts, and that the suspect or suspects killed him
and decimated the bank interior in a search for something that
was not there."

The investigation continues. Sergeant Bennett and his six-man
team will spearhead the drive to apprehend the slayer or slayers
of Lionel D. Thornton. A backup investigation will be fielded by the

Los Angeles Office of the Federal Bureau of Investigation, supervised by Special-Agent-in-Charge John C. Leahy.

<u>DOCUMENT INSERT</u>: 3/12/71. Verbatim FBI telephone call transcript. Marked: "<u>Recorded at the Director's Request/Classified Confidential 1-A: Director's Eyes Only.</u>" Speaking: Director Hoover, Special Agent Dwight C. Holly.

DH: Good morning, Sir.

JEH: It is decidedly not.

DH: Sir?

JEH: The Resident Agency in Media, Pennsylvania, was burglarized Monday night. A great many files were stolen.

DH: Is it secured, Sir? And forgive my ignorance, but I don't know where Media is.

JEH: It's a two-man office space near Philadelphia. The file bank holds overflow from the New York, Boston and Philadelphia offices. The break-in occurred while local police officers were at Shakey's Pizza Parlor, watching replays of the Cassius Clay–Smokin' Joe Frazier Battle of the Apes.

DH: Sir, is it secure?

JEH: It is. The break-in was discovered by the agents themselves. They bypassed the Media PD and called the Philadelphia SAC. Media has not yet made the media.

DH: The files, Sir?

JEH: Bland, by your Los Angeles Office standards. Damning by the standards of addlepated civil libertarians. We lost adjunct surveillance files, tap files and <u>COINTELPRO</u> addendum sheets.

DH: It's a shocking breach, Sir.

JEH: You are muddle-headed and swoony with emotion today, Dwight. Extended stays in sanitariums undermine strong people. They confuse their emotional states with the world.

DH: Yes, Sir.

JEH: That's better. The old "Enforcer." Hard-edged and submissive.

DH: Yes, Sir.

JEH: Better yet.

DH: Yes, Sir.

JEH: I'm sure we're thinking along similar lines. Which lunatic fringe group will claim credit? Will they release the files? Which treasonous leftist rag will they release them to?

DH: How many agents are on it, Sir?

JEH: Forty-six, full-time. Of course, there are no witnesses and the thieves left no physical evidence.

DH: I'll query my informants, Sir.

JEH: Do that. Offer cash incentives and employ your generally intrusive methods with my full sanction.

DH: Yes, Sir.

JEH: I have sent out a general memo to all our field offices. The file sections are being security enhanced at this very moment.

DH: Yes, Sir.

JEH: Do not underestimate my resolve to forestall future break-ins. Do not underestimate the robust state of my health. My physician, Dr. Archie Bell, considers me to be an outstanding specimen.

DH: Yes, Sir.

JEH: President Nixon is mentally ill. He refuses to inform me that he will reappoint me as director after his fait accompli reelection next year. I'm telling it like it is, Brother Dwight. Tricky Dick has asked me to black-bag the major Democratic candidates, which I have declined to do. I'm dragging my heels. Nixey boy is starting to sweat.

DH: I can dig it, Sir.

JEH: I'm sure you can. And your mental health? Have you regained your brusque grasp of life?

DH: In spades, Sir.

JEH: We lost some files, but we will prevail in the end. The files in my superbly secure basement would bring down the world.

DH: Right on, Sir.

JEH: Good day, Dwight.

DH: Good day, Sir.

DOCUMENT INSERT: 3/12/71. <u>VERBATIM STAGE-1/CLOSED CON-TACT/TOP-ACCESS ROUTING telephone call transcript.</u> Closed file #48297. Speaking: President Richard M. Nixon and Special Agent Dwight C. Holly, FBI.

RMN: Good evening, Dwight.

DH: Good evening, Mr. President.

RMN: It's been too long, my friend.

DH: I agree, Sir.

RMN: Are you keeping busy?

DH: I certainly am, Sir.

RMN: That's the ticket. Keep going until your hat floats.

DH: That is very sage advice, Sir.

RMN: It is. On that note, I would have to say that you-know-who must be very busy fretting over that break-in.

DH: He is, Sir. We were discussing it this morning. May I ask if he was the one who informed you?

RMN: The attorney general called me. He said, "The old girl may have her dick in the wringer."

DH: May I be blunt, Sir?

RMN: By all means, Dwight. Why mince words? I only call you when I've been belting a few and I've got a yen for bluntness.

DH: The burglars will or will not claim credit and may or may not leak the files. Parenthetically, I would add that Media, PA, is the Siberia of file holes and that all the data in the files pre-dates your administration.

RMN: I like that.

DH: I thought you might, Sir.

RMN: Here's my fear. I'm thinking what's-her-name may be infirm to the point where she'll deploy her files on me to keep her job.

DH: You'll be reelected next November, Sir. Inauguration Day 1973 sounds like a good time to cut your losses.

RMN: I like that.

DH: I thought you might, Sir. And please let me add that should the break-in be claimed and the files go out resultantly, it will make you-know-who quite circumspect about releasing files in any sort of derogatory manner.

RMN: Dwight, you my main man.

DH: Thank you, Sir.

RMN: Per next year's election, then. The old girl has been dragging her heels on a certain front. "Black-bag job." It's got soul as a concept, don't you think?

DH: Frankly, Sir, it's ghetto. I appreciate it that way myself.

RMN: Dwight, you're a sketch. Let's talk about that again next time.

DH: Yes, Sir.

RMN: Anything I can help you with?

DH: One thing, Sir.

RMN: I'm listening.

DH: The L.A. Office is security-fitting the file section. The agents are afraid you-know-who will show up unannounced before it's finished. Will you get me his travel schedule from someone at Justice?

RMN: Sure, Dwight. On the QT, baby. Just like all our chats.

DH: Thank you, Mr. President.

RMN: Straight ahead, kid.

100

(Los Angeles, 3/13/71)

Scotty doodled.

His cubicle was three-wall-wrapped. He drew little emeralds. He added that Greek gender symbol. It meant *"Who's the Woman?"*

It was early. The night-watch shift left a mess. He connived the job. He sent his backup guys down dead-end roads. He oversaw the first forensic. They covered their tracks. The tech team got no leads off one walk-through. That meant one more to go.

They stole the Tiger Kab receipts and no more. Jack Leahy was running point, FBI-adjunct. Mr. Clean was a Fed snitch. Circle-jerk aspects overlapped.

That hidden vault. So far, unfound. The conduit. Brother Bowen, hanging in strong.

Scotty scanned a list. Fred O. telexed it. The Tiger Kab fight guests, alphabetized.

Milt C. and Fred T. Lenny Bernstein and Wilt Chamberlain. There's Sal Mineo—c/o Peeper Crutchfield. Sissy Sal was supposed to meet Macho Marsh that night.

Scotty skipped down the list. Aha: Marcus and Lavelle Bostitch.

They lived in Watts. They had a squatter's shack behind Mumar's Mosque #2. Junkies, heist guys, pedophiles. Nobel Peace Prize candidates.

The Bostitch boys bopped carless. They were legendary that way. They rode Schwinn Sting-Rays with gooseneck risers and banana seats.

The bikes were gone. The door was unlocked. The mosque Moors were loudly absorbed with Allah. Scotty walked right in.

He brought an evidence kit. He carried a pocketknife and three tiger-band cash rolls. He brought print cards, print tape, print powder and six plastic bags.

The pad stunk. It was junkie stench. Poor hygiene and suppuration. He walk-tossed the place. No guns on the premises. That meant nothing.

Two upholstered chairs, linoleum floor, one mattress. No bathroom, kitchen, cupboards or shelves.

Let's work.

Scotty slit the bottom of the mattress and tucked three cash rolls in. Scotty opened a plastic bag and sprinkled wall debris from the bank. Scotty pulled kinky hairs off a window ledge and bagged them.

He print-dusted the doorways and four touch-and-grab planes. He got two latent print sets. He card-compared them. The Bostitch boys, ten points apiece.

He tape-transferred them and secured them in print tubes. He bagged chair fibers and more hair. He bagged dirt and dust residue. He tucked a throwdown gun in a mattress slit.

The heathens were still chanting. Scotty walked by the mosque and shagged his car. A spade in a fez prayer-bowed to him. Scotty prayer-bowed him back.

Crime scene: LAPD/FBI. Yellow tape and point guards all around the bank.

Scotty badged the door guy. The guy let him in. The floors were drop-clothed. Sifting screens were stacked waist-high. Collected grit filled giant Baggies. The teller's cage reeked of Luminal. They were going for blood type. Maybe Thornton cut the killers as they cut him.

Wrong.

Scotty walked into Mr. Clean's office and inside-locked the door. He transferred the print strips to wall surfaces and shelves. He sprinkled hair, dirt and dust. He tucked a bloody C-note under a carpet pad.

He unlocked the door and walked outside. A lunch truck was feeding the point cops. Jack Leahy was lounging in a Fed sled.

Scotty walked over. "Let me guess. The Laundryman had some connections you need to be wary of. Mr. Hoover said take a look-see."

"In a nutshell, yes."

"It's a mess in there. SID got nothing on the first roll. I've ordered a second."

Jack said, "You were always thorough that way."

Scotty smiled. "Mr. Clean deserves the best. I won money on Frazier, so I'm feeling generous."

Jack polished his glasses. "Suspects?"

"Two male Negroes. They were at Tiger Kab for the fight. I think they followed Thornton here and jumped him."

A jalopy rolled down the street. Two brothers clench-fisted the fuzz.

Scotty laughed. "This is starting to remind me of the Fred Hiltz job."

Jack said, "I'll concede that."

"You took that one over, but I won't permit it here."

Jack said, "For now, I'll concede."

"Hiltz was a Bureau informant. I'm thinking Mr. Clean was, too."

Jack said, "No comment."

Mumar's Mosque was closed for the night. The two Schwinns were outside.

Jungle rides. Mock-croc saddlebags and mud flaps. Cheater slicks and aaa-ooo-gaaah horns.

Scotty looked in the window. Ah, brothers—how kind of you.

They were insensate. They were tourniquet-tied and nipping at Neptune. Spoons, spikes and white horse were out in plain view.

Scotty put on gloves and walked in. Marcus and Lavelle dozed in side-by-side chairs. Scotty pulled out two throwdowns. Marsh shot Mr. Clean with gun #1. Gun #2 was a dope-bust steal, circa '62.

Peace, brothers.

Scotty placed gun #1 in Marcus' right hand and laid his right forefinger on the trigger. He raised the gun and placed the barrel against Marcus' right ear. He placed his own finger over the trigger and squeezed.

The shot was loud. Marcus pitched back, dead. The bullet stayed inside his head. Scotty let his gun arm drop. The gun fell close to his hand.

Scotty placed gun #2 in Lavelle's right hand and laid his right forefinger on the trigger. He raised the gun and placed the barrel against Lavelle's right ear. He placed his own finger over the trigger and squeezed.

The shot was loud. Lavelle pitched back, dead. The bullet stayed inside his head. Scotty let his gun arm drop. The gun fell close to his hand.

Nice powder burns. Empirically correct and textbook-consistent. Nice mouth trickle. Late seepage out through their eyes.

101

(Los Angeles, 3/14/71)

FBI/48770.

Blend in. You're a worker. You'll make it fly.

He studied the crew yesterday. They wore jumpsuits and lunch-boxed it on the Fed Building lawn. Agents head-counted them in the a.m. The afternoon—nix. You're just another tool-belted geek.

Clyde said the Feds got B&E'd outside Philly. It mandated a file-room blitzkrieg. Clyde said five-digit numbers were snitch codes. Shit/fuck—let's try.

Crutch ate a salami hero. The crew guys ignored him. *It is all one.* Mr. Clean dies. Marsh with bloody hands. Scotty gets the case, junkie suicides, case closed.

A whistle blew. The crew stood up and stretched. Six guys plus him. Please, no head count.

Crutch blended in. Nobody said boo. He had a two-day growth and a painter's cap pulled low. He paint-smeared his face.

They entered the lobby. A Fed keyed the elevator. Crutch crouched between two fat Polacks. Nobody said shit.

The elevator stopped at floor 11. The Fed led them down a hallway. Dwight Holly walked by, with a clipboard. He didn't see shit.

The file section was off the main squadroom. It was airplane hangar—size.

The Fed waved bye-bye. The crew dispersed. They went around unscrewing shelf runners. Crutch moved six aisles down and mimicked them.

He worked slow. The other guys schlepped around panels. *Now I get it. Cover the file shelves. Gain access by lock and key.*

File shelves, file banks, file rows. Chained binder directories. "CBI." Abbreviated Fed-speak: "Confidential bureau informants."

The real workers *worked.* Panels and lock placements went up *faaaaast.* Crutch quick-walked. Look officious now. Tighten some screws.

He walked away from the other guys. He flipped open binders. He hit sixteen file rows. Abbreviations blurred. Number 17: "CBI/00001."

He gulped. He looked up. He counted numbers and shelves to the ceiling. Motherfucker—the high-4 series was up at the top.

No shelf ladders here. You've got to shimmy up.

He climbed. The shelves wobbled. He fucking monkey-grabbed, hoisted and pulled. He reached the summit. The ceiling loomed.

He crawled. He ate dust, rubber bands and age-old dead bugs. He peeked over the side and saw file tabs. He got the 4–5's, the 4–6's, the 4–7's. He stifled sneezes. The shelf shimmy-shimmied. He hit the 4–8's. He saw the red tab for the *one.*

He plucked it.

He read the first page.

The Black Pride Laundryman—craven Fed snitch.

He snitched heist guys exclusively. He reported to the office boss, Jack Leahy. The relationship started back in '63. The robbers' names were inked over. *It's all too close, it's all as one.* Nothing's tangential—it's all right here in my fist.

The shelf wobbled. Crutch almost blew lunch. Robbery rat-outs. Dissemination and disinformation. It had to be.

Crutch sneezed. The shelf dipped. He almost dropped the file. A page fell out. He saw a black-inked paragraph. God spoke to him: Jack Leahy redacted Joan Rosen Klein.

102

(Los Angeles, Rural Mississippi, 3/15/71–11/18/71)

he Operation.
They never named it. They didn't need to or want to. They never exchanged memoranda. There was no need to paper-reference their tasks. Acronyms were self-indulgent and satirical. They reeked of puerile Feds fucking the disenfranchised for kicks.

He worked his file-room job in a perfunctory manner and worked the Operation full-tilt. A Nixon aide sent him Mr. Hoover's travel list. The old girl was frail. She was traveling less. There were no planned L.A. trips this year.

His sleep was good. His nerves were sound. He chucked his booze and sleeping-pill stash. He imagined spot tails. He took evasive action. The tail cars disappeared. It was just residual fear.

The old girl trusted him. The Operation was secure. The fallback was inviolate. There was no surveillance.

He gave up the tail checks and drove place to place. He was post-crack-up now. He went task to task, un-paranoic. The Operation was incomprehensible. Nobody would suspect their goal or dispute the outcome. A paper avalanche would follow. Media preannounced it. The Event was inevitable.

Joan worked with him, task by task. She understood the level of detail required. They talked, they plotted, they built a giant paper maze. Joan refused to embellish her astonishing statement.

"I've wanted to kill him since I was a child, and I won't tell you why."

He did not ask her again. He did not ask Karen. He ran more records checks on her known family members. Every file had been lost, misplaced, diverted, destroyed or stolen. He gave up. He wasn't supposed to know. She'd tell him or she wouldn't. He found himself less curious. The Operation was theirs. Its brutal scope was their bond.

The Media break-in worked. Karen and her team stayed anonymous. She leaked files through a series of cutouts. The *Washington Post* hit on March 24. The *New York Times* and *Village Voice* followed. A hue and cry escalated. Karen attributed the leaks to the "Citizen's Committee to Investigate the FBI." Joe Public got a gander at bland surveillance files. Jane Public got hip to COINTELPRO. Mr. Hoover made flabbergasted remarks. The prez was relieved. The files revealed only pre-Nixon chicanery.

It worked. Joan conceded the point. The event faded in and out of public play. Lefty journos kept teething on it. COINTELPRO was subtextually planted. The Event would etch the concept in blood.

Work was tense. The Operation sustained him ideologically. The Operation drove Joan in a wholly vindictive manner. She saw it as a vendetta. She would not reveal the origin of her journey of revenge. She was running haggard. Lionel Thornton's death disturbed her. He was a money washer at worst and a political bagman at best. Joan wouldn't talk about it. She always said what she always said: "I'm not going to."

Joan slept with him in hotel suites and worked with him at the fallback. She stayed in safe houses the nights he slept with Karen. She was worried about Celia. She was making phone calls and trying to find Celia in the D.R. She refused all his offers to help.

She'd sit by herself on the terrace. She'd sip tea and take herbal capsules. He stole a few and had them analyzed. They were Haitian fertility potions. Joan was almost forty-five and was trying to get pregnant. Her child, his child—it astounded him. There was no chance of conception. He knew it. He never said it. He never mentioned the potions. He watched her face recast itself as she tried to will her body. He reveled in the mad task and in her obduracy.

Karen's house was down a steep hillside. He trained his binoculars and watched the girls play. Karen debriefed him on Media and told him no more. They formally terminated their snitch relationship. He accepted it. Karen described Media as a debt to Joan and him and respectfully asserted that she had paid it. He said she had. She never returned to the fallback. He carried the picture of her with the girls. She sent him coded night messages. She'd sense him on the terrace and blast Beethoven string quartets. She'd leave a kitchen light on to pinpoint the sound.

The music invaded his dreams. Wayne replaced Dr. King. Crocodiles and rivers in Haiti. Explosions in the D.R. and gaunt black men with wings.

The Operation proceeded. Convergence remained the one obstacle. He flew to Mississippi four times. Bob Relyea remained committed. Bob was training. Bob would keep his mouth shut. Bob would not know the target until hit day.

He B&E'd Marsh Bowen's house six more times. He searched for a hidden diary and found none. Joan was certain that Marsh kept a candid daily journal. His actor's self-absorption fairly screamed it. Their fake diary was the deus ex machina of the Operation. They had to be certain that a real diary would not be found.

Marsh worked night-watch shifts and gave motivational speeches. Dwight black-bagged him and prowled. Trash runs, desk and drawer runs, fake-panel taps. Numerous art books and Haitian travel brochures. No diary yet.

The file section was now security-fitted. It was a post-Media precaution. It didn't matter. He was an FBI agent. He had file-shelf keys. Marsh Bowen was now deeply file-inserted. Sergeant Bowen was injudiciously promiscuous. Sergeant Bowen was politically unstable, going back years.

He spent late nights at the office. He chatted with the mordant Jack Leahy. Jack was fixed on the old girl in gasping decline. Media was a pisser. Jack considered it predictable. He was pension-secure and raucous by nature. He didn't seem to give a shit.

Dick Nixon got raucous behind two highballs. He called Dwight twice a month. Mr. Hoover called twice as much. Nixon was Hoover-tweaked. Hoover was Nixon-tweaked. The prez got half-gassed and vented his frustration. Hoover raged for reassurance amid mental gaffes. Both men found the Enforcer consoling. He was the gunslinger, back from a crack-up.

His consolation? Marsh's diary.

He's creating a world of troubled men in extremis. He attributes his dreams to Marsh. Marsh's discourse is shaped by his discourse with Karen and Joan. Marsh's diary feels almost utopian. It rebuts the world that is and prophesies the world that could be. The entries cover the inception of BAAAAD BROTHER and run to the present. Marsh carries guilt for exploiting the "Black-Militant Blastout." He is determined to kill J. Edgar Hoover. His cop-actor's role won him glory and spawned death. His moral confusion counterpoints his tortured inner life and day-to-day indulgence of perversion.

He's added details from his own breakdown. Marsh's crack-up is his crack-up, hyper-radicalized. He's created a Holly-Bowen bond that did not exist. The two men discuss crack-up as a call to violent arms and the means to transcend self-serving pathology. He portrays public policy as private nightmare and vehicle of atonement. What it's like to have to *do* something so you won't go insane. His story and Marsh's story regained.

He's come to care for Marsh. He won't regret killing him.

103

(Los Angeles, 3/15/71–11/18/71)

Frustration. Fucking ceaseless, day by day.

The county grand jury nailed the Bostitch boys posthumous. Scotty breathed easy then. The brothers snuffed Mr. Clean and formed a suicide pact. Nice, but the heist gig was stalled flat.

Who's the Woman?

She was Thornton's emerald conduit and cutout. A *Woman* pervaded the Jomo offshoot. Marsh perks when he says *Woman.* Marsh comes on bifurcated. He's solid *and* untrustworthy.

Who's the Woman? His notion: she was in with OPERATION BAAAAD BROTHER. Dandy, but:

He can't brace Dwight Holly. Dwight is dead smart and subtle and would brace him right back. He can't brace Jack Leahy. Jack knows about BAAAAD BROTHER. Jack is dead smart and subtle and would brace him right back.

Frustration. Mind-bending, night after night.

They stole the emerald-disbursement clip file and the coded ledger. He tried to crack the code. He spent months on it. He thought about hiring a cryptographer. A pro might crack the code. He finally nixed the idea. The code guy would *know* then. One more loose end would unfurl.

Federal bank examiners tossed the Peoples' Bank. Scotty went with them and Jack Leahy. They tore the walls, floors and roof to shreds. They found the vault from Mr. Clean's drawing. Inside: a dope stash and $89,000.

Cat's-paw. Long-term stopgap. A hedge against possible exposure.

The money and remaining emeralds were stashed elsewhere. Thornton was smart. He didn't give up the vault. He played the "I don't know" card. He knew he was dead, anyway. Theory: the money and gems *were* in the vault. The heist guys knew it. They pulled them before the bank team went in.

Where's Reggie? *Who's the Woman?* Who'll disburse the emeralds with Mr. Clean dead?

Frustration. Night sweats. *Woooooo,* toss the sheets.

Marsh was frustrated. He's read all their files. He reads them and nitpicks the details. They're the world's greatest rogue cop salt-and-pepper team. They're years in and still short of the rainbow.

Frustration meant backlash. Scotty fucked his wife and girlfriends more and lived for stakeouts. He nailed two cholos outside a Boyle Heights bodega in May. Marsh loved it—at least they weren't black. He 86'd two neo-Nazis a week later. They robbed a black-owned market on Vermont. He blew one cracker's arm off. He pulled a black tot to safety. Marsh *loooooved* it. Marsh had clout with the NAACP. They might give him a medal.

Marsh let steam off *his* way. Do your own thing? Sure. Marsh vanished three times in eight months. He *said* he took car trips, to re-wire his head. It had to be fruit shit. Fruit junkets, fruit trysts, fruit excursions.

Frustration. You want *gooooood* booty? Let Pastor Bennett and Peeper Crutchfield pimp for you.

Sissy Sal crush-crawled all over Macho Marsh. Marsh won't jump his bones back. It was driving him *nuts.* Ditto Peeper, Fred T. and Fred O.

Frustration. *Who's the Woman?*

He's sniffed all over darktown. He's gotten nothing substantive. The description rings bells. Some geeks seem slightly spooked. One guy said she might be black militant–connected. He queried his Panther and US contacts and got shit. The BTA and MMLF geeks were all off in prison. He couldn't brace them there. His visits would be noted. Stray talk would disperse.

The case was all *Her.* The woman with the gray-streaked hair was *Everything.*

DOCUMENT INSERT: 11/18/71. Extract from the privately held
journal of Karen Sifakis.

Los Angeles,
November 18, 1971

Media was eight months ago. My comrades and I have
remained unapprehended; no one has broken ranks; the FBI's
illegal surveillance of political organizations, civic groups and
protest-inclined individuals has been revealed in a flurry of news
reportage, angry editorials and television and radio airtime. The
revelation has come and gone. The concept of the COINTELPRO has
been introduced to the American people, who have largely chosen
to ignore it. The FBI's more draconian undercover operations were
not mentioned in any of the released files. Dwight and Joan
seemed pleased by this. I am quite capable of discerning Dwight's
unspoken thoughts. He's happy that the FBI's specific war on the
civil rights movement and black-militant groups has not been
preemptively placed under the COINTELPRO umbrella.

I don't want to know what Joan and Dwight are planning; I
suspect that I will learn of it in the public arena and am beginning
to nurture a sense of it as a grandiosely large event. Media was a
diversionary tactic and/or a setup. The ramifications of my one
proactive salvo for Dwight and Joan will become apparent over
time. I don't want to know. They know that and withhold their
plans from me. I have prayed over this and have made a vow to
continue to love them, regardless of any horror and chaos they
may perpetrate.

We never meet as a group of three. Joan has resurfaced in my
life; we meet for coffee or lunch two or three times a week, always
here in Silver Lake or Echo Park. We discuss politics incessantly.
Nixon, Vietnam, labor issues and the black-militant movement in
decline can engross us for hours. Joan is gaunt and speaks in
nervous, yet fully coherent bomb bursts of invective, with percep-
tive flows of political monologue mixed in. The lovely and defining
gray patches in her hair are turning white and are streaking
through the overall black. I'm afraid she's becoming paranoid—
she says she's had an intermittent sense of being followed—and
she often speaks of her lover/comrade Celia, out of touch in Haiti

or the Dominican Republic. Celia once told Joan not to try to find her should she go missing. How many times has Joan told lovers or lover/comrades the same thing? Now, Joan is the one bereft, and it is her bond with Dwight Chalfont Holly that has taken her to this point where she cannot suppress grief.

Joan smokes constantly and drinks pots of self-brewed Haitian herb tea. She swallows Haitian herb capsules with all her meals, at precisely timed moments of the day. I asked her about it. She said she was trying to get pregnant. She wanted to have a child.

I didn't question her motive. I knew not to ask "Why?" Joan would simply say, "I'm not telling you." A woman her age cannot will a child. Joan doesn't seem to know how improbable it is. It continues to remain unspoken, albeit ineluctably true. She wants to have this child with Dwight.

Joan and I have always withheld from each other. We are individually compromised and duplicitous; we live in a mendacious world we have been morally charged to undermine and subvert. I could tell Joan the one thing I have never told Dwight. It might or might not hurt her. I know what it would do to Dwight. I fear the further breakdown that it might engender and the deep resolve it would certainly create.

DOCUMENT INSERT. 11/18/71. Extract from the journal of Marshall E. Bowen.

Baldwin Hills,
11/18/71

I thought the murder would hurt me more and would more hurtfully invade my body and mind. It hasn't. I assumed the role of murderer and behaved in the manner of a first-time killer determined to survive. It took a few days for my mental equilibrium to adjust. I mindscaped the possible upshot of my actions as Scotty took care of business. I met him for a series of late-night dinners at Ollie Hammond's. We boozed a bit and ate steak sandwiches. Scotty preached. In the end, you'll survive. You did what was necessary; you'll do it again if you have to. Feel better now?

I did then, I do now. I have the upper hand in the partnership. I know two things that Scotty doesn't: Reginald Hazzard and the emeralds are in Haiti. The woman is Joan Rosen Klein.

My life is a series of shadow plays and non sequiturs. I work the detective bureau at Hollywood Station. I go to movie-biz cocktail parties and enjoy the ambivalent responses that my presence there provokes. Three years ago, I was a policeman who had been beaten, ostracized and converted to the black-militant faith. *That* inspired film-biz cachet. Now, I am a policeman revealed to have been a planted informant; a policeman who extolls authoritarian values in prestigious speaking engagements and stands tall in LAPD dress blues. The film-biz folks would love to hate me as a sellout, but they can't. I won the game and I look too good.

I've been party-hopping and meeting people, including the very attractive actor Sal Mineo, who starred in several notable angry teenager films in the '50s. Sal has the Bent and has determined that I share it. Sal's tweaked on me; we run into each other; we talk on the phone, flirt, go out for coffee, but don't *do* it. Sal's very persistent, *and* he's a sweetheart, but my plate is too full to accommodate a part-time or full-time squeeze. It's funny. It's mindscape. I talk to Sal and hang up; Scotty calls five minutes later. Scotty took care of the Thornton/Bostitch brothers business with great panache and leaked a series of Intelligence Division files showing Mr. Clean to be, in fact, a mob stooge. Crusading journalists picked the story up; articles have appeared in Los Angeles and have gotten prominent nationwide ink. Scotty slanders our dead as we grasp for leads on our living. We've considered making an attempt to grab Thornton's Fed-snitch file, but Scotty thinks it's too risky. *I've* thought about trying for an independent look, but haven't figured out how.

I'm holding back Reggie in Haiti and *the Woman* as Joan. She's Dwight Holly's lover. That makes her unapproachable. Dwight Holly fucked with could blow our deal sky-high.

Mindscapes: feints, jabs, withholdings and deceptions.

I'm holding back from Scotty. I've made stabs at getting *full* customs files on Reginald Hazzard and have failed. Access requires legal warrants. My hold-backs are motivated by pure hubris and pure race hate. I learned some things from <u>OPERATION BAAAAAD BROTHER</u>. Kudos to Mr. Holly: I did, in part, transcend my self-serving actor's pathology. I *did* become radicalized.

Scotty Bennett represents the white world out to level me with indifference. I cannot let that be. Scotty is the white oppressor, and I will not knuckle down to him. Scotty will not split the money and emeralds. I must get to them first and kill Scotty before he kills me.

I've made three trips to Haiti. I've synced them to Scotty's boozy weeklong fishing trips with his cop pals. Sal had been to Haiti on a film shoot and shared his knowledge of that wondrous and atavistic place. I flew to Port-au-Prince. I toured Haiti as a middle-class, French-fluent black man. I displayed my Reggie Hazzard photograph and asked questions. I learned nothing substantive and smelled the obvious fact that Reginald had to be here.

Haiti was primitive and seductive. I felt like I was regressing. It was an actor's immersion process. I visited voodoo-sect taverns and drank klerin alcohol. I dreamt of armless men with wings. I attended a few voodoo ceremonies and ate handfuls of herbs. I came out of trances and found myself dancing with wooden-masked men. I awoke from an herb trip and saw that I had blood on my hands. The man in bed beside me said I had eaten a fresh-killed chicken.

My shape-shifting personality served me well in Haiti. I pretended to be a French tourist, which assisted me in my queries on Reginald. Nobody knew Reginald. Many people told me tales of the late Wayne Tedrow and his brave pro-Haitian acts. What would poor Wayne say to that? People walk around with photographs of him attached to their necks. I heard the story of Wayne's death twenty or thirty times. The details varied. Several people told me that winged men came for him. Wayne and I shared the dream-state concept. He related it to chemistry. It was all about fated souls in flux.

I've been to Haiti three times. I'll be back. Reginald Hazzard has to be there.

104

(Los Angeles, 3/15/71–11/18/71)

P*eeper.*

It's his old name and his new name re-discovered. Guys used to call him Dipshit and *pariguayo.* He asked Clyde about it. Clyde said, "You've been around awhile. People in The Life know you. There's rumors about you. Some guys believe them, some guys don't. If a handle sticks to you, you've got to figure there's some truth in it."

He let it go. He didn't mention his JFK/MLK/RFK hit knowledge. He didn't mention his Commie kills or his case. He didn't mention his nightmares or the shit he saw and did on that island.

Peeper—sure, it's true. Peeper—it's okay for now.

He tail-jobbed for Clyde and Chick Weiss. He entrapped cheating spouses. He kicked in doors and peered in windows.

Peeper, sure. Reader, too. Part-time student—that fits.

He read some more chemistry books and left-wing-theory books. He mixed a sulfur paste and blew up a street sign at 1st and Oxford. He learned about the Wobblies and the *L.A. Times* bombing. He mixed fertilizer paste and blew up a VIVA VIETNAM sign.

There was a dream movement inside of him. It was like he was becoming Reggie and Wayne.

He studied. He learned. He part-time Tiger-kabbed. He drove to Vegas and tried to find the Haitian herb man. The guy was gone. He asked around and found some other herb guys. None of them knew Reggie. They all knew how to cook herbs and induce wild shit.

They said they'd teach him. He spent two weeks in Vegas and learned tricks. They taught him how to mix toad organs and blowfish toxins.

They showed him how ferns and tree-frog livers caused heart attacks. He learned zombification. He mixed grand mal seizure potions. He learned some dope-trip formulas. He bought herbs, tubes and beakers. He learned some Kreole French.

He blew up a Nixon sign in East L.A. He popped herbs, drove around and peeped windows. He tried leapfrogging Dwight Holly again. Dwight lost him three times running. He lucked out on tail #4.

Dwight drove to a bungalow in Silver Lake. He perched and peeped. Dwight stayed inside for long stretches. Dwight took breaks and walked to a house down the street. A tall woman and two little girls lived there. A part-time hubby showed on occasion. He checked house-sale records and got the woman's name: Karen Sifakis.

He did more checking. He stiffed a call to Clyde. Clyde said Karen S. was a college prof and a Fed snitch. She was Big Dwight's lover. Big Dwight back-doored the hubby. It was going on five or six years.

He popped herbs and surveilled the bungalow. It was file-packed, like his pads. He thought about breaking in. He couldn't do it. The thought immobilized him. He'd learned all this new shit. It made him sit still and just *look*.

Then she was there.

She was older and more gray and even more fierce. Her glasses still fit crooked. Her slouchy walk was the same. He perched out of sight and watched her arrive for twenty days straight. He anticipated what she'd wear. Some days he saw her knife scar, some days he didn't. He still had the 6/14 scar on his back.

He watched her come and go. He started to get a sense of what it all meant.

He's the nexus of great and startling events. Nobody knows and nobody cares. He has linked a series of baffling crimes. Nobody knows and nobody cares. Scotty Bennett and Marsh Bowen killed Lionel Thornton and are chasing the armored-car swag. He knows this. Nobody else knows and nobody else cares.

Scotty distrusts Marsh. Scotty is levying a fruit squeeze. Sal cannot seduce Marsh. He knows this. Nobody else knows and nobody else cares.

Jack Leahy redacted Joan Rosen Klein's file. Nobody knows and nobody cares. He tailed Joan to Jack and surveilled three of their lunch dates. He hovered close by. He heard them discuss Celia, lost in the D.R. He heard the word *Haiti*. Reggie was living in Haiti. He sensed it quite strongly. Reggie sends out the emeralds. Nobody else knows and nobody else cares.

He's alone in his quests. Joan and Jack were in on the heist. He accepts that conclusion as fact. Marsh and Scotty know more and less than he does. He has worked this case for a very long time. It is all unprovable. His paper trials are logically inviolate and specious. It is all in his head.

The island terrifies him. He's afraid to go back. He might become that monster child again and lose everything he has.

He's a kid chemist and a kid Red now. He reads files and books and passes out in paper. His mother's file, Wayne's file, the file on "Tattoo." He gets lost in logical surety and inconsistency. Nobody knows how hard he works and nobody cares.

Tattoo wanted to meet film-biz men. He didn't know *who* she met. His suspect pool was large. Joan did not kill Tattoo. It consoled him. It allowed him to track her and live that much more with her.

Joan has lunch with Karen Sifakis. He observes them. He knows they share a love for Dwight Holly. They never mention Dwight. He's the third party hovering. Only peepers know how this works.

He follows Joan. He lives in the hope that she will lead him somewhere. It must justify all the time he has spent with her. She must do something or say something that will let him rest and give this all up.

I have been following you for three years, four months and twenty-nine days. I know you have a story you can only tell to me.

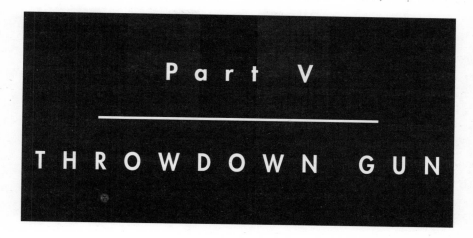

Part V

THROWDOWN GUN

November 18, 1971–March 26, 1972

105

(Puckett, 11/18/71)

"So, who'm I gonna kill?"

"You'll know him when you see him."

"You picked a date yet?"

"Next summer's our best shot. It has to happen in L.A."

"These political hits stir up lots of shit. Various patriotic groups get scrutinized pretty good."

The kampground was krowded. *Mi kasa es su kasa.* The Exalted Knights invited some kolleagues. Sleepover kamp. Klan klods, Cuban exiles, South American *fascistas.*

The bunkhouse was full. The gun range did brisk biz. The county sheriff dressed a four-point elk. His deputies built a cook pit.

Bob said, "You *want* the conspiracy talk. I'm just afraid my name'll pop up on the suspect list."

Dwight shook his head. "It won't. The fall guy's taking all the bows on this one. Nobody will want to look past him. We've built him from the ground up. The more you look, the more you'll want to keep looking."

Bob got sulky. He scooched low in his chair. His sheet brushed the dirt. It was mid-fall hot. Dusk came on. Exiles propped up arc lights. Some beat-on Klan frau prepped a buffet.

Dwight shut his eyes. It cued Bob to split. You're a loser assassin, please go away.

Bob meandered. Dwight opened his eyes. The kampsite was deklassé. His daddy's Klan was high-swank compared to this. Indiana, the '20s. Nativist gabfests and pyramid schemes. Eugenics readings. A ladies' string kwartet.

Full night hit. Bugs bombed the arc lights. The roast elk smelled good. The nuts hit the snack buffet for sour mash and Cheetos.

Dwight walked away from the party. The arc lights glowed wide and hot. The kampsite was dirt-floored. The Klan klowns mingled. Their sheets were soiled to the knees.

Joan worried him. She was haggard. She was chain-smoking and knocking back double scotches at night. She was vicious per Mr. Hoover. It was un-utilitarian and very un-Joan. She refused to explain her invective. She stonewalled his queries with looks and "I'm not telling you." It was frustrating. Their time frame was "insanely protracted." She knew Mr. Hoover was elderly and traveled far less. He had been somewhat discredited. He did fewer public gigs. Doctor's visits preempted his recent jaunts. The White House was telexing an updated schedule. Joan was worried about Celia. He stiffed an unscheduled call to the prez and requested help. Nixon rebuffed him. "You've been to that well, kid. You can't keep coming back."

Odd things moved her. Lionel Thornton's death stuck and held. She refused to say *why*. Scotty Bennett worked the case and closed the case, toot sweet. Scotty vaguely troubled him. Scotty had a tweaky friendship going with Marsh. Peeper Crutchfield reported it before the "Blastout." Marsh's life would be fine-tooth-combed postmortem. It begged a question: should they insert Scotty in the fake diary?

Flying bugs bombed the arc lights. The nuts ate, drank and ignored him. They knew he was FBI. Their bias was misdirected. They were punk punsters. FBI: Federal Bureau of *Integration*.

The diary defined the Operation. He worked on it while Joan or Karen slept. He utilized Marsh's verbal style and emphasized a political language he'd evolved in his head. He attributed his own childhood memories to Marsh. Alchemy and transposition. He was a sand-kicking Klan kid. Marsh was a sand-kicked-in-the-face black boy. He was building a sympathetic portrait. He was creating Marsh's non-existent crush on Agent Holly himself. It was distorting Marsh's work on OPERATION BAAAAAD BROTHER. He knew nothing of the Marsh-Scotty relationship. The diary must etch Scotty with verismo. The Scotty sections must withstand public scrutiny and Scotty's bellicose rebuttals. The theme should be authority. Marsh hates it ideologically, but cannot let it ago. He's like his old chum Mr. Holly that way.

The Klanfest picked up steam. Story fragments drifted over. Emmett Till was a Commie agent. Rosa Parks turned tricks for a Zionist cabal. Dr. King was a hermaphrodite.

A Klan tot brought Dwight food and a Jax lager. He thanked her and watched her skip off. Fat spritzed off the elk meat and killed his appetite. He lit a cigarette.

Joan kept taking the fertility pills. He never told her that he'd had them analyzed. She turned forty-five last month. It couldn't happen. He fucked with the notion, despite that. It was a pipe dream. It felt good for a while. It ran in shorter and shorter arcs. It reminded him what his life was. It took him to Karen's kids and dropped him somewhere cold in the rain.

Klan kliques pulled chairs up nearby him. They balanced paper plates and told tales. A guy sold Che Guevara's dick to Josef Mengele. The Fourth Reich would rise from Paraguay. A guy told a story of right-wing coups and mystic emeralds.

Joan drank tea in bed. The herbs flushed through her skin, bitter. He noticed new gray in her eyebrows.

Her robe was open. The herbs made her sweat. Dwight kissed the sheen off her breasts.

"Tell me what you're thinking."

"That I should relent. That you should call your phone pal and have him make some calls for Celia."

Dwight shook his head. "I called from Mississippi. He said no."

Joan rolled away from him. He pulled off their robes and curled around her. She put his fingers in her mouth for a second and tucked his hand under her head.

"It's all taking too long."

"He'll probably be in L.A. next summer. I'll be getting his revised schedule soon."

"Suppose he doesn't stay at the Beverly Wilshire?"

"He will. We'll have to lease the perch soon, and start laying in the evidence."

Joan coughed. "The black kid who leases it will be a witness."

"We'll work him through a cutout. If he comes forward, he'll be considered a nut. People want to crash history. There were four-thousand-odd false witnesses on Jack alone."

Her pillow was sweated through. Dwight pulled it out and tucked a fresh one under her head.

Joan grabbed a capsule off her nightstand. Dwight passed her his water glass.

She swallowed the capsule. Her hair was wet. Dwight stroked it dry with a bedsheet.

She started dozing. She fell asleep tucked into his hand.

. . .

He worked late. Midnight meant Marsh-as-me time. He recalled a cop barter, 1953. Cleveland PD wanted a Fed file. A grand larceny suspect was Red-tinged. The SAC refused a file trade. The PD sent a cop's ex-wife to lube the Enforcer. She liked random men. He liked random women then. They spent the night at the Shaker Heights Plaza. She brought champagne. He brought the file. They enjoyed each other. She read the file in the morning. Cleveland PD nailed the guy—six-count indictment.

Okay, now—Marsh Bowen's perspective.

The time was now. Marsh is working the Hollywood night car. He's alone. He's trolling. Marsh shits where he eats. He spots a hunky male prosty. He pat-searches him and gets a hard-on. The prosty notices it.

Marsh F.I.-cards the kid and warrant-checks him. He comes back dirty: possession and deuce. Marsh says, "How do you want to handle this?" Fade to the crude back-alley embrace.

He couldn't sleep. Joan was dead out. Marsh was sleeping over in Ventura. The Black Leadership Council brought him up. Keynote speech: "The Minority Officer's Role in Team Policing."

It was 2:14 a.m. He got in with tungsten bolt-snaps and wore infrared shades. He carried his Minox mini. He prowled in rose-tinted dark.

He opened drawers and tapped panels. He got status quo. He scanned the bedroom walls. Marsh had a new Rothko print. He checked the stereo rack. New sides by Chet Baker and the Dresden Stattskapelle. He checked the kitchen trash. Marsh had a new yen for gourmet TV dinners. There's an airline boarding ticket. Marsh recently traveled to Port-au-Prince, Haiti. Educated guess: he shits *out* of harms way. Afro fruit retreat.

Dwight walked back to the living room. More status quo. The steel-brushed frames, the neat work desk, the address book by the phone.

He skimmed the pages. Ah, at *B:* Scotty's home and work numbers. He skimmed *C* to *M*. Ah, there's a new one.

Sal Mineo. A West Hollywood–prefix listing.

Logical: Sal's a fag, Sal's a horndog, Sal's got a well-traveled chute.

But:

He deployed Sal in a fruit squeeze, four-plus years ago. He saw Sal's name on a Bureau snitch roster.

Status quo? Probably, but—

One agent dozed in the squadroom. The file keys were hooked to a corkboard. Dwight grabbed them and walked straight back.

The CBI files were five-digit-coded and ran ceiling high. Dwight skimmed the directory. There: "Mineo, Salvatore"/02108. There: third shelf up, two rows over.

Dwight unlocked the panel, stood on his tiptoes and snagged it. It was skimpy. Four pages total. Simple narrative gist.

August, '66. Sal's got a co-star gig. He's the sidekick in a crime turkey. It's called *Southside Crackdown*. It plays low-rung drive-in circuits and disappears. It's loosely based on the famous 1964 heist.

So far—snore.

Jack Leahy visits the set. Jack braces Sal and the rest of the actors and crew. Suspicious guys loitering? Suspicious queries on the real-life heist?

Sal knew *buppkes*. Ditto everyone else. Jack charmed Sal and popped his snitch cherry. Sal ratted out queer actors for occasional chump change.

Snore, yawn, status quo—but don't dismiss it yet.

Dwight stood there. Dwight heard a whole box of pins drop.

The Bureau worked the heist *for ten seconds*. It was LAPD's case and Scotty B.'s fixation. Scotty and Marsh, tight now. The heist: Clyde Duber's soft-line fixation. Marsh worked for Clyde. Scotty grilled Jomo C. about the heist. It made no sense then. It might make sense now. Jomo killed Fred Hiltz, Jomo's a heister. There's Joan hovering. She false-snitched Jomo. She ratted Marsh's fruitness. What do Marsh and Scotty want? Red file tab, red flag. The Marsh-Scotty bond must not impede the Operation.

Dwight put the file back. The pin drop went to pins and needles.

Sicko Sal never slept. He closed fruit bars and debriefed in coffee shops. His milieu was the pre-dawn hen party. The fry cook at the Klondike said try Arthur J.'s.

Dwight bombed over. Sodomy Sal was ensconced with three trannies. He was tattling. I browned James Dean on *Rebel Without a Cause*. He was hung like a light switch. I packed him the pork till he squealed.

The trannies tittered. Salacious Sal ragged on Rock Hudson. He was hung like a microbe. I tickled his tonsils till he trilled.

Dwight loomed by the table. The trannies gulped and get-awayed. They left their coffee and pancakes. Dwight helped himself.

Sal fondled his spit curl. "Hello, Mr. Holly."

"What's shaking, Sal?"

"Not you again, I hope."

Dwight poured coffee. "Nothing like that."

"No entrapment? No victimizing some poor champion of social justice who just happens to dig boys?"

Dwight wiped lipstick off his coffee cup. "Summer '66. You were working on *Southside Crackdown*. Jack Leahy came around with some questions."

Sal buttered his hash browns. "So? We're dealing with ancient history. That flick was a loser. I had to sue to get my per diem."

"You started informing for Jack."

"Well . . ."

Dwight snagged a bread stick and scratched his neck. Redd Foxx and that shyster fuck Chick Weiss walked in. A Tiger Kab geek propped them up.

"So, I'm assuming there's more to the story. 'Jack Leahy came around.' You take it from there."

Sal shrugged. "So, another cop comes around, asking the same kind of questions."

Dwight said, "Scotty Bennett?"

Sal rolled his eyes. "Oh, yes. Scotty."

Dwight snapped the bread stick. "Let me drop a name on you. I want to see how you react."

"It's a little *early* for name games, but I'll play."

Dwight said, "Marshall Bowen." Servile Sal seized up and queased up. Oh, yeah—he's green at the gills.

"Tell me about it."

Sal fucked with his spit curl. "Why should I?"

"I'll buy you breakfast if you do. I'll hang stat rape on you if you don't. There's a perv honking boys at Berendo Junior High. You match the description."

Sal popped a Valium and coffee-chased it. Sal took a get-it-over-with breath.

"Okay, sweetie. I've got another fruit shake going. Freddy O. recruited me. A cop's bankrolling it, but I don't know his name. Bowen's the mark, but I *cannot* get him to loosen his wig and rock 'n' roll with me. Some guys are just like that. I'm *dying* to give up some prime slash, but the boy just will not bite."

Scotty B. Marsh. Running ubiquitous now.

"Who else is in on it?"

"Fred T.'s the bug man. The charmless Peeper Crutchfield is watchdogging me."

"Bowen. What's going on there?"

Sal rolled his eyes. Sal tossed his spit curl. Sal did fag exasperation shtick.

"He just won't *biiiiite*. I've got plenty to bite onto, but he just *woooooooon't*. It's *craaaaazy*. Marsh is sure-as-shit gay, but he just won't *plaaay.* He's *sooooo* weird. He just sits there or runs all these weird riffs on *Haiti,* of all fucking places."

Dwight rubbed his eyes. His feelers twitched. More pins dropped, more pins stuck and held.

Okay, Jack Leahy. He knows about Marsh and BAAAAAD BROTHER. Jack's tweaked on Mr. Hoover. It's untoward and impolitic. He just B&E'd Marsh Bowen's pad. He saw plane tix to *Haiti.* Joan's *Haitian* herbs. The recent shit in the D.R. and *Haiti.* Celia's there. Peeper Crutchfield *was* there. The persistent Peeper rumor: he's searching for some runaway woman. She bilks men. She may have *Red* ties. Peeper's a loser, let him do his own thing.

Tie-in: Celia as the bilker. Toss the net, take the leap. Wider now, say it.

Joan's 211 background. The things she won't say. Wider, now: Jack redacted Joan's file. They were in on the armored-car heist.

A rainstorm hit. The windows drummed. Raindrop-pins fell. Three drag queens walked in. They wore soaked-through prom dresses. Their chest hair showed. They saw Sal and waved. They saw Dwight and ran away.

Sal pouted. Sal scolded Dwight with his fork.

"Mr. Holly, you are fucking with my love life."

106

(Los Angeles, 11/22/71)

The bar TV blared. America mourns JFK, eight loss-looped years later. We were innocent then. The world hates us now.

Scotty signaled the barman. The barman switched channels. Bucky Beaver huckstered Ipana toothpaste. Scotty resignaled the barman. The barman pulled the plug.

Marsh said, "You're fried, brother. Go out and waste a few heist guys. You'll feel better then."

The Kibitz Room at Canter's Deli. The 6:00 p.m. clientele: alky hebes bopping home from shul.

Scotty lit a cigarette, took two hits and snuffed it. Scotty ate a bite of kreplach and pushed his plate back.

"We keep hitting dead ends."

"Scotty, it's over. The bank examiners got the vault stash, and they're not letting on. We can't find Reggie, we can't find the emeralds, and there's nothing more we can do."

"*It's not over.* We've got to find the woman. We brace her, she'll talk, we'll take it from there."

Marsh shook his head. Condescending, patronizing, noble-negro shit.

"You check steamship companies. You go through their work passage lists. You work it from spring '64 through the end of the year. You work every major port and overseas destination. You fucking do it, and you fucking do it now."

107

(Los Angeles, 11/26/71)

A box arrived at the Vivian. It was parcel-posted Las Vegas. The contents rattled. It weighed a fucking ton.

He paid off the postman and lugged it inside. Return address: Mary Beth Hazzard, P.O. Box 19. An envelope taped on.

Fuck—she answered his queries. Fuck—she found more—

He opened it up. Mary Beth Hazzard wrote:

Mr. Crutchfield,

A police officer in Cleveland, Ohio, sent this in response to one of Wayne's numerous queries. It is an updated FBI file on a woman named Klein that Wayne was suspicious of. As you can see, apart from the heading and various routing numbers, the actual text has been blacked out. Wayne told me that he had had very limited success in chemically stripping ink, but I have included the tools and chemicals he told me he used.

My best to you,
M.B.H.

The file was updated: 12/8/68. <u>SUBJECT KLEIN, JOAN ROSEN,</u> routine numbers, adios. Six full redacted-ink pages.

One file. Sent to a dead man. The fucking genius chemist: "Very limited success."

And a spectroscope.

And a fluoroscope.

And high-pH hydroxic acid.

And Wayne's notes on contrasting-ray bombardment.

He laid everything out. He skimmed his chem books and got proportion stats on hydroxic acid. He got zilch on spectroscopes and fluoroscopes. He hooked the gizmos up to a wall plug and positioned them on his desk. He grabbed some Q-tips and put on rubber gloves. He laid out the inked pages.

He hit the On switches. Blue and pink lights beamed. *"Bombardment"*—huh?—you mean mix and match?

He tried it. He craned the gizmos and let the beams crisscross. The first four times, it blackened the black. The second two times, it lightened the black. He dabbed *smiiiiidgens* of hydroxic acid on the lighter ink. It burned the paper through to his desk.

Re-adjust the beams. Dab the dark ink now.

He did that. He dabbed heavy, he dabbed light. He burned the paper through to his desk.

He stopped. *Deep breath now.* He tried the blue-beam gizmo and heavy dabs. He burned the paper through to his desk. Let's start over. He tried the pink-beam gizmo and light dabs. He burned the paper through to his desk.

His hand jerked. The bottle fell. Acid spilled out. Four full pages burned through to his desk.

Start over. Deep breath now. Brother Wayne, I'm trying. We've got two pages left.

He blotted up the acid spill. He crisscrossed the beams again. He got *all* lighter-type lines. He dabbed them *exxxtra light.*

The paper sizzled and bubbled. The lines burned all the way through to his desk.

Last page.

His desk was burn-scarred. He toweled it off. He centered the page. He futzed with the beams. He got some all-new pink-blue hybrid. He got dark-ink lines and light-ink lines and saw something else.

Little typewriter marks. Right there under the ink.

He squinted at them. He got his magnifying glass and held it down close. He couldn't make out the ink-covered words.

Deep breath now. Don't dab, daub, burn, scald, scorch just yet.

Yes, try this.

He walked into the kitchen. He emptied out a spritz bottle of Windex window spray. He rinsed the inside with mild detergent. He let it dry. He carried it into the living room and placed it on his desk.

He poured in the hydroxic acid. He screwed on the top. He test-spritzed the acid and got a fine mist.

The air stung his eyes. He let the mist dissipate. He centered the page under the pink-and-blue beams. He *very lightly* sprayed the ink lines, top to bottom. The ink dissolved in random streaks. He saw words and word fragments underneath.

"SUBJECT JOAN ROS"/"has dep"/"various ident"/"Williamson, Margaret Susan/Broward, Sharon/Goldenson, Rochelle/Faust, Laura"/"B," "D," "L," "Q," "A," smudged word stew.

"Suspected of participation"/"payroll," smudges, "eries," "since 194," "donated," smudges, "wing causes."

"SUBJECT JOAN ROSEN KLEIN," parenthesis, smudges, parenthesis. "Celia Reyes, aka Gretchen Farr"/"6/14 Movement," smudges and blurred text. "As of this (12/8/68) writing SUBJECT REYES-FARR reported by CBIs to be searching for assumed killer of Dominican-Haitian woman known as 'Tattoo' (no real surname known) allegedly missing in Los Angeles since summer '68. Also reports that SUBJECT REYES-FARR enlisted aid of (assumed black militant) LEANDER JAMES JACKSON in this venture."

"SUBJECT," smudges, "EIN," "susp," "rev," smudges, "ment," "Algeria," "Palest," "Carrib."

Oh, shit. There's full lines. Addresses in Spanish. Safe houses in the D.R.

"One persistent rum," smudges, "alleg," "seeking to interdict a flow of contraband emeralds rumored to have financed," smudges, smudges, "coups."

The print started fading.

He lost letters and whole words A sentence blurred to white. He blinked. He rubbed his eyes. He lost a whole paragraph. He lost the word "JOAN."

He sprayed the page. He sprayed too hard. The mist came out a gush. Words vanished. The air burned. The page went aflame.

108

(Los Angeles, 11/26/71)

The plane rolled in. Dwight had a crimped center seat. Dogdick, Mississippi, and back in seventeen hours.

The trip was ad-lib. Bob Relyea threw a fit. Dwight, a man likes to know who he's killin'. Bob, I ain't sayin'. Here's five grand. Go push some hate tracts and clout some pharmacies.

The gate was by the parking lot. Dwight deplaned, got his car and cut for the freeway. It was 9:16 p.m. Joan was at the fallback. Marsh was in Oxnard. The Black Pride Caucus invited him. That Brother Bowen—he can speechify.

Dwight swung over to La Cienega and climbed the Stocker Pass. He was frayed. His bad nerves and bad sleep had reprised. The Sal Mineo deal head-slapped him. He hadn't seen Joan since then. They hadn't talked at all. He was full-court-pressing. The prez was sending a Hoover travel update. He had to go to D.C. Nixon wanted a black-bag summit. The Enforcer and Howard Hunt, old Agency hand. Karen and her kids would be there then. Show the girls some monuments. Teach them explosives later.

The Joan/Jack Leahy theory torqued him. His first Joan suspicion: she's got a Fed friend. Three years later, he *tenuously knows.*

Peeper Crutchfield torqued him. The meddlesome little cocksucker. Fucking prescient and super-human persistent. *They let him live.* He knew everything *then.* Who knew what he knew *now?*

The big issue: convergence. The sub-issue: the Marsh-Scotty bond. The big question: does the fruit shake mean we abort?

Dwight chased three aspirin with coffee. Auspicious: his first migraine since Silver Hill.

The bolt slides always worked. The oil coating never left tool marks. His shades supplied haunted-house light.

Dwight locked the door behind him. The living room smelled ripe. Incense dregs lingered. Marsh splurged on a new Kandinsky. It fucked up the north-wall symmetry.

Dwight prowled. It was B&E #6,000. Futile repetition cop work—he loved that shit.

He tapped panels, he opened drawers, he reached under couches and rugs. He saw dust leak from a ceiling beam. The beam was smooth-finished. That shouldn't be.

He pulled a chair over and stood on it. He squinted. He saw faint markings on one side of the beam. The dust leaked from a near-invisible seam.

He pushed against it. The wood piece opened inward. A tiny hinge and runner squeaked. The door was near invisible and rectangular. The dimensions were eight by ten.

Paper scent. Right off—the very first thing.

He reached in. It was leather-bound. Stylish Marsh—raw-cut pages.

He pulled it out and stepped off the chair. He prepped his Minox. He carried it to Marsh's desk and read.

He *knew* Marsh. The diary confirmed it straight off. Their narrative styles were similar. They both knew how smart they were. They both had the same dry wit. They both worshiped ruthlessness. Marsh was new to it and in awe of it. Oh, you kid. Oh, my brother. You don't know what it costs.

It was 10:21. He had twelve rolls of film. He could shoot most of the text.

It was cumbersome. Fold the pages, aim the camera, shoot. He got in close and read as he snapped. It was all there. It was his world and Brother Bowen's world combined.

The heist as Holy Grail. His kid crush on D. C. Holly. His duplicitous union with Scotty B. Wayne Tedrow and long-lost Reggie. Reggie as heist survivor and emerald conduit. The Lionel Thornton snuff. The three Haiti trips. Marsh ID's Joan as the Woman. He withholds it from Scotty.

He shot seventy-three pages. He ran out of film. He memorized most of the text. He replaced the diary and cleaned up the dust. He left the room pristine.

His migraine was gone. The Operation was in jeopardy. He felt calm and light and something else.

The fallback was dark. Joan was out. Karen played the *Grosse Fuge* at full volume. He walked to the terrace. Karen's bathroom light was on. The music roared from a bright little square.

The darkroom was fully equipped. Joan developed film better than he did. He knew the basic drill. He red-lit the space, filled the trays and unfurled his film rolls. It was four full hours' work.

He cut film strips, dunked them and pinned them up. He watched words on paper appear. He took a break and called Peeper. The punk never got a word in. He dropped hints about emeralds, Joan Klein and the heist. *Do nothing, Dipshit. Do you understand?*

Peeper gulped and said, "Yes." Dwight went back to work.

He finished the film dunks. He clotheslined all the photos and let them drip dry. He pulled them and carried them into the living room.

Let's create a narrative. Let's expose it eye level. Let's shape a scan-and-read.

He pinned the photos. It told Marsh's story and their story. He told it in three around-the-wall strips.

The photos were slightly dark and buckled. It didn't matter. The living room lights were fine.

He walked out to the terrace. Karen's bedroom light was still on. He trained his binoculars. Dina ran into the room, crying. Karen picked her up and held her. Dear child, bad dream.

The lights went out. He waited for the bathroom light and more music. He didn't get it. Skyscraper lights blinked downtown.

A key went in the front-door lock. The door swept and slammed. Her footfalls were too light. She didn't hurl her handbag.

He waited. He scanned the sky and saw City Hall. It was '51. LAPD was headquartered there. He saw a young cop manhandle a suspect. Six-five, crew cut—Scotty B. presaged.

He saw her shadow and smelled her hair. He leaned into the terrace rail. She walked up and leaned into him.

"I haven't ever lied to you or betrayed you."

"I know that."

"Marsh has put a good deal of it together."

Dwight turned toward her. She embraced him. His chin brushed the top of her head.

"I recruited Reginald Hazzard. Jack and I have been friends for many years. We planned the robbery together. Reginald has been in Haiti for a very long time."

Dwight touched her hair. Last week's black was gray and gray was white.

"The heist gives this a whole new dimension. Scotty knows that Marsh is not the lone-assassin type. It's a level of scrutiny we can't afford. Scotty will know that we're behind it in a heartbeat."

Joan said, "I disagree."

Dwight shook his head. "They're shafting each other. Scotty's pulling a sex shakedown on Marsh. Marsh knows your name and knows that you were my informant. They killed Lionel Thornton. Marsh is not going to walk into a sniper's perch with all this going on."

Joan said, "I disagree." Dwight balled his fists. Joan cupped them and placed them on her chest.

"It densifies every level of our subtext. It indicts Scotty Bennett and facilitates the need for an LAPD cover-up, which will extend the paper trail and greatly increase the degree of public exposure. We can combine the diaries. We can remove the references to Jack Leahy, Reginald Hazzard and me. We can edit out the references to Lionel Thornton, so that his people don't get hurt. Think of this as a social document that unfailingly takes us back to Mr. Hoover and every evil thing that he's done. The heist will muddy the trail and enhance the overall readership and scholarship. The Bennett-Bowen friendship explicates every point about hatred and greed that I've ever wanted to make."

Dwight pulled away. Karen's bathroom light went on. He strained his ears. No music played.

"Tell me about Lionel Thornton."

"He was a comrade of sorts."

"He laundered the money for you and Jack."

"Yes."

"Jack went in with the bank examiners. He got the basic sum out beforehand. He left some money behind to be found."

Joan said, "Yes, you've got all of it, but there's the thing you haven't said and the question you haven't asked."

Dwight looked at her. "I don't blame you for any of it. Given what I've done, I simply can't."

"And the question?"

"The question is, 'Who got the money?' The answer is, 'It's all been going to the Cause.' "

The music started low. Dissonant strings. It was very late. She wanted them to hear it soft.

Joan said, "I don't want to lose this."

Dwight strained for the music. A low wind obscured it.

"Marsh knows about you, Scotty *could* learn about you. You'd be in danger then, and your name would be revealed in the end."

Joan shook her head. "Scotty doesn't know about me. Marsh won't tell him or anyone else. He's a greedy, covetous little man. He wants everything for himself. *You* saw the diary pages. No one else did. I'll be kept out of it, and no one will believe anything that Scotty says about you. He's the faggot nigger's white cop buddy, and you're the government's star witness who cracked up and has to confess."

Dwight brushed tears from his eyes. Joan squeezed his hands, white-knuckled.

"Tell me what Mr. Hoover did to you."

Joan said, "No. I'm not going to."

DOCUMENT INSERT: 12/3/71. Telex communiqué. Marked: "Access Code 1-A/Recipient's Eyes Only. Destroy Upon Reading." To: SA Dwight C. Holly. From: Travel-Scheduling Office, Central Communications Center, Washington, D.C.

Sir,

Per your last telephone request, please be informed that SUB-JECT'S travel schedule has been reduced, due to recent recurrences of poor health. As of this date, SUBJECT will be traveling to Miami on 4/14/72, Cleveland on 5/5/72 and Los Angeles on 6/10/72. Any changes or updates will follow, per your request. As always, please destroy upon reading.

DOCUMENT INSERT: 12/4/71. Official FBI telephone call transcript. Marked: "Recorded at the Director's Request/Classified Confidential 1-A. Director's Eyes Only." Speaking: Director Hoover, Special Agent Dwight C. Holly.

JEH: Good morning, Dwight.
DH: Good morning, Sir.
JEH: (Coughing fit: twelve seconds.)
DH: Good morning, Sir.
JEH: Don't repeat yourself.
DH: Yes, Sir.
JEH: I don't know why I continue to talk to you.
DH: Yes, Sir.
JEH: Stop repeating yourself. I'm not senile. I'm in perfect health.
DH: Yes, Sir.
JEH: You did it again. Stop it. I'm telling you not to respond. (Silence: fifty-three seconds.)
JEH: Slippery Dick asked me to black-bag the Watergate Hotel. I declined. I'll keep my job as long as I string him along. I'm a cock-tease. I'm stringing that cocksucker along. He called me a sissy. He called my hemorrhoid surgery a "hysterectomy."
(Coughing fit: nine seconds.)

JEH: I've got a file on Slippery Dick. He called me a sissy. My basement is reinforced with Kryptonite. No file thief on earth could break in.

(Coughing fit: sixteen seconds/phone transcript terminates here.)

109

(Los Angeles, 12/5/71)

"Sal, you're a cute side of beef. Why can't you land this chump in the sack?"

Fruit squeeze summit #2. Sergeant Robert S. Bennett, presiding. Also there: Sal, Fred O., Peeper Crutchfield.

"Listen, there's guys who just won't bite. Sometimes they're Little-Miss-Hard-To-Get, sometimes they just don't crave stick."

The Silver Star on Western. Scotty dined gratis there. The owner was stickup-prone. He called Scotty direct.

A waiter served gin fizzes and pretzels. Their booth faced the door. Scotty insisted. He knew faces quicksville. He had cop total recall.

Fred O. picked a hangnail. Peeper scratched his balls. Silky Sal was depressed. He was a coal burner. He craved Marsh's deep mine shaft.

The waiter split. Sal said, "I met you before, Sergeant. It was on this movie shoot."

"I know. *Southside Crackdown.* I took my kids to see it. My daughter had the hots for you. I told her, 'That guy's a fruit fly, you're shit out of luck.' "

Sal yukked. Fred yukked. Peeper did not. Peeper was always off in his head. Yonder windows loomed.

Scotty snarfed pretzels. "Lay it on me. Why won't this stupe come around?"

Sal shrugged. "Marshey's a tough nut. He's got his tight little world all figured out, and he doesn't appreciate interruptions. He's got his cop thing and his speech thing and his art thing. And now all he talks about are these trips he took to Haiti."

Hel-lo.

Softball. Easy lob, easy catch. Marsh was holding back. Haiti adjoined the D.R. The emeralds shipped from there. Haiti meant Reggie and the stones.

Sissy Sal blathered. Scotty tuned him out. Peeper fidgeted. Note the sweaty hands and neck.

Scotty chugalugged his drink. "You keep pressing, Sal. I'll get you some Quaaludes. A little Soul Train on the stereo and va-va-va-voom."

Sal tee-heed. "It's not like *I* don't want it. Marshey is a stone fox. I call him 'the African Queen.' "

Fred O. clutched his belly. Peeper howled out loud. Pretzel gack flew.

Scotty said, "This is all between us white men. You cannot go to Dwight Holly. This is *our* fruit shake. *His* fruit shake is old news."

Hel-lo.

Sal flushed at "Dwight Holly." Peeper residual twitched.

Sal twirled his spit curl. "I only saw Mr. Holly way back when. *My* Fed guy was always Jack Leahy. He was bugging me with questions on *Southside Crackdown.* Remember, Sergeant? You were, too. Armored-car heist this, armored-car heist that, as if this girl would know *anything* about that kind of action."

Hel-lo.

Peeper blinked at "Leahy." Peeper blinked at "heist." There's Peeper's darty eyes and light sweat.

Scotty glared at Sal. Sal wet his lips and smirked. Fred O. picked his hangnail. The charged air whizzed by *him.* Peeper gulped and *re*gulped. His Adam's apple did the Frug and the Peppermint Twist.

Scotty walked to the can. The cold tiles beckoned. He leaned his head on the wall. Okay, okay, okay—let's logic this out.

Leahy. Heist questions *then.* Peoples' Bank ruckus *now.* Jack went in with the bank team. He was in on the heist. He's got the big money now.

"Haiti" meant Marsh goes.

110

(Los Angeles, 12/5/71)

Dashboard frieze: all-new photos. His ink-scorch spree got him one hot lead and four fake IDs. He tracked the names to mug-shot numbers. He got four new Joans.

Williamson, Goldenson, Broward and Faust. Joan in 1949. Joan three, five and seven years later.

She's younger, she's darker-haired, she's still short of fierce. She's always defiant. She's blinky-eyed sans glasses. Her shoulders are smoother. Her jaw hasn't set in as harsh.

Crutch stared at the pictures. The summit just concluded. He tracked Scotty's brain waves. Scotty picked up on Haiti and Marsh.

He kicked the key and cruised south. Clyde had work. He had Tiger Kab gigs. His case was breaking out and breaking back in on him.

Dwight Holly called and warned him. Do nothing, Dipshit. Celia was looking for Tattoo's killer, just like him. Scotty was going after Marsh, post-fucking-haste.

He drove through Hancock Park. He daylight-peeped windows. There was no kick extant.

Christmas was coming. His mother would send a postcard and a five-spot. He'd buy Dana Lund a gift.

He drove by the wheelman lot. Phil Irwin and Buzz Duber waved. Chick Weiss pawed a mulatto whore.

The babe limped to the service bay. Mud-shark Chick scowled at her. Crutch pulled up and idled. Chick leaned in the car.

"You look blue, boychik. You should join Voyeurs Anonymous."

"Fuck your mother."

"I tried to once. She rejected me and packed me off to law school."

A warm wind kicked on. Crutch aimed the AC vent at his balls.

"Get me a rope job."

Chick said, "Nix. Phil's my guy. I've got that donkey-dick Filipino on retainer, so I can't stretch my overhead to accommodate your ennui."

Crutch laughed. Chick said, "Get out of here. Do something dumb and brave, so the world will think you get laid."

He drove by Tiger Kab. LAPD had some jail trustys there. They wore tiger-striped jumpsuits. They did coerced wash-and-wax jobs. Redd Foxx served them soul-food plates.

He was avoiding it. He couldn't just let it go.

Milt C. saw him and waved. Junkie Monkey waved one paw. Crutch waved back and cut west to Stocker.

The pad was nice. Baldwin Hills was top-end colored. Ray Charles and Lou Rawls lived down the street. He Tiger-kabbed them both.

Crutch got out and rang the doorbell. Marsh Bowen opened up. He was in uniform. His Medal of Valor pin glowed.

Marsh did a double take. Oh, yeah—Clyde Duber's kid.

Crutch said, "Scotty knows you went to Haiti. I think you'd better run."

111

(Washington, D.C., 12/7/71)

Harvey's was packed. He waited at the bar. Howard Hunt was late. The lunch crowd table-hopped.

Ted Kennedy and John Mitchell. Veep Agnew with a multi-table joke. Dwight caught fragments. A lion was fucking a zebra, ha ha.

He was jet-lagged and up-for-days shot. He had lunch with Jack Leahy yesterday. It was nails-on-blackboard raw. They did not discuss the Operation. Joan told him about it. He approved of it and wanted it. His looks signaled sanction. That much was clear.

Jack came to talk—his terms solely. He said he went back with Joan. He said he got the money out. They did not discuss the heist. Jack said he hated Hoover like Joan did. Dwight asked him why. Jack said, "I'm not telling you."

Hunt was late. It pissed him off. Karen and the kids were here. Dwight sipped coffee and scanned the restaurant. Ronald Reagan walked in. He got ooohs, aaaahs and jeers.

He'd worked three days straight with Joan. They combined the fake-diary excerpts with Marsh's real-life text. It was now seamless. They deleted the Lionel Thornton murder. It would throw huge heat on Scotty and induce him to talk. The omission might convince him to stay silent. Joan had been close to Lionel Thornton. The omission would spare his family.

The new text revealed Marsh's heist fixation. He partnered up with the equally fixated Scotty and pursued fruitless leads. Marsh was now all greed and perversion. He came to political grievance late. He was pawn and puppetmaster. His psyche had disarticulated sixteen million ways. Cops took him in and gave him an identity. Cops told him to retain it while he assumed an antithetical one. The search for the money and emeralds went nowhere. He didn't know who he was, where he was or what to do. He decided to kill a public figure to make it all click.

Howard Hunt walked in. Dwight waved him over. The barman saw him and built a martini.

He took two sips and packed a pipe. He cleaned his glasses with his necktie.

"I can't stay for lunch."

"I didn't expect you to."

"It's warm out. The spring's going to be a bear."

Dwight passed him an envelope. Hunt palmed it and lit his pipe.

"So?"

"This summer. The Watergate. Your call on the exact timing and the personnel."

"The old girl turned him down. I've heard rumors."

"The Man likes me. Let's leave it at that."

Hunt drained his martini. "You're in charge?"

Dwight shook his head. "Look in the envelope. There's a drop-phone you can call. The Man has a thing for Cubans. You've been here before. It's all drops, cutouts and flash paper. I'm walking away from it now."

Hunt put down a five-spot. Dwight handed it back.

"It's on me."

"Dwight 'the Enforcer.' Ever the gent."

"Nice seeing you, Howard."

Hunt put on a golf cap and walked outside. The door swung wide. Sunshine hit the bar and the table floor. Two big guys ushered in a frail old man.

He shuffled. His clothes fell off him. His glasses slipped down his nose. Liver spots, palsy, slack neck. Half-inch mincing steps.

The old man looked over and saw him. He had filmy dark brown eyes. Nothing clicked outward. Dwight blinked and refocused. Mr. Hoover dead-eye stared.

The bodyguards eased him to a table. It took three minutes to walk fifteen yards. He looked around the restaurant, unfocused. Nobody noticed him. People table-hopped around him. A waiter brought pre-cooked food out.

Dwight had him head-on. A short space stood between them. He stepped away from the bar. He built a big, simple frame.

Mr. Hoover looked over. Dwight waved. Mr. Hoover stayed blank.

One bodyguard cut up his steak. One bodyguard fed him. Ted Kennedy noticed him and looked away. Ronald Reagan smiled and waved his way. Mr. Hoover dead-eyed it. Saliva dripped down his chin.

Dwight walked three steps closer. It built a clearer frame. Mr. Hoover coughed. Saliva pooled on his plate. A waiter pounced and snatched it. Dwight stepped forward. He hovered now. Mr. Hoover was very close. He looked straight at Dwight and never saw him.

The girls skipped around the monument. Dwight and Karen held hands on a bench.

"Have you told them Washington was the father of our country?"

Karen smiled. "Your American history is not my American history."

"I might dispute that now."

"Given recent events, I might concede the point."

The lawn was full of nannies with strollers and kids kicking balls. A little boy saw Dwight's belt gun and grinned.

Karen said, "We've been together for seven years."

"I know. You'll be forty-seven in February."

"Take me somewhere for a weekend. I'm bracing myself all the time. You're doing something irreparable. I want a few moments with you first."

Dwight tucked a knee up and faced her. Karen looked at him. He held her face. Some tears rolled. He brushed them off with his thumbs.

"I'm not doing it."

Karen leaned away from him. Her tears rolled crazy. She took off her sweater and blotted her eyes.

The mauve cashmere cardigan. His first Christmas gift. She'd said, "What? You didn't buy me *red*?"

"Why?"

Dwight said, "Nobody dies."

He had a big suite at the Willard. Bureau-vouchered digs. The bathroom featured a walk-in shower.

Room service sent up a bottle of bourbon. It made him salivate. He carried his briefcase and the jug into the bathroom. He dumped the diary pages in the shower and poured the bourbon on top.

He lit a match and dropped it. The shower stall contained the blaze. He let the flames leap way up.

The nozzle dangled outside the stall. He kicked on the water and sprayed it all out. The pages crackled down to black muck.

A wall phone was clamped above the toilet. Dwight dialed the fallback direct. He got three rings and "Yes?"

"We're pulling out. I can't do it."

Joan said, "No," and hung up.

DOCUMENT INSERT: 12/8/71–1/17/72. Extract from the journal
of Marshall E. Bowen

I always know when something has ended. I opened my door,
saw that silly boy on my porch and realized that many threads of
my life had fully run their course. I did not ask him to elaborate
on his statement; I did not tell him that I had glimpsed him here
and there enough to know that he had to be a deft surveillance
artist with considerable knowledge of me. His car was parked in
my driveway. I walked over to grab the day's newspaper off my
lawn and saw that the boy had photographs of Joan Rosen Klein
taped to the dashboard. In that instant, I knew: it is over.

He drove off. I grabbed my journal from its hiding place, liquidated my bank account, packed a bag and flew here. I doubted that
Scotty would come here or risk exposure of our many crimes by
siccing the LAPD on me. Instinct told me that the money was in
Los Angeles and Reginald and the emeralds were here. Thus, I got
on an airplane and flew to Port-au-Prince.

It is very black. I am a French-fluent black man, an American,
a policeman. I have the gifted actor's flair for assimilating language. I could never pass myself off as purely Haitian, but I have
become proficient in Kreole French. Native people feel honored
when foreign rubes attempt to speak their tongue and actually
succeed at it. My proficiency and natural charm have given me
carte blanche to indulge and observe.

I travel by foot and bicycle and stay in small hotels. I ask questions about Reginald Hazzard in French and English wherever I go.
I describe the young black man with the burn-scarred face; I sometimes display my police credentials. Many people recall having
seen Reginald, but no one knows where he is. I have all the time
in the world to find him. I am not going back to America.

The Tonton Macoute has surveilled me on many occasions and
has interrogated me four times. My American-cop status flum-
moxes them. They are *all* rogue cops and sense that I am one, as
well. They have seen me distribute cash for tips on Reginald. I am
certain that they know who he is and perhaps where he is now.
Tonton men have told me the cautionary tale of another American
policeman who felt compelled to explore rural Haiti. Wayne
Tedrow was white and lacked my protective coloration. The Tonton

men have never threatened me; they have implied that black Americans with financial resources can buy their way into anonymous security and live safely in Haiti as long as their money holds out. They have further implied that this may be the case with Reginald Hazzard and have yet further implied that perhaps I should go home.

I'm staying. The Tonton men accept it with some reluctance—because Haiti is a dangerous place, I'm a black cop who speaks their language with no small flair and because they seem to like me. A Tonton man told me that LAPD had queried them about my whereabouts. The Tonton had not yet responded. It had to be a secondhand query initiated by Scotty. I gave the man some money and told him to rebuff the query. He told me he would.

I am always jaunting about Port-au-Prince, the larger nearby towns and more remote villages. I drink klerin and trip on all manner of Haitian herbs. I herb-tripped and retraced Wayne's last day on earth. A *bokur* mixed me a potion named after Wayne. It is the most breathless mindscape. I often see faces out of my past in entirely altered forms. I think of my life as a middle-class black kid, a left-wing poseur, a policeman, a homosexual, a faux black militant and a killer. I live in a contemplative and unburdened state. February 24, 1964, and everything I have done to claim profit from it feels entirely irrelevant.

I occasionally think of Scotty. I think of Wayne frequently and Mr. Holly most of all. I loved him in the manner that the morally afflicted love those people who most exemplify their complex will to assert and to survive. I think we knew each other. In the end, it led to nothing more than that. Given who I am, he is and we are, it was a bond of some solvency—and, on my part, affection. I am oddly nurtured by it now.

Rural Haiti compels me. It is akin to a rough-trade zone in East Hollywood. I have attended a number of voodoo ceremonies. I have seen men and women zombified. Groups of men follow me sometimes, but I never feel threatened. I think of Wayne and our discourses on the dream state. I want to be physically immobilized so that I can be utterly still and devoid of the will to summon conscious thought and reaction. I have a stash of wildly powerful herbs and blowfish toxin that I've been saving for a special occasion. I carry it with me at all times. I seek stimulation and stimulation seeks me. I want to be chemically prepared to enhance any state of revelation that I may find myself in. I often recall my first conversation with Mr. Holly. It was during the Chicago police riot

of summer '68. I was in a southside lockup, a racist-cop casualty
who also happened to be a cop. Mr. Holly was in the early stages
of entrapping me for OPERATION BAAAAD BROTHER. He quoted
"a very wise woman," whom I later learned was his Quaker leftist
girlfriend. " 'Take note of what you are seeking, for it is seeking
you,' " Mr. Holly said to me. It was an immediate recognition of
my life to date and a spellbinding prophecy of my future. I was
sitting on the bench at Cayes-Jacmel yesterday. I was mindscaping
that very thought and looking out at the Caribbean. It was sunny
and not quite hot. A vendor had sold me a shaved-ice treat laced
with klerin liqueur. It was fruit-sweetened, with a bitter after-
taste. Reginald Hazzard walked up and sat down next to me.

I recognized him from that day nearly eight years before.
Wayne's photograph was a flat, pre-disfigured image. This man
was the man my doctor neighbor and I rescued from the robbery
and the vicious police aftermath.

We said hello to each other. Reginald's burn scars had faded
and had left his dark skin blotched pink-white. He thanked me for
saving him and told me he had heard rumors that a policeman had
been asking questions. I was pointed out to him three weeks earlier. He had been following me since that time. He knew who I was
at once. It took a long period of study for him to determine that I
meant him no harm.

He had a bottle of klerin. We passed it back and forth. I did not
press him for details on the robbery; he did not press me for
details on my police career or my recent hometown celebrity. He
knew a great deal about me. I sensed it readily and knew it would
be ungracious to seek affirmation or in any way pry.

I asked Reginald if he felt safe in Haiti. Reginald said that he
did, but added that he missed his mother a great deal. I did not
mention his father's death in the summer of '68, with Wayne
Tedrow very much in its orbit. I did not mention Wayne as Haitian
folk hero. I did not mention Wayne's union with Mary Beth Hazzard or his quest to find the boy who so easily found me. He knew
all of it, none of it, part of it or most of it. I understood that and
again behaved decorously.

The sun fell low on the water. We sat silently much more
than we talked. Reginald asked me if I had met Joan. I said that
I had. Reginald placed an emerald in my hand and told me it
was the very last one. I thanked him. He got up and walked away
from me.

.   .   .

I bicycled into the Haitian interior. Villages were scattered along low mountain ridges and brush-covered plains. Fallen branches and sharp rocks shredded my tires. I continued on foot. The night grew darker. I sensed groups of men following me.

The moon gave me sight at odd moments. I got glimpses of far-ranging crocodiles and blood-marked trees. I felt the groups behind me expanding. I came up to a small village with a very small hotel. Car lights strafed me. I waved to the driver. He was wearing a white wooden mask.

I swallowed my special stash of herbs and entered the village. A dog wearing a pointed hat ran up and bit me. I walked into the hotel and spoke French to the desk clerk. He rented me a second-floor, street-facing room.

It was low-ceilinged and narrow, with just a sink, a chair and a bed. I turned the lights off. I held Reginald's emerald and stood in front of the window. The herbs took effect. The moon made the green stone a prism. People passed in and out of the rays and said astonishing things to me.

A group of men is forming outside now. They are looking up at me. There are three of them. They are carrying machetes in scabbards. They have left arms and wings where their right arms should be.

I'm becoming immobilized. My thoughts are dispersing as I start to form them. I will drop the pen I am writing with in a moment. The winged men are entering the hotel now. I have left the door unlocked for them.

112

(Los Angeles, 1/22/72–3/18/72)

He got the word late. It knocked him down. It sent him sideways. He'd spent weeks running one way. It sent him running back and running out and sitting still to think. He missed him more than anything. He had a friend in this. The friend fucked him and ran. He missed him anyway.

Marsh got snuffed in Haiti. He knew that he'd fled there. He stiffed an LAPD query and got a late response. *He* couldn't go there. His white-pig status would deep-six him. Extradition was out. Marsh was AWOL, but Marsh was clean. IA cops searched his house. They found fruit-bar listings in his address book. They interviewed Scotty. You and Marsh clashed in '68—tell us about it.

He tattled Marsh's Fed-plant deal. The IA guys jumped on it and braced Dwight Holly. Dwight told them Marsh did an outstanding job. The IA guys laid out dumb-ass theories. Marsh ratted black militants. It might be belated revenge.

Scotty pooh-poohed it. Haiti—who cares. Let it go. Call it a fag junket. Don't reveal his fruitness. Don't soil LAPD. Don't shit on his elderly dad.

Marsh might have left a diary. That prospect gored him. He tossed his crib and found a stash hole in a ceiling beam. It reeked of leather and paper. Obvious—Marsh took the diary with him. IA decided to drop the case. It was best all around. The "Black-Militant Blastout" cop's a swish. He won the Medal of Valor—go figure *that.*

The news curveballed him. He'd been hamstrung and schizzed all the preceding weeks. He brooded in his den. He worked stakeouts. He took Ann and the kids to Disneyland. He took four of his girlfriends to Vegas on consecutive weekends. He spread tip cash around darktown and waited for callbacks. Who's the Commie woman?

Marsh was always secretive. They pulled outrageous shit together. Marsh rabbited *and* held his mud. He respected him for it. *He* walked on their shit. Marsh died behind it. Fucking Haiti—flying centipedes and voodoo. Marsh was a closet mystic. He talked that jive sometimes. Reggie and the emeralds—a dead-issue bust. The money was another thing.

Somebody tipped Marsh. The fruit summit had just ended. Suspects: Sal M., Fred O., Peeper C. Sal and Fred had no motive. That left Peeper. He spent weeks thinking it through.

Peeper was ubiquitous. He drove around and peeped and kept his yap zipped. Fred O. implied that he *knew* things. He's *seen* shit and *done* shit—don't short-shrift that kid.

Peeper lived in his head. So did he, lately. The heist lived all in his head now. Marsh was *there* that day. So was he. *They* knew what it meant and why they had to have it. No one else did.

He postponed the Peeper issue. He cruised by the wheelman lot and induced fear. Pieces fell together at the summit. It came down to this:

Jack Leahy worked the heist. The details didn't matter. He went in with the bank team. He got the money out first.

It's a soft confrontation. He'll see the light and okay the split.

He saturated the southside. Mr. Scotty *spreeeeads* that long green. He got big consensus leads last week.

The probable call: Joan Rosen Klein. She's got a hard-Left pedigree. There's missing cop files. There's 211 rumors. She's a Federal informant. She might be Big Dwight's squeeze.

He tallied all his tip sheets. He chewed breath mints and worried it. It felt kosher. She's Red, she's wrong. She's been margin-hopping black-militant shit since '68.

She mandates a rogue-cop summit. One order of business: the extended cash split.

It supersedes all agendas. It's essentially left-wing. Let's share the wealth. I don't want to cause pain.

He taps Dwight. Dwight taps Jack and Joan. The dollar count depletes. It's big coin just the same.

He missed Marsh. It stuck with him. He did this grand-gesture thing.

The fruit gig went kaput. Fred O. returned half of his money. He cut a check and sent it to Marsh's dad in Chi-town.

Hey, pops. Our deal went south, but I was fond of your kid.

113

(Los Angeles, 1/22/72–3/18/72)

*S*afe House.

It's a radical term. It's Joan Zone nomenclature. He's got his own variation on it.

He needed a safe house. He was a half-assed Red. He had spooky knowledge and a chemistry set. He had some new ideas. He had a right-wing white man out for payback.

Scotty came by the wheelman lot and winked at him. Scotty got his bruiser sons part-time Tiger Kab jobs. Bruiser One and Bruiser Two were Scotty-sized. They winked *and* smirked.

Dipshit, Peeper, *pariguayo*. Add "snitch" to that. Scotty knew he'd tipped Marsh Bowen. The winks meant you're dead—but not yet.

Safe House.

He rented a shack in the Hollywood Hills. He stored his files, books, herbs and chemical gear there. It's *safe* there. He's not *safe* there. He flops at the Vivian and his downtown pad sporadic. He sleeps in his car. He rents motel rooms ad hoc. He does rope gigs for Clyde and Chick. He feels *safe* when he's following people. He feels *un-safe* when he stops.

Marsh went somewhere. He cruised Baldwin Hills all winter and saw surveillance traffic galore. Scotty staked out Marsh's house. Dwight staked out Marsh's house. Some IA cops scoured the crib in late January. Dwight warned him: Do nothing, Dipshit. Dwight knew most of what he knew. Dwight might or might not kill him. Scotty sure as shit would.

Safe House.

Deferred execution.

He couldn't run. L.A. was L.A. He only felt *safe* here. His case was *here.* He kabbed people and followed people *here.* He blew up right-wing street signs *here*. He knew how to live *here*. He couldn't run anywhere else. L.A. always gave him urgent shit to do.

Gretchen/Celia tried to track Tattoo's killer. The late Leander James Jackson helped her. He found four of Jackson's known associates. They said Leander was hipped on the case. They said he kept no records. A chick named "Celia" shared his fixation. They phone drop–communicated. The Tattoo deal commenced with bad Haitian *gre-gre*.

Safe House.

His gear is safe there. He's not. It's funny and fucked-up. He just turned twenty-seven. He looks way older. He's got gray-streaked hair and a Commie brand on his back. He can't talk to the people he cares for. He follows them instead.

He follows Dwight Holly. Joan seems to have left him. Dwight sits in the pad near Karen's house, for days at a stretch. The boxes and gear are gone. Dwight waits by the phone. He picks up the receiver every half hour. He watches Karen's house with binoculars. He lights up on her little girls.

Dwight stays immobile. He's got to stay moving. He follows Karen sometimes. She's led him to lunch dates with Joan.

Following was easy. Mobility was his strong suit. Cars were camouflage. His zhlubby kid look supplied cover. Bug-tap jobs were easy. He knew how to drill, bore and thread. Eavesdropping was tough. People could see you and sense your intent.

He got close to Joan and Karen. They sipped coffee and chain-smoked at a joint on Hillhurst. Joan said she had "the money." That encouraged her. She was worried. Celia was lost in Haiti or the D.R. Joan had severed ties with Dwight. It pertained to "the Operation." The phrase made Karen wince. Joan said "safe house" twice. Joan said Dwight would never be able to find her.

They were such good friends. He heard New York in their voices. Karen was red-haired and didn't look Greek. It was cold lately. Joan wore sweaters. He couldn't see her knife scar.

He snapped a sneak photo. Joan was forty-five years, four months and seventeen days of age.

He taped it to his dashboard. He's always moving. All of his pictures are safe.

114

(Los Angeles, 1/22/72–3/18/72)

Gone.

Joan took their forged documents and marking tools. Jack retired from the Bureau. He posted his resignation letter in the squadroom. It was respectful. It thanked Mr. Hoover and praised his leadership. Please send my pension checks to my P.O. box in rural Oregon.

Marsh ran to Haiti and was murdered there. LAPD IA questioned him. He did not mention Sergeant Robert S. Bennett. He praised Sergeant Bowen's performance on OPERATION BAAAAD BROTHER. The cops said Marsh was a homosexual. Dwight acted surprised.

They're gone. She's gone. She cleaned out the fallback and left the phone line intact. It's a bootleg listing. She's the only one with the number. If the phone rings, it's her.

Tell me things.

Tell me what that man did to you.

No, I'm not going to.

Her hatred superseded the heat of his conversion. Jack held whatever hate he had close. Their rage eclipsed his shame and guilt. Their hurt cut deeper. He couldn't kill the man. They went off to do it their way. They couldn't use Marsh. They'd find a new fall guy or do it sans subtext. He won't intercede. They know it. If Joan calls, he'll say it.

He black-bagged chez Marsh one final time. He checked the hidey-hole. The diary was gone.

He called Bob Relyea and told him they'd aborted. Keep the money and buy yourself a new sheet. Bob was relieved. Dwight, it had snafu written all over it. Bubba, it's still percolating. Stick close to your TV.

He kept replaying D.C. It helped that Karen was there. He saw Mr. Hoover. He forgave Marsh for what the man made him. *Nobody dies* was no leap.

He goes to the office. The fallback phone and the drop-front phone never ring. Mr. Hoover hasn't called. Nixon hasn't called. Peeper Crutchfield tails him and loiters outside. The kid knows everything except *It's All Over.* Son, I don't have the will to kill you.

He took Karen away for her birthday weekend. They stayed at a cottage and made love a great deal. She'd seen Joan. He knew it. She never mentioned her name.

She plays the string quartets every night. He stands on the terrace and listens. He holds Joan's red flag. Karen leaves a light on for him.

115

(Los Angeles, 3/19/72)

Sultan's Sam's. The Sandbox at 8:00 a.m.—far-out surreal.

Scotty had a key. Sambo snitched for ATF and LAPD. Sambo hosted retirement bashes. Redd Foxx performed for instant bail release. Redd worked the room like a mofo. He was a closet white-pig groupie.

The booth section needed a sweep-up. The bandstand was a scrap heap. The Soul Survivors left all their shit onstage. The walls were lime velour. They absorbed cigarette smoke. The rugs were deep shag. They absorbed piss.

Keep it short. Summitry was brevity. Hold your nose, shake hands and split.

Scotty sat in a back booth. He lit a cigarette, took two hits and snuffed it. He left the door ajar. Dwight Holly walked in.

The dim light hit him. He eye-adjusted in the doorway. He got his bearings. He saw Scotty and joined him.

Their knees brushed under the table. They scooched around and created some space.

"Thanks for coming."

"I wouldn't have missed it."

"It won't take long."

Dwight said, "We're both good negotiators. I think we'll get there fairly quick."

Scotty twirled an ashtray. Leftover butts spilled.

"You've told the others, right? You're negotiating for them?"

Dwight shook his head. "We'll cut the deal. I'll make sure that they accept it. We all know it has to end. If you're reasonable, we'll get it done today."

Scotty tipped his hat. "I thought you'd pat me down for a wire."

"I thought you'd feel me up for an ankle piece."

Scotty laughed. "It took so goddamn long for it all to fall together."

"Mr. Hoover got some things going. I'll concede that."

"Just to let me know I'm not crazy. The heist was Jack Leahy, Joan Klein and that burned-up colored kid. It was all nutty political shit."

Dwight smiled. "That's about it."

Scotty said, "I'm giving you a walk on the emeralds."

Dwight said, "That's white of you."

"Leahy got the cash out."

"Yes."

"How much?"

"Slightly more than seven million."

Scotty cracked his knuckles. "It's all been washed? There's no more ink stains?"

Dwight nodded. "Clean, non-consecutive bills. Fives up to hundreds. It's the best-looking money you've ever seen."

"I want half."

Dwight shook his head. "40%."

Scotty said, "45."

Dwight said, "Deal."

The room felt itchy and toxic. The velour was shredded. Scotty felt particles eat his skin.

"Let's talk about Peeper. He's a side issue here. I think he knows a lot of it."

Dwight said, "I'm sure he does."

"He's been around forever. He knows all the players. He's potential grief we don't need."

Dwight nodded. Scotty said, "He goes." Dwight said, "No sale. I'll up you to 50, but I don't want him hurt."

"Lets rethink this. The 50 is generous, but I have to insist."

"No sale. I'll give you another concession, but I'm not folding on him."

A horn blared outside. Dwight jerked a bit. He was thin. His chest was bulked off-size. Odds on a load-stopper vest.

"We can't have him peeping around and coming around with his hand out. The little fucker just will not desist."

Dwight said, "No." He jerked a little. His shirt stretched. The vest fabric showed underneath.

"I have to insist. It's a rough go now, but you'll thank me some day."

"No. Let's start over again. I'll up you to 55 and give you one more free one. I step up, you step back, it all works."

A horn blared. Dwight jerked. His hand dipped under the table. Scotty gripped the table ledge. Dwight watched his hands. Scotty read his mind. *He's thinking cross-draw or side-draw/vest or no vest?*

Their eyes clicked. Their eyes held. Their hands disappeared.

Dwight fired. The shot ricocheted under the table. A seat cushion exploded. Scotty ducked and rolled low. He saw Dwight's legs and gun hand. He pulled two throwdowns. Dwight fired twice. He hit the booth post and Scotty's vest. Scotty flew back and bounced forward. The impact double-visioned him. He pushed the table up and over. Dwight fired. The bullet caromed and tore out his neck. The table fell on him. He gouted blood and shot wide. Scotty rolled out of the booth and fired two-handed. He hit Dwight in both legs and the groin. He shattered Dwight's gun hand.

Dwight fired. A wall section ripped. Dwight dry-fired. His fingers didn't work. The gun didn't work. Blood covered the cylinder and the trigger. Scotty rolled close and kicked the gun out of his hand.

Dwight spat blood in his face. Scotty pulled his vest up and gut-shot him. The air was cloud-thick. The cordite fumes stung.

Scotty got his breath and his legs. He pat-checked himself. Okay—no grazes, no hits. They both shot revolvers. No stray shells extant.

He pulled out a roll of tiger-band C-notes. He tucked it in Dwight's coat pocket. He rubbed his own chest. He felt the slug vest-embedded. Okay—you can walk now.

He did it casual. He *stroooooled.* He saw the mailbox on the corner and dropped the envelope in.

Snitch-out. Anonymous. Written in ghetto-ese. The L.A. Office would get it. Jack Leahy would *see* it. Rogue Fed D.C. Holly. He suborned and offed the Bostitch brothers. Look close, don't act. The Enforcer's good for the Peoples' Bank.

Low clouds over darktown. Powder fumes out the door. A rainbow due south.

Lawdy—it's 2/24/64 redux.

116

(Los Angeles, 3/19/72)

He was running prone or rolling aloft. His back grew legs and propelled him. He didn't know how this could be.

Green walls tumbled. A red film held his eyes away. His right arm pulsed. A green man ran with a bottle and stayed in front of him.

I think I get it.

He remembered crawling and the sidewalk and the old black guy. The picture in his pocket. Her phone number on the back.

The green walls grew white lights. His legs were wheels. The red film dissolved and let faces in. More green men with bottles. Not the faces he wanted to see.

You know who you are. One last time, please.

He started grabbing and blinking. The red returned. He brushed things and knocked over things. He heard them crash. His hands were weightless. They were more like wings.

His legs stopped rolling him. Someone wiped the red away. Someone grabbed his hands and squeezed life in them. He saw river borders around Karen.

She said, "They are your children, Dwight. I swear it is true."

The rivers compressed and swam over her. She pushed through them and held in close. He reached for it and found it and got it out full voice.

"Do you love me?"

The rivers came in darkening. The green walls faded to pinpoints. She said, "I'll think about it" as the lights stopped.

117

(Los Angeles, 3/23/72)

Uncle Gibb's Liquor—*again.*

The southside record holder. Twenty-nine 211's since 1963. Old Gibb always shook his head. "Mr. Scotty, I gots a dark cloud over me."

The tip came in an hour back. It was a solid phoner. A colored lady heard street talk. Two no-good boys with shotguns. Mr. Scotty, you stop this.

Scotty perched in the alley. The back door was adjacent. He brought his civilian wheels. He'd bag them going in.

His letter ploy worked. Dwight Holly's death went unreported. The bank cash and Jack Leahy, the Enforcer's low-down past. As planned—the Bureau buried it.

Joan soon. She'd be tractable. He'd sidestep Jack and approach her direct. She'd see the sense in the split.

It was misty. The windshield beaded over. Scotty kicked the ignition key and ran the wiper blades.

A woman walked up. She was tall and red-haired. She didn't quite look lost. She looked darktown-out-of-place.

He rolled down his window. She came around the car and leaned in. He prepped a baby-you're-lost spiel. She put her hand on the window ledge. She clicked as off-kilter then.

She raised a little snubnosed revolver. She shot him six times in the face.

DOCUMENT INSERT: 3/24/72. Extract from the privately held journal of Karen Sifakis.

The following pages will serve as my confession, should it come to that. I am not going to run. I am not going to lie if I am officially confronted. I am not going to offer personal or political justifications for the horrible thing that I did. I did it because I loved Dwight Holly to the bottom of my soul and because the other children's name.
woman he loved lacked the will to do it. I am determined to survive without Dwight and pray for the strength to do so, in our

I performed the act in a state of rage. I did not pause to pray or summon moments of reflection. I walked to Dwight's little bungalow and found a single throwdown gun in a box. I killed in the spirit of wanton apostasy. I refuse now and will always refuse to abdicate my personal responsibility for this act. Dwight scuttled his operation and spared a life. My persistent preaching of nonviolence influenced his decision. His deeply sure rebuke of his own vile deeds compelled me to violently acknowledge the price he paid to revoke his past and seek transcendence. I could not have lived with myself had I not formed a circle back to that brave man and the woman I sent forth to teach him. The bond of the three of us must continue to flourish within me. My action was an attempt to settle all debts and hold us together, with one of us now incapacitated and one of us dead. I see through the grandiosity and speciousness of these statements even as I write them. I am past caring at this moment. I will always stand by what I have done.

I feel the urgency of Dwight's patrimony now. I will not dwell on whether I should have told him earlier. He knew for a conscious flicker and he will know in the world that follows this one. I will change our daughters' names to Holly at an appropriate time.

Dwight cared more for Marshall Bowen than he ever admitted. Bowen died in Haiti a few months ago. I am going to have his body shipped to the States and interred with Dwight's. I will be sure that they are laid to rest near some tame goats.

118

(Los Angeles, 3/26/72)

She was inside. She never left. He'd been watching for days.

He talked to Clyde last night. Scuttlebutt was raging. Dwight Holly was dead. Some heist men shot Scotty. Clyde ran down all the theories. They were bogus. *He* had X-ray eyes. Only *he* knew what it meant.

She stayed inside. He slept in his car and watched the windows. He saw her once, two days ago. She looked in the closet where the boxes used to be. She wore frayed jeans and one of Dwight's suit coats.

He started counting the days since he first saw her. He stopped at one thousand. He looked at the dashboard pix and got all raw. He ran up and jiggled the door.

It swung open. She was sitting on the floor. Her face was blotchy and tear-streaked. She'd twisted some strands of her hair out. Her wrists were blood-crusted. A knife was stuck in the far wall. She wrote the word *No* in blood beside it.

He almost stepped on her glasses. She squinted at him. He picked her glasses up and walked over. She pushed herself away from him and braced her back on the wall.

He handed her the glasses. She put them on. Her eyes focused past her tears. She looked up at him.

"Miss Klein, my name is Donald Crutchfield. I've been following you for a very long time, and I'd be grateful if you'd talk to me."

Part VI

COMRADE JOAN

March 26, 1972–May 11, 1972

Joan Rosen Klein

(Los Angeles, 3/26/72)

She'd seen him. He was a pop-up face and a blur, persistent. It was intermittent. He felt like a shape-shifter. He'd go away and reappear, changed.

So I'll tell you. It's the story I should have told him.

She cleaned up and bundled into Dwight's tweed coat. She made them a pot of tea. Clouds rolled in low. A spring storm hovered.

It began with the stones. "Green Fire," "Green Death." Colombia, mid-15-something. Spanish settlers conquer the Muzo Indians and rape their emerald mines. The Spanish become Colombians. The Muzos become slave labor. The tradition extends to now. Mining companies rape the Itoco Mountains. They're near Bogotá.

Her grandparents were German-Jewish émigrés. They came to America and settled in New York. Isidore Klein traveled to South America and became immersed in Green Fire lore.

He was a borderline mystic. He was every inch a Red.

Red bandits hit the Muzo Valley mines. The men called themselves *quaqueros*. It meant "treasure hunters." They dug tunnels into the mining companies' tunnels and dug out stones for themselves. They warred with company goon squads. They looted emeralds routinely and were routinely trapped, tortured and killed. There were dozens of *quaquero* bands. Some were politically identified. Isidore Klein bought his emeralds exclusively from them. He earmarked a portion of his ultimate profits to South American insurgent groups. He sold his emeralds in fine jewelry stores

throughout the United States. He grew wealthy. He gave away small for-
tunes to anarchist cabals and left-wing labor organizations. He lived comfortably. He lived more modestly than other immigrant arrivistes. His rise
to wealth matched a young lawyer's rise to power. The man's name was
John Edgar Hoover. He was a Justice Department drone. He was brilliant
and sensed opportunity in wildly unfolding events.

The post–World War I Red Scare granted him History. The attorney
general's home was bombed. Hoover took it from there.

The Red Raids. Civil liberties suspended, abrogated, quashed, interdicted, suppressed. First Amendment rights shat upon. Political roundups, false imprisonings, deportation at whim. A concurrent resurgence of
nativist groups and the Klan. John Edgar Hoover saw the force of fear and
exploited it. His power grab succeeded commensurately.

Isidore Klein had one son. His name was Joseph. He was born in 1902.
Isidore raised him *RED*. Joseph married Helen Hershfield Rosen in 1924.
Helen had been raised *RED*. Their daughter Joan was born on Halloween
night, '26. Her parents and grandfather raised her *RED*.

The FBI was recently chartered. The old Bureau of Investigation had
been deemed moribund. J. Edgar Hoover took over. He was an organiza-
tional genius and a PR whiz. His mandate was smother dissent. He honed
his techniques during the madcap boom decade. He understood the metaphysical value of the Enemy. He knew that Reds could serve in that capacity. Gangsters were picaresque touchstones for the public imagination.
They lacked the pervasive force of the Reds. The boom became the
Depression. The American Left mobilized. Hoover sensed an insurgent
shift and reacted. He stepped into the public arena with flair. He preached
an anti-Red message and ignored organized crime. He made himself a
national hero. He unleashed a tidal wave of illegal surveillance, official
scrutiny and false arrest. Isidore Klein took full notice of him.

The name Hoover reigned ubiquitous. He recalled the name spoken by
savaged comrades in 1918. He began to study Hoover. He developed a
sense of Hoover as his personal enemy. He acted in the public arena. He
utilized the stones.

He bought subversives out of stir. Small and large emerald gifts
unlocked jail doors. Emeralds supported Joseph, Helen and the child
Joan. They camped in socialist meeting halls and distributed leaflets in
bread lines. They housed and fed fugitive leftists. They skirmished with
goons on picket lines and endured three- and four-day detentions. They
fought *their* war. Isidore Klein fought an increasingly recognized war
against J. Edgar Hoover.

His weapon was words. Emeralds bankrolled the clandestine publish-
ing of anti-Hoover tracts. Isidore Klein pushed the tracts in significant

quantity. Mr. Hoover took enraged note of it and began a lockstep surveillance. Isidore's printing operations were repeatedly raided and Isidore was repeatedly jailed. Emeralds bought him out of custody. The stones were trinkets, talismans, keepsakes and bribes. The Depression raged. A small emerald carried a cop's family for months. Green Fire was the flame of magic and revolution. Mr. Hoover knew it. He failed to interdict the flow of the emeralds and thus the flow of the tracts. He believed that Isidore Klein held an emerald stash at his home on East 63rd Street. He ordered a squad of New York City agents to ransack the house and steal them. It was 1937. Joan Rosen Klein was ten years old.

The squad was led by Special Agent Thomas D. Leahy. He was a widower with a sixteen-year-old son named John. The squad tore Isidore's home apart. They found twenty-three pounds of the highest quality Muzo emeralds and stole them. Isidore arrived later that night. He discovered the theft and suffered a fatal heart attack.

Joseph and Helen Klein were now without resources. They knew that Hoover directed the burglary and told Joan the story in full detail. Hoover kept the emeralds. He dispensed small quantities to his toadies as quid pro quos. The *quaqueros* found less controversial gemstone importers. Hoover emerald-gifted strikebreak captains and subversive-group infiltrators. He hoarded the sum of the stones for himself.

Isidore Klein's death devastated Tom Leahy. He became horrified of Mr. Hoover. His fear and revulsion ran equal with his guilt and self-disgust. A gear clicked the wrong way or the right way inside him. He became radicalized.

He covertly assisted left-wingers and warned them of impending Fed raids. He acted with great caution and covered his tracks. Agent Tom became a cherished secret of the leftist underground. The Kleins had heard of him. No one knew that he'd led the emerald raid. Hoover had quashed all public mention of it. Agent Tom confessed the deed to Joe and Helen Klein and their daughter. Joe and Helen forgave him. A deep friendship evolved. Agent Tom took their forgiveness to heart. It spawned inspiration. He was a gifted lawyer and criminal investigator. He knew how to log information and build information to the indictment stage. He decided to build a massive file on J. Edgar Hoover and take it public.

He queried other agents, Hoover's minions, law-enforcement colleagues and rivals. He took depositions from witnesses to Hoover's negligence and planned obfuscation. The file grew to several thousand pages. It catalogued covetousness, pettiness, the large-scale violation of civil liberties and rampant power abuse. Joe and Helen Klein read the file. The young Comrade Joan read the file and became enraptured and enraged.

It was now fall 1940. Joan was fourteen. Tom Leahy's son Jack was now almost twenty. Tom Leahy was a Red with an FBI badge. He was grooming Jack to become a cop revolutionary. Mr. Hoover was forty-five years old. He had the emeralds. He was ascendant. He possessed the power he had always craved.

He had created a myth. Newsprint and radio waves spread it for him. He adroitly read the times he lived through. He created a tale of moral sureness and his own supremacy. It was tailor-made for the Depression and the onset of World War II. It posited the unseen other as epidemically everywhere. It vouchsafed the FBI and his stewardship for as long as he could render the myth real.

Hoover had informants everywhere. He learned of Red Tom's betrayal and the anti-Hoover file. He heard that Leahy was off taking depositions. Leahy was isolated at a leftist campground in the Catskills. The moment was perfect.

He paid off a squad of New York State troopers. They were expedited with parcels of emeralds, no cash. The troopers raided the campground. Several inhabitants resisted. The troopers rounded them up and burned down the women's bunkhouse.

Joseph and Helen Klein resisted. They were arrested and severely beaten at a state police jail near Poughkeepsie. They died from their injuries.

Joan was home in Brooklyn that weekend. A veil of rage and horror fell over her.

New York City agents stormed Tom Leahy's apartment. They found his file. Hoover read it and burned it. His informants helped him build a sedition case against Tom. The war was newly raging. Hoover played a trump card: "national security." He had Tom Leahy arrested and tried sub rosa. Tom was convicted by a hastily impaneled judge and jury. He was sentenced to six years at Sing Sing.

Tom Leahy's file was comprehensive. It was diligently annotated and superbly constructed. It begat Mr. Hoover's devouring file lunacy.

FBI paperwork accrued to ten tons yearly. Tom Leahy died in prison in 1943. He drank himself dead on rotgut toilet brew. He had been repeatedly beaten. The guards who beat him all wore emerald rings.

Tom's son Jack disappeared and lived anonymously. He attended college and served in the U.S. Navy. He entered Notre Dame Law School. He was wholly and committedly *RED* and equally committed to sustained vengeance. He laid out a paper trail of obscure name changes and came all the way back to the defiant John Leahy. The trail was built from his date-close birthday up. His father's file taught him how to build paper. His father's access to Hoover's files taught him to build paper fraudulently.

He got through the FBI background-check process. He was appointed to the Bureau in 1950.

Special Agent John C. Leahy—*RED*.

He worked routine Bureau assignments. He kept up with his father's subversive friends. He covertly redacted his comrades' files and diverted FBI interference. Jack Leahy: Fed toady by day. Jack Leahy: *RED* provocateur by night.

Jack reconnected with Joan. She had gone underground and gone criminal. Her sense of vengeance had gone scattershot. She had remained fixedly *RED*.

She recruited on college campuses. She proudly retained her own real name, much as Jack did. The sporadic use of aliases muddied her trail. She met Karen Sifakis. Their deep friendship began. A floating dialogue defined it. Karen advocated non-violence. Joan nearly always disagreed.

A strikebreaker pulled a gun on her. She hit him with a two-by-four. She sustained a scarring knife wound.

Two Legionnaires cornered her at that Paul Robeson concert. She took a savage beating. She waited nine years. She shot and killed the two men in their sleep.

She loved the thrill of armed robbery. She planned the jobs and steered clear of the jobs as events. She was conscious of herself as a woman. She crouched in certain shadows as she raged *RED*.

Jack fed her inside scoop on payroll jobs and bank vaults. She always donated her heist takes to the Cause. Joan and Jack became comrade-lovers. They shared a family story and a family hatred. They moved together and in circles overlapping. Joan became Williamson, Goldenson, Broward and Faust and always returned to Klein. Jack remained a G-man under his real and entirely fictive name. Jack got Joan out of jail. Jack utilized municipal PD contacts for criminal-records deletes. Joan conceived two textile-plant jobs in L.A.—'51 and '53. Dragnets caught her up. Jack got her out and blitzed file reports. Joan conceived a heist in Dayton, Ohio. Jack bought off key investigators and got most of the paperwork expunged.

Joan roved and toured revolutionary hot spots. It was a breathless errand and a blood duty of great urgency. Her dialogue with Karen Sifakis curtailed her worst urges. A lust peaked and sent things bad: '51, '56, '61. Only Karen knew the details. Only Karen knew the price she paid to continue at her mad pace.

She moved heroin to finance left-wing coups. She fomented revolt in Algeria and Cuba. She was heedless, reckless, vindictive and in many ways ideologically unsound. The death of her great love Dwight Holly taught her things. Her arc left matched his arc right in hate and specious rigor. She should have told him that before she ran from him.

She roved. She ran from and toward J. Edgar Hoover. She thought about the emeralds near constantly. She heard out rumors and cribbed lore and supposition. She exerted common sense and followed the trail.

Jack followed it with her. They shared information and came to this:

Hoover sold the stones to a Paraguayan fascist after the war. It was greed and political payback. *El jefe* hid Nazi scientists the U.S. wanted. *El jefe* knew brilliant gemologists. They knew *of* the stones and had their own designs.

They studied the emeralds. Their findings comprised a thesis on exploitative mining techniques. A straight bore-through-rock technology evolved. It was successfully employed and brought an end to the *quaquero* raids. *El jefe* was afraid of overt *quaquero* vengeance and ordered massacres. Scores of *quaqueros* were slaughtered.

The bore-through-rock technology caused massive worker layoffs. Enhanced emerald profits financed right-wing coups throughout South America and the Caribbean.

Green Fire served to sustain Rafael Trujillo's power. The Goat became obsessed. He had to own the initial Muzo-Klein stones outright. The provenance consumed him. He wanted the story to end with him.

Trujillo hoarded Dominican money and grabbed Haitian-owned land. Papa Doc Duvalier had been emerald-financed and wanted the gems for himself. Trujillo and Duvalier hated each other. Trujillo murdered Haitian refugees. Duvalier enacted reprisals. The two führers discovered their mutual longing. They decided to trust each other on the acquisition of the stones and nothing else. Joan tracked the arc of the emeralds to this point and no further. She went to the D.R. in early '59.

She found a country ripe for revolt. She found Celia.

A leftist network supplied the introduction. Celia was a gone-bust United Fruit heiress. She was half American, half Dominican, all old money. She used her father's surname of Farr and her mother's maiden name of Reyes interchangeably. Gretchen and Celia came and went at whim. Joan preferred the latter name. Celia was a casualty of revolution, left- and right-wing. Castro nationalized the cane fields and bankrupted her father. The Goat robbed her mother in a recent land grab. Celia was a nationally ranked polo player and a bunco artist extraordinaire. She was omnivorously intelligent and not quite brilliant. Joan considered her ripe for conversion. One thing told her this.

The emeralds. Celia was crazed over them.

They became comrade/lovers. Celia was headstrong and tractable, independent and willfully submissive to the concept of revolt. Celia was a mystic. Joan was not. Celia dabbled in Eastern philosophy and more than dabbled in voodoo. Celia believed in the spiritual force of the emeralds. Joan did not. They reconciled their differences and traveled to Castro's Cuba. They began plotting the 6/14 invasion.

The invasion failed. A rebel named María Rodríguez Fontonette betrayed the Cause. A Tonton Macoute man named Laurent-Jean Jacqueau assisted the Cause. Jacqueau secretly emigrated to America and changed his name to Leander James Jackson. Joan and Celia were captured, imprisoned and bribed free. Joan had stashed a robbery take in an L.A. bank vault. Jack Leahy tapped the cash and found the right officials.

Joan and Celia flew to America. The Goat was assassinated. Juan Bosch and Joaquín Balaguer succeeded him. They were repressive and much less garish rulers. Balaguer inherited the Goat's emerald fixation. He was then a government lawyer eyeing the presidency. Papa Doc remained in power and remained emerald-fixed.

The men found each other. They collaborated and cut a side deal. They learned the identity of the Paraguayan *el jefe*. They gave him a down payment on the Muzo-Klein emerald stash. *El jefe* was near-broke and in poor health. He wanted to sell. It was December '63. Fate intervened and fucked it all up.

Balaguer had a financial setback. Papa Doc had a financial setback. They lacked the cash to outright buy the stones. They looked for a rich American to consign them to.

The right-wing grapevine supplied a name: Dr. Fred Hiltz. He was a hate pamphleteer and an emerald-myth worshiper. They contacted Dr. Fred. He paid off *el jefe* with a bank draft. The stones were messengered to Santo Domingo. Balaguer and Papa Doc met there *just to touch them.* They did not trust messengers to hand-deliver the stones. Dr. Fred insisted on an armored-car drop. A Haitian man was hired to fly the emeralds to L.A. It was now 1/16/64. He could not leave until 2/21/64. Balaguer and Papa Doc enjoyed the delay. *They got to touch the stones more.*

SUDDENLY:

A Tonton Macoute thug learned of the shipment. He contacted his old Tonton *frère* Leander James Jackson. Leander knew his old comrades—Joan and Celia. Serendipity: Celia's brother Richard Farr worked at Wells Fargo in L.A.

Jack Leahy ran the FBI's L.A. Office. Richard knew the armored-car route. Richard predicted the cash take along with the stones. Jack knew expendable criminal scum to leave dead at the scene. The greatest hurdle was obscuring their IDs. Joan knew a brilliant chemist named Reginald Hazzard. She had mentored him at the Freedom School. She had bailed him out of jail the month before.

The plan was developed. Reginald concocted a bone-deep burning solution. Jack recruited an expendable Klansman named Claverly and an expendable hood named Wilkinson. The plan was now fully formed, *but:*

Reginald wanted to *be there.* He told Joan and Jack this. Joan and Jack conferred and tried to dissuade him. Reginald insisted. He thought his chemical expertise marked him invaluable and immune to deceit. He was right and he was wrong. Joan and Jack argued. Jack argued for compliance as Joan argued for termination. Jack won. Reginald would go in and Reginald would survive. The plan was now fully formed, *but:*

Reginald feared a double cross. Reginald harbored a hurt-child resentment. His comrades trusted him to develop deep-burning compounds, but not to be there. *He was there that day.* He impulsively popped a bank tab and let loose jets of ink. Jack impulsively shot him.

His flame-retardant precautions saved his life. Soft-point bullets hit him, regardless. His chemical compounds worked erratically. The palliative pellets in his mouth circumvented damage. The anti-flame chemicals enhanced flames paradoxically.

So he lived. So Marsh Bowen and the doctor saved him. He grabbed handfuls of inked cash as he went down. He gave them to the doctor.

He hid in East Los Angeles. Scotty Bennett led the LAPD Task Force. Jack worked FBI-adjunct. The newspaper accounts and crime-scene reports shocked him. There were *two* dead robbers at the scene.

Jack wanted to find Reginald and kill him. Joan told him, "No." The debate raged for days. Comrade Joan won. She searched for Reginald and found him. She begged for his forgiveness. He told her he wanted to live in Haiti and study herbal chemistry. She gave him the emeralds and told him to serve the Cause.

Joan and Jack now possessed millions of dollars. A dozen ink bindles had leaked. Stains rendered the cash unpassable for some time. They waited. Jack heard a rumor: pilfered heist cash had been laundered through the Peoples' Bank. He told Joan. She asked around about Lionel Thornton. She learned that he was mobbed up. She learned that he came out of the Detroit labor struggle, circa '40. She arranged a meeting with him.

The meeting went well. It was instinctively collaborative. A level of trust built both ways. Thornton was politically versed and self-interested. Joan got dirt on him as an insurance policy.

She gave him the stained and non-stained cash. Reginald developed a compound to obscure the ink markings. She let Thornton trade the money up, down and sideways. The base sum grew in a hidden bank vault. She let him implement Reginald's emerald-disbursement plan. The green stones formed a circuit back to Isidore Klein and his struggle. That gave Joan a bare semblance of peace.

Thornton did his job and kept his word. Scotty Bennett and Marsh Bowen killed him. He did not reveal Jack's name or hers.

Reginald remained in Haiti. He was still there. His exact whereabouts were unknown. He forgave Joan and Jack. He was nineteen, he was eager, he was easily led. He was passively complicit and as guilty as they were. He bought revolution unblinkingly and never saw through to the cost. Joan understood a bit of that now. She was thirty years in the game.

The heist aftershocks subsided. Joan rode the '60s zeitgeist. Jack stayed with the Bureau. He disseminated information. He redacted and misplaced their comrades' files. Joan kept up with Karen Sifakis. Karen described her love affair with a rogue Fed named Dwight Holly.

Dwight did terrible things for Mr. Hoover. Dwight was dead-wrecked in the spring of '68. Tommy Narduno sensed the FBI behind the King hit. Tommy saw Dwight in Memphis a few days before. Joan kept Tommy's thoughts from Karen. Karen said Dwight was planning a COINTELPRO. He needed an informant. Joan knew it had to be her.

BAAAAAAD BROTHER entered the planning stage.

A non sequitur clash occurred. Jack called Joan and reported rumblings.

It was Dr. Fred. He put together some leads on the heist, gleaned from Clyde Duber's file. He wasn't looking for revenge. Balaguer and Papa Doc had refunded his money. He wanted a second shot at the stones.

Hiltz wanted to run his heist leads by Mr. Hoover. He was a trusted CBI and a Hoover phone-chat pal. Joan summarily acted.

She knew about Dr. Fred's bomb-shelter stash. Leander knew of Jomo Clarkson, via the black-militant grapevine. Joan cutout-worked Jomo and fed him the plan. Steal Dr. Fred's money. Don't hurt him. Scare him into silence per 2/64. He'll fold off that.

She didn't want more death. She got it anyway. Jomo and his partner killed Dr. Fred. The partner absconded. Jomo found him and killed him.

BAAAAAAD BROTHER went forth. Joan became Dwight's informant and lover. The wild-card clash of Marsh Bowen and Scotty Bennett occurred. Joan and Dwight did not know the extent then.

Marsh and Scotty wanted the money and the emeralds. They colluded and betrayed each other and died for *their* cause. Dwight and Joan colluded and conspired. She betrayed him only by her silence. They had crafted an operation that would serve to right all their wrongs. Dwight pulled out, unilaterally. Their paperwork was stashed at a comrade's house. She'll honor Dwight's decision to abort their plan. She lacks the requisite will.

Celia was lost on that island. La Banda and the Tonton had *X*-marked her. The warrants derived from her work with Wayne Tedrow. Celia was past reason in some regards. María Rodríguez Fontonette was almost certainly murdered in L.A several years back. Celia felt complicitous. She had hexed Tattoo. It was preposterous. Voodoo was barbarous capitalism cloaked in magic. Celia thought otherwise. It didn't matter. Celia was courageous beyond ideology. Belief works that way.

She should have told Dwight the story. One thing hexed her, still. Her last word to him should not have been "No."

The clouds broke and spilled rain. The boy looked different. The length of her tale matched the breadth of his surveillance. That pop-up face always there.

I know you want to touch me.

So I'll let you.

He caught the signal and leaned in. She thought he'd be clumsy. He brushed dried blood off her wrists and kissed the part in her hair.

120

(Los Angeles, 3/27/72)

T*HE ELECTRIC CHAIR, THE HANDS AND FEET, THE EYE.*

The fried skin, the stumps, the flamethrower stink. Cinerama and Smell-O-Vision. Wait—there's a dog in a voodoo hat and a palm tree on fire.

Crutch woke up. The barking dog was a dog outside. The flames were a 6:00 a.m. sun.

He got his bearings. It was pad #3/safe house #1. Scotty was dead. He didn't have to hide.

You have to go back. There's where she took you. It cost her everything. She punched your surveillance card. You clocked out at three years and nine months.

Crutch made coffee and wrote out a question list for Celia. She knew things about Tattoo. He wondered if she still cared.

He fucked with his chemistry set. The story kept re-spooling. The tape jammed here and there.

The Operation. Joan and Dwight's plan. It could only be *That.*

Crutch drove to Clyde Duber Associates and let himself in. It was 7:10. He could log private time.

He read Clyde's heist file and Marsh Bowen's personnel file. He had Joan's story now. Facts clicked in, redundant. Who gives a shit?

Farewell tour. You can't peep and prowl paper the rest of your life. You're fucked-up in the head.

Crutch split and cruised by the wheelman lot. Phil Irwin and Bobby Gallard snoozed in their sleds. Clyde was throwing a wake bash for Scotty. The lot would be tartan bunting–draped and lit up.

Joan had gotten a second wind and riffed before he left. She told him about the blacklist and all the people Hoover trashed. He memorized their names. He wanted to touch her scar and show her the scar on his back.

He cut east. He parked in front of the fallback and walked up the steps. The buzzer didn't work. He knocked a bunch of times, loud. The lock was too lame not to pick.

She'd made a nest on the floor. Dwight's jackets and sweaters, Dwight's Fed suits. He smelled her cigarette smoke and Dwight's after-shave. The suits were blotched up with it. She'd doused them good.

Crutch walked out to the terrace. A cool pair of Bausch & Lombs sat on the ledge. He adjusted the sights and looked down at Karen's house. Karen and Joan were burning paper in the backyard bar-b-q. Joan had bandaged up her wrists.

The little girls played catch. A blood-crusted towel was draped over a chair back. He zoomed in very close. Joan almost smiled and laughed.

He got *AN IDEA*. He didn't hex it by stating it, inside or outside of his head. His chemical shit was stashed at pad #3. He Walpurgisnacted and worked till he dropped.

Blowfish toxin and stinging nettle. Tree-frog livers from his icebox. Rigorous formulas, potpourri and improvisation. Three hot plates boiling and mushroom clouds like Hiroshima.

Build, reduce, enhance, revise, re-calculate and re-try. It's like Bryl-creem: "A little dab'l do ya." Re-formulate and get it down to sub-atomic size.

He got close. Eyedrop portions burned paper and wood. He re-calculated and re-tried. He futzed with endless molecular strings and brought down the dose. He thought he got sub-ultra-close and miscalculated. He got closer than that first close and yelled *Halt!* before he collapsed.

He squeezed a particle on a piece of cheese and left it on his back porch. He popped two red devils and slept it all off.

Sedation. No nightmares. No Zombie Zone flashbacks.

Bird noise de-comatized him. He lurch-walked out to the back porch.

There's the cheese and a dead rat. A minuscule nip chilled his rodent ass flat out.

121

(Los Angeles, 3/28/72)

"Who killed Scotty Bennett?"

"I'm not telling you."

"I remember the first time you said that."

"It was 1944. You asked me if I was sleeping with the boy from the Young Socialists' Alliance."

"Were you?"

"I'm not telling you."

They sat in Jack's car. Elysian Park was still rain-wet. She met Dwight there early on. Stone's throw: the LAPD Academy. Dwight's intimidation spot.

Jack said, "Did you destroy the file?"

"Karen and I burned it yesterday."

"Had she read it?"

Joan lit a cigarette. "She didn't have to. She knew it couldn't be anything else."

A black & white rolled by. Joan watched it. Jack said, "We could have leaked some pages on Bowen and BAAAAD BROTHER."

"Not without hurting Dwight."

"Dead's dead. Lost comrades serve the Cause from the grave routinely. 'Don't mourn. Organize!' Don't tell me you haven't heard that one."

"Things have shifted."

"You and the 'Enforcer.' "

" 'Some people you wait your whole life for.' Wayne Tedrow told me that."

Jack lit a cigarette. The sun hit his eyes. He pulled the visor down.

"IA's buried Scotty. They found his file, with Bowen all over it. They made Scotty and Bowen for the Thornton job, belatedly. We weren't in the file. I'd have heard if we were."

Joan cleaned her glasses on her shirttail. Jack did the same thing. She remembered the first time: Brooklyn, '46.

"We have seven million dollars."

"I know."

"I miss Celia. I'm too well known to go back to find her."

Jack said, "She knew the risks. You instilled them in her. She told you not to find her if this happened. You have to respect that. It's how our world works."

Joan tossed her cigarette. "You could go back."

"I'm not going to."

"On principle?"

"Yes."

"Solely on principle?"

Jack squeezed her arm. It hurt. It was a jilted comrade/lover's move, '46.

"*You* called off the Operation. *I* did not. *You* had a sentimental lapse. *You* put a personal relationship before a duty, and *I* did not."

Joan looked out her window. A young cop waved to her. She waved back.

Jack said, "I picked up a tip."

"I'm listening."

"Dwight put a black-bag team together for Nixon. We could capitalize on it."

"No."

"Why?"

"I'm not telling you."

Jack laughed. Joan dry-popped two pills.

"We should have had a child together."

Jack squeezed her arm, soft. "I remember the first time you said that."

"When was it?"

"Fall '54. The Army-McCarthy hearings were on TV."

"Why do we remember things that way?"

"Pure arrogance. We're self-absorbed and confuse our lives with History."

Joan smiled. Jack opened his briefcase.

"I've got a file on your new friend. It was in Dwight's desk. Clyde Duber built it. He thought the kid might get out of line one day."

· · ·

DONALD LINSCOTT CRUTCHFIELD. Born Los Angeles, 3/2/45. Brown hair, brown eyes, 5'9"/158.

Joan read at the fallback. The clothes nest smelled like her now. She caught less and less of Dwight.

Clyde Duber cribbed from PD reports and typed in his own notes. A Fed CBI carbon was clipped at the back. The persistent blur takes shape.

The racetrack-bum father. The missing mother. The boy at age ten. She sends him five dollars and a card every Christmas. The boy investigates.

Clyde Duber's postscript:

He located Margaret Woodard Crutchfield, May '65. She drank herself to death in Beaumont, Texas. He couldn't break the kid's heart. He tapped old pals nationwide. They continued the Christmas-gift tradition. The search gave the kid a non-perv task.

The kid was deft. "Voyeurs make good wheelmen and sometimes good investigators." Clyde got the kid out of trouble and gave him work. He noted his intransigence and invisibility. He feared his "weird tendencies." He noted the Dr. Fred Hiltz/Gretchen Farr case.

So it started then. You found me there.

Celia was Gretchen that summer. She was near mad in that guise. She was bilking men and taking drugs and transporting cocaine in rented airplanes. She was off in a mystic phase. Revolution bored her. King's death and RFK's death produced vile hippie pranks. She was worried about Tattoo. She had hexed and de-hexed her. She devoutly believed that Tattoo was in jeopardy. *Summer '68. The boy sees you.*

The Duber typescript ended. Joan hit the CBI report. The boy knew a wheelman named Phil Irwin and a divorce lawyer named Charles Weiss. Irwin was an FBI informant. He snitched cheating spouses from his rope jobs. His FBI handler quoted him:

"Yeah, I'll admit it. My buddy Chick and I like to peep. We studied under the best, Crutch Crutchfield. There ain't a window in Hancock Park that that twisted cocksucker ain't put his snout up to. He never knew it, but Chick and I used to tail him and study his technique. Chick said he 'scaled the Peeper Parthenon,' whatever the fuck that means."

Three muni PD file notes were listed below. Santa Monica PD: Irwin and Weiss questioned for loitering, 9/67. Beverly Hills PD: Irwin and Weiss questioned for loitering, 4/68. LAPD file note, 5/68: Realtor Arnold D. Moffett questioned per "porno parties."

She remembered the name. He rented "Gretchen" a house.

LAPD dropped the inquiry. Porno parties—so what? A KA list was footnoted: four names, plus Charles Weiss. "Mr. Weiss shares Mr. Moffett's penchant for bizarre Negro art."

Joan thought about the boy. Show him the file? Maybe, in part.

She found her pocketknife. She blade-redacted the lines on Margaret Woodard Crutchfield. The knife fit her hand precisely. She'd stabbed a picket-line goon with it in 1956.

122

(Los Angeles, 3/29/72)

Redd Foxx said, "Scotty was fucking a porcupine. I gots to tell you motherfuckers that it was a *female* porcupine, so I don't see nothing perverted in it."

Yuck, yuck—the crowd laffed, misty-eyed. Some coons offed Scotty—let's get zorched and mourn.

The wheelman lot. Early Christmas lights and plaid bunting. Booze and jelly bean–jar pharmaceuticals. You gots to love it.

Crutch, Clyde, Buzz, Phil Irwin and Chick Weiss. Milt C. onstage with Redd and Junkie Monkey. Ex-governor Pat Brown and numerous pigs. Fourteen Black Panthers. A colored heist guy turned TV evangelist. Frau Scotty and six of his girlfriends.

Junkie Monkey said, "Scotty popped my simian ass for a chump-change 211. I stole six moon pies, four bags of pork cracklings, a case of T-Bird and ten cartons of Kool king-size. Scotty saw that I had *soul* and let me live. We consumed all that motherfucking shit on the premises and went out lookin' for bitches."

Yuck, yuck—we're grief-struck, but it's fun. Frau Scotty passed a joint to Girlfriend #4. Girlfriend #5 nibbled a hash brownie.

Redd Foxx said, "Scotty was out searchin' for this brother name of Cleofis. He was a stickup man and a booty bandit. He was robbing liquor stores with a sawed-off shotgun and banging Scotty's bitches with a piece of hard black steel ten times that size."

Girlfriend #3 roared. Girlfriend #2 hugged Frau Scotty. Phil Irwin popped a Quaalude in the air. Chick Weiss caught it with his mouth. Pat Brown blinked—*Why am I here?*

The bash noise bashed him. He'd spent the day re-memorizing and phone calling. The parlay: D.R. safe houses and Hoover victims.

He re-memorized the CIA-safe-house list. He re-memorized the safe-house list from Joan's file. He got on the horn at pad #3 and called folks.

They vibed him as fuzz more than comrade. Joan's name got him some trust. It was name stew out of Joan's story and monologues. He ran phone checks and got numbers. He called and schmoozed the folks. He got updates and little tales back. J. Edgar fucked you—tell me about that.

They grapevined him. Jail terms, suicide, despondency. Early death and harassment. Lots of rat-out-your-pals barters—some succumbed to, some not.

He kept calling. The fuckers kept talking and feeding him numbers. He ran up his phone bill. The bad news avalanched him. Feds lurking at your window and your kids' school. You ragged Gay Edgar, loose chitchat, *now we'll get you.*

It got to him. It re-fueled *That Idea.* More suicides. More vanished loved ones. The grief had him earthquaked and tidal-waved.

Frau Scotty hopped onstage and got schmaltzy. It cued the Panthers to waltz. Junkie Monkey leered at Girlfriends #1 to #6. It cracked them up.

Crutch veered to the pay phone. It was still early. He could log more call-outs and more fuel. He coin-checked his pockets. Zilch on dimes and nickels. He pulled this sparkly emerald out.

His good-bye embrace. She slipped it to him then.
Babe, you didn't have to. You already sent me Red.

Sills Tip-Top was North Vegas. The drive sapped him. She called it her lucky-charm place. If you have to come, meet me there.

It was a bum-fuck coffee shop near Nellis AFB. The a.m. crowd was enlisted geeks and lounge-act debris. He made it on time—snatch-hair margin.

She waited in a back booth. The joint was integrated. Minimal tension buzzed.

He sat down. Mary Beth said, "You always look like you're out of breath."

A waitress poured him coffee. Crutch guzzled it and burned his mouth.

"I'm always running here to tell you something. I called ahead this time, though."

Mary Beth sipped coffee. "You always look different. Maybe it's because I only see you at intervals and always in such distress."

Crutch fumbled at his cup. Coffee spilled. Mary Beth wiped it up.

"You remind me of Wayne."

"I'm so goddamn sorry for that."

"Wayne made his bed. I was grateful to share it for a while, but it had to end the way it did."

An air force chump evil-eyed them. Crutch hard-eyed him back.

Mary Beth said, "Don't. Look where big gestures took Wayne. Try to be more prudent. You'll be better served in the end."

Crutch got a late road cramp. He stretched his legs and bumped Mary Beth. It jittered him. She sat still and let his fluster subside.

"I'm good at finding people."

"You told me that last time."

"I'm better now. I've learned some things."

"You look different. I'll concede that."

The waitress freshened their coffee. Mary Beth rolled up her blouse sleeves. She wore a silver bracelet with a single emerald inset.

"Your son sent you that stone."

"How do you know that?"

"I'm not telling you."

Mary Beth looked out the window. Crutch tracked her eyes. She studied a RE-ELECT NIXON sign.

"I know where your son is."

"How do you know that?"

"I'm not telling you."

She touched his hand. "I'm not going to ask you for it. You'll do whatever you're going to do, regardless of my wishes. The only thing I ask is that you don't attribute all your foolishness to some perceived debt to Wayne."

The waitress walked up. Crutch jittered. Mary Beth laced their fingers. The waitress caught it and zoomed.

Mary Beth covered his hands and held them to the table. He saw the green flecks in her eyes.

"Why do you do these crazy things?"

Crutch thought about it.

Crutch said, "So women will love me."

The herb guys lived close by. They shared lab space at this cat François' garage. Crutch showed up with beer and pizza. He caught a boil-and-sluice session in full swing.

The guys broke for a nosh-and-brew. Crutch said he had *An Idea*. I want to char-blacken paper short of combustion and flame.

Okay, baby boy. We work, you watch, you learn.

He explained Wayne's redaction work and his own mixed results. He said he could carry liquids or powders, but no ray gizmos. He ran down all the molecule charts he'd just memorized. The guys jabbered in French and told him to watch.

Three boil plates ran overtime. He lost track of the proportions and the reduction process. François dumped piles of typing paper on the garage floor. The other guys filled Windex bottles with liquid. Crutch counted six bottles and paper piles. François walked pile to pile and spritzed.

Pile #1 sat there, wet. Pile #2 bubbled and dripped. Pile #3 exploded. Two guys stamped the fire out.

Pile #4 curdled and crackled and cut loose a black haze.

123

(Los Angeles, 4/1/72)

Ella missed Dwight.

She told her stuffed animals. She didn't tell Karen. Plush *alligators*—Dwight's gifts to her.

Joan watched. Ella perched the gators on the picnic table and stage-whispered. She was three. She was developing stoic qualities and playing to adults. She'd learn to parcel information soon.

Dina darted into the house. Karen said, "I've decided to vanish. Too much has happened here. I'm going to take the girls and just go."

Joan rubbed her wrists. They were healing. She removed the bandages last night. New scars were forming.

"Your husband?"

"I'll leave him a note. He's too self-interested to look for me. He'll miss the girls for a while and move on."

Joan said, "I can give you some money. You won't have to teach."

"I'd appreciate that."

The gators were scuffed. Ella was rigorous and assigned them tasks. She didn't say much. She listened and acted. She was dogged and circumspect. She'd become calculatedly blunt.

Karen said, "I want to build some paper. I'll keep my first name and concoct a persona from there."

"Jack can pull mug shots and fingerprint cards. Your name will show up in KA files, but you can limit your exposure."

Ella snatched her gators and ran inside. Joan looked up at the fallback.

"Is there a genetic link to the virtue of persistence?"

Karen pointed to Ella's shadow. Joan smiled. Sun shards hit the yard. Karen covered her eyes.

"We're being surveilled."

"Yes, I know."

"Is he harmless?"

"I'm not sure. He's a convert of sorts, and he tries to be kind."

"My husband gave me those binoculars. He'd die if he knew where they've been."

"Leave them with the note. They'll make a good paperweight."

The light swerved. Joan waved and gestured *Come Here*.

The girls inspected him. Ella *studied* him. Dina covered her mouth and ran. Ella ambled and peered over her shoulder.

Karen said, "The coffee place on Hillhurst. You were always there."

The boy said, "I follow people. I make my living that way."

Joan heard Dina crying. Karen went *excuse me* and ducked into the house. The boy was fit. He had small brown eyes and a gray-flecked crew cut. The style was fuck-this-era defiant.

"Your wrists are better."

"Yes."

"I hope I'm not bothering you and your friends."

"You make your living that way."

He smiled. "I'm good at finding people."

Joan smiled. "We've discussed your prowess before."

"I'll find Celia. I'll get her out and bring her back."

Karen scolded Dina. Their voices carried. The boy disturbed the child. Dina tossed a fit.

"Maybe I should go."

"You don't have to."

"I'm bringing Reginald back. I may as well bring Celia, too."

"What do you want?"

"I don't know. That's my way of saying 'I'm not telling you.' "

They walked to the fallback and talked up through dusk. The boy described his craziness in the D.R. She fortified her capsules with Haitian tea. They left the terrace door open for breezes. She took her temperature covertly and counted days.

She put candles down. He said he liked the flame light on her hair. She tossed her hair. He said he saw sparks.

Their feet bumped. She looked at him. The look said *Yes, now.* He kissed her. It was soft. She kissed him back hard. It said *Don't Be Scared.* He popped a blouse button. He put his hands on her breasts.

She pulled his shirt off and saw the scar. He started to tell her the story. She shushed him. It said *I know.* It brought back all of Dwight.

He pulled off her boots. She braced herself on the floor. Her blouse was up. Her jeans were loose. He ran his mouth over the gap. She arched. He pulled off her jeans and underwear and kicked off his own shoes and pants. Her blouse was half-buttoned. He popped the last three. The floor was cold on her back.

The candlelight and shadows set up *something.* Their heads converged in a weird way. She calculated the age-space between them. Telepathic tabulation. Eighteen years, four months, five days.

She rolled onto the mattress. Dwight's smell was still there. The boy kneeled and cramped up. She rubbed his legs and made him stretch and un-jangled him. He kissed her legs. She opened up for him. Little nose rubs parted her. She liked him for that.

A cold wind gave her goose bumps. He got protective then. He wrapped himself all over her. *Be safe/be still/I'm here.* She eased him back. She let her hands dance.

Her hair fanned as she touched him. He pulled himself up to *watch. Be still/don't look/I'm here.*

Her hands played rougher and harder. Their heads clicked in again. He fell back and shut his eyes. He made hurt sounds she'd never heard before.

Candlelight swerved. Shadows formed on the walls. He opened his eyes and saw her profile. Their heads clicked again. *We* haven't seen this before.

He tried to roll her. She didn't let him. She fit herself over him. She let him look and willed his eyes shut. She moved and took them someplace. It went for a while. The candles burned down to nubs.

"You're determined to do this?"

"Yes."

"There's a safe house in Borojol. The small building by the open-front bodega. You might get leads there."

"I've got some addresses memorized."

"There's a doctor named Esteban Sánchez. He moves his office around. He and Celia are close. He might know where to look."

"I've got some ideas. I know some people there."

"Are they bribable?"

"Yes."

"I'll give you some money."

"It scares me. You know what I saw there."

"You went looking for it and it found you. It always does."

"Will Celia know where Reginald is?"

"Possibly. They're comrades."

"It scares me. The place itself. It scares me more than anything that might happen there."

"What were you looking for?"

"Everything."

"What did you find?"

"A picture of you on a beach and a ticket back here."

"Was it worth it?"

"You don't have to worry about me. I know what shit costs."

"No, you don't. You can't run at his pace forever, because one day it just stops."

"Don't tell me that. I'm just getting started up."

124

(Santo Domingo, 4/7/72)

The Zombie Zone, distilled. Plain fucking *MORE*.

More street rousts, more toxic rodents, more Haitian dispossessed. More sap-twirling *fascistas* and more skin-color gaps.

More heat. More flying insects. More stump-legged black guys on rolling planks. No casino-build cosmetics. More *baaaaad* juju and less dissent.

Crutch cabbed into Borojol. He had four hundred K and a silencered piece. Customs let him in easy. He wasn't red-tagged. He had his memory lists. Joan got him two forged passports: one for Celia, one for Reggie.

Too familiar meets evil. Everything brought back something he tried to forget. He passed the golf course. His X-ray eyes revived. There's the torture bunker and the electric chair.

The *New York Times* diverted him. Doofus Democrats and Nixon. J. Edgar's latest gaffe. A street flash de-diverted him. Surging fuzz crush a leaflet-passing cabal.

He'd spent four nights with Joan. They talked and made love. He'd leave for short stretches, just to take deep breaths. He didn't mention His Idea. He couldn't risk the word "No." He didn't sleep much. He curled around her and smelled her hair on the pillow. She held his hands to her breasts.

The cab pulled into Borojol. The More got Worse. More iron-heel bullshit. More skateboard beggars. More barefooted Haitians traipsing through rat dung and broken glass.

There's the open-front bodega. There's the safe house.

Crutch paid the driver and got out. The safe house looked innocuous.

He knocked and got no answer. No footsteps inside and no sounds of flight.

He shouldered the door. Sunlight through broken glass supplied the upshot.

The walls were bullet-holed. Spent shells covered the floor. One wall was blood-sprayed and pellet-flecked, all laced with dark hair.

Flies buzzed around a doctor's smock, soaked red on a chair.

Stay awake. It's a last look. Go get more of the More. Lefty lifestyle rules curtailed him. Joan knew her comrades mostly by first names. Dr. Sánchez had no phone listed. That meant drive and peep.

Crutch rented a junker and cruised the safe-house list. He'd memorized fourteen addresses. He started in Gazcue and worked west.

The first three pads were empty. He door-knocked to no avail and broke in. He saw telltale cleanup signs. He smelled ammonia with blood undertones. He ran his penlight and saw the casings the cleanup guys had missed.

Santo Domingo by night: 82° and still fascist-oppressed.

He drove around. He got lost in the details. He saw three women he'd peeped a while back.

The black kids eating boat chum in the Río Ozama. The old casino sites with squatter bands and cracker-box cribs going up.

He hit four more addresses. Two houses weren't there. He talked to a street fool. The guy said La Banda torched them. It got to him. He wanted them to be speakeasies. Knock, knock. A peephole slides. He says, "I'm a friend. Comrade Joan sent me."

He looped around. He hit the next seven places. He met two square families at the outset. We just rented the dump. We don't know no Celia, no Reds.

He cruised the last five pads. He got one torch job and four clean-outs. A wino said those La Banda humps were fucking firebugs. He saw pellet pocks and maggot mounds on gristle. He saw a shot-to-shit Afro wig.

He got Another Idea.

Ivar Smith said, *"Hola, pariguayo."*

Terry Brundage said, "I never thought we'd see your peeping ass back here."

The bar at the El Embajador. 8:00 a.m. Bloody Marys affixed with celery sticks. Both guys had aged. Both guys looked prematurely sclerotic.

Crutch cleared table space. Brundage Tabasco'd his drink. Smith pointed to the briefcase.

"*¿Qué es esto?*"

Crutch said, "Four hundred G's."

Brundage said, "Oh, shit. He's working for the Boys again."

Smith said, "As if Wayne Tedrow and the Tiger Krew weren't enough."

Brundage said, "Just what we need. More mob grief and Commie sabotage."

Smith said, "Wayne killed Mormonism for me. I used to think they were all good right-wing white men."

Brundage noshed his celery stick. "I hate fucking wops."

Smith noshed his celery stick. "I hate fucking left-wing converts with chemistry expertise."

Crutch flashed his show pix: Reggie and Celia Reyes.

Brundage said, "Who's the chiquita? I dig her eyes."

Smith said, "Sambo looks like Chubby Checker. 'Come on, baby. Let's do the Twist.' "

Crutch dipped into the briefcase and tossed them both ten grand. Smith gagged and almost sprayed. Brundage dropped his celery stick.

Crutch said, "They're Commies, sure as shit. I want to find them and take them back to the States."

Brundage fanned his cash stacks. "Why?"

Crutch said, "I'm not telling you."

Smith fanned his cash stacks. "Put motive aside for a moment. How much of the money do we keep?"

Crutch patted the briefcase. "All of it. You pay everybody who needs to get paid, and you keep the rest."

Brundage said, "Explain this to me. I'm not saying no, but give me more of a hint."

"I'm all out of leads. You've got the files, the informants and the manpower. It's a roundup. You find them or you find the Commies who know where they are."

Brundage salted his drink. "Detentions."

Smith peppered his drink. "Interrogations. We bring in La Banda."

Crutch said, "They could be in Haiti."

Brundage rolled his eyes. "That means the Tonton."

Smith rolled his eyes. "Evil, chicken-fucking primitives, who do not work cheap."

Brundage chomped his celery stick. "Papa Doc will want a taste."

Smith chomped his celery stick. "So will the Midget."

Crutch fanned a cash roll. "It's a lot of money."

Brundage said, "I've got Jew blood. We'll do it for five."

Smith said, "I'm getting more Jewish by the moment. Five closes the deal."

Crutch shook his head. "Four hundred big ones, over and out."

Brundage sighed and looked at Smith. Smith salted his drink and sighed back.

"This could get raw. You're dealing with hard-core subversives."

Crutch tapped the show pix. "I don't care, as long as they don't get hurt."

He stayed awake. Sleep scared him. His nightmares would eclipse shit that flared real-time. He copped dexies at a quick-script *farmacia*. He leveled his fuel with klerin-laced sno cones. The fruit base cut down dehydration.

Smith and Brundage culled files and built a name list. The cash split went down. Papa Doc and the Midget hogged the green. They got a hundred each. Smith and Brundage got fifty each. The rest went for ops costs and goons. La Banda and the Tonton supplied shake-the-trees guys.

Flying squads: the D.R. and Haiti. Rural-jail detention sites flanking the river. Polygraph machines, Pentothal, coercion. Hard boys with phone books and saps.

The planning took three days. Smith's office served as command post. Crutch stayed awake and sat in. Brundage and Smith scanned KA lists. They found nineteen Celia listings and zero Reggie listings. That limited their targets. Smith said, let's keep it tight. Detain, interrogate, press and/or release. Brundage disagreed. The Reds all know each other. Let's build a big snitch-out pool.

The argument extended. Crutch sided with Brundage. More was better. Smith argued for a less-meets-more combo. Don't overcrowd the jails. Don't let the fuckers huddle and collude. Weed out the lice who don't know Celia or Reggie at the get-go. Offer rat-out cash. Restrict the interrogations to likely suspects.

They agreed on thirty-four names. Twenty-three lived in the D.R., eleven lived in Haiti. They had four La Banda teams with squad cars. They had three Tonton teams with squad cars. The jail sites were mid-island, near Dajabón. A walk-bridge provided foot access. The Plaine du Massacre was croc-infested there. The fuckers dined on dumped garbage and errant Haitians on voodoo-herb trips.

The polygraphs were hooked up. The Pentothal was laid in. The interrogators stood ready. Both jails were two-way-radio–rigged. The squad cars had two-ways. The system was spiffy.

Smith called the shots. Crutch joined him at the D.R. jail. Crocs lounged on the riverbank. They were groovy. Crutch stared out the window at them.

Clock it: exactly 7:00 a.m.

Smith radioed the cars. The cars rogered back in English and French. Mug shots were wall-pinned: thirty-four comrades, total.

Crutch read their files last night. They were mostly kids his age. They looked like kids. He didn't. He had gray hair and posterior scarring. One non-kid exception: Esteban Sánchez, M.D. He looked battle-aged. Joan had called him "a seasoned Red Brigade warrior."

The callbacks hit: got them, got them, got them. Smith manned the radio. Crutch heard sputter and squawk. Some Reds resisted, some didn't. We're coming in now.

Crutch walked outside and waited on the bridge. Crocs sunned and swam below. He tossed them handfuls of beef jerky. They snapped it off the water. Their teeth flashed. Their snouts veered toward the bridge.

Joan.

Every thought now. Cutting through his case and his idea. Cutting through to *This*.

She raises her arms. He kisses her there. She says, "You're insanely durable and persistent." She harps on that. She talks about the gene of persistence. He asks her what she means. She says, "I'm not telling you."

Hours whizzed by. Crutch stayed in the Joan Zone. He ate dexies. He watched the crocs. He heard incoming calls on a loudspeaker. Yeah, we got Reds—but no Reggie or Celia.

The squad cars showed. Muffler noise announced them. Whoosh—dual-court press—both riverbanks. It felt synchronized. Crutch had a two-river view.

Eyes right—Tonton guys and black Commies. Eyes left—La Banda with Reds black and brown. Crutch stood on the bridge and head-counted. The D.R.: eighteen total. Haiti: nine of eleven. No Reginald Hazzard, no Celia Reyes.

The comrades were handcuffed. Crutch counted twenty-four men and three women. The goons shoved and pushed them. A few dragged their feet. Little sap shots got them back going.

They entered the jails. Two-river view. Out and in, instantaneous.

Nothing showed through the windows. Crutch stood on the bridge and fed the crocs. He was weavy and dingy. Spots popped in front of his eyes. He'd been up since L.A.

A croc leaped way high. Crutch reached down and scratched his nose. A man screamed in the D.R. jail, up close. A man screamed in the Haiti jail, faint.

It went on for ten seconds. Crocs swarmed under the bridge. *Feed me that shit now.*

Crutch tuned it all out. The crocs dispersed. Time dispersed. He popped more dexies, he got more dingy, he saw more spots. Joan takes off her glasses and rubs her eyes. He kisses her arms. He yanks at her boots. She laughs and resists. He falls on his ass.

A man screamed in the D.R. jail. Two men screamed in the Haiti jail, faint. It went on for half a minute and stopped.

Crutch re-tuned it out. His arms tingled. He felt sunstroked. He saw spots. His pants felt slack. The spots started to look like bugs.

A man screamed in the D.R. jail. It went on and didn't stop. He conjured Joan harder. She touched Dwight's clothes and cried. He told her he'd look after her. She said, "You can't."

A woman screamed in the D.R. jail. It went on and didn't stop. Crutch covered his ears. That didn't stop it. He turned his back and got more distance. That made it worse. His ears hurt. The spots grew into grids and reframed everything. The screams got louder. He turned around and sprinted up.

The front door was open. Kids were shackled to drainpipes and benches inside. The sound reverbed down a back hall.

Crutch ran. The spots became figures. He knocked down a Tonton dude and a La Banda guy with a Sten gun. He hit a connecting corridor. He saw mirror-paned sweat rooms on both sides. Kids resisted poly tests. Goons cuffed kids to chair backs. Goons waved phone books and hose chunks.

The woman screamed louder. Crutch nailed the sound and kicked in the door. She was chair-cuffed. Her arms were bloody. A Tonton fuck had a barbed-wire sap.

She saw him and screamed louder. The Tonton guy stepped up. Oh, no, baby boy—this is mine.

Crutch arm-barred him. His throat bones cracked. Crutch elbow-slammed his nose and broke it. The Tonton guy grabbed at his throat and convulsed. The woman screamed. Crutch pulled off his shirt and showed her his scar.

Smith ran into the room. The Tonton fuck puked bone chips and blood. Crutch weaved and saw spots. The woman looked at his scar. Their heads converged. She said something in Spanish. Crutch thought he heard "Celia" and "Port-au——"

Two Tonton guys drove him. Brundage and Smith frosted the dustup. You was over-zealous. You over-reacted. Thanks for the bread.

The car was a voodoo barge. A '63 Impala, lowered and chopped. Bizango-sect flags. Cheater slicks and baby-moon hubcaps. Dashboard pix of dogs in pointed hats.

Crutch weaved in the backseat. Those spots kept swirling. He broke his L.A. record for staying hot-wired awake. The Tonton guys dug him. The torture guy fucked the driver guy's wife. That be bad juju. You a righteous white boy.

The barge was air-cooled. Tinted windows shaded all the *pauvre* shit outside. Little villages and big signs extolling Papa Doc. Blood-marked trees ubiquitous and geeks in chicken-head hats.

The people faded into spots and vice versa. The Tonton guys spoke half English, half French. The roundup made them each a C-note. La Banda skirmished with some Reds in Santo Domingo. That be bad *gre-gre*.

Port-au-Prince was Shitsville with a Sea Breeze. Rocky beaches, stucco cubes and eroded buildings older than God. The barge stopped at a lime green pad raised off the street on pylons. Crutch said bye-bye and lurched up the steps.

He knocked. The door opened. Celia Reyes leaned on the jamb. She said, "I've seen you before." He said, "Everyone has." The spots cohered and made everything black.

Lieutenant Maggie Woodard, USNR.

She wore the winter blues and the summer khakis. Her name tag read WOODARD. She never married Crutch Senior. She drank too much and got pissy or effusive. She stayed in the reserves after the Big War.

She wore her uniform on weekends. He watched from doorways. She tipped highballs and played Brahms on a scratchy phonograph. She chain-smoked. She dangled her brown uniform shoe off her left foot. She dangled her black uniform shoe off her right. She caught him lurking and laughed. She fed him maraschino cherries out of her glass.

Fading in and dispersing. Blackout sketches into spots.

We're in Ensenada. You've got an earache. I can't stand your hurt. I hit a farmacia and shoot you up.

We're in L.A. Your father blows our money. We scrounge empty pop bottles and splurge at Bob's Big Boy.

We're in San Diego. Your father is elsewhere. You're out roving, as you always are. You come back unexpectedly. You catch me with a lover at the El Cortez Hotel.

You're always watching me. I leave that day. You stand at the window, waiting. I never saw it, but I know.

. . .

"You undressed me."

"You were delirious. You weren't making sense at all."

"How long was I out?"

"Two full days."

"Jesus. Everything looks different."

"Then maybe it is."

The robe was too big. He'd lost twenty pounds, easy. She cooked a big breakfast. The smell repulsed him. The kitchen was cramped. Everything was off-scale. Dishes covered the table and sent weird fumes up.

Celia said, "Joan sent you."

"How did you know?"

"I found a picture of her in with your clothes."

"What else did you find?"

"A Saint Christopher medal, a .45 automatic and a list of meticulously prepared questions."

Crutch re-focused. Four years, then to now. Hollywood to Haiti. She hadn't changed. Everything else had.

"I hope you'll be willing to answer them."

Celia sipped coffee. "I don't think I care like you do."

"I don't understand."

She smiled. "I'm saying I've changed. My beliefs have solidified. I'm not that reckless and vindictive person so determined to avenge Tattoo."

Crutch weaved. The off-scale room contracted. He felt kitchen heat and started to sweat.

"I'd appreciate it if you could tell me what you know and what you remember."

Celia buttered her toast. She wore a knee-length shift. Her hair was cinched tight by a barrette.

"Tattoo was a voodoo priestess. I held to her beliefs much more then than I do now. She was wild and I was wild, and I was trying to manipulate a man who worked for Howard Hughes. I wanted to see those casinos built in my country. Joan and I thought we could shape that event to benefit the Cause."

Crutch poured coffee. "I know that part. I know about the hex you placed on Tattoo and how you wanted to revoke it. What concerns me is the specific details of that sum—"

"I was wild. She was wild. We were caught up in large things together. I had summoned a curse on her because I believed in those things then. We reconnected that summer. It was a dangerous time in the world. I wanted to hurt Tattoo and save her, all at once. She had made a pornographic film with a voodoo theme. A sleazy realtor arranged for screenings of it around the time Tattoo disappeared. Things connected. The realtor knew the man who worked for Howard Hughes. It all felt mystical. Joan humored me and allowed me to rent a house from the man. Tattoo was crashing in a house nearby. Joan had told her about the place. It stayed vacant for long periods. Joan and some comrades had used it as a safe house years before."

Convergence, confluence, coincidence. Arnie Moffett, Horror House, the Commie meeting notes. A time loop: '68 to 12/6/62.

"The realtor's name was Arnold Moffett."

"Yes, that sounds right. He had a vague connection to the Caribbean. I think he was involved in Haitian import-export."

Re-convergence. Arnie Moffett in '68: my pads are fuck-film sets.

"You knew Sal Mineo. You asked him to set Tattoo up with some movie-business men. He'd referred you before. You wanted to revoke the curse. Tattoo had done penance and bought her way out of the book of the dead. She—"

Celia clamped his hands. He was racy and sweaty. He let her anchor him.

"Sal called it 'fantasia' then, and I'm calling it that now. *Tattoo was wild, I was wild. We were wild like you're wild now.* Tattoo reconciled with the 6/14 people and did favors for Joan. Joan said, 'Sweetie, stop this foolishness. Tattoo will be better served if you let all this go.' "

Crutch pulled his hands free. "And you *did*? And you're telling me that's *it*?"

Celia nodded. "I'll grant you this. Tattoo disappeared, and I had a legitimate premonition that she had been killed that summer. For what it's worth, I still have it. I had it later that year, and I talked to a friend about it, and—"

"Leander James Jackson, who—"

"Who is dead now himself. *He* asked around about Tattoo. *He* talked to the realtor, and *he* got nowhere."

Crutch rubbed his legs. His limbs felt numb. His brain re-spooled, re-started, re-stopped and re-fed.

"You're saying that's it?"

"Yes."

"You're saying you don't remember the men you set Tattoo up with?"

"Yes."

"You're saying you don't know who attended the screenings?"

"Yes. I have a copy of the film, but Leander and I never identified the other actors."

"You're saying that Jackson braced Arnie Moffett on the screenings and got nothing, and that from there you just let it all slide?"

Celia touched his arm. "You're resourceful and persistent, or you wouldn't have found me. If you're as anxious to please Joan as I think you are, you can find better ways to serve the Cause."

Re-feeding, re-spooling, stop/start, squelch/sputter/off.

"Do you know where Reginald Hazzard is?"

"Yes. He lives a mile from here."

Crutch laughed. "Just like that?"

She took a napkin and wiped his face. Sweat trickled into his eyes.

"I'm taking you back to Joan."

"No, you're not. I'll write a note to her."

The film can was heavy. The envelope was sealed. C.R./J.K. was printed on the back.

He decided to walk and re-scale things. It didn't work. He felt *re*-railed, not *de*-railed. He had the Arnie Moffett *re*-lead. He still had That Idea.

He called Ivar Smith from Celia's place. They made travel plans. Tonton shuttle to Santo Domingo. L.A. from there. Stiff the Vegas call and pray it plays out.

His fingers were paper-cut. File reads did that sometimes. They tingled. His brain just re-signaled him the pain.

Sea spray and humidity. Spice in the air. Black folks speaking French.

He tossed Celia's passport in a trash can. He swiped a banana from a fruit stand and snarked it. Some kids played a portable radio. Memory Lane: Archie Bell and the Drells with "The Tighten Up."

There's chez Reggie. It's Caribbean Day-Glo green.

The door was open. A torn-up screen was stuck in place. Crutch reached through a hole and un-latched it.

A lab and a file trove. Bottle rows and stacked folders. Chem texts, beakers, burners and pots. Some nifty molecular charts.

His fingers stung. He scanned shelves and played a hunch. There's *ocimum basilicum*. Sure, why not?

He dipped his left-hand fingers in the bottle. They re-tingled and un-stung. He pulled them out. The cuts disappeared as the skin puckered up.

"Do you believe in Haitian chemistry?"

He turned around. Nix on Chubby Checker. Reggie looked like Harry Belafonte with white splotches and a Fu Manchu stash.

Crutch said, "I believe in everything."

Sleep found him and won. He wanted to see it all one more time and say good-bye to Wayne. He got a blackout curtain and cigarette backdraft.

He smelled the airport. Jet fuel and scorched rubber. He heard chants right after that.

"*Muerto,*" La Banda, "Raids" *en español.*

He opened his eyes. He saw kids with black-bordered placards. A photo of a swarthy guy. ESTEBAN JORGE SÁNCHEZ, 1929–1972.

He shut his eyes again. Reggie said, "Don't go to sleep. We're here."

The Midget flew them first-class. Reggie was tall. The legroom jazzed him. Crutch tried to conjure Joan and got Esteban Sánchez non-stop.

Reggie was Mr. Quiet. It all oozed fait accompli. He didn't niggle, question, protest. Reggie, the doofus genius with the hellbent past.

Crutch stayed awake. The nightmare potential re-vitalized him and kept him up. Reggie read chemistry books and over-ate. His burn scars looked exotic. The stewardess dug on him. Reggie, the socially unkempt and angelic savant.

Crutch got mad out of nowhere. The jet engine throb got lodged in him somehow. He got dizzy. Sleep fought him and won.

"Sir, we've arrived."

The stewardess jostled him. First class had filed out. Reggie was gone. *No, not yet. Please, God—let me see—*

He jumped up. He grabbed his bag and shoved people out of the way. His coat flapped. People saw his gun and got panicked. He shoved his way down the ramp. He elbowed some hippie fools and a nun. He made the runway. He saw Reggie and Mary Beth lock in an embrace.

The kid was sobbing. Mary Beth held his head down. She looked up and saw Crutch. She gave him her green-flecked eyes for a moment and walked her son off.

125

(Los Angeles, 4/13/72)

Joan built identities.

She worked at Dwight's desk. Klein and Sifakis were verboten now. Too much had happened. She'd overused Williamson, Goldenson, Broward and Faust.

They needed birth certificates. Forest Lawn sent her a plot list. It included names, dates of birth and dates of death. She thumbed through it. The decedents were alphabetized. They needed two women. 1920s DOBs, one ethnic/one not. She was Jewish and looked it. Karen was Greek and did not.

She scanned columns. The correct-age name selection was scant. They needed solitary women. Scant family or none. That required backup research. From there: driver's licenses, Social Security cards, official file plants.

The names bored her. She sipped tea and lit a cigarette. Her wrist scars itched. She glanced around the fallback.

An envelope by the door. Expensive paper. It barely fit under the crack.

She got up and reached for it. She saw the set of initials on the back. She slit the top and read the note attached.

Mi Amor,
   Me quedo. Por la Causa. Con respeto al regalo que eres tú.

She'd kissed the page below her signature. Her lips had left an imprint bright red.

126

(Los Angeles, 4/14/72)

R oll it.

Clyde and Buzz were out. Crutch worked the briefing-room projector. He spooled in the film and matched the sprocket holes. He killed the lights and pulled down the wall screen. He centered the beam and got *Action*.

Color footage, grainy stock. He jiggled dials. Better now—a clear image.

Fade in. There's a panning shot. There's a living room. The camera catches a window. It's light outside. The room is small and cheaply furnished. It's not Horror House.

A shot holds: the living room, close in. Five people walk into the frame. There's three women, two men. They're all naked and body-painted. Voodoo symbols, head to foot. The two men are black. Two women are white. They all wear wooden masks. The other woman is unmasked and wildly tattooed. She's María Rodríguez Fontonette.

Crutch straddled a chair. The camera swerved through the living room. There's the window again. The street is visible, it's Beachwood Canyon, we're *near* Horror House.

The camera re-centered. The actors swallowed brown capsules. Haitian herbs, yes. Cut to a close-up. There's María. There's the tattoo on her arm. The severing bisected the artwork soon after. She had lovely hands. They'd be severed. She moved gracefully. The killer cut inside of her. All that lithe movement, quashed.

Crutch watched. He felt compressed. Summer '68. Tattoo crashes in Horror House, Tattoo dies there. Arnie Moffett's rental houses. Joan and

Celia rent one. The rental-house screenings. It's all compressed. He was close at the start of it and never since. Warning click: there's something you missed.

Jump cut: we're in a bedroom now. There's an uncovered water bed, jiggling. The actors mill around. They talk to someone offscreen. Their lips move soundless.

Crutch stared at Tattoo. She's beautiful, she's alive. She betrayed 6/14 in '59 and reconciled later. "It was a wild time." Celia said that. He couldn't reconcile the Cause with a fuck flick. It offended him.

The men trembled and shook. They fell on the bed. Their backs arched. Their legs spasmed. The potions took hold. They were early-stage zombified. They dumped their masks and gasped for air. They sweated the voodoo paint off their bodies.

Tattoo whipped them. Soft shots, for show. The two white girls started trembling. Their movements were puppet-string jerky. They got on the bed and stroked the guys hard. They all seized and thrashed. They all did grand mal shit, out of body. The men thrashed prone. Their movements slowed. The white girls straddled them and pulled them inside. The camera got insertion-close.

Different herbs. The women contorted at a hyper-pace. They pinned down the men. Their hips and arms moved in counterpoint. Their heads moved on some spazzy axis. The camera caught the men close. Their eyes were open and dead. Tattoo soft-whipped the women. Their contortions accelerated.

Tattoo stepped out of sight and stepped back in the frame. She held a fireplace tool, shaped like a phallus. The cock tip glowed. It was near white-hot. She touched the carpet with it and got combustion. The women thrashed and opened their mouths. She fed them the cock head. They sucked it and displayed no pain. They removed their mouths and pressed the cock head to the bedstead. The fabric sizzled and burned down to the springs.

The men were zombified. The women voodoo-fucked them. Tattoo grabbed the burning cock and burn-carved the wall. Crutch *got it*. He *knew* the markings. Tattoo drew them at Horror House. Tattoo drew them in fire on a fuck film–set wall.

The sprocket holes jammed. The screen went all white. The film died at just that spot.

Convergence. Connection. Confluence. Clyde's line: *It's who you know and who you blow and how you're all linked.*

Warning click: something's missing. You don't know who killed Tattoo. You don't know who glued all this up.

Crutch drove up Beachwood Canyon. It was all tight. There's Horror House. There's the house Joan and Celia rented. There's Arnie Moffett's other pads. Your four-years-back memory holds.

He zigzagged side streets. He calibrated the view out the fuck-film window. There it is, intact. The same palm trees and driveway across the street. A Moffett Realty sign.

Still all tight. Stone's throw here, stone's dribble there. Who/what started it and made it all cohere?

Celia said Arnie Moffett ran an import-export biz. Click—we're back *there* again.

Confluence. It's who you know and who you—

Crutch drove downtown. Clyde had pull at the L.A. License Bureau. File access cost you fifty clams and a wink.

The duty clerk recognized him. Import-export from a while back? The boxes in Room 12.

The room was a musty paper swamp. The boxes were marked by years. No pull tabs, no alphabetizing. Real paper digs.

He started at '66 and worked backward. He hit at '63.

Arnie had a low-rent biz going. "Arnie's Island Exotics, Limited." Curios, knickknacks, *connection.* Imports from: Jamaica, Haiti, the D.R. closer now. Where's that little link-it-all click?

The same office. The same next-door deli. "The Home of the Hebrew Hero."

He brought a pint of Jim Beam. Arnie was a lush. The booze softened the beating then. It might work now.

Crutch walked in. A bell jingled. Arnie sat at the same desk. His bowling shirt was green today. He picked his nose and read *Car Craft.*

Crutch took the client's chair. Arnie ignored him. Crutch placed the jug on his blotter.

Arnie glanced at it. Crutch said, "Summer '68. What's the first thing you think of?"

Eyes on the jug. He considers, *re*-considers and *re*-cogitates. Aaah, he gets it.

"The first thing I think of is all that political *tsuris.* The second thing I think of is you."

Crutch cracked the jug and passed it over. Arnie chugalugged.

"The third thing I'm thinking is that you look a lot older. The fourth is that I hope you ain't still on that crusade. If it pertains to my houses, Gretchen Farr, Farlan Brown or Howard Hughes, you heard everything I got."

Crutch said, "Leander James Jackson."

Arnie *re*-chugged. "Say what?"

"The other guy who came around asking questions. That woman 'Tattoo,' your fuck-film set, the house you rented out for the screenings."

Arnie picked his snout. "We got two different agendas here. Where they connect, I don't know. You had your Gretchie crusade, he had his thing for Tattoo. He's dead, by the way. He got offed in that 'Black-Militant Blastout.' And, by the way, I didn't hold nothing back from you. I told you I rented my cribs as porno-film sets, but you didn't ask me no questions about Tattoo."

Re-convergence, *de*-convergence. So far, Arnie played kosher. Shit hovered close.

"Tell me about Tattoo."

"What's to tell? I knew somebody who knew somebody who knew her. I heard she was on the skids. She heard I used to run an import biz out of her shitty country. She wanted to make some *farkakte* voodoo-smut film, and she needed a place to screen it. We talked on the phone. I gave her some leads. They were all pervy-type guys off my old import-customer list. She cold-called them, which ended our brief and borderline profitable encounter."

Crutch rubbed his eyes. "Were you there for the film shoot?"

"No."

"Did you meet the camera crew or the other actors?"

"No."

"Have you seen the film?"

"*Nyet.* Porno ain't my bag. I like the real thing there in the sack with me. I'm an in-and-out kind of guy. Ten minutes of bliss and I'm back watching *Bowling for Dollars* on Channel 13."

Crutch rubbed his neck. He was all knots and kinks.

"Who went to the screenings? Give me some names."

Arnie sucked on the jug. "I don't know. I sent Tattoo a mimeograph copy of my list."

"She was murdered that summer. How does that sit with you?"

Arnie made the jackoff sign. "It don't sit with me one way or the other. That Haitian guy thought she'd been clipped, so I'll tell you the same thing I told him. Bobby the K. and that civil rights *macher* just bought it, so it's not like some stray piece of island gash carries all that much weight with me."

Crutch saw *RED*. Just like *then*. No, don't do it.

"Where's the fucking customer list?"

Arnie popped a zit on his neck. "It's in my garage, if it's anywhere. The key's on the hook by the john. Have fun, but don't come back in another four years and put me through this shit again."

Dust, mildew, cobwebs, spiders' nests, mice. Oil cans, dead batteries, a cracked engine block. *Car Craft* back to '52. Forty forged Sandy Koufax baseballs.

Arnie Moffett's garage, Mar Vista.

Stolen prescription pads. The full run of *Food Service Monthly*. A photo of Marlon Brando with a dick in his mouth. Four BB guns, two defunct lawn mowers, the skeletal remains of a cat.

Crutch worked. He dug through pack-rat shit to get at a pile of boxes. He hit the first box row. Arnie's résumé expanded. He sold French ticklers, he sold rosaries, he sold the Donkey Dan Dong Extender. He sold counterfeit football tix. He ran the Debra Paget Fan Club. He mail-ordered JFK and Jackie K. dolls. He drop-shipped amyl-nitrate poppers to fag bars. He owned an employment agency for wetback kitchen help.

There—"Arnie's Island Exotics."

He ripped the box open. An invoice stack popped out. He dumped the box on the floor. Gotcha—"Customers/'59–'63."

Four stapled pages. A fuckload of names.

Crutch scanned alphabetic. The names and addresses meant greek. He got to the last page. He scanned the *T*s to *Z*s. He stopped dead at:

"Weiss, Charles. 1482 North Roxbury, Beverly Hills."

Chick: divorce lawyer. Chick: wheelman consort. Chick: Phil Irwin's best pal. Phil: hired and fired by Dr. Fred Hiltz—find me Gretchen Farr. Chick: dope fiend and mud shark.

And . . .

There's . . .

The . . .

CLICK.

Chick's office. Rope-job strategy. The three-phallus statue. The open-legged Negress. Imports—all voodoo vile.

He needed a throwdown. The fallback was close. *Cold pieces.* Dwight might have left some.

It was dusk. He floored it northeast. He looped by Karen's place en route. Window view: Karen and Joan in the living room. The girls acting rambunctious.

The fallback lights were on. Crutch snagged the key under the mat and let himself in. A file was propped up on the desk. Joan had left him a note.

D.C.,

A friend found this. The Feds have paper on you. I thought you might like to see it.

J.K.

CRUTCHFIELD, DONALD LINSCOTT.

Clyde Duber–culled reports. Knife-redacted paragraphs. Clyde's assessments: "Voyeurs make good wheelmen." "Weird tendencies." The kid was working the Farr case. He was too tweaked on it.

A CBI report: Phil Irwin, Fed snitch.

"My buddy Chick and I like to peep. We studied under the best, Crutch Crutchfield. There ain't a window in Hancock Park that that twisted cocksucker ain't put his snout up to. He never knew it, but Chick and I used to tail him and study his technique."

PD reports below: Phil and Chick popped for loitering. KA Arnie Moffett questioned per "porno parties." Arnie shares Chick's love of "bizarre Negro art."

He saw *RED*. He couldn't breathe. He gulped sink water and coughed it out. He got some wind back.

Dwight had left a goody basket in the closet. He found a throwdown, handcuffs and a roll of duct tape.

Phil was a car-dweller. He crashed in his Tiger kab most nights. He usually parked in the wheelman lot, away from the street.

Crutch drove over. The station was closed. A Tiger stretch was parked by the toolshed. Phil was sleepytimed in the backseat. His arms dangled out the window.

Snores. Booze breath wafting. Phil's head propped on the window ledge.

Crutch parked and walked up. Phil dozed on. Crutch opened his cuffs and snapped Phil's left wrist. Phil dream-yipped. Crutch cranked the ratchets and spare-cuffed the doorpost. Phil grimaced and snored.

Crutch yanked the door wide. The cuff chain gouged Phil and pulled him up and out of the seat. He roused. He hit the world on his knees. He didn't get it. I can't move. My arm's above my head *and it hurts*.

He shrieked. He blinked and saw Crutch. He said, "Hey, Peep—"

Crutch kicked him in the balls. Phil hurled booze laced with peanuts.

He tried to stand and get some chain slack. Crutch re-kicked his balls. Phil re-hit his knees.

He screamed. The cuff gouged him tight. Blood leaked down his arm. Crutch said, "Summer '68. You got the Gretchen Farr gig first, I got it second. You went on a bender, I took over then."

Phil tried to sit down. The cuff chain dug tighter. Phil tried to stand up. Crutch kicked him in the balls. Phil hit his knees, harder.

He screamed, he coughed, he dribbled puke. He lolled his head on his chest and panted.

Crutch said, "You and Weiss. The peeping, Arnie Moffett, that voodoo film."

Phil lolled his head. Crutch slapped him. Phil ducked and tried to bite his hand. Crutch pulled the throwdown and held it out eye level.

"I'll run the radio. No one will hear the shot. You work Tiger Kab. You're all over darktown. You're fucking half the black chicks south of Washington Boulevard. How much time will LAPD give it?"

Phil took some breaths. Phil scooched around on his knees. His eyes got snitch-darty. Blood ran down his arm and soaked his shirt.

"So, we like to peep. You like it, I like it, Chick likes it. He knew this Arnie guy. Chick used to buy knickknacks and shit from him. Arnie owned party cribs and showed movies at them. Chick saw this weird-ass flick and got hipped on some babe in it. He heard she was living in some empty house around there, and my guess is he peeped her."

Crutch said, "And that's it?"

"You want more?"

"Yes."

"Okay, you've got it. We peeped you peeping, so we learned from the King. Whatever you're in a lather over came straight from you."

Crutch pulled out his duct tape. Phil squirmed and thrashed his head. Crutch grabbed his hair and mummy-wrapped him. He left a nose hole open. He covered his mouth, his head, his ears. He pulled him off the ground and kicked him into the backseat. The cuff ratchets gouged him. His bones showed plain. The mock-tiger seat covers shed all over him.

Hash smoke. Follow the trail. The wife's car is gone. He's tripping back by the pool.

Crutch walked down the driveway. The backyard was dark. The pool supplied shimmer light.

Olympic-size. Artful nudes scrolled on the bottom. Picasso on LSD.

Chick sat by the deep end. He rocked his chair and toed the diving board. The fumes got stronger. He had a little mesh-spouted pipe.

Crutch pulled a chair up. Chick focused in on him.

"You're supposed to call first. Clyde knows that."

"Does Phil have to call first?"

"Phil's a special case. Clyde knows that, too."

Crutch flipped his chair and straddled it. The hash smoke burned his eyes. He smelled Hai Karate cologne.

The pool water rippled. Chick took a hit and offered the pipe. Crutch shook his head.

"I've put some things together. I'd appreciate your comments."

Chick re-lit the pipe. The little mesh glowed.

"There's something portentous about this visit of yours. It's starting to bum me out."

"You killed a woman named María Rodríguez Fontonette. I'd like you to tell me about it."

Chick grinned and winked. It was practiced. Chick had studied the late Scotty B.

"There's not much to tell, although I have to credit you with an assist on that one."

"Have there been others?"

"A few, here and there."

"You peep, you see something you like, and you kill them?"

"More or less."

"Tell me about María."

Chick took a hit. His eyes were red, his pupils were dots.

"I peeped her. She dug voodoo, I dug voodoo, we both dug voodoo art. We ate some herbs and rapped about Haiti. Everything's cool, until she lays out this guilt trip about some Commie invasion she betrayed. It was a bummer. It brought me down, until I started thinking, you know, you're here in this abandoned house, you've always wanted to do it, she's a nigger fly-by-night that nobody will miss."

Crutch pulled his chair up. "So you did it."

"Yeah. I bisected the body and cut off her hands. She told me all these emerald stories, so I ground up some green glass and stuffed it in with her wounds. I started having these fantasies about five years earlier. I bought a set of surgical tools and kept them in the trunk of my car, but I never thought I'd have the nerve. Well, the moon was in Scorpio that night, and I guess I just did."

Crutch looked at the moon. It was slivered and half-eclipsed.

"You're vibing judgmental, Peeper. That cracks me up."

"Oh?"

"I always thought you had a surfeit of balls and a shortage of brains. Now, I have to add 'hypocritical mind-set' to that."

Crutch reached in his pockets. Chick took a hit and blew smoke in his face.

"You can't put your nose to windows and come away blood-free. Inspiration's inspiration. It's like that guy King said. 'I have a dream.' You just never know who's been watching you or who's kicking around in your head."

Crutch pulled out the capsules and displayed them. Chick said, "What have you got?"

"They're Haitian. It's an up trip. You'll fly for a day and a half."

Chick went *May I?* Crutch went *Sure.* Chick dry-swallowed the capsules and re-lit his pipe.

Crutch leaned closer. "Tell me about the other ones."

"What's to tell? They looked good, and I was bored."

"Just like that?"

Chick took a hit. "Yeah, 'Just like that.' It's the '70s, baby. 'Do your own thing.' "

Crutch looked around. The pool, the moonlight, the moment. A bird flutter overhead.

Chick looked at him. A few seconds passed. His gaze glazed. Green foam poured out his eyes, nose and mouth. His arms spasmed and constricted. Bones shattered. Crutch heard the breaks. Chick stood up and staggered. Foam bubbled out of his ears.

Crutch stuck a leg out and tripped him. Chick fell into the pool. Crutch watched him thrash and float facedown.

127

(Los Angeles, 4/17/72)

"Don't give me a surname. There's one I'm considering."

"Dare I guess?"

"Let's just say it honors the past several years, as well as runs from them."

The backyard was Ella's gator farm. Clouds brewed and promised rain. Joan rounded the stuffed creatures up.

Karen said, "Literary executor. What do you think? All our files, diaries, memoranda. Everything we've put together."

Joan looked up at the fallback. "He'd be good. He's quite the hoarder."

"What would he do with it?"

"He'd read through it and look for answers. He'd see things that no one else has seen and impose his own logic on it. If he grows up, he'll understand what it all means."

The girls bombed around the house. Joan peered through windows. Dina watched TV cartoons. Ella snuck up, pulled the plug and laughed.

Karen said, "I miss Dwight."

Joan said, "Something's changing with my body."

The rain kept up. A strong wind came with it. Joan anchored her paper stacks with throwdown guns and Dwight's knickknacks. She wanted the wind. The boy loved her hair aswirl.

Mixed blessing. The wind gave them the backdrop. Gusts snuffed the candle flames.

He was there with her and off somewhere. He kept his eyes open. She kissed them shut and held them shut and caressed a neck vein pulsing. He made sounds she'd never heard before. He had a kid-sound repertoire. The sounds pushed his tears back. He burrowed into her hair, so she wouldn't see.

It took a while. He'd drift someplace and touch her from a distance. He'd spend time away from her and roll back. He saw what he saw or thought what he thought and come back to her. He put a knee between her legs and kissed her underarms. He forced the fit. She rolled and kneeled over him. His eyes looked crazy. She covered them. He kissed her palms and held her fingers in his mouth.

"Tell me what you've been doing."

"I can't."

"Have you been thinking about the island?"

"Yes, in part."

"I heard that Esteban Sánchez had been killed."

"Yes, he was."

"Were you complicit?"

"Yes."

"Trust the purity of your intent. There will always be casualties, and there will always be fewer of them if you act boldly."

"There's something else."

"Tell me about it."

"I'm not going to."

"Were you complicit?"

"Yes."

"Did you act boldly?"

"Yes."

"Did you realize that you had to act, because no one else would?"

"Yes."

"Are you comforted by that now?"

"No."

"Your options were do everything or do nothing. You made the correct choice."

"How will I know when I've done the wrong thing?"

"When the result is a catastrophe that will in no way subside."

"What do I do then?"

"Reach for a deeper resolve and try to be stronger and smarter next time."

"There's something kicking around in my head now."

"Tell me about it."

"I can't."

"All right."

"Tell me why you redacted my file."

"I'm not going to."

"I don't think I'll ever feel safe again. I'll always be looking for something that may or may not be there."

"You've always been that way."

"Is there a way to run away from all this?"

"Not for you or me. We might run, but we'll always run back."

128

(Los Angeles, 4/18/72–4/30/72)

He worked at pad #3. He closed the curtains, shut the drapes and ran the air conditioning. He shut off all the clocks. He unplugged the phone. He turned day to night and night to day.

It was a controlled burning. He emptied out his file trove at the Vivian. He boxed up all his file shit downtown. He had the liquid-herb formula and the syringe. He had written formulas from his herb guys. Burn your mother's file, burn Wayne's file, burn your case file. Build your paper bombs and gauge the results.

He stole Dwight Holly's bolt-tappers. Pre-oiled tungsten cut through anything. He had his plane tix, his fake facial hair, his bogus ID. He had everything. He had to act, because no one else would.

He emptied out the boxes. The paper piles ran ten feet high. He dumped out his case file last. The murder occurred a heartbeat away. He should have known then. He figured it out late. He acted, because no one else would.

He saved Joan's mug shots. He nailed them to the back basement wall. He clamped his Saint Christopher medal to the nailhead.

The herb guys gave him crib sheets. He brewed liquids and filled eyedroppers. He squeezed droplets on blotter paper. He cross-checked molecular charts. He refined the burn words/retain paper effect.

File paper stripped. File paper blackened, curdled, crisped. Smell and haze—but no smoke outright.

He brewed six full bottles and baffle-wrapped them. He placed three Windex empties in his knapsack. He bought forty mesh laundry bags. He jammed them all paper-full.

Paper balls, paper pods, paper cylinders. Hold for the spritz.

He filled Windex bottle #1. He sprayed his Paper Parthenon life's work. It curdled, bubbled, singed, reduced and vaporized text. It sent up a stink. It produced eye irritation. The paper nests vibrated. The little mesh nets snapped. Wordless paper scraps whirled.

Crutch walked to the back wall. Joan's mug shots were dust-coated. He wiped them off. He placed the Saint Chris around his neck.

I will avenge you.

I will honor the great gift of you.

You faltered and gave me your flag for safekeeping. I will carry it for you now.

129

(Los Angeles, 5/1/72)

May Day.

Red flags swirled up Silver Lake Boulevard. Political banners were mixed in. END THE WAR, BLACK PRIDE, WOMEN'S RIGHTS. Marchers diverting traffic. Pissed-off cops working overtime.

Joan watched from the terrace. Dwight's binoculars got her in close. She recognized faces from Free the Rosenbergs, twenty years ago.

She'd be leaving soon. Their paper was built. She'd start out again as Jane Anne Kurzfeld. Karen was set to go. She wouldn't reveal her surname. They'd communicate through phone drops.

She had a good sum of money. She gave Karen an equal amount. Jack would administer the rest.

Cars skirted the parade route. Some drivers honked for peace. Some drivers lobbed balloons filled with piss and flipped off the marchers.

The boy disappeared. Something was distressing him the last time they met. Karen agreed with her. He's persistent and rich in synchronicity. We'll leave him our paperwork.

Joan lit a cigarette, took two hits and snuffed it. She shouldn't. That change in her body had persisted. *Yes, I'm sure this is it.*

130

(Washington, D.C., 5/1/72)

May Day.

Red flags and yippies, aging peaceniks galore. Boocoo banners and causes. Mounted cops like Chicago in '68. Nowhere near the bloodshed.

A few skirmishes, a few chases, some tramplings. Goofballs with red spray paint, ghouls in Nixon masks.

He blended in. He wore paste-on hippie hair. His mustache and beard itched. His headpiece fit askew. His overstuffed knapsack enhanced the effect.

He flew in two days ago. He pseudonymed his ticket and his hotel-stay stats. He cruised the target three times. The basement door looked impregnable. The basement fuse box looked easy. The laundry-room window was always ajar.

No live-in help. No stakeout Feds parked outside. No watchdogs.

She'd ask him if he did it. He'd wink like Scotty Bennett. He'd say, "I'm not telling you."

The day marches became night parties. He hung out at Lafayette Park. The White House was across the street. He got Tricky Dick elected. The Frogman assisted. It was a billion pre-Red years ago.

Hippies smoked weed and cavorted. A few chicks went topless. Cops made pro forma passes through.

Crutch ambled off to Rock Creek Park. D.C. was full of squares and renegades. Nobody noticed him.

He hit a Texaco station and changed back to his normal duds. He cut up his camouflage threads and hair and flushed them. He walked into the park and found a quiet spot. We're on-go for midnight.

The L.A. papers tagged Chick Weiss a drug OD. Phil Irwin held his mud. He remembered some things Joan told him. Esteban Sánchez kicked through his head.

It was muggy. Night insects bombed him. He was secluded. Fireworks popped on the other side of the park.

The countdown was endless. His watch hands got de-sprung. Midnight hit finally. He was woozy up to 12:03. Bam—reserve adrenaline popped on.

He walked, he ambled, he strolled. Nice night, nice neighborhood. I'm a nice kid lugging school clothes home to my mom's.

There's Northwest Thirtieth Place. There's the driveway. There's the neo-Georgian house.

Por la Causa. Be brazen, be bold.

The window was unscreened and ajar. He walked over, pushed the sill up and vaulted in. He hit the floor light on his feet.

The downstairs lights were off. The kitchen smelled like Lemon Pledge. He'd seen photos in *Antique Monthly* and diagrammed floor plans. He pulled his penlight and walked to the basement door.

It was locked. He inserted a #6 pick and popped the tumblers. Outside access was impossible. Inside access was easy.

He walked down the stairs. He narrow-dialed his beam.

It was his file space and Wayne's file space and Reggie's lab gone mammoth. The basement ran the length and breadth of the house. The ceiling was raised for more paper. The shelves topped Mount Matterhorn and almost scraped clouds.

He had forty-four paper bombs, mesh-netted and screw-topped. He uncinched the duffel bag and placed them shelf by shelf. He got to the bottom. His heart-attack potion had spilled. His syringe had been crushed.

He stood there. A million voices said, "*Dipshit, Peeper, pariguayo.*" He covered his ears. It didn't stop them. The voices beat on him. He sat on the floor and let them yell themselves out.

He put on his gas mask. He ran through the basement. He popped all forty-four screw tops.

The fumes went up.

Colored clouds rose.

The walls contained them.

Paper singed, curdled, crackled and charred. Little explosions went off. The file shelves rattled. Paint peeled off the walls. The fumes turned re-colored: dark/light, dark/light. Paper flecks vaporized in thin air.

Crutch walked up the steps and shut the door behind him. The kitchen light snapped on. Mr. Hoover stood by the fridge.

Crutch reached in his pocket and pulled out the emerald. Mr. Hoover trembled and homed in on it.

The sparkle was incessant. It eyeball-magnetized. The green glow grew and grew. Mr. Hoover weaved and drooled. Mr. Hoover clutched his chest and staggered upstairs.

131

(Los Angeles, 5/3/72)

I t was headline news. Heart attack, seventy-seven.

She felt nothing. The obits would extoll and defame. Dwight had ripped him out of her. She didn't care anymore.

Joan parked in front of the house.

A newscast blared next door. TV rays bounced out a window. The boy called the place "pad #3." His souped-up car was gone. She opened the door with a bogus credit card and let herself in.

The living room was messy. A breeze swirled paper scraps. The air smelled odd. The walls were soot-flecked.

A stack of car magazines. Test tubes and chemical bottles. Notes scrawled on scratch pads. A sawed-off shotgun.

She opened her purse and pulled out the camera. She rolled up her sweater to show him how she'd changed. She held the camera at arm's length and snapped the picture.

The print popped out a minute later. The image faded into focus. She placed it on the front window ledge.

Your resolve resurrected my resolve.

I can't imagine who you'll become.

I'm grateful this happened with you.

DOCUMENT INSERT: 5/11/72. Extract from the privately held
journal of Karen Sifakis.

Los Angeles,
May 11, 1972

I'm leaving. This will be my last journal entry. The house has
been sold, the car has been packed. The girls are tucked safely in
the backseat, along with Ella's stuffed animals. I will never have
to teach college again. Profits from a hellishly violent robbery will
support me for the rest of my life.

For the time being, I possess no surname. I have resisted all
the false identities offered to me. It's a risk, but I'm taking it
gratefully. At the proper time, I will tell the girls the entire story
and how I came to the name Holly.

I locked the house and took one look up at the fallback; I made
sure all the car doors were secured. Dina pouted a little; Ella
grinned at me. I noticed the little red flag attached to the seat.

I looked around. I wanted to see her one last time or at least
catch a breath of her smoke. She was gone. She had always held
that farewells were mystical and presumptive. Comrades should
be ready to reunify or lose each other forever. Belief works that
way.

NOW

The photograph has been preserved. History stopped at that moment thirty-seven years ago. History reconvened with the first batch of paper.

Documents have arrived at irregular intervals. They are always anonymously sent. I have compiled diary excerpts, oral-history transcripts and police-file overflow. Elderly leftists and black militants have told me their stories and provided verification. Freedom of Information Act subpoenas have served me well.

I found the journals of Marshall Bowen and Reginald Hazzard. I found Scotty Bennett's notebooks. Joaquín Balaguer was surprisingly candid. The Richard M. Nixon Library provided perfunctory support. The J. Edgar Hoover Library was resistant. Hoover spokesmen have consistently denied the charred files in his basement and refuse to link the event to Hoover's death that night.

I interviewed numerous comrades of Joan Rosen Klein and Karen Sifakis. Their recollections form a great contribution to this narrative. They refused to reveal Joan's and Karen's new identities. My attempts to bribe and coerce them have roundly failed.

My own memory rages in sync with everything I have described. I have not forgotten a moment of it. Forty thousand new file pages buttress my recall. I burned all of my original paper. I built paper all over again, so that I might tell you this story.

Most of the people are dead. Sal Mineo was murdered in a botched stickup. Booze took down Phil Irwin. Tiger Kab went bust. Freddy Otash had a fatal heart attack. Dracula died in '76. Farlan Brown died a year later.

Clyde and Buzz are gone. The mob guys are dead. Mary Beth is still alive. Reginald Hazzard returned to Haiti. Daná Lund died in '04. Jack Leahy has vanished.

I was the youngest of us all. I remain in fine health. I run a successful detective agency in Los Angeles. My firm bodyguards celebrities and verifies stories for tabloid tell-all rags. I am a frequent guest on scandal-mongering TV shows. My employees utilize cutting-edge technology. I reap profit from their efforts. It allows me to relive History and continue my search for Joan.

I know she's still alive. I know that Karen and her daughters are alive and thriving. All my hunter's prowess has not led me to them.

God gave me a restless temperament and a searcher's discipline. My unruly rover's drive now veers toward the good. I look for lost loved ones and bring them home. I do it constantly and anonymously and at my own cost. I have found a great many lost people and quite a few lost dogs. This book encapsulates four years and circumscribes many arcs of magic. Wisps of that magic have come to reside in me. I listen, I look, I cull files. I follow people to people and bring them back to the people who most love them. The process fulfills a sacred trust and takes me breathlessly close to Joan.

She's eighty-three now. Our child is thirty-six. Instinct tells me it's a girl. My mother is ninety-four. She still sends me a card and a five-dollar bill every Christmas.

"Your options are do everything or do nothing." Joan told me that. I have paid a dear and savage price to live History. I will never stop looking. I pray that these pages find her and that she does not misread my devotion.

I have toured the world's revolutionary hot spots. I have been to Nicaragua, Grenada, Bosnia, Rwanda, Russia, Iran and Iraq. I have drawn pictures of Joan and aged her in my mind's eye. I read newspapers and magazines and search for her actions in ellipsis. I see women who might be her and follow them until their auras disperse. I have paid out millions of dollars in tip cash. I hear of car bombings and arms deals and scan computer photographs. I have a lab filled with photo-enhancing equipment. Correspondents send me footage every day. I stare at crowd scenes and hold my breath for the moment it's her.

Her picture. My gene of persistence.

My options often fluctuate between Then and Now. I live in the latter with reluctance. I live in the former with kid-convert rectitude.

There's a party at Tiger Kab. A strange island beckons me. I'm chasing a killer to a self-indicting end. I'm making friends and enemies and roving at full speed. I've got that license to steal and that ticket to ride.

It's always there. It's always unfurling. It's always teaching me new things. I give you this book and anoint you my comrade. Here is my gift in lieu of a reunion—my lost mother, my lost child and the Red Goddess Joan.

A Note About the Author

James Ellroy was born in Los Angeles in 1948. His L.A. Quartet novels—*The Black Dahlia, The Big Nowhere, L.A. Confidential,* and *White Jazz*—were international best sellers. His novel *American Tabloid* was *Time* magazine's Best Book (fiction) of 1995; his memoir, *My Dark Places,* was a *Time* Best Book of the Year and a *New York Times* Notable Book for 1996. His novel *The Cold Six Thousand* was a *New York Times* Notable Book and a *Los Angeles Times* Best Book for 2001. He lives in Los Angeles.

A Note on the Type

The text of this book was set in Cheltenham, a typeface originally designed by the architect Bertram Grosvenor Goodhue in collaboration with Ingalls Kimball of the Cheltenham Press of New York. Cheltenham was introduced in the early twentieth century, a period of remarkable achievement in type design. The idea of creating a "family" of types by making variations on the basic type design was originated by Goodhue and Kimball in the design of the Cheltenham series.

Composed by North Market Street Graphics,
Lancaster, Pennsylvania
Printed and bound by Berryville Graphics,
Berryville, Virginia
Designed by Virginia Tan